P9-DUF-726

MODERN MANORS

MODERN MANORS

WELFARE CAPITALISM SINCE THE NEW DEAL

Sanford M. Jacoby

PRINCETON UNIVERSITY PRESS PRINCETON, NEW JERSEY

Published by Princeton University Press, 41 William Street,
Princeton, New Jersey 08540
In the United Kingdom: Princeton University Press, Chichester, West Sussex

Library of Congress Cataloging-in-Publication Data

Jacoby, Sanford M.
Modern manors : welfare capitalism since the New Deal / Sanford M. Jacoby
p. cm.
Includes bibliographical references and index.
ISBN 0-691-01570-8 (alk. paper)
1. United States—Economic conditions—1945– 2. Welfare state.
3. Capitalism—United States. I. Title.
HC106.5.J33 1997
330.12′2′0973—dc21 97-7835
CIP

This book has been composed in Times Roman

Princeton University Press books are printed on acid-free paper and meet the guidelines for permanence and durability of the Committee on Production Guidelines for Book Longevity of the Council on Library Resources

http://pup.princeton.edu

Printed in the United States of America

1 2 3 4 5 6 7 8 9 10

TO ALEX, MAGGIE,
AND SUSAN

Contents

Acknowledgments

I AM DEEPLY GRATEFUL to many individuals who helped me write this book. Research assistance was provided by a fine group of students, including Gordon Betcherman, Richard Copeland, Seongsu Kim, Kim Kurtzberg, Richard Lester, and Maury Pearl. Travel and research support came from UCLA's Academic Senate, the Anderson School at UCLA, the UCLA Institute of Industrial Relations, and from the National Endowment for the Humanities. Thanks to Harry Katz, David Lipsky, and Nick Salvatore for helping me spend a productive NEH year at Cornell's School of Industrial and Labor Relations.

Among the libraries and their staff who assisted me were Baker Library of the Harvard Business School, the Labor-Management Documentation Center at Cornell, the Hagley Library, the Herbert Hoover Presidential Library, the Eastman Kodak Archives, the Newberry Library, the Regenstein Library at the University of Chicago, the Reuther Library, the special collections department of the University of Rochester Library, the Sears Roebuck Archives, the State Historical Society of Wisconsin, UCLA's University Research Library, and the Western Reserve Historical Society. Two dedicated UCLA librarians—Bob Bellanti and Roberta Medford—were always ready to answer my requests. I also wish to thank several individuals who shared their private materials with me, including John Jeuck, Anil Verma, and James Worthy.

Drafts of various chapters were read by Hal Barron, Stan Engerman, Nancy Fitch, Doug Flamming, Jacqui Greenberg, Darryl Holter, John Laslett, Daniel J. B. Mitchell, Jill Quadagno, Steve Ross, Bob Slayton, George Strauss, Frank Stricker, and Leila Zenderfeld. Tom Kochan and Daniel Nelson gave the final manuscript a close read, and Eric Monkkonen and Charles Romney provided useful advice. I am indebted to all of them, and to many others.

I owe special thanks to Suzanne Wagner, who expertly edited the manuscript; to Sheenah Bell-White, Wilma Daniels, Cornelia Marsh, and Rose Pressey, who helped prepare the manuscript for publication; and to my editors at Princeton University Press—Jack Repcheck, who first expressed interest in the project, and Peter Dougherty, who wisely shepherded it through the publication process.

The years during which I labored on this book saw the deaths of three dear relatives—Hugo Kanter, Leo Meyer, and Edith Weissfeld—who, among other things, taught me the value of hard work. These years also brought the births of my wonderful children, Alexander and Margaret. In their captivating way, they encouraged me to keep work in perspective. And throughout it all there was Susan, whose love and support sustained me, and always will.

Abbreviations

AAWA	Automotive and Aircraft Workers' Alliance
ACTU	Association of Catholic Trade Unionists
ACWA	Amalgamated Clothing Workers of America
AFL	American Federation of Labor
AIC	Associated Industries of Cleveland
AMA	American Management Association
APW	Automotive Parts Workers
AT&T	American Telephone and Telegraph
AWA	Aircraft Workers Alliance
BAC	Business Advisory Council
BIW	Brotherhood of Independent Workers
BPUR	Lawrence Bachman Papers, University of Rochester
CED	Committee for Economic Development
CEO	Chief executive officer
CER	Committee of Employee Representatives
CIO	Congress of Industrial Organizations
CUOHP	Columbia University Oral History Project
DCCU	Labor-Management Documentation Center, New York State School of Industrial and Labor Relations, Cornell University
EEOC	Equal Employment Opportunity Commission
EI	Employee Inventory
FBI	Federal Bureau of Investigation
FPUR	Marion B. Folsom Papers, University of Rochester
HEW	U.S. Department of Health, Education, and Welfare
IAM	International Association of Machinists
IBM	International Business Machines
ILWU	International Longshore and Warehouse Union
JCWP	James C. Worthy Papers, Northwestern University
JMBP	James Madison Barker Papers, Newberry Library, Chicago
KA	Kodak Archives, Eastman Kodak Company, Rochester, N.Y.
KEA	Kodak Employees' Association
LRA	Labor Relations Associates
LRC	Labor Relations Council
M-form	multidivisional
MPC	Michigan Plant Council
NACA	National Advisory Committee for Aeronautics
NASA	National Aeronautical and Space Administration
NAM	National Association of Manufacturers
NICB	National Industrial Conference Board
NLRB	National Labor Relations Board

NRA	National Recovery Administration
NWLB	National War Labor Board
PSAC	Profit Sharing Advisory Council
RCIA	Retail Clerks International Association
RCIAP	Retail Clerks International Association Papers, State Historical Society of Wisconsin, Madison
REWP	Robert E. Wood Papers, Herbert Hoover Presidential Library, West Branch, Iowa
RLR	Retail Labor Report
RP	Rosenwald Papers, University of Chicago
RWDSEA	Retail, Wholesale, and Department Store Employees Association
SCC	Special Conference Committee
SR Archives	Sears Roebuck Archives, Chicago
SREC	Sears Roebuck Employees' Council
SPP	Studies in Personnel Policy
SRA	Science Research Associates
SUB	Supplementary Unemployment Benefit
TAPCO	Thompson Aircraft Products Company
TPEA	Thompson Products Employees' Association
TPP	Thompson Products Papers, Baker Library, Harvard Business School
TRW	Thompson-Ramo-Wooldridge
TRWP	TRW Papers, Western Reserve Historical Society, Cleveland, Ohio
UAW	United Automobile Workers
UE	United Electrical, Radio, and Machine Workers of America
URL	University of Rochester Library
WRC	Workers' Representative Committee
YMCA	Young Men's Christian Association

MODERN MANORS

Introduction

DURING THE EARLY TWENTIETH CENTURY, one of America's leading employers was S. C. Johnson & Son of Racine, Wisconsin, makers of floor wax and other household products. Samuel C. Johnson, who founded the company in 1886, plied his employees with recreational facilities, a profit sharing plan, paid vacations, group life insurance, and myriad other benefits. Samuel's son, Herbert, followed in his father's footsteps. During the First World War, he stabilized the company's erratic employment levels by hiring more full-time workers and then training them to perform several jobs, so they could be rotated around the company. Then, in 1922, he started what was to become a highly publicized private unemployment insurance plan. As Herbert Johnson told Congress in 1929, he felt "there should be something more permanent and more definite for the average working man." To reformers concerned about the "labor question" of the early twentieth century, companies like S. C. Johnson offered a distinctively American answer: the business corporation, rather than government or trade unions, would be the source of security and stability in modern society. This approach was dubbed "welfare capitalism."

Today, S. C. Johnson continues to win accolades for its progressive employment policies. A leader in the corporate child-care movement, it has day care facilities for children from infancy to adolescence and a summer camp for older children. JoAnne Brandes, a company manager and founder of the child-care program, says, "This isn't a benefit—it's a good business decision because we want to attract the best." Although innovative, S. C. Johnson has a strong sense of tradition. In a recent interview at Johnson headquarters, an impressive building designed by Frank Lloyd Wright, the firm's chairman recalled that his great-grandfather Samuel Johnson "laid the first building block for the first Y.M.C.A. in Racine. Our company's social involvement grew out of this early sense of local community involvement. My great-grandfather had a sense that there had to be a fair way to do things." The company currently provides profit sharing, child care, an aquatic center, and other benefits because, says the chairman, they create "a family atmosphere within the company. We all sit on the same side of the table, so to speak, so we don't have a confrontational environment between the various groups of people who work here. As a result, we have very low employee turnover and no unions," the same desiderata sought by welfare capitalism since its inception.[1]

The origins of welfare capitalism lie in the nineteenth century, when people began moving in large numbers from rural to urban areas. This transformation forced people to seek new ways of dealing with the uncertainties of life. City-dwelling workers could not rely on home-grown food to get them through a spell of joblessness. The elderly, who were an important part of rural family life, found that industrial corporations were reluctant to employ them. Young unmarried women began to work outside the home, raising parental concern for their morals. Meanwhile, dangerous factories and crowded cities brought on occupational injuries and other health problems.

One response to these problems was a recrudescence of market individualism: workers saved as best they could while taking fierce pride in the independence and employability that came from having a well-rounded set of skills. Another strategy was to form mutual benefit associations to provide savings funds, health plans, and burial benefits. The associations sometimes grew into trade unions that negotiated risk-sharing arrangements with employers. An alternative to individualism and mutualism was government, which increasingly sought to minimize risk through protective legislation or to redistribute it via mandatory social insurance. The latter approach reflected the logic of the European welfare state: to pool risks by providing all citizens with unemployment, sickness, and old-age security. A fourth option was to have corporations reduce risk or indemnify their employees against it. This, essentially, was welfare capitalism.

By the end of the nineteenth century, welfare capitalism could be found throughout the industrialized world, but it was especially popular in the United States. Not only did American employers favor welfare capitalism because they thought it would inhibit the growth of unions and government, they also saw it as an efficient alternative to market individualism: training would be cheaper and productivity higher if employees spent their work lives with a single firm instead of seeking their fortunes on the open market. Also impelling welfare capitalism was a moral impulse: self-made business owners felt a sense of stewardship and paternal obligation to their employees. But virtue was conveniently conflated with strategic considerations, as when American employers convinced themselves that welfare capitalism constituted the best defense of freedom against laborism and statism. In short, welfare capitalism was a good fit for a distinctive American environment composed of large firms, weak unions, and small government.

Welfare capitalism was an influential movement for the first three decades of this century. It was embraced by employers as well as by intellectuals, social reformers, and political leaders, all of whom shared the belief that industrial unrest and other problems could best be alleviated by this distinctively American approach: private, not governmental; managerial, not laborist. To put its ideas into practice, employers cleaned up their factories, constructed elaborate recreational facilities, launched "company" unions, and even built housing for their employees. Like S. C. Johnson, they turned casual positions into career jobs offering health, pension, and other benefits. By the 1920s, welfare capitalism reached millions of workers at thousands of firms. It was an impressive if imperfect system, one whose notions of order, community, and paternal responsibility recalled the preindustrial household economy. The firms pursuing welfare capitalism were, in effect, industrial manors.

But the edifice crumbled during the Great Depression. Companies cut wages, instituted massive layoffs, and discontinued most of their welfare programs. Economist William Leiserson, who earlier had been dazzled by welfare capitalism, wrote pessimistically in 1933 that the Depression had "undone fifteen or so years of good personnel work." In its wake, workers searched for alternatives to safeguard their security. They voted for the Democratic party, supported the New Deal, and enthusiastically joined unions. Welfare capitalism appeared to be dead and gone.[2]

Or was it? In fact, welfare capitalism did not die in the 1930s but instead went underground—out of the public eye and beyond academic scrutiny—where it would reshape itself. Without doubt, welfare capitalism *had* to change if it were to survive what was becoming a hostile climate, one in which company unions were unlawful, collective bargaining was public policy, and a nascent welfare state promised to shield workers from the uncertainties of industrial life. In response to these challenges, welfare capitalism gradually was modernized by a group of firms that had been spared unionization and the ravages of the Depression. Studies of three of these companies—Kodak, Sears Roebuck, and Thompson Products—form the core of this book. The three companies were exceptions to the "rise and fall" story of welfare capitalism: each one made major contributions to welfare capitalism's modernization between the 1930s and 1960s, the high point of labor and government activism in the United States.

In their attempts to build "modern manors," these companies retained many of the elements of earlier welfare capitalism. Kodak, Sears, and Thompson still provided generous welfare plans, though now the benefits were cast as supplements to Social Security and other public programs. And each company still asserted that it was a corporate community whose cohesion stood in opposition to the occupational and industrial solidarity of the labor movement. But the events of the 1930s forced employers to do a better job of bolstering words with deeds. Workers took seriously the idea that they were part of the corporate community and demanded more of the privileges that previously had been reserved for salaried employees. Modern welfare capitalism responded by becoming less tolerant than its predecessor of the foreman's coercive "drive" system. And paternalism itself was redefined during the era. Companies still drew attention to their lord of the manor—the CEO—but they also tried to routinize paternalism by offering insurance instead of discretionary benefits and by educating managers about human relations.

With modern welfare capitalism, then, the emphasis shifted from control to consent; this was a kinder, gentler sort of paternalism. One reason for the change was the Wagner Act, which, along with labor's newfound strength, made it more difficult for employers to resort to force majeure when threatened by an organizing campaign. Coercion did not disappear, but large nonunion companies had to rely on persuasion to carry more of the load. The emphasis on persuasion mirrored changes occurring in the realm of production, where the "carrot" of a career job system was displacing the "stick" of close supervision. Thus, modern welfare capitalism was controlling yet consensual, coldly efficient yet cozily humane.

Mixed motives like those represented in modern welfare capitalism have never been handled well by social critics and historians. Liberals focus on workplace conflict, while conservatives emphasize the harmony between labor and capital. But in reality, workers and managers simultaneously have opposing *and* shared interests. They disagree over issues such as the split between profits and wages while at the same time they depend on each other for their livelihoods, a point that Emile Durkheim made a century ago when he observed that the division of labor creates a shared interest in the enterprise as an economic commonweal.[3]

Within the industrial community, workers not only relied on management for their livelihoods but shared skills and technical expertise with their employers. Hence they tolerated, even respected, managerial authority. As for managers, they depended on workers' expertise, intelligence, and discretion—whether in service industries, where managers sought but could not command consummate performance, or in mass-production manufacturing industries, where labor ostensibly no longer needed to be skilled. Mutual dependence between workers and managers created a consensus regarding rights and responsibilities at work, so when conflict occurred—as it often did—the dispute was likely to be over the specific terms of agreement rather than its fundamental axioms.

Managers and workers also shared cultural aspirations. Even the lowliest manual laborer had middle-class yearnings: to own a home, be comfortable, and obtain respect in the community. Even if people did not personally identify with successful businessmen, a sizable portion of the population hoped that they would someday have their own businesses or that their children would. Workers held fast to the idea that it was within their power to succeed and, in fact, it was not unrealistic for them to expect some amount of advancement in the career-type jobs offered by welfare capitalism. Here in the realm where hope and reality mingled lay the "reefs of roastbeef" that, according to Werner Sombart, had beached American socialism. None of this is to deny the truth that social class constituted a cultural divide. But class barriers could be bridged by bonds of shared belief, ethnicity, and gender, as often they were in America's modern manors.

More than a few workers were indifferent or opposed to unions even before they entered the workplace. During and after the 1930s industry was filled with cantankerous individualists, Black Legionnaires, and skilled workers who "boasted of their superior experience, dedication, and loyalty." Not all anti-union workers were ideologues, though; some were merely fearful, or caught up in the economic anxieties of daily life. Others, like African-American workers, were skeptical of both sides but willing to give management the benefit of the doubt so long as it kept its promises, especially about employment security, a critical issue for all workers who lived through the Great Depression.[4]

Workers who were indifferent or unresponsive to unions are invisible in much of the scholarship on American labor history, which frequently ends with a surge of solidarity in the 1930s and 1940s. But even then, labor's victory was neither stable nor complete. At its peak after World War II, the labor movement represented less than a third of nonagricultural workers and its strength was concentrated in only a few regions and industries. Just three sectors—construction, manufacturing, and regulated transport and energy utilities—accounted for more than 80 percent of organized labor at its peak. Although much has been written recently about union losses in representation elections, this trend actually started during World War II.

What stopped labor's rise? First, by the mid-1940s the most easily organized workers had already been signed up. Second, problems festered inside the house of labor, ranging from factional schisms to an inability to broaden unionism's appeal beyond certain well-defined types of workers. Finally, welfare capitalism killed unions with kindness and occasional ferocity. Even the most progressive nonunion employers were willing to spend enormous sums both in the factory and in Congress to stave off unions. Costs aside, it was simply an article of faith that unions were anathema. Employers who acknowledged that collective bargaining might be beneficial—either as a stabilizing force in competitive industries like apparel or as a prop to oligopolistic pricing practices in industries such as steel—were a distinct minority. In steel, Myron C. Taylor of U.S. Steel failed in the late 1930s to convince fellow steelmakers Tom Girdler, Ernest Weir, and Eugene Grace that the virtues of price stabilization outweighed the vice of recognizing unions. Each of these men saw their companies organized against their wishes during World War II, along with holdouts from many other industries. That left a small group of sophisticated nonunion companies to develop the strategies that checked labor's growth in the postwar decades.

In contrast to employers in other industrialized nations, these modern manors preserved an American tradition of vehement employer opposition to organized labor. With its roots in America's distinctive social and economic history, employer exceptionalism remains a relatively unexamined counterpart to the labor exceptionalism about which scholars have written so much. Explanations of labor's weakness in the United States often fail to mention that employer policies as well as worker attitudes were a key determinant of union strength. These policies set a ceiling on unionization during labor upswings (the early 1900s, late 1910s, and the 1930s and 1940s) and hastened the erosion of unionism during downswings (the 1920s and today). While this book is about management, in its reverse image one can trace the fortunes of the American labor movement.

Although there is a sizable literature on welfare capitalism during the first three decades of this century and an abundance of articles about today's progressive nonunion employers, the pickings get slim when one seeks information on such companies during the intervening decades, the heyday of organized labor in America. Explanations for this gap are not hard to find. Industrial relations experts were preoccupied during the 1940s and 1950s with forging a new labor relations system based on collective bargaining. Dedicated pluralists, they saw organized labor as a vital challenge to management's power in the economy, the polity, and the workplace. They thought collective bargaining would protect individuals from the political power of business and from the psychological demands of bureaucratic work organizations, and thereby preserve freedom in the modern world. By investing the labor movement with such an important historical function, liberal academics inevitably treated nonunion companies as socially retrogade and thus undeserving of scrutiny.

A result of this scholarly blind spot was the erroneous impression that organized labor had achieved greater stability and acceptability than was actually the case. Thus a distinguished group of economists asserted in 1956 that American businessmen had "come to accept the legitimacy and respectability of labor unions." The claim was not entirely without justification, since managers from unionized companies often sounded as if they had agreed. John E. Rovensky, a prominent industrialist, said in 1952 that "All sound-thinking businessmen today recognize the right of labor to collective bargaining. Unions are an absolute necessity." But Rovensky's words masked a disjunction between management's public pronouncements and its private beliefs. Pluralism did not have deep roots in management circles, even during the period of its purported hegemony, from the 1940s through the 1960s. Two speakers made this exceptionally clear at a 1957 meeting of the Industrial Relations Research Association, when they cautioned that "if American management upon retiring for the night, were assured that by the next morning the unions with which they dealt would have disappeared, more management people than not would experience the happiest sleep of their lives."[5]

There was, however, one group of managers who would not have slept well if unions had disappeared: the thousands of new personnel and labor relations specialists whose expertise lay in administering the increasingly abstruse world of collective bargaining. For if organized labor had vanished overnight, most of these managers would have been jobless the next morning. As a group they had a vested interest in collective bargaining, even in preserving its technical complexity. Those who strongly felt this way were likely to attend professional events where they rubbed shoulders with, and molded the perceptions of, labor economists and other industrial relations experts.

But the vast majority of managers, although demoralized by the New Deal, eventually regained their self-confidence and took aggressive steps to contain union inroads. The effort to get the Taft-Hartley Act passed was one example; another was seen by the actions of General Electric. The firm had ostensibly accepted industrial unionism in the mid-1930s, but began to move plants to the South in the 1950s while taking a more combative stance toward its remaining unions. GE managers, and others following them, looked for inspiration to those progressive employers who had never been organized by unions, firms like Du Pont, Eli Lilly, IBM, Procter & Gamble, S. C. Johnson, Standard Oil, and the companies examined in this book.

Until the 1960s, modern welfare capitalism was confined to a minority of large nonunion companies. Though the practitioners were well known in their regions and industries, their practices spread at a slow pace. Organized employers such as General Motors found that their unions either resisted the introduction of modern welfare capitalism or sought to control it and take credit for it. Smaller nonunion employers were skeptical of welfare capitalism or else lacked the necessary resources to pursue it; hence they stuck to traditional approaches. But in the 1960s and 1970s modern welfare capitalism began to spread rapidly, not so much because managers modified their views of it, but because of changes in the economy and society that supported it, such as the shift away from mass production, the growing importance of educated workers, and the decline of organized labor. Labor's fading strength encouraged employers to deploy the anti-union tactics developed by welfare capitalist companies after World War II. Put more positively, modern welfare capitalism's emphasis on commitment proved well suited to managing college-educated workers, who were fast becoming dominant in the labor force, and it meshed neatly with the participative principles that were supplanting traditional Taylorist approaches to work organization. Thus was modern welfare capitalism transformed into the "new" nonunion model of today.

Magazines and academic journals lately are filled with articles about "the modern American workplace." Few of them, however, can tell us what makes the workplace "modern" or "American." We are all familiar with the latest crop of model employers, companies like Microsoft and Motorola, Nucor and Nordstrom, yet we have little idea how these "new" companies came to be what they are today. Some managers even think they invented the world as it is. Thus the history of welfare capitalism, while fascinating in its own right, can also be read as a cautionary tale about the present.[6]

Pundits tell us we are living in a postmodern age in which the institutions that fueled America's postwar prosperity—mass production, labor unions, and the Keynesian welfare state—have been replaced by a new set of sensibilities: postindustrial, decentralized, and privatized. If one measures present circumstances against the activism of the New Deal or the optimism of the 1960s, it is easy to conclude that we have entered a new age that breaks with the past. But if one looks back beyond the Great Depression, other interpretive possibilities arise, and the present seems less like a break than a rerun. Immigration restriction is again a national obsession; entrepreneurs are lionized by the media; and creationist biology is back in the schools. The labor market also looks like an atavism. The United States once again has one of the lowest unionization rates and one of the most miserly social insurance programs in the industrialized world. As in the 1920s, the workforce increasingly is split between the "have-nots" and the "haves," who will spend most of their careers working in modern manors like S. C. Johnson or Microsoft.[7]

Yet things are not exactly the same this time around, and too much can be made of the parallels. Public confidence in business is not as strong now as it was in the 1920s, nor are major corporations as stable as they used to be. Indeed, welfare capitalism today is undergoing its first major crisis since the Great Depression, reflected in "downsizing" at blue-ribbon firms like IBM, a pervasive sense of insecurity among American workers, and a growing national debate about corporate responsibility. Clearly, employers are reluctant to shoulder as much risk as they once did. On the other hand, many Americans still look first to corporations to meet their needs, rather than to government or organized labor. How we reached this point—how welfare capitalism re-emerged as an alternative to liberalism and laborism—will become evident in the chapters ahead.

One

The Coming of Welfare Capitalism

AT THE BEGINNING of the twentieth century huge corporations dotted America. Inside them, workers labored under the "drive system," which economist Sumner H. Slichter described as "the policy of obtaining efficiency not by rewarding merit, not by seeking to interest men in their work . . . but by putting pressure on them to turn out a large output." The system depended on fear of job loss to ensure obedience, and employers did not hesitate to fire workers. Those who were dissatisfied had few alternatives other than to seek their fortunes on the open market. High quit rates contributed to the overall instability of the workplace, which made unemployment a recurring fact of life.[1]

Although European workers faced similar problems, they were supported by a spreading web of institutions that tempered the insecurity produced by the market: labor unions, protective legislation, and social insurance. These institutions were more elaborate and encompassing than those that existed in the United States. Indeed, in the early 1900s the United States had the smallest welfare state and the lowest unionization rate (when adjusted for per capita income) among the industrialized nations.[2]

There were pockets of stability scattered throughout the American labor market, however. White-collar employees enjoyed privileges such as paid vacations, pensions, and exemptions from nightwork and layoffs, all of which were unavailable to blue-collar workers. When the employees were female, companies added an additional layer of paternalism—nicer restrooms, lunchrooms decked with flowers, social clubs—which, says historian Alice Kessler-Harris, had the effect of "reinforcing [women's] sense of obligation." White-collar employees received these perquisites because their positions were considered a fixed cost and because employers entrusted them with cash and company secrets.[3]

Also enjoying favorable employment terms were skilled craftsmen, whose unions sought to regulate the drive system and close the gap between salaried and hourly employment. Union rules ensured that equitable procedures rather than a foreman's whim governed pay and promotion decisions. The union shop undermined a key assumption of the drive system: that employment was a relationship of limited duration terminable at the employer's will. Instead, trade unions held that employment was a permanent relationship between the union—a set of workers—and the employer—a set of jobs; the union behaved as if it owned those jobs in perpetuity. Under the "guild" system, jobs spanned company boundaries, permitting versatile craftsmen to move from shop to shop; under a newer system, "guild manorialism," they were restricted to a single employer. Guild manorialism was found in medium- and large-sized firms operating on a year-round basis, such as meatpacking and printing. Here workers adhered to craft customs while also establishing rules to govern career-type jobs.

Although European employers saw collective bargaining and the welfare state as antidotes to class warfare, American employers, with their strong belief in individualism and free enterprise, reacted vehemently whenever "outsiders" (either government or unions) bothered them. They asserted an absolute authority to control their businesses. According to historian Philip Taft, this attitude resulted in "the bloodiest and most violent labor history of any industrial nation in the world."[4]

Here it is important to keep in mind labor's powerlessness in the United States as compared to the situation in the nations of northern Europe, where craft and class loyalties supported an interlocking structure of labor unions and working-class political parties. On the employer side were numerous small and medium-sized firms, often family owned, specializing in skill-intensive, customized products. To gain control of the shop floor and to allay larger threats to the economic order, these firms formed employer associations that agreed to union recognition and industrywide bargaining in return for labor's support of management rights. The employer associations reduced the cost of union recognition by moving bargaining from the shop floor to the industry level and standardizing labor costs.[5]

These gains, however, were hardly a clear-cut victory for employers. In Britain and other countries where craft unionism was deeply entrenched, industry-level bargaining could not erode craft control of production. And even when employers succeeded in displacing bargaining to higher levels, the outcome was not inconsistent with labor's objectives. Industrial bargaining—especially when combined with extension of contracts to unorganized workers—promoted worker solidarity, legitimated unions as social actors, and made it easier for unions and their affiliated parties to pressure governments to expand the welfare state.[6]

The situation in the United States was different. Working-class parties and the labor movement were weak, and so were craft traditions. There was little in Pittsburgh or Peoria that could compare to the complex and long-established craft communities in Europe. With many trades only lightly organized, the cost of union recognition to a single firm was substantial, including an increase in relative labor costs and possible loss of managerial prerogatives. Such costs could have been mitigated through multiemployer bargaining, but it was difficult to get American employers to form associations because unions were neither strong enough nor radical enough to pose a threat like that which spurred European employers to band together.[7]

The sheer size of American companies was another factor. On average, American firms were larger than those in Europe and were heavier users of mass production technology, a combination of traits the Europeans called

"Fordism." Mass production made American firms less dependent on skilled labor and, together with their size and labor's weakness, made them better able to resist unionism. For defense and attack American firms could rely on company guards, on armed strikebreakers, and even on private arsenals.[8]

American employers also had easier access to public police forces. Each state and town had its own militia and police agents, and because labor disputes often were local affairs, employers could rely on local units to act on their behalf. The judiciary, with its "constitutional supremacy over labor legislation," also played an important role.[9] Few judges were friendly to unions, as demonstrated by a steady stream of decisions enjoining strikes, boycotts, picket lines, and other collective actions. The courts refused to enforce collective bargaining contracts and held unconstitutional most legislative attempts to regulate workplace conditions. Although there were instances when the federal government acted to protect organized labor, such efforts were limited to key industries such as coal and the railroads, or were temporary wartime provisions.[10]

No industrial country was as successful as the United States in suppressing organized labor. Rather than stirring revolt, repression reinforced the American labor movement's weakness and conservatism. By the 1890s, Samuel Gompers, who had earlier sympathized with many socialist positions, had become wary of revolutionary goals and increasingly saw trade unionism as an end in itself. Recalling how the police violently broke up a Tompkins Square labor demonstration in New York City, he wrote that the episode taught him how "radicalism and sensationalism" inevitably led to repression which "nullified in advance [any] normal, necessary, activity" on the part of organized labor. Gompers thought that to achieve even limited economic goals, American labor would have to appear sober and respectable, thus garnering support from middle-class allies. Under Gompers, the American Federation of Labor (AFL) pursued a conservative form of job-control unionism, but that strategy had the ironic effect of reinforcing opposition from employers.[11]

An American Alternative

Even as American employers tried to maintain power, they nevertheless felt the need for a more positive response. Thus they fashioned an alternative—welfare capitalism—whose main idea was that corporations would shield workers from the strains of industrialism. Originating in the 1880s as "welfare work," the movement grew to encompass most branches of American industry. By 1914, the National Civic Federation counted twenty-five hundred firms pursuing a gamut of welfare activities, from cafeterias, gardens, and profit-sharing plans to company housing, magazines, and athletic facilities. Welfare work was not uniquely American. Profit sharing was first popularized in France, and elaborate welfare schemes existed in companies throughout Europe, including Krupp, Le Creusot, Cadbury's, and the textile houses of Lancashire, but it was more pervasive in the United States than elsewhere.[12]

Welfare work initially prevailed in companies controlled by their founders. Observing that their firms had grown large and impersonal, these men hoped welfare activities would reproduce the close ties that had existed when they knew each of their employees by name. Company growth had also brought great personal fortunes to these men, and they saw welfare work as a way of responsibly sharing their wealth and discharging the moral obligations that it imposed. Religious beliefs often reinforced these motives. Quaker businessmen started some of the earliest welfare experiments, as did employers imbued with mainline Protestantism's "Social Gospel." The ethical impulse, however, included no small measure of self-interest. It created company bonds that undermined trade unionism and quieted public critics of concentrated wealth.[13]

Welfare work was as diverse as the situations that spawned it. In isolated company towns—particularly in the textile and mining industries—welfare work verged on a feudal system whereby the employer controlled most aspects of a worker's life. As in preindustrial master-servant relations, deference was combined with paternal obligation and prerogative. Closer to urban areas, welfare work was infused with communitarian ideals adopted from utopians like Charles Fourier, Robert Owen, and John Humphrey Noyes, and, later, from thinkers such as the pragmatist John Dewey. Reverend Josiah Strong founded the League for Social Service in 1898 to promote industrial welfare programs, which, he said, enhanced the "oneness of society" and its "interdependent organs."[14]

The company towns built throughout the United States between 1880 and 1915 were characteristic settings for welfare work. Places such as Pullman (Illinois) and Wilmerding (Pennsylvania) were living experiments in paternalistic social engineering. Employers designed every aspect of the industrial community—from leisure activities to architecture to landscaping—to match the putative harmony inside the workplace. With profit sharing, even the worker's pay package was not immune to this encompassing organicism. But communal harmony did not come cheap, if it came at all. Model towns were expensive to build and maintain and, as demonstrated at Pullman, they offered no guarantee of labor peace. Besides, profit sharing and other welfare activities could just as easily be pursued in a conventional factory setting.[15]

As welfare programs became more complex and costly, employers sought to systematize their administration. Among the first companies to hire a specialized manager to oversee welfare programs was National Cash Register. NCR's welfare secretary sought to "restore the old-time 'personal touch'" by counseling employees at work, organizing social activities, and visiting the sick at home. These home visits revealed mixed motives: while they extended a friendly hand from an otherwise impersonal corporation, they often served as occasions for a patronizing lecture on proper housekeeping or a chance to see if the employee was really sick.[16]

Filene's, the Boston department store, took a different approach to managing its welfare programs. It placed the administration of its loan fund, medical clinic, and recreation clubs in the hands of elected employee representatives. Constituted in 1905 as the Filene Cooperative Association, this group of elected representatives was the first major company union in the United States. By giving workers a stake in corporate decisions, management hoped to widen the circle of common concerns while shrinking the distance between itself and the employees.[17]

Welfare work was frequently condescending and manipulative. The hope was that firms could recast the intemperate, slothful worker or the ignorant immigrant in a middle-class mold: uplifting him, Americanizing him, and making his family life more wholesome. The most paternalistic programs were directed at immigrants from eastern and southern Europe and also at women. Skilled workers—who were almost always men, either native born or from northwest Europe—were likely to be offered more straightforward economic incentives for loyalty, including wage bonuses, deferred compensation, and profit-sharing plans.

The relationship between welfare work and unionism was not a simple one. In England, iron and cotton manufacturers combined paternalistic welfare programs with trade-union bargaining. That mixture was rare in the United States, although some American employers were willing to try company unions. The years before World War I saw experiments in industrial democracy at a number of influential companies, including Filene's, Joseph and Feiss, Leeds and Northrup, the Plimpton Press, and Dennison Manufacturing. Avoiding "outside" unions was not always the motive for experimenting with company unions; several of the firms came from industries in which trade unionism was weak or nonexistent.[18]

Welfare work primarily concerned employees' lives off the job; inside the workplace, employment policies often remained crude. Given an abundance of immigrant labor, at least until World War I, employers were reluctant to tamper with the drive system as applied to the mass of semiskilled workers. Between 1900 and 1920, however, some employers began to devise stable, structured employment systems, initially for their skilled workers. The systems combined policies pursued by craft unions, such as seniority rules, with enticements offered to salaried employees, chiefly deferred compensation in the form of pension benefits and stock bonuses. The railroads were pioneers in this area, followed by industrial giants such as U.S. Steel, Baldwin Locomotive, and International Harvester. Because the benefits could not be enjoyed if a worker was dismissed, they raised the cost of engaging in union activity—an intended effect.[19]

By tying skilled workers to the firm, employers hoped to weaken craft traditions, speed the pace of work, and hasten the introduction of new technologies. In effect, employers sought to take the guild out of guild manorialism.

Piece-rate and other incentive wage devices were part of this strategy, especially in the metalworking industries, where Frederick W. Taylor's ideas were popular. However, the importance of incentive pay can be overstated. Employers started to realize that incentive pay sometimes produced undesirable results. Because it rewarded proficiency in a given job, incentive pay made employees reluctant to accept technical innovations or job transfers, either of which might cause earnings to decline.

Other, more career-based workplace policies—promotion ladders, seniority rules, and dimissal restraints—began to supplement incentive wage systems. These policies were administered by new employment departments whose job was to keep watch over foremen and other line managers. Gradually the drive system started to give way to more enduring work relationships, intertwined with employer-provided welfare services outside the workplace.[20]

The pioneers in these developments were mid- to large-sized firms serving the national market, companies like Dennison Manufacturing, Goodyear, and National Cash Register. Such firms had the resources to establish career employment policies, a major resource being their managerial hierarchies. To keep pace with company growth and increasing organizational complexity, turn-of-the-century corporations were impelled to adopt systematic planning, accounting, and management methods. Initially these methods were applied to sales and production; managerial rationalization only later spilled over into the employment sphere. Thus, while welfare capitalism emerged as a solution to the problems of modern industry, it was modern industry itself that made welfare capitalism viable.

Welfare capitalism also drew heavily on developments outside of industry. The decades after 1890 saw American society caught up in a "search for order" led by a new class of professional problem solvers—educators and economists as well as social workers and psychologists. Although their specific prescriptions differed, they embraced the idea of deliberate social engineering conducted by benevolent professionals. Scientific administration—order guided by knowledge—was seen as the best hope for stabilizing an industrializing society.[21]

John Commons and Meyer Bloomfield in the United States, and Beatrice and Sidney Webb in England, took these ideas and cast them in terms appropriate to the workplace. The work reformers conceived of industry as the site of reconcilable differences between workers and management, a place where competing interests could be bridged by people skilled in the art of mediation and compromise. At the center of this approach was the impartial professional, trained to prescribe administrative solutions to workplace problems. Where unions were present, these professionals would serve as arbitrators, the approach developed by Louis Brandeis for the New York clothing industry. In the absence of unions, newly created personnel departments would, it was hoped, bring to unorganized employees some of the same benefits as unionism.[22]

Despite a penchant for top-down social engineering, these reformers hoped to create institutions that would encourage democracy as well as efficiency. "Consent of the governed" was necessary to avoid the resentment bred by autocratic hierarchies. Here the reformers drew on a set of common ideals inspired by Progressive pragmatism: that individuals are capable of making choices, that differences can be solved through open communication, and that democracy would emerge from decentralized problem solving. Characteristically American in its optimism was the belief that modern industry could avoid the deadening rigidity of bureaucracy by applying what John Dewey called the "science of participation."[23]

For those reformers concerned with industrial democracy, these ideas pointed in the direction of trade unions, which were seen as the only genuine vehicle for realizing citizenship norms within industry. The "new" unions in the needle trades were viewed as the exemplar of a laborist alternative to welfare capitalism. The new unions were promoting modern management methods and joint problem solving, while also building worker-run schools, banks, and other institutions to serve their immigrant membership. Reformers were enthralled at the prospect of foreign-born workers being educated to participate in industrial as well as civic democracy.[24]

Other reformers rejected laborism in favor of a private corporatism that elevated enterprise ties over those of craft or class. For the corporatists, modern industry was viewed as a vast experiment in cooperation. Managers, technicians, and workers had what Dewey called a "genuinely shared interest in the consequences of interdependent activities." Only by thoroughly involving workers in production—through company unions, shop committees, and the like—could industry realize its cooperative ethos, what Dewey called "reciprocal solidarity." These corporatists were liberals, but they were wary of what they perceived as Luddite tendencies within the labor movement. They also were skeptical of legislative responses to social problems, preferring instead to rely on private solutions—especially programs associated with welfare capitalism—although some saw a government role in coordinating the economy through trade associations and industrial planning.[25]

The Taylor Society (originally the Society for the Promotion of Scientific Management) was a hotbed of liberal corporatism. By 1915 it had been taken over by progressive engineers sensitive to the criticism that scientific management "had not fully caught the organic nature of human relations in industry." As currents of reform passed through the Taylor Society, they produced a fascination with the idea that industrial democracy was the key to industrial efficiency. Company unions, works councils, and employee participation in time studies were justified as stimulants to productivity.[26]

The Taylorists also were captivated by the idea that unemployment—perhaps the most pressing problem of the day—could be mitigated through the application of scientific management techniques by private employers. The Taylorists believed that market analysis and production planning could stabilize fluctuations in employment, thereby removing a major cause of joblessness. Stabilization would also make employees more willing to participate in works councils and more tolerant of schemes to raise efficiency.

After World War I, some laborists were drawn to scientific management and to the idea that "microregulation," as historian Steven Fraser calls it, would efficiently reduce unemployment. But the group—including Sidney Hillman, Mary van Kleeck, and John Commons—continued to believe that collective bargaining was the best way to achieve microregulation. As proof they pointed to union efforts to rationalize production and reduce seasonality in the clothing industry by hiring industrial engineers, cooperating with management in redesigning wage systems, and negotiating joint unemployment insurance plans. In contrast, the employers who moved in the Taylor Society's orbit—liberals like Henry S. Dennison, Henry P. Kendall, and Richard Feiss—criticized the drive system and saw trade unions as a reasonable corrective, but held traditional unionism to be inferior when measured against their own brand of enlightened management. Their synthesis of personnel administration, employment stabilization, welfare work programs, and company unionism served as a model for other employers to follow.[27]

The welfare capitalist model, however, was not entirely free of kinks. Although personnel management was intended to resolve conflicts between workers and foremen, welfare programs implicitly denied that such conflicts existed. Meanwhile, employer paternalism contradicted the citizenship ideals informing employee representation. These tensions—between authority and democracy, efficiency and community—would strain industrial relations in progressive companies for years to come.

Before World War I, companies like Henry Dennison's constituted a distinct minority within American industry. Although numerous employers adopted welfare work programs, few combined them with systematic personnel administration, and fewer still had company unions. But the war changed all that. After 1916, the combined pressures of labor shortages and labor unrest produced a rapid expansion in all manner of workplace reforms. By 1920, more than half the firms with five thousand or more workers had established personnel departments.

The war also saw a proliferation of welfare work programs. Much of it was of the uplift variety: such things as Americanization classes and glee clubs. With time, employers gradually relinquished these activities to groups like the Young Men's Christian Association (YMCA) and began to direct more attention to insurance plans, pensions, and profit sharing. Financial benefits were less paternalistic and intrusive than other welfare activities, and they could be keyed to specific workplace needs such as retention, recruitment, and union avoidance. In 1918, Standard Oil of New Jersey—a bellwether among the Rockefeller companies—initiated a comprehensive package of financial benefits that included health and accident insurance, pension and stock ownership plans, and mortgage assistance.[28]

During the war, workplace reforms were motivated by rational calculations made in the face of labor shortages and encroaching unionism. This was particularly true at large companies, which had long known about personnel management and employee representation but, with some notable exceptions, had done little to support them. In a flash, the titans of American industry set up personnel departments and representation plans: in 1918 at Bethlehem Steel, Jersey Standard, and Western Union, and in 1919—when strikes and union membership reached peak levels—at American Telephone and Telegraph (AT&T), Du Pont, U.S. Rubber, and Westinghouse. To justify these reforms, managers at companies such as AT&T began to use a sophisticated set of ideas drawn from the new discipline of industrial psychology.[29]

The impetus for change sometimes came from below, as when striking General Electric workers demanded that the company hire a "Manager of Man Power." And here and there managers could be found who envisioned the firm as a democratic community, men like Morris Leeds of Leeds and Northrup and Gerard Swope of General Electric. Swope was an exemplar of liberal corporatism, having spent his youth living and teaching at Hull House, the renowned settlement house in Chicago.[30]

As before the war, corporate reforms were often contradictory. On the one hand, the new personnel departments sometimes were as vigorous as any trade union in standing up to foremen and pursuing rule-bound employment practices. Grievance procedures in employee representation plans had the potential for restraining arbitrary, egregious supervisors, and sometimes acutally did so. A few firms even had company unions coexisting with craft unions.[31]

On the other hand, employers hoped that workplace reform would cause employees to see themselves as an integral part of the enterprise—siding with management rather than against it. Issues of power and conflict were downplayed in the hope of fostering a sense of community. But although picnics and parties served to create a harmonious family atmosphere, other policies such as company unions could serve either unitary or power-balancing ends. Most managers were unconcerned by these inconsistencies, yet they did not go entirely unnoticed.

One influential observer was Mary Parker Follett, a management theorist who drew her ideas on democracy from pragmatic philosophy and the "new psychology" of industry. Follett, a former settlement-house worker, was friendly with such liberal Boston employers as Edward A. Filene and Henry S. Dennison. Seeking to counter what she saw as modern society's anomic individualism, Follett advocated group participation—in communities and in industry—as a democratic solution. Although Follett idealized the solidarity of groups and organizations, she nevertheless was a trenchant critic of power balancing. Follett argued that a fundamental problem with trade and company unions was their insistence on "drawing an absolutely sharp line between management and labor." This distinction resulted in an emphasis on "grievances instead of problems" and on bargaining instead of "integrative unity."

Follett endorsed various postwar experiments in union-management cooperation such as those pursued by the Baltimore and Ohio Railroad and its shopcraft unions, but she thought that company unions were more capable of achieving the desired end of "integrating relations."[32]

Follett also urged employers to adopt modern psychological techniques to assess worker attitudes and bring them into alignment with the ideas of upper management. Her industrial psychology was one branch of a wider movement—including advertising and opinion polling—that sought to incorporate the masses into modern industrial society by manipulating their preferences from above. Although some liberals, like Walter Lippmann, were horrified by this kind of social engineering, other liberals—including John Dewey, Charles Horton Cooley, and Follett herself—saw "positive, democratic possibilities in the social construction of human desires and interests."[33]

Characteristically pragmatic was Follett's belief that orderly and lawful employment relations would emerge from regular deliberations between managers and workers. Although Follett was more interested in achieving unity than in resolving conflict, she was at pains to point out that "integrative unity" did not deny workers an independent voice. Nevertheless, her view of what this meant in practice entailed employees presenting to management "the workers' point of view of what is best for the plant as a whole."[34]

Welfare Capitalism Takes Hold

Follett's ideas presaged the approach to welfare capitalism taken by progressive employers in the 1920s, when cutting-edge companies moved away from heavy-handed paternalism and also from the power-balancing approach. The 1920s were more conservative and less uniformly prosperous than the decades that preceded them. Employers who saw welfare capitalism as nothing more than a roadblock against unions were reluctant to pump money into expensive expedients. Welfare capitalism was more prevalent in large firms than small, although there were many exceptions. Some large companies adopted only bits and pieces of welfare work; others undermined their welfare programs with harsh shop floor practices. Comprehensive welfare capitalism—including financial benefits, career jobs, company unions, and supervisor training programs—was limited to an elite group of companies employing at most a fifth of the industrial labor force. The movement's impact, however, was greater than this figure alone would suggest. Welfare capitalism drew attention from academia and the press because it was concentrated among the nation's most prosperous companies: science-based firms in the electrical and chemical industries and highly visible "modern" producers of mass consumer products. By pursuing welfare capitalism, they endowed the movement with an aura of technological inevitability. Thus, despite its shortcomings—coverage was limited and benefits meager—welfare capitalism came to be seen as America's future.[35]

A shifting political climate and a steep decline in union membership also contributed to the perception of welfare capitalism's inevitability. Although many former laborists would have preferred larger roles for trade unions and government, they deferred their desires or came to share the corporatist view that individuals were best cared for by their employers. John Commons, a prominent prewar laborist, became resigned to private regulation after the Wisconsin legislature repeatedly refused to pass an unemployment insurance bill in the early 1920s. A discouraged Commons wrote in 1923, "Only from the large establishments, and not from the smaller establishments, nor from employees, nor from the state, can any material progress be made towards prevention of unemployment." Though a stalwart friend of the AFL, Commons now argued that workers could thrive under company unions so long as these unions rested on "the integrity, capability, and good judgment of the workers."[36]

From the intertwining of liberalism's laborist and corporatist strands emerged a new consensus. Welfare capitalism, company unions, and corporate efficiency were seen as complements rooted in the logic of mass production and consumption. Here was a distinctively American response to the "labor question."

Welfare capitalism's corporate core in the 1920s was the Special Conference Committee (SCC). Executives from ten of America's leading companies founded the committee in 1919 to coordinate their labor relations and personnel policies. The SCC had close ties to the Rockefeller interests; until 1933 it was chaired by Clarence J. Hicks, former head of the personnel department at Standard Oil of New Jersey. In addition to Jersey Standard, other members included Bethlehem Steel, Du Pont, General Electric, General Motors, Goodyear, International Harvester, Irving National Bank, Standard Oil of Indiana, and Westinghouse Electric. U.S. Rubber joined the group in 1923 and AT&T in 1925. (U.S. Steel, a laggard in most respects, did not join until 1934.) The upshot was a tilt in corporate policies toward greater integration and consistency.

In 1920 the SCC adopted a set of principles, the heart of which was the belief that, as John D. Rockefeller, Jr., put it, "the only solidarity natural in industry is the solidarity which unites all those in the same business establishment."[37] Corporatist cohesion was intended to supercede other forms of collective identity: workers were expected to eschew trade unions and instead to identify with their company; in return they would receive steady jobs and welfare benefits. The SCC approach was more enlightened than the unbridled repression of the American Plan, a coordinated employer campaign to break the AFL unions at the local level. Although repression was not entirely absent from SCC companies, it played a shadowy, secondary role in the 1920s. The prominence of the SCC companies and their control of organizations such as the American Management Association ensured that the SCC approach had considerable influence on the conduct of industrial relations at other large companies.[38]

A key part of the SCC approach entailed placing the personnel department under the control of line management. With personnel managers taking their orders from production officials instead of the other way around, there was little chance that line managers would be questioned or overruled, especially in cases of discipline and dismissal. The idea was to replace centralized power-balancing on the employee's behalf with integrative practices on management's terms. Rules would continue to be promulgated—in fact, the 1920s saw growing adherence to the seniority principle in employment decisions—but they would be interpreted and enforced by line managers.

More than a few personnel specialists had a hard time adjusting to the new realities. Humble Oil, a subsidiary of Jersey Standard, fired its personnel manager in 1922 for being overly zealous and "tactless" in urging the company to adopt an eight-hour day. Even at progressive companies outside the SCC nexus—such as Leeds and Northrup in Philadelphia—personnel departments were abolished in favor of less conflictual methods of restraining line officials.[39]

One such method was to instruct foremen in the psychology of work relations. In classroom courses and at weekend retreats on "the new foremanship," participants were taught "teamwork," "cooperation," and how to be "both big brother and boss to [their] people." That leadership styles might affect employee attitudes was an idea industrial psychologists had recently begun to explore. Industrial psychology had achieved national prominence during the war, when the army began giving intelligence and vocational aptitude tests to new recruits. Industrial psychology's technocratic ethos—that scientific methods could simultaneously improve both human welfare and human efficiency—appealed to managers in technology-based companies like AT&T. Early in the 1920s, AT&T aided efforts to create the Personnel Research Federation, a consortium of about a dozen companies interested in industrial psychology. The federation disseminated research on psychological approaches to work problems such as employee selection, wage administration, and supervision. Federation members also teamed up with university-based psychologists to conduct applied research in these areas. Leadership studies were done at several sites, including a Kimberly-Clark plant in Wisconsin and various AT&T facilities, notably the Western Electric plant outside Chicago.[40]

Central to the SCC approach was employee representation, which, according to the committee, formed "the practical application" of its philosophy. Company unions were supposed to provide a forum for cooperative problem solving and the airing of grievances. Since many worker complaints concerned supervision, foremen were adamantly opposed to employee representation, "feeling that their authority was being curtailed and their discipline slipping away." Reluctant to upset existing disciplinary regimes, the two most conservative companies belonging to the SCC—General Motors and U.S. Steel—eschewed company unions in the 1920s. International Harvester adopted a works council plan in 1919, but company foremen "resented the authority that the [council] exercised and took steps to combat it." Later in the decade, as complaints from foremen persisted and the union threat faded, Harvester clipped the wings of its councils. At Du Pont, management simply began ignoring its councils; by the early 1930s they were moribund.[41]

Many company unions deserved their poor reputation. Samuel Gompers lambasted them as a "pretense admirably calculated to deceive," an opinion shared by other AFL leaders. Yet here and there company unions could be found that had support from management as well as from employees. Medium-sized innovators like Dennison Manufacturing and Leeds and Northrup, as well as large SCC members like AT&T, Goodyear, General Electric, and Jersey Standard, all had such unions. Goodyear's Industrial Assembly included joint worker-management committees to deal with issues ranging from time-study standards and transfers to plant safety and sanitation. At GE's Lynn works, says historian Ronald Schatz, by 1926 management "had won the loyalty of the plant's former labor leaders—not through use of threats, for none were employed—but by education. At meetings of the Plan of Representation, management disclosed financial data to the workers' leaders, showing them the plant's costs, its return on various products, and its problems. They frankly sought the representatives' advice, while simultaneously expressing a willingness to adjust grievances as they arose."[42]

Active works councils like these were a far cry from the rough-and-tumble world of the drive system. Not only did they shrink the gap between managers and managed, they proved capable of solving a variety of local problems. Moreover, as managers at Jersey Standard and General Electric were quick to point out, their company unions included immigrants from diverse ethnic backgrounds as well as blacks and women—groups neglected by most AFL unions. Like John Commons, some laborist liberals decided in the 1920s that company unions were preferable to the AFL or were a realistic alternative to no representation at all. Others saw company unions as a transitional form that could serve as "education for democracy" until workers were ready to run their own unions. William Leiserson, an economist with close ties to the AFL, predicted in 1928 that active company unions would evolve "in quite unforeseen directions," possibly becoming "more and more like trade unions." But any such evolution was cut short after 1935, when most company unions were taken over by national unions or disestablished by the Wagner Act, which created a regulatory framework for labor-management relations.[43]

A common objection to company unions was their inefficacy in the economic realm. To avoid controversy and to retain control over compensation decisions, managers steered company unions away from pay issues, or they limited pay discussions to internal wage inequities. Pay cuts, however, were considered a legitimate subject; company unions were pressured to ratify cuts at International Harvester and other companies, especially those that hastily adopted representation plans after passage of the National Industrial Recovery Act in 1933.[44] None of this is to deny that some company unions did bargain over wage increases—even, until the mid-1920s, at International Harvester.

And at Goodyear, after electing new officers in 1922, the company's Industrial Assembly demanded a 15 percent pay raise. Management vetoed the raise but then assented to it after the assembly overrode the veto. In 1926, the assembly voted to adjourn after the company turned down its request for higher pay, resulting in the only recorded company union "strike" during the 1920s.[45]

Still, even progressive employers like Goodyear were dismayed by pay disputes and saw them as evidence that employee representation had failed. For this reason, several of the decade's most liberal firms—including Eastman Kodak—rejected company unions while searching for less conflictual methods of achieving "integrative unity." These employers held the belief (not entirely naive) that distributive conflicts could be minimized through a combination of premium wages and profit sharing, which could amount to as much as 10 to 12 percent of base pay.[46]

A problem with profit sharing occurred when it was used to raise inadequate pay levels to the market average, a practice condemned as "illegitimate" by Dennison and others. Another problem stemmed from the formula used to determine the share workers would receive. Although one employer touted profit sharing as "a bridge across the natural chasm between the management and the rank and file," most companies kept the determination of relative shares a management prerogative. Workers had no voice in setting the formula. However, a few companies—including Dutchess Bleachery, Leeds and Northrup, Simplex Wire, and Procter & Gamble—made the profit share a subject for deliberation by the works council or company union. A manager at Dutchess cautioned that "books must be kept open to workers" if they were to become "partners in industry."[47]

SCC and other companies also adopted a slew of welfare programs that provided monetary benefits: pensions, stock ownership plans, paid vacations, mortgage assistance, and health insurance. The SCC believed that such benefits "establish a mutual interest between management and the employees." Although some historians claim that the growth of welfare capitalism slackened by the late 1920s, the evidence shows that this was true of meddlesome activities like home visiting but was not true of financial benefits. The provision of financial benefits had various objectives, but the most important was to create a body of stable, loyal, and productive employees. The logic was the same as that behind the pecuniary benefits earlier devised for salaried and skilled employees.[48]

Benefit plans contained various incentives to increase employee stability and loyalty: only workers with a minimum level of tenure were eligible to share in profits or belong to company unions, and insurance and pension programs had a "continuous service rule" that linked receipt of benefits to unbroken tenure, thus making dismissal more costly for workers. Yet these incentives also imposed costs on the employer. With service restrictions came seniority rules that prevented workers from being transferred, laid off, or fired at will. Profits had to be shared with eligible workers, and employee representatives had to be heard.[49]

Welfare capitalism in the 1920s resembled earlier paternalist experiments. As before, employers offered security to their core employees while using economic and cultural controls to get workers to identify with the firm. There were, however, some significant changes. The ties binding workers to the firm had become more bureaucratic and impersonal, with managers taking care to distinguish between an employee's work life and home life. Managers were more sensitive to workers as individuals whose "personality and dignity, whose attitudes and inner feelings, must be respected." Unlike turn-of-the-century paternalists who believed they knew best, employers in the 1920s began to probe the opinions of workers to find out what they wanted, relying on psychologists and employee representatives to convey this information to them.[50]

Because welfare capitalism denied or suppressed conflict, some historians have characterized it as a system whose "central purpose" was identical to the American Plan—"the avoidance of trade unionism." But in contrast to the American Plan, welfare capitalism reached its goal in an ironical fashion: by reproducing within the firm the same regulatory structures sought by trade unions, a phenomenon Mary Follett called "the anticipation of conflict." In other words, it achieved its goals by an elaborate system of employer self-restraint.[51]

Such paradoxical dynamics were hardly new. Just as a master's paternalism had given slaves "their most powerful defense against the dehumanization implicit in slavery," and just as nineteenth-century English employers found that paternalism was "the prison of the rulers as of the ruled," so, too, did welfare capitalism bind the employer along with his employees. American employers did not go the European route—containing worker radicalism by recognizing national unions—but they did engage in their own kind of buyout: guild manorialism was preempted in favor of a top-down, nonunion version. The savviest managers came to realize, as John Commons claimed, that most American workers wanted "nothing more than security in a good job with power to command respect."[52]

Yet even those employers who grasped Commons's point did not always follow through on it. Some firms gave their all and others gave only lip service. For example, although the 1920s saw operatives and laborers included for the first time in benefit programs, status differences remained large. Vacation plans were limited to salaried employees, who were also given better cafeteria facilities and more regular work schedules than hourly employees. At the bottom of the ladder were semiskilled and unskilled workers, especially women, who were more likely to quit or get laid off than other employees. As a result, they often failed to qualify for benefits requiring continuous service.[53]

Though meant to be an enlightened alternative to trade unionism, welfare capitalism retained a primitive underside that surfaced whenever workers showed union sympathies. At these times, few managers could resist turning to coercive practices such as spies, injunctions, and dismissals. These tactics rarely blemished welfare capitalism's reputation during the 1920s only because labor was unable to penetrate the new mass production and distribution industries. Yet even with labor quiescent, welfare capitalism still rested on a questionable premise: that it was efficient, even moral, to give employees what they could obtain for themselves. To critics, this was social engineering of a kind that was inimical to democratic principles. As Sumner Slichter asked, "Is it not, in general, desirable, that men be encouraged to manage their own affairs rather than that they be deliberately and skillfully discouraged from making the attempt?"[54]

The Vanguard, the Laggards, and the Traditionalists

The 1920s were a period of economic transition during which consumer-goods companies eclipsed producer-goods manufacturers, the giants of the first industrial revolution. One result of these changes was that interfirm differences in labor policies—already substantial—became even more skewed. Employers were arrayed on a continuum stretching from a vanguard who practiced full-blown welfare capitalism, to a group of laggards whose efforts were less comprehensive, to traditionalists who adopted few or none of the reforms. Vanguard firms shared a number of features, not least important of which was their size. Whether measured by pension plans, company unions, or other programs, large firms were more in the vanguard than small ones.[55]

Although size mattered, its effects were mediated by other factors. Some large companies saw welfare programs as a waste of money. One firm with 28,000 employees had neither a personnel department nor welfare programs because, said a top manager, all employees were "co-workers," so they needed "no personnel or 'Santa Claus' department to hand out goodies to them." Even Sumner Slichter thought that close supervision and high turnover could be "profitable" and "practical" for employers "dealing with some classes of workers." But, he warned, because the drive system "wears workers out" and "intensifies class consciousness," what was privately profitable could have dire consequences for "the class interests of [all] employers."[56]

Initially, that very concern brought together the firms constituting the SCC and similar organizations. But as the 1920s wore on and labor unrest receded, broad visions faded away. Employers who maintained their commitment to welfare capitalism did so less out of a fear of unrest than a conviction that it paid. George F. Johnson of Endicott-Johnson said, "Democracy in industry is possible *and* it's good business," while Julius Rosenwald of Sears Roebuck put it more bluntly: "Don't imagine that anything we do for our people . . . is done from philanthropic motives—not in the least. Whatever we do for our employees we do because we think it pays, because it is good business." Surveying the scene in 1929, Slichter was impressed by the shift in management thinking since the war. What had changed, he said, was a growing number of managers (and Slichter himself) who had come to believe in "a close relationship between industrial morale and efficiency." That belief provided the impetus for continued experimentation with welfare capitalism.[57]

Putting beliefs into practice was easier in privately owned firms. Among the decade's most innovative employers were some mid-sized, privately held companies such as Columbia Conserve and Leeds and Northrup. Ownership allowed visionary employers like William P. Hapgood and Morris Leeds to pursue their inclinations over those of more conservative stockholders and managers. Ownership played a role in large firms, too. Part of the vanguard consisted of large but tightly held concerns, including Du Pont, Jersey Standard, and Procter & Gamble. A study of forty-seven large firms with sales over $500 million in 1929 found that owner control—by the founder or his heirs—had a positive association with spending on welfare activities that year.[58]

When enlightened owners lost their grip, however, it could mean a reversion to more primitive practices. Welfare capitalism at Filene's was largely the work of Edward A. Filene, a practical idealist who justified his pursuit of innovation "not from an idealistic social motive but simply because it will be the best policy." He shared majority ownership with his brother A. Lincoln Filene, although the two did not always see eye to eye on personnel policy. Among other things, Lincoln was concerned that Edward's programs were undermining employee discipline, since more than half of the company's Cooperative Association arbitration rulings on discipline and dismissal went against management in the early 1920s. Although the two brothers agreed never to vote their holdings against each other, Lincoln grew tired of Edward's experiments and in 1928 decided to put a stop to them. He wrested control of the store away from his brother, merged Filene's into the Federated Department Store chain, quashed the profit-sharing and stock plans, and gradually cut back on other programs. Edward never spoke to Lincoln again.[59]

Keeping a company on the progressive cutting edge required more than vision. Also necessary were economic resources, without which an employer may have had the will but not the way. One permissive factor was low labor costs relative to overall costs. Firms with low labor-cost ratios could afford to spend more on personnel programs because such spending brought only a small increase in total costs (a case of what the economist Alfred Marshall dubbed "the importance of being unimportant"). During the 1920s, low labor-cost ratios were found in capital-intensive, continuous-process industries such as soap making, sugar and petroleum refining, and food canning. These industries were home to a number of vanguard firms, including Procter & Gamble, California and Hawaiian Sugar, Standard Oil, and Columbia Conserve. Numerous progressive companies did not have low labor-cost ratios, however, so generalizations based on this factor should be made cautiously.

Another factor was profitability. Profits provided funds with which to finance personnel programs and they also encouraged innovation by serving as a cushion against the uncertain results of personnel experimentation.

Among industries with above-average profits nearly every year between 1919 and 1929 were scientific instruments, motor vehicles, electrical machinery, food products, paint, department stores, and public utilities. As the list suggests, some of these emergent industries were science-based, while others saw their profits originate outside the laboratory—in marketing and organizational innovations that propelled the rise of a mass consumer economy during the 1920s.[60]

Stable profits were related to a third factor: steady product demand, which stabilized not only profits but employment as well. A sizable number of the vanguard came from industries whose product demand was relatively stable over cycles and seasons: either service providers like Macy's and Irving National Bank, or nondurable-goods producers in industries such as chemicals, petroleum refining, public utilities, and food and tobacco processing. Firms with steady demand could offer commitments to their work force—such as guaranteed employment—that would have been quite costly for less stable companies. However, firms had to minimize layoffs during downturns to make such commitments credible by producing for inventory, by sales planning, and by training workers to be versatile.

Throughout the 1920s, a number of companies consciously pursued such stabilization programs, including Columbia Conserve, Hills Brothers, Dennison Manufacturing, Eastman Kodak, and Procter & Gamble. Packard Motor, known in the automobile industry for its advanced welfare policies, was able to minimize layoffs by refusing to adopt the new marketing strategy of annual model changes. By and large, though, stabilization remained a rarity in the auto industry and in other durable-goods industries.[61]

Firms seeking to stabilize usually weren't unionized, or they came from industries where craft consciousness—identifying with one's trade—was weak. A 1929 study told of a nonunion candy manufacturer whose product mix and employment levels varied seasonally. To reduce seasonal layoffs, the firm cross-trained its workers and moved them around to different jobs. A nonunion corset manufacturer trained workers in a variety of operations to facilitate rapid transfers in response to style and product changes. And the H. H. Franklin Company, an early practitioner of scientific management, rewarded such cross-training by paying workers an additional 4 percent for every new process they learned.[62]

Craft unions were leery of these practices. In the 1920s, the eight separate unions representing workers in the New York printing industry prohibited an employer from transferring a worker into another union's jurisdiction and forbade workers to hold membership in more than one union. Although many printers had multiple skills or could easily learn them, the unions insisted on strict demarcations between trades. The unions preferred to handle layoffs by relying on guild manorial rules specifying that layoffs be made in reverse order of seniority. Industrial unions (about 15 percent of union membership in 1929) were more flexible on these matters. Yet even the clothing and garment unions disliked transfers because they weakened the union's job control system linking job titles to pay and seniority.[63]

One requirement for membership in the vanguard was to have a centralized personnel department. Forty percent of industrial firms of more than one thousand employees (accounting for approximately a quarter of the industrial workforce) had such departments in 1929. Other features of welfare capitalism were less frequently adopted, however. In the mid-1920s, the National Industrial Conference Board, an employer-funded research organization, could find only 245 firms with active pension plans and 399 with company unions. As for stabilization, only 26 companies offered income or employment guarantees in 1929 (although 28 percent of firms surveyed by the Conference Board said that they were "definitely endeavoring to overcome seasonal variation.")[64]

Companies that had personnel departments but not a full ensemble of welfare programs were the laggards of welfare capitalism, a motley group. Most lacked company unions and did little to encourage stability. They made haphazard attempts to restrain foremen, avoid layoffs, and follow seniority rules. With few programs to administer and little authority over foremen, personnel managers in laggard firms had little to do besides hiring employees and administering the payroll. One study found that "many personnel departments are what one executive described as 'mere fronts.' "[65]

During World War I, managers of some laggard firms had aspirations to become part of the vanguard. After 1921, however, rising unemployment and labor's loss of momentum caused a reversion to prewar practices, especially with regard to the foreman's drive system. The companies that had faced the greatest union threat during the war years shifted to bellicose anti-union programs like the American Plan. Most of the vanguard, however, was found in sectors where organized labor had been, and remained, relatively weak.[66]

Laggards often came from durable-goods industries—autos, nonelectrical machinery, rubber, and steel—that were greatly affected by seasonal and cyclical fluctuations in demand. Such sensitivity made it costly for laggard firms to extend career employment policies beyond an elite minority. Given market volatility, they found it cheaper during downturns to rely on layoffs than on stabilization. Further hindering employment stability were capital-intensive technologies—such as blast furnaces—that did not allow for gradual reductions in output during slack periods. Incentive pay, which linked wages to specific tasks and was widely used in heavy industry, had similar effects: it inhibited transfers and thereby promoted layoffs.[67]

Circumstances peculiar to the 1920s, notably deflation and excess industrial capacity, had the additional effect of making production (and employment) less stable in capital-intensive industries than during earlier years. Such instability did not mean a shortage of profit; the automobile industry, for example, saw sharp fluctuations in production during the 1920s yet was among the decade's most profitable industries. But instability did have serious consequences for the quality of employment. Auto workers experienced periodic layoffs, a decline in the number of full-time jobs, and gradual abandonment of welfare programs. Another example was the rubber tire industry, where production instability inhibited the creation of stable jobs for more than a minority of rubber workers. Historian Daniel Nelson terms this "the failure of career employment" in the industry.[68]

Layoffs could have been less devastating had companies carried them out with the assurance that workers eventually would be rehired. A few durable-goods manufacturers took steps along these lines during the 1920s—notably, General Electric, Goodyear, Otis Elevator, Studebaker, and Westinghouse—but even these firms limited their seniority and rehiring commitments to employees with more than five to ten years' service. Elsewhere, however, layoff decisions were less orderly and equitable. While about 40 percent of large firms surveyed in 1927 made seniority a factor in determining layoffs, use of seniority as a determining factor was itself a seniority benefit: many workers were not eligible for it because of their unstable work histories. Even in firms with personnel departments, foremen remained responsible for deciding dismissals.[69]

Laggard firms exemplified the gap between the rhetoric and reality of welfare capitalism. Employers held out the prospect of pensions and other rewards to tenure, but made it hard for workers to be eligible for them. Little was done to relieve the instability and insecurity of employment. Workers heard high-minded speeches about the social responsibilities of business but then failed to qualify for welfare benefits or found them meager. International Harvester's vacation plan was so restrictive that not a single production worker at the firm's Fort Wayne plant qualified for it in the early 1930s. Off the shop floor, workers participated in programs like profit sharing and group insurance, but on the shop floor they were still goaded by barking foremen.[70]

Traditionalists were firms whose personnel policies were much the same during the 1920s as they had been thirty years before. Many of these companies were smaller concerns that lacked formal procedures and programs. (In 1929, fewer than 3 percent of firms with under 250 employees had personnel departments; almost none of them had pension plans or company unions.) Working for a small company had certain advantages, though. Owner-managers frequently knew employees by name, provided for them during hard times, and did what they could to offer year-round employment. Philadelphia, for example, had numerous small firms that lacked bureaucratic personnel systems but nevertheless pursued an informal yet conscious sort of paternalism. But smaller firms were often the locus for paternalism of a less benign variety, where employers clung stubbornly to the belief that benevolence on their part would undermine the work ethic.[71]

Puritan rigor hardly was limited to small firms. Based on field research conducted during the mid-1920s, J. David Houser, a psychologist, identified a group of large but traditionalist firms in which he found "the callousness so characteristic of many controlling executives. The general manager who paid lip service to the obligation for treating men 'decently' but who felt there was nothing for a man to do when he had a grudge (to which the foreman would not listen) except to 'stick around for a while and finally quit' is one example." Along with such coldness came strict policies of union suppression, the kind associated with the National Association of Manufacturers and the National Metal Trades Association. John Commons called the steel industry's approach to union avoidance "the low road"—keeping ahead of unions "not by doing better than the unions . . . but by doing worse, and doing it under the name of liberty and the open shop." Commons thought that "only the big stick of unionism or legislation" would bring an end to the industry's harsh conditions.[72]

Traditionalism resulted from economic pressures in industries where demand was elastic and changes in labor costs quickly affected a firm's ability to compete. The lowest profits and highest bankruptcy rates in the 1920s were in such industries as steel castings, coal, clothing, rubber products, leather, and wool. Mature industries that had begun to stagnate during the 1920s also experienced problems, including cotton textiles, railroads, and railway equipment. A few employers in these industries pursued experiments in union-management cooperation to raise productivity and stave off bankruptcy. Most, however, responded to their problems by intensifying the drive system and by hawkishly pursuing the open shop. More than half the judicial injunctions issued against unions between 1880 and 1930 were granted during the 1920s; antitrust suits against unions also reached a peak. Operating on thin margins, traditionalists did not have the luxury of pursuing more enlightened policies. For these firms, the downturn that started in 1929 made a bad situation even worse.[73]

The Death of Welfare Capitalism?

The historical literature on welfare capitalism tells a common story: the movement peaked during the 1920s, disintegrated during the Great Depression, and was followed by the rise of the modern labor movement and the welfare state. Subsequent interpretations build on this basic theme, differing only on issues of timing and in their appraisal of the significance of welfare capitalism for the events of the 1930s.

One perspective, associated with the historians Irving Bernstein and Stuart Brandes, asserts that welfare capitalism was already unstable, even dying, during the 1920s; the Depression simply knocked over a fragile structure. In his masterpiece, *The Lean Years*, Bernstein argues that welfare capitalism was "an unstable equilibrium" whose "cornerstone, the company union, had an inherent propensity to disintegrate." Similarly, Brandes claims that there was a "levelling off of interest" in welfare capitalism during the 1920s because "as corporations became larger and larger, their managements became so distant that they lost all contact with their employees."[74]

These interpretations capture aspects of welfare capitalism—indeed, it was rather rickety in laggard firms—yet they exaggerate the movement's instability. Part of the problem stems from lumping together disparate companies; the varieties of welfare capitalism make it hazardous to generalize about the movement as a whole. Another problem is the failure to recognize that employers in the 1920s consciously rejected older forms of paternalism in favor of more impersonal, pecuniary programs.

David Brody and Lizabeth Cohen offer a different perspective on the fall of welfare capitalism: that it was very much alive during the 1920s and might well have become the norm in American industry had it not been for the Depression's severity. Although we may prefer to think that welfare capitalism was "never a success, never persuaded workingmen that they were best off as wards of the employer, and never took deep root," the facts, says Brody, "suggest otherwise." The evidence—most recently compiled by Cohen—shows that before the Depression, industrial workers reacted favorably to welfare capitalism.[75] Because workers took welfare capitalism to heart, they felt all the more abandoned by their employers when the Depression struck, says Cohen. Yet even as workers looked in new directions for security—to unions and to government—they continued to believe in the potential for a "moral capitalism, born out of the promise of employers' welfarism in the twenties."[76]

This interpretation is a powerful one, but it fails to distinguish between vanguard and laggard employers. Although the Depression did force companies to shrink their work force and trim their welfare programs, the worst cuts were felt outside the vanguard—at cyclically sensitive companies that had long been ambivalent toward welfare capitalism. Here, inconsistent policies that rankled during the 1920s became a source of deep bitterness in the 1930s. Brody cites U.S. Steel and Ford as firms where "welfare capitalism had exhausted its credit" by the early 1930s, yet both were actually laggards in the 1920s. So were several of the Chicago employers studied by Cohen, including Armour Company and U.S. Steel's South Works. International Harvester, another of Cohen's companies, began the 1920s as a vanguard firm but gradually lowered its standards. Foremen regained control of the shop floor at Harvester's huge McCormick plant by the late 1920s. In these laggard companies, workers turned to unions in the 1930s not to reinstate moral capitalism but to transform employers' overblown rhetoric into reality.[77]

Complicating matters was the fact that laggard companies were among the hardest hit by the Depression. Durable-goods industries, where the laggards were concentrated, had to make deep cuts in employment between 1929 and 1932, far deeper than those of nondurable-goods manufacturers (50 percent versus 25 percent). Instead of feeling grateful, those who kept their jobs remained anxious that their fate rested in the hands of powerful and capricious foremen. *Fortune* magazine reported in 1936 that "steel workers are filled with stories of money lost to foremen after a better-than-usual pay, of minor officials who have small business interests that the men patronize in the hope of getting more work." Younger workers watched with guilt and smoldering anger as their elders—fathers and mothers, aunts and uncles—fell victim to a managerial belief that workers over the age of forty were too slow. At one steel mill where older workers with good service records were being dismissed—many of whom were immigrants who could not read English—the company justified the firings on the grounds that a state safety law prohibited workers unable to read English from operating cranes. Workers waited and watched for a chance to redress their grievances. When the opportunity came—in the form of mass unions—workers from heavy industry were quick to join, pushing their unionization rates far above those in the nondurable-goods and service industries.[78]

Of course, events of the 1930s were not determined strictly by economic factors. Had a larger number of firms adopted vanguard practices, they would have stood a better chance of delaying unionism or of acceding to it on their own terms, as did General Electric and Goodyear. Despite a severe slump in sales after 1929, Goodyear tried to preserve jobs and welfare benefits. The company's efforts—and its previous history of progressive policies—gave it a huge reservoir of goodwill to draw upon even as the work week dropped to 18 hours in 1931. More than a third of Goodyear's work force consisted of company loyalists who refused to support the Rubber Workers union and kept it in a precarious position until well into the 1940s.[79]

Because some vanguard companies (such as AT&T, Du Pont, IBM, Procter & Gamble, and Standard Oil of New Jersey) did not feel the Depression's full fury, however, it was easier for them to avoid layoffs, maintain welfare programs, and deter national unions. Western Electric, a subsidiary of AT&T, was one such place where welfare capitalism survived the Depression. The company bent over backwards to avoid layoffs and provide material aid to workers who lost their jobs. When union organizers arrived at Western Electric's Hawthorne works, employees remained loyal to the company union. Western Electric's experience was similar to that of other vanguard companies who were spared the brunt of the slump. Brody and Cohen are right—workers did turn to national unions when their employers failed to keep promises—but not all employers reneged, and among those who did, half-hearted promises angered workers more than sincere but failed attempts.[80]

A third perspective, that of economist Richard Wilcock and historian Howell Harris, asserts that prior experience with welfare capitalism did not have much influence over employers' responses to unionism in the 1930s. Wilcock and Harris distinguish four groups of companies. In the center were "sophisticates" who, like Du Pont, opposed unions but eschewed armed guards and brute force, and the "realists" who, like General Motors, recognized unions but did so with reluctance and only because resistance was seen as too costly. At the ideological poles were two smaller groups: the "belligerents," who violently opposed unions and were willing to fight bloody battles—as at National Steel—to fend them off, and the "progressives," chiefly U.S. Rubber, General Electric, and Crown Zellerbach, the only firms that immediately accepted national unions and strove to cooperate with them. The typology does not explain why companies selected one policy over another, although it implies that such choices were reactive rather than strategic.[81]

Another look at the 1930s, however, suggests that employer attitudes were heavily influenced by choices made in earlier years. Ostensible "realists"—General Motors, Allis-Chalmers, and Chrysler—were laggards that had dabbled in welfare capitalism during the 1920s, taken a bad bounce in the early 1930s, and then found themselves facing a majority of employees who supported national unions. The "sophisticates"—AT&T, Du Pont, Goodyear, and Jersey Standard—all had been part of the corporate vanguard during the 1920s, an experience that provided the know-how needed to pursue sophisticated anti-unionism in later years. Also, the vanguard's reliance on career policies in the 1920s helped to create a cadre of senior workers whose loyalty in the 1930s reassured company managers that sophisticated belligerence was sustainable.

Finally, the economy left its own mark on later events. Vanguard firms most affected by the crash—like Goodyear and International Harvester—had a hard time staving off national unions, although neither firm turned "realistic" until the Second World War. On the other hand, vanguard firms that weathered the Depression often were able to remain unorganized and to continue practicing welfare capitalism well beyond the 1930s.

Bear in mind that employer strategies and economic conditions are best thought of as probabilities that inclined industrial relations in particular directions without automatically determining their outcome. Whether a company stuck with welfare capitalism depended on a host of contingent factors—like luck and timing—that mediated the impact of history and markets. Attitudes mattered, too—those of management as well as of workers, not all of whom, it bears reemphasizing, favored unions and their social agenda. Working-class Black Legionnaires and Coughlinites staunchly opposed organized labor on ethnic and political grounds. Other workers viewed unions as a threat to their skill or hard-won perquisites.[82]

Still, even the luckiest of vanguard firms could not mechanically chug along tracks laid out in the 1910s and 1920s. The world changed too much after 1930 to permit that kind of stability: company unions became unlawful, collective bargaining was supported by a Congressional mandate, and Social Security seemed more reliable than private programs. Employers—whether vanguard companies or sleepy traditionalists roused by an organizing drive—needed new ideas. Coming out of the Depression, the most astute employers realized that welfare capitalism had to be reshaped to fit modern realities.

Two

Modernizing Welfare Capitalism

THE 1930S MARKED A TIME of rapid growth for the American labor movement and an unprecedented threat to the practice of welfare capitalism. Welfare capitalism faced challenges not only from militant labor but from a ravaged depression economy and a vastly expanded federal government. This baptism of fire, embodied in the experience of three firms—Kodak, Thompson, and Sears—provided the setting for the modern manors that would emerge strengthened after the war.

Union membership rose from less than three million in 1933 to almost fifteen million in 1945. After the Second World War, membership increased more slowly, to a little over eighteen million in 1960. Measured as a proportion of the private-sector labor force, union density peaked during the war at 40 percent. Throughout the late 1940s and 1950s, it fluctuated in a narrow band between 33 and 38 percent. The end of this "great upswing" came around 1960, when private-sector density started a decline that continues to the present day.

During the upswing, organized labor gained not only new members but public approval and political influence as well. The combination of economic and political power created the impression of an indomitable social movement. Belligerent employers who earlier had resisted unionism—big companies like General Motors and Bethlehem Steel—were compelled to concede a role for collective bargaining. Although relations were not cordial, they were becoming regular, even ritualized. If there were limits to labor's newfound power, the pundits did not perceive them.[1]

Despite rapid growth, unions remained concentrated in the construction, transportation, and manufacturing industries, and in the Midwest and on the coasts. This was well known in the 1940s and 1950s, but misconceptions clouded contemporary views of the situation. One fallacy was the belief that labor was about to burst beyond the firebreaks and spread to new regions, occupations, and industries. Another was the assumption that, within its sectors of strength, collective bargaining was the dominant mode of industrial relations. Although this was true in a strictly quantitative sense, observers failed to appreciate how important the exceptions were—the large northern firms that managed to stay partially or totally nonunion during the great upswing. Large nonunion firms followed wage and benefit patterns established in the union sector, a phenomenon that received considerable attention from economists in the 1950s. But these firms also set patterns (norms of conduct, personnel innovations, modes of employee relations) for their unionized counterparts to imitate, thus demonstrating how welfare capitalism—properly reconceived and reconstructed—could be an exemplar for a new era.

Welfare capitalism had to surmount challenges on several fronts: from the Depression, which created an obsession with security while throwing in doubt welfare capitalism's ability to provide it; from Congress, where the LaFollette Committee hearings on employer misconduct exposed welfare capitalism's harsher side; from the White House, whose social insurance programs made employer-provided benefits appear obsolete; from the new labor boards, which aggressively pursued allegations that employers were engaged in unlawful practices such as company unionism; and, finally, from a revitalized labor movement itself. Not only were unions forcing laggard companies to live up to their promises, but even when unions did nothing more than formalize existing procedures by writing them into their contracts, they undermined the claim—central to welfare capitalism—that the corporation was the worker's primary source of security.

As workers abandoned welfare capitalism, so did the intelligentsia. As during World War I, corporate and laborist liberals parted company over the issue of employee representation. Corporatists—including liberal intellectuals such as the economist Leo Wolman and the New Deal labor official Donald Richberg—felt that company unions still had a role to play and insisted that this option be permitted to appear on the ballot in representation elections. Laborists castigated company unions for being insufficiently democratic, and cast their lot with a resurgent labor movement.[2]

Reinforcing the laborist position was an economic critique of welfare capitalism. In the early 1930s, prominent economists asserted that the Depression had been caused by a lack of purchasing power—what they termed "underconsumption"—a claim that immediately became popular with liberals and later was systematized by John Maynard Keynes. According to the theory, government could more reliably redistribute income to the unemployed and the aged than could individual employers; private benefit programs might be efficient for the employers who had them but they did not guarantee macroeconomic health. Underconsumptionists favored anything that bolstered the share of income going to consumers: minimum wage laws, collective bargaining, and transfer programs such as unemployment insurance. The theory also revealed what many saw as the Achilles heel of company unionism: its inability to tolerate aggressive wage bargaining. Senator Robert F. Wagner, a key figure in the laborist network, forcefully argued in a 1934 article that the company union "has failed dismally to standardize or improve wage levels, for the wage question is a general one whose sweep embraces whole industries or States, or even the nation."[3]

With welfare capitalism's legitimacy shaken by the Depression and labor's reawakening, some corporatists—including Mary Follett and Arthur H. Young—were drawn to statist, even fascist, models of integrative unity. Others remained sympathetic to the vision of the 1920s. Yet the farsighted among them understood that welfare capitalism would have to change. Somehow it would have to acknowledge its adversaries while conceding as little as possible to any of them.[4]

The Experiences of Three Nonunion Companies

Energy for reforming welfare capitalism came primarily from large nonunion companies that had both the resources and the room to maneuver. Three such companies—each of whom made distinctive contributions to the modernization of welfare capitalism—were Eastman Kodak, Sears Roebuck, and Thompson Products.

Eastman Kodak's key product was photographic film, the demand for which grew steadily as amateur photography, movies, and X-rays became essential features of modern life. With a near monopoly on film manufacturing, Kodak generated enormous profits for its founder, George Eastman, and for its stockholders, many of whom were Kodak employees. The vast majority of Kodak's employees were located in Rochester, New York, where the company manufactured film along with related products like cameras and photographic chemicals. Of the three companies, Kodak changed least over the course of the great upswing. Stability, Kodak's most striking characteristic, stemmed from the fact that the company was, in many respects, sheltered. It had little competition in its product markets, was unscathed by the Depression, and faced only one serious organizing attempt between 1930 and 1960. In this environment, Kodak held fast to the welfare programs initiated by George Eastman and lobbied to prevent them from being displaced by the Social Security Act and other legislation.

Sears Roebuck was the nation's largest mail-order company from the 1890s through the 1920s. From its headquarters in Chicago, Sears shipped everything a farm family might need: livestock to linens, pants to pails. During this time, Sears did not have a single retail store; everything was sold out of its famous catalogue. But in the 1920s, as the nation's population became increasingly urban, Sears shifted its emphasis from mail order to retailing. By 1940, two-thirds of its employees were in its retail division and the company had stores across the nation, mostly in large towns and cities. Like Kodak, Sears belonged to the pre-1930 vanguard and was relatively sheltered from the turbulence of the 1930s. Beginning in the 1940s, however, Sears and Kodak followed divergent paths. Employment at Sears more than doubled between 1945 and 1960, while Kodak's employment barely changed. As retailing unions flexed their muscles in the 1940s and 1950s, they repeatedly made organizing attempts at Sears's far-flung facilities. To cope with this pressure, Sears initiated a series of innovative policies grounded in the behavioral sciences. When these company reforms failed to sustain worker loyalty, however, Sears played tough. It pioneered the use of management consultants to ferret out labor-law loopholes and to squelch employee dissent.

TABLE 2.1
Domestic Employment: 1935–1960

	Kodak	*Sears Roebuck*	*Thompson Products*
1935	17,840	49,500	2,510
1940	28,100	82,520	6,800
1945	45,000[a]	103,100	9,000
1950	46,400	154,620	13,400
1955	50,900	178,800	21,220
1960	45,860	207,000	22,970[b]

Sources: For Kodak and Thompson: *Moody's Manual of Investments: Industrial Securities*, various years. For Sears: Boris Emmet and John Jeuck, *Catalogues and Counters: A History of Sears, Roebuck and Company* (Chicago, 1950), 595 and company data.

[a] Estimate.

[b] Figure is for 1958, before merger with Ramo-Wooldridge.

Thompson Products was a gritty producer-goods company. At factories in Cleveland, Detroit, and elsewhere, Thompson manufactured precision automotive and aircraft parts using mass-production techniques. Thompson was best known for its valves, which were found inside many of the engines powering motor vehicles and airplanes. Thompson was the smallest of the three companies (see Table 2.1), although it was still large compared to most other U.S. firms. Heavy wartime demand for Thompson's aircraft, truck, and tank parts caused the firm to mushroom in size during the early 1940s. In the 1950s, it diversified into rockets, satellites, and other sophisticated products for the Air Force, eventually changing its name to TRW (Thompson-Ramo-Wooldridge). Unlike Kodak, Thompson had no formal welfare programs in the 1920s. Beginning in the 1930s, however, the company started benefit programs and company unions at all its facilities and kept them alive long after the Wagner Act. Even in the 1950s, company unions were set up at every new plant Thompson opened, this at a time when most employers had given up on them. Unlike Sears, Thompson had a blue-collar workforce concentrated in the Midwest's industrial heartland. Yet Thompson resembled Sears in its pursuit of innovative tactics. Using the behavioral sciences, it developed new ideas about employee involvement and small-group activities, while in the legal arena it aggressively tested the limits on employer behavior. Frederick C. Crawford, the company's president during this period, was a hero to the employer community and led the campaign that culminated in the anti-union Taft-Hartley Act of 1947.

The main operations of all three companies were centered in metropolitan areas of the Northeast and Midwest, where unions—and the working-class communities that nurtured them—remained vital forces in the 1940s and 1950s. Thus the companies stayed unorganized in spite of geography, not because of it.

The companies were not always similar in their technological and demographic characteristics. Sears had a large number of facilities; employment at

Kodak and Thompson was concentrated in just a few plants. And only Kodak relied on continuous-flow technology. Its huge investments in equipment also made it the only firm to have below-average ratios of labor costs to total costs.[5]

Kodak and Thompson—the two manufacturers—employed fewer unskilled laborers and more craftsmen and semiskilled operatives than the average manufacturing firm. Laborers were usually drawn to industrial unions, and their scarcity at Kodak and Thompson may have made it slightly easier for those firms to fend off unions. As for operatives, it is hard to generalize about their loyalties. On the one hand, they owed their wage premiums to training provided by employers. On the other hand, they typically stood at the top of the layoff list. The same ambiguity holds for skilled craftsmen. Depending on circumstances, they were among the first (the automobile industry) or last (the rubber tire industry) to join industrial unions. In any event, nothing in the historical record suggests that skill—its presence or absence—affected industrial relations at Kodak and Thompson (or Sears, for that matter).[6]

When it came to ethnicity, race, and gender, all three companies periodically played one group off against another. Sears, for example, reserved its best jobs for married men, Kodak preferred hiring native-born workers, and Thompson made a special effort to employ blacks at a time when many Cleveland unions refused to admit them.[7]

Because divide-and-conquer was a risky tactic, employers supplemented it with other strategies that tied employees to the company and, through the company—but *only* through the company—to each other. Just as in the 1920s, the strategies resulted in an elaborate array of welfare programs, both "soft" (company athletics, newspapers, and such) and "hard" (pecuniary benefits such as pensions); the precise mix varied from company to company. Because of its small size, Thompson offered fewer "hard" programs than Sears and Kodak, who were masters at conjuring new benefits that mixed economic and ideological objectives. Kodak tied its profit-sharing plan to stock dividends, thus concretizing the credo that employees had the same stake in the company as did shareholders. Sears, however, obliterated the distinction between employees and shareholders by investing its profit-sharing fund entirely in company stock. By the 1950s, Sears employees owned nearly a third of the company.

"Hard" benefits were intended to heighten the distinction between insiders and outsiders, between the firm and the labor market. Key to this distinction was the presumption of employment security—that maximum benefits would be paid to those who remained with the firm until retirement. Stable markets permitted Sears and Kodak to make implicit (and occasionally explicit) promises of employment security (in contrast to the income security provided by unionized firms). Once inside Sears or Kodak, employees could anticipate steady work and the first crack at internal vacancies. Pay, however, fluctuated somewhat more than in unionized firms (due to profit sharing) and employees were expected to move around the company, if needed. Sears's philosophy was to pay the person, not the position; it prided itself on having "interchangeable employees" who were not pigeonholed to the same extent as in other companies.[8]

Thompson was a bit different. Though it promoted from within, it made no promises concerning layoffs. Its employment system was more like that of a conventional manufacturer, with wages attached to jobs and cyclical adjustments occurring via layoffs. On the other hand, after layoffs in 1931 and 1932, Thompson experienced steady job growth during the rest of the 1930s and on into the postwar decades. With this stability came the same clannishness found at Sears and Kodak. Thompson was proud of having managers who had come up through the ranks, and it worked hard at softening status distinctions inside the firm: the firm even encouraged workers to call managers by their first name.

By focusing on employment security, these companies surely intended to shield themselves against national unions, yet, as in the 1920s, pursuing stability had other purposes as well—purposes rooted in consent rather than control, in productivity growth instead of cost reduction. The notion was to develop an industrial community, a Gemeinschaft, that would be an alternative to Taylorized bureaucracy and to market contractualism. Managers at all three companies believed that instability corroded institutional cohesiveness and that arm's-length relationships bred resentment and withdrawal. Anything that added to the web of ties binding workers and managers—even profit sharing—would make the organization more cooperative and thus more productive. These same ideas had been espoused by Henry Dennison and Mary Follett in the 1920s; now Elton Mayo and Chester Barnard reinterpreted them for a new generation of managers.[9]

Of the three, Sears came closest to discovering how the pieces fit together, that is, how integrative policies pointed the way to a more fluid and productive workplace. Sears's precocity stemmed from its personnel research program, which was created with help from leading university-based behavioral scientists. Initially a response to an upsurge in retail unionism, the program later took Sears far away from conventional labor-relations concerns.[10]

Sears was more sophisticated than Kodak and Thompson, yet they all moved in similar directions. Kodak's welfare plans originally were adopted to ward off external threats like unions and antitrust suits, but the company came to believe that stable jobs and generous benefits also had positive internal effects, which managers referred to as "cooperation." A common word in the Kodak lexicon, *cooperation* implied that management could be trusted to treat employees fairly and that employees would reciprocate in myriad ways: by keeping trade secrets, accepting transfers, and acquiescing to technological change. Thompson Products, the last of the three to adopt formal welfare policies, also became convinced that a cooperative ethos would promote desirable outcomes, even in situations where unionism was not a problem. Thompson installed at its research facilities in California, where unions were not an issue, the same programs developed for its blue-collar auto workers.[11]

Creation of a friendlier workplace was viewed suspiciously by unions. They were quick to criticize "human relations" programs, branding them as attempts to undercut unions (which they often were). On the other hand, managers at nonunion companies observed their unionized competitors (or, in the case of Sears, its unionized facilities) and saw how difficult it was to maintain trust in workplaces divided between "us" and "them." Efforts to promote hierarchical solidarity thus generated a self-confirming logic: there could be no place for unions in the enterprise community.[12]

The dynamics of corporate solidarity could also be seen outside the workplace. Ideological egalitarianism ("we are all middle class") had long been part of mainstream American culture, as sociologists Robert and Helen Lynd discovered at "Middletown" (Muncie, Indiana) in the 1920s. When they revisited Middletown in the 1930s, the schools and newspapers were still asserting the city's classlessness. One editorial even claimed that "there is no permanent class of hired laborers amongst us." Despite the polarized climate of the 1930s, the Lynds found Middletown's blue-collar residents receptive to such bromides, more so than workers in the big cities, where the working class ostensibly was "tainted by a foreign element with the stereotyped slogans of . . . radicalism."[13]

Yet neither Middletown nor nonunion companies were able to realize their own equally stereotyped slogans of unity and democracy. Welfare capitalism brought workers closer to management, but management still had the final say on most issues (just as the wealthy "X family" still called the shots in Middletown). Here lay the Gemeinschaft's darker side, where coercion was used in pursuit of positive ends like community. To justify coercion, company managers turned to the rhetoric of relationship: unions were tagged as "outsiders"; those who supported them were said to be harming the enterprise community. After all, nonunion firms were planned communities; dissent was not easily tolerated.[14]

Another feature distinguishing Kodak, Sears, and Thompson was the absence of an armory. With the exception of one incident at a Thompson subsidiary in 1935, no use was made of tear gas, guns, strikebreakers, militias, or other physical threats. Indeed, the companies' ability to resist unions was aided by the realization that belligerence had become a losing strategy. Violence not only provoked unwanted scrutiny from government agencies but it hardened attitudes at work and in the community as well. And if there was one thing these companies understood well, it was that attitudes—of employees, government officials, and the public—were key to maintaining control.[15]

In the battle for employee loyalty, companies relied on everything from attitude surveys and nondirective interviewing to sociometry and new methods of mass communication. Each firm also had staff specialists who counseled employees about on-the-job problems, while surreptitiously identifying potential troublemakers. Social conformity was encouraged by the insular atmosphere of these companies. Sears, for example, refused to discuss employee relations with outsiders despite the fact that the firm was continually in the news, and secretive Kodak shut itself off behind what employees jokingly called "the silver curtain."

Although the new pressure tactics were legally dubious, employers boldly continued to test the limits, especially on issues such as employer free speech and company unions. Thompson kept its company unions alive despite numerous orders to disband them, whereas Sears flouted the labor law by relying on the Teamsters Union and professional labor "consultants" to sow confusion during organizing campaigns. Both companies also tried to expand the legal limits. Frederick C. Crawford, Thompson's president, led the the National Association of Manufacturers in the fight for passage of the Taft-Hartley Act, and Sears lobbied for legal reform through its leadership role in the American Retail Federation. Kodak was less aggressive simply because it faced fewer challenges from unions. It did join other companies in efforts to make the law more favorable to employers, however, and was represented on every major labor relations lobby of the 1940s. In short, the companies did not consistently pursue a single strategy. They worked hard to develop cooperative norms inside the workplace but, like Janus, showed a belligerent face to the outside world and to those who violated company norms.

The 1947 Taft-Hartley Act is often pointed to as a reason (if not *the* reason) for the end of the great upswing. Yet even before its passage, Thompson and Sears—as well as other companies—were violating the law with impunity, and did so because they understood and exploited flaws in the Wagner Act. The Wagner Act's enforcement machinery, housed in the National Labor Relations Board (NLRB), was complex, slow, and poorly equipped to terminate illegal behavior in flagrante delicto. By the time the NLRB acted, an organizing drive could have long since lost its momentum. Also, the NLRB's penalties were quite mild. The benefits to employers of breaking the law usually exceeded the costs. And because the NLRB lacked direct enforcement powers, companies like Thompson and Sears found themselves in appellate courts that often were more sympathetic to employers than the NLRB, even on seemingly straightforward issues like company unionism. Finally, the NLRB itself became increasingly conservative over time. When Taft-Hartley was enacted, several of the act's provisions already were de facto practices of the board; in these areas, Taft-Hartley simply ratified the status quo. Put another way, the law was symbolic as well as causal; it registered the outcome of earlier economic and political struggles between unions and management. Although it is impossible to construct a counterfactual scenario to demonstrate how labor relations might have evolved without Taft-Hartley, it is important to remember that the union success rate—as measured by the number of NLRB elections won by labor—started to decline during World War II, that is, *before* Taft-Hartley became law.[16]

Regular engagement with the outside world distinguished modern welfare capitalism from its earlier forms. Given the large role government was playing in labor relations and labor markets during the great upswing, employers of necessity became more politically active. Kodak, Sears, and Thompson were heavily involved in efforts to pass Taft-Hartley; such political mobilization by employers checked labor's own legislative efforts and, in the long run, proved as important as Taft-Hartley itself. Thus, whenever labor attempted to press for a more generous and comprehensive welfare state, it found itself facing stiff opposition from employers, especially nonunion companies seeking to preserve an arena for private welfare programs. Kodak's treasurer Marion Folsom was a key figure in the battle to design a welfare state that would complement modern welfare capitalism.

Another facet of welfare capitalism's external orientation was its reliance on the social and behavioral sciences. Linkages between industry and academia had started in the 1920s, encouraged by support from the Personnel Research Federation, the Rockefeller Foundation, the Social Science Research Council, and others. But the Depression cut short these efforts. The big move in this direction did not come until the 1940s, which were a time of great intellectual ferment in the behavioral sciences. During World War II, government agencies—especially the army—hired thousands of psychologists and other behavioral scientists. After the war these experts readily found jobs as independent consultants, corporate staff specialists, and university-based researchers; the result was an intricate network linking corporations to academia and the military.[17]

Before the war, industrial psychology was narrowly focused on hiring methods and supervisor training. Despite John Dewey's belief in psychology's liberating potential, its industrial practitioners took a highly mechanistic approach, which, as one critic put it, "sought to apply the concepts and methodology of engineering to the problems of human organization. There was a narrowness of outlook and literalness in translation that often produced sterile results." But after 1940, the applied behavioral sciences became more dynamic as a result of infusions from social psychology, anthropology, psychiatry, and other fields. Elton Mayo's renowned studies of group behavior at Western Electric's Hawthorne plant were partly responsible for this change; they led many to use the terms "human relations" and "behavioral science" interchangeably.[18]

At the center of the human relations movement during these years were large nonunion companies like Sears, whose personnel research department was highly visible in the academic community. Unionized firms had a hard time getting human relations techniques to take root in their polarized organizations. The link between the behavioral sciences and nonunion status also was causal: companies taking the lead in this area found that the new techniques helped build employee loyalty and identify union supporters—which is precisely why critics condemned industry's use of the behavioral sciences.[19]

The critics—labor economists and sociologists—faulted the behavioral sciences for suppressing conflict at the workplace. The critics were sympathetic to organized labor and were disturbed by the anti-union thrust of the new techniques. They saw open expression of conflict—especially through collective bargaining—as healthier and more democratic than the integrative methods of human relations, and they charged Mayo and others with obscuring hierarchy and engaging in manipulative social engineering; this was a reprise of the conflict between liberal corporatists and laborists that first had surfaced in the 1910s.[20]

Behavioral scientists defended their approach by arguing that consensual forms of persuasion were preferable to the drive system and to the spiritless ideas—such as Taylorism—that underpinned it. Proponents of human relations believed that their methods would force managers to treat employees as "flesh and blood men and women, with sentiments, ambitions, and needs of their own ranging far beyond the confines of the organization." As for unions, they were held to be necessary only where managers ignored the individual or hewed to the Taylorist dogma that workers cared solely about money.[21]

In retrospect, it is clear that each side in the debate over human relations exaggerated its claims. The critics underemphasized the positive contributions of human relations to personnel management: respect for the individual, sensitivity to emotions and personality, and a concern with fairness. The human relationists, however, consistently minimized the ways in which their methods slighted power relations at work and, therefore, helped management to undermine independent unions. To say that unions were necessary only to combat the effects of Taylorism was doubly wrong: it misconstrued the purposes of unionism and exaggerated the virtuousness of post-Taylorist management.

In fact, organized labor was most successful where Taylorism was strongest. Confronted with scientific management as a fait accompli, the new industrial unions pragmatically constructed their regulatory systems around the division of labor wrought by the Taylorists. Hence unionism's contractual restraints reinforced Taylor's unimaginative approach to work design. In contrast, the behavioral sciences were sensitive to the shortcomings of Taylorism. James Worthy, who headed the personnel research department at Sears, castigated Taylorism for its "efforts to separate the 'thinking' part of the job from the 'doing' parts." The result, he said, was "an organization where there are many layers of supervision [and] employees feel restricted, controlled, and policed. There is little opportunity for creative effort and the development of ideas." Although Worthy's rhetoric was more attractive than were actual working conditions at Sears, it nevertheless pointed the way to a powerful critique not only of scientific management but also of modern unionism.[22]

In the 1920s, welfare capitalism had been able to ignore developments in the union sector. The AFL's unions were cautious, exclusive, and situated in older industries; they rarely presented a major threat to managerial capitalism. Not so during the great upswing, when personnel managers were forced to pay close attention to the labor movement. Unions began to offer an inspiring and legally sanctioned alternative to welfare capitalism. They regularly won new rights at the bargaining table—from seniority to health benefits—and championed a slew of social legislation.

To meet the challenge, nonunion employers monitored collective bargaining in their own markets and in bellwether industries like steel and automobiles. Union wage patterns kept nonunion companies alert to pay issues whether or not an organizing drive was under way. Kodak, for example, repeatedly pumped managers at a General Motors plant in Rochester for information on impending developments with the United Automobile Workers (UAW). Even companies suffused by the human relations approach did not for a moment risk acting on the assumption that employees would trade economic rewards for emotional ones. As Sears chairman Robert E. Wood said, "I think the secret of proper relations with labor is always beat them to the gun. . . . I mean we keep track of that cost of living just as carefully as the government did, and when we saw it going up, we gave the men and women raises across the board. . . . Well, they felt management was looking after their interests, and we were. The result is that labor relations in Sears have been very, very happy."[23]

Benefit patterns were watched as closely as wages. Because benefits (by then called "fringes") were central to welfare capitalism, nonunion employers were reluctant to cede leadership on this issue to organized labor. The result was a kind of leapfrogging between nonunion employers and unions. Kodak's Marion Folsom recalled that when General Motors and the UAW came out with a noncontributory health plan in the 1950s, Kodak "had to fall in line. . . . As long as there's somebody else in the world has got it a little bit better, the industrial relations people say we have to go along." Imitation extended even to minor benefits. When Sears had to decide whether holidays should be considered as time worked when computing weekly overtime, it resolved the question by surveying major union contracts.[24]

Even the contractualism associated with collective bargaining was, to some extent, reproduced within large nonunion firms. By the 1940s, supervisors of nonunion workers were required to follow complex rules regarding promotions, layoffs, and dismissals. The rules assigned heavy weight to seniority and made use of job evaluations, which, by tightening the link between job titles and pay levels, further constrained the autonomy of line managers. The codification spree caused employee handbooks at nonunion companies to begin to resemble collective bargaining agreements both in size and complexity. Kodak, for example, consciously modeled its "Code of Industrial Relations" after a union contract; at Sears, the personnel manual grew from 36 pages in 1932 to 105 pages in 1939, with the latter edition divided into 51 separate subjects.[25]

Imitation became controversial and potentially unlawful when employers unilaterally established unionlike mechanisms for employee representation. Only Thompson went so far as to create full-fledged company unions that negotiated over a wide range of subjects. Kodak and Sears limited representation to particular issues: at Kodak, employees at every plant elected coworkers to administer the company's recreational programs; at Sears, regional elections were held to select delegates to the Profit Sharing Advisory Council, a group that met several times a year to convey employee sentiments to the plan's trustees. Sears claimed that the council offered a "sense of participation," though actual participation was more circumscribed than under collective bargaining.[26]

Despite such imitation, large nonunion companies did not exactly copy the union sector. Grievances, for example, were handled less formally, with personnel managers taking an almost therapeutic approach to resolving conflicts between employees and supervisors. Reward systems also were relatively informal and individualized. Although seniority was a factor in promotions, it was applied less rigorously than in unionized firms, with greater weight given to merit, ability, and other factors. Nonunion firms made fewer across-the-board pay increases; their wages were more dependent on "the individual and merit," as a Sears executive said. But while managers at nonunion firms liked to boast of their respect for the individual, much of that rhetoric was a defensive necessity. An emphasis on merit—and the use of objective merit-rating procedures—created the impression that rewards were given fairly, thereby undercutting demands for strict seniority rules. Employees at Thompson Products were in the midst of an organizing drive when management introduced a merit-rating plan in response to charges that foremen were capricious. The company said that the plan would be "of untold value IF at some future date" stricter seniority rules were demanded.[27]

The two sectors also approached economic security differently. The typical unionized firm used a layoff/rehire system that allowed for periodic joblessness while providing income (both public and private unemployment insurance) to tide workers over. In contrast, large nonunion firms sought to avoid layoffs by a maximal reliance on transfers, retraining, and work sharing (cutting hours in lieu of layoffs). One exception was Thompson, whose seniority-based layoff system was "unionesque," at least on paper, although the firm laid off few employees during the 1940s and 1950s.

To sum up, a major change in welfare capitalism was its heightened responsiveness to the outside world. Before 1929, welfare capitalism was rather insular and politically unsophisticated, even though it pronounced itself a superior alternative to social democracy and trade unionism. But the Depression dealt a severe blow to this claim, while giving rise to movements that challenged the rationale for welfare capitalism. Nonunion employers responded to the surge of labor and legislative activism by becoming more cosmpolitan and by reaching beyond the confines of the firm: to engage in political struggle, to forge ties to the media and the intelligentsia, and to emulate labor's achievements.[28]

Cents and Circumstance

Money and managerial talent were critical resources for companies trying to modernize welfare capitalism; they gave ambitious firms the means to proceed. Another critical resource was the goodwill of workers—their readiness

TABLE 2.2
Net Income as a Percentage of Sales

Period	Chemical Industry	Kodak	Auto Parts Industry[a]	Thompson	Retail Industry	Mail-Order Industry	Sears
1936–40	15.77	15.52	8.84	6.34	3.76	4.72	5.54
1941–45	9.71	9.66	4.40	2.52	3.11	3.18	3.76
1946–50	12.62	12.80	6.70	4.90	4.22	3.72	5.64
1951–55	10.36	9.58	4.96	3.72	3.00	2.91	4.32
1956–60	9.80	12.74	3.96	2.94	3.08	2.98	4.60
1961–65	10.22	14.32	2.22	3.20	3.24	1.70	5.16

Source: Standard & Poor's *Industry Surveys*, various years. Note that "Industry" data are derived from the fifteen largest firms in each industry, excluding the target companies.

[a] From 1959 onward Thompson becomes TRW and industry figures are for aerospace.

to trust their economic fate to management. Although the Depression deeply tested that trust, the companies examined here fared better than most, which conferred an advantage that lasted for years. Of course, the success of new programs also depended on chance and timing, factors over which managers had little control.

Of the three companies, Kodak and Sears were the most profitable, both in an absolute sense and as compared to their industrial competitors. Thompson Products was in a lesser class; in some years it was less profitable than major competitors like Dana, Bendix, and Eaton. Yet it consistently operated in the black and was well regarded by investment analysts (see Table 2.2).[29]

Although financial resources were necessary to modernize welfare capitalism, they were not sufficient; companies also had to be willing to spend their money on employee programs. Despite the occasional Cyrus Ching (at U.S. Rubber) or Joe Wilson (at Xerox), employers fought fiercely—and spent freely—when faced with an organizing drive. The difference came during quieter times, when a concern with unions, and with employee relations as a whole, faded from the minds of most executives. Thus, when the tide turned against labor in the early 1920s, many firms slashed their personnel expenditures. The same thing happened after the Second World War, when companies again cut back on welfare programs like employee counseling and attitude testing, which, as one observer reported, were "suspected by top management and the budgeters as being a luxury and a 'newfangled' idea."[30]

Such cuts never occurred at the companies examined here. For them, employee relations remained a priority whether or not unions were knocking at the company gates. This priority stemmed not only from anti-unionism, which was widespread in the business community, but also from top management's belief that the corporate Gemeinschaft possessed moral worth, boosted productivity, and aligned employee interests with those of management. Corporatist values, in other words, strengthened the commitment to fight unions.

In all three companies, those values were embedded in the managerial hierarchy. Each company's top personnel executive was a powerful individual, a member of the corporate policy group who had direct access to the chief executive officer. This set up a self-reinforcing cycle: a powerful personnel function kept the companies open to new ideas and sent a signal down the ranks that employee relations would not be subordinated to other goals. As a result, the companies were better able to create structures that unions found tough to crack.

A high-powered personnel function had its virtues but it also created knotty problems: close control from above annoyed local managers and made them overly cautious; on the other hand, if headquarters didn't scrutinize local employee relations, there was the risk that an inept manager might create a situation conducive to unionism. Each company came up with its own response to this paradox. Thompson, the smallest of the three, followed the most traditional path. With the bulk of its plants located in the Cleveland vicinity, headquarters staff could directly monitor shop-floor relations without the clutter of bureaucratic controls found in more dispersed organizations. Sears and Kodak took a somewhat different approach. Sears gave its store managers considerable autonomy while regulating their behavior through unobtrusive controls such as employee surveys, a strong corporate culture, and a centralized managerial promotion system. Similarly, Kodak's plant personnel managers had a strong tradition of independence but were kept in line by the company's inbred managerial culture.

This approach was consistent with the multidivisional (M-form) structure pioneered by Du Pont, General Motors, and Jersey Standard in the 1920s, whereby corporate divisions were allowed to maintain their operating autonomy so long as they met targets set by company headquarters. The M-form structure was still a rarity in the 1930s and 1940s; only in the 1950s did it become well established in American industry. Companies lacking the M-form either had weak central personnel staffs or went too far in the opposite direction, clamping down on local operations when unions became a threat. Thus, without the M-form, large companies found it difficult to strike the sort of balance achieved at Kodak and Sears. Had the M-form diffused at an earlier date, American management's response to the great upswing might have been more effectual. How different the results would have been is hard to judge: although M-form pioneers such as Jersey Standard and Du Pont remained nonunion, General Motors did not. Also, Kodak and Sears were not thoroughbred M-form companies; they relied more on psychological controls and strong corporate cultures than the typical M-form organization, with its thick bands of middle management.[31]

Here and there, managerial capitalism created a new breed of executives who, though they retained a distrust of outsiders, conceded a role for government and pragmatically accommodated to unions when cost-benefit calculations told them to do so. Such was the case with Gerard Swope of General Electric and Myron C. Taylor, head of U.S. Steel, whose background was in Wall Street finance rather than steelmaking.

Nevertheless, other companies retained a mind-set from the era of proprietary capitalism, when the reigning doctrine had been the "freedom to control" (the employer's right to run his business without interference from unions, government, or other outsiders, who sometimes included Wall Street financiers). The doctrine reappeared in the 1940s as "management rights" and was aggressively promoted by the National Association of Manufacturers (NAM). Although some NAM members came from smaller, often family-owned, enterprises, by the 1940s the organization was dominated by large industrial corporations, including the firms examined here.[32]

None of the firms in this study was family owned or operated, none was small, yet all preserved the anti-union mentality of proprietary capitalism. One reason for this was the persistence in these firms of a founder's culture. At Kodak, this culture developed during the forty-year reign of its founder, George Eastman, a conservative, reticent man who identified with his Yankee work force. When Eastman died in 1932, he left behind two generations of inbred managers, men who continued to run the company into the 1960s. Eastman's protégés shared his commitment to welfare capitalism as well as his view that unions were anathema and an affront to private property. Although these were the beliefs of a self-made man, they guided Kodak long after it had become a managerial organization. It was well understood by Kodak managers of the 1950s that a sacred tradition would be broken if a union came into the company on their watch.[33]

At Sears and Thompson, the founder's culture had different origins. Initially, Sears stood in the welfare capitalist vanguard as the result of policies established during the long reign of its founder, Julius Rosenwald. But the Rosenwald era had a declining influence on Sears after the mid-1920s, when an outsider—General Robert E. Wood—took over the company. Wood led Sears into retailing, which soon supplanted mail order as the company's dominant business. Wood also rid Sears of Rosenwald's friends and family and replaced them with his own management team. The one family member who remained active in Sears—Rosenwald's son, Lessing—cut all ties to Wood in 1940, when Wood refused to condemn publicly the anti-Semitic speeches of his fellow isolationist Charles A. Lindbergh.[34]

Strategically and managerially, Wood created an entirely new company. He was the "founder" of the modern Sears Roebuck, a role he played to the hilt. He enjoyed being seen as the benefactor of his employees and, like Eastman, kept his hands on the corporate reins for a long, long time. Even after his formal retirement in 1954, Wood remained on the board of directors—which selected Sears's chief executives—until 1966, a career of nearly four decades. The men Wood picked as protégés shared his vision and values, including his conservatism and his deep aversion to unions.

Much the same story can be told for Thompson Products. After Frederick C. Crawford took over from Charles Thompson, the founder, in 1933, he thoroughly transformed the company. By the 1960s, the once-small producer of auto parts had become a "Fortune 500" diversified manufacturing company. Crawford initiated the transformation during the 1930s, when he vastly expanded the company's production of aircraft parts, a less cyclical and more rapidly growing business than auto parts. After the war, Crawford diversified into related "high tech" products such as missiles and avionics, setting the stage for Thompson's merger with Ramo-Wooldridge in 1958. At that point, after twenty-five years at the helm, Crawford retired, but he stayed active in company affairs, as did his personnel chief, Raymond Livingstone, and his legal adviser, J. David Wright, both of whom remained corporate officers through the 1960s.

By recasting their companies' business strategies, both Wood and Crawford became de facto corporate founders. Both were in office for several decades—a long time by managerial standards—which gave them the chance to turn their personal views on labor issues into corporate policy. Both men also were passionate ideologues: deeply conservative, active in right-wing causes, hostile to the cultural and financial elites of the East, and willing to take great risks to keep unions out of their companies. Neither man would have said, as did one employer in the late 1930s, "I'll go along with the union as long as it's top dog here. My idea is to stay out of trouble."[35]

Crawford and Wood, despite their conservatism, were populists—charismatic, plain-talking leaders who seemed genuinely to enjoy mingling with employees. Crawford was trained as an engineer and had an affinity for shop culture. (The same was true of Frank Lovejoy, Eastman's successor.) Wood's background was military rather than technical, but he was an odd sort of military man, someone who abhorred bureaucracy or anything else that threatened the small-town values he sought to preserve at Sears. Unlike noblesse oblige, the paternalism of Crawford, Lovejoy, and Wood was vertically inclusive; managers and workers were all just plain folks. There were, however, two anomalies—nonwhites and women—who remained second-class citizens in these corporate communities. Neither Kodak nor Sears had an appreciable number of nonwhite employees, nor did Thompson until World War II. And although Kodak and Sears employed many women (unlike Thompson), all three firms directed most of their generosity to male employees. Corporate populism, then, was primarily for white men; the industrial community was a brotherhood in which race and gender reinforced the ties between managers and workers.

The Great Depression was a crucible through which few firms passed unscathed. Employment and wages dropped precipitously between 1929 and 1933, and recovery was slow and erratic. The 1938 recession was a painful reprise of the decade's early years. Many firms did not return to pre-Depression employment levels until the 1940s. Hardest hit and slowest to recover were older industries, like textiles, and newer industries in the transportation-equipment sector: cars, trucks, glass, rubber, and primary metals. At steel blast furnaces, for example, more than half of all production jobs were lost between 1929 and 1933, a problem compounded by the industry's "chunky"

TABLE 2.3
Production Employment, Selected Industries and Firms

	Percentage Change, 1929–1933	*1935/1929*	*1939/1929*
All Manufacturing[1]	−31	.85	.96
Blast Furnaces[2]	−52	.61	.78
Cars & Trucks[2]	−46	.87	.88
Chemicals[2]	−17	.95	.90
Food Products[1]	−10	1.08	1.18
All Retail Stores[3,4]	−29	.91	1.07
Chain Stores[4]	−1	1.09	1.24
Kodak[5]	−17[a]	1.19	1.89
Sears Roebuck[5]	+10	1.19	1.75
Thompson Products[5]	−56	1.09	1.74

Sources: [1] U.S. Bureau of Labor Statistics, *Handbook of Labor Statistics* (Washington, D.C., 1975), 105; [2] U.S. Census Bureau, *Census of Manufactures: 1954*, vol. 2 (Washington, D.C., 1958), tables 28–3, 33A–4, 38B–3; [3] David M. Polak, "Evidence Study of Retail Trade," National Recovery Administration, Division of Review (Washington, D.C. 1935), 8–11; [4] U.S. Census Bureau, *16th Census of the United States, Manufactures: 1939* (Washington, D.C., 1942), 19; [5] *Moody's Industrial Manual*, various issues; and company data.

[a] Data for 1929–1933 are for Rochester only.

technology. By 1939, the hard-hit industry had refilled only about half of the jobs that had been there a decade earlier (see Table 2.3).[36]

Companies with massive layoffs and subsequent slow growth were not happy places in the 1930s. Those who lost their jobs underwent great hardship and found their careers permanently impaired. The experience created a lifelong preoccupation with security and stability. The same was true of workers who held on to their jobs. For them, the discrepancy between present and past, between the promise of the 1920s and the hardships of the 1930s, remained a bothersome reality. Interviewing blue-collar workers in the mid-1930s, Helen and Robert Lynd uncovered an overwhelming sense of "fear, resentment, insecurity and disillusionment." The Lynds, however, thought these feelings were "an individual experience for each worker, and not a thing generalized by him into a 'class' experience."[37]

As the Lynds suggested, it was the individual worker's sense of betrayal and injustice that provided a rallying point for America's bread-and-butter unions. Unions promised to protect the individual worker's sweat equity—what labor economist Selig Perlman called "property rights in the job"—an entitlement that had been nurtured by welfare capitalism in the 1920s. When workers rebelled in the 1930s, says the historian Lizabeth Cohen, it was not against the class structure so much as against "what they perceived as shortcomings in welfare capitalism." Workers still believed in welfare capitalist values, a faith, she says, that "could be seen in the distinctions they themselves made between companies. Despite frustrations with program failures, workers considered some employers to be better welfare capitalists than others. The criteria they used to make those judgments were derived from welfare capitalist ideals."[38]

Who were these "better welfare capitalists"? They were employers who kept their work force and welfare programs relatively intact during the 1930s. Typically they came from industries in which contraction was less severe than average; these were the same industries in which recovery was most rapid. These "dynamic" industries, as Michael Bernstein calls them—on which the postwar economy was based—included food processing, appliances, chemicals, and services. Kodak and Sears were located in this privileged sector, on top of which they both showed steadier and more rapid job growth than the average firm in their industries.

Corporate policies contributed to steady employment during the Depression. Both Kodak and Sears tried to mitigate layoffs through cuts in hours and planned transfers. The firms also stabilized jobs through their profit-sharing plans, which shifted the adjustment burden from employment to wages. As General Wood explained, "The greatest advantage in a profit-sharing plan is that it is flexible. It is very difficult to reduce a high wage once established. It becomes a fixed charge and when bad times come along, it eventually hurts both industry and the worker. But profit sharing goes up and down with the profits." And so it did at Sears and Kodak in the early 1930s.[39]

Again, the Thompson experience deviates a bit. Auto parts were cyclically sensitive, and Thompson had neither a profit-sharing plan nor a legacy of stabilization. Hence Thompson workers were vulnerable to job cuts in the early 1930s. Nevertheless, in the midst of the Depression, Thompson adopted an aggressive diversification program that moved it into the growing replacement parts market and into aircraft parts manufacturing. As other auto parts manufacturers languished, Thompson enjoyed extremely rapid job growth. Come 1935, employment at Thompson surpassed its 1929 levels, a performance matched by few manufacturing firms. Thompson continued on this trajectory through the postwar decades.

Although not determinative, these economic trends nevertheless were important to workers at Thompson, Kodak, and Sears. Like other people, they interpreted their Depression experiences not only through economic logic but in accordance with social norms, including those established by welfare capitalism. Unstable employers were judged harshly, while stable companies came off looking quite good. The latter apparently had kept their promises and had done so when other firms—even from the vanguard—broke theirs. Managers at Sears and Kodak were quick to claim credit for the low rate of layoffs, even though it had more to do with sectorial conditions than managerial skill or morality. Such claims, however, were no different from the blame unions heaped on cyclically sensitive companies for economic outcomes beyond employer control. In both cases, the arguments were persuasive.

As for Thompson, although its layoffs were heavy in 1932, it had made few promises in the 1920s regarding stability, and beginning in 1933, Thompson workers saw their job opportunities expand rapidly while the rest of the region stretching from Buffalo to Chicago was held back by the slow-recovering steel and automotive industries. Credit for exceptional growth redounded to the benefit of Thompson's management, as at Sears and Kodak. Also, being employed by a thriving company had the effect of cutting off Thompson workers from others in the region. While most industrial workers remained out of work or stuck in sluggish firms, Thompson employees enjoyed steadily growing opportunities. With this came a sense of separateness from the Depression-based "culture of unity" that in other places served to unite diverse workers and to give the CIO its vitality.[40]

This is not meant to imply that workers at Thompson—or at Kodak and Sears, for that matter—were unaffected by the Depression. They were, though the Depression reinforced rather than ruptured the ties binding them to their employers. One might say that ties at these companies formed a vertical culture of unity in contrast to the horizontal solidarity of the labor movement. Grateful for a safe harbor, one Sears worker said in the 1940s, "I value security above everything else, and this job offers security more than any other I know of. As I see it, this is a necessary job. They'll always have to have people doing this kind of work [even] in case of another depression." Managers were aware of these feelings, believing, as one executive said, that "this deep-seated sense of insecurity is unquestionably responsible for much of the behavior of labor which has been so distressing for management in recent years."[41]

Recently, Glen Elder and other sociologists have found that an obsession with security was characteristic not only of Depression workers but also of children raised in those years, the cohort that began entering the work force during World War II. After the war, despite the prosperity around them, working-class youths raised during the Depression shared the anxieties of their parents, a burden they carried throughout adulthood. Of particular interest is the finding that these "children of the depression" attached special value not only to economic security but also to their families and to the familial atmosphere provided by large, paternal employers. This gave an obvious advantage to companies like the three examined here, which could—and did—offer stability to their risk-averse employees. As a Sears manager said in 1948: "Management has a tremendous responsibility in the years ahead for restoring the confidence of its workers in its ability to provide them with immediate and long-range job security. . . . Regardless of the general level of employment, the worker needs to feel secure in his own individual job, to be able to plan for his own individual future."[42]

During the 1940s, the CIO's Depression-born culture of unity fissured along several fault lines. Racial, gender, and ethnic tensions resurfaced in the workplace, while factionalism fragmented the labor movement. Organized labor found itself slipping from the moral high ground on which it had stood in the 1930s, when it was seen as the underdog battling for basic rights. The

Cold War and the return to prosperity gave new life to old charges that unions were radical, irresponsible, inefficient, and bureaucratic—in short, that they were un-American. It is impossible to say how much damage these events inflicted on labor's organizing prospects, but they definitely braked the movement's momentum, even before World War II was over. Employers now had the upper hand and they used it. Taft-Hartley was one result; so was the return of more belligerent anti-union tactics.[43]

By the mid-1950s, anti-labor passions had cooled somewhat, in part because of the CIO's efforts to establish its respectability. It purged several Communist-dominated unions from its ranks and, in 1955, merged with the AFL, ending two decades of internecine conflict. Unionized employers made it clear they were seeking less conflictual and more orderly labor relations, not, as in the 1920s, a return to the open shop. After a drop from its wartime high, union membership stabilized in the 1950s. Despite some annual fluctuations, the same proportion of workers belonged to unions in 1960 as a decade earlier, about 31 percent of the nonagricultural labor force.

But this seeming stability masked serious problems. Nonunion employers were taking a harder line than ever before, a fact reflected in union organizing statistics: after an initial drop in 1943, the union "win" rate in representation elections moved steadily downward during the rest of the 1940s and 1950s. Although there were some annual fluctuations, the trend was unmistakable, with the rate falling more than twenty percentage points during the 1950s alone. Even as industrial relations scholars wrote approvingly that a new "maturity" was being achieved in union-management relations, nonunion managers quietly crowed over their improving fortunes. In 1949, Clarence Caldwell, the top personnel manager at Sears, sent a memo to the company's president in which he observed that unions "may continue to grow in terms of total membership but it is very doubtful that the rate of growth will exceed the rate of population growth. Organizing activity has progressed beyond the point of diminishing returns." Caldwell was prescient; by the end of the 1950s most executives had come to share his point of view. When Robert L. Heilbroner analyzed speeches given by major business leaders in the late 1950s, he found "a more realistic assessment of the diminished threat offered to the business community by organized labor during the postwar era." The great upswing that had started in the 1930s was just about spent.[44]

For Sears, Kodak, and Thompson, these trends were, to say the least, highly favorable. None of the three experienced a major organizing drive in the 1930s, when labor was at its peak, and Thompson was the only one to face a major campaign during the war. The CIO's Thompson campaign, however, dragged on into the postwar years, when it was torn apart by factionalism and unfavorable rulings from an increasingly conservative judiciary. At Kodak, the United Electrical Workers (UE) suffered from similar bad timing. The UE launched its Kodak campaign in 1947, just when the FBI, the House Committee on Un-American Activities, and the Association of Catholic Trade Unionists began their own drive to discredit the union's Communist leadership. Meanwhile, the CIO's retail affiliate (the Retail, Wholesale, and Department Store Employees Association), which was judged the one retail union capable of organizing a national department store chain like Sears, decided to target Montgomery Ward first, a strategic error. By the time the union turned to Sears—after World War II—its treasury was nearly empty and it was embroiled in the same kind of factional disputes that paralyzed the auto and electrical unions. The AFL's Retail Clerks did not attempt a campaign against Sears until the late 1950s; by then time was on the company's side and it easily thwarted the union.

In short, all three companies were lucky. In the 1930s, they recovered rapidly from the Depression, managed to escape major labor confrontations, and began to reconstruct welfare capitalism—developments that were all closely related. By the end of the war, they were well situated to withstand challenges from the labor movement, which, though it had gained organizational resources, was beginning to lose some of its moral stature and cohesion. Thus, when unions finally started to organize these firms, the tide had begun to shift in management's favor. This is not to say that everything, everywhere, depended on good timing. In the postwar years, labor continued to make inroads at firms with regressive policies and unsophisticated management, though there were fewer such firms than before. This, too, was an important change: not only had labor lost momentum but unorganized firms had become more confident in applying the model developed by Kodak, Thompson, and Sears. In the memo he sent to the president of Sears, Clarence Caldwell analyzed these trends with startling clarity:

> Management has learned a great deal in the past fifteen years—about how to retain the loyalty and good will of their employees, and about how to combat outside organizing efforts. During the thirties and continuing through the war, much of management was "off balance" in the struggle with unions. This is no longer the case, and the competitive advantage now lies on the employer's side. This shift in power relations is not the result of the Taft-Hartley Act. . . . It is a result of far more deep-seated forces and hence is likely to be little influenced by any further changes in legislation.
>
> Any company which has been able to keep free (or relatively free) of organization up to this point can undoubtedly remain so provided it does a reasonably good employee relations job and keeps a cool head in handling any crises which may arise.[45]

Before turning to the individual company histories of Kodak, Sears, and Thompson, there is one last issue to consider: are these companies what statisticians would call a representative sample? That is, were circumstances at Sears, Kodak, and Thompson Products similar to those at other large nonunion firms? There is reason to believe they were. Looking at the period's other major nonunion firms—companies like Delta Air, Du Pont, IBM,

National Cash Register, S. C. Johnson, Procter & Gamble, and the Standard Oil companies—one finds many of the same conditions and outcomes, despite differing corporate attributes.

The major nonunion companies all had progressive employment and benefits policies, often dating back to the pre-1930 period of welfare capitalism. (IBM borrowed many ideas from its upstate neighbor, Eastman Kodak.) These companies also were quick to adapt welfare capitalism to changing circumstances. Procter & Gamble and Du Pont, for example, let their company unions lapse in the late 1920s, but then—like Thompson Products—revived them in the 1930s and kept them going long after the Wagner Act. Second, many of the companies came from emergent industries with cyclically stable and steadily expanding product demands, and the Depression did not hit them as hard as it did other firms. Third, several benefited from the good luck of facing relatively weak unions or of not having to confront unions at all until after World War II. Finally, the companies were run by their founders or by powerful leaders who created a modern corporatist culture. Men like Richard Deupree (Procter & Gamble), Thomas J. Watson (IBM), and C. E. Woolman (Delta) shared a commitment to reconstructing welfare capitalism, took personnel management seriously, and favored the creation of a corporate Gemeinschaft. They also personally detested labor unions, to the point of spending more on wages and welfare programs than it would have cost to sign a union contract.[46]

Kodak, Sears, and Thompson were selected for this study for several reasons. The firms represent a wide variety of technological, demographic, and market characteristics; such diversity assures that the chosen firms are typical of the range of variation in other major nonunion companies. Also, although the firms are diverse, they do overlap. For example, Kodak and Thompson are both manufacturing firms, Sears is not; Sears and Thompson had to contend with numerous organizing drives; Kodak did not. These pairings permit me to form some modest generalizations about outcomes.

Finally, although neither Sears, Kodak, nor Thompson has previously been studied in any depth, historical materials were available for each of them. Obtaining those materials, however, was no easy trick. Corporations are loath to make records available to historians. The direct benefits are outweighed by the potential costs: negative publicity, sullied reputations, even lawsuits. And few issues are more sensitive to a company than the recent history of its employment and labor relations policies. Ironically, most of the companies that modernized welfare capitalism and opened it up to the outside world remain reticent in baring their records to public scrutiny. The following chapters, however, give a good sense of what those records might contain.

Three

Preserving the Past: Eastman Kodak

"BIG YELLOW," as Kodak employees called their company, referred to its colorful film cartons and generous benefits. A pioneer in the employee welfare movement, by the 1920s Kodak was a prominent member of welfare capitalism's vanguard. Along with company housing and health insurance programs, it had an elaborate production planning system to minimize layoffs. Once hired into the "clan," employees often remained with Kodak their entire working lives. Profit sharing kept wages up and, if there were layoffs, Kodak paid jobless benefits out of its own private fund. Here was proof of the corporatist credo that the business enterprise should be the industrial worker's primary source of security.

Kodak did not use its welfare policies to reshape workers' private lives, as, for example, Ford Motor's Sociological Department had attempted to do. Kodak had an Anglo-Saxon work force that was largely native born. With no need to "Americanize" his workers, George Eastman, Kodak's founder, built Kodak's programs around a cash nexus that was relatively impersonal and unintrusive. Eastman gave employees the same things that the company's owners were after—a share of Kodak's fabulous profits.

Eastman had a deep-seated fear that disgruntled workers might sabotage or shut down the company's gargantuan film-making factory in Rochester. Rather than simply bribe employees with high wages, the company's approach was more strategic. Funds were channeled through specific benefit programs intended to harmonize employee interests with those of management. But a more immediate problem was the U.S. Justice Department's antitrust division, which repeatedly investigated Kodak's monopoly in the film industry. Kodak's widely publicized benefit programs were meant to create the impression of a "good trust," one that jurors would treat sympathetically if the firm found itself in court.

Like Eastman, the engineers who ran Kodak attributed the firm's continuing profitability to its technical prowess. Company managers were imbued with the ethos that social problems were amenable to the same scientific methods Kodak applied to its research and production problems. Kodak's blend of mass production, scientific management, and financial benefits gave a technocratic twist to welfare capitalism. Other science-based firms pursued similar policies in the 1920s, inspiring lofty hopes that technologists would create a new kind of capitalism, as in economist Thorstein Veblen's "Soviet of the Engineers."

What made Kodak distinctive was its ability to stay on this trajectory well into the 1960s. The New Deal dramatically transformed industrial relations for American employers, even large techno-corporatist companies like Du Pont, General Electric, and Westinghouse. But Kodak remained remarkably unchanged. For one thing, most of its work force still was concentrated in Rochester, a conservative city where unions had difficulty organizing. The CIO did not come to Rochester until World War II, and even then the workers who signed up were more "ethnic" than Kodak's. Also, Kodak was spared the worst agonies of the Depression. Relatively few layoffs occurred there, and welfare programs were kept intact. Even before the Depression ended Kodak was introducing new benefits, keeping up the pace of the 1920s. The company followed this pattern through the ensuing decades, so that by the 1960s it had become a sort of corporate coelacanth—a living example of what welfare capitalism might have looked like had the Depression, the welfare state, and mass unionism never occurred.

The Company before 1930

In March 1932, the industrial world was stunned by news that George Eastman, founder and chairman of the Eastman Kodak Company, had committed suicide at the age of seventy-seven. The event occurred at the nadir of the Depression, a time when magazine cartoons depicted managers leaping from Wall Street ledges. Yet Eastman's suicide was prompted by his own poor health, not that of the company he left behind. Under his leadership, Kodak had grown from a small factory employing six people in 1881 to one of the largest and most profitable firms in the United States. In 1929, it ranked sixtieth in assets among American industrial companies and employed nearly 24,000 people worldwide. The year of Eastman's death, Kodak reported profits of $6 million, while two-thirds of all U.S. firms showed losses.[1]

Kodak's early growth was propelled by a marriage of mass production to mass distribution. Whereas photography had once been a difficult and cumbersome process, George Eastman simplified it in the 1880s by introducing roll film and lightweight roll-film cameras. Both were manufactured in large quantity but with careful attention to quality, thus providing inexpensive and accurate photographic equipment to the amateur market. Kodak's chief distribution outlets were the drugstores found in every American city and town. Low prices and clever advertising ("You press the button. We do the rest.") formed the link between production and consumption.[2]

Kodak was a highly integrated company—horizontally, vertically, and spatially. During the 1890s and 1900s, Eastman acquired various firms in the film, paper, and camera industries to protect and expand Kodak's patents. At the same time, Kodak expanded vertically through purchase or construction of its own supply sources. In an antitrust era, this was less controversial than horizontal integration and it gave Kodak control over quality and costs. A small chemical plant was opened in 1898, followed by a box factory, printing facility, gelatin plant, lens factory, and distillation-chemicals factory (the Tennessee Eastman division, purchased from the government in 1920). Except for Tennessee Eastman, Kodak's domestic facilities were concentrated in Rochester, which by the early 1900s had become the center of the nation's photographic industry. From 1900 to 1930, over 80 percent of Kodak's domestic employees worked in Rochester.[3]

The company's flagship was its giant Kodak Park facility, opened in 1891. The plant was a behemoth of capital-intensive mass production. It made all Kodak's photosensitive products, including film and paper. Kodak Park covered 230 acres and employed about 7,000 people. Nearby were Kodak's Camera Works (employing more than 2,000 workers) and the small Hawk-Eye lens factory. By 1896, the company had made its hundred thousandth Kodak camera and was churning out miles of film and paper each month. Thus, Kodak perfected the techniques of mass production well before Henry Ford brought them to the automobile industry.

With the exception of machinists and emulsion makers at Kodak Park, and some lens grinders and metal finishers at the other plants, Kodak's production workers were largely semiskilled. Many were women. In 1927, women accounted for 30 percent of Kodak's domestic employees; the proportion was even higher at Kodak Park.[4]

In 1912, the company opened a research laboratory at Kodak Park, where engineers, chemists, and other scientists developed or refined products such as X-ray and motion picture film. But the making of film emulsion, which was Kodak's core process, was as much art as science. The emulsion makers were an elite group—no more than 2 percent of the Kodak Park workforce—with long training and experience. The emulsion formula and many of Kodak's other production methods were closely guarded secrets.[5]

Kodak had a centralized management structure in these years. Eastman, said historian Blake McKelvey, "kept a tight hand on his firm. He had little patience with directors' meetings and made most decisions himself." Although Henry A. Strong, one of Eastman's early backers, was the company president from 1884 to 1919, Eastman retained for himself a more powerful position as president of Kodak's holding company. As late as 1913, Eastman still owned 25 percent of the company's stock. Gradually he loosened his grip, giving vast quantities of stock to employees and various philanthropies. Other changes followed a 1919 Price Waterhouse report that recommended a reduction in presidential control as well as greater staff involvement and autonomy for Kodak's factories. Around this time, Eastman handed over the reins to a group of younger managers headed by Frank W. Lovejoy. In charge of Kodak Park since 1903, Lovejoy became vice president in 1919 and general manager in 1925. The three main Rochester facilities and Tennessee Eastman were given considerable independence—from each other and from Kodak's head office.[6]

Kodak occasionally found itself charged with patent infringement and related offenses. By purchasing other film and camera companies, it avoided such problems and availed itself of its competitors' trade secrets. And Kodak's dominance in photographic film and its soaring profits made a tempting target for antitrust prosecution. The government focused on the lack of competition in Kodak's photographic markets and on the company's distribution methods, which included exclusive dealerships and fixed prices. In 1911, a complex antitrust suit was filed against Kodak. The charges were dropped when Kodak signed a consent decree in 1921.[7]

Yet antitrust remained an abiding concern. Because an unfavorable ruling could have decimated Kodak, legal strategies permeated Kodak's business decisions. To protect against being broken down into smaller units, Kodak was prepared to claim that, for technical reasons, production of photographic goods required close physical and administrative coordination of its various operations. The claim was probably true of sensitive goods like film and paper, where there existed economies of scope and scale, but it made less sense for products like chemicals and cameras. Nevertheless, by keeping most facilities in Rochester, Kodak protected itself from government efforts to split it up.[8]

By the early 1920s, Kodak was far and away the city's largest employer, with 20 percent of Rochester's work force on its payroll, so involvement in local affairs was motivated by self-interest as well as civic duty. Eastman believed that what he gave to the community ultimately would redound to Kodak's benefit. Speaking of his gifts to the University of Rochester, Eastman said, "From the Kodak point of view I consider it a very highly desirable thing to have a good college here, not only to help train good men but also to make Rochester an attractive place for Kodak men to live and bring up their families." Though Rochester was too large to be called a company town, Kodak was the city's center of gravity. A 1924 article observed that Kodak's location "in a moderate-sized, homogeneous community, whose social and community life it shares and from which it largely draws its personnel, is a factor in developing that close community of interest which is generally recognized as the family spirit."[9]

Other companies in Rochester were owned by local men who took their cues from Kodak. Even the city's smaller employers were known for their progressive policies, from nonunion Bausch and Lomb to the unionized clothing industry, which had an elaborate arbitration plan and employment bureau. Eastman's efforts spurred other businessmen to become involved in local activities, including the chamber of commerce and the Industrial Management Council. A few employers privately complained that Eastman was a despot, which was not entirely untrue. For example, he decreed a music appreciation course for chamber of commerce members and "virtually required all of Rochester's lesser businessmen to attend every excruciating class."[10]

Eastman was an ascetic, taciturn, and distant man, but his philanthropy enhanced his reputation. With the exception of some enormous gifts to the Massachusetts Institute of Technology, most of his money went to the University of Rochester and other local projects such as the Eastman Theater, the Mechanics Institute, Rochester City Hospital, and the Children's Dental Clinic. After 1915, he took an increasingly active role in Rochester civic affairs.[11]

The local community—including the trade unions—respected Eastman for his rectitude. Although rarely active in partisan politics, he was a staunch Republican and conservative. He called antitrust laws "socialistic" and inserted a codicil in his will cutting off the local YMCA because a socialist once gave a speech in its auditorium. Like many others, Eastman saw socialism as an alien and un-American philosophy. This view was reinforced by his observations of Rochester's clothing companies—the city's second-largest industry—whose unionized workers were mostly Italians and Jews and included socialists. Eastman was discomfited by foreigners who could not speak English, and in the 1920s he became a supporter of the National Eugenics League.[12]

Yet Eastman stressed to Kodak managers the importance of treating employees fairly and avoiding personal favorites. This opinion had its roots in Eastman's own experience as a bank clerk, a job he took at age fourteen and held for ten years. When his immediate superior resigned, Eastman expected a promotion, but he was passed over in favor of a bank director's relative. Years later Eastman recalled, "It wasn't right. It wasn't fair. It was against every principle of justice." The experience sensitized Eastman to the importance of making employees "feel that the fair thing was being done."[13]

When Kodak Park began hiring workers in 1891, there was nothing unusual about its employment policies, but by the 1920s Kodak had become a prominent member of welfare capitalism's vanguard. The first step in this direction came in 1897, when Eastman set up an employee suggestion system after hearing a speech by John Patterson of National Cash Register, a pioneer in the industrial welfare field. Monthly prizes were awarded to the best employee proposals. Kodak later introduced a slew of traditional welfare activities for men and women—dining halls, smoking rooms, reading rooms, recreation programs, and an assembly hall for concerts and dances. Eastman, a lover of classical music, had string quartets come out to Kodak Park and serenade employees at lunch. In 1910 Kodak established the Athletic Association, which elected its own officers and charged a membership fee of only one dollar. In return, members could use the company's tennis courts, baseball diamonds, cinder track, and basketball gymnasium. Activities were hierarchically inclusive: production workers sang and played alongside foremen and managers.[14]

Although its facilities and the funding for them were impressively lavish, Kodak was best known for its copious financial benefits. On three occasions—in 1899, 1911, and 1919—Eastman gave large amounts of his own wealth to company employees. The 1899 "divvy" came when Eastman made a fortune on the London stock market after launching Kodak Ltd., the firm's British subsidiary. Twelve years later, Eastman endowed an employee welfare fund by donating stock worth over $1 million, an enormous sum. The fund compensated sick and injured workers and offered emergency loans to employees in need. In 1919, Eastman sold to employees another chunk of stock priced substantially below market value.[15]

Each of these gifts solidified Eastman's reputation as a model employer. The 1919 stock sale brought him accolades from the national press, including a laudatory article in the *New York Times*. By the early 1920s, the Kodak Employees' Association (KEA) ran one of the nation's most comprehensive private welfare programs, including retirement bonuses in the amount of one week's pay per year of service; disability and accident insurance; and sickness benefits.[16]

On top of this, in 1912 Kodak started a profit-sharing plan covering all employees. Payments were based on Kodak's stock dividends, hence the name Wage Dividend Plan. Tying the plan to stock dividends prevented erratic swings in bonus payments, because dividends fluctuated less than profits. Also, the link to dividends reminded employees that they had a stake in the company similar to the shareholders'. The plan did stipulate that wage dividends would not be paid to employees if stock dividends fell below a specified level, but this proviso was invoked only once in the company's history, in 1934.[17]

The amount a worker received was based on earnings and tenure, with the maximum reached after five years. Annual payments were large, averaging about a month's wages for employees with five years' service. Instead of saving their dividends, most Kodak workers spent the money on major consumer goods like automobiles and appliances. On dividend payment day, auto dealers lined the streets in front of Kodak Park selling new cars for cash. That workers treated the dividend like regular income was attributed by one manager to "the fact that [the plan] has paid cash since 1912 without interruption." As a result, "most employees look upon its payment as practically assured, the only question being the rate." Kodak did not try to force workers to save the wage dividend by investing it in company stock or holding it until they had been with the firm for ten years or more, both common features of other profit-sharing plans. This policy stemmed from Eastman's reluctance to "put any string on the money. The employee is either entitled to it or not."[18]

International Harvester, National Cash Register, and other large companies designed their welfare programs to weaken existing craft unions, but this was not a primary motive in Kodak's case, since almost none of its craft workers were union members. Kodak's managers had no desire to see the company organized, but they were less immediately concerned with union deterrence than were other industrial employers since, with one exception, Kodak's domestic plants had no contact with organized labor until after the Second World War. The exception came in 1901, when Samuel Gompers visited Rochester at the invitation of the Central Trades and Labor Council. While in town, he encouraged polishers and platers at the Camera Works to organize a union. In August, thirty-four of Kodak's forty-five polishers walked off their jobs and asked Mr. Brownell, head of the Camera Works, to recognize their union. Brownell refused, but rather than aggravate the situation he made a unique proposal: the men should set up their own cooperative, which Kodak would equip and supply with orders on a contract basis. The workers agreed and thus was born the Union Polishing and Plating Company. Although the venture was successful, in 1904 several of the original founders bought out their partners and shed the cooperative form. This episode set a pattern of strategic divestiture that Kodak would follow in later years.[19]

Eastman admired the AFL's trade unions more than most employers of his day. He was even friendly with a few local union leaders, who agreed to have him arbitrate several wage disputes in the early 1920s. But he drew the line at allowing unions inside his own plants, because he thought that unionism—particularly the AFL's craft-based form of it—would interfere with Kodak's technologically advanced manufacturing system. Construction of new facilities posed a special problem, since Rochester's building trades were heavily organized. In the early years, Kodak managers met with local union leaders, negotiated terms (which Kodak called "understandings"), and hired union builders on the condition that no written agreements would be signed. But eventually management thought this too risky. In 1921 Kodak started its own building division—Ridge Construction—whose nonunion employees worked for Kodak year-round. Ridge had its own apprenticeship programs and matched or exceeded union wages and working conditions. The firm also kept its work force lean, so that employees almost never were laid off, unlike unionized workers in the seasonal construction industry.[20]

Kodak's other wage rates were also above average for similar work in Rochester, in keeping with the firm's obvious ability to pay. More than profits propped up wages, however. Pay levels also reflected Kodak's low labor-cost ratios. In the capital-intensive photographic industry (which included smaller and less mechanized firms than Kodak), production-worker wages constituted 27 percent of total value added versus an average of 37 percent in other industries.[21]

Although unions were a distant threat, Kodak nevertheless had reason to be concerned about them. Despite the growth of overseas production during the 1920s, in 1930 Rochester still accounted for more than half of the company's employees worldwide. Of these, the vast majority worked at one facility—Kodak Park. The plant's film-making machines, which turned out Kodak's most lucrative product, were costly to stop and start, and thus operated continuously. Were a labor dispute ever to have shut down the plant, it could have inflicted serious damage to Kodak's revenues and profits. Further, Kodak's production technology made the firm vulnerable to sabotage on the part of disgruntled employees. At Kodak Park, "much of the work was done in dark rooms where there could be no direct supervision. An employee could spoil in a day materials worth what was paid him in salary over an entire year. There was no way to inspect the results of the individual employee's work."[22]

These factors led Kodak to spend substantial sums to secure its workers' loyalty. The company's generous financial benefits, particularly the wage dividend, were supposed to demonstrate that Kodak was fairly dividing the huge surplus that flowed to it. The benefits were also intended to foster a sense of obligation and reciprocity. Eastman made a point of telling employees that the 1899 divvy was not a gift but "extra pay for extra work." Twenty years later, much the same was said about the stock plan, which, declared Eastman, proved "that those who have shown their fidelity to the Company will be fully warranted." Finally, Kodak's wage dividend and other cash bonuses raised the potential cost to employees of losing their jobs. By being munificent, Kodak deterred disloyalty and indiscipline, an effect that was useful in situations where workers could not be monitored directly by management. One manager said that it all boiled down to having workers "keep off lawns" without posting signs telling them to do so.[23]

Kodak's welfare programs were also a reaction to external economic pressures. Financial houses were reluctant to recommend Kodak stock because Eastman owned so much of it. Investors worried that if anything happened to Eastman, it would hurt Kodak's share value. By giving stock to employees, Eastman reduced his personal holdings and eased these concerns. Putting large chunks of stock on the market also held share prices down and kept the antitrust lawyers at bay: high stock prices were sure to attract the lawyers' attention, as were large earnings, which the wage dividend plan helped reduce. Two years before starting the plan, when Kodak profits had reached record levels, Eastman wrote Henry Strong, "I am sorry we had to declare the extra dividend. It seems necessary on account of the accumulation of ready money." The following year, the U.S. Supreme Court ruled against Standard Oil's holding-company structure and ordered the dissolution of the American Tobacco trust. Kodak already had been investigated by New York's attorney general, and Eastman worried that the firm might soon come under federal scrutiny. "The power of this popular uprising against trusts," he wrote, "is a thing that has to be now taken into calculations by anyone whose business comprises any large part of the total output in any given line." His fears were well founded: the Justice Department launched an investigation of Kodak in 1912, the same year that Kodak paid out its first wage dividends.[24]

By emphasizing cash benefits instead of in-kind services, Kodak's welfare programs were less manipulative and moralistic than those at other companies. The pecuniary approach can be traced to Eastman, who, like Frederick W. Taylor, thought that what mattered most to industrial workers was money. "You can talk about cooperation and good feeling and friendliness from morn to midnight," said Eastman, "but the thing the worker appreciates is the same thing the man at the helm appreciates—dollars and cents." Eastman believed that programs like profit sharing "make the worker feel that he belongs to the success of the plant. When the dividend on stock is high, his wage dividend is high; when stock dividends are low, his wage dividend slumps. Ergo, what do we get? High production and fine quality of output."[25]

Kodak also had less need of aggressively paternalistic programs because it employed relatively few immigrants. Hardly any Italians, Jews, or Poles worked at Kodak Park, although a few held jobs at the Camera Works. Most Kodak workers were either native white Protestants (often from farm villages near Rochester) or German-Americans from Rochester's sizable German community. By hiring only high school graduates, Kodak Park's employment department kept out most immigrants and nonwhites. A Kodak manager wrote approvingly of "the high average intelligence of [Kodak] workers. Their native-born tastes and conservative habits of thought have been highly favorable to economic experiment and to the development of the company's ideals."[26]

Kodak's family hiring system reinforced these attitudes. It was common for two or three generations to be employed at Kodak, with mothers and daughters or fathers and sons often working side by side. Not only did family hiring literally make Kodak workers a clan, it also was a subtle way of maintaining discipline and avoiding workers from union-loyal families.

On a more philosophical level, Kodak's hiring practices corresponded with Eastman's larger vision of the company as an industrial community. The company's "ideals" (today these would be called its "culture") harked back to nineteenth-century republicanism, marked by small-town virtues, communal solidarity, and ethnic homogeneity. Yet Kodak was hardly a hamlet of yeoman smallholders; most of the company was owned by Eastman. Hence producerist rather than property-owning values infused this updated version of republicanism. Eastman liked to describe himself as an inventor rather than a marketing genius, and he wanted the company run by engineers rather than financiers. This was a scientized sort of producerism in which engineers made key decisions that clean-clothed workers carried out in return for stable jobs and a high standard of living.[27]

Eastman enjoyed working with his hands and respected men like Thomas Edison and Henry Ford who could combine tinkering with scientific knowledge. As a youth he spent his free time mixing up dry plate coatings on his mother's stove. The men Eastman hired from schools such as MIT shared his infatuation with rational, systematic methods of administration. Eastman's technocratic orientation fueled his interest in such things as eugenics and the thirteen-month calendar.[28] It also attracted him to psychological testing, which was supposed to enhance social efficiency by directing individuals to the jobs that best suited them. During the First World War, Kodak began giving aptitude tests to prospective clerical employees and to people (mostly women) being considered for jobs in the film-finishing department. The results were so promising that in the early 1920s testing was extended to all factory applicants and to prospective supervisors as well. Kodak was one of eight corporate sponsors (along with Western Electric and AT&T) of the

Personnel Research Federation, established in the 1920s to promote the application of psychology to industrial management.[29]

Kodak's production planning system was the company's prime example of how technocratic methods could enhance employee welfare. In the 1890s, photographic film had a shelf life of only a month or so. Because amateur photography was a highly seasonal business, so was film production. Output reached peak levels in the spring and summer and then dropped during the fall, when Kodak would lay off up to 40 percent of its force. Although this meant that the firm incurred rehiring costs, the main expense lay in idle physical capital. Kodak had an enormous investment in its film-making machines, which were underutilized during the off season.[30]

At the turn of the century, attempts by Kodak and other companies to rationalize such fixed costs led in two directions. Across firms there was a wave of mergers in capital-intensive industries, while within firms industrial engineers experimented with new methods of systematic management. As a chemical engineering student at MIT, Frank Lovejoy had been exposed to these methods and began to apply them after arriving at Kodak. Working with the company's master emulsion maker, Lovejoy created a film in 1903 that could stay fresh for months. After making careful estimates of future demand, Lovejoy leveled off film production so that Kodak Park could operate year round. By producing for inventory during slack months, he eliminated the need for extra capacity to meet peak levels of demand. The new system also allowed Kodak to cut its seasonal force and provide year-round jobs for most workers. Training costs were reduced and workers benefited from more stable employment. To ensure the success of its new approach, Kodak began to advertise the joys of winter photography.[31]

This experience helped solidify the Kodak ethos that both employee and company interests were best served by maintaining Kodak's technical prowess. During the 1910s, Kodak gradually extended Lovejoy's planning methods to the manufacture of other photosensitive goods. Because this required the analysis of an enormous amount of data, Eastman turned to the new Harvard Business School in 1914 to recommend someone capable of managing Kodak's information flows. The school suggested Marion B. Folsom, a Georgia native and M.B.A. honors graduate. Folsom headed Kodak's new Statistical Department, which put out a steady stream of data for production planning. (At Eastman's request, the department developed a thirteen-month calendar to govern Kodak operations and also devised an organizational chart to manage Eastman's twenty-eight-person household staff.) By the 1920s, the company had become so proficient at sales planning that employment levels at Kodak Park varied by less than 1 percent annually. Kodak was even able to reduce production during the peak summer months to accommodate employee vacations.[32]

Kodak found it difficult to stabilize production at the Camera Works, however, where sales fluctuated with economic conditions and the product line went through frequent style changes. Heavy layoffs at the Camera Works during the 1921 depression revealed the Achilles' heel of the stabilization approach—its inability to shield workers from cyclical, as opposed to seasonal, instability. In the midst of the depression, Marion Folsom attended a lecture by B. Seebohm Rowntree, a progressive English employer, and was struck by Rowntree's claim that Britain's unemployment insurance program had saved the country "from something like a revolution." Folsom discussed the lecture with Eastman, whose dread of social unrest had been rekindled by a wave of strikes in Rochester the preceding year. Folsom proposed that Kodak set up its own unemployment fund to deal with cyclical layoffs, reminding Eastman that "fear of unemployment . . . is one of the most potent causes of labor unrest." Eastman liked the idea and told Folsom to proceed.[33]

An unemployment committee chaired by Kodak's industrial relations director met weekly during the winter of 1921–1922 and then presented its findings. Noting that "unemployment is primarily a problem of management," the report prescribed better planning and an unemployment reserve fund that would build during normal times and pay out benefits if Kodak had to lay off workers.[34]

Eastman liked the technocratic logic of the reserve fund, but Kodak's plant managers vetoed the Folsom plan, claiming it would make other employers reluctant to hire unemployed Kodak workers. Had Kodak adopted the plan, it would have joined an elite group—including Dennison Manufacturing, Dutchess Bleacheries, and Leeds and Northrup—that guaranteed income security to its workers in the 1920s. Folsom raised the idea again in 1927, but without success.[35]

Nevertheless, the management literature touted Kodak for being among the nation's first companies to offer career employment to its manual workers. Along with year-round jobs, Kodak promised to promote from within whenever possible. In 1920, it adopted a formal system by which workers could be "interchanged between departments and promotions made for higher positions within the organization." Kodak's career policies made it easier for the firm to move workers around. In addition, as Lovejoy told Eastman, the policies gave Kodak "the whole-hearted interest and cooperation of the worker . . . [and] a satisfied, contented, and permanent body of employees."[36]

When describing these policies, Kodak relied on the same family metaphors used by other practitioners of welfare capitalism—including upstate New York firms like Endicott Johnson, IBM, and Solvay Process. But unlike its neighbors, Kodak worried about being excessively paternalistic. It warned managers that workers were "suspicious of 'welfare' benefits," changed the name of the Welfare Fund to the Kodak Employees' Association, and began to use the term "clan" instead of "family." The changes were, in part, a cosmetic response to a postwar surge in worker assertiveness, but they also connoted the kind of organization Kodak was striving for: a stable industrial community held together not by loyalty to George Eastman but by a common commitment to corporate growth. The ends were those of welfare capitalism; the means were supplied by scientific management. If workers were offered the same incentives as managers, they would start thinking like them.[37]

George Eastman abhorred the strikes that hit Rochester and other cities in 1919, seeing in them the beginnings of "Bolshevism or Anarchy, born twins, just the same." An August strike at Bausch and Lomb, a neighbor of Kodak with similarly progressive policies, touched off rumors that the Sheetmetal Workers were trying to organize Kodak's Camera Works. In response, Kodak launched the Anti-Bolshevistic Program, which included mass meetings of Kodak workers, posting of "anti-Bolshevistic bulletins," and distribution to all employees of a letter from Eastman. The letter warned that professional agitators were ready "to fasten the poisoned talons of anarchy upon the whole community." It urged employees to "see to it that the disciples of anarchy do not influence the foolish and the thoughtless." After all, Eastman reminded them, "your comfort and prosperity and the growth and prosperity of the company are inter-dependent."[38]

Although nothing came of the purported drive, Eastman was sufficiently shaken that he approved some immediate changes in Kodak's personnel program. One was the stock sale, proceeds from which were deposited in the Welfare Fund. Another was the creation in 1919 of a corporate industrial relations department. Although Kodak had employment departments at each plant, these were responsible for little more than hiring and record keeping. The new department administered companywide welfare programs and provided staff assistance to the plants. Initially it was headed by W. H. Cameron, formerly with the American Council on Safety. In April 1920, Cameron was replaced by Harry D. Haight, who remained in charge for the next twenty years. Unlike Cameron, Haight had long experience in the photographic industry, having previously owned a small camera company.[39]

Cameron's main accomplishment during his tenure (and the reason for its brevity) was to start a controversial employee representation plan at the Camera Works in February 1919. Support for the plan came chiefly from the Camera Works' managers, who thought it would "anticipate unrest by providing a vehicle for expressing the desires of labor." Managers at other Kodak plants felt the plan was an overreaction to temporary conditions and warned that it would be hard to get rid of if it was found unsatisfactory. Managers from Kodak Park were unanimously opposed because, they boasted, their employees were "high class, better educated and better paid" than those at the Camera Works.[40]

Under the plan, elected representatives met with camera works management to discuss worker grievances. The head of the shop committee (whose salary was paid by Kodak) was Charlie Rogers, formerly a bartender at a saloon near the plant. Rogers knew many of the workers personally, which helped him win the post. In a newspaper interview, he said that at first he viewed the plan as "an effort to stop the workers from organizing into unions.

I was wrong. I take it all back. The men in these shops wouldn't gain a thing by organization. We're always a lick ahead of organized labor."

In its early years, the committee was quite active, negotiating over piece rates, shop conditions, and a 1921 work-sharing plan. Although Eastman said little when the committee was first set up, by 1923 he publicly opposed what he called "industrial representation. By that is meant giving the worker some sort of vote in the running of the business. I do not agree that a program of that sort is advisable. That is not evolution in industry. That smacks more of a revolution." The plan ceased to exist in the mid-1920s.[41]

Under Haight, the industrial relations department introduced other power-balancing reforms of a more lasting nature, particularly those limiting foreman discretion. Among its changes, the department prohibited foremen from directly firing workers. Instead, workers were to be sent to the employment manager with a written disciplinary report. The manager was allowed to rescind the discharge and reassign workers to other jobs. The department also initiated a complaint system by which, said Lovejoy, "the employee can freely state and discuss any complaints or grievances and whereby same can receive considerate, unprejudiced, and prompt attention." Workers were encouraged to bring complaints to the plant manager or the industrial relations department.[42]

To win support for these changes, the industrial relations department started a foreman training program. Plant managers were amenable to the idea, feeling, as one of them said, that "the majority of foremen do not get close enough to their men." The program combined group discussion with textbook readings on personnel management. In 1930, Allen B. Gates, formerly of Western Electric, was hired to fill a new position as director of training. Kodak was praised by a Wharton School expert for its "carefully designed and administered" training program. Indeed, when other firms with similar programs reversed course in the 1920s and returned disciplinary powers to their foremen, Kodak bucked the trend. It upgraded the foreman's job by recruiting and training college graduates for supervisory positions.[43]

Haight also expanded Kodak's welfare benefits during the 1920s. As before, these benefits focused on the employees' financial security instead of their moral fiber. A new sickness plan insured against illness or accident off the job, and also enlarged Kodak's medical department to include four full-time doctors, ten visiting nurses, and eye and dental clinics. Housing needs were met through two new institutions: the Eastman Savings and Loan Association, which provided mortgages to employees, and the Kodak Employees' Realty Corporation, which sold vacant lots to Kodak workers. The Realty Corporation built several housing developments in and around Rochester that were keyed to different corporate strata—from the inexpensive homes of the Koda-Vista subdivision near Kodak Park to the more elaborate homes in suburban Meadowbrook. Eastman told Haight that "employees should be encouraged to buy their own homes. Nothing stabilizes a working force like having them own real estate."[44]

By the late 1920s, Kodak was, if anything, too successful at stabilizing its work force. Good pay, benefits, and steady work made Kodak a "sticky" company, with turnover rates well below the U.S. average. But in solving one set of problems related to security and motivation, Kodak unwittingly created another: older workers, who received the highest relative pay, were reluctant to retire. This raised costs while blocking promotions for younger workers. Kodak managers were reluctant to dismiss older workers even though they privately complained of "privileged senility" and "deadweight." Compounding the problem was the absence of a formal pension plan. Eastman opposed the idea of pensions, believing that workers should fend for themselves with funds saved from profit sharing. "Set [the money] aside for a rainy day or for your old age," he told them. Few did so, however. In 1927, Folsom—by now fascinated with welfare issues—investigated corporate pension plans and went to Europe to study social insurance policy. Upon returning, he and an insurance executive designed a pension plan for Kodak, which they persuaded Eastman to accept because it would "retire workers after . . . their period of usefulness and replace them with more efficient workers." It went into effect in January 1929.[45]

Along with retirement annuities, the plan included disability and life insurance. The annuities were the most innovative and costly part of the plan. Although pension plan details are not usually of much interest today, matters were quite different in the 1920s. Of the roughly four hundred pension plans then in existence, the vast majority were discretionary and unfunded. Even before the stock market crash, some firms abandoned their plans because of financial problems. Kodak caught the industrial world's attention by being the first major employer to adopt a pension plan that was contractual, nondiscretionary, and fully insured. Other features included vesting after twenty years and careful actuarial projections. The plan was featured in the *New York Times* and analyzed at a special session of the American Management Association. Folsom was proud that it placed Kodak "in the vanguard of the leading American corporations."[46]

Thus, on the eve of the Depression, Kodak offered its employees an impressive array of welfare programs. The company combined traditional paternalism with financial benefits like the wage dividend, sickness insurance, and a pension plan. Complementing these programs were the planning and personnel methods that made Kodak jobs relatively stable and secure. Folsom was not exaggerating when he said that Kodak workers with more than five years' tenure had "permanent employment." In 1929, few American manufacturers could match Kodak's advanced policies. The company was a paragon of welfare capitalism.

This is not to say that Kodak had no labor problems in the 1920s. Its restrictive hiring policies rankled members of Rochester's various ethnic communities. And a Bedaux wage incentive plan, introduced in 1921, led to periodic disputes over time-study standards. In February 1928, a Communist party-affiliated group calling itself the Workers' Nucleus began to distribute a newspaper, *The Kodak Worker*, outside the gates of the Camera Works. It attacked the Bedaux system for causing speedups and for offering workers "nothing but pay held back and used as a means of preventing us from quitting our jobs. We are employed only in order to make profits for our bosses and thrown aside when we no longer are a source of profit to them." The paper demanded a reduction in work hours from forty-seven to forty-four per week, a change in point standards, and two weeks' vacation with pay (a benefit that Kodak workers did not yet have). In May, *The Kodak Worker* took credit for a retiming of jobs in the buffing department at the Camera Works. Shortly thereafter it ceased publication.[47]

This episode suggests that, although Kodak's factories were hardly free of friction during the 1920s, the company's problems were sufficiently minor to leave its reputation unsullied and its workers uninterested in unionism. Yet the 1920s were a time of high profits and steady employment growth for Kodak; if the Workers' Nucleus had appeared in the 1930s, would events have turned out differently?

Kodak during the Depression

Kodak was in the midst of a sales surge when the stock market crashed in 1929, and initially the Depression had no effect on Kodak. More than eleven hundred new employees were hired at Kodak Park between June 1929 and August 1930, during which time Kodak also inaugurated an extensive building program. Even as business began to taper off, Kodak kept construction going.[48]

Camera sales were the first to falter, whereas film and related products were less affected. At Kodak Park, which accounted for over two-thirds of Kodak's Rochester workforce, the layoff rate in 1930 was the same as in the late 1920s. When the winter of 1930–1931 arrived, nearly all the employees who had been with Kodak in June 1929 were still there. Benefit programs remained intact and a huge wage dividend was announced in February 1931. To the average industrial worker that year, Kodak must have seemed a peaceful haven. In March, the Camera Works played a basketball game against the Rochester Police Department, and a nine-hole indoor putting green was installed at Kodak Park's Assembly Hall. Meanwhile, nearby paternalist companies like Endicott-Johnson were laying off workers and slashing benefit programs.[49]

Kodak management was quick to take credit for the firm's performance. W. G. Stuber, the company's president, went on local radio in January 1931 and attributed Kodak's enviably low layoff rates to new stabilization techniques adopted during the 1920s. That was why the company had heavy layoffs in 1921 but not in 1931, said Stuber. In fact, Kodak's stabilization methods hardly changed at all during the 1920s, but by 1931 the nation was eager to hear success stories, so no one challenged Stuber's claims.[50] Kodak helped keep Rochester's economy afloat during the Depression, while other upstate cities such as Buffalo and Syracuse suffered greatly. Rochester hardly was immune to the economic crisis, however. Against a backdrop of rising unemployment, a mass protest was held at City Hall in March 1930. That same month, a coalition of Rochester organizations formed the Rochester Civic Committee on Unemployment. Most of the committee's board was made up of businessmen (including Marion Folsom), although it also included local clergy, politicians, and the AFL, which was given one seat. Kodak's success in averting layoffs enabled Folsom to persuade the committee to create a task force on employment stabilization, which issued a report urging local firms to adopt work sharing along with more permanent measures like production planning. Later that year, the U.S. President's Emergency Committee for Employment praised the Civic Committee for its prompt relief work and stabilization efforts, which dovetailed with the Emergency Committee's emphasis on local, voluntary efforts to combat unemployment.[51]

Other examples of voluntarism praised by the Emergency Committee included two private unemployment insurance plans initiated in 1930: one at General Electric, which was headquartered in Schenectady, and the other a joint effort by the Rochester Clothiers Exchange and the Amalgamated Clothing Workers of America. Thinking that Lovejoy would want to keep up with the competition—both locally and across the state—Folsom again raised his previously aborted plan for a Kodak unemployment fund. Although Lovejoy was in favor of it, Haight raised the same objections as before. To get around this impasse, Lovejoy told Folsom to get other employers involved. Folsom agreed to explore the idea, but warned Lovejoy, "I doubt if many firms will be interested."[52]

For once Folsom turned out to be wrong. In February 1931 the Rochester Unemployment Benefits Plan was announced, a cooperative effort by fourteen local companies, including Bausch and Lomb, Taylor Instrument, the Gleason Works, and Kodak. In normal times these firms employed 26,000 people, about half of whom worked at Kodak. Each firm agreed to have separate but similar reserve funds to which they would contribute up to 2 percent of their payroll. Having separate funds permitted a company's contributions to be tied to its layoff history, a practice known as "experience rating." This kept costs down for stable firms like Kodak while providing an incentive for unstable firms to rationalize their employment practices and reduce layoffs. Because of experience rating, said Folsom, "greater effort is made by the entire company to plan better, to spread work, and to adopt other means to prevent layoffs."[53]

To businessmen worried that the Depression would lead to compulsory welfare legislation, the plan appeared a stroke of genius. It covered firms of varying size and, because endorsed by Rochester community groups, came wrapped in the civic virtues of American voluntarism. *Forbes*, the business magazine, hailed it as "one of the landmarks of 1931. In these days of confusion and stress, it has the merit of being purposeful, well planned, well coordinated, and voluntary." But this favorable publicity came as no surprise to

Folsom. As he told another employer, it was "our intention in drafting the Rochester Plan . . . to get up a plan which could be recommended generally." That summer, Folsom addressed a gathering of progressive employers at the Silver Bay Industrial Relations Conference and urged them to start similar plans as an alternative to the "compulsory legislation" then being considered by the states. Private experimentation, said Folsom, would provide "experience [from which] it can later be decided what legislation, if any, is necessary."[54]

Under the plan's original guidelines, participating firms were to endow their reserve funds gradually and start payments in 1933. Folsom hoped that by that date enough new firms would join the plan so that at least half of Rochester's labor force would be covered. But the Depression proved this hope to be overly optimistic. After 1931, instead of growing the plan shrank, promised benefits were cut, and only seven firms remained when the first benefits were paid in January 1933. Folsom privately admitted that "no one expected [in 1931] that the depression would be so deep or of such long duration."[55]

The Rochester Plan's poor showing did not dampen Folsom's enthusiasm. In hearings on the Social Security Act in February 1935, he boasted to Congress about the plan's achievements. Thirteen thousand workers were covered by the plan in 1934 (about 80 percent of them Kodak employees), yet compensable layoffs totaled only 477 in 1933 and 1934 combined. Folsom attributed this impressive record to Kodak's long history of stabilization and to the plan itself, which induced companies to stabilize "in order to avoid paying unemployment benefits for which nothing is received in return."[56]

Folsom conveniently ignored the fact that Kodak went into a brief tailspin in mid-1932, several months before the plan went into effect. Camera sales dropped by about 60 percent in 1932; film sales also declined, although less sharply. To its credit, Kodak did everything it could to preserve jobs. As chairman of the regional Share-the-Work Committee, Lovejoy set an example by closing Kodak Park on weekends. This brought the average work week down from forty-six hours in 1929 to thirty-six hours at the end of 1932. Kodak's only wage reduction came in June 1932: a 5 percent cut for those earning less than fifty dollars per week and a 10 percent cut for those earning more than that. Kodak claimed these measures saved hundreds of jobs, but they were not enough to prevent layoffs in December 1932, which pared the Rochester work force down to 8,694 workers, a drop of 12 percent from a year earlier and 24 percent from 1929. Early in 1933, however, sales and employment revived. By June, Kodak's average work week was back up to forty-one hours. When the photographic industry adopted an NRA code in August, Kodak raised hourly pay by 10 percent across the board. Recovery continued steadily thereafter.[57]

Contrary to Folsom's 1935 testimony, low layoff rates in 1933 and 1934 reflected the fact that Kodak in those years was recovering from its 1932 losses. The Rochester Plan helped to keep those losses in check, but it could not have helped a great deal since there were other companies that took precisely the same steps yet suffered a good deal more. Stabilization had little effect on the demand for Kodak's products, yet consumer demand, more than any other factor, determined the company's employment levels. Luckily for Kodak, demand for its products was relatively inelastic. Although domestic sales sagged in 1932, they fell less sharply than at other U.S. manufacturers, and although many manufacturers stayed in the doldrums throughout the 1930s, Kodak surged ahead. The company's sales in 1934 matched those of 1929, and in 1937 Kodak had its most profitable year ever, with sales nearly 40 percent above the 1929 level.[58]

The international markets kept Kodak afloat during the 1930s. Film production in Rochester fell 50 percent between 1929 and 1932, but total world sales dropped by only 25 percent in the same period. Another positive factor was Kodak's increasingly diversified product line. Tennessee Eastman underwent a major expansion during the 1930s and grew to 3,600 workers by 1939. It developed a new plastic material—Tenite—that became widely used in the automotive industry. Sales of motion picture film also rose sharply during the 1930s, helped along by new products such as Kodachrome color movie film and by Kodak's willingness to loan money to ailing movie studios. By 1939, motion pictures brought in 16 percent of Kodak's revenues, while chemical products accounted for another 20 percent. New facilities in Tennessee, Hollywood, and elsewhere reduced the proportion of Kodak's U.S. work force employed in Rochester from 82 percent in 1930 to 67 percent in 1940.[59]

In theory, Kodak's wage dividend plan should have been a factor in the company's performance during the early 1930s, since profit sharing makes wages more sensitive to economic conditions, which, in turn, shields employment levels during hard times. But Kodak's wage dividend in a given year was based on stock dividends from the preceding year, meaning that the wage dividend lagged behind economic conditions. As a result, Kodak did not pare its wage dividend until 1933, too late to help employment levels in 1932, although the relatively small wage dividends paid between 1933 and 1936 helped Kodak generate capital for expansion, thus providing a timely shot in the arm for a company that scrupulously avoided debt.

Kodak's post-1932 expansion faltered only once—early in 1938—when the nationwide recession caused a temporary drop in Kodak sales. In a letter to employees, Kodak finally admitted that its planning and stabilization methods "can not prevent those fluctuations caused by general business conditions and declining sales." Kodak's layoff rate in Rochester rose to 15 percent in 1938, with most of the cuts concentrated at the lens and camera plants. Yet this was far below the U.S. manufacturing average.[60]

Kodak's stable jobs and reliable welfare policies made it an island of security in the midst of a turbulent sea. From 1935 to 1939, the average annual separation rate (the sum of quits, layoffs, dismissals, and retirements, divided by employment) at Kodak's Rochester plants was 11 percent, compared to 45 percent for U.S. manufacturing as a whole. In other words, even during the volatile 1930s—with mass layoffs and labor migration around the country—Kodak remained a sticky company. Thirty-five percent of the employees on its payroll in 1937 had been with Kodak for ten years or more; 51 percent had been there for at least five years, a remarkable record. Meanwhile, during the early 1930s the city of Rochester experienced its most rapid population turnover since the 1860s, with only 58 percent of those listed in the 1930 city directory still appearing there in 1935.[61]

These features would undoubtedly have helped Kodak's management stave off unions, but there were none to deter. Beyond the building and clothing trades, Rochester was largely untouched by labor organizing drives during the 1930s. In a study published in 1940, economist Frederick C. Mosher observed that "the nature of the city's industries has discouraged any very potent labor movement. A number of trade unions, affiliated with the American Federation of Labor . . . are well established in certain of the crafts and offer a rather conservative labor influence in the political life of the city. The only important affiliate of the Congress of Industrial Organizations in 1938 was the Amalgamated Clothing Workers Union, by far the largest, the most powerful, and the most left-wing union in the city." Because it was the largest industrial union in town, the Clothing Workers attracted a motley group of members from Rochester's smaller factories—including macaroni, paper box, and pretzel workers. It also signed up about three hundred workers at Haloid, a small photographic paper manufacturer that was renamed Xerox in the 1950s. Most of these firms were poorly managed and paid low wages. The Clothing Workers did not attempt to organize local companies that were better managed, such as Bausch and Lomb and Kodak. No other unions tried either, at least not until after World War II.[62]

The War and After

Like other large manufacturers, Kodak converted a considerable amount of its capacity to war production. By 1942, over half of its photosensitive-goods output went to the military for use in training films, aerial photography, and industrial X-rays, a new application of an old technology. The camera and lens factories were given over to the manufacture of military products. Employment in the company's Rochester plants swelled from less than 19,000 in 1940 to more than 31,000 in 1944, a more rapid increase than in industry as a whole.[63]

Kodak made its most important military products in Tennessee. On behalf of the War Department, Tennessee Eastman ran the Holston Ordnance Works, the largest explosives factory in the world. About one hundred miles from Holston was Oak Ridge, which in 1943 became the site of an enormous nuclear weapons facility. Kodak was one of three companies asked by the government to assist in the development of Oak Ridge. It built and ran the Y–12 plant, which used electromagnetic processes to produce fissionable material.[64]

Toward the end of the war, Kodak's statistical department began preparing estimates of peacetime sales, which it forecast would hit new highs. Kodak thought that pent-up demand for photographic goods, which accounted for 70 percent of revenue in 1939, would make markets strong after the war. No cameras had been made for civilian use since 1942. Kodacolor film (the first to permit color negatives in ordinary roll-film cameras) had been ready for the amateur market in 1941 but had to be diverted to military use. Moreover, Kodak faced little competition in the photographic market.[65]

As predicted, peace brought prosperity to Kodak. Between 1945 and 1959, the company's sales grew twice as fast as American national income. Rapid growth was fueled by demand factors—the baby boom and expanded leisure time—and by new products such as color film and inexpensive home movies. Fearing that the golden goose might someday give out, Kodak tried to diversify by pumping large amounts of money into new, capital-intensive businesses like petrochemicals, plastics, pharmaceuticals, and synthetic fibers. Yet the new ventures sent a substantial portion of their output to Rochester, where Kodak used it as feedstock for sensitized goods: for example, much of the polyethylene made at the giant chemical complex built by Texas Eastman, a new division started in 1950, ended up in Rochester. As a result, photographic goods accounted for about 65 percent of sales in 1959, only slightly less than before the war.[66]

Kodak's attempted diversification was held back by the enormous profit still to be reaped from photographic film, a market in which Kodak had a near monopoly. In the United States during the late 1950s, Kodak sold about 80 percent of all amateur film, rising to 90 percent for color film. Kodak's hold on the camera market was more limited. The four largest firms in the photographic film industry accounted for 96 percent of sales but this concentration ratio dropped to around 60 percent for photographic equipment. Yet Kodak did not worry much about this. As one Kodak executive quipped, "A lot of people think of us as a camera company. But it's like Gillette: it ain't the razors but the *blades* that make the big money." Kodak did not release disaggregate profit figures, but *Forbes* estimated Kodak's return on capital in the film business to be at least 25 percent in 1962.[67]

The profitability of Kodak's core business also reduced the incentive to innovate. Although Kodak had an enormous laboratory for basic research, on several occasions it missed out on new products that proved highly profitable: the Polaroid Land camera in 1946, zoom lenses in the early 1950s, and dry office photocopying in the late 1950s. Reinforcing the company's stodginess was its inbred management; no major mergers or acquisitions occurred during the 1940s or 1950s. Another reason for Kodak's cautiousness was the company's continuing concern with antitrust. Management feared that Kodak might end up in court if it aggressively deployed cash reserves to purchase Polaroid or Xerox. These risks were not imaginary. In 1948, after a lengthy investigation by the Justice Department, Kodak signed a consent decree acknowledging its attempt to monopolize the color movie-processing business.

Another decree was signed in 1954, this one over Kodak's domination of amateur color-film processing.[68]

In short, Kodak's corporate strategy did not change after the war. Most of its profits still came from the photographic industry, antitrust problems persisted, and Rochester remained the firm's primary location. The same proportion of Kodak's U.S. work force was employed there in 1966 as in 1936 (65 percent), even though Kodak's total U.S. employment more than doubled in those years. During the Second World War, some Kodak managers worried that with so much productive capacity concentrated in Rochester the company was vulnerable to attack by enemy bombers. After the war, similar concerns were expressed about strikes, which would cause major losses were Kodak Park forced to close. In each case, however, Kodak decided that the risk was small relative to the cost of dispersing production.[69]

When it came to industrial espionage and sabotage, Kodak refused to take risks. In the 1950s, Kodak lost a plant manager to GAF, an upstate competitor, causing top management acute anxiety lest key technologies be divulged. To prevent such an occurrence, almost no one at Kodak had complete knowledge of any production process. The Kodak handbook warned employees not to discuss confidential work and strictly forbade taking photographs on company property. Although there were no recorded incidents of sabotage, Kodak managers constantly worried about it, since company products were easily ruined. In the late 1940s, damage amounting to over $300,000 occurred when an operator accidentally transferred hair tonic residue from his hands to some film machinery.[70]

Like its business strategy and management structure, Kodak's labor policies remained the same after the Depression. One policy that Kodak consciously sought to preserve was its reputation for innovative and generous welfare benefits. There was a management consensus that Kodak should maintain national leadership in this area. Other employers who spent heavily on welfare benefits were, like Kodak, capital-intensive firms with low labor-cost ratios, but Kodak's benefit levels were higher than can be accounted for by these factors alone. In 1949, benefit expenses per employee in the chemical and petroleum industries ($523 and $590 respectively) were ahead of the national average ($424). At $822 per employee, however, Kodak was in a league of its own. The same held true more than a decade later. Whereas chemicals and petroleum still ranked ahead of other manufacturing industries in the proportion of payroll spent on benefits (28 percent versus 23 percent), Kodak spent nearly twice as much (45 percent), a level few companies could match.[71]

The gap between Kodak and unionized firms narrowed during the 1950s as the labor movement put health and welfare benefits at the top of its bargaining agenda. Yet here, as elsewhere, Kodak maintained its lead. Although most unionized workers had basic life and health insurance by 1958, only about half were covered by pensions and very few received two-week vacations after one year of service, all standard Kodak policies. Unions in the 1950s prided themselves on regularly winning new welfare benefits for their

TABLE 3.1
Employment Benefits at Kodak, 1950–1959

	New Benefits	*Revisions*
1950	30–60 plan for retirement	Annuity supplement
1951	Blue Shield coverage	
1952		Group life waiting period eliminated
1953	Quinby stock purchase plan	Blue Cross/Shield premium shared Vacation plan liberalized
1954	Relocation expense reimbursement Company-paid retiree health insurance	Sickness allowance extended
1955		Holidays increased to 7 Tuition aid liberalized
1956	Survivor income plan	
1957	Deferred compensation plan	
1958		Holidays increased to 8
1959	Tax-deferred savings & investment plan	Eastman Savings & Loan mortgage lending reaches $8 million

Sources: Eastman Kodak, "Chronology of Changes: Benefit and Employee Relations Plans," (n.d.), Kodak Archives; *Kodakery* 18 (21 January 1960).

members, what economist Sumner Slichter called the "rapid and continuous revision" of benefit plans. Yet benefit changes came primarily at contract renewal time, so unions or employers could take credit for improvements only at three-year intervals. Kodak, however, did not face this restriction. New or improved fringes were announced at least once a year, which gave the appearance of a regular "delivery" of benefits (see Table 3.1).[72]

Kodak set the pattern for this behavior back in the 1930s, when it first revised its health and pension plans. The benefit changes then were notable in that they came at a time when welfare programs at other firms were still reeling from the Depression's impact. Kodak, however, was determined to maintain its commitment to welfare capitalism and its reputation as an innovative employer. In 1935, it announced a hospital insurance program that was a precursor to the modern Blue Cross system. As with the Rochester Plan, the program was drawn up and run by a group of local companies led by Kodak. Although it was noncontributory, over 60 percent of Kodak workers subscribed to it by 1939. Employees could easily have purchased similar protection from a private insurer, either directly or with Kodak's assistance, but Kodak felt that "a company-administered plan is preferable to one handled through an insurance company from the point of view of maintaining direct contact with employees without the introduction of any outside organization."[73]

In 1937, Kodak made the first of several changes in its pension plan. It increased life insurance coverage and raised disability benefits. A year later it announced a vacation plan for hourly workers, this being the last major benefit that Kodak had previously given only to salaried employees. Actions of this sort continued throughout the 1940s, 1950s, and 1960s: Kodak made regular, incremental improvements to benefits that had originated in the Eastman years, while periodically forging ahead with new policies. Even before the rapid reforms of the 1950s, the company's lead was assured. A 1949 article in *American Business* praised Kodak's employee welfare program as "one of the most thorough in all industry."[74]

Of its various fringe benefits, Kodak spent the most on wage dividends, pensions, and paid vacations, in that order. The wage dividend alone accounted for 10 to 15 percent of Kodak's annual payroll. By the 1940s, it had become a corporate totem, symbolizing Kodak's prosperity and its willingness to share the wealth with employees. Kodak paid the dividend to every employee who had been with the firm more than six months, regardless of occupation, corporate division, or geographic location. This created a bond among Kodak employees throughout the world, although symbolic unity came at a high price. While Kodak was still enormously profitable, market maturity made it somewhat less of a money-making machine than it had been in Eastman's day. Also, the wage dividend raised the ire of Kodak's stockholders, who complained that it cut into their returns. Some wanted to get rid of the plan, but doing so would have been quite difficult. Moreover, Kodak could easily afford the plan and most managers thought it worthwhile.[75]

Other problems with the wage dividend stemmed from its formula, unchanged since 1929: "For each dollar per share of dividends declared on Kodak common stock during the preceding year, over and above $3.50 per share, the wage-dividend rate is one-half of 1% [multiplied by] total wages for the last five calendar years." In other words, the wage dividend was only indirectly related to profits. It was also determined by an employee's past earnings (the wage base) and by the stock dividend rate. Hence the formula brought about an intertwining of corporate finance and employee compensation.[76]

Kodak kept a stable ratio between wage and stock dividends, aiming to split corporate earnings over $3.50 per share evenly between employees and stockholders. Until the early 1940s, Kodak was able to maintain the ratio. After the war, however, things got out of joint. High profits boosted the stock dividend rate while inflation and new hiring swelled the wage base. By 1947, the ratio was over 60 percent. At that point, brokerage houses began to recommend against purchases of Kodak stock.[77]

The logical response would have been to revise the wage dividend formula. But—and this is key—management was deathly afraid that employees would misunderstand such a change and feel that Kodak had reneged on a deal. Instead Kodak engaged in some clever financial legerdemain that pleased the brokers without upsetting employees. Almost every year in the late 1940s and early 1950s, it paid shareholders extra dividends in stock instead of cash. This held down the wage dividend, which was affected only by the dividend *rate*, and raised potential shareholder returns by increasing the amount of stock in circulation. For the same reason, in 1947 Kodak announced a five-for-one stock split. These actions lowered the ratio, but it did not fall far enough. So in 1953 management held its breath and put a cap on the wage dividend payout rate. With great relief it discovered that this brought few complaints from Kodak workers, who, it turned out, judged the adequacy of their wage dividend by measuring it against their earnings, a ratio unaffected by the cap. (Wage dividends still averaged about 15 percent of annual pay.) Emboldened by the experience, Kodak capped the wage dividend again in 1956 and once more in 1960. By taking these steps, Kodak effectively unhinged the wage dividend from corporate earnings, ratifying its status as a pay supplement. In the palmy 1950s, the lack of contingency did not matter a great deal, but it would cause problems for Kodak in later years.[78]

In strict economic terms, Kodak's fringe benefits were simply a monetary exchange between the company and its employees, but by tying benefits to specific employee needs, Kodak could portray itself as acting from moral concerns rather than a cold cash logic. Ever sensitive to charges of paternalism, the company downplayed the dependency inherent in its benefit plans and emphasized their communal aspects. Thus, instead of taking paid vacations alone with their families, Kodakers regularly traveled to Europe and elsewhere on group trips arranged by Kodak. Retirees receiving pensions met for daily recreation activities organized by the company. Along with sports scores, wedding announcements, and obituaries, the company newspaper regularly reported on new benefit programs. Benefits thereby reinforced the impression that Kodak employees were part of a Gemeinschaft, an industrial community of fate. Paternalism was further softened by Kodak's heavy reliance on the helping professions—nurses, doctors, even psychiatrists—in the administration of its welfare programs. In earlier years, pensions were offered because Eastman or Lovejoy personally thought it a wise thing to do. Now Kodak held counseling sessions where trained professionals gave advice on retirement and handed out booklets like "You and the Years Ahead."[79]

In addition to financial benefits, Kodak continued to organize recreational programs on a grand scale. Whereas other firms let such programs die out in the 1930s, Kodak kept its own going full blast. After the war Kodak built an eighteen-hole golf course and a 300,000-square-foot recreation center. The rec center included three cafeterias, meeting rooms, bowling alleys, squash courts, pool tables, a gymnasium, retiree lounge, pistol range, and auditorium that showed movies daily. Popular clubs included the Kodaskaters and Kodactors. Each plant had its own athletic association whose teams played others in interplant leagues. Sports news regularly made the front page of the company newspaper, as when Kodak Park won both the league golf championship and bowling tourney in 1958. These were the most popular sports at Kodak in the 1950s; between them the Rochester plants had twenty bowling leagues and thirty-five golf leagues whose teams contained a mixture of manual and white-collar workers. This sent a powerful message of corporate unity.[80]

Salaried "secretaries" ran the plant athletic associations. Their duties also included counseling employees and selling Kodak products to them at a discount. To fill these jobs Kodak picked "father confessor types," people with whom workers could discuss personal and work-related problems. Assisting the secretaries were nonsalaried officers elected annually by the members. (Kodak Park alone had twenty-four such officers.) The company administered the elections, which usually drew several candidates for each office. Having employees involved in the associations was another way to defuse charges of paternalism, just as company unions had done earlier in the century.[81]

Why did Kodak spend so much time and money on its welfare programs? Like other employers, the firm was swayed by economic considerations—such as economies of scale and tax incentives—that made it cheaper to give workers fringe benefits than to have them purchase it privately. Beyond this was Kodak's implicit contract with employees: in return for steady work and excellent benefits, the company asked employees to keep company secrets, accept technological change, trust their supervisors, and stay away from unions. One Kodak official said privately that, although the company's wage dividend plan was costly, stockholders failed to realize that it was cheaper than fighting labor unions. Kodak's innovative benefit policies kept it several steps ahead of organized labor, which meant that unions had little or nothing to offer Kodak workers in this area.[82]

Benefits also were a subtle way of blurring the distinction between labor and management upon which unionism was premised. Welfare benefits—whether athletic facilities or cash dividends—were companywide and cut across the ranks. Benefit programs also served more mundane but no less important ends to do with efficient personnel management. On the one hand, being a national pacesetter in benefit spending made it easier for Kodak to recruit and retain the best people. On the other hand, programs like pensions and retirement counseling helped Kodak to ease out employees who were thought to be superannuated. Because of these push-and-pull factors, Kodak's Rochester operations in 1950 employed a greater percentage of prime-age workers (twenty-five to fifty-four years old) and fewer workers over the age of fifty-five than were in the local labor force.[83]

In return for its spending, the company boasted that it received "a spirit of cooperation . . . reflected in attitude, efficiency, and longer service." Undoubtedly there was truth to this claim. But how much of a return on the implicit contract did the company get? Kodak simply had no idea. As one manager was forced to admit, "It is not possible to measure the results [of Kodak's benefit program] in dollars, nor can we say how much of the success we may have had has been due to any one part of the program." Kodak could have conducted cost-benefit analyses of its welfare spending, but it never did so. This points to the basic reason for the company's munificence: between high profits on the one hand and low labor-cost ratios on the other, Kodak could well afford to shower its employees with benefits, even if the payoff—in commitment, loyalty, or stability—did not clearly warrant the company's level of spending.[84]

The same was true of wages and salaries. In the 1940s and 1950s, Kodak had a policy of paying wages at least 10 percent above the median of its labor market competitors. This was intended to smooth recruitment, raise morale, and deter unions. Kodak carefully monitored wage bargaining between the Autoworkers and General Motors, and in England it kept pay increases in line with those negotiated by the Cinematograph Technicians Union. Kodak's wage leadership was facilitated by its continuing low labor-cost ratio and by its relatively small blue-collar workforce. Hence, while all Kodak employees received relatively high pay, the premium was largest for production workers. On top of this, new technology steadily boosted Kodak's labor productivity. During the war, Kodak shifted to mass production of lens and camera parts that had previously been fabricated by skilled craftsmen. The trend continued after the war, when sales per Kodak employee rose from $8,435 in 1947 to $15,792 in 1957.[85]

High wages and benefits kept Kodak workers from quitting. As in the 1930s, the company's separation rates were extremely low, running at 13 percent in 1956 as against 50 percent for U.S. industry in general. Long-term jobs were common at Kodak, where, despite the war, nearly one-third of all employees in 1956 had been with the company for fifteen years or more. Other reasons for Kodak's continued stickiness included its internal promotion practices and the policy of avoiding layoffs whenever possible. Although Kodak's postwar stabilization practices were more sophisticated than they had been under Lovejoy, the basic principles remained the same. The statistical department made one- and five-year sales forecasts that formed the basis for detailed production planning. Kodak had an amazing ability to shift among product lines and to alternate between stock and sales production. As a result, seasonal and cyclical employment variation was slight and there were few part-time workers.[86]

Because of Kodak's steady postwar growth, the company could usually absorb its surplus workers. Employees displaced by technological change had the option of taking early retirement or being trained for other jobs in the company. When automation became a national concern in the late 1950s, Kodak workers were assured by the company that "everything is done to hold layoffs to an absolute minimum. In fact, Kodak's experience has been so favorable we can say that layoffs hardly ever occur because of mechanical processes." Ironically, one year after issuing that statement, cessation of a naval contract forced the company to lay off several hundred workers in the Rochester area. Over a third of those eligible chose to take early retirement; the remaining workers were rehired within the year. But this was a "blue moon" event for Kodak, the only major layoff to occur between 1940 and 1975.[87]

In contrast to fringe benefits, Kodak carefully analyzed the savings brought about by stabilization, but the measurements related chiefly to the more efficient use of capital that stabilization permitted. When it came to Kodak's layoff-avoidance policy—an offshoot of stabilization—no evidence was gathered to prove the policy was worth the cost. Nevertheless, it was an article of faith for Kodak managers that the layoff policy was the primary reason for the firm's nonunion status. Managers knew how much the policy meant to Kodak workers who had experienced the Depression. If employees ever worried whether Kodak's security commitments were credible, they would have been reassured by the company's ubiquitous ceremonies and awards in recognition of long service: watches, dinners, field trips, and the publication in *Kodakery* of employee "anniversary dates" and stories about old-timers. The continuation of Eastman-era hiring practices further reinforced perceptions of stability. Entire families (such as the Inghams—husband, wife, and six sons) could still be found at Kodak after the war. Although there was an increase in the number of white ethnics, Yankees and German-Americans remained the dominant groups. Few blacks worked at Kodak, even in menial jobs.[88]

Kodak encouraged employees to think of themselves as an elite, and they did. Among Rochesterians, Kodak workers had a reputation for being a bit snide and superior. In 1957, the local journalist Curt Gerling wrote that "association with the giant business octopus has come to carry with it a certain class distinction. . . . From the cradle infants are impressed with the fact that 'daddy is a Kodak man'; inferentially this compares with 'your father is a 33rd Degree Mason.'" Along with elitism came what Gerling called "a certain conformity." Workers were expected to adjust to Kodak's genteel paternalism, while Kodak hired only workers whom it thought could fit in. The problem with people of southern or eastern European descent, said a Kodak manager in the 1950s, was that "they are too emotional and more likely to join unions." Prejudice was one of the less laudable legacies of the Eastman years. When Kodak sought a site for its Texas plant in the late 1940s, it first considered the Gulf Coast, where other chemical companies had located. But management was bothered by the large number of Mexican-Americans there, so it built the plant in Longview, a costlier site but one with more Anglos in the area.[89]

Despite all this, Kodak was the employer of choice for Rochester workers of the 1940s, 1950s, and 1960s. Pay, benefits, and security were excellent. The factories were air-conditioned and modern, and most of Kodak's manual jobs were clean, if at times difficult or dangerous. In contrast to Rochester's automotive and machine workers, whose clothes were stained with grease and dirt, film makers at Kodak dressed entirely in white—hats, pants, and shirts. Because of the preponderance of clean jobs, Kodak attracted a large number of women. It also exempted women from night work, which was an additional draw. Like other firms, Kodak hired more women during the Second World War, although this produced less dramatic changes than elsewhere. In fact, the percentage of women at Kodak—about one-third of the work force—changed little between the 1920s and 1950s. And although Kodak employed more women than the typical U.S. manufacturer, its work force was proportionately less female than the Rochester average, which was boosted by the city's numerous clothing and garment factories.[90]

Kodak's personnel policies were lavish and costly, but there was always a risk of having them undermined by inept supervision. A worker's relationship to his or her supervisor was a daily affair, whereas welfare benefits and job stability had less immediate consequences. Although this observation may seem perfectly obvious, many companies did not act on it. Personnel managers could change policy by fiat, but getting line managers to change their behavior to match the new policy was more difficult, especially when a belief in the virtues of harsh discipline was deeply engrained. Large companies that ignored this problem in the 1920s began to grapple with it during the 1940s. Often the advent of a union was the spur to action. Kodak had a different experience, however, because it had never pursued the drive system and, relatedly, because it had longstanding programs for foreman training.

The training course designed by Allen B. Gates in the 1930s emphasized formal relations of authority, such as the role of line versus staff and the delegation of responsibility. The course was well regarded and well funded, but it was completely redesigned at the end of the Second World War, when human relations ideas began to seep into industry. During the war, Kodak had used the government's Job Relations Training program, which was based on the human relations approach. Favorably impressed by the program, in the fall of 1945 Kodak commissioned a clinical psychologist to design a new foreman training course dealing with "the nature of human nature."[91]

The course consisted of twenty-four sessions combining role-playing, discussion of filmed case studies, and readings. Foremen were told that "the Company's idea [is] that feelings are important" and that their job was "to make feelings work FOR rather than against the employee and the Company." The course explained how to recognize "common evidences of anxiety or worry" and when to provide "emotional first aid." Often the advice for foremen consisted of nothing more than cliches like "add a 'personal touch' when dealing with people." But the manual could be more sophisticated, as when it instructed foremen to "appeal to the things the employee values [and] avoid threatening those things." Critics charged that the human relations approach was manipulative. But Craig P. Cochrane, the head of industrial relations for Kodak, argued that it satisfied "a deep yearning for recognition [and] a sense of participation" while providing "opportunities for self-development on a meaningful job."[92]

Kodak insisted, somewhat defensively, that the course was "not a sudden thing developed to meet some current situation," although the course happened to be initiated at a time—the late 1940s—when Kodak faced its first major union activity. One Kodak manager later justified the money and effort spent on supervisory training as a legitimate response to "salesmanship" on the part of labor unions. "But we can sell too," he said. "We try to treat people fairly, with integrity, with decency, with honesty, because this is the way people deserve to be treated. And we feel that if we do the best we possibly can, the salesmanship on the part of the union organization will have to take care of itself."[93]

Human relations training was frequently ineffectual. As historian Howell Harris says, "It could produce verbal acceptance of the principles of 'leading, not bossing,' etc., but had little apparent effect on foremen's actual behavior in the workplace." At Kodak, however, such training did have an effect. Kodak was renowned for the excellence of its supervision; its training course was filmed and sold to other companies. But the secret of the program's success was Kodak's personnel staff, who kept an eagle eye on foremen and were ruthless with them when an employee problem occurred. Every foreman at Kodak, said Craig Cochrane, would receive credit for good relationships in his group, but "if poor relationships exist, then he must [also] be held largely responsible." Any such "failure," said Cochrane, "cannot very well be tolerated."[94]

An unusual way Kodak kept track of its foremen was through its suggestion system, which consisted of blank forms and locked boxes for depositing them; the boxes were placed throughout each plant. Kodak workers were never told to turn in suggestions about supervision, but the company did nothing to discourage the practice. In a memo to managers, Kodak said that "a suggestion which calls attention to a condition without offering any constructive idea would not normally be considered a suitable subject. Yet we must remember that such a suggestion might offer an employee his only means for getting action on the matter." In fact, complaints about foremen constituted a substantial number of the "suggestions" turned in each year. Kodak's plant personnel managers were always alert to comments about supervision. As a company manual put it, "it is greatly to [the foreman's] credit when suggestions from his men indicate that he has developed a sound and effective organization and a general attitude of cooperation."[95]

Given all this pressure, Kodak foremen suffered their own morale problems. The Clothing Workers' Rochester office periodically received calls from disgruntled Kodak foremen who would ask about joining the union. Kodak bent over backward to compensate for on-the-job stress with after-work diversions at the foremen's club, where dinners, smokers, and musical entertainment were regularly provided.[96]

In the classical organization model, personnel managers, whether at the corporate or plant level, are supposed to serve in an advisory capacity to line management. Kodak's plant personnel managers, however, did not adhere to a strict separation between policy conception and execution. They took over duties that, at least in theory, were the province of line management—such things as resolving employee complaints and disciplining supervisors. As one manager described the Kodak approach, "Each plant has its own industrial relations department reporting to the plant manager. These groups *carry out* the industrial relations plans and procedures." Kodak's powerful plant personnel staff not only checked the company's foremen, but they were also proof of the importance Kodak attached to boosting employee morale and, moreover, to avoiding unions. Only that sort of external threat could justify Kodak's approach.[97]

The power of Kodak's plant personnel staff also came at the expense of the corporate industrial relations department, which did little more than handle companywide benefit policies. Each of Kodak's major plants was, as one manager put it, "almost a law unto themselves." Plant managers distrusted the corporate industrial relations staff for their liberal arts degrees and lack of line experience. The prejudice was even shared by some of the company's top executives. Much of this can be traced to Kodak Park, which dominated the scene in Rochester and did not want corporate staff meddling in its affairs. Other Kodak divisions took their cues from Kodak Park. While this arrangement pushed the personnel function down to the plant level, where a close watch could be kept on employee relations, it created problems: for example, no one could tell plant personnel managers to lighten up on foremen if need be.[98]

Keeping Unions at Bay

Kodak managers attributed the absence of unions to the company's high pay and good supervision. The head of Kodak's British subsidiary, who spent his entire career with the company, said that he had "always been brought up to understand that the primary objective of a trade union was to see that a group of employees collectively got a fair deal, and that the companies' standards are good in every conceivable way. . . . We have a reputation of very high standards and very good industrial relations." The implication of this remark was clear. At Kodak, *management* saw to it that the employees got a fair deal, and if a union came in, it was management's fault. For that reason, Kodak executives were embarrassed and their pride badly hurt when a small chemical union organized a Kodak plant outside Toronto shortly after World War II. This was the only Kodak facility in North America ever to be unionized. Since the plant had the same personnel policies as other Kodak units, Craig Cochrane had to rationalize the Canadian experience by blaming a local plant manager for his "stubborness and arbitrariness."[99]

Under certain conditions, however, the company was willing to tolerate collective bargaining. In Britain, in 1951 Kodak set up Workers' Representative Committees (WRCs)—company unions that were an offshoot of the production councils created by the wartime government. Although Kodak's British managers were opposed to bargaining with craft unions, they negotiated with WRCs and claimed they would do the same with an industrial union if it could prove majority support. As compared to craft unions, industrial unions were said to be "the lesser of two evils."[100]

Despite these few exceptions, opposition to unions was engrained in Kodak's corporate culture. Even employees received pamphlets entitled "Why Are There No Unions at Kodak?" Unions were based on a conflict of interests, said Allen B. Gates; management, however, had the ability to recognize "conflicting *and* common interests" and so, Gates concluded, "collective bargaining [is] unnecessary." In a nutshell, this was the corporatist philosophy. Kodak managers quickly learned that it would be considered a major failure if unionism were to take hold under their guard.[101]

While other firms were transformed by the rise of "big labor" and "big government" in the 1940s, Kodak stuck to the approach developed under Eastman. Since Kodak was profitable and experienced few organizing attempts or other problems, management saw little reason to make major changes. The foundations laid in the Eastman years were solid; even in the 1960s, few employers could match Kodak's array of benefits and job security. Stability also had a human dimension. Long after Eastman's death, Kodak managers remained loyal to his memory. Curt Gerling, the journalist, was not entirely joking when he advised Kodak employees that "the founder should always be referred to as Mr. Eastman. Try to get a touch of reverence in your intonation." Yet because Kodak was such an insular company, few employees snickered at this ancestor worship. Low turnover, family hiring, and managerial inbreeding created a corporate culture with a strong sense of tradition. Frank Lovejoy, who ran Kodak after Eastman's death, once gave a speech to employees in which he asked, "What is 'The Company'?" The company, he said, was "the accumulation of precedents and principles, growing with the years, that have come to animate the organization—perhaps the spirit that permeates it. At any rate, that is what I mean when I say to myself, 'The Company can't do that,' or 'The Company should do this.'"[102]

This is not to say that Kodak rested on its laurels, oblivious to the changes going on around it. As described earlier, Kodak kept close track of wage and benefit negotiations in the union sector, and after 1940 it began to shower employees with publications that boasted of the advantages the company offered. *Kodakery*, the employee newspaper, was started during the war because management realized the potential for "a confrontation with third parties and [it] wanted a vehicle to get into the home so that not only the head of the house but his family would get our story." After the war, Kodak began mailing quarterly "Statements of Your Personal Situation," which showed the value of an employee's current and accrued fringe benefits.[103]

Kodak's major innovation during these years was its Code of Industrial Relations, which contained an item-by-item listing of Kodak's policies on supervision, promotions, layoffs, wages, and benefits. The code was Lovejoy's idea and came to him on a train ride from New York City to Rochester in 1937. The U.S. Supreme Court had recently upheld the constitutionality of the Wagner Act, a ruling that touched off a surge of contract negotiations. Lovejoy wanted Kodak workers to have something like a union contract—a written document—that laid out for them "the principles which determine the way of life at Kodak." On the train with Lovejoy were Kodak's other top executives. After a lengthy discussion, they decided on the code's basic language. Copies of the code were distributed to every Kodak employee.[104]

The heart of the code was a complaint system known as the Open Door. Workers could take up grievances with their foremen; in turn, Kodak expected foremen to "make it clear that group action is not required to get attention and action on an individual complaint." Each foreman was told to be sympathetic to employees, prompt in resolving complaints, and vigilant in "safeguarding the rights and interests of his group." Having to fill contradictory roles as counselor and shop steward—and doing it with grace and empathy—was yet another reason Kodak's supervisors sometimes felt overwhelmed. On top of that, workers were permitted to bypass their foreman and take complaints directly to the division or plant personnel manager. If a foreman had erred, the plant manager faced the sticky situation of correcting the problem without embarrassing the foreman.[105]

Kodak workers most commonly complained about performance appraisals, time study, and promotions. These were the same grievances raised in unionized plants but with one difference: dismissal complaints were less common at Kodak, because relatively few workers were dismissed. One reason for this was structural: since the 1920s, only plant personnel departments—not foremen—had been permitted to fire Kodak workers. Yet this was the same department that was supposed to be the final step in the Open Door procedure. Plant managers resolved the contradiction in being both judge and jury by erring on the side of leniency and giving workers a second chance.

Although precise statistics on usage of the Open Door were not kept, company managers admitted that Kodak workers were less likely to file complaints than the average worker in a unionized firm. This probably reflected workers' fears of being stigmatized as complainers should they press an issue too assertively, not an unreasonable concern in a conformist company like Kodak. Thus, Kodak's Open Door provided employees with fewer "voice" opportunities than did a union grievance procedure, but discipline was more lenient and there were stricter limits on the foremen's discretion than in a unionized setting.[106]

Despite these concessions to unionism, the overall situation at Kodak between the 1930s and 1960s was one of stability, even of complacence and staidness. Stability allowed Kodak to project a corporate image of self-confidence and integrity, which undoubtedly contributed to its capacity to remain unorganized. Paradoxically, however, Kodak's stability owed a great deal to the infrequency of its contacts with organized labor. From 1930 to 1960, only three organizing drives took place at Kodak facilities in the United States. Of these, just one occurred at the company's home base in Rochester.

Kodak's first encounter with the modern labor movement came during Operation Dixie, the CIO's ambitious Southern organizing drive. Launched near the end of the war, Operation Dixie targeted large employers such as Burlington Mills and the coastal petrochemical industry. The drive drew on the efforts of more than a dozen unions and employed nearly 250 organizers, yet it succeeded at only a small number of companies, often in communities where employers had difficulty mobilizing public opinion and police support. One such place was Oak Ridge, Tennessee, a town that sprang up during the war under federal government supervision. Along with Kodak, the prime contractors at Oak Ridge were Union Carbide and Monsanto. Of the 70,000 workers there, each firm employed about one-third, making Oak Ridge an enticing concentration of potential union members. In 1946, Operation Dixie set up the Atomic Workers Organizing Committee when the government lifted its wartime ban on union organizing at Oak Ridge. Along with the AFL, Operation Dixie launched intensive campaigns at the three companies.[107]

Only a few hundred of Kodak's Oak Ridge employees had previously worked for the company. Most of the supervisors also were new, so Kodak had to improvise crash training programs for them when the facility was set up. Of the three firms at Oak Ridge, Kodak was said to have the best-trained supervisory force. When the organizing drive got under way, Kodak relied on these supervisors to convince workers to remain nonunion. Working and living conditions at Oak Ridge were primitive, though, and they provided a potent organizing issue for the unions. At Union Carbide, a majority voted for the CIO, and Monsanto workers decided in favor of an AFL affiliate. Kodak was the only facility where a majority voted no union. Kodak managers were elated with this result, but the campaign had given them the jitters. There was always a chance some union would return to Oak Ridge for another try. If the union won, Kodak might have a hard time keeping unions out of its nearby Kingsport and Holston Ordnance facilities. It was rumored at the time that Operation Dixie officials were planning a drive at these plants, which, like Oak Ridge, were part of the Tennessee Eastman division. Rather than take the risk, Kodak sold the Oak Ridge facility to Union Carbide in 1947.[108]

Shortly after the Oak Ridge election, the CIO again confronted Kodak, this time on Kodak's home turf. Although labor relations in Rochester were relatively peaceful before the war, the city got caught up in the nation's 1946 strike wave. Walkouts by the Steel Workers and the Electrical Workers (UE) idled several thousand in Rochester that year, including workers at American Brake Shoe and General Motors-Delco. The city's most dramatic strike came during an organizing effort by Rochester's municipal trash collectors. To prevent a union from forming, the city manager fired 489 workers and transferred the city's garbage services to private haulers. The next day, the Rochester AFL and CIO affiliates, which previously had never cooperated, formed a joint committee to plan protest activities. Representing the AFL was Tony Capone, a popular Teamster official; the CIO was represented by an official of the Clothing Workers and by Hugh Harley, chief organizer for the UE in Rochester. Two weeks later, after police arrested several hundred picketers for blocking entrances to city garages, the committee called for a general strike.[109]

A one-day protest strike paralyzed Rochester in late May. Picketing occurred at most of the city's unionized workplaces and the Teamsters refused to make local deliveries. An estimated 35,000 workers stayed home and numerous employers shut down for the day. When the city agreed to reinstate the trash collectors, the dispute ended. Local labor activists were thrilled by these events. A Communist party publication said that "in the Rochester strike, the masses learned very quickly, grasping the political nature of their struggle," while a labor newspaper predicted that "the fruits of victory will not only be plucked by the city workers but will also serve as a spur to the majority of unorganized workers in Rochester to organize."[110]

Among those emboldened by the strike was Hugh Harley. A Dartmouth graduate, he had become a UE organizer in 1940. After working in Pittsburgh and New England, Harley arrived in Rochester in September 1945 to oversee the UE's five area organizers. The UE had previously organized General Motors' Delco plant and, in a long report written in October 1945, Harley discussed organizing strategies for a dozen other local targets, including General Railway Signal, Bausch and Lomb, and General Motors' Rochester Products plant. Although Harley mentioned Kodak workers as potential UE members, he did not include Kodak in his list of targets. But a year later, in the aftermath of the general strike, the UE secretly began an organizing drive at the Camera Works. This was a wise choice—the Camera Works paid less and was less stable than Kodak Park, and during the war it had begun to hire large numbers of "ethnics," particularly Italians from the surrounding community.[111]

The UE's initial target was the three-hundred-worker automatic screw department, which recently had hired a third shift to meet the demand for Kodak cameras. Some of the new hires were UE activists "boring from within." In January 1947, the UE brought the drive aboveground. It started distributing leaflets each day in front of the Camera Works, using striking workers from nearby Liberty Tool to help with this and related activities. By February, Harley felt he had "solid control" of the department and issued a list of ten demands. Along with union recognition, the major issues were wage standards and job security.[112]

Eighteen years earlier, the Workers' Nucleus had also targeted the Camera Works. Although there was no direct connection between the two campaigns, both focused on the fact that the camera workers—semiskilled assemblers and machine operators—had jobs that were dirtier, noisier, and less secure than those at Kodak Park. As in the 1921 depression, the Camera Works bore the brunt of Kodak's layoffs in the 1930s. Postwar shift workers worried whether they would keep their jobs if the boom petered out. Also, the camera workers were still on the Bedaux wage-incentive plan, whose standards periodically became a contentious issue.

Kodak managers were shaken by news of the organizing drive. According to Harley, "they moved their industrial relations setup with extraordinary speed." There were no threats or dismissals, none of "the heavy stuff," as Harley called it. Instead, Kodak sent in teams of interviewers from the corporate industrial relations department to find out what the matter was. Harley disparaged this move as "sweet talking," although it led to some immediate changes. In late February the company retimed work standards and raised wage rates by 5 percent, this on top of a 10 percent increase previously set for March. A UE flyer denounced management for "their usual practice of attempting to buy out the workers away from the union" and took credit for the raise.[113]

Next, all camera workers received a letter from Kodak's president, T. J. Hargrave, that sought to refute the union's charges. It asked, "Do these outsiders design cameras and other products? Do they get the customers' orders for them? . . . You know that they do not and cannot do these things. They are also the only things that make jobs secure." As for wages, the letter said that Kodak's postwar wage increases had come without a long and costly strike like the UE's recent five-month walkout at Westinghouse. Finally, Hargrave ticked off Kodak's numerous benefit programs and asked "Did these outsiders have anything to do with bringing [them] into existence? I know, and I am sure you know, that they did not." The letter closed with a call for continued "mutual respect and cooperation." Kodak's swift actions undercut the union's support. Meanwhile, the company kept up its usual whirl of activities. In March, the Camera Works won the Kodak bowling prize, a new cafeteria was opened, and the company paid a record wage dividend. The drive ended the following month and nothing more was heard of the UE at Kodak.[114]

The UE's failure was largely the result of Kodak's soft touch and deep pockets, but not entirely. For one thing, Rochester was a conservative city, where, said one observer, "the business ideology—as expressed in the Chamber of Commerce, the Rotary Club, the Real Estate Board, the Citizen's Tax League, the Gannett papers—provides the prevailing tenor of the town." After the UE targeted Kodak, other employers in the community were quick to lend support to Kodak. When the *Rochester Sun* reported on Hargrave's letter, it printed a side bar listing in bold type each of Kodak's benefit programs and the year it was initiated. Local employers provided Kodak with information about the UE, some of it gleaned from the FBI. Ever since the 1946 general strike in Rochester, the FBI had been closely monitoring the city's labor scene. In 1947, the FBI approached Russell McCarthy, head of Rochester's Industrial Management Council, and questioned him about Harley's activities. McCarthy immediately went to Kodak and reported everything the FBI had told him.[115]

Such cooperation was not uncommon. Compared to other industrial cities in the region, Rochester had fewer branch plants and fewer unionized companies. Whereas branch plant managers had to carry out labor relations policies set in Pittsburgh or Detroit, Rochester's locally owned firms could steer a more independent course. Bausch and Lomb, Rochester's second-largest firm, was completely nonunion, as were Taylor Instrument, Ritter Dental Supply, and Gleason Works.[116] Whenever a local employer contemplated signing a union contract, other businessmen closed ranks and pressured him not to do so. For example, an engine manufacturer on the verge of recognizing a union was threatened with a service cutoff by the bus company that transported workers to its plant.[117]

Also contributing to the UE's defeat were the union's innumerable internal problems. Although 1946 had been a banner year for the UE, 1947 was quite different. Like other unions, the UE was torn apart by factional fights that were intensified by passage of the Taft-Hartley Act in June. Little more than a year later, the CIO expelled the UE and then helped its anti-Communist wing launch a rival union, the International Union of Electrical Workers (IUE), whose predatory tactics consumed the UE's energies. Even if the Camera Works could have been organized, the UE was probably the wrong union at the wrong time.[118]

The only other postwar organizing drive at Kodak came in 1956 at its Los Angeles film-processing plant. About two hundred people worked at the plant, which developed film for the motion picture industry. The Film Technicians Union, which represented other photofinishers in the city, claimed its members received higher wages than Kodak paid its workers. Kodak countered with its own figures, which showed higher total compensation at Kodak. Kodak officials privately blamed the drive on local management, citing the case of a Los Angeles supervisor who allegedly had used company employees to build an addition on his house. The campaign was straightforward, with the exception of a National Labor Relations Board ruling in favor of Kodak's definition of who was eligible to vote in the election. Had the election at the plant been close, the ruling might have hurt the union, but Kodak won by a majority of nearly three to one. Despite the small size of the unit, Kodak officials took the drive seriously, not wishing to see any chink opened up in Kodak's nonunion armor.[119]

There was one U.S. case in which Kodak tolerated collective bargaining. This was at Kodak Park, where, from the 1910s through the 1950s, the photoengraving department employed a handful of workers belonging to the AFL's Photo-Engravers' Union. Kodak accepted them because the union effectively controlled entry into the trade. Although the company refused to sign the union's contract with local employers, it adhered to its terms. Relations between Kodak and the union remained friendly until the late 1950s, when a new union leader began pressing Kodak to sign the multi-employer agreement. Kodak responded with its by now customary divestment strategy: it sold the photoengraving operations to Case-Hoyt Company, which in turn set up a division known as Empire Graphics. This division received most of its business from Kodak.[120]

All in all, union organizers felt that they had few material benefits to offer Kodak workers. A combination of corporate characteristics—including stability and steady profits—was translated into job security, high wages, elaborate benefits, and esprit de corps, which helped Kodak combat unionism when other companies failed. This is not to say that an experienced organizer could have found no weak spots. Kodak's Open Door procedure, for example, was inferior to the typical union grievance system. Employees received no assistance when pressing complaints, and neutral parties were unavailable to ensure impartiality. Yet even here there were counterweights. Kodak carefully monitored its supervisors and trained them to be lenient, in contrast to union-sector foremen, who relied on tight discipline to suppress union challenges to their authority. According to a local labor arbitrator, only gross malfeasance would have gotten someone fired from Kodak's Rochester plants in the 1950s and 1960s. People with problems, like alcoholics or heart-attack survivors, were offered counseling or transferred to easier jobs. Kodak was a good example of what sociologist Alvin Gouldner called "the indulgency pattern," in which employers use disciplinary criteria "applicable to friends and neighbors, rather than . . . a business and industrial context." Such lenience, said Gouldner, disposes workers "to trust their supervisors."[121]

Paternalism—the absence of an employee voice—was a more serious weakness. Kodak claimed it was sensitive to workers' needs and as far back as 1944 called its suggestion system a form of "employee participation, providing the opportunity for self-expression through submitting ideas to management." Yet this was hyperbole, to say the least. Kodak never encouraged workers to offer nontechnical suggestions, nor did it provide any open forums for dialogue between workers and management. To determine what workers wanted, management relied on informal channels: close contact with employees, supervisors, and recreational secretaries. Kodak managers boasted of their ability to "anticipate the needs of the individual. This is the secret of how we are in advance of anything a union can do for our employees." That view harked back to the 1920s, when Mary Follett had urged "integration [via] the anticipation of conflict." Follett wrote, "It isn't enough merely to study the actual relations of your employees; you must anticipate their reactions, beat them to it." Yet this sort of paternalism, no matter how benevolent or responsive, missed a point that some employers began to grasp in the 1960s: that self-expression was not only meaningful for employees but also a cathartic way of easing conflict in the workplace.[122]

Still, one wonders how many Kodak workers nodded in agreement when the UE criticized Kodak for its paternalism, or were stirred when John L. Lewis attacked General Motors' haughty managers as "economic royalists [with] their fangs in labor." This was powerful rhetoric, but Kodak did not have the social chasm separating workers and managers that existed at firms like General Motors. To reduce status distinctions, Kodak refused to pay special bonuses to managers, ran all benefit programs (including time off) on a companywide basis, and taught supervisors to say "so-and-so works 'with me,' not 'for me.'"[123]

Even as Kodak's clannishness bridged the internal chasm, it widened the gap between the company's workers and the rest of the Rochester working class. Members of the the Clothing Workers—the largest industrial union in Rochester—had little in common with Kodak workers. Not only were they paid less, but the union was multi-ethnic and in the 1950s still had separate locals for members who spoke Italian, Yiddish, Lithuanian, and Polish. Other unionized Rochester companies had pay levels closer to Kodak's but few could match Kodak in all respects. Opinion polls showed that even union members considered Kodak the best place in town to work. Hence Kodak workers were unlikely to feel that the labor movement supported their standard of living.[124]

Kodak had succeeded admirably in making its workers feel greater loyalty to the company than to other workers in the community. Lifetime employment prospects, benevolent management, and cradle-to-grave benefits made "Big Yellow" a desirable place to enter and a difficult place to leave. The company had been a forerunner in pursuit of welfare capitalism and never abandoned its progressive programs as many other companies did, particularly during the Depression. By the 1960s, Kodak was so identified with its employment policies that management would not risk alienating its workers by revising them, even though the company was less profitable than it had been in the 1920s. Eventually—in the 1980s—Kodak was forced to make a series of traumatic layoffs. Yet even so, the basic structure of the company's employment policies remained intact. Despite changing times, Kodak chose—once again—to preserve tradition.

Four

Changing Styles: Sears Roebuck

A MAGAZINE ARTICLE once asked, "Which company do you think has the most stores, the most customers, the most sales, the most profits—and at the same time is the most loved, the most far-flung, the most *American* institution ever to charge two bucks for a bottle of snake oil?" The answer, of course, was Sears Roebuck.[1]

Sears Roebuck had its start in 1886, when a Minnesota railway agent named Richard W. Sears began selling pocket watches and trinkets to other station agents and then to local farmers through the mail. A year later Sears moved to Chicago, joined up with a watchmaker named Alvah C. Roebuck, and expanded his mail-order line to include clothing and household goods for farmers. Sears was a marketing genius, but he lacked the managerial skills needed to handle efficiently the growing volume of orders. Julius Rosenwald, a successful Chicago clothing merchant, bought into the company in 1895 (Roebuck sold out for a pittance shortly thereafter), slashed costs, and gradually wrested control from Sears.[2]

Over the next three decades, Sears Roebuck grew rapidly. Until 1920 more than half the U.S. population still lived in rural areas, where Sears made most of its sales. Its mail-order catalogs offered everything a farm family might need, from furniture to farm implements to shoes (its most popular item). Whereas mass production had made Kodak an industrial giant, Sears built its reputation as "merchant to the millions" on its prowess in mass distribution. By 1929, Sears ranked thirtieth in total assets among the top one hundred American industrial corporations; Kodak was farther down the list, in sixtieth place.[3]

Like Kodak, Sears was an exemplar of welfare capitalism in the 1920s. But whereas Kodak stayed the course after 1930, Sears fashioned a new approach, welding welfare capitalism to modern personnel techniques both "soft" (behavioral science) and "hard" (aggressive union avoidance). That Sears was more dynamic than Kodak comes as no surprise. For one thing, Sears was repeatedly confronted with union organizing drives from the late 1930s to the late 1950s. For another, Sears was less geographically and socially integrated than Kodak. Headquartered in Chicago, the company had units in hundreds of cities and towns across the nation. With neither community nor ethnic ties to hold it together, Sears found substitutes in gender (its core work force was mostly male) and in its carefully contrived corporate culture. Sears confronted a more volatile business environment than Kodak. In the late 1920s Sears jumped into retailing, which brought a revision of business strategy and a change of chief executives. Julius Rosenwald, who had built Sears into a mail-order giant, handed over the reins to Robert E. Wood in 1928. Known as "the General," Wood turned Sears into the nation's largest department store chain.

Sears' empire of stores was vast and complex, a nightmare for centralized management. By 1950, Sears had three times as many employees as Kodak, and unlike photographic film, retailing was a highly competitive industry offering fewer surplus profits. Also, whereas Kodak workers never had to meet the people who purchased their products, contact with customers was a critical part of retail salesmanship. As a result of all these factors, Sears was forced to move far beyond the kind of welfare capitalism that served Kodak so well. Necessity, as the cliché has it, impelled Sears to invention.

From Mail Order to Retail

To succeed in the mail-order business, Sears constructed a behemoth mail order plant on Chicago's West Side in 1906. With more than ninety acres of floor space, it was then the largest business building in the world. By 1926, similar branch plants had been built in Atlanta, Dallas, Kansas City, Seattle, and Philadelphia. The plants were marvels of modern scientific management whose scheduling systems resembled automotive assembly lines. After the post office delivered the orders in huge sacks, they were sent through a device that date-stamped each envelope and slit it open at the rate of 450 envelopes per minute. Then the money was removed, the order was scrutinized to determine if special handling was required, and it went to the scribing department, where lading bills and box labels were printed. From there the order went to the index routing department, where card files showed the best route for shipping the order. In the schedule division the order received tickets showing the exact time its component parts had to clear each merchandise department so as to simultaneously arrive in the assembling room. To quicken the flow, heavy use was made of horizontal conveyors, vertical belts, and spiral chutes. At the Chicago plant, over fifteen miles of pneumatic tubes—the largest system of its kind in the world—sped order forms around the building.[4]

For workers, periodic analyses by management to eliminate "useless motions," as well as incentive wages tied to production speed, added to the pressure of precise scheduling. Because the work was so physically demanding, Sears preferred hiring young workers. Quit rates were high, but employees were easily replaced, so management didn't mind. Most jobs were semiskilled and, said one manager, it took "just a few days to get [a new employee] up to maximum speed." Seasonal hiring and a reliance on temporary workers also contributed to the high turnover. Like factory work, mail-order jobs were monotonous and enervating. After visiting Sears' Chicago plant in 1925, a German journalist wrote, "Day in and day out they stand and pack, year in and year out. Others copy letters containing orders, but each one always the same, day in and day out. The ghost of standardization stands like an Alp over the entire business. . . . Only an iron will and a tireless energy suffices for this mill."[5]

Yet there were notable differences between mail-order and factory work. Mail-order jobs were comparatively clean and safe—like office work, but more routinized. Many of the jobs were held by women, who did most of the order filling, wrapping, and clerical work. In the 1910s, between 55 and 60 percent of the employees at Sears were female, typically young and single. Hiring young women kept labor costs down, but in 1913 the strategy backfired and caused a major scandal. During the early 1900s, efforts to pass protective legislation for women led reformers to investigate the link between low wages and prostitution. A commission on vice reported in 1910 that prostitution was a $15 million industry in Chicago, attributable to the low wages earned by the city's young women. Julius Rosenwald—president of Sears, benefactor of Hull House, and supporter of progressive reform activities in Chicago—sat on the commission. Nothing was done about the report until 1913, when an ambitious attorney general set up a state committee to investigate white slavery. The first employer called to testify was Rosenwald, who was grilled by the committee about wage rates at Sears. When Rosenwald was asked if he thought low wages had anything to do with "the immorality of women and girls," he replied, "I think there is no connection between the two." The remark caused a sensation in the press, as did Rosenwald's testimony that Sears employed more than fifteen hundred young women earning less than $8.00 per week, said to be the minimum necessary to live in Chicago. In his defense, Rosenwald said that those women paid less than $8.00 all lived at home, and other evidence showed that wages at Sears—where the average woman earned $9.12 per week in 1913—were within the range paid by comparable employers. Yet the overall impression was that Sears mistreated female workers.[6]

This episode was deeply embarrassing to Rosenwald, a friend of Chicago's leading social reformers (once during a clothing workers' strike he had his chauffeur drive Grace Abbott to the picket line) and renowned for his philanthropy. Over the years Rosenwald had given millions to various causes, including the Tuskegee Institute and other black educational institutions. Now he was vulnerable to charges that his fortune was ill-gained. The state committee's chairman brought out the fact that net profits at Sears were $8 million and he forced Rosenwald to admit that Sears would be able to pay large stock dividends even if it gave employees a quarter of its profits. Later that year, a fellow trustee from Hull House suggested to Rosenwald that he consider a profit-sharing plan for Sears workers. In 1916 Rosenwald created one of the nation's most generous and publicized profit-sharing plans.[7]

The "Savings and Profit Sharing Pension Fund of Sears Roebuck" paid out about 10 percent of net profits each year, somewhat less than Kodak's wage dividend. But Kodak's dividend was a wage supplement intended to boost current earnings, whereas the Sears Fund was a pension plan designed to encourage savings and stability. Employee and company contributions were deposited in personal accounts and most of the money was invested in Sears stock. Employees could not touch the funds until they left the company, and even then they could not take the company's contribution unless they had been with Sears for at least ten years. Only regular employees with more than one years' service could participate in the plan. Ironically, then, the plan's prime beneficiaries were not women but men, who had lower turnover rates and were more likely to be employed on a regular basis. One concession Sears made to women was permitting them to withdraw the company contribution after five years' service instead of the usual ten, but only if a woman quit to get married. Other personnel policies also favored men. For example, Sears gave "special consideration to the financial responsibilities of married men," a policy that widened the gender gap in earnings. None of this, however, was inconsistent with social norms. Women at Sears received the same second-class treatment as at other large companies.[8]

Even before profit sharing, there had been other career-oriented policies at Sears, including vacation (1907) and illness (1912) plans (again favoring long-service workers) and yearly bonuses based on tenure (1912). But Sears was slow in developing its personnel staff. It did not have a central personnel department until the 1930s, although each mail-order plant had a hiring manager and the company's early use of monetary benefits to stabilize employment anticipated personnel management reforms of the 1920s.[9]

Going back even farther—to the late 1890s and early 1900s—Sears had experimented with more traditional welfare work. Elmer Scott, who joined Sears in 1895 and became general manager of the Chicago plant, was responsible for most of these programs. Scott started an employee magazine, *The Skylight*, and set up social groups such as the Seroco Club. A follower of Jane Addams, the founder of Hull House, he brought YMCA speakers to the plant to give noontime talks on "character training" and arranged for the Chicago Public Library to distribute books there. Although some of Scott's reforms were superficial—buzzers that signaled shift changes were replaced by colored lights—others were more substantive, including the Mutual Benefit Association for employee health expenses. Scott's crowning achievement was the new Chicago mail-order plant, which was surrounded by sunken gardens, athletic fields, tennis courts, and a branch YMCA building. Inside were several restaurants serving low-cost meals and a small hospital that gave free treatment to the plant's ten thousand workers. Taken as a whole, these reforms placed Sears in welfare capitalism's vanguard, along with companies like Kodak, Filene's, and National Cash Register. Seeing Sears' reputation tarnished was another reason Rosenwald was so distressed by the 1913 hearings.[10]

Rosenwald's concern with public relations was more than personal vanity. As early as 1897, independent Southern merchants threatened by Sears' growing success began circulating rumors that Richard Sears and Alvah Roebuck were black. The fact that Rosenwald and other top officers at Sears were Jewish, and that Rosenwald gave millions to black colleges, only made matters worse. Merchants in one town urged local residents to burn their Sears catalogs in the public square. Elsewhere, store owners called the company "Shears and Sawbuck," linking Sears to cheap merchandise and deceptive advertising. As Sears grew ever larger, so did the tide of opposition from independent merchants. To improve its image in rural areas, Sears established the Agricultural Foundation, which supplied farmers with information on modern agricultural methods. Sears also organized national seed-corn shows; donated money to help rural areas hire extension experts; and started the radio station WLS—World's Largest Store—to broadcast crop and weather information to Midwestern farmers. These efforts did little to allay complaints from local merchants, which rose to a fever pitch when Sears began opening retail stores.[11]

Sears was spurred to move into retailing by Montgomery Ward, its archrival. In 1920, sales at Sears were more than twice those at Ward's, but the gap between the two firms narrowed after the 1921 depression. One reason for Ward's growing success was its new vice president, General Robert E. Wood, who previously had been in charge of supplies for the Panama Canal and for the U.S. Army during the First World War. At Ward's, the general proved himself to be a merchandising genius. Realizing that automobile owners constituted a lucrative new market, Wood heavily advertised replacement tires and raised Ward's tire sales tenfold. He also urged Ward's to enter retailing on a large scale; the firm was willing to open a few stores in and around its mail-order houses, but Wood clashed with Ward's president over retail strategy and left the company in 1924. Several months later, he joined Sears Roebuck and was able to put in place his ideas about retailing. As at Ward's, he first opened retail stores inside mail-order plants and in cities where those plants were located. Once these stores were established, Wood moved rapidly on to other cities. By 1929, Sears had 319 stores, which accounted for almost 40 percent of the company's sales.[12]

Julius Rosenwald, by then the chairman of Sears and still a powerful figure there, went along with Wood's retail drive. Wood convinced Rosenwald that the time was right to diversify into retailing because the decline of the farm population and the growth of urban areas implied a shrinking market for mail order. Also, the automobile made farmers less dependent on mail order but created new markets such as auto supplies and home repair items for suburban homeowners.

To avoid competition with its mail-order business, Sears opened retail stores in large cities, targeting those with at least 100,000 inhabitants. Montgomery Ward's favored smaller towns, which was another reason Sears went after big cities. By 1930, Sears had twenty-three large stores in cities with populations over 300,000; Ward's opened only one such store. Sears built its stores on the urban fringe, where land was cheap enough to construct ample customer parking lots, a simple idea that nevertheless was critical to the company's long-term success.[13]

Another distinctive feature of Sears stores was its product line. Sears avoided the "stylish" items and high levels of service found in department stores. Instead it offered standardized but high-quality products. Most profitable for Sears were "hard goods"—automobile supplies, hardware, sporting goods—particularly "big ticket" items like furniture and home appliances. Forty percent of Sears retail volume came from such items and an additional 30 percent from other hard goods. Five-and-dimes and variety chains—stores such as Woolworth's, W. T. Grant, J.C. Penney, and Kresge—had been selling a mixture of hard and soft goods since the late nineteenth century. But their merchandise consisted mainly of low-quality dry goods (that is, no furniture or major appliances). By offering variety and quality at low cost, Sears spanned a more diverse clientele than department stores or other chains.[14]

Sears had three store sizes. The small "C" stores sold only hard goods, usually tires and batteries. Targeted for the suburbs, Wood envisioned these stores as catering primarily to men. The large "A" stores were as big as department stores and, like them, carried a mixture of hard and soft goods. In between were the "B" stores, which sold only hard goods but had a wider selection than the "C" stores. Until Sears came along, most hard goods were carried by independent furniture, appliance, and hardware stores. Sears could undercut their prices because it had a more efficient distribution system and because it received volume discounts from suppliers. Sears nurtured long-term relationships with its suppliers, which gave the company the advantages of vertical integration without the risks of full ownership.[15]

The "A" stores did not compete directly with existing department stores. Soft goods, chiefly apparel, constituted only 20 percent of "A" store sales, whereas in department stores they accounted for 75 percent of sales. One reason Sears stayed away from apparel was that seasonal style changes precluded volume discounts based on long production runs. Sears management admitted that apparel was the weakest point in the "A" stores, although the company did manage to steal other profitable soft lines from department stores, including bed linens and bath towels. With their mix of hard and soft goods, the "A" stores represented an entirely new concept in retailing: serving men and women under one roof.[16]

Thus, Sears differentiated itself from other retailers by its products, customers, and buying tactics. The companies that most resembled Sears were Ward's and J.C. Penney, although Sears had several advantages over them, notably its store locations and management policies. By stepping up its retail expansion after the Second World War, Sears was able to pull far ahead of the competition. A few weeks after V-J Day, Sewell Avery, the head of Ward's, had lunch with General Wood. Like many other businessmen, Avery predicted a "tremendous depression" and told Wood, "I'm going to stop all expansion, accumulate cash, and be ready." Wood, however, was gambling that pent-up consumer demand would fuel a postwar boom, and he told Avery, "I'm going ahead at full speed." During the next eight years, Ward's closed several dozen stores, while Sears opened 134 new stores and expanded or relocated 232 others. The Sears stores were well situated to profit from the postwar surge in suburban homeownership. Sears targeted California, Texas, and the South, correctly guessing that these areas would experience rapid growth in the postwar period. Indeed, Sears outpaced all other large retailers during the 1950s. Although Sears retained its mail-order units, retailing became far and away its primary business.[17]

Although Sears' postwar growth was remarkable, the company's resilience during the Depression was as important to its growing strength. Mail orders dropped right after the crash, but rising retail sales buoyed Sears, and the company showed a profit in 1930 and 1931. Luckily, Sears had slowed the pace of new store openings in 1929. After the crash, Sears continued to open new stores but was able to lease them at rock-bottom rents, while Ward's—which expanded full tilt in 1929—was stuck with paying boom prices.

1932 was a different story. For the first time in its history, Sears showed a loss. It reduced its mail-order force by nearly three thousand workers (about 15 percent) and instituted a companywide wage cut. However, retail sales did not suffer nearly as much as mail order. Stores were put on short hours, but only four were closed completely; the retail work force was not cut. By 1936, when Sears celebrated its fiftieth anniversary, the company was in good shape and sales were recovering vigorously. Mail-order employment was back to its pre-crash levels, and total employment far surpassed the previous peak. That year Sears paid a Golden Jubilee bonus of two weeks' extra pay in recognition that "employees had suffered during the depression."[18]

Even during the Depression, Sears outperformed other retailers. From 1929 to 1933, total Sears employment rose 10 percent while U.S. retail employment declined 29 percent. Net sales fell at Sears during this period, but the drop was smaller than the national retail average. Thus Sears was gaining a growing piece of a shrinking pie. From 1929 to 1933, its percentage share of total U.S. retail sales increased from 0.9 to 1.1, largely at the expense of smaller, independent stores. After 1933, when Sears resumed its retail expansion, it continued to gain market share and by 1939 controlled 1.5 percent of total retail sales. By then Sears was taking business away not only from small merchants but from department stores as well.[19]

Other chain stores also expanded during the 1930s, a phenomenon that touched off a nationwide anti-chain-store movement. Opposition came from independent merchants as well as local politicians seeking new revenue sources. Chains were accused of stealing away the community funds that previously had gone to local businesses and tax coffers. The movement's populist strain was picked up by Huey Long and Father Coughlin, who portrayed the merchant's plight as symbolizing the decline of small towns and the loss of old-fashioned community values. In 1933, the movement's peak year, more than two hundred anti-chain tax bills were introduced in state legislatures. Although aimed primarily at grocery store chains, they also affected Sears. So did the fair trade laws passed by Congress and the states, which struck at the heart of Sears' buying strategy by prohibiting sales at prices below "cost." In 1936, the Federal Trade Commission enjoined Goodyear from selling tires to Sears at volume discounts.[20]

Sears fashioned a two-pronged response to the anti-chain movement. The first part was a major lobbying effort conducted through the National Chain Store Association and the American Retail Federation, both of which had Sears managers on their executive committees. At the state level, Sears worked hard to make friends in high places, including governors, legislators, and other officials. The second part was a public relations campaign to convince consumers that Sears was not just a store but an American institution worthy of their support. This message was aimed at rural areas and the South, since this was where anti-chain feelings ran deepest. Sears used its mail-order catalog to "strike a warmer, friendlier tone, to show readers that the great mail-order house had a deep and abiding interest in their welfare." General Wood, a conservative Republican, surprised his friends by backing the early New Deal, especially its agricultural support policies. The 1933 Sears catalog featured a letter from U.S. Secretary of Agriculture Henry A. Wallace thanking Wood for his interest in the farmer's prosperity.[21]

To show that it had "heart," the company spent millions on agricultural scholarships and other programs for 4-H and Future Farmers of America. Of greater importance was the involvement of local managers in community activities. Sears permitted managers to purchase store supplies from local companies and to donate Sears money to the local Red Cross and community chest. A 1941 survey showed that Sears managers were active in service clubs like the Rotary and in other organizations like the YMCA, Boy Scouts, and Camp Fire Girls. The unifying theme behind these efforts, said Wood, was to prove the company's "good citizenship in all of the cities and states where its stores are members of various communities." The efforts paid off. Sears was rarely mentioned by the anti-chain forces.[22]

Working for Sears, 1935–1960

Compared to other retailers, Sears offered relatively good jobs and could afford to treat employees well: operating costs were lower and productivity higher than in old-style department stores. Further, Sears was growing rapidly, which ensured career opportunities and job security. Although other chains had high growth rates, few had sales per employee or margins as high as at Sears. Also, whereas most chains—and particularly the five-and-dimes—had never done much in the way of welfare work, Sears executives could speak proudly of a legacy dating back to its pre-retail era. But more than tradition kept welfare programs thriving at Sears.[23]

In urban labor markets, Sears competed head on with department stores, which were trendsetters for the retail industry. These stores were roughly the same size as Sears' "A" stores and the largest of its "B" stores. Department stores had such lavish welfare programs that one critic charged they had carried welfare work to "unwarranted extremes." To match the competition, Sears was forced to maintain costly welfare programs in its retail division.[24]

TABLE 4.1
Employment Composition of Sears Retail Stores and U.S. Department Stores, 1939–1940 (percentage)

	Department Stores	*Sears Retail*
Part-time female	7	16
Full-time female	59	23
Part-time male	13	17
Full-time male	20	43

Sources: *16th Census of the U.S., Census of Business*, vol. I, "Retail Trade: 1939," pt. 1 (Washington, D.C., 1943), 57–58, 79–80; Sears Roebuck, Department 707, "Educational Background of Retail Timecard Employees," Special Report no. 54, August 14, 1941.

In other respects, though, Sears and the department stores were fundamentally different operations. Sears relied more on part-time employees and also employed relatively few women. The key to this seeming paradox is that men held the majority of full-time jobs at Sears (65 percent), whereas in department stores most full-time jobs were filled by women (see Table 4.1). A department store was a woman's place, where women waited on other women. Sears, as General Wood put it, was "a store for the family," with a mixture of male and female customers and salespeople.[25]

Men and women held different jobs at Sears, however. The big-ticket and hard-goods departments had been a male preserve since the 1920s and remained so through the 1970s, when the Equal Employment Opportunity Commission (EEOC) filed a lawsuit against Sears. A variety of factors might account for such occupational sex-typing. First, Sears had numerous male customers, many of whom preferred purchasing masculine articles—such as guns, tools, and boots—from other men.[26] But this explanation has its limits, for when it came to gender-neutral items like furniture or major home appliances, the customers were often female yet the salespeople almost never were. A better explanation, then, might be labor market factors: when Sears first filled these jobs, the only experienced hardware and appliance salespeople were men.[27] Over time, however, one might have expected Sears to train women and substitute them for men. Yet except during the Second World War, this rarely happened. Big-ticket men, who earned almost twice as much as other salespeople, tried to preserve these lucrative jobs for other males, even against the company's wishes. On those occasions when a woman was hired to sell big-ticket items, she encountered solid, open resistance. As one executive explained, "In one furniture division, there was a woman handling the unpainted furniture. Whenever unpainted furniture of any value appeared on the floor, one of the men would simply put a 'sold' tag on it and that was that."[28]

Sears managers ignored such behavior because their toleration bolstered the salesmen's loyalty and because managers themselves believed that men made better big-ticket salespeople. Company manuals on hiring described the ideal big-ticket salesperson as a "man," someone who was "socially dominant," "aggressive," and "not a wall flower." Filling big-ticket jobs with men was also an effective way of limiting the spread of commission selling. Sears worried that other salesworkers (many of them female) might some day demand commissions, so it consciously kept small- and big-ticket salespeople from mingling with each other. The groups had different working hours and took breaks at different times. Thus gender was another way of deterring horizontal solidarity while promoting vertical ties between male managers and male salesmen.[29]

Keeping women out of big-ticket sales jobs also was consistent with a long-standing Sears policy of favoring married men. As in earlier years, Sears paid wage premiums to men—but not women—with families. When Sears adopted a national pay system in the late 1930s, it prescribed the highest rates for married men with family responsibilities. Single men received less, while the lowest rates went to boys and women, regardless of family responsibilities. Although the Depression gave new legitimacy to these practices, Sears maintained them even after the return of prosperity. During World War II, "father's allowances" were paid to male employees with families when they entered the armed services but not to females who did so. After the war, married men were given first crack at the company's full-time jobs *and* they were paid more. One angry woman said at an employee meeting that Sears was "prejudiced" because its policy was "to keep women at the same financial level as when they started with the company, when responsibilities have increased, while this is apparently not true of men."[30]

During the Second World War, shortages of both male workers and male customers drove Sears to employ more women in full-time jobs. By hiring women, Sears could meet its labor needs and at the same time attract more female customers to its stores. The company told local managers that women "prefer to be waited on by other women rather than by men. They feel—and rightly so—that women will be able to visualize their needs more accurately than men and are better able to assist them in selecting merchandise to meet their needs." Store managers were supportive of the new hiring strategy. Not only were women cheaper but, as one manager said, "they are good housekeepers by home training who do much to tone up the appearance of their departments. They often are far better at detail work than men and have a higher degree of customer consciousness." The number of women working in Sears retail jobs rose steadily, from 39 percent in 1940 to 65 percent in 1945. By the end of the war, women had even made inroads into the big-ticket and hard-goods departments, although they still were assigned to the least lucrative lines, such things as cutlery, floor wax, lightbulbs, and baby chicks.[31]

After the war, Sears went back to its previous policy of favoring men for full-time jobs. By 1948, the proportion of women had fallen to 47 percent. This was a bit higher than prewar levels but well below the ratio at department stores, which were about 75 percent female in 1950. The company attributed the reversal to its policy of rehiring veterans into their old jobs. Even if returning servicemen are excluded, however, men still made up over 60 percent of new hires at Sears between 1945 and 1948. Sears' ambitious postwar growth plans provided one more reason to hire men: the company anticipated severe shortages in its managerial ranks, which were heavily male, and hiring men for full-time jobs became a way of expanding the pool of potential managerial recruits.[32]

These new policies were less explosive than might be expected. Postwar employment growth allowed Sears to both rehire veterans and recruit new men without laying off women. Also, there was a high turnover of women in full-time jobs, since Sears still gave preference to single women when filling such jobs and expected them to quit upon marriage. Just to make sure they would not stay on, Sears explicitly reserved the right to fire a woman when she got married. Thus full-time women tended be young and single, while full-time men were older and married.[33]

This pattern was completely reversed in the case of part-time employees. Sears considered "housewives" to be the most desirable part-timers and avoided hiring men for such positions, with the exception of mature high school students and insurance agents, who were thought to make good part-time appliance salesmen. Sears assumed that men took part-time work only because they couldn't get full-time jobs. In the company's eyes, this was "indicative of their poor qualifications." Also, these men were thought to be susceptible to unionism. A company report said, "If they remain as parttime workers for any period, they become bitter and lose their self respect [and] fall in line with any movement which they think may assist them in gaining full-time employment."[34]

Chain stores typically used more part-timers than did traditional department stores. Sears' "A" stores had twice as many part-time employees as the typical department store (40 percent versus 20 percent), which helped Sears reduce its labor costs. Part-timers who worked fewer than twenty hours per week were entitled neither to insurance benefits nor profit sharing. Also, using part-timers made it easier for Sears to provide stable jobs to full-time employees. And part-timers—if carefully selected—were less interested in unionism than full-time workers. When directly threatened by a union, Sears would hire additional part-timers for four-hour shifts; they were eligible to vote in National Labor Relations Board (NLRB) elections, yet few were pro-union. For this reason, the Retail Clerks union favored a ban on part-timers voting in elections.[35]

Employment stability was another factor differentiating Sears from department stores, whose jobs were more seasonally variable than Sears'. At department stores, December peaks were higher, while July troughs dipped lower. Seasonality reflected both consumer buying patterns and department stores' emphasis on stylish goods, the consumption of which was less regular over the course of the year than the consumption of staples. Also, because styles changed frequently, department stores could not risk purchasing large orders in advance and therefore could not make future commitments to suppliers or employees.[36]

By basing its retail stock on staples, Sears was able to establish stable, enduring relationships with suppliers. Among the company's eight thousand suppliers in 1946, more than seventeen hundred had been selling to Sears for fifteen years or more. Sears owned several factories outright and had partial ownership of many others, which gave it tighter control over inventories and product quality than was the norm in retailing. In the 1930s, Sears began employing economists to predict future demand and it set up the Economic Research Office to coordinate and review operating data. The upshot was that Sears, unlike most retailers, could plan annual employment growth and make long-term commitments to full-time workers. Already buffered by the part-time force, these full-time workers ended up with quite secure jobs. Even some part-time workers benefited from the stable environment Sears created.[37]

In the 1930s, Sears had minimal layoffs in its retail stores because staple consumption held up better than the purchase of stylish items. Also, its size and flexible jobs allowed it to transfer employees if their line was discontinued. Finally, Sears was on a roll. The Depression slowed but could not halt the company's retail expansion. With growth came an ability to make good on promises of promotion. Sears had a policy of hiring from within and practically all vacancies were filled internally, including management slots, so that by the 1950s many employees had spent most of their working lives at Sears. Other stores offered good career opportunities, but Sears had an outstanding record in this area. Thus, a relatively favorable Depression experience separated Sears workers from those around them.[38]

Mail order was a different kettle of fish. Pay rates were lower than in retail and, since there were few good jobs, advancement was slower. To fill vacancies, Sears looked for energetic young people, not too educated or ambitious. Most of all, the company preferred unmarried women. Two-thirds of mail-order employees were female in the 1940s, a higher proportion than in the 1910s, before Sears entered the retail business. In fact, transfers to retailing served as an escape hatch for mail-order workers seeking advancement. Annual reviews determined whether an employee would be promoted, either to a better mail-order job or to retailing. One management consultant commended Sears for providing opportunities for upwardly mobile working-class males whose blocked aspirations, he said, might otherwise find an outlet in union organizing. Despite dead-end jobs, Sears proved more career-oriented than other mail-order houses.[39]

Internal surveys consistently found Sears employees to be enthusiastic about their career opportunities, although men were more positive than women. The motto of the company's management training program—"Sears Jobs for Sears Men"—made it clear for whom the program was intended. While there is little hard evidence, remarks by employees suggest that Sears may have had a glass ceiling blocking women from rising above entry-level management positions. As early as 1934, Sears women complained about the lack of opportunities; twenty years later the same criticisms could be heard. Women said it was difficult for them even to become buyers or sales managers, jobs that other retailers often gave to women. One female employee asked General Wood at an open meeting, "Is it fair to have brought women into the company with promises that real careers for women could be found at Sears, only to find now that it is the exception for women at Sears to have anything above the mediocre?"[40]

Such complaints might have made a potent union organizing issue were it not for the fact that career-oriented women made up only a small portion of the labor force. Most of Sears' full-time women were young and single and, according to union organizer Myrna Siegendorf, they viewed their jobs as an interlude between high school and marriage. That attitude also shaped their views of unionism. During a wartime organizing drive at Montgomery Ward, Siegendorf found that younger women were not anti-union so much as indifferent.[41]

Men at Sears faced a different situation. Most held stable full-time jobs with good promotional opportunities (which were enhanced by the lack of competition from women). Just as Kodak workers were grateful that "ethnics" were kept out of Kodak Park, Sears men appreciated the fact that the company reserved its best jobs for them. Along with gratitude, however, there was also some fear. Although the majority of middle-aged men never made it into management, few wanted to jeopardize their chances—or their profit sharing—by getting involved in union activity.[42]

Older women holding full-time jobs were less prone to these fears. Unlike their male coworkers, dissatisfied older women often became intensely active in unions. However at Sears, relatively few such women held full-time jobs, while elsewhere they made up a sizable chunk of the retailing labor force. One department store manager said after a strike that these women were "among the foremost trouble makers." The Depression had made older women fearful of losing their jobs to younger ones. Also, these women often had employed spouses, which made them less timorous about taking risks that might cause them to get fired. In the 1940s, Siegendorf found them to be quite feisty: "The older women give the impression of being rather quiet and prim . . . that is, until you see them with their dander up." On the picket line, they "marched stubbornly and told nonstrikers exactly what they thought of them in no uncertain terms."[43]

When it came to paying women, there was little Sears could be faulted for. Wages were higher there than in most women's retailing jobs, and the same was true for men. Sears had a corporate policy of paying at the high end of the scale, which shielded it from unions and anti-chain sentiments. Even in mail order, where wages generally were low, Sears paid more than its competitors, including Ward's. As for the pay ratio between women and men, Sears matched the national retailing average and in some instances exceeded it. A national survey of department stores in 1948 found few women selling major appliances; those who did earned only 43 percent as much as their male counterparts. Although it was equally unusual to find women selling major appliances at Sears, those who did earned 63 percent as much as big-ticket men.[44]

The same was true of Sears' welfare benefits—they were above average for women in retailing—although the average Sears woman received fewer benefits than the average Sears man, since benefits rose with seniority and full-time status. Sears devoted about a fourth of its payroll to benefits in the 1950s, a smaller share than at Kodak, although Sears matched the national manufacturing average and was ahead of most retailers. Other chain stores—like Grant's and Woolworth's—offered few benefits, while neither Penney's nor Ward's had anything to compare with Sears' profit-sharing plan (not even pensions). The same was true of department stores. Fewer than half had formal health or pension plans, although most offered company nurses, country outings, and good dining facilities. Department stores pursued these programs as part of a Pygmalion strategy to make working-class salesgirls more like their well-heeled clientele. However, Sears shied away from heavy-handed uplift programs, avoiding what it called "a paternalistic influence over the private lives of employees."[45]

The Sears approach to benefits was a sophisticated twist on the ideas of Elton Mayo, the Harvard professor who ran the Hawthorne experiments at Western Electric. Mayo contended that workers expressed deep-seated psychological needs in economic terms; managers, he said, erred when they ignored the latent causes and symbolic aspects of economic discontent. Sounding like a true Mayoite, Clarence B. Caldwell, the head of Sears' personnel department from the 1930s to the 1950s, said that welfare benefits were "tangible evidence of management's concern for the welfare of employees." Caldwell cited studies showing that "employees respond primarily to the evidence of concern and only secondarily to the economic values." Yet Caldwell did not entirely eschew financial considerations, noting that if benefits had been less substantial, "their value as symbols and as an earnest expression of management's attitude would be correspondingly diminished." Paying hefty benefits, then, allowed Sears to "demonstrate the sincerity and weightiness of its concern."[46]

By far the "weightiest" benefit program was profit sharing, which accounted for nearly half of total welfare spending. With more than $100 million in assets in 1950, the sheer size of the fund was impressive, as were the benefits paid to retiring employees. General Wood raised the payout from 5 to 10 percent of profits and extended the plan to cover all Sears employees, not just those in mail order and retail. According to Caldwell's assistant, James C. Worthy, Wood made skillful use of the profit-sharing plan as "the central unifying symbol around which the entire organization revolved." To enhance the fund's image as a symbol of corporate unity, Wood placed an annual limit on the amount an employee could contribute and pegged this limit to nonmanagerial salaries. In other words, top executives and rank-and-file workers received similar benefits if they had worked for the company the same number of years. Wood saw the plan as proof that no significant conflict existed between managers and workers or between those who owned Sears and those who labored there. With profit sharing, employees were said to be "working for themselves." In all its facilities, Sears put up signs showing its current price on the New York Stock Exchange.[47]

Despite the hoopla, the main purpose of profit sharing was to keep employees around until mandatory retirement and then ease them out the door with an annuity. To discourage employees from quitting, the plan gradually increased the company's contribution from 100 percent of the employee's contribution (for those with less than five years' tenure) to 400 percent of the employee's contribution (for those with more than fifteen years' tenure). In the top bracket, annual dividends plus company contributions totaled more than half of an average employee's salary; those with over twenty-five years' service often received more from profit sharing than from wages. Although the plan obviously was lucrative, some workers nevertheless felt trapped by it. As an employee told an interviewer in the late 1940s, "The profit sharing system is really something. It's a damn good thing, but they take advantage of it terrifically. They know damn well that that's the only thing that keeps most of the people on here. If it weren't for that the turnover would be terrific. But after you've been here for a couple of years, your profit sharing mounts up, and it's damn hard to break away."[48]

Because extras and those with less than a year's service were ineligible for the profit-sharing plan, only about 50 percent of Sears employees participated in it. The chief beneficiaries were long-service workers, typically married men. As one employee said, "Everyone, without exception, thinks profit-sharing is a wonderful thing. However, the people who follow it most closely are the married men with families." Almost half of the participants had less than five years' service (vesting occurred at five years), so most of the company's contributions went to a minority of senior workers. Moreover, these workers benefited when a nonvested employee left Sears, because the latter's share of company contributions reverted to the general fund. These so-called lapse earnings made up about 3 percent of the cash going into the fund each year, essentially a transfer payment from unmarried women to married men.[49]

Profit sharing was a relatively risky way to provide pensions. With 80 to 90 percent of its assets invested in Sears stock, the fund was not diversified and its value fluctuated along with Sears' stock prices. During the 1930s and early 1940s, Sears stock was quite volatile. There were several years when the company made additional contributions to compensate for underfunding, although there were no formal guarantees for such payments. Stock gyrations eliminated short-term incentive effects while making the value of a retiree's annuity highly dependent on the share price on retirement day.[50]

Sears was honest with employees about profit sharing's financial risks yet never did much to eliminate them. One reason was that the plan helped to prop up stock prices, making Sears more attractive to owners and investors. Sears purchased shares for the plan when prices were low and waited if the price was high. Further, the plan gave management effective control over the company. In the 1950s, the profit-sharing fund held over 25 percent of all Sears stock. When employee private holdings were added to this, the total came to over a third, a deterrent to outside pressure. Sears also freely turned to the fund to finance its expansion. Cash from selling stock to the fund was plowed back into the company. And when Sears needed quick cash, it borrowed excess reserves from the fund. Top managers did worry about the appearance of impropriety, and the head of the finance committee warned General Wood in 1953 to be on guard against "possible arguments of the government, or our competitors, or labor agitators that Sears was using the fund as a mere adjunct to its business operations and for Sears' own profit."[51]

In light of all this, one might think profit sharing would have made employees anxious or caused them to distrust the company's integrity. Yet precisely the opposite was true. Attitude surveys showed that employees liked profit sharing more than anything else about Sears. The reason is not to hard to discern. After the turbulent 1930s, Sears share prices raced steadily upward in the 1940s and 1950s. By 1957, stock values had risen eleven times over their 1932 nadir, dwarfing the rise in the Dow-Jones index. The company was rife with miraculous stories about humble workers who retired with giant pensions. Although some of these tales were apocryphal, many were true. As one employee, a veteran of the armed services, said, "Outside of the Army this is the only place I know of that offers anything that even comes near it in the way of security. You never heard of a man doing a menial job like a janitor being able to retire with $2,500 put away. But I know of one janitor here who did just that. I don't think he made more than $40 a week, tops. And he raised a family of six or seven kids. A man like that working anywhere else wouldn't have a cent to his name."[52]

On the other hand, the fact that older workers felt trapped by profit sharing suggests that the plan gave management too much control over their actions. Sears was not above playing on workers' insecurities, and in the 1940s and 1950s, the employee newspaper repeatedly warned that if a union organized Sears, employees might lose the profit-sharing plan. One labor organizer caustically disparaged profit sharing as the "golden handcuffs approach," although union officials misgauged the depth of employee enthusiasm for the plan.[53]

Other Sears benefits were quite conventional. Like most large retailers, Sears provided paid vacations and employee discounts, policies that went back to the Rosenwald era. The 1940s were a time of change, however, when Sears' benefit costs per employee more than doubled. Although this put Sears at the front of the retail pack, the company failed to keep up with large unionized firms like Bethlehem Steel and General Motors. Concern about this gap caused continued increases in welfare benefits in the 1950s.[54]

Clarence Caldwell and other top officers feared that employees might perceive the company's largesse as "some kind of management fast trick" or as an attempt to "buy" their loyalty and goodwill. To avoid this, said Caldwell, "management must be sincere. The adoption of a program of employee benefits is very likely to fail if management's real aim is the undercuttting of a tendency toward unionization rather than a sincere desire to provide needed benefits." Caldwell's assistant, James Worthy, similarly argued that there was no simple cause and effect relation between welfare spending and employee loyalty. Alluding to differences between Sears and Ward's, Worthy said that identical benefit plans "installed in organizations already enjoying good employee relations are greeted with favor [while] plans installed in organizations where relations are poor are greeted with resentment." This line of reasoning pointed to employee attitudes as the key factor determining how employer actions would be interpreted.[55]

External Pressures

Although Sears offered relatively good jobs for a retailer, its version of modern welfare capitalism was more rudimentary than Kodak's and less daunting to union organizers. By the late 1930s, Sears had already experienced several major organizing drives, causing management to cast about for new defenses. Out of this search developed Sears' attitude survey program, which became one of the largest and most sophisticated applications of behavioral and social science research to personnel problems in industry. Using questionnaires and nondirective interviewing, Sears continuously surveyed thousands of its employees, gathering data on their attitudes toward the company and other matters. The program attracted a stellar array of anthropologists, psychologists, and sociologists, and put Sears at the center of the human relations movement in the 1940s and 1950s, a position formerly held by Western Electric. Although the Sears program grew out of Western Electric's, it differed from its predecessor in two respects: its longevity (the survey continues to this day) and its integration into company efforts to forestall unionization.

The initial attitude surveys at Sears were conducted by a consultant named J. David Houser, who headed the eponymous Houser Associates. Houser was a pioneer in the use of sophisticated sampling and interviewing techniques to gauge employee opinion, and he was the first to take a quantitative approach and demonstrate its utility to employers. While a Wertheim Fellow at Harvard in 1924–1925, Houser interviewed top executives at major corporations and found that few of them knew with any accuracy how their employees felt about their jobs, what Houser termed "employee morale." Such ignorance was unfortunate, said Houser, because low morale caused workers to "express resentment through sabotage, 'soldiering' in their work, wage demands, and strikes." There was, he added, "a direct ratio between morale and the amount of output, the quality of work, and other factors."[56]

To gauge morale, Houser asked employees a set of standardized questions about factors in their work environment. Responses were coded on a scale from 1 to 5, with each number corresponding to an equal increment of feeling, ranging from enthusiasm through indifference to hostility: for example, "I'm in a fierce rut! No chance to learn!" would have been coded as a hostile response to the question, "How much do you feel that you are growing on the job?" From the answers to these questions, Houser computed an overall "morale score": a single number that, when averaged over all employees in a unit, allowed for comparisons across departments or firms.[57]

Publication of Houser's book *What the Employer Thinks* in 1927 was followed by a rush of academic research on morale and job satisfaction, blending theoretical concerns with practical advice to managers. Psychologists were inclined to rely on standardized questionnaires, whereas sociologists and anthropologists favored more qualitative information of the sort obtained in the Hawthorne studies. To shed light on the link between supervision and morale, Mayo and other researchers at Western Electric's Hawthorne plant had developed the method of nondirective interviewing, which encouraged workers to discuss freely with an interviewer whatever was on their minds. Between 1928 and 1931 more than 21,000 interviews were conducted at Hawthorne. Beyond the specific information obtained, the interviews were found to have a cathartic effect on workers.[58]

Industry initially was slow to adopt employee surveys, but interest picked up during the late 1930s when private consultants, including Houser Associates, promoted the technique as a way of avoiding labor unrest. In a 1938 book, Houser warned that "the gates are open too wide to a flood of unionization" because management "[has] dangerous and costly misconceptions [concerning] the motives of men in their work." Like Mayo, Houser said that managers overemphasized pay and misjudged the importance to workers of fair supervision, interesting work, and participation in workplace decisions. By using surveys, business could get a "true picture of workers' desires" and thereby avoid "the dangers inherent in unionization." Houser's analysis appealed to employers because it suggested, first, that surveys could uncover relatively inexpensive ways of deterring unions and, second, that union demands for wage increases did not reflect workers' true desires. "Management alone can satisfy the most vital of these desires," said Houser, "through the methods provided by modern psychology."

In the late 1930s, Houser Associates was the leading consultant in the employee survey field. In addition to utilities like AT&T, its clients included several retailers. One of the psychologists on Houser's staff, Arthur Kolstad, developed a psychometrically sophisticated questionnaire specifically designed to assess retail employee attitudes. His work brought the firm to the attention of Sears. Early in 1938, Houser made a presentation to Sears' top managers, during which he repeatedly mentioned "industrial unrest," "human friction," and "labor unions." Shortly thereafter, Houser received an enormous consulting contract from Sears.[59]

Houser had made his pitch to a receptive audience. The previous year, in 1937, unions had begun to organize department stores on a wide scale. The CIO's new retail affiliate (the Retail, Wholesale, and Department Store Employees Association or RWDSEA) aggressively went after retail and warehouse employees in the East and Midwest. Taking an industrial-union approach and relying on militant tactics like sit-down strikes, the RWDSEA signed up some of the largest stores in New York—including Macy's, Gimbel's, and Woolworth's—and in more than a dozen other cities. In 1937 alone, the union organized more workers than the AFL's Retail Clerks had done during the previous twenty-five years.

The Retail Clerks were a lethargic union made up mostly of grocery clerks. With a craft-union focus on merchandise handlers and with a largely male membership, the Clerks were ill suited to the complex job structures and feminized, white-collar atmosphere of the department store. Making matters worse, the union entered the 1930s in a state of disarray: from a peak of twenty thousand members in 1920 it had shrunk to only five thousand in 1933, and no conventions had been held since 1924. Dissatisfaction with this state of affairs led several rebellious locals to bolt from the Clerks and form the CIO-affiliated RWDSEA in 1937. But instead of weakening the Clerks, the secession galvanized them into action. A group of activists led by James Suffridge opposed the old guard and began to concentrate on organizing chain grocery stores. By 1940, Suffridge had built up the union to more than seventy thousand members; it continued to grow steadily in the 1940s and 1950s. To accomplish this feat, the Clerks—like their CIO rival—relied heavily on support from the Teamsters. On their own, retail workers rarely had the strength to shut down a store. But when the Teamsters blocked deliveries, a store could not hold out for long. The Teamsters often had hopes of organizing a store's truck drivers and warehouse workers, and frequently they exacted a high price from other unions for their cooperation.[60]

Sears had little experience with unionism before the 1930s.[61] Then, suddenly, in the spring of 1937, strikes occurred at two Sears mail-order plants: one an eight-day walkout in Minneapolis and the other a short sit-down strike in Chicago. The strikes came as a shock to management. Also in 1937, the RWDSEA made inroads at Sears stores in Detroit, while the Clerks won a multi-employer contract covering department stores in San Francisco, including Sears.[62]

Of greatest concern to Sears were its nonselling occupations, such as stock clerks and warehouse workers. Employees in these jobs were accessible to organizers and had lower status than other workers. Sears advised its managers to "involve these employees in broader store activities" and to "cut down the isolation that presently exists among them." Sears viewed big-ticket salesmen as another "potential hot spot." Although they earned more than other salesworkers, they were paid on commission, and commission rates were directly affected by management decisions in areas such as hiring, product lines, and advertising. Anxious to have a say in these issues, big-ticket salesmen sometimes turned to unions for help. Clarence Caldwell feared that if these high-status employees formed unions, it would encourage other workers to do the same. Caldwell also worried that employees in heavily unionized places like Gary, Indiana, might succumb to community pressure to join a union.[63]

Opposition to unions was ingrained at Sears from the top down. General Wood was a deeply conservative man: an ardent isolationist, a supporter of right-wing causes, and a committed adversary of organized labor. Writing to President Roosevelt in 1937, Wood argued that organized labor was growing only because it used physical force to intimidate workers into joining unions. Caldwell, who had been appointed by Wood, said in a private memo that Sears was prepared to offer last-ditch resistance: "Whatever the cost, it will be less expensive than the permanent burden which capitulation would involve." In Caldwell's view, the burden would include lower productivity, higher labor costs, periodic strikes, and "constant bickering." But the main reason for fighting unions, said Caldwell, was that "if we are ever organized to any substantial extent, most of the atmosphere, the spirit, the tradition that has been uniquely Sears, will be lost. We must not lose sight of the fact that our interests and those of our employees are identical."[64]

Along with the usual employer reasons for disliking unions, chain stores had a few of their own. Chief among these was the threat of contagion: by capitulating to unionism in one city, a precedent might be set for stores in other places. This was a serious problem for Sears, which had hundreds of operating units, as well as for Ward's. Indeed, the best-known dispute between a retailer and a union came during the RWDSEA's drive against Ward's, a long and ultimately unsuccesful effort that depleted the union's treasury before it could take on Sears. Sewell Avery, president of Ward's and a member of the archconservative Liberty League, mounted a militant defense that included bitter battles with the government. Ward's was involved in forty NLRB disputes between 1937 and 1947 and was charged with unfair labor practices in half of them. On three separate occasions during World War II, Avery defied federal orders to negotiate an interim agreement, even disobeying a direct request from President Roosevelt. Exasperated by Avery, in 1944 Roosevelt ordered the army to seize and operate Ward's main warehouse and ten of its retail stores. When the army arrived, they found Avery barricaded in his office. Newspapers from coast to coast carried photographs of him being forcibly removed by a group of soldiers, and the incident became a lightning rod for Roosevelt's enemies.[65]

Although economics and ideology can explain why Avery and Wood were so devoted to fighting unions, they do not account for the different tactics on which each man relied. That Wood's approach was less combative than

Avery's was due partly to differences in personality. Intellectually, Wood was more flexible than Avery: for example, Wood started out an isolationist but later became an ardent war supporter, even lending Roosevelt several of Sears' top managers to be dollar-a-day men in Washington (including Donald M. Nelson, who was chairman of the War Production Board). Wood was also a more flexible manager. Whereas Avery ran Ward's like a petty dictator, causing a steady exodus of managerial talent, Wood decentralized authority and gave considerable responsibility to lower-level managers. Finally, Wood had a better appreciation of public relations, in part because the anti-chain-store battles had shown him how vulnerable retailers were to bad publicity. Within Sears, he championed personnel management as a form of internal public relations, while Avery paid little attention to "people" issues. Not until 1946 did Ward's hire a high-powered personnel officer.[66]

When unions came knocking at Sears' door in 1937, Wood realized that the company's welfare policies had to be augmented. Nine months after the 1937 strikes, he approved the hiring of Houser Associates to conduct a morale survey at the Atlanta mail-order plant and subsequently at other sites. Between 1939 and 1942, Houser surveyed some 37,000 Sears employees in 150 retail stores and 10 mail-order plants. When the war forced Sears to suspend the program, Houser was in the midst of a second round of surveys. The national personnel department (known in Sears parlance as "Department 707") was responsible for the survey program. In charge were James C. Worthy, formerly a labor relations manager in a department store, and David G. Moore, who previously had counseled employees at the Hawthorne plant.[67]

The heart of the survey program was a questionnaire. Sixty multiple-choice questions probed employee attitudes toward supervision, salaries, and other workplace conditions. There was also a ten-item scale that asked employees to compare Sears to other firms. Responses to the ten questions constituted the employee's "morale score," with a "perfect" score scaled as 100. When analyzing a unit, Houser took questionnaires from the top and bottom deciles of the morale scale and compared them to see which workplace practices determined morale.[68]

For employees, a survey was like a cross between an examination and an election. Groups of twenty-five to two hundred workers were surveyed in a cafeteria or meeting room. To reassure workers about anonymity, no supervisors were allowed in the room and completed questionnaires were placed in a locked box marked "Houser Associates." After the questionnaires had been scored, members of Worthy's staff met with local managers to discuss their findings. Later a report was written up, and copies were sent to the store manager and Caldwell. The report would analyze the overall situation at the unit, the unit's morale scores as compared to those of other units, and ways to remedy problems uncovered by the survey. Store managers were expected to devise a plan for correcting problems and to send copies of the plan to

Caldwell. Because there were no formal mechanisms for monitoring the plans, however, remediation was the survey program's weakest link.[69]

Research was the program's strong point. Worthy's staff prepared numerous studies of worker attitudes and summaries of morale scores broken down by occupation, sex, tenure, age, marital status, and other factors. One might think managers would have little interest in reading survey statistics, but this was not the case. As Caldwell explained, "Executives in the retail business, and I imagine in most other businesses as well, have a great respect for figures. The statistical reports . . . are a highly effective means for bringing to their attention the need for greater awareness of the factors likely to influence the attitudes and morale of the organization."[70]

Worthy found that the three items most strongly correlated with high morale were a belief that Sears dealt fairly with employee complaints, that it offered a satisfactory future, and that it provided interesting work. Pay, on the other hand, ranked eighth, confirming the Mayo-Houser claim that managers and unions attached too much importance to money. Economic factors, said Worthy, "are not enough; they are only the beginning. If the only basis management can conceive for employee loyalty and cooperation is the pay envelope and the short workweek, there can never be enough money or short enough hours to do the job." Worthy, like Mayo, was critical of scientific management's economic approach to motivation and instead stressed employees' expressive needs and the manipulation of social factors to fill them. In later years, the Sears researchers admitted they may have overemphasized the significance of social factors because they were trying too hard "to develop a theory of motivation that would leave out money altogether."[71]

Other research findings were less interesting, and when a peculiar pattern did turn up, Worthy's staff often was unable to provide a good explanation for it. This failure stemmed from weaknesses in Houser's survey instrument, which provided little basis for teasing out and corroborating causal relationships. It was, at best, an imperfect diagnostic tool. Nevertheless, when judged by the standards of American business in the late 1930s, the program was sophisticated and prescient. Moreover, its scope was unprecedented. Until the U.S. Army surveys during the Second World War, the Sears program was the most extensive organizational morale survey ever carried out.[72]

Between 1943 and 1946 the survey program was suspended. During this period, Sears experimented with nondirective interviewing as a way of assessing employee attitudes. Whereas Houser's questionnaire could be analyzed with simple statistical tools, nondirective interviewing required an interpretive framework to make sense of the ambiguous qualitative data that it dredged up. This framework was supplied to Sears by Dr. Burleigh B. Gardner, a social anthropologist who was a consultant to Department 707. Gardner familiarized Sears managers with cutting-edge ideas in the behavioral and social sciences. He also put Sears on the intellectual map by linking its programs to the resources and prestige of the University of Chicago, where he was a professor.

While a graduate student at Harvard in the 1930s, Gardner had attended seminars conducted by Mayo and by Lawrence Henderson. Later he was one of the interviewers hired by William Lloyd Warner for his massive study of social class in Yankee City (Newburyport, Mass.). Under Warner's supervision, Gardner went on to do a field study of social relations in Natchez, Mississippi, a site chosen as a matched comparison to Newburyport. Gardner's study employed the same methodology as was used in Yankee City, including "free associative interviewing," a refined version of the nondirective interviewing technique first developed at Western Electric. Through Warner, who had left Harvard for the University of Chicago, Gardner found a job in Western Electric's employee counseling program in 1937. After working at Hawthorne for five years, Gardner wrote a book, *Human Relations in Industry*, based on his experiences there.[73]

The book, which went through several editions and became a standard business school text, showed the influence of Mayo and Warner on Gardner's thinking. From Mayo came a focus on work groups and informal organization and also an eagerness to apply psychoanalytic concepts such as latency and catharsis. But while Mayo often reduced workplace dynamics to psychological factors, Warner sensitized Gardner to the importance of class, status, ethnicity, and the outside community. In his book, Gardner analyzed how a company's occupational ranking system shaped worker outlooks, and in other writings he attributed the unionization of foremen to their status anxiety. Gardner's attention to social class was a departure from Mayo, as was his approach to why workers joined unions. Gardner's analysis—that unions sped up complaint systems and made workers less fearful of using them—was a sympathetic account compared to Mayo's. Gardner used the concept of equilibrium, which Mayo had adopted to support a conservative social view, to show how unions arose to restore an industrial balance that had been disturbed by autocratic managers and technological change.[74]

Though not an especially original thinker, Gardner was a superb teacher and instilled enthusiasm for his ideas in the people around him. One of the counselors Gardner trained at Hawthorne was David G. Moore, who, after moving to Sears in 1941, repeatedly told his new boss James C. Worthy that the Houser surveys were simplistic and that the only way to understand worker attitudes was to uncover the "deep stuff" then being mined at Hawthorne by Gardner. At Moore's instigation, Worthy met with Gardner to discuss personnel research at Sears. The two men hit it off, which was hardly surprising. Gardner was an intellectual, but he had an entrepreneurial bent and industrial experience, while Worthy was a would-be academic who appreciated the practical potential of esoteric concepts like catharsis. Worthy hired Gardner in 1942 to demonstrate how nondirective interviewing might be used as an adjunct or alternative to the Houser survey.

Gardner distanced himself from Mayo's therapeutic conception of nondirective interviewing and instead used it primarily as an information-gathering tool. Top management encouraged this because it viewed morale problems as inherent "in the structure of relationships within the organization and not [as at Hawthorne] in the individuals who comprise the organization." According to Worthy, Sears placed the burden of change on management rather than on the individual employee, who "is never guided or directed [by the interviewer] into what are considered to be the proper channels of activity." This was a bit disingenuous; Sears well understood the cathartic effects of nondirective interviewing and used it to modify employee behavior. Nevertheless, the nondirective interviewing program at Sears was less overtly manipulative than Western Electric's.[75]

Gardner's first assignment was to investigate problem units: those with low morale, high turnover, or union proclivities. His projects included a study of the status system in a retail shoe department and another that compared the social structure of selected departments in Sears' Chicago-area stores. His main project was a study of the white-collar employees who prepared the catalog, a high-turnover group that had the lowest scores on Houser's morale scale. Gardner interviewed everyone in the department, starting at the top and moving down the ranks. He also interviewed the buyers, a group that worked closely, but not always smoothly, with the catalog employees.[76]

In applying nondirective interviewing, Gardner said that he listened with interest, never argued, looked for omissions and hesitations, and periodically summarized for the employee what had been said, thereby "reassuring the employee and carrying him far into the interview."[77] Even before the project was finished, the interviews began having an effect: turnover fell and morale improved. Gardner attributed these changes to the catharsis achieved by interviewing: "Emotional stress is relieved and the individual is able to think more objectively about his problem and ceases to act in erratic or ineffective ways. In many cases a person who before the interview had been noticeably worried or depressed . . . will afterwards seem relieved and cheerful and return to the job with renewed vigor." Nondirective interviewing was also credited with giving the department's top managers a chance to discuss their problems with a neutral confidant and come to a clearer understanding of how to resolve them. "Executives both in and above the department had an opportunity, possibly for the first time, to really talk through their problems as they saw them. There are many things about a job a man cannot talk over with his wife or others outside the company."[78]

In line with his human relations approach, Gardner told Sears that departmental morale could be raised by changing "social conditions," everything from job titles to the leadership style of department managers. But little was said about economic issues or the physical work setting. Gardner, for example, did a study of two Sears warehouses—one with high morale, the other low. Although the latter had poor working conditions and low wages, Gardner concluded that these factors were not nearly so important as the fact that employees were never given positive goals. For Gardner, the fundamental determinant of job attitudes was social needs, "the things involving the individual's relations with others on the job." Gardner's report made a deep impression on Sears management and cleared the way for wider use of nondirective interviewing after the war.[79]

In 1945, Sears was poised for an expansion that would add more than 45,000 retail employees over the next five years. Company executives knew that growth of this magnitude would bring a host of problems, including tussles with organized labor. In preparation, Worthy and Caldwell began planning to revive the large-scale survey program. Houser Associates tried to renew its contract, but the Sears managers most closely connected to the survey—Moore and Worthy—were confident they could develop and administer a survey program on their own. In 1946, Sears inaugurated a new program created by Worthy and Moore known as "the organization survey," a name chosen to emphasize the company's intention to measure morale not as an end in itself but as a means of diagnosing the problems of the organization.[80]

The new survey had two parts. First was a questionnaire, which was similar to Houser's although it took a different approach to defining morale and calculating morale scores. Sounding every bit like Mary Follett, Gardner and Moore held that "If employees follow the leadership and identify their personal interest with the aims and goals of the organization, they may be said to have high morale." In this unitary view of the world, there was little room for the clash of interests on which unionism thrived.[81]

Nondirective interviewing (or as Sears called it, "employee-centered interviewing") formed the second part of the new program. After the questionnaires had been filled out, the survey team left the site, scored the forms by hand, and identified departments in which the "feeling tone" was "negative." They then returned to the store, usually within several hours, and interviewed selected employees from those departments. The employees were given a general picture of what the interviewer wanted them to talk about and were encouraged to say whatever was on their minds. Said Worthy, "They often find themselves talking to the interviewer about personal fears and anxieties which they would never otherwise discuss. The kind of information gained through such interviews is invaluable because it is the basic personal stuff out of which grievances and demoralization grow." To reduce the employee's anxiety, no notes were taken during the interview. Afterward, the interviewers wrote a word-for-word transcript to the best of their memories and rated the employee's attitudes based on the same set of factors measured by the questionnaire. They also filled out special forms designed by Gardner and Moore that asked about the department's status system, cliques, "resistance groups," and informal leadership.[82]

The new survey program brought together the quantitative, closed-question format of the questionnaire and the more open, qualitative approach of the interviews. The methodologies complemented each other: the questionnaire was speedy, objective, and relatively inexpensive, whereas the interviews filled in interpretive gaps and uncovered rich psychological material not ordinarily revealed by other methods. At Sears, the questionnaire was distinctly secondary and viewed as superficial and difficult to interpret. In describing their survey methods, the Sears managers used revealing metaphors. They called the questionnaire "a kind of crude thermometer" whose function was to assess a unit's "general feeling tone," establish rapport with employees, and prime them for nondirective interviewing, which was seen as a more precise process, like that of a physician diagnosing the cause of a feverish patient's "negative feeling tones." If Moore and Gardner could have had their way, Sears would have relied exclusively on nondirective interviewing, but Worthy deemed that too costly.[83]

Selecting units to be surveyed was the critical part of the process. Typically Sears took a "firefighting" approach and surveyed units thought to be potential union organizing sites. Units were selected by the territorial zone managers—who traveled from store to store—based on evidence of poor management and employee complaints. Location in a heavily unionized community was another consideration. Sears was proud of the fact that its stores in places like Pontiac, Michigan, and Gary, Indiana, were unorganized, and in 1946 those stores were test sites for trial runs of the new survey program. Store managers themselves could request a survey if they thought things were going awry, although Department 707 refused to conduct a survey if an organizing drive was in progress because this could be held to be an unfair labor practice. On average, each year from 1946 to 1952 Sears surveyed 6 to 7 percent of its employees, most of whom worked in "problem stores."[84]

Those in charge of the new survey claimed it could accurately forecast union activity in a particular department or store. According to Gardner, "You could see it coming as clear as day . . . [and could] predict trouble in six months unless you acted." Managers of units showing an average morale score below 35 on a scale of 100 were advised to "start looking where your trouble is and start figuring out how to do something about it." A typical survey report would warn local managers of trouble spots and suggest ways to improve morale: through better communication, more personal contact, breakfast meetings, or the transfer of employees to departments with higher morale. Some stores with low scores were turned over to Sears' labor relations "adviser," Nathan Shefferman, who used informants and other techniques to detect and snuff out incipient unions.[85]

Tied to the firefighting effort was an active research program. Studies were made of employees prone to unionism, including service and warehouse workers and big-ticket salesmen, whose morale scores were lower than those of other selling groups. Not all the research was related to labor relations, however. Included in the occupational studies were low-morale groups like control buyers, who were part of management. The research produced some important findings that obtained academic exposure and legitimacy for the survey, although the bulk of Sears' resources went into defusing troubled units rather than into the research.[86]

In the 1950s, attempts were made to decentralize nondirective interviewing and fit it into the routine of the "A" stores and mail-order plants. The plan was to have area assistants—members of the local personnel staff—interview every employee at least once a year using nondirective techniques. Those picked as area assistants were supposed to be friendly, poised, and able to put others at ease. These were the same "father confessor" types used in Kodak's recreation programs, although there was a higher level of psychological sophistication at Sears: for example, the assistants were told to let employees talk freely and never to argue or give advice. An employee might say, "You know I have no parents. I was brought up in an orphanage. I'm all alone in this world. In case of a layoff, what would I do?" The assistant was supposed to respond, "The possibility of a layoff frightens you because you feel so alone in this world." The point of this, said Sears, was that "rather than giving reassurance, which is always easy but does not reassure, the interviewer offers simply a genuine understanding which helps the girl face up to her own problems more clearly."[87]

Despite the survey program's tendency to emotional manipulation, management described it as "democratic," "flexible," and consistent with American values like "freedom of expression." The democratic rhetoric extended to rights, one of which, said Worthy in a 1948 speech, was the right of each employee to "fairness, justice, and . . . a voice in his own affairs." Worthy's speech was taken seriously by General Wood, who sent copies to every Sears executive along with a cover letter complimenting Worthy for "having put his finger on the greatest weakness of large industrial organizations in this country."[88]

Worthy's speech harked back to the 1920s, when managers freely relied on democratic metaphors to describe company unionism—as employee representation, constitutional government, and industrial democracy. But that kind of talk died down in the 1930s, when organized labor appropriated the democratic mantle for itself. Worthy and others wanted it back, and their "managerial" democracy was supported by academic researchers like Kurt Lewin, who, in a series of influential workplace experiments, showed the superiority of democratic leadership over more autocratic forms. Worthy and Gardner were familiar with Lewin's research and found its larger implications congenial: democracy, it implied, was as likely to trickle down from enlightened managers as to bubble up from disgruntled workers.[89]

Yet democracy, human relations style, was pretty thin gruel. At the time Houser was first hired, Sears established both the Employee Forum and the Profitsharing Advisory Council. The forum was a mass meeting of employees, held annually, where Wood and other top officers gave speeches on the company's future plans and then fielded questions from the audience, many on topics such as executive pensions, unions, and the treatment of women. Predictably, Worthy said that the forum "symbolizes the democratic spirit of Sears," although a memo from the treasurer James M. Barker may have been closer to top management's true feelings. With condescension Barker wrote, "Very few of the questions submitted indicated any understanding of the explanation made, but the meetings have always been enthusiastically attended because the employees enjoy the chance to see a great personality in action and to fire questions at him."[90]

The Profitsharing Advisory Council (PSAC) consisted of nineteen delegates elected by Sears employees throughout the country. The PSAC met twice a year with the trustees of the profit-sharing fund to convey nonbinding ideas and suggestions. Such representation was not unusual—nearly half of the firms with profit-sharing plans in 1948 provided it—but Sears was one of only a handful whose representatives were elected.[91] Although company managers boasted that the PSAC provided a "psychological sense of participation," they admitted privately that the PSAC was more symbol than substance.[92]

Other retailers regarded the forum and PSAC as innovative, since retailing was a sector in which formal structures like company unions were rare, even in the 1920s. The behavioral scientists working on the survey paid little attention to either of them, however. Compared to attitude surveys, neither offered much opportunity for scientific research. Management, too, preferred the surveys, since they met many of the same objectives as the forum and the PSAC without whetting appetites for more active forms of participation. Despite the rhetoric, then, there was not much democracy at Sears. Tellingly, an employee interviewed in the late 1940s said, "They never ask your opinion around here when they want to make changes. They just go ahead and make them. They all think they know what's best." Still, the surveys made management more sensitive to employee views, even when those views were considered important not as ends in themselves but only insofar as they contributed to predetermined company goals, such as corporate cohesion or union avoidance.[93]

Keeping ahead of unions in the 1940s and 1950s usually meant focusing on security, since workers of that era had all been touched, if not scarred, by the Depression. At Sears, the survey showed that a basic reason employees liked the company was the protection it offered against old age and unemployment: profit sharing took care of old age, while steady growth was important for avoiding unemployment. "The best thing about the company," said one retail worker, "is that every day I am sure I will work." To complete the package, Sears—like Kodak—replicated union-style safeguards against job loss, chiefly a "progressive" discipline system adopted in 1939. Store managers could no longer dismiss someone unless the employee had been told twice what was wrong; if the employee had more than four years' service, the store manager had to have proof that proper warnings had been given.[94]

For employees seeking redress, Sears relied on an informal "open door" approach. Management rejected a more elaborate system on two grounds: first, such a system would be a bureaucratic encumbrance and, second, unions might ridicule it as a pale imitation of a grievance procedure. Yet there was no evidence from the attitude surveys that the absence of formal procedures created dissatisfaction at Sears. The surveys found Sears to be a relatively open company where employees felt comfortable bringing complaints to their store manager or regional representative.[95]

To give employees someone to turn to, Sears asked certain nonmanagerial employees to be "sponsors." In addition to their regular responsibilities, sponsors were expected to show new employees the ropes and to counsel them when problems arose. For sponsors, this was a way of getting more pay without a promotion; for employees, the sponsors served as ersatz shop stewards to whom they could confide or complain. Local managers were wary of the system: since they never knew exactly what sponsors told employees, there was a risk that sponsors might become advocates rather than mediators for aggrieved workers. This risk kept Sears from using the sponsor system in all its units, and where it was used, Sears carefully selected the sponsors, choosing only "employees whom local management has confidence in."[96]

Internal Pressures

Throughout the ebb and flow of union organizing, Sears remained vigilant, regularly checking for chinks in its armor. During a quiet spell in the early 1950s, Clarence Caldwell sent a memo to the company's managers reminding them to "continue to look at all our policies with the question: Are they likely to keep out the union?" Even after Wood stepped down in 1954, top management retained a deep aversion to unionism, which permeated Sears and boosted the personnel department's status within the company. Caldwell, the head of the department, had the rank of vice president, and several other key executives came out of personnel as well, not usually a route to the top. But antiunion animus alone does not explain why Sears took the personnel function so seriously.[97]

Part of the answer lies in corporate structure. Sears had to redesign its structure completely when it shifted from mail order to retailing in the 1920s, something no other major retailer except Ward's was forced to do. Mail order had been amenable to a centralized approach, whereas mass retailing—with hundreds of stores in a variety of settings—required decentralization. This was not so easily accomplished; Sears needed some kind of organizational glue to hold a decentralized empire together. One place it turned was to the personnel department, which, by selecting and monitoring store managers, ensured consistent standards at the local level. Another binding agent was a set of companywide personnel policies ranging from profit sharing to a folksy work culture.

Sears opened nearly four hundred retail stores between 1925 and 1931. To secure the retailing skills he so desperately needed, General Wood hired managers from other retailers and even considered a merger with J. C. Penney. However, most of the store managers came from the company's mail-order plants, which staffed and supervised retail stores in their region. The logic behind this decision was that retailing bore a resemblance to mail order: consumers could purchase the same goods from retail stores as from the catalog, and Sears initially saw retailing as a way to dispose of surplus mail-order goods.[98]

But the link between mail order and retailing proved superficial at best. Mail order was impersonal and mechanistic (one executive called it "a horrible example of hardening of the arteries, overspecialization, and lethargic giantism"). Retailing was precisely the opposite; its profitability hinged on direct contact with the customer. People shopped at stores for a variety of reasons: to examine goods before purchase, to get information and reassurance, to participate in a social ritual, or simply to get out of the house. These psychological factors were critical, yet few mail-order managers could assess them or teach employees to be sensitive to them. They knew little about "Remembering Names and Faces" or "Tested Sentences that Sell" (titles of Sears training films). Mail order was an old business whose managers still relied on scientific management and military discipline to get the work done. The problem with such an approach in retailing, as Caldwell pointed out, was that there was "no way to organize or rationalize the relation between the salesman and the customer."[99]

To get retailing out from under mail order's thumb, Wood decided to revamp Sears' organizational structure. Following the recommendations of George Frazer, a management consultant, Wood brought retail under the purview of two new management layers—four territorial offices and thirty-three retail districts. More middle managers were needed because retail talent was "too thinly spread for local store managers to be trusted with discretion." Introduced in 1930, the new structure was logical but fraught with problems. Territorial offices were understaffed, while the district managers were overzealous, causing store managers to chafe under the increased scrutiny. When the Depression worsened, Wood scrapped the Frazer plan. In 1932, he gave control of the retail stores to James M. Barker, former head of the eastern territory. Barker abolished the territories and instructed all the company's "A" stores to report directly to him. The "B" stores—the least profitable—were initially left under district control. As "B" store managers grew more seasoned and efficient, Barker gradually removed them from district purview. In Sears parlance, they were then "reporting direct to Chicago." Most "B" stores improved their performance after being weaned from the district, so Barker also got rid of the district structure in 1935.[100]

From 1935 to 1948 Sears was a paradox. Its short hierarchy made it appear highly centralized, but the profusion of stores effectively decentralized the company. Top managers could not keep close tabs on the far-flung retailing operation, which by 1940 comprised more than six hundred stores. Though officially reporting to Chicago, store managers had enormous freedom to run their stores without supervision from above. General Wood, who abhorred bureaucracy and wanted store managers to be entrepreneurial, was pleased with the resulting administrative system in which responsibility was widely diffused: "Detailed controls are kept to a minimum," said Wood, "and maximum reliance is placed on the initiative and judgement of those closest to the scene of the action."[101]

The system changed after World War II, when Sears reintroduced a territorial system. On paper, after this change Sears conformed to the multidivisional (M-form) structure found in other big firms, but in practice it was an unusual M-form company. Despite its territorial divisions, Sears remained a relatively flat organization, with only three or four layers between the president and store employees. And those layers stayed thin: middle managers were assigned more stores than they could keep close track of. Again, the idea was to encourage entrepreneurialism by checking the accretion of territorial staff. Also, a sparse hierarchy freed up funds that Wood used to sweeten store managers' salaries. His successor, T. V. Houser, said in 1957 that Sears was evolving to the point where each store would operate on an independent profit-and-loss basis.[102]

In his landmark study, *Strategy and Structure*, the historian Alfred D. Chandler, Jr., criticized Wood and other Sears executives for placing too much faith in personal ability and for failing to appreciate the value of systematic organization. But for Wood's "distrust of bureaucratic procedures," argued Chandler, Sears could have worked out an M-form structure back in the early 1930s. Moreover, Wood's minimization of middle management prevented Sears from taking full advantage of the company's size, even after it reintroduced the M-form. Chandler's analysis had the ring of truth when it was published in 1962, a time when firms like General Motors set the standard for efficient management practices. Today, however, management experts are less confident that such bureaucracies are unambiguously efficient. The new wisdom is that of the "lean" organization, which keeps itself vital by pushing responsibility down to the lowest ranks. The trick is to get economies of scale without sacrificing flexibility and ambition. Wood had much the same idea back in the 1930s, and although he did not master the trick, he was ahead of his time in grappling with it.[103]

Like Robert Michels, the sociologist who first described the "iron law of oligarchy," General Wood thought large organizations had a fatal tendency to "centralize controls, establish rigid rules of procedure, [and] build up staffs which arrogate all thinking [and] treat the great mass of employees as robots." If Sears adopted "too elaborate a system of checks and balances," Wood warned, it would "only be a matter of time before the self-reliance and initiative of our managers will be destroyed." Wood's faith in men rather than systems infused his political beliefs as well as his business practices. A conservative populist, Wood attacked big government in the same terms he applied to big business—it was overly centralized, out of touch with the citizenry, and too reliant on "rigid controls." His aversion to systemization also had a personal side. At West Point he had been nominated the sloppiest cadet in his class, and in later years he showed up for work in rumpled clothes and unshined shoes. He discouraged the dissemination of organization charts, which, said T. V. Houser, made Sears "the despair of scientific management students who constantly come to look us over."[104]

Wood was not blind to economies of scale, however. All the company's buying was handled through offices in Chicago and New York, which gave it enormous leverage when making purchases from suppliers. The powerful merchandising department formulated procedures for stores to follow in sales techniques, layout, and operating methods. Yet with these important exceptions, store managers were on their own. They could decide which items to sell and how to price them for local markets. They were free to define the responsibilities of their staff. And as the point men for Sears' public relations strategy, store managers had control over their cash, dealing directly with local banks and donating more than other firms when natural disasters struck. Compared to most chain-store managers, they had greater leeway to run their stores and were better respected by the communities they served.[105]

For local autonomy to succeed, said James Barker, Sears' architect of decentralization, the company needed managers "who do not have to be ordered what to do in detail, once they have passed the training stage." It is here that the national personnel department played a critical role; Barker gave Department 707 control over the Reserve Group Program, started in 1933 to meet the company's insatiable demand for managers. The Reserve Group Program trained thousands of prospective managers; by 1939, two-thirds of all stores were run by the program's graduates. Sears prided itself on having managers who had risen through the ranks. Thus the Reserve Group Program enhanced Sears' image as a store for the "great middle-class buying public," where social distinctions were blurred in both employment and consumption.[106]

Department 707 relied on its field representatives to keep track of promising employees. When promotions were made, the field man usually was the only person familiar with all the candidates being considered, which gave him considerable clout. When it came to executive promotions, Caldwell was the powerful figure, a fact that was formalized in 1946 when 707 took charge of a new Senior Reserve Group Plan. Caldwell's ability to make or break executive careers forced others to give lip service—and usually more—to his belief that good managers should have "a friendly attitude" and practice "good human relations." Just to be sure, Caldwell intertwined career development and the survey program as a way of exposing managers to human relations ideas. Store survey teams included reserve group members from other parts of the country who were trained to conduct nondirective interviews and analyze survey data.[107]

Local managers were suspicious of the survey program and worried that it signaled doubts about their abilities. These fears were not unfounded, since the survey team's final report became part of a manager's permanent record. Indeed, the survey was consciously intended to identify and weed out problematic managers. Sears knew it was possible for a store manager to mistreat employees and still show high profits and low quit rates (profit sharing tended to keep turnover down). In other words, standard indicators might not signal a problem until an organizing drive or some other crisis occurred. Companies normally relied on middle managers to track such problems, but that was not an option for a radically decentralized company like Sears. Hence the survey became an important "control device," as Worthy called it, for monitoring managers, and this reinforced 707's role as an organizational linchpin.[108]

To minimize the chance of hiring bad managers in the first place, Sears engaged L. L. Thurstone, an eminent University of Chicago psychologist, to develop a test of managerial ability. Thurstone spent more than five years analyzing psychological profiles of successful Sears managers. The result was the Executive Battery, a three-hour test that screened for such traits as sociability, emotional stability, and agreeableness—all indicators of the friendly, easygoing personality Sears wanted its managers to have. By the late 1940s, more than fifteen thousand employees had taken the battery.[109]

Despite these efforts, Sears was perpetually short of managers, so after World War II it expanded what previously had been a small college-recruiting program. Ever fearful of breeding an elite, Sears recruited at state universities like Illinois and North Carolina and stayed away from the Ivy League and other prestigious private schools. Even at the state schools, however, Sears avoided students whose fathers were doctors, lawyers, or other professionals. Instead it went after lower-middle-class students from small towns, young men who would "experience no sense of social degradation in working for an organization catering to mass needs."[110]

By reducing the social distance between managers and workers, Sears hoped to create an amiable and cohesive work culture. The effort was often successful. Surveys documented a widespread feeling that Sears was a friendly place to work: as one employee said, "The executives all recognize you, when or where they meet you, in or out of the store." Another worker said, "In my opinion, the people I work with are the friendliest crowd of folks I have met." Outside research corroborated these findings. A Michigan State University study found that, although tensions existed at Sears, they were defused by an easygoing climate and relaxed supervision. Ironically, Caldwell's minions regularly pressured store managers not to pressure employees. Sounding like Kurt Lewin, a 707 report criticized managers of low-morale stores for being "rather distrustful, feeling that people had to be watched and checked closely." The best managers were those who could relax these controls, even for unskilled stockroom workers, and "capitalize on their initiative and good sense."[111]

All of this made Sears different from the typical department store, where social class and gender created a chasm between managers and workers. The owners of department stores were highly visible public figures, influential not only as businessmen but as trendsetters, charity leaders, and symbols of their cities, and class snobbery filtered down the management ranks from them. Macy's and Marshall Field's recruited their managers from the Ivy League and were less likely than Sears to promote from within. Department store managers were expected, as historian Susan Benson puts it, "to be at home with urban gentility." This reassured customers that a department store and its management had good taste.[112] These customers were either from the upper class or wanted to be treated as if they were. The problem for store managers, then, was that the selling staff was predominately working class. Elaborate training programs and dress codes helped to erase the typical saleswoman's class identity and make her more cosmopolitan and subtle, yet despite such efforts class remained an irritant for employees. There were constant reminders of the staff's social inferiority—the lavish lifestyle of the store's owners; snide remarks from managers; even separate stairways, elevators, and bathrooms. On top of this, customers usually demanded deference and regularly reminded the saleswoman of her subordinate status. To deal with these indignities, department store workers developed a culture of resistance, which union organizers successfully tapped in the 1930s and 1940s.[113]

In contrast to department stores, Sears sold to a wide spectrum of customers. Like General Wood, with his prairie populism and unshined shoes, Sears was the workingman's friend, but it also was "respectable enough in most locations to be the somewhat 'messy' friend of the cost-conscious local physician." It had neither the *hauteur* nor the stylish goods found in department stores, and with many items standardized and well labeled, Sears had little need for the costly services other stores offered to gratify customer vanity, nor did it rely on the high-pressure tactics associated with direct selling. The salesperson was expected only to be "pleasant, helpful, and reasonably familiar with his own line of merchandise." In this setting, a customer's social class rarely mattered.[114]

Sears tried in many ways similarly to diminish status distinctions in the workplace. The company newspaper, designed to look like an urban tabloid, made a point of treating top corporate managers in an irreverent and humanizing fashion. To prevent executives from looking like "fat cats," General Wood kept a lid on their salaries, leading *Fortune* magazine to conclude that, compared to other large firms, executive salaries at Sears were "not excessive." While many employers commonly used fringe benefits to confer special advantages, Sears did not. The profit-sharing plan had egalitarian features, and employees with the same seniority received the same vacation and illness-allowance benefits regardless of rank. An exception was made for performance bonuses, which only salaried employees were eligible to receive, although 92 percent of salaried employees ranked below store manager, so it really wasn't an upper-level-only benefit.[115]

The consultants employed for the survey program imbued the company with a sociological acuity rare in American industry. Burleigh Gardner's reports repeatedly referred to status anxiety and the dangers of excessive status differentiation; these concepts became familiar not just in 707 but in other parts of the company as well. Gardner held seminars for top executives on "Social Structure in Industry," while David G. Moore, Gardner's protégé, promoted the use of rituals in which employees "laugh together, grow sad together, and in general *feel* together."[116]

The search for social integration led Sears to focus on store size, which the survey had shown to be inversely related to morale. Worthy made this finding the basis for a powerful, if not entirely original, critique of scientific management's preoccupation with the efficiency of large organizations and a detailed division of labor. He argued that smaller stores had higher morale because they had simpler social systems and lacked hierarchy. Relying on face-to-face relationships rather than formal controls, smaller stores could more easily get employees to identify and cooperate with management. Worthy extended this proposition to the community surrounding a store, since surveys showed that stores located in large, industrial cities had low morale. Worthy attributed this to the "fairly high degree of social disorganization characteristic of the great metropolitan agglomerations," which, he said, produced "sharp cleavages between workers and management." There is no evidence that Sears changed its policies on store size or location in response to Worthy's findings, but the company was alerted to the dangers of excessive formalization. For example, when office automation was first discussed in the early 1950s, Caldwell told Sears' president that the company had to be "careful about the way we routinize and mechanize our large-scale activities. It is playing with dynamite to over-systematize and over-regiment our white-collar workers as though they were unskilled mass production workers in a factory."[117]

These ideas provided intellectual support for General Wood's overall approach to corporate organization. The major contribution of the Sears researchers came in demonstrating how radical decentralization could allow a giant like Sears to capture economies of scale without sacrificing the relational advantages Worthy had found in smaller stores. Warner and Gardner praised Sears for its minimal formalization and flat hierarchy, which, they said, placed a premium on managers with strong social skills. In contrast, companies like General Motors and Ward's were faulted for their "tall, rigid" structures, "a division of labor gone wild," and a "low degree of integration." According to Warner, "in a large percentage of these tall organizations opposition groups form. Out of such groups grow unions."[118]

For Warner, unions were a symptom of a dysfunctional organization. The implication was clear: so long as Sears did everything necessary to maintain morale it would remain free of unions. But for top executives at Sears, unions were more than just a sign of problems; they were the very antithesis of the company's core values. A 1951 report said that unions fostered "a reliance on system rather than the individual; overdevelopment of organizational procedures; and creation of a rigid and bureaucratic type of organization structure." With so much at stake—even the company's unique corporate structure—top managers felt justified in taking extreme steps whenever organized labor began to make inroads. Prevention was Sears' primary union policy, but it kept a stick in the closet just in case.[119]

The Shefferman Alliance

Testifying at the McClellan Committee hearings on labor racketeering in 1957, Wallace Tudor, then head of personnel at Sears, was grim but contrite: "In our relations with the unions, we have made some errors. Certain actions were taken on our behalf which were mistakes, which never should have happened and which will never be permitted to happen again." Tudor's confession was deeply embarrassing to Sears, which never had expected that its labor relations policies would be scrutinized by the U.S. Senate, although Robert F. Kennedy, counsel to the committee, had been equally surprised when his investigation of the Teamsters led him to one of the nation's most respectable corporations. The link between the Teamsters and Sears was one Nathan W. Shefferman, a labor relations consultant who had worked for Sears since 1935.[120]

Sears management had always boasted openly that unions never made much headway at Sears. In 1957, the year of the McClellan hearings, only about 2 percent of Sears domestic employees were represented by the Clerks, 5 percent by the Teamsters, and less than 0.5 percent by other unions. This put Sears well below national unionization rates, which ranged from 10 to 22 percent for department store employees and 19 to 27 percent for drivers and warehouse workers.[121]

From 1935 to 1948, Sears handled labor relations in a peculiar manner. "Employee Relations" was part of Department 707, which relied on progressive welfare policies to ensure disinterest in unionism. But the moment an organizing drive occurred, no matter how tentative, the problem was referred to Department 731—"Labor Relations"—which was headed by Nathan Shefferman. When Shefferman reached mandatory retirement age in 1948, Sears disbanded Department 731. According to formal policy, labor relations became the joint responsibility of Department 707 and the new territorial personnel departments. In practice, however, organizing attempts were still referred to Shefferman and his consulting firm, Labor Relations Associates.

Shefferman was a colorful figure. Voluble, charming, and articulate, he was a regular speaker at management conferences and Teamster conventions, where he would wax eloquent about the wonders of free enterprise and the mutual dependency of workers and employers. The speeches were funny but full of banalities like the oft-repeated "Ode of Protest," the first lines of which are: "Capital and Labor, Why this senseless strife? Capital and Labor, You are Man and Wife." In contrast to the University of Chicago experts who consulted for 707, Shefferman came from the hucksterish, pseudoscientific side of the personnel management movement. Born in 1887, Shefferman's first job was with the American Institute of Phrenology, which classified personalities according to head size. After that he worked for Katherine Blackford, who developed a system for selecting employees based on their handshake and nose shape, and then for Arthur F. Sheldon, a pioneer in the field of "scientific salesmanship." During the First World War, Shefferman worked for the efficiency engineer Harrington Emerson, whose flamboyant schemes to gain money and status prefigured Shefferman's own career. Later, Shefferman wrote one of the nation's first personnel management textbooks.

After the personnel fad faded in the 1920s, Shefferman ran a company called Ideas Inc., which helped inventors bring their products to market. When the Depression killed the business, he found a job with the radio station WMCA in New York. Every morning, Shefferman was the anonymous "Friendly Voice" offering inspirational and self-help messages to a wide audience. He reentered personnel work in early 1934, when he found a job mediating disputes for the National Labor Board, predecessor to the NLRB. Shefferman rose to become supervisor of regional boards, at which point he met Lessing J. Rosenwald, who recently had succeeded his father as Sears' chairman. Rosenwald asked Shefferman to help Sears create a federation of company unions like AT&T's. In 1935 Shefferman made the fateful move to company headquarters, where he reported directly to Rosenwald and General Wood.[122]

In 1939, Wood and Donald M. Nelson, then executive vice president, asked Shefferman to offer his services to Sears' suppliers as well, including companies in which it had ownership interests. Shefferman agreed and formed Labor Relations Associates (LRA), a consultancy with offices in Chicago, New York, and Detroit. Sears provided the initial capital, and Wood, Nelson, and other Sears executives recommended Shefferman to prospective clients. LRA's first president was General William J. Westervelt, formerly head of Sears' product-testing laboratory and a West Point classmate of General Wood.

Shefferman recruited LRA staff from two sources. First there were the attorneys, men familiar with the new and arcane complexities of labor law. Like Shefferman, many had previously worked for the government. Then there were the personnel experts and several industrial psychologists. With backing from Sears, LRA grew rapidly. By the 1950s, its clientele numbered more than three hundred, including Schaefer Brewing, Macy's, and Sears suppliers like Whirlpool and Englander Mattress.[123]

Shefferman spent most of the late 1930s traveling from one Sears hot spot to another. The worst year for the company was 1937, when strikes occurred at the Minneapolis and Chicago mail-order plants. The Chicago drive was thwarted after Shefferman began spying on the union's organizing committee. The committee met on Saturdays in the offices of a health faddist specializing in heat treatments. Shefferman arranged to have treatments every Saturday afternoon and "toasted comfortably while listening to plans for conquering

Sears float over the roofless sides of [his] booth." The organizers eventually gave up on Sears and shifted to Montgomery Ward.[124]

Although subterfuge was always part of the Shefferman approach, he applied a more original tactic in Minneapolis, San Francisco, and Seattle, strong labor towns where, Shefferman felt, some degree of unionism was inevitable. Consequently, he convinced General Wood to follow a "containment" policy in these cities. Sears would negotiate with the Clerks or the Teamsters in order to avoid more militant CIO unions like the RWDSEA and the Longshore and Warehouse Workers (the ILWU). The Teamsters were the key to the containment policy. They were the only union powerful enough to stop the ILWU's "march inland" from the docks to onshore storage, trucking, and mail-order facilities. And the Teamsters could make or break an organizing drive in almost any branch of the retail industry. The problem was getting the Teamsters to cooperate with Sears instead of deploying its considerable resources against the company. For Shefferman, the answer was simple: Dave Beck.

With Seattle as his base, Teamster leader Dave Beck organized much of the West Coast trucking industry in the 1930s. During the war, he began to play a major role in the union's national affairs, making key decisions behind the back of the aging Teamster president Dan Tobin, whom he replaced in 1952. Beck was the epitome of the conservative trade unionist. "I run this place just like a business," he said, "just like the Standard Oil Company. Our business is selling labor." Among employers, Beck had a reputation for being tough but fair. One Seattle executive said he was the only union leader "who ever showed any sympathy with the difficulties faced by the businessman." Beck's standing in the business community was boosted by his crusade against communism and the CIO. In Seattle, employers lauded him as the bulwark protecting the city from Harry Bridges and the ILWU.[125]

It was in Seattle in the late 1930s that Shefferman first met Beck, when the city's retailers and the Clerks were negotiating an industrywide contract. Reassuring to Sears and other employers was the fact that Beck controlled the Clerks' Seattle locals; indeed, he dominated their lives. He negotiated their agreements, chose their leaders (the treasurer was his wife's cousin), gave them offices in the Seattle Teamsters' building, and managed their funds. Although the Clerks' national officers were painfully aware of the situation in Seattle, they were unable to stop Beck, whom they called "Brother Rat."[126]

In private, Shefferman backed Beck's multiemployer retail contract, since it held the CIO at bay while preventing the Clerks from playing the larger stores off against each other. Publicly, however, Sears had an official policy of refusing to sign union contracts; it also refused to collect any union dues from its employees. So Shefferman cut a deal with Beck: in lieu of signing the multi-employer contract, an attorney present during the negotiations would send a letter to Sears and to the Clerks describing the terms of their agreement. And instead of the union shop, Shefferman and Beck worked out an arrangement whereby every Sears unit in Seattle had a person known as a "union coordinator," whose job it was to get employees to pay dues to the Clerks.[127]

With Beck's assistance, Sears and the Clerks settled on a similar compromise in San Francisco.[128]

Shefferman and Beck both were clever, pragmatic, and venal, and they became close friends. Their relationship was no secret. The two went off on family vacations together and boosted each other's careers whenever possible. After he became the Teamsters' president, Beck hired Shefferman to develop a modern filing system for the union and a new type of dues book. And when the union built new marble headquarters in Washington, D.C., Beck cut Shefferman in on a deal that paid him a $12,000 commission for the purchase of the building site. Beck regularly asked Shefferman to speak at Teamster conventions and even helped Shefferman's son, Shelton, obtain a contract to sell toy trucks sporting the Teamster logo to union members.[129]

Considerable sums also flowed from Shefferman to Beck, most of them financed by Sears. Among the entertainment expenses Shefferman incurred on Beck's behalf were dinners at Maxim's, a deep-sea fishing expedition, a trip to attend Dan Tobin's funeral, and a Hawaii vacation taken by Beck, Shefferman, and their wives. Sears reimbursed Shefferman for all these expenses and also allowed him to purchase for Beck vast quantities of goods at wholesale prices—mundane items like Coldspot refrigerators, a chestnut divan, and bow ties. Beck set up a special Teamsters account in Los Angeles to cover these purchases, which totaled $96,000 between 1949 and 1953.

Shefferman bestowed similar favors on other Teamster leaders, from obscure local presidents in Ohio and Michigan to top officials like John English, Harold Gibbons, and Jimmy Hoffa. In fact, many union leaders—including Matthew Woll of the AFL and Walter Reuther of the Autoworkers—took advantage of Shefferman's ability to "get it at wholesale," though no evidence suggests that company or union funds covered purchases for these men. But the center of Shefferman's attention was Beck, whose vanity, Shefferman knew, was as great as his greed. Before Beck became a national figure, Shefferman tried bribing a *Business Week* columnist to do a story on the Teamster leader. And when Beck planned a trip to Tokyo in 1949, Shefferman got General Wood to give Beck a letter of introduction to General Douglas MacArthur, who was Wood's old army friend. Two years later, Shefferman took Beck to Hawaii and Wood instructed the Sears manager in Honolulu to "extend any social courtesies to Mr. Beck . . . for while he is on the other side of the labor fence, he has on the whole been a good friend of Sears."[130]

Exactly how good a friend Beck was will never be known, since the McClellan Committee treated Sears with kid gloves and did not delve deeply into its internal affairs. But it is no coincidence that after Shefferman met Beck, the Teamsters became the linchpin of Sears' CIO containment policy, which was, as it turns out, quite successful—not only on the West Coast but in Minneapolis and Dallas (against the ILWU)[131] and in Detroit and Philadelphia (against the RWDSEA).[132] By 1950, Sears had only one CIO contract left, covering thirty-three warehousemen. The AFL's Teamsters represented nine thousand Sears workers that year, but this was almost entirely the result of their having opposed or displaced some other union; from 1933 to the McClellan hearings in 1957, the Teamsters never made an independent organizing attempt at Sears.[133]

Having brought the CIO threat under control, Sears found itself facing organizing attempts from AFL unions, chiefly the Clerks.[134] To squelch these drives, Shefferman developed a whole new bag of tricks, which were laid bare by the McClellan Committee. The hearings examined in detail more than a dozen organizing campaigns thwarted by LRA between 1948 and 1956. The majority of cases involved Sears: either its stores, its subsidiaries, or its suppliers. LRA's activities at Sears' Boston store provide a revealing picture of Shefferman's modus operandi, although it took longer to put down the union there than at other sites.

In 1938, Shefferman set up the Sears Roebuck Employees' Council (SREC) at the company's large Fenway store in Boston, where workers had begun to join the AFL's Retail Clerks. Although this company union had no written contract, its charismatic president, Roy Webber, was able to wrest concessions from Sears by periodically threatening to call in the Clerks. In 1949, the Clerks took Webber seriously enough to send an organizer, who signed up many of the SREC's members, including Webber. Shortly before the NLRB election, Sears offered Webber a generous raise. He switched his support back to the SREC, a reversal that cost the Clerks the election. Sears then negotiated a written contract with the SREC covering four stores in the Boston area, but two years later Webber again felt that Sears was ignoring him and the SREC, and he approached John Lind, an organizer for the Clerks, who suggested that the SREC directly affiliate with the union. At a January 1953 meeting, SREC members voted 470 to 76 in favor of affiliation. The Clerks then mounted a major campaign overseen by Samuel J. Meyers, the union's regional organizing director. But Meyers was no match for Shefferman, who stalled the NLRB election until May 1955, when the Clerks lost by a wide margin.[135]

Throughout the thirty-month campaign, LRA engaged in two types of activities to defeat the Clerks. The first was what might be called "dirty science": using interview and survey techniques to identify union supporters, who subsequently would be coerced into withdrawing from the union or be dismissed. While it was unlawful to poll employees during an organizing drive, and Sears never conducted surveys at those times, 707 officials had no inhibitions about letting LRA do this work for them. When Sears developed a new survey form in the early 1950s, Clarence Caldwell, head of 707, transferred one of his assistants over to LRA to explain how to use it. In 1953, LRA sent this man to administer the survey in Sears' Boston-area stores.[136]

Another technique developed by Sears and applied by Shefferman in the 1950s was the rotating committee, in which groups of employees met with management, either on a one-time basis or repeatedly, to discuss problems like warehouse safety or store operations. Sears did not make much use of these committees but LRA did, both in Boston and other Sears locations. As one LRA official explained, the rotating committee was a way of getting people to relax and talk openly, thus revealing—as with nondirective interviewing—sentiments they might otherwise withhold. "The idea is," he said, "when you get people around the table and get them relaxed and don't put any bars on what they talk about, they will talk about anything. It uncovers a lot of personal feelings and you can get a lot of information no matter what the original subject was." After committee meetings, LRA officials would scribble on note cards such things as "not a leader" or "talked to boy's mother and father; will talk to Dick. Parents will talk to Dick."[137]

LRA had its own staff psychologists. Originally they included Richard L. Hull and Arthur Kolstad, two noted psychometricians and former partners of Houser Associates. Most other LRA psychologists, however, had neither the research orientation nor stellar credentials of these men or of Sears' in-house staff. For example, Dr. Louis Checov, who worked for LRA in the 1950s, was the inventor of something called the "Human Equations Test," which only he was capable of scoring. Officially described as a measure of employee adaptability, Checov later admitted that the test was designed to uncover "general feelings and sentiments pertaining to unions and collective bargaining." During the Boston campaign, LRA had Checov and another psychologist conduct personal interviews with employees, ostensibly to discuss their feelings about Sears' upcoming anniversary, although the interviews were really intended to reveal pro-union attitudes.[138]

Shefferman himself liked to dabble in this sort of science. He created "The Chart of Relationships," a sociometric matrix showing, for each pair of employees in a department, the frequency of their interaction. From the charts, Shefferman developed "The Spheres of Influence," a listing of opinion setters and "ring leaders" inside the workplace, who were then ranked on "The Confidence Index," a subjective measure of loyalty to management. Those who lacked "confidence" were approached by their supervisors and subjected to what Shefferman euphemistically called the "power of personal persuasion"—everything from friendly hints and bribes to transfers and dismissals.

LRA staffers would apply intense pressure to "ring leaders." In Boston, Roy Webber was offered a better job—at a Sears store in South America. When he refused to go, LRA sent a private detective to Boston to investigate reports of "sexual perversion." Several months later, Webber was fired. Although he was reinstated by the NLRB, his dismissal had a chilling effect. After the election, Samuel Meyers attributed the union's loss to the fact that Sears was "firing our active members so cleverly that we could not get a single one back on the job (although we won the Webber case). It does not appear that we have much chance to win elections in Sears . . . because of the use they can make of FEAR and because of the deadly efficiency with which they operate."[139]

LRA's other major activity consisted of campaign tactics intended to sow confusion and slow momentum. Some were lawful (filing numerous NLRB objections and appeals), while others were not (creating and funding pro-management employee committees). In Boston, LRA secretly funded three different employee groups to fight the Clerks. The first appeared after the SREC decided to affiliate with the Clerks, when LRA confusingly set up *another* SREC opposed to affiliation. This "independent" SREC consisted of a small group of pro-management SREC activists who received all their literature and legal advice from Sears via LRA. Never certain of their loyalty, LRA showered these committee members with cash and steak dinners—and even installed Coldspot air conditioners in their homes for free. To spur support for the independent SREC, LRA arranged for it to take credit for a hefty wage increase and for reinstating some previously dismissed employees.[140]

To further complicate matters, Shefferman lured away one of the Clerks' key organizers, John Lind, and got him a job with the Laundry Workers, a union controlled by the Teamsters. Lind told LRA everything he knew about the Clerks and then started a diversionary organizing drive financed by LRA. One of Lind's more inventive tactics was to make the Clerks look like thugs by staging an attack on a car belonging to a pro-Teamster employee: while the car was parked outside the Boston store, its windshield was smashed and its tires punctured with an ice pick. Ever thoughtful, Shefferman later arranged to have the car's owner receive free replacement tires from Sears. The Laundry Workers disappeared before the union election, but at the last minute the Teamsters themselves filed a petition to represent the warehouse workers.[141]

The third group was the "vote no committee," handpicked by local management for their opposition to any form of unionism. With LRA help and LRA money, the committee hired an attorney and put out a steady stream of anti-union literature urging employees to vote "no union" (a choice on the NLRB ballot). One pamphlet ridiculed Samuel Meyers with subtle anti-Semitic gibes intended to appeal to the predominately Catholic workforce. By financing three separate groups—the independent SREC, the Laundry Workers, and the vote no committee—all of whom had a place on the NLRB ballot, LRA made it difficult for any union to obtain a majority in the election.[142]

Shefferman was also a master at using legal appeals to enervate a union drive, which is why it took more than two years for an NLRB election to be held in Boston. The Clerks considered filing an injunction against Sears but decided against it, citing lack of support from the Eisenhower administration.[143] Instead they petitioned the NLRB to force Sears to bargain with the original SREC and disestablish the independent one. Both requests were upheld by the NLRB's trial examiner. At this point Shefferman made a brilliant move and cajoled Louis Becker, the NLRB's executive secretary, into quitting his job and joining the Sears legal defense team, something Samuel Meyers called a "treacherous turncoat transformation." When the case finally went to the NLRB, newly appointed by Eisenhower, the members found nothing wrong with Sears' conduct during the campaign and overruled the trial examiner on all charges. Two years later, when the McClellan hearings revealed new evidence, the NLRB's general counsel recommended that the Boston case be reopened, which would have allowed similar moves against Shefferman in other cases. The board said no, to the great relief of Sears and Shefferman's other clients.[144]

The McClellan hearings raised several questions about Sears. For one, how was it that a respectable company came to rely so heavily on an outfit like LRA? Sears had a lot going for it—not just good wages and excellent benefits but also an innovative company structure and a bevy of sophisticated programs to maintain morale. In cities like Seattle and San Francisco, Sears even had learned how to live with unions, albeit in a peculiar fashion. In front of the McClellan Committee, Wallace Tudor pinned most of the blame on his predecessor, Clarence Caldwell, who, he said, showed poor judgment in giving Shefferman "too much latitude." (Caldwell had retired in 1956 because of health problems and he never testified at the hearings.) As for Shefferman, Tudor called his practices "disgraceful" and claimed Sears had recognized his deficiencies long before the McClellan hearings. Ever since Shefferman retired in 1948, said Tudor, Sears had "seldom utilized" his services and then only for "isolated episodes." Thus, by making LRA appear a rogue operation that was no longer used or condoned, Tudor won absolution for Sears from Robert F. Kennedy: "Mr. Tudor's attitude and forthright admission blunted the sharp criticism the company might otherwise have received from the Committee," said Kennedy. "When someone says mistakes have been made, asks for no sympathy, and pledges in good faith that the errors will not be repeated, it is difficult to be critical."[145]

The truth is, as Shefferman bitterly pointed out in his memoirs, that Sears terminated its relationship with LRA not in 1948 but in 1957, right before the hearings began. Even then, both Tudor and Sears' counsel Arthur M. Wood promised Shefferman he would be rehired after the hearings were over. Moreover, the "isolated episodes" of which Tudor spoke were actually the major organizing drives directed against Sears between 1948 and 1957, including those in Boston, Pittsburgh, and Indianapolis. Finally, responsibility for the Shefferman fiasco lay farther up the hierarchy than Caldwell. In effect, Tudor made Caldwell the fall guy for General Wood.[146]

Wood had been an admirer of Shefferman from the moment the consultant first joined Sears. Part of the attraction was ideological. By the late 1930s, Wood had become quite conservative, generously supporting right-wing fringe groups. Like others who relied on the General for support, Shefferman played to his conservatism. Shefferman always sent Wood copies of his speeches, which had titles like "Let's Not Be Easy on Marx" and "Property Rights are Human Rights." Wood relished Shefferman's glib rhetoric in defense of minimal government and free enterprise. In a letter to the head of the National Association of Manufacturers, he endorsed Shefferman as a "realist" who "speaks fearlessly and freely to America's top union leaders."[147] Wood was also a shrewd businessman and appreciated Shefferman's ability to keep unions away from Sears, particularly the Teamsters. In a memo authorizing a check to Shefferman, he called LRA "a good investment." But not everyone in the company valued Shefferman's services. Local managers in Boston and Indianapolis protested LRA's presence in their stores, but to no avail. Despite the company's vaunted principle of store autonomy, Wood judged labor relations too important to be left to local managers.[148]

The hearings raised another question: if Sears had chosen to fight lawfully, without LRA, would the outcome have been any different? The answer to this question came after the hearings, when the Teamsters and Clerks poured all their resources into national campaigns against Sears. The Teamsters announced their intentions first, in the fall of 1957, just as the revelations about Beck and Shefferman were coming out. The union's timing could not have been worse. That fall, Beck resigned from office after being indicted for tax evasion, and the AFL-CIO expelled the Teamsters. With the drive stalled, the union spent most of 1958 marshalling its forces. By December, they recruited two hundred organizers, printed an organizing handbook, and formulated plans to target Sears in more than seventy locations. The ultimate objective was a national contract like the one they had signed with Ward's. In January 1959, the drive itself finally got under way. The union distributed a pamphlet titled "An Invitation to a Better Life," which made vague promises to Sears employees of higher wages and better benefits. A Teamster official predicted that Sears would be fully organized within two years.[149]

Although Sears was outwardly confident, news of the Teamsters' drive sounded alarms throughout the company. Sears still regarded the Teamsters as the one union with enough strength to force concessions from it. The company responded on three fronts. First, it initiated an employee relations campaign, including a "Benefits Bonanza Contest," which awarded prizes to employees who could answer detailed questions about Sears' benefit programs. Also part of the campaign was a film of Wallace Tudor's speech at the 1959 Sears Forum. Shown at every Sears unit in North America, the film stressed that Sears' wages, benefits, and promotion opportunities were better and more flexibly applied than those at unionized companies. Equating security with profit sharing, the film raised old fears that unionization might damage the plan—an unlikely prospect but one that unnerved Sears' employees. Second, Sears sweetened various benefits and boosted wages in selected locations. Decisions about where to raise pay were guided by the third defense: an intensified use of morale surveys. In 1959 Sears conducted an unprecedented national survey of all 205,000 employees, using a questionnaire designed specifically to predict union proclivities. Surveying on this scale was made possible by new technologies such as the computerized scanning and scoring of questionnaires. In subsequent years, Sears regularly surveyed one-third of its units, followed by nondirective interviewing at units whose morale score fell below 35 percent.[150]

The Teamsters' drive was a failure. Between 1959 and 1961, only a half-dozen NLRB elections were held at Sears units. The union lost all of them, with the exception of one at a Fresno warehouse employing thirty-five workers. The Teamsters had to contend not only with Sears but with their own poor image as well. Long after Robert Kennedy finished with Shefferman, he continued to investigate the Teamsters and their new president, Jimmy Hoffa. The steady stream of stories about Hoffa's Mafia connections did serious damage to the union. Sears, on the other hand, was virtually unscathed by the hearings. When the company commissioned Burleigh Gardner to do a public opinion survey, he found that few people were aware anything in particular had happened. Among those respondents who admitted knowing about Shefferman's practices, many thought he was backed by Ward's—stunning proof that Sears retained an untarnished reputation. Said one respondent, "Yes, I heard something about some funny goings-on but Sears isn't the kind of company that would do that sort of thing. It must have been Montgomery Ward."[151]

Despite public confusion about Shefferman, the Clerks made him the centerpiece of their campaign at Sears. Right after the Shefferman story broke, a union official advised all locals to contact Sears stores to check if employees were interested in a union. Somewhat wishfully, he said that the "Sears-Shefferman arrangement . . . should make it obvious to the employees that Sears' paternalism is tainted with selfishness." The Clerks did not actually initiate a campaign until the Teamsters announced theirs. Taking a page out of Sears' book, the Clerks tried to pinpoint trouble spots by handing out surveys asking Sears employees how much they were paid and whether they liked local management. Like the Teamsters, the Clerks promised better pay and shorter hours, and they spiced up their campaign literature with copies of a *Fortune* magazine article on Shefferman and the Teamsters, entitled "The Creature that Works in the Dark."[152]

Sears was harsh in its response. It immediately began pressuring Clerks' locals in Seattle, San Francisco, and other cities where Sears had regularly negotiated with the union since before the Second World War. The message was clear: unless the Clerks backed down, they risked losing more than they might gain. The company's tough approach signaled its contempt for the Clerks and an eagerness to squelch any impression of post-Shefferman weakness. In Seattle, Sears played hardball. It repudiated the union shop arrangement, withdrew from the employers' association, and stalled on contract negotiations. Privately, the Clerks feared that Sears was "neutralizing and breaking unions without saying so." In several places, there were decertification elections (employees voting to remove an existing union), which the Clerks said were illegally spearheaded by Sears' management. The most provocative event occurred in May 1960, when Sears fired 262 of its San Francisco employees for refusing to cross a Machinists' picket line.[153]

Instead of retreating, the Clerks responded with a national consumer boycott of Sears. Ostensibly a protest against the San Francisco firings, the boycott's real purpose was to help the union's organizing campaign. After Sears reinstated the fired employees, the Clerks vowed to continue the boycott until

Sears eliminated "all Shefferman-type coercion and corruption in company labor relations." Samuel Meyers was in charge of the boycott; five years earlier he had recommended one as the only way to bring the Clerks into Sears. Meyers infused the boycott with a vengeful moral passion fed by anger at Sears' dirty tricks in Boston. Millions of pamphlets emblazoned "The Shame of Sears" were handed out to shoppers. One flyer even asked shoppers to send a postcard to Sears demanding a public apology to all of organized labor. Demonstrations were organized around the country: there was an anti-Sears oompah band in Duluth and a parade of protesting clowns at the Miss America Pageant. A "memo" to Sears' stockholders appeared in the *Wall Street Journal*, and the AFL-CIO sent a letter to President Kennedy asking him to stop Sears from participating in a trade fair in Peru.[154]

Despite these efforts, the boycott had little effect on Sears. Most NLRB elections involving the Clerks were to remove the union (decertifications), not to add new members. By 1963 Sears was not even mentioned in the union's annual organizing plans. Eventually, the Clerks' own members lost interest. Support was erratic and reluctant locals had to be prodded into action. Even union members and pro-union liberals went back to shopping at Sears. Another problem was the boycott's obsession with Shefferman. As late as 1964, the Clerks were still tagging Sears as "the outfit that put the notorious Shefferman into business," although Sears had long since repudiated Shefferman and most people had no idea who he was. After gradually reducing expenditures, the Clerks quietly ended the boycott in 1967. Meyers explained, "It had become apparent that a boycott would never be substantially effective against a monster with such resources."[155]

Thus even without LRA, Sears was capable of repelling major campaigns by two of the nation's largest unions, and it is likely that Sears would have done nearly as well without Shefferman in the pre-McClellan decades. Against the company's many strengths the unions had numerous weaknesses, the most important being a profound lack of understanding of Sears' management policies and labor force. Operating in the dark, the Teamsters and the Clerks could not plan an effective organizing drive. Neither union grasped how the attitude survey worked; one Clerks' official believed that it was designed to elicit only favorable responses.[156] The Teamsters made the mistake of regularly attacking the profit-sharing plan, a tactic that played right into management's hands.[157] And although the Clerks understood grocery workers, they had a hard time appealing to Sears' relatively privileged salesmen and, for different reasons, to its saleswomen.[158]

It helps to put Sears into perspective by comparing the La Follette and McClellan hearings, which occurred roughly twenty years apart. The La Follette hearings had exposed the underside of traditional welfare capitalism—its willingness to use brute force—and had portrayed labor as the suffering victim. With the harsh light of publicity shining on the once-private world of labor relations, employers realized that their sullied reputations could only be restored by adopting more lawful and less conspicuous methods for staving off unions. It was hardly surprising, then, that Sears—ever sensitive to public relations and faced with persistent union challenges—became a pioneer in developing these methods.

One key method was the attitude survey. The program clearly was deceptive and manipulative (nondirective interviewing, for example, sought to change an employee's behavior without his or her knowledge or consent). It was not, however, an effort to frustrate union organization as such but rather an attempt to deal with problems before they kindled pro-union sentiments. The program did deter unions, but it did so by improving the already high quality of management at Sears: it gave top executives reliable indicators of how employees perceived company policies and practices, and by quantifying intangible concepts like morale it cast workplace issues in terms skeptical managers could understand. Finally, by forcing management to be responsive to employee opinion, surveys helped to improve working conditions and keep Sears several steps ahead of the unions.

If attitude surveys were the anti-union high road, Shefferman was the low road. Shefferman's activities were despicable; even Sears' own store managers disdained them. But Shefferman's tricks were not always illegal; in fact, he exploited to full advantage the many grey areas in the legal framework governing labor-management relations. Shefferman also took advantage of the fact that, as the labor movement became more successful in the 1940s and 1950s, it also became more internally divided, less zealously reformist, and more corruptible.

By the time of the McClellan hearings, the tables had turned: now labor was the party on trial, not management. Even though Sears was mortified by the hearings, it suffered few consequences as a result of them. Public opinion polls showed that a majority of Americans viewed the hearings—possibly even Shefferman himself—as an indictment of labor's corruption, not of management's shortcomings.[159] Moreover, at its worst Sears looked a lot better than the ruthless employers exposed by the La Follette Committee, and at its best Sears appeared to be a model employer: progressive, enlightened, and successful.

Sears was not nearly so wealthy as Kodak; margins were much thinner in retailing than film manufacturing. For a retailer, however, Sears offered excellent employment conditions: everything from profit sharing and good benefits to stable jobs and a chance to advance. And partly because Sears was a successful retailer—skilled in tugging at the consumer's emotions—it was way ahead of Kodak in applying behavioral science to the workplace: not just attitude surveys but a panoply of management techniques ranging from small-group activities to companywide efforts to create a uniform, yet friendly, internal culture. Producing this kind of industrial community in a sprawling chain retailer was no small accomplishment; other chains lagged Sears by twenty years or more.[160] Thus even though Kodak was kinder and, because of its isolation, gentler than Sears, it was Sears that took the lead in modernizing welfare capitalism.

Five

Recasting Company Unions: Thompson Products

In 1929, on the eve of the Depression, Thompson Products appeared ill equipped to cope with the events that lay ahead. It employed more than two thousand people but lacked most of the features characteristic of progressive management in the 1920s. It had no personnel department, few welfare benefits, and nothing so sophisticated as an employee representation plan. Although several Cleveland manufacturers, including General Electric and White Motors, were part of welfare capitalism's vanguard, Thompson Products was not among them. Thompson's managers could be kind, even generous, but their paternalism was old-fashioned and provincial. In this respect Thompson resembled other small and medium-sized companies.

During the 1930s, most of these middling firms stuck to their traditional management styles. Despite a changing environment, they started and ended the decade with few of the accoutrements of the progressive approach. Although a number of them launched representation plans in the wake of the 1933 National Industrial Recovery Act, the plans typically were ineffectual; they also were "as ephemeral and short-lived as their World War I predecessors."[1] When confronted by restive workers or union organizers, midsized companies often regressed to primitive forms of resistance. In doing so they took their cues from organizations representing American industry's *Mittelstand*, outfits like the National Association of Manufacturers and its local affiliates. These groups offered no positive alternative to unionism; their approach was simply to stand fast, to fight hard, and, whenever they thought they could get away with it, to ignore the law.

Though it came from this milieu, Thompson Products charted a different course in the 1930s, one that put it on a distinctive trajectory for years to come. Thompson's exceptionalism can be traced to Frederick C. Crawford, the man who took over as company president in 1933. During the Depression, Crawford turned the company's labor policies upside down. He started a personnel department, a representation plan, and new welfare programs. But Crawford was determined to learn from the past, not simply to repeat it; he added new ingredients to welfare capitalism, including semiautonomous company unions and a bevy of human relations programs. To get his ideas across, Crawford relied on modern communications techniques and on the force of his magnetic personality. Accessible and garrulous, Crawford gave workers the kind of attention they rarely received from top management. Such attentiveness, together with homespun touches, made Crawford extremely popular with employees. Out of this came a loyalty to "Fred" and the "TP Family," which union organizers consistently underestimated.

How was Thompson able to adapt so quickly to the changing environment of the 1930s and 1940s? As the economic historian Alexander Gerschenkron once pointed out, backwardness has its advantages. When a late-developing firm decides to improve itself, it can leapfrog past more successful companies by copying their successes and avoiding their mistakes. Late developers also have an easier time reacting to a new environment because they lack the rigidity that comes from having a financial and organizational stake in a given way of doing things.

Yet there was a darker side to Thompson that showed itself during union organizing campaigns. When first confronted by unions in the 1930s, the company adopted the heavy-handed tactics that made Cleveland employers infamous, and in later years management walked a fine line between persuasion and coercion. Union activists were harassed and Crawford himself tested the legal limits on employer involvement in representation elections. Crawford's repeated clashes with the NLRB made him a hero to other employers and led to his being named head of the National Association of Manufacturers in 1943.

Thompson Products eschewed the elaborate dissimulations orchestrated by Sears, however. A producer-goods company, it did not have to worry about offending pro-labor customers; hence there was no need for arm's-length relationships with consultants like Shefferman to ensure what we today would call plausible deniability. Also, being head of a relatively small company, Crawford was deeply involved in day-to-day plant affairs and took personal responsibility for the company's reputation. Crawford believed that Thompson's growth depended "not just on money and machinery but on people—the key to success." For a medium-sized parts supplier operating in highly competitive markets, this was a reasonable belief. Then, too, Thompson had fewer opportunities for deceit. Until the late 1950s it never had more than a dozen plants, each under the constant scrutiny of the NLRB and aggressive unions like the Automobile Workers (UAW). Thompson would have had a hard time getting away with Shefferman-type tactics even if it had tried to use them.[2]

In place of a Shefferman, Thompson relied on its company unions to help defeat organizing drives by "outsiders." The company-union formula worked so well that Thompson stuck with it long after World War II. Every new facility that Thompson opened in the late 1940s and 1950s had a plant union as well as elaborate human relations and welfare programs. The plant unions were a curious breed: though cooperative, they were not entirely lacking in adversarial mettle; though concerned about wages, they were actively involved in many aspects of factory management. Thompson actually encouraged its workers to participate in plant affairs, so long as an AFL-CIO union was not the medium. By the 1960s, Thompson (by then known as TRW) was well positioned to become a leader in the employee involvement movement, thus forming a bridge between traditional and modern welfare capitalism.

The Company and Its Workers

Founded in 1901 in Cleveland, Thompson Products grew up alongside the motor vehicle industry, manufacturing auto parts (valves, pumps, and chassis components) for the original-equipment and replacement markets. The Cleveland auto industry can be traced back to Alexander Winton's Motor Carriage Company, which sold its first automobile in 1898. Three years later, Charles E. Thompson, W. D. Bartlett, and two other men founded the Cleveland Cap Screw Company to produce valves and fittings for automobiles and light machinery. "Charley" Thompson, a New England-born tinkerer, had invented a welding process to hold together a nickel steel engine valve and a carbon steel stem. Winton was impressed by the new valve and began using it in his engines, and in 1905 he bought a controlling interest in Cleveland Cap Screw.

In 1915, Charley Thompson bought out Winton and twice renamed the firm: first as the Electric Welding Products Company and later as the Steel Products Company. To better supply auto manufacturers in Detroit, Thompson purchased two plants in that city and began manufacturing a variety of automotive parts. As the automobile industry expanded during the First World War and again in the 1920s, so did the Steel Products Company. Employment at its Cleveland plant (the "Main" plant on Clarkwood Road) reached eighteen hundred during the war, then fell back to twelve hundred, and rose to more than two thousand by 1929.

The company's growth was aided by its development, around 1920, of a new high-resistance valve. Made of a chromium, nickel, and silicon alloy, by the end of the 1920s nearly all American cars used it in their engines. (So hard was the alloy that machinists called it "the Devil's steel.") The 1920s also saw Thompson enter the replacement-parts business. Initially it manufactured replacement valves, bolts, and starting cranks, which it distributed through its own network of suppliers under the brand name Thompson. To draw attention to the brand and to honor its founder, the company was renamed Thompson Products in 1926.[3]

A fateful change came during the First World War, when the company successfully applied its valve technology to airplane engines. Aircraft-engine parts became an important part of Thompson's line over the next twenty years; by 1940 it derived equal revenue from its three divisions: original auto parts, replacement auto parts, and aircraft parts. Other Cleveland companies followed Thompson's lead and the city became a major producer of aircraft parts. In 1943, Cleveland accounted for nearly one-fourth of the nation's wartime production of aircraft parts, much of it supplied by Thompson. The firm mushroomed during the war and for a while was Cleveland's largest employer. High in demand were its sodium-cooled aircraft valves, which it made under a license from Eaton Corporation.[4]

Until the 1950s, engine valves were welded by hand, a slow and labor-intensive process. Thompson's genius was to manufacture these (and other) precision parts using semiskilled workers, mass-production methods, and a high division of labor. Manufacture of aircraft valves, for example, was done in 180 separate operations, from initial bar stock to the finished valve (including cutting, forging, milling, pointing, heat-treating, grinding, and polishing). During the war, Thompson's largest plant produced more than 200,000 valves daily on fifteen continuous production lines. Thompson used this same method—which it called "precision mass technology"—to manufacture a vast array of automotive parts such as water and fuel pumps, pins, locks, caps, rods, sleeves, and bolts.[5]

The bulk of Thompson's work force comprised semiskilled workers who received their training from the company. Training occurred either on the job or in a "learners" program. The company's machine tool jobs could be learned in eight weeks, though some of the more complicated operations required from four to ten months to learn. Thompson also employed a small but vital group of skilled craftsmen, including master machinists, pattern makers, electricians, and tool and die makers. To meet company needs—and to circumvent local craft unions—Thompson set up a four-year apprenticeship program in 1936.[6]

While superior technology aided Thompson's sales, its success in the aircraft-parts market depended on two additional factors that also figured in the company's labor relations strategy. One was Charley Thompson's appreciation of the adage that "good publicity is good for business." After Charles Lindbergh's 1927 transatlantic flight, the company heavily advertised the fact that the *Spirit of St. Louis* was powered by Thompson valves. Two years later, Charley Thompson made a successful bid to hold the National Air Races at the Cleveland airport. Lindbergh sat next to him in the reviewing stands, and when the race was over the winner received an elaborate prize known as the Thompson Trophy. What came to be known as the Thompson Trophy Race was held annually during the 1930s and brought national attention to Thompson Products.

The other factor boosting sales was Thompson's early recognition that the federal government would be a major player in the aviation industry, both as a purchaser of planes and as the sponsor of aviation-related research. Much of the credit here goes to Frederick C. Crawford, who succeeded Charley Thompson. As head of Cleveland's chamber of commerce in the late 1930s, Crawford successfully lobbied the National Advisory Committee for Aeronautics (NACA) to select Cleveland as the site for its Aircraft Engine Research Laboratory. The facility, opened in 1940, contained a wind tunnel for studying jet propulsion, and Thompson closely followed its neighbor's research activities, which helped the company make an early transition from piston to jet engine valves. The company's familiarity with NACA (later to become NASA) also helped it get in on the ground floor of the missile, rocket, and satellite industries in the 1950s. In 1953, Crawford helped to fund a small West Coast missile manufacturer, the Ramo-Wooldridge Company. The company grew so rapidly that by 1958 it merged with Thompson to form Thompson-Ramo-Wooldridge. This later was shortened to TRW, which is what the firm is called today.[7]

During the 1920s and 1930s, most of Thompson's workers were white males. Although blacks accounted for 10 percent of Cleveland's population in the 1930s, none worked at Thompson. Such discrimination was not unusual: in 1940, fewer than 1 percent of Cleveland's auto workers were black. Thompson had a few female employees, nearly all of them young and unmarried. Pay rates were very low for these "girls," who worked in Thompson's packing department. Like other firms of its day, Thompson prohibited the employment of married women, and single women had to quit if they married.[8]

Thompson's white males were ethnically diverse, like Cleveland itself. The city was one of the most heterogeneous places in the nation. The largest groups were the Slovaks and Poles, followed by Italians, Germans, Hungarians, Slavs, and Russians. Each group occupied a particular section of Cleveland's metropolitan area, forming a patchwork of insular enclaves. Studies of Slavs and Italians, for example, show that well over half of the second generation married inside the group. Although immigration to Cleveland slowed to a trickle in the 1920s, 25 percent of the city's population was still foreign-born in the 1930s.[9]

Ethnic animosity was a recurring problem at Thompson's small piston Pin plant on Detroit Avenue. Thompson bought the facility in 1929 from John R. Cox, a tough entrepreneur whose foremen ran the factory along drive-system lines. Although Thompson's other plants were managed less autocratically, Cox was allowed to stay in charge of the Pin plant after Thompson bought him out. In crude divide-and-conquer fashion, Cox built the workforce of 150 employees out of two distinct groups: Irish workers from the city's Westside area and Polish workers from the Scranton Road area. When a company union was set up at the plant in 1934, the Irish workers joined immediately, whereupon the Polish workers instinctively avoided it. Shortly thereafter, the machinists' union (IAM-AFL) began organizing at the plant and signed up about a third of the workers, nearly all of them Poles. Cox repeatedly refused to recognize the IAM, leading to a three-week strike during the summer of 1935, the first in Thompson's history.[10]

At the Main plant, Thompson Products pursued a different strategy—hiring workers from more than a dozen ethnic groups—which prevented any one of them from constituting a majority. Shortly after the Pin plant strike, Thompson's personnel manager, Raymond S. Livingstone, wrote a memo reassuring top management that "we are attempting to hire friendly, congenial workers in order to keep this a friendly place to work. . . . We are trying to avoid running too strongly to any one nationality, cliques, friends, or relatives." Throughout the 1940s, the company stuck to what it called a "percentage [hiring] policy with respect to all nationality and religious groups."[11]

World War II changed some hiring practices. First came a rapid increase in the number of women, notably married white women, at the company. By 1942 roughly 10 percent of the company's Cleveland production workers were female; the proportion doubled in 1943. After the war, however, Thompson shed many of these women.[12] A more lasting change was Thompson's hiring of black men to work as machine operators. Thompson was first among the city's major manufacturers to make a concerted effort to hire black workers, earning the company accolades from the African-American community. Employment of black workers peaked in 1943 at about 10 percent (this was Livingstone's "percentage" quota), making Thompson the city's largest employer of blacks in relatively high-paying semiskilled jobs. (Republic Steel employed a greater number of black workers but relegated them to laborers' tasks.) The company deserved the praise it received, although it was not above playing on racial animosities when faced with labor unrest.[13]

Hiring from a multitude of groups was a more effective divide-and-conquer tactic than John Cox's dichotomized approach at the Pin plant. Yet such diversity made it difficult for Thompson to identify a majority whose loyalties it could depend on. To create a loyal majority out of an ethnic hodgepodge, some companies turned to "Americanization" programs, but Thompson rejected the melting pot in favor of a different strategy: recognizing diversity while identifying commonalities that would bind workers to management.[14]

One such unifying force was God. According to a company survey, the average Thompson worker had "a sense of spiritual values and supports the church of his faith." Thompson sprinkled biblical sayings throughout its employee publications and made its facilities available after hours to fraternal and religious groups like the Knights of Columbus. Assistance to these groups started in the 1930s and continued through the 1950s, though in later years some employees began complaining that too much consideration was being given to them.[15]

Another unifying force was the image of Thompson as a brotherhood, a group of hard-working men bound together by economic fate. As Crawford said in a 1935 speech to employees, "All of us in this room are friends. We are all workmen. We all come in the morning and punch a clock and go to work and we all go home at night." In other words, work and family responsibilities were shared by everyone; class was less significant than the affinities of gender. Raymond Livingstone claimed that it was company policy "to eliminate class lines and have our relationships on a first-name basis." He was known as Ray to workers, while Crawford was known as Fred. Having masculinity serve as a basis for cooperation between employers and workers was not unusual: other companies—such as Ford, Reo Car, and Sears—made imaginative use of gender. Masculinity could fuel opposition to employers (as with the "manly ethos" of nineteenth-century craft workers), but, as historian Patrick Joyce has remarked, it also could be "a force for all sorts of understanding with the employer (a 'boss' in his sphere as was the worker in his home and work functions)."[16]

Thompson's camaraderie had deep roots. Though the firm had little in the way of a formal personnel program in the 1920s—workers then were hired at the front gates by foremen—a friendly atmosphere differentiated Thompson from drive-system companies of the day. Guided by the firm's production manager, Thompson workers and managers would pool their money to organize bowling and baseball leagues and other group activities. The production manager was remembered by Crawford as "a man of big heart [who] loved men and machinery, spent his time in the plant. Employment was never so large but what he knew them all personally. He loaned them money, helped them when they were sick." Crawford himself was then a manager at the company's factory in Detroit, where he established a reputation as a personable leader who could "talk straight" with shop-floor workers. To boost production, he would hold mass meetings with workers every sixty days: "I'd call them in and tell them what we were doing and what our challenges were. The response was amazing." Crawford's success in Detroit, which he attributed to "decency and good communications," hastened his ascent up the ranks.[17]

Two other policies originating in the 1920s—group bonuses and seniority privileges—had the same effect of tying employees more closely to the company and to each other. The group bonus plan worked as follows:

> A price range is set up for each job, based on the company's wage policy, and each employee is given a rate within this range depending on his ability to produce. This rate is called the basis rate. Employees doing similar or related work within a department are classified into groups. The work produced by the entire group is counted, and the efficiency of the group figured against a fair standard. An individual's earnings are then determined by his base rate multiplied by his group's efficiency. . . . Whether the employee receives more or less than his base rate depends on whether the total group efficiency is over or under 100 percent.[18]

Groups covered by a common incentive typically included 60 to 125 workers, though some had as many as 400 workers. There were two types of groups: colonies and lines. Colonies were made up of workers doing similar tasks, such as heat-treating or grinding; finished work moved in batches from colony to colony. Lines were assembly lines, where each piece went through a series of operations as it moved from worker to worker within the group. Also covered by the bonus plan were nonproduction workers, including truckers, sweepers, and maintenance crews.[19]

By the 1940s, group bonuses accounted for more than 20 percent of employee earnings. This, and the company's policy of matching union wage increases, raised earnings to the point where Thompson employees ranked among Cleveland's best-paid manufacturing workers. Not everyone liked the group plan, however. Common complaints were that learners "penalize the whole group," that "too many of us are dependent on each other," and that "the loafer gets the same bonus as a good worker." Indeed, group bonus plans were quite rare in American industry: only 4 percent of workers on incentive pay were covered by them. Managers disliked the plans because of their complexity and technical requirements. Also, said one consultant, "managers have raised the objection that the formation of groups tends to organize workers in a way that may prove embarrassing."[20]

Despite this risk, Thompson had several reasons for sticking with the group plan. For one, it reduced the need for close supervision; as an observer noted, "Social pressure within the group encourages slackers to increase output." (Some groups even planned their own work in an attempt to raise group efficiency.) Another advantage was that the plan facilitated on-the-job training, forcing seasoned workers to bring learners up to speed so as not to jeopardize the bonus. Finally, Thompson favored the plan because it created a collective production ethos, which was known as "the Thompson spirit." Explained one manager, "We like the system because it is the teamwork way of running the business. We produce as a team, sharing our good and bad luck together, dividing our bonus earnings." Said another manager, "I think most of our people are pleased to think that they belong to a *team*. That may seem trite or inappropriate but it really describes the spirit and relationship that we have within the company."[21]

Also dating from the 1920s was systematic recognition of seniority. Employees of any rank who reached twenty-five years' service would be called into Mr. Thompson's office to receive a check for 25 percent of their salary. Mr. Thompson would sit with them, smoke cigars, and discuss old times. The emphasis on seniority deterred employees from quitting, while at the same time creating a bond between older workers and managers. An article in the company newspaper boasted that "every executive and every department head has made his way up through the ranks. No outsiders have been brought in. Continuity of service brings friendships; in a company where men strive together friendships are made which are lasting and make daily duties pleasant. Thompson is a company of this kind." Long-service workers often were loyal workers, a tendency Thompson sought to encourage through an organization called the Old Guard. After five years at the company, employees could join the Old Guard and participate in its social activities. During the Depression, the company tried to prevent the layoff of any Old Guard member. As seniority became more important in determining layoffs, a special committee of the Old Guard was formed to help the company set up precise seniority records. In cases of doubt—for example, when a service break was disputed—workers could present their story to their peers on the Old Guard committee.[22]

The Old Guard symbolized stability. To a generation that had weathered the Depression, such symbols meant a lot. When asked in 1947, "What is the one thing you fear most in life?" the vast majority of Old Guard members replied, "insecurity." Members praised Thompson for the security it provided: "steadiest job I ever had," "no layoff in 14 years," "off 1 week in 17 years," "it couldn't be steadier." This is not to say Thompson workers had an easy time of it during the Depression. However, by shielding Old Guard members from layoff, the company enhanced its reputation and that of the Old Guard. In exchange, management asked Old Guard members to "exert all of their influence in helping shape proper opinions in the minds of new employees."[23]

Although cigars no longer were smoked in Mr. Thompson's office by the 1940s, the Old Guard remained a masculine organization in which age and gender bridged the fissures of ethnicity and class. Women were permitted to join the Old Guard, but because of marriage bars and postwar layoffs, few of them were able to achieve the necessary seniority: the average Old Guard member in 1947 had been with the company for nine years, a span that exceeded most women's tenure. A postwar survey of twelve hundred Old Guard members made this discrepancy clear. When asked about their hobbies, the top response was "participating in sports"; the favorites were fishing, golf, bowling, and hunting.[24]

The Depression Years at Thompson

The Depression hit Cleveland hard. The industrialist Cyrus Eaton thought that Cleveland was more severely affected than any other city in the United States. A year after the stock market crash, one-third of the city's workers were unemployed, and more lost their jobs in the next two years. With its economy based on metal working, Cleveland was slow to recover. Unemployment remained a serious problem until the beginning of World War II.[25]

Like other Cleveland manufacturers, Thompson Products shrank during the Depression's early years. With few people buying new vehicles, orders for parts plummeted, as did prices. To keep their factories running, the big auto companies made their own parts instead of buying them from independent suppliers, many of whom went out of business. Thompson was lucky in this regard. Though its sales fell it didn't lose any major contracts. The company was helped by Charley Thompson's friendships with several auto moguls and by its reputation for providing quality parts at a reasonable cost. Even so, employment fell by more than 50 percent between 1929 and 1933.[26]

In coping with the downturn, Thompson consistently favored its senior workers. Layoffs were made in reverse order of seniority (no one in the Old Guard was laid off for any length of time) and men with dependents were given preference when deciding who should stay. Those who held on to their jobs saw their hours and wages sharply reduced, however. To cushion such cuts, the company created a fund to loan employees money for purchasing coal and clothes, for paying off credit at grocery stores, and for other needs.[27]

A turning point for Thompson Products was 1933. Charley Thompson died that year, leaving behind a company entangled with his personal estate. Immediately after assuming the presidency, Fred Crawford moved quickly to wean the company of its dependence on Charley Thompson's buddies in the auto industry. Through clever marketing, Crawford expanded the company's replacement-parts business. He built a network of more than 3,000 jobbers who sold Thompson replacement parts directly to garages. Whenever a garage placed a major order, it received a manual showing every vehicle built in the last twenty-five years and the Thompson parts needed to service them. The 1930s were a good time to go after this market, since most people were choosing to repair their old cars rather than replace them. In 1935, Crawford purchased the Toledo Steel Products Company, which had a small plant in that city, and started a second line of parts under the Toledo brand name.[28]

With its parts business rapidly expanding, the company was able to rehire many of the workers previously laid off. By mid-1934, half the jobs lost since 1929 had been refilled. Despite a slump in the fall of 1934, employment in 1935 surpassed Thompson's 1929 peak; by 1939, the company was almost twice as large as it had been a decade earlier. Thompson's growth outstripped that of most other local manufacturers. In steel—a major Cleveland industry—nearly a quarter of the jobs existing in 1929 still had not been recreated by 1939.[29]

In 1933, also, Cleveland autoworkers began to organize. At White Motor Company, a young activist named Wyndham Mortimer was signing up workers for the Communist-affiliated Auto Workers Union. The union was attacked by the AFL's Cleveland Metal Trades Council, which urged workers to "join the only bonafide *American* labor union . . . the AFL." Eventually Mortimer brought the White Motor workers over to the AFL and was granted a federal charter. Similar charters were issued to unions at other local auto companies—including Fisher Body, National Carbon, and Willard Storage Battery—and during the winter of 1933–1934, several strikes broke out. Although the fledgling auto unions were weak (out of seven thousand workers at Cleveland Fisher Body in 1935, only three hundred were dues-paying union members), their existence troubled the city's employers.[30]

As was his nature, Fred Crawford decided to meet the problem head on. Despite his Brahmin roots, Crawford was a feisty extrovert who was both familiar and comfortable with shop culture. Educated at Harvard, where he took two degrees in civil engineering, Crawford's first job came in 1916, when he went to work for Charley Thompson's Steel Products Company. To learn about the firm from the bottom up, Crawford started out as a millwright's helper. After service in the Navy Aviation Corps during World War I, he returned to Steel Products, which was the only company he ever worked for.

A diehard Republican, Crawford was deeply conservative, but receptive to new ideas. Despite his dislike of the Roosevelts (in his office in the 1930s hung a picture of Franklin D. Roosevelt, upside down, and another of Eleanor Roosevelt, with a pipe in her mouth), Crawford believed that the New Deal marked a major shift in social values that businessmen had to acknowledge. As head of the National Association of Manufacturers during World War II, Crawford transformed the hidebound organization into an advocate of labor law reform and progressive personnel management. Though critical of government, Crawford recognized the possibilities inherent in the emerging military-industrial complex. His knowledge of Washington's inner circles brought contracts to Thompson Products and also helped his efforts to amend the Wagner Act. On top of all this, Crawford was a natural leader and gifted speaker—handsome, articulate, self-assured, yet unpretentious.[31]

High on Crawford's agenda after becoming president of Thompson Products was the labor situation. Determined to preempt unionism before it had a chance to take root, Crawford moved quickly to shake the company out of its complacent paternalism. One of his first steps was to ask Raymond S. Livingstone to create a corporate personnel department. Livingstone was a young journalist who had been hired in 1929 to run Thompson's public relations programs. Although he lacked experience in personnel management, Livingstone saw employee relations as the internal analog of public relations. A personnel manager, he said, "must be a salesman at heart [with] a flair for the dramatic." Like Crawford, who was his close friend, Livingstone was an engaging speaker. Their friendship—and Crawford's determination to keep unions out of the company—put Livingstone's personnel department on an inside track.[32]

Livingstone's first year as personnel director was a frenzied rush to build the programs that other firms had experimented with during the previous two decades. Livingstone created a code of personnel policies, a centralized hiring department, an employee records office, and two new membership organizations. One of these was the Thompson Products Employees' Association, a company union started in January 1934, ostensibly by the employees themselves, although Livingstone and a company attorney conceived the idea and loyal members of the Old Guard carried it out. The other was the Social and Recreation Club: members paid dues of twenty-five cents per month and elected officers to oversee an orchestra, a picnic committee, and a variety of clubs—motorcycle, baseball, bowling, golf, hiking, and shooting.[33]

Livingstone also reorganized the Old Guard in 1934. A constitution was drafted and secret-ballot elections held to select officers. An Old Guard committee took charge of social events, which were expanded from what the company had done in the 1920s. The main event was the Old Guard picnic, open to all employees and their families; at its peak in 1944 the picnic drew close to fifty thousand people. Also popular was the Old Guard banquet, first held in a cleared area adjacent to the toolroom and later in a local hotel. These were raucous affairs, lasting from six in the evening to midnight or later. There was an orchestra, food, dancing, beer, stronger liquor brought by the guests, and, at some point during the festivities, speeches by Crawford and Livingstone. Public address systems were still a novelty in the 1930s; on one occasion, several Old Guard members "seized the mike and became enthralled with the sound of their own harmony booming from the speakers." Two other important Old Guard activities were the seniority committee and the welfare committee, which took over from the company the giving of aid and interest-free loans to destitute employees. Livingstone arranged for the loan fund to be subsidized with money earned from plant vending machines and with "contributions" from employees who forgot to bring their badges to work.[34]

Having the Old Guard help needy workers was a way of minimizing overt paternalism without severing the link between the company and kindness. But any impression of an arm's-length relationship between the Old Guard and management was misleading. Because the Old Guard was open to all ranks, supervisors and managers made up a good chunk of its membership (27 percent in 1947). The Old Guard's first president, in 1934, was Lee Clegg, a high-ranking company manager, and Livingstone served as an officer for more than twenty years. Having managers in the Old Guard made them part of the "family" while also giving management some leverage with the company union, to which only nonsupervisory employees could belong. Several company-union leaders got their start as officers of the Old Guard and one individual, Frank Manning, simultaneously served as head of both organizations in the 1950s.[35]

In the early and mid-1930s, a time when other companies were getting rid of their welfare programs, Thompson was a beehive of activity. There were clambakes, picnics at Geauga Park, and boat rides on Lake Erie. The company started a newspaper, *The Friendly Forum*, and encouraged employees to serve as reporters. Although Thompson lacked Kodak's lavish facilities and benefits, its programs had the same objectives as Kodak's: to get workers to feel good about their jobs and feel committed to the company. Still a relatively small firm, Thompson's general manager in 1936 nevertheless reported that "we are budgeting an appreciable amount of money for personnel work and for other department activities that were not in effect in 1929."[36]

Instead of merely duplicating 1920s-style welfare capitalism, Livingstone looked critically at other companies and tried to avoid the mistakes they had made. Take, for example, his design of the company union. In a 1934 manual he explained to supervisors "the reasons why some employee representation plans have failed or will be likely to fail." Citing the experiences of laggard firms, the manual predicted that "a plan which provides only for meetings in case of grievances will soon deteriorate." It also warned against tying employee representation to profit sharing because, as the Depression had demonstrated, such a linkage would "last only as long as the financial return is satisfactory."[37]

From the beginning, Thompson's personnel department considered the legal consequences of its activities. They worked closely with the company's attorney, J. David Wright, and with its outside counsel, Stanley and Smoyer, on the increasingly important legal aspects of labor relations. Of course, Livingstone was not interested in the law simply because he wanted to comply with it. He regularly probed the new legal structures for loopholes and weak spots, aggressively challenging the government at every step. Although Livingstone's truculence was not unique, it was precocious: Thompson's first confrontation with the NLRB came only thirty days after passage of the Wagner Act.[38]

Also novel was Thompson's sensitivity to worker attitudes and desires. Like Sears, Thompson relied on a bevy of communications programs to assess—and shape—the way employees thought. Central to this effort were the behavioral sciences, although the impetus to apply them originated in Crawford's faith in the power of persuasion and Livingstone's meticulous concern with "preventing rather than settling labor disputes after they had arisen." Inside the company the two men, and other top managers, were omnipresent. Much time was spent mingling with employees at social events and chatting on the shop floor. Livingstone referred to the latter as "walking." It gave managers a chance to see at first hand what was happening and gave employees a chance to tell them. Walking, said Livingstone, was the keystone of Thompson's personnel program.[39]

The UAW took a cynical view of these activities, saying that Crawford was "very loquacious and never miss[ed] a chance to preach to his workers." Nevertheless, Crawford's regular visits to the shop floor created a folksy atmosphere—and kept foremen on their toes. According to Livingstone, workers were made to feel that "little things which might be taken advantage of by the supervisor will come to the attention of the president. They also want him to drift up and say hello so they can go home and say to their wives that night, 'the president was through the shop tonight and he said hello to me.'"[40]

Walking was not as simple as it sounded; its success required a friendly style and a sense of humor. Like Will Rogers, Crawford had these in abundance. He could give almost anything a humorous spin, even his own walking philosophy. As he told a group of executives in 1943:

> Going down to a shop cafeteria one day to have a cup of coffee, I found a group of men together, and over on one side, seated on a barrel, was a young man with very dirty hands having his cup of coffee. I went over and sat on the next barrel and shook hands. He didn't want to shake hands at first, but I said, "Hell son, you've got to get dirty to run this world. How long've you been here?" He said, "Ninety days." I said, "Like it here?" "Oh yes, I like it here. It's a fine place." "Where do you live?" and so on. Well the incident passed in ten minutes. But two months later a minister told us that the members of his parish sang the praises of my particular company as being a human company. I said, "What does your parish know about my company?" He said, "They have the most wonderful institution. Whenever a worker has been with the company for ninety days the president comes down to have lunch with him to see how he is getting on."[41]

Thus Crawford practiced "human relations" long before he knew it had a name. He believed in the power of emotions and was skeptical of bureaucratic controls. Like Robert E. Wood of Sears, Crawford eschewed organization charts because, he said, they hampered cooperation and fluidity. At some point in the early 1940s, Crawford began reading Elton Mayo and other human relations writings and felt, not surprisingly, that he had discovered "an answer to the ills that beset our economic system."[42]

The Mayoites provided Crawford with an intricate set of ideas whose impact could be seen in two realms: first, in Thompson's heavy reliance on behavioral consultants (psychologists helped the company with everything from its attitude surveys to Muzak to productivity-enhancing color schemes in the factories); and second, in Thompson's corporate philosophy, which was more coherent and sophisticated than that guiding most companies of the 1930s and 1940s. For Crawford and Livingstone—as for Mayo—human relations was both an industrial psychology and a social vision.

One element of Crawford's corporate philosophy can be termed "authoritarian Mayoism." This is the belief that employees want more from their jobs than just money—they also want personal recognition and to be treated as intelligent adults. Underlying this belief, however, is the assumption that workers are followers, eager to attach their loyalties to strong institutions and leaders. As Crawford put it, "The working man today, more than ever before in this emotional age, wants someone interested in him, and if he thinks you are not interested in him he turns instinctively to find someone outside your plant who is. . . . The worker doesn't care about his pay and plant conditions. It is what he thinks about the honesty and square-shooting and directness of the boss who is over the plant, and his ability to meet him, talk to him, and know him." But, said Crawford, the worker ". . . has one great weakness—he is far too susceptible to emotional leadership. He will fall for any emotional bandwagon that comes along [because he is] starved for understanding and friendship and for the truth. He is tremendously confused right now . . . and is eager to be taught and led."

Crawford sought to exploit that weakness by spending much of his time speaking to employees, projecting the force of his ideas and personality. Like Livingstone, he intertwined employee relations and public relations. Once he boasted to an audience of managers, "I would almost be willing to take a bet that if you will give me six weeks' time and a soap box, I will stand in front of your employment office, and at the end of six weeks I will have the employees throwing rocks at you or I will have the employees working all night without overtime, and wearing an American flag, depending on what is said from the soap box."[43]

Taking their cues from Crawford, managers at all levels of the organization regularly walked the shop floor, dispensing a gospel of friendliness and good feelings. Beneath all the patter, however, a serious claim was being made: that workers and managers held common values and a common economic fate. Such an assertion of solidarity—what may be called industrial "communitarianism"—formed the second element of Crawford's philosophy. As Crawford told a group of workers, "We both want lots of business; we both want lots of money; we both want the plant fixed up; we both want success for Thompson Products; we both want our pay raised; we both want our hours shortened. . . . None of us is wholly satisfied."[44]

On Crawford's corporate island there was no room for organized labor. Unions were viewed as bureaucratic interlopers who propagated artificial conflict. In a debate with A. E. Stevenson, a Cleveland CIO official, Ray Livingstone disparaged what he called "the outside professional union organizer":

> His interest is not at all concerned with trying to build a better business so that there will be more to divide. His interest is in building a union. . . . Union heads meet in oak-paneled rooms. In these offices are big maps, and through the cigar smoke, union leaders point to them and say, "This plant must be organized. That plant must be struck. . . . Then, wires crackle all over the United States and edicts go forth to local union officers, and workmen in the plants have nothing to say at all about the making of such decisions.[45]

Government was tarred with the same brush. Crawford and Livingstone believed that Roosevelt's labor policies were consciously designed to make it difficult, if not impossible, to maintain welfare capitalism. In the mid-1930s, Crawford angrily called for an end to "the remote control of local relations . . . imposed by national labor boards, whose efforts now invite and incite conflicts between labor and management." Over a decade later, Livingstone used passionate hyperbole to make the same point: "Ever since 1933," he exclaimed, "the CIO and the New Deal have been destroying all forms of man-to-man relationships."[46]

Despite their hostility to government and "outside" unions, Crawford and Livingstone were willing—even eager—to deal with "inside" unions. Company unions were easily assimilated into Thompson's corporate community; conversely, the solidity of that community bolstered Thompson's ability to propagate company unions. Not only in the 1930s but during the 1940s and 1950s as well, company unions appeared at Thompson facilities around the country. Although disestablished by the NLRB and subject to stiff competition from the UAW, Thompson's company unions proved remarkably resilient, in part because of how they evolved over time.

The First Company Unions

The collective bargaining provisions of the 1933 National Industrial Recovery Act sparked a wildfire of labor organizing. To contain it, employers dug numerous firebreaks, the most elaborate of which were the company unions that sprang up in 1933 and 1934. Whether a lethargic laggard or a hidebound traditionalist, employers now rushed to set up representation plans for their employees. Bethlehem, the only large steel company with company unions in the 1920s, was suddenly joined by U.S. Steel, Republic, Jones and Laughlin, and the industry's other major employers. Much the same occurred in autos, where General Motors—which had spurned employee representation in the 1920s—now led the industry in setting up works councils at its major facilities.

Smaller companies were equally bold. The National Association of Manufacturers distributed sample company-union constitutions to employers around the country. Finally, companies that had let their 1920s-style representation plans lapse into desuetude took steps to revive them. Du Pont had discontinued employee representation in the late 1920s, but within two weeks of the Recovery Act it had set up works councils at more than sixty-five plants. By 1935, somewhere between two and three million workers were covered by company unions, more than double the coverage in 1932.[47]

Many of the new company unions—especially in smaller firms—existed only on paper. Others were tightly circumscribed by management. Fully 50 percent of the company unions surveyed by the U.S. Bureau of Labor Statistics in 1935 did not engage in collective bargaining; another third practiced only a few of the activities that unions normally carried out. There were other problems. General Motors failed to take its works councils seriously, while at Jones and Laughlin, employee representatives were bribed by the company to do its bidding. Because of these shortcomings, company unions fared poorly in representation elections, winning only 30 percent of the total votes cast between 1933 and 1935.[48]

Yet despite their low win rate—or perhaps because even 30 percent was seen as too high a share—the drafters of the Wagner Act aimed to legislate company unions out of existence. The circle of intellectuals around Senator Robert F. Wagner—and Wagner himself—loathed company unions, seeing them as barriers to industrial democracy and economic revival. The act did not specifically outlaw company unions, but Senator Wagner made it clear that the law would not tolerate a "company-dominated" union. Strict rules prohibited employers from dominating employee organizations; management was not supposed to participate in founding them, funding them, or running them. A third of the National Labor Relations Board's decisions in its early years involved company unions; of these, nearly 90 percent found individual company unions in violation of the law.[49]

Not all company unions were mere shells, however. As a result of legal scrutiny and the need to compete with national unions, some company unions began to evolve into more independent organizations. By 1935, more of them permitted employee representatives to hold separate meetings and also provided for arbitration of grievance disputes. The number of employee representatives increased—at Goodyear it tripled—while written agreements grew more common. A labor economist, David Saposs, argued that "a brand new type of company union is coming into existence. . . . This one approaches the characteristics and collective bargaining practices of trade-unions." In its survey, the Bureau of Labor Statistics estimated that about 15 percent of company unions were "seriously attempting to function in those fields commonly ascribed to collective bargaining. They represent the interests of the workers with a vigor not entirely attributable to management."[50]

Several such company unions—at Goodyear, International Harvester, and U.S. Steel—became the nuclei around which national unions formed. The

CIO's strategy for organizing U.S. Steel was to "capture the company unions from within" by recruiting disaffected employee representatives to the CIO side. As control was wrested away from company loyalists, pro-CIO representatives voted to affiliate U.S. Steel's company unions with the Steelworkers' Organizing Committee. Leaders of the company unions at Goodyear were similarly split between loyalists and rebels. The CIO's strategy was to court disaffected leaders and rely on them to attract others.[51]

Elsewhere, however, as company unions grew less dependent on employers and modeled themselves on trade unions, they proved tough adversaries for national unions. Workers had various reasons for supporting these revivified company unions. Some saw them as less corrupt and less radical than national unions. Others supported them out of a sense of loyalty—either blind or calculated—to management. Finally, skilled employees, especially in high-wage labor markets, were drawn to company unions because they feared that industrial unions would shrink wage differentials through policies of geographic standardization and skill compression; this was the case, for example, with Bell System workers in New York and Chicago (though it was not much of a factor at Thompson).[52]

Yet even when employees seemed to prefer a company union, the NLRB was reluctant to grant their wishes. The board's rationale was that a fear of management retaliation might be motivating employee preferences, an argument originally put forth by Senator Wagner. The NLRB also worried that employees would not be able to discern subtle types of employer domination and might support a company union without realizing its liabilities. Thus, in cases where company unions had become more independent but had not established a clean break or "cleavage" from an employer-dominated predecessor, the NLRB ordered their disestablishment and barred them from appearing on election ballots.[53]

Despite the threat posed by national unions and the NLRB, in 1947 there remained several hundred company unions, with roughly 470,000 members. These survivors included several company unions dating back to the 1920s or earlier (at AT&T, National Cash Register, Procter & Gamble, and the Standard Oil companies). Others were of more recent vintage, including company unions at large firms such as Du Pont and Sun Oil, as well as at numerous small to middling firms like Dow-Jones, Weirton Steel, Stromberg-Carlson, and Zenith Radio. Company unions at smaller firms occasionally joined together in federations like the Philadelphia-based National Independent Union Council. Most company unions, however, did not have formal ties to others. This was the case at Thompson Products, which by the end of the Second World War had become a bellwether for what remained of the company-union movement.[54]

Thompson's company unions first appeared in January 1934, when the officers of the Old Guard called a meeting of Main plant workers interested in forming "an organization for all employees, no matter the length of service, who could present their problems to management; such matters as wages, hours, and working conditions." A week later three hundred blue- and white-collar employees met in the company cafeteria and formed the Thompson Products Employees' Association (TPEA). They immediately elected a committee (headed by Bill Hoffman, a company auditor) to draft a constitution outlining the TPEA's structure.[55]

Under the constitution, Thompson's Cleveland employees annually elected seven people to the Committee of Employee Representatives (CER). The elections took place during working hours with ballots supplied by the company. After the second election in 1935, the company issued a manual to prepare new representatives for their posts. It warned: "Your job will not be an easy one. . . . On many occasions you will have to tell your fellow constituents that some of their requests are unreasonable, that is, if you perform your function fairly. On other occasions you will be called upon to press your beliefs and viewpoints firmly when they do not find a ready reception with management." The employee representatives and an equal number from management made up the Joint Council, which met monthly and whose executive secretary was the omnipresent Ray Livingstone.[56]

Like other post-Recovery Act company unions, the TPEA gave workers some formal rights that had been absent from earlier representation plans: these included the right to ratify the constitution (80 percent approved it); to vote for employee representatives; to have the option of membership in the TPEA (no dues were collected or membership meetings held, although there were numerous TPEA social events); and to present grievances to an outside arbitrator. Under the new grievance procedure, employees took their complaints to delegates appointed by the CER and, if the grievance could not be resolved by the worker's delegate and his foreman, it went to a CER member and his paired management representative. The third step in the procedure was the Joint Council, followed by outside arbitration if the council could not resolve a grievance, although that never occurred.

The TPEA was hardly a trade union, though. Its constitution barred strikes "or other independent action taken by employees or their representatives." Although the TPEA negotiated collective agreements—unlike 85 percent of the company unions surveyed by the Bureau of Labor Statistics in 1935—these contracts contained little of substance. Each was written by management and presented to the CER for inspection and signing. None mentioned wages; wage bargaining was the TPEA's greatest weakness. Two of the three major pay increases between 1934 and 1937 coincided with outside union organizing—in 1935 when the Machinists struck the Pin plant and in 1937 when the UAW first appeared at Main.[57]

The TPEA had a better record when it came to grievance handling and cooperative problem solving. The company provided forms for filing grievances, and the Joint Council kept track of their disposition. Most concerned transfers, bonus pay, or safety issues. Grievances that went as far as the council usually were settled in the worker's favor, although the council upheld several dismissals without comment, as, for example, when a worker was fired for stealing a pair of pants. On occasion, however, it saw fit to say more, as in 1936, when it approved two dismissals but told the foreman to give workers adequate warning of performance problems.

The council spent the bulk of its time discussing plantwide issues. Although some TPEA representatives' proposals were refused by management, others resulted in joint policy announcements (on such topics as toilet facilities, drinking water, and the rotation of employees for weekend work). The council also had joint subcommittees that periodically conducted studies on plant safety, sanitation, bonus pay, and area wage rates. Finally, management used the council as a means for sharing information with employees on its expansion plans or for announcing new policies in areas both major (compensation) and minor (nurses at company sporting events).[58]

Despite its limitations, the TPEA was more active than many of the company unions reviewed by the Bureau of Labor Statistics. It discussed a wide variety of issues and was kept informed by management of decisions affecting the work force. Sometimes the employee representatives got feisty, especially when management reneged on implicit promises of security. In 1934, for example, the accounting department filled several job vacancies from the outside. Bill Hoffman interceded on behalf of current employees who had been passed over, creating what Ray Livingstone termed a "touchy" situation. Livingstone attributed Hoffman's assertiveness to the fact that he was running for TPEA reelection and stood a chance of being defeated.[59]

On other occasions the TPEA's officers were extremely cooperative, even obsequious. In an editorial in the company newspaper, Hoffman acknowledged a strike going on at the nearby Fisher Body plant and warned members that "one of the quickest and surest means of endangering your job and pay envelope is to permit strike talk." The TPEA, he said, would never cause Thompson to lose business to competitors; it had a "keen interest . . . in the welfare of the company."[60]

Management was pleased with the TPEA, enough so that it created representation plans at other facilities owned by Thompson in the 1930s: in Toledo, Los Angeles, and Detroit. None of these proved to be as energetic as the TPEA, although all of them were modeled after it. The largest and oldest of the three was the Michigan Plant Council (MPC), established in August 1934, officially by the Michigan Old Guard, although that organization had been in existence for less than a month. The evidence strongly suggests that Livingstone, in cooperation with loyal employees in Detroit, set up the MPC, whose constitution and organizational structure were similar to the TPEA's.[61]

Thompson's Detroit plant had one thousand employees making steering and chassis parts for cars and trucks. The plant was situated in a major manufacturing zone on the edge of Hamtramck, right behind the Dodge factory. Because this was fertile territory for the UAW, one might think that Thompson would have given the MPC at least as much attention as the TPEA. This was not the case. Livingstone and Crawford left day-to-day management of the Detroit plant—and the MPC—in the hands of two ineffectual local managers: Matt Graham, the head of production, and Tom Colbridge, Graham's newly appointed head of personnel. Neither seemed to understand how executives in Cleveland wanted the MPC to be run. When Livingstone visited the Detroit plant in 1936, he was dismayed to find the MPC being kept under tight controls. Privately, Livingstone complained that the MPC did "not seem to be functioning as an agency for the free exchange and discussion of ideas by the management and employees. This will prove fatal to the council," he predicted.[62]

The year 1937 was a fateful one for automotive workers. The famous Flint sit-down strike took place in January, followed by a wave of strikes throughout the industry. In March, General Motors signed a historic agreement with the UAW that brought trade unionism into the heart of America's mass-production sector. Three weeks before the signing, Thompson's Detroit plant was itself rocked by a couple of sit-downs. The first was a one-day strike on February 20, when fifty-six workers on the night shift pulled all the switches and sat down. That evening Matt Graham was alone in the plant. Feeling that he had to concede something to end the strike, Graham initialed a six-month contract with the UAW, the first signed agreement in the UAW's history. Afterward Graham was remorseful. He offered to resign and to apologize personally to Ford's Charlie Sorenson for what he had done, but Livingstone persuaded him to do neither. When wage negotiations broke down on February 26, a second sit-down strike occurred. Seven hundred workers—most from the day shift—refused to leave the plant. Tom Colbridge, the plant personnel manager, was immediately fired and replaced by J. David Wright, the company's chief attorney, who came up from Cleveland to take over the negotiations. On March 4, Wright gave a five-cent raise to the union, Local 247 of the UAW. Later that month, the UAW organized a local at Thompson's plant in Toledo. The big question then was what would happen in Cleveland.[63]

The heart of the UAW in Cleveland was Fisher Body. Several top-notch Communist organizers, including Wyndham Mortimer and Paul Miley, had helped to build a strong union there. At Christmas in 1936, Fisher Body workers in Cleveland held a spontaneous three-day sit-down strike (this was two weeks prior to the more famous sit-down at the sister plant in Flint). In March 1937, when the UAW's national settlement with General Motors was announced, Fisher Body workers marched through Cleveland's streets, touching off a CIO organizing drive in the city.[64]

Things started to cook at Thompson's Main plant in late March, when the UAW began a campaign there under the direction of an energetic twenty-one-year-old radical named Bert Cochran. Flyers appeared in the plant urging Thompson workers to "win the prize of collective bargaining and industrial democracy." In early April the UAW held its first open meeting for Main plant workers. Ignoring a group of hecklers, Cochran promised to abolish the group bonus plan and pointed with pride to what "our boys in Detroit" had won: a signed agreement, time and a half for overtime, strict seniority, and a nickel raise.[65]

After management gave the TPEA a wage increase equivalent to what the UAW had won in Detroit, the UAW asked, "why the sudden generosity on the part of the company?" Management, said the UAW, "thinks it will buy the men off with a few nickels." Yet despite the UAW's tough sarcasm, and despite auspicious circumstances, all three UAW drives—in Cleveland, Detroit, and Toledo—eventually ground to a halt. Thompson's carefully timed wage increases were part of the reason. Equally problematic for the UAW was the recession that began in the fall of 1937. Layoffs decimated many fledgling UAW locals, including those at Thompson. The company had its first layoffs in September, followed by two more rounds in November and December. Although work sharing mitigated the recession's impact, Thompson's business remained slack for more than a year.[66]

Another problem for the UAW was Thompson's tough response to the organizing drives. Thompson was a member of the Associated Industries of Cleveland (AIC), an anti-union employers' group that grew out of the open-shop movement of the early 1920s. Because Cleveland lacked a unifying financial group like the Mellons or a single dominant employer like Kodak, it fell to the AIC to bring together heads of local corporations to coordinate their labor policies. In charge of the AIC was William Frew Long, who personally saw to it that Cleveland employers were well supplied with spies, provocateurs, and armed thugs. Most of the clients of the Corporation Service Bureau, an anti-union agency headquartered in Cleveland, also were members of the AIC. William Long liked to boast that "where the people of a city or town rise in righteous indignation about a situation they don't like, it is a very healthy sign." With numerous midsized companies run by reactionaries like Thomas Girdler of Republic Steel, Cleveland proved fertile ground for the AIC approach.[67]

Back in 1933, when the Cleveland labor movement began to heat up, Long had advised Ray Livingstone to get in touch with the Corporation Service Bureau. Livingstone hired a spy from the bureau to work as a millwright at the Main plant, a job that allowed the man access to all parts of the facility. Thompson's first use of weaponry came during the Pin plant strike, which occurred ten days after passage of the Wagner Act. The Machinists, who had been demanding a contract for several months, threw a picket line around the plant to force Thompson to recognize the union. John Cox immediately hired a group of men from the Service Bureau to guard the homes of company executives, to spy on the strikers, and to intimidate workers on the picket line. This went on for three weeks. Then Cox organized a back-to-work movement to end the strike. A group of twenty-five tough Service Bureau "guards" and seventy-five loyal workers—some from the Main plant—cut through the picket line and reopened the Pin plant. Picketing continued for several more days; in one incident, a group of mounted police charged a crowd of strikers and picketers. Within a week the strike came to an end.[68]

Another violent incident occurred in Detroit in 1937. After the UAW sit-down in February, John Cox—who was now in charge of security for all of

Thompson Products—hired guards from the O'Neil Industrial Service of Detroit. For undercover work, Cox turned to some Service Bureau men from Cleveland, who were led by one Arthur Beaudry (also known as "Slim" Brody and A. M. Brodie). Beaudry and another man were told by Cox to purchase tear gas and launchers and bring them up to Detroit. In May, a series of events occurred—possibly provoked by the company—that culminated in the firing of the tear gas. First a factional dispute rocked the Detroit plant's UAW local; several founders of the local—who later became company loyalists—were expelled from the union. Next the UAW attempted to renegotiate its contract, only to be stonewalled by the company. At this point the union staged a sit-down. The strike, unlike earlier ones, was broken up by Beaudry and his tear gas in fifteen minutes, making the UAW appear reckless and impotent.[69]

To deal with the UAW in Cleveland, Cox organized an undercover squad of around eight or nine Service Bureau men. The group met weekly in different spots around town, practicing what it would do in case of a sit-down at the Main plant. When Bert Cochran held the UAW's first meeting near the plant in April 1937, the squad was there to catcall, hoot, and heckle with questions such as, "What kind of racket are you running? Why don't you go back to Russia where you belong?" Although they had stink bombs, the squad never got to use them because the meeting broke up so quickly. Nevertheless, there was time enough to notice who was there and to pass their names along to Thompson management. Three workers were dismissed several days later.[70] The UAW was quick to fight back, however. Five days after the dismissals, the union filed NLRB charges alleging that Thompson had fired the men because of their union proclivities. The board upheld a trial examiner's recommendation that all three men be rehired with back pay, a victory the UAW crowed about.[71]

Thompson's repressive tactics were never severe enough to create the kind of paralyzing fear that existed at some other AIC companies. Although Thompson belonged to the AIC, it did not slavishly follow all of William Frew Long's suggestions, such as his idea of having employees sign loyalty oaths. Nor was repression at Thompson as elaborate as at Ford Motor and U.S. Steel (both of which had private police forces) or as violent as at the "Little Steel" companies, including Republic and National. Republic, with plants throughout the Cleveland area, was armed to the teeth with billy clubs, rifles, and tear gas; it also had an airfield for bringing supplies in to struck facilities.[72]

Even before the LaFollette committee's revelations about the AIC and its members, Thompson had begun to shift away from physical coercion. The undercover squad at the Main plant was dismantled in the fall of 1937 and never reformed. And after the LaFollette hearings, John Cox played an increasingly smaller role in the company's labor relations until, in 1939, this "direct and two-fisted guy" left the company for good. Meanwhile, Thompson's strategies became ever more attuned to the intricacies of the labor laws.[73]

The law became the new arena in Thompson's fight against organized labor. Management's first victory came in the case of the three workers fired from the Main plant in 1937. Thompson boldy disobeyed the NLRB's order to reinstate the men, at which point the board asked the Sixth Circuit Court of Appeals to enforce the order. Like most appellate courts, however, the Sixth Circuit was a far more conservative body than the NLRB. In what proved to be the first of several highly publicized defeats for the NLRB in its fight with Thompson, the court in 1938 not only refused to enforce the order but criticized the NLRB for promoting "discord among employer and employee" and for failing to provide more than "a scintilla" of evidence to sustain the charges against Thompson. A few nights later, the NLRB chairman J. Warren Madden was forced to go on national radio to defend the board's decision in the Thompson case. Crawford basked in the glory of vindication while the NLRB, which unsuccessfully tried to reopen the case in 1939, was—along with the UAW—handed a major defeat.[74]

Another factor inhibiting successful organizing at Thompson in the 1930s was factionalism, within both the labor movement and the company work force. The Cleveland Federation of Labor was riven by disputes between traditional craft unionists and those favoring industrial unionism. The federation condemned the sit-down strike at Fisher Body and refused to lend its support to the organizing drive at Thompson. Two years earlier, the business agent for the Machinists attributed the union's defeat at the Pin plant to the "deplorable fact" that the Federation did not support the drive.[75]

In Detroit, Thompson's new UAW local was itself split into factions, including a group of older workers, led by Foster Martin, who were dissatisfied with the Michigan Plant Council but favored a go-slow approach, and a more militant, younger group led by Charles D'Annunzio, who was only twenty-three years old. In a bitter contest, D'Annunzio defeated Martin to become the local's first president. Instead of healing the rift, D'Annunzio widened it by seeking to abolish the Social and Recreation Club, a move that irked the plant's older workers. Here the record becomes murky. It appears that management struck some kind of deal with Martin and his followers: the MPC was replaced with a new and more assertive company union, the Automotive Parts Workers (APW), whose first president was Foster Martin. Meanwhile, the inexperienced D'Annunzio was under tremendous pressure. The tear-gassing of the May sit-down was followed by months of fruitless negotiation over a second contract. Members drifted away from the local, while UAW headquarters pressed D'Annunzio for dues. In November, D'Annunzio resigned and turned over all records of Local 247 to the company.[76]

The transformation of the MPC into a more independent organization was not an isolated event, but instead part of a nationwide push by employers to make company unions conform more closely to the provisions of the Wagner Act. The effort began in 1937, when Roosevelt's reelection and the *Jones & Laughlin Steel* decision convinced managers that the New Deal and a strong labor movement were here to stay. *Jones & Laughlin*, in which the U.S.

Supreme Court upheld the Wagner Act's constitutionality, gave the NLRB license to proscribe company unions more aggressively. The trick for employers was to dissolve their old company unions and reconstitute them as "independent" unions without being involved in the process, at least not noticeably. The National Association of Manufacturers sent guidelines to its members explaining how to effect such transformations; meanwhile, the shadowy Independent Organizations' Service was formed to help workers set up independent unions. A large number of company unions failed to make the transition and were replaced by regular trade unions. Of the company unions remaining in existence in 1939, nearly all had been initiated or reconstituted after *Jones & Laughlin*.[77]

From Company Union to Independent Union

As it had done at the Michigan plant, Thompson in 1937 thoroughly overhauled its Cleveland company union, the TPEA. This reorganization—more than any other single factor—would make Thompson's Cleveland plants a tough nut for the UAW to crack during the critical stretch from 1937 to 1947.

Shortly after the *Jones & Laughlin* decision in April 1937, Bill Hoffman met with Ray Livingstone to discuss bringing the TPEA into compliance with the Wagner Act. Under subpoena at an NLRB hearing in 1940, Hoffman recalled Livingstone saying to him, "We will certainly have to do something, because [previously] we always told the representatives how to conduct themselves in their capacity as representatives." Events happened quickly: the TPEA's officers met with a Thompson attorney; Livingstone resigned as council secretary; Hoffman and other TPEA officers stepped down; and new officers volunteered to replace the old ones. At the suggestion of a TPEA delegate, the new officers hired a local attorney, Milton A. Roemisch, to give them legal advice.[78]

Roemisch was part of a breed of lawyers who emerged during this period as advisers to, and often de facto leaders of, independent labor unions. Roemisch represented independent unions at a number of Cleveland-area firms, including Ohio Tool, Sherwin-Williams Paint, and Ohio Crankshaft. In the early 1940s he tried, unsuccessfully, to affiliate twenty-six of these independents into a federation called the National League of American Labor. Roemisch served his clients not only as legal counselor but also as organizer, publicist, and banker, loaning fledgling independent unions his own money to help them get off the ground. Although dapper, Roemisch was hardly a high-powered attorney. He lived in the same neighborhood as several Thompson workers, including "Bud" Anderson, the TPEA delegate who recommended hiring him.[79]

After the UAW filed charges against Roemisch, he acquired the dubious distinction of being the first union attorney ordered by an NLRB official to cease and desist from "instructing and coercing" employees. The NLRB trial examiner considered Roemisch to be an employer because he "worked hand in glove with the company." Yet there was no evidence against Roemisch other than the fact that he represented an independent union charged with being company-dominated; a year later, in fact, the NLRB dismissed the charges.[80]

Roemisch was an ardent believer in independent unionism, which, he thought, provided the only way to defend workers' rights while preserving "American Democracy." In a speech to Thompson workers, Roemisch told them, "You people among yourselves have enough brains to run your own union without paying some person interested in extorting money from you to represent you. . . . Now, don't get the idea that independent unions are any "finky, stinky" shop organization. An independent union . . . must be an aggressive, militant organization that is interested in the workers' rights and the workers' rights only."[81]

In May 1937, Roemisch changed the TPEA's name to the Automotive and Aircraft Workers' Alliance (AAWA), wrote a new constitution, and then incorporated the organization with his own funds. He asked the TPEA's old officers to solicit AAWA membership cards, but warned them not to do so on company time. By June, Roemisch had authorization cards signed by more than 60 percent of Thompson's Cleveland employees; in July, management recognized the AAWA and negotiated a new agreement. A heftier document than the old TPEA contract, it contained several new features: a plan for seniority-based layoffs by department (something the UAW had been demanding) and provisions allowing AAWA representatives to caucus privately at council meetings. There were also some changes in the union itself. It began collecting monthly membership dues and in August held a mass meeting at a nearby theater, where Roemisch explained the new contract and presided over a ratification vote.[82]

Over the next four years, the AAWA's monthly council meetings addressed the same types of issues as had the TPEA's. Little was said about discipline or discharge. Discussion focused on relatively uncontroversial matters like rate adjustments, complaints about new foremen, inadequate locker space, and poor ventilation. Management continued to make AAWA representatives privy to the firm's financial affairs and occasionally sought their advice on details of personnel policy, such as whether to rehire workers who had previously been dismissed.

Though it was deferential to management and tamer than most national unions, the AAWA occasionally displayed an independence that the TPEA had lacked entirely. It gathered its own data, caucused at council meetings, and regularly sought Roemisch's advice on legal, tactical, and economic issues. One of the AAWA's first actions was to demand a closed shop and automatic deduction of dues from members' paychecks, both of which management declined to do, on the grounds that "it is both an American principle and a Company principle that a man has the right to work in an establishment whether he belongs or does not belong to a labor organization. . . . Payment of union dues is a personal matter, and one in which the company wishes to take no part." The AAWA dropped the request, but on other issues it doggedly persisted, more willing to challenge management than the TPEA had been.[83]

One of these issues was vacation pay. In 1936, Thompson and the TPEA had negotiated a vacation plan for employees with more than five years' service; management abandoned the plan in 1937 when business conditions worsened. In March 1938, an AAWA representative asked Thompson to revive the plan and extend it to workers with fewer than five years' service. Speaking for management, Lee Clegg said that the request could not be granted because business remained poor; he offered to show the company's books to the AAWA. Another AAWA representative insisted that the plan was part of the AAWA's contract with Thompson, but Clegg denied this, saying that vacations were given at management's discretion. After someone from the AAWA called this "unfair," the matter was tabled. The AAWA, however, brought the issue up again at the council meetings in April and June; on both occasions management said it still did not have the funds, even bringing in Fred Crawford to address the council on the company's financial problems. Clegg then offered to authorize vacations but not to those with under five years' service. He asked the AAWA to go along with this proposal and to record its acceptance in the minutes. The AAWA reluctantly agreed, although Roemisch said that "the Alliance resented the acceptance portion of the statement read into the minutes by Mr. Clegg and asked that this part be omitted." Early in 1939, the AAWA again raised the issue. Management asked for time to respond, and two months later it offered a liberalized plan, but one that still did not include junior workers. After caucusing, the AAWA accepted management's offer. Both sides then expressed their "appreciation" for each other's patience and understanding. In 1940 the same thing happened: the AAWA asked for a more inclusive vacation plan and the company said it could not afford it. This time an AAWA representative presented data on other Cleveland-area firms that showed that many of them gave vacations to junior workers. At the next meeting, management agreed to grant vacations to those with more than three years' service.[84]

This episode shows that, on the one hand, the AAWA had some degree of autonomy and was ready to press an issue, at least until a compromise could be reached. On the other hand, it demonstrates that the AAWA had little bargaining power unless outside pressure could be brought to bear on Thompson management. In the case of vacations, Thompson adopted the new plan less than a month after the UAW had started a second organizing drive under the leadership of Paul Miley, one of the militants from Cleveland Fisher Body.

The record on wage bargaining clearly demonstrates the role of external forces in the relationship between Thompson and the AAWA. In 1939, when the UAW had only a scant presence at Thompson's Cleveland plants, the AAWA asked for a wage increase of five cents. The company refused but told the AAWA it was willing to pay a special bonus instead. When the AAWA's representatives asked for time to caucus and to consult Roemisch, management testily told them they had three hours to take the offer or lose it; the AAWA quickly accepted. In the summer of 1940, after the UAW reappeared at Thompson, the AAWA again asked for a five-cent increase. Livingstone responded with a study of area wages that showed Thompson's pay to be competitive if the group bonus were taken into account. In October the AAWA wrote a letter to management protesting the unfairness of including incentive pay in the survey data since the bonus was "a gratuity given by the company for the extra benefits [received] by reason of employees overextending themselves as a group in the interest of the company." The AAWA raised its request to seven cents, saying that "the union wishes to point out to the management that we are in a rising labor market, and that the law of supply and demand holds good as to labor as well as to production." Although the AAWA hinted for the first time that it might go on strike, the company turned down the request. A day later the NLRB announced that it would soon hold hearings to determine if the AAWA was a company-dominated union. At the next council meeting, management offered an increase of five cents and the AAWA promptly accepted it. The AAWA boasted that it won the increase "in a true American way, without a strike," although the UAW was nearer the truth when it claimed in a handbill that "we of Local 300 have been partly successful in our drive for higher wages."[85]

In March 1941, an NLRB trial examiner held the AAWA to be an employer-dominated organization. He told Thompson to disestablish the AAWA, which meant that the union could not appear on the ballot in NLRB elections. The NLRB sustained these orders in August, finding the AAWA to be "merely an advisory agency supported by the management for adjusting differences with the employees within management limitations." More serious for the NLRB was the fact that the AAWA had sprung, without cleavage, from the TPEA, an organization clearly initiated and controlled by management.[86]

One could argue that the NLRB applied its cleavage rule too mechanically, failing to give sufficient consideration to how the AAWA was evolving into a more independent organization. Indeed, around 1944 the NLRB opted for a less rigid approach: in cases where the only charge was no cleavage and where the parties had been bargaining for at least two years, it would permit a previously dominated company union to appear on the ballot if employer domination had ceased. It is conceivable that the AAWA would have appeared on the ballot had it been tried under this rule. But in 1942, before the new rule emerged, the Sixth Circuit enforced the AAWA disestablishment order, stating that "a company-created union could not emancipate itself from habitual subservience to its creator without being completely disestablished."[87]

Despite its legal victories, the UAW made little headway at Thompson's Cleveland plants in 1940 and 1941. Business—and hiring—were booming as Thompson shifted more and more of its production to military contracts. Due to extensive overtime, earnings were among the highest in Cleveland. Thompson Aircraft Products Company (TAPCO), a new subsidiary, was getting ready to occupy a huge government-owned plant—the largest in Cleveland—under construction in Euclid, a nearby suburb. Designed for mass valve production, the plant was an industrial showcase whose "beautiful" landscaping, "modern" air conditioning, and "unexcelled" recreational facilities harked back to the heyday of welfare capitalism. Another problem for the UAW was Crawford, who again was refusing to obey the NLRB. Crawford's obstinate refusal to sever ties to the AAWA was front-page news and it aroused the admiration of the business community. Unlike Sewell Avery, however, Crawford eventually complied with the law when ordered to do so by the Sixth Circuit.[88]

The UAW's organizing drive began to gain momentum after Ed Hall took over the campaign from Paul Miley late in 1941. Hall, who had been with the UAW since its earliest days, was a savvy organizer and union strategist. Although he probably never was a party member, Hall allied himself with the Communist faction in the UAW hierarchy and was a close friend of Wyndham Mortimer. Described as heavy-set and loquacious, someone who "carried the colorful language of the factory into his union work," Hall could match Fred Crawford point for point in charisma and machismo.[89]

Initially Hall erred by asking Mortimer to assist with the Thompson drive. Back in June, the UAW had fired Mortimer for his role in the North American Aviation strike, in which President Roosevelt used national troops to reopen the plant. When word got out that Hall had rehired Mortimer to help organize Thompson, the local newspapers blasted the UAW for its "dangerous irresponsibility." "Real Americans," said one editorial, "will not stand for it." More adroitly, in January 1942 Hall began weekly radio broadcasts over station WADC in Akron, urging Thompson workers to join the UAW. That month he also asked the newly formed War Labor Board to enforce the NLRB's disestablishment order and blasted Crawford for disobeying the law.[90]

Crawford and Livingstone were annoyed when the War Labor Board agreed to examine the Thompson case. They were convinced that the UAW had pulled strings to get Labor Secretary Frances Perkins to certify the case to the board, even though it was still under review by the courts. With characteristic lack of diplomacy, Crawford excoriated the board for being "interested solely in a CIO victory." The situation became more volatile in February, when Thompson dismissed seven UAW supporters for pasting swastika-shaped stickers on unused equipment; the stickers said, "This Idle Machine Works for Hitler." The War Labor Board dispatched a mediator to Cleveland. Describing the situation as "tense . . . with danger of interference with all our war production," the board ordered the reinstatement of all seven workers and scheduled May elections at the Main plant and at TAPCO. Behind the scenes, Walter C. Teagle, the employer representative on the board, pressured Crawford to take the workers back. When this failed, Crawford and Livingstone were summoned to Washington to meet with Dr. Frank P. Graham, the board's chairman. According to Crawford, Graham "gave an eloquent sales talk on the satisfaction of dealing with international unions, how reasonable and cooperative they can be," and then told Crawford, "I shudder with fear at the thought if we ever go into another depression and don't have strong international unions to control the people." According to Crawford, at the end of the meeting Graham accused him of being "a labor hater," while Crawford complained of the board's "absolute pro-labor bias." Nevertheless, in April Crawford reinstated the men "out of respect for the War Labor Board." On his radio show, Ed Hall took credit for getting Thompson to back down and urged listeners to vote for the UAW in May.[91]

Throughout this period, Thompson workers were bombarded by flyers, newspapers, and posters issued by the UAW on one side and Thompson and the AAWA on the other. The UAW hammered away at the AAWA, accusing it of being a shill for management; its newspaper, *The Thompson Products Organizer*, gave the AAWA's leaders nicknames such as "Goonie" Musto, "Gyp" Kenna, and "Weasel" Wrost. The UAW stressed economic issues, promising to raise wages and to abolish the group bonus in favor of straight piecework. Workers like Al Penko, a grinder at the Main plant, appeared on Ed Hall's radio show saying that the UAW would see to it that workers got a larger share of Thompson's profits. On election day, *The Thompson Products Organizer* printed a tantalizing front-page headline saying, "THIS CHECK IS YOURS! BY VOTING UAW-CIO." Below it was a check made out to "Thompson Worker" for $307.30, the average pay increase the UAW was promising to garner after the election.[92]

To rebut the UAW's charges, the company issued a regular bulletin, *Let's Have the Truth!*, which was festooned with small American flags. Always referring to the UAW as the CIO, the bulletin said the union's allegations were "either based on abysmal ignorance or else carefully planned to breed distrust between men and management. This is not helping the war effort!" In a curious role reversal, the UAW emphasized economic issues while the company hammered away at the UAW's alleged lack of democracy, accusing its leaders of being outsiders who wanted workers' dues in order to finance a secret agenda. This put the UAW on the defensive and forced Hall to devote several radio broadcasts to explaining how the Thompson local would be run and what its relationship would be to the parent union. Hall reassured his audience that international representatives like himself would have "nothing to do with your organization or its affairs, other than to be helpful in assisting you, and counsel and advise you from time to time."[93]

With management staking the high ground, the disestablished AAWA was free to roll in the mud. By 1942 it was the second-largest company union in the nation (behind AT&T's) and the largest dues-paying local in Cleveland. Defying the NLRB's order to stay out of the campaign, the plucky union instead played a major role: it issued bulletins with headlines attacking the UAW ("Swat the Pest," "Ruled by Gangster Methods") and the NLRB ("the leading organizer of the CIO"); raised its dues to five dollars a year to finance these activities (still a low amount); staged incidents such as one in which a group of AAWA activists refused to work alongside a known UAW supporter; and continued to bargain with Thompson for a night-shift bonus and a wage increase, both of which were granted shortly before the election. Although even its supporters were unhappy that it never held membership meetings and annoyed that its representatives received special favors from management, the AAWA was quite popular at Main.[94]

The UAW, on the other hand—despite a two-year campaign—had little to show for its efforts. When elections finally were held it received only 33 percent of the vote at Main and TAPCO. After a long, expensive, and highly visible campaign, the results were, as a local newspaper put it, "a severe blow for the UAW." The UAW filed objections with the NLRB, claiming that management had illegally interfered with the election by distributing *Let's Have the Truth!* bulletins, by hanging posters at Main plant reading, "the election affords an opportunity for employees to accept or reject the present bargaining relationship" (that is, the AAWA), and by allowing AAWA representatives to roam freely about the plant on election day.[95]

Yet the election proved a Pyrrhic victory for the AAWA. At first it was elated and sold tickets to a victory party sponsored by the Social and Recreation Club. The euphoria was short lived, however, for the AAWA was forced to dissolve three months later, when the Sixth Circuit upheld the NLRB's disestablishment order. The AAWA did not appeal the order; instead it posted notices saying that "neither the courts nor the Labor Board has ever criticized the effectiveness, sincerity, or honesty of the bargaining of the AAWA, even though it has been slandered by international, communistically-controlled organizations." That night, management treated all AAWA officers to dinner at a local restaurant and thanked them for their "cooperation."[96]

The Battle Continues, 1942–1947

Independent unionism was far from dead at Main, however. In September 1942, Milton Roemisch organized a meeting at an American Legion hall for employees interested in forming a new independent union. One of the speakers was a worker named Tony Laurenti, who never had held a post in the AAWA. In an interesting twist, Laurenti told the audience of fifty that he wanted a new independent union because he did not want to be "dominated" by an "outside organization." He also called for the new union to have three times as many stewards as the AAWA, arguing that this would spread the union "from a few favorite individuals to a representative body." Sounding almost syndicalist in his calls for direct democracy, Laurenti ended by saying: "We don't have to call anybody in from the outside to organize for us. We can do our own organizing. We all have confidence in our own ability to meet daily problems, and by the same token we have confidence in our own ability to meet the problems that face us in our workday lives."

Another speaker was Roemisch, who gave a speech denouncing the UAW for being "full of communists" and "hungry [for] dues because all of the officers are on salary." But, he said, workers did need some kind of organization: "It is impossible for management sitting up in the front office with their Carrier air conditioning systems, away from you workers, to know intimately your problems, your heartaches, your troubles that happen down in the sweltering heat of the forge department and . . . other departments. They would take advantage of you, maybe not willfully or maliciously, but they wouldn't know and understand your problems." Those present voted on several names for the new union, finally deciding to call it the Brotherhood of Independent Workers (BIW).[97]

Roemisch was careful to paint the new union with a coat of legality. He convened BIW meetings at neutral sites and advised former AAWA officers not to play an active role. Although management told one of the BIW's organizers that it was "behind [the BIW] 100 percent," it, too, was cautious not to do anything that might be construed as illegal support. When Roemisch carried signature cards to Livingstone and asked for recognition, he was rebuffed and told to get the BIW certified in an NLRB election. Several months later, Ed Castle, a BIW leader, approached Lee Clegg for money to help defray union expenses, but Clegg refused. Despite these precautions, or perhaps because of them, the BIW failed to get off the ground. It never participated in an election, nor did it ever obtain a contract.[98]

Despite the BIW's problems, its leaders were committed to making the organization an active, if moderately aggressive, union, not unlike the AAWA in its final days. Ed Castle, an electrician, said that he "hoped the BIW would gather enough strength that it could lay it on the line with management and become a real organization." Castle took his job as a BIW representative seriously. But when some foremen agreed to redress grievances and then later reneged, Castle said, "After a few sessions like that, it commenced to put me in a light as a stooge for management, and I just couldn't take it." He resigned from the BIW's grievance committee, telling other members, "The only condition I would go back . . . is that they back me 100 percent, and we go in there slugging, and force the management to give us a fair decision on our grievances, and give us proper recognition." In a meeting with Clegg and Livingstone, Castle fell back on the AAWA's old trick of using the threat of outside unionism as leverage against management: "If the grievances aren't settled with some degree of fairness," said Castle, he and the other BIW leaders would "put on CIO buttons and take this whole damn plant CIO." Castle then gave Livingstone a ten-day ultimatum to pressure recalcitrant foremen to cooperate with the BIW. A few months later, Castle resigned from the BIW to head the Machinists' organizing committee; another BIW officer quit and became a UAW steward.[99]

The BIW never recovered from Castle's departure. The final blow came in 1944, when the NLRB distestablished the BIW, contending that it was "infected from the outset with the virus of [employer] control." Cognizant that Castle and others were trying to create a genuine alternative to the UAW, the NLRB nevertheless took a hard line: "That certain members of the BIW . . . were earnest and sincere in their efforts to make the BIW a bona fide and strong labor union, cannot operate to absolve management from its illegal practices and conduct. Seldom does the domination and interference with employee representation take the form of threats or coercion. More often it is to be found in the guise of friendly cooperation." Although the *Plain Dealer* ran an editorial saying that "apparently it has not occurred to the NLRB that some workers would prefer not to belong to either the AFL or the CIO," the disestablishment was never contested and eventually the BIW disappeared from the Main plant.[100]

Meanwhile, Thompson completed its giant TAPCO facility in the fall of 1941 and started hiring nearly a thousand people per month to staff it. (At its peak in 1943, TAPCO employed more than ten thousand workers.) In a brief filed with the War Labor Board, Ed Hall charged that the company was handpicking AAWA supporters for transfer to the new plant and that no UAW members had been sent there. One of these transferees was George Wrost, a former secretary of the AAWA. With Roemisch's assistance, Wrost started a new company union at TAPCO called the Aircraft Workers Alliance (AWA). Management recognized the AWA in December 1941, when there were still only 265 workers on the payroll. The AWA lost no time establishing itself at TAPCO. It negotiated a contract providing for seniority rights, a grievance procedure (delegates now were called stewards), and a joint council similar to the AAWA's. After defeating the UAW in May 1942, the AWA demanded a 9 percent wage increase. When management offered only four cents an hour, the dispute went to the War Labor Board, which refused to grant any pay increase at all. The AWA then threatened to conduct an illegal strike. Despite all this, and despite a loosening of its cleavage rule in some other cases, the NLRB disestablished the AWA in 1944, contending that it was an extension of the AAWA, hence "stamped with the imprimatur of company domination." (In a fit of pique, the NLRB chided the AWA for being "a docile child which never got out of hand.") Unlike the BIW, however, the AWA spent three years fighting the disestablishment order, during which time it remained active at TAPCO.[101]

Notwithstanding its losses in 1942, the UAW tried for five more years to organize Thompson's Cleveland plants. It spent large sums on elections—held in 1944, 1945, and 1947—and on legal expenses. During the 1944 election, Crawford and Livingstone snubbed the NLRB by delivering so-called captive-audience speeches in which they compared the UAW's "parade of Communist leaders" to Thompson's record of job security, no strikes, and "the best God damn wages in town." Because of these speeches, the NLRB invalidated the election. In 1945, the UAW's campaign came under the direction of Bill Grant, who recently had been voted out as president of Local 600 at Ford's giant River Rouge plant in Detroit. Grant asked for a new election at Main (but not at TAPCO, where UAW support had dwindled). Shortly before voting day in 1945, when it became clear that management again was taking an active part in the campaign, the NLRB went to the Sixth Circuit for an injunction barring the company's officers from "interfering with the election." Unfortunately for the NLRB (and the UAW), the request did not come at a propitious time. The public mood was turning increasingly conservative and sympathetic to employer demands for "free speech" during union campaigns. Three days before the election the court turned down the NLRB's request without comment. The *Plain Dealer* ran a headline reading, "NLRB Takes Licking." In the vendetta between the NLRB and Thompson, however, the decision proved an empty victory for the company; the NLRB simply overturned the election when it was over.[102]

Besides captive-audience speeches, Thompson pursued other, more clearly coercive, tactics. Dismissal of UAW activists was a regular occurrence during organizing drives at the Main plant. (The company's attempt to fire twelve UAW stewards at Main in 1943 led to the war's first authorized wildcat strike.) Inside the plant, pressure on union activists was relentless. UAW supporters testified that they had been offered raises or extra overtime if they would quit the union; those who refused to go along sometimes found themselves transferred to less desirable jobs. When Ed Castle was head of the BIW, one of his stewards, Blanche Picklo, complained that she couldn't sign up any BIW members in her department because Anna Haddad, a UAW supporter, was very popular with the other workers. Castle arranged with Haddad's foreman to have her transferred to another department that very evening.[103]

Thompson worked closely with its company unions to gain support from crucial swing groups, including black workers hired during the war. Management pressured the BIW to increase the number of black employees and suggested that the BIW hold a recruitment meeting at the "colored YMCA" instead of at the tavern the BIW had originally selected. To help the BIW gain black support, management told Ed Castle to file a grievance saying that the dust bags in the plant needed to be cleaned more frequently. Then, when the company hired some "colored girls" to empty the bags—something it was planning to do anyway—the BIW could take credit for introducing the women into Main.[104]

The UAW played the same game: it tried to win over black workers by making exaggerated claims of managerial discrimination. Yet most black workers stuck with the company unions: out of gratitude for being hired by Thompson, out of concern that the UAW's strict seniority rules would hurt them after the war, and out of a belief that the UAW, at least at the local level, was no less racist than the company union. This notion stemmed from events like the 1943 wildcat strike led by Tony Mazeo, a UAW committeeman. Mazeo worked in the all-white mirror polishing department, which held some of the Main plant's best-paying jobs. When Thompson tried to upgrade blacks into the department, Mazeo called the strike.[105]

Given Crawford's interest in "human values," working at Thompson Products was, to put it mildly, an emotional experience. Crawford and Livingstone expected all supervisors to do as they did: to walk the shop floor regularly and chat with employees. "Good feelings," said Livingstone, "start with the boss. If the boss is affable, if he says 'Good morning,' smiles, and looks approachable, the men begin saying 'Good morning' and 'Hi-yah,' and camaraderie develops." Foremen were told to read textbooks on psychology and never to miss an opportunity to make friends with an employee.[106]

As Thompson mushroomed during World War II, it created a new position—the personnel representative—who was supposed to keep an eye on the shop floor and correct problems before they got out of hand. Workers could go to their "rep," whose office was in the plant, to complain about foremen, to get legal advice, or even to get a parking ticket fixed. The rep was a throwback to the welfare secretary of the 1910s, but with two key differences: first, Thompson's reps were part of line management, with authority to tell foremen what to do, and second, Thompson consciously avoided hiring college graduates to serve as reps, preferring instead those with a background in production work (including former company-union officers). As a key link in the communications system, Thompson expected its reps to "become intimately acquainted with as many employees as possible" and to keep abreast of labor sentiments by reporting to top management on "trends of thought developing in the organization." In contrast to the spying done in the 1930s, however, Thompson's turn toward Mayoism allowed the reps to do their work openly, even affably. One UAW activist testified that Sam Lazzaro, a personnel representative at Main, was "always kidding me about our paper and the work we were doing [and] said I would get along much better if I would join [the company union]."[107]

Thompson, like Sears, was a pioneer in the use of large-scale employee attitude surveys. In the first of several surveys conducted in the 1940s, questionnaires were mailed to more than sixteen thousand employees along with a letter from Fred Crawford disarmingly describing the survey as a way for him "to get into the shop and swap ideas." The UAW had little to say about the survey, although the Machinists composed a parody of Crawford's letter in which a Thompson worker writes back to Crawford saying, "Sometimes a man in your position can't get the truth. So I'm writing this to let you know that your employees don't trust you. Not even to the extent of filling out an anonymous questionnaire. . . . They know about other employers who used tricks like this one to find out which employees were union-minded in order to get rid of them at the first opportunity." The IAM could only hint at reprisals, though; it couldn't specify—and may have had no idea about—how the company intended to use the survey results. Although the survey analysis did identify particular departments and demographic subgroups that were dissatisfied, the company's major objectives were promoting catharsis ("getting things out in the open") and creating the impression that malcontents were a minority. The latter was accomplished by feeding back the survey results to employees in the form of a seventy-page booklet full of cartoons, humorous quips, and data. The results showed that the "overwhelming majority" of employees (80 to 90 percent) were pleased with Thompson and their jobs.[108]

Older forms of welfare work meshed smoothly with Thompson's increasingly sophisticated approach. Thompson indulged employees with all kinds of privileges, from smoking on the shop floor to time off for a death in the family. The Old Guard, the Social and Recreation Club, and other activities continued on a daily basis. Monday was bingo night, with movies and ice cream provided for the children. The TAPCO orchestra, under the direction of Jimmy Cagno, a toolroom worker, played every Wednesday during the first shift's lunch period. And more than ten thousand employees ate turkey at the company Christmas dinner while watching vaudeville acts and glee clubs from local high schools. On a rotating basis, workers and their spouses attended annual dinner meetings at a local hotel, where they shook Fred Crawford's hand and listened to him discuss the company's financial condition and field questions from the audience. There were, however, some changes from the 1930s: financial benefits (including pension and home-buyer assistance plans) loomed larger in the company's welfare package, and the company described itself less often as a "family," preferring the more egalitarian "team," as in "TAPCO Team" and "Thompson Team."[109]

The human relations movement was closely related to the emerging fields of opinion research and mass communications: all shared a concern with assessing and influencing group attitudes, whether employees', consumers', citizens', or soldiers'. Thompson management considered communications to be a key part of its personnel program; both internal (employee relations) and external (public relations) activities were handled by Livingstone's office. To get its point of view across, management relied on a variety of media. Each plant cafeteria had a public address system that carried announcements, headline news, and music all day long. Throughout the plants there were distribution boxes for the company newspaper, *The Friendly Forum*, and numerous bulletin boards displaying posters and press releases. Annual reports to employees, first issued in 1940, contained economic data on the company, such as charts showing how "little" went to profits and how "much" to wages. During the war, Thompson produced a forty-five-minute movie, "Men, Management, Production," which was shown to every new employee.[110]

Thompson's communications machinery shifted into high gear during organizing drives. To counter union charges, the company issued blunt rebuttals in *Let's Have the Truth!* ("dedicated to Truth, Understanding, and Real

Americanism: There is no place for hate, lies and misunderstanding in American industry"). Thompson's tactics were notably daring, deft, and swift. For example, when the NLRB announced late one Friday that it was setting aside recent election results at the Main plant, Thompson published the news in special flyers that were immediately posted around the plant. On Monday, when UAW organizers handed out leaflets hailing the decision, a journalist reported that "Thompson people shrugged it off as 'old stuff.'" On other occasions, letters from Crawford were mailed to each employee's home; Livingstone believed that involving spouses and other family members had a conservatizing influence on the employee.[111]

Capping it all off were Crawford's captive-audience speeches. These were delivered at huge gatherings that Crawford himself described as "emotional": "Here were five thousand people together, all looking in one direction, all thinking the same things, and they responded. The value of the mass meetings was that I was able to show the employees that I had their interests at heart, as well as my own. . . . We were all friends." Crawford was a spellbinding speaker, someone with a natural talent for entertaining and persuading. A local newspaper said of Crawford, "He has all the qualities of the truly great orator and can shape mass psychology so shrewdly that you're not aware of his artistry. There is something hot in his heart and he wants to get it into yours, and he does." Although the NLRB repeatedly censured Crawford for inserting himself into the election process, Crawford convinced many employees—and eventually Congress—that he was merely exercising his rights to free speech.[112]

Defeating the UAW

The UAW's final Thompson drive of the 1940s started at the Main plant late in 1946, led by Paul Miley. The campaign was marred by intense factionalism within the UAW and sharp anti-Communist rhetoric on the company's part. Two weeks before the May 1947 election, the AWA negotiated a hefty wage increase at TAPCO, as if to signal what it could accomplish at Main. Crawford gave several captive-audience speeches, while the company churned out its usual anti-UAW letters and bulletins. Once again the UAW lost, but this time the NLRB did not sustain any of the union's objections and in July it certified the results. The NLRB's sudden turnaround came on the heels of a major rebuke from the Sixth Circuit, which in June had overturned the NLRB's 1944 disestablishment of the AWA. Not only did the court hold the AWA to be lawful, but it also sharply criticized the NLRB's "dictatorial" approach to regulating management conduct at Thompson. A year later the AWA was recognized at Main after it submitted authorization cards to a local accounting firm. This time neither the NLRB nor the UAW said a word. In fact, the UAW did not reappear at Thompson's Cleveland plants until the early 1960s, and even then the AWA continued to represent TRW's Cleveland-area workers until the plants were sold in 1986.[113]

But did Thompson's Cleveland workers freely choose to reject the UAW, or did management coerce them into doing so? There certainly is evidence to support a charge of coercion: the company bombarded workers with propaganda, forced them to listen to Crawford's speeches, harassed UAW activists, and gave special favors to AWA leaders. Moreover, the AWA's cooperation and close identification with management may have undercut its effectiveness without employees even realizing that this had occurred. As the NLRB chairman Paul Herzog said during the Taft-Hartley hearings, the board's policies were based on the idea that, when management bargains with a dominated union, it finds itself on both sides of the table. Workers might vote for such a union but do so out of a "mistaken continued belief that the company-dominated organization affords a genuine agency for collective bargaining." Although the AWA was eventually exonerated of domination charges, it obviously was a different breed of union than the UAW, namely, less independent and less adversarial.[114]

It does strain credulity, however, to say that Thompson workers were unaware of the differences between the two unions, or that they rejected the UAW only by compulsion. After a decade of campaigns and six NLRB elections in Thompson's Cleveland plants, employees were well informed about the faults and merits of both the UAW and the company union. During the Taft-Hartley hearings, one congressman cited the Thompson election record and then asked an NLRB official if he thought Thompson workers were "that easily influenced and their minds poisoned, and that dumb and stupid, that they cannot go in and exercise a reasonable intelligence and have their votes counted and recognized by established agencies?" Not only the election results but also data from the company's own attitude surveys show that Thompson workers had few serious gripes about management and, although not enthusiastic about the AWA, "generally regarded [it] as the lesser of two evils. The CIO is considered more distasteful than the independent union."[115]

That Thompson workers might prefer a company union to the UAW was hard for NLRB officials and other liberals to accept (as it still is today). Yet circumstances other than coercion helped shape this preference. First, Thompson workers had an unusually high degree of loyalty to management as a result of the company's steady growth, its brand of modern paternalism, and its charismatic leadership. Second, the AWA and its predecessors did an effective job of handling grievances, while contracts consistently followed the UAW pattern. AWA members received these benefits for only a fraction of the cost of UAW membership (UAW dues were about six times higher than the AWA's) and without any losses due to strikes. Third, the AWA offered a more immediate and less bureaucratic form of democracy than a national union. All of the AWA's officers—from the president on down—came from the plant and were well known by the members. Elections were hotly contested and highly publicized, and unlike an affiliated local of a national union, the AWA was the master of its own fate. It did not have to answer to a higher authority or conform to policies that were not of its choosing. Because it had no staff and only a simple hierarchy, the AWA tended to be less formal and legalistic than a national union, and although the UAW faulted it for failing to hold regular meetings, the AWA's small size and numerous social activities kept its officers in close touch with the rank and file. The AWA's claim to be "your union" may have conjured up a more appealing image than the UAW's promise of providing "one big union, coast to coast." (Realizing this, the AWA referred to the UAW as "the octopus" and warned Thompson workers not to feed it.)[116]

Not all of Thompson's company unions were as successful as those in Cleveland. In Detroit and Toledo—where Thompson made the same products as in Cleveland—workers rejected company unions in favor of the UAW. The Detroit story is complicated. Briefly, the company union (now known as the Society of Tool and Die Craftsmen) won an NLRB election in 1941, lost by a wide margin to the UAW in a second election held in 1943, and lost again in a third election held in 1945. The UAW continues to represent the plant to this day.[117] In Toledo, where Thompson employed about three hundred workers, the company union, formed in 1937, was easily defeated in 1942 by the UAW's Local 12, a spunky amalgamated (citywide) local. Thompson did not even attempt a second election, although it later shut down part of the plant.[118]

The failure of company unionism in Detroit and Toledo reflected, in part, the strength of the UAW in those cities. By the end of the war, UAW members accounted for 24 percent of Detroit's population, as opposed to only 5 percent in Cleveland. Equally important was the fact that Crawfordism got off to a slow start outside Cleveland. Prior to the war, the Toledo and Detroit plants were managed locally. The production manager in Toledo, a rugged individualist, was slow to adopt the personnel policies initiated in Cleveland. Not until workers struck the Toledo plant in 1937 was a company union established there. As for Detroit, it too lagged behind its sister plant in Cleveland. Matt Graham, the manager in charge, never made employee relations a high priority. The personnel manager, Tom Colbridge, did not even have his own office—his desk was next to a vending machine—while the company union, the MPC, was an ineffectual organization. (The UAW called it "dead.") When shown the minutes of Cleveland's Joint Council, Colbridge told Ray Livingstone, "You fellows really discuss things in Cleveland, don't you!" In short, what was distinctive about Cleveland was not coercion (each plant had its share of dismissals and captive-audience speeches), but a more sophisticated and comprehensive style of personnel management and company unionism.[119]

The UAW also was a victim of its own success. During the war the union repeatedly told Thompson's Cleveland workers they were paid less than other UAW members (a comparison group that included high-wage auto assembly workers). After the UAW negotiated a contract for Thompson's Detroit plant, however, workers in Cleveland had a more accurate standard for judging the

UAW's claims. Because management kept Cleveland wages equal to or above those at the Detroit plant, the UAW's promise that it would boost wages in Cleveland was no longer meaningful. Although hyperbole, the company had a point when it said, "the CIO can't get anything [Cleveland] workers don't already have."[120]

The UAW's failures at Thompson's Cleveland plants were not preordained, however. Around the middle of the war, when the AWA was getting off the ground and the Main plant had no company union, the UAW appeared to have a chance of winning. Like the NLRB, the War Labor Board considered Thompson one of its primary antagonists and kept close watch over the company. Right from the start the board was quick to reinstate UAW activists and, in November 1942, it ordered Thompson to adopt a grievance plan at its Cleveland plants. Under the wartime plan, the company was required to grant recognition to the UAW and the IAM for grievance-handling purposes. Workers could select a steward from any union (including the company union) and file a grievance under a multistep procedure ending in external arbitration. The board's grievance procedure gave UAW stewards a visible presence on the shop floor—at the Main plant the UAW had a network of seventy-eight stewards and committeemen—and provided an opportunity for the union to prove its mettle. Indeed, in the plan's first year the UAW filed hundreds of grievances—far more than any other union—and was the only union to press its grievances all the way to arbitration. The UAW used the procedure not only for disciplinary issues but also to check management's anti-union activities. After the UAW filed a grievance charging that plant bulletin boards were "championing the AWA," the arbitrator ordered the company not to encourage approval of any particular union. And when the UAW complained that misleading statements had appeared in *The Friendly Forum*, the arbitrator told the company it had a legal and moral obligation to make truthful statements in its publications. Although the U.S. Army sometimes bent over backwards to shield major contractors from the labor boards, this did not occur with Thompson. If anything, the government leaned in the opposite direction.[121]

Despite government support, the UAW's campaign increasingly was hindered by political disputes within the union. The people in charge of the campaign—Ed Hall, Wyndham Mortimer, Bill Grant, and Paul Miley—all were affiliated with the UAW's left-wing faction. Their adversaries were in a middle-of-the-road group led by Walter Reuther, who built his reputation by attacking the left over incentive pay and other issues. By 1945, the feud had split the UAW national office into warring camps—including even the office's typists—and polarized the union right down to the local level. When Elizabeth Hawes, a UAW international representative, visited Cleveland in 1944 and again in 1945, she found the Thompson campaign stalled by what she called "chop chop" (internal union disputes). Campaign staffers bitterly complained that the "Reutherites" had tried to send an inexperienced organizer to lead the drive in the hope that his failure would discredit the left.[122]

When Reuther became UAW president in 1946, he continued his attack on the left. Rather than making the hackneyed charge that the Communists took orders from Moscow, Reuther criticized them on the more pragmatic grounds of squandering the union's money. As proof, he pointed to a fruitless strike at Allis-Chalmers and to the ten-year campaign at Thompson. Speaking to the 1947 UAW convention, Reuther castigated the Thompson drive as "a glaring example of . . . mismanagement and waste of funds." Claiming that money had been misused for "factional purposes," Reuther cited the case of an unidentified Thompson organizer (Ed Hall), who had taken 183 trips away from Cleveland while running the Thompson drive in the early 1940s. The split within the UAW encouraged Thompson and the AWA to step up their anti-Communist rhetoric. The company warned that the UAW's "Communist contamination" was "something no true American wants to be aligned with," while the AWA called the UAW's stewards "babes in the woods with noble motives who [are having] clever webs spun upon them."[123]

As an explanation of the UAW's failure at Thompson, Reuther's charge of financial impropriety was wide of the mark. Yet the judgment of the leaders of the Thompson drive was occasionally clouded by ideological fervor. For one thing, the UAW consistently failed to recognize Fred Crawford's enormous popularity inside the plants. When describing Crawford, the union's rhetoric was overheated, overdone, and probably counterproductive. UAW publications described him as "the No. 1 fascist in America," "a Pro-Axis enemy of our country," and "a man bordering on degeneracy, such as Hitler." Similarly, the UAW refused to acknowledge that workers might have good reasons for supporting a company union and thus found itself on the defensive when issues like democracy or localism were raised. Instead of addressing such issues, the UAW simply blasted company unionism with the same hypermilitant bombast it aimed at Crawford. Workers were urged to "march over the rotting, decaying corpse of the company union and trample the remains into oblivion under the banner of the CIO."[124]

Another UAW error was its excessive reliance on the labor boards to make up for its weakness inside the plants. In the beginning, having the government on its side gave the UAW tactical advantages and allowed it to project an image of strength. The strategy, however, had two pitfalls: first, the NLRB—and, by extension, the UAW—were shown to be impotent when they ran up against an implacably conservative court like the Sixth Circuit; second, the NLRB itself gradually became more cautious and less willing to serve as the UAW's battering ram. Under pressure from the courts and Congress, the NLRB in the 1940s adopted a more "balanced" approach to a variety of issues, including employer free speech and company unions. One of the board's chief critics on these issues was none other than the Sixth Circuit, which overruled the NLRB in decisions involving Thompson's Cleveland plants and in other major cases as well. Thus the UAW's myriad political difficulties—both internally and in Washington—weakened its position and strengthened the AWA's at a critical moment in the contest between them.[125]

Company Unionism in the 1950s

As a result of the NLRB's more permissive policies, company unions began to win a growing number of elections and were disestablished less often. Accelerating these developments was the Taft-Hartley Act, which contained several provisions favorable to company unions. Following passage of the act in 1947, there was an upsurge in the number of company unions (technically "independent labor unions"), and company-union membership rose by 50 percent between 1947 and 1953, faster than either AFL or CIO membership.[126]

Thompson contributed to this phenomenon by propagating company unions at the plants it built or acquired between 1947 and 1958 (when it became TRW). Of eight such plants, Thompson started employee organizations at seven. About half of these were full-fledged company unions modeled after the AWA, which by the late 1940s had turned into a more autonomous and active organization than its predecessors. As such, it did not correspond to the unfavorable picture of "independents" painted by labor relations experts in the 1950s. This is not to say that the AWA (or Thompson's other company unions) came to resemble militant CIO locals; if anything, the AWA's cooperative and occasionally subservient relationship to management made it more like some AFL affiliates of the time. Despite any similarities to the AFL or the CIO, however, the AWA developed according to its own inner logic and to situational incentives beyond the control of either the union or management.[127]

A distinctive feature of the AWA was that it never struck or even threatened to do so. It had no strike funds and boasted to its members in 1954 that the absence of strikes "contributes in large measure to the Thompson company's success. They can accept orders with firm delivery dates and their customers have sufficient confidence to place large orders. This guarantees steady work for you." Even though it eschewed strikes, the AWA was not without bargaining power: there was always the possibility that if management and the AWA did not satisfy the employees, the latter could defect to a national union like the UAW. The seven campaigns conducted by the UAW between 1942 and 1967 had the unintended effect of giving the AWA strong leverage in bargaining with management. Nearly every drive was accompanied by negotiated wage increases and other gains. As one worker said, "As long as we manage to defeat the CIO's attempt to unionize this place—but not by too lavish a margin—we can be sure of getting better than union rates." Although nonunion workers also had such leverage, AWA members were in a stronger position because of the greater risk that they might defect to a national union. They had already made a psychological break by becoming (company) union members; voting for the UAW would have meant only a change of representatives and not a whole new system. And even when no drive was actually under way, AWA members could still signal their dissatisfaction in ways unavailable to nonunion workers, as they did in 1955 when they rejected a proposed contract for being insufficiently generous on wages.[128]

Throughout the AWA's early years, its leaders relied heavily on the attorney Milton Roemisch for guidance. Although Roemisch helped to plot the AWA's tactics during UAW organizing drives, his assistance went far beyond campaigns. He took the lead in wage negotiations, marshaling facts and arguments to back up the AWA's demands, and explaining how to comply with legal directives on overtime pay. Roemisch was usually polite to management and careful to point out that his proposals were "realistic," unlike the "pie in the sky demands" made by national unions. But he could also be combative, especially if he believed the company was making decisions behind the AWA's (and his) back. To some extent, then, Roemisch served as a technical adviser of the kind available through a national union's research staff. Other company unions (such as those at AT&T) also relied on advisers outside their ranks, although this sort of arrangement was unusual.[129]

As time went on, the AWA developed a cadre of leaders who were adept at contract administration and bargaining. An important source of their experience was the War Labor Board's grievance plan. To compete effectively against the UAW, AWA stewards had to learn basic labor law and aggressively tend to grievances. After the war, stewards were usually conscientious in looking out for the job rights of "their people." Aside from cases of discipline and discharge, the bulk of the AWA's grievances involved wage standards, occupational nomenclature, work conditions, seniority, and demarcation (for instance, whether a job would be performed by pipe fitters or by mold maintainers). In other words, the AWA—like most national unions of its day—fought to preserve a workplace structure built around seniority rights and job classifications. Yet internal labor markets at the Cleveland plants remained a bit more flexible than those found in comparable industrial-union plants, with about one-third fewer job classifications than the latter.[130]

Another difference between the AWA and an industrial union was that the AWA never pressed a grievance through to outside arbitration until the 1960s. Thompson management had a strong aversion to arbitration; it did not want to establish any precedent for its use and was able to persuade the AWA to yield on this issue. Management did pay a price for the AWA's acquiescence, however. Over the years, the AWA pressed a number of grievances to the fifth and penultimate step in the procedure—a hearing by the Thompson vice president Lee Clegg. In theory, Clegg was supposed to stick to the facts of a case, but he was vulnerable to horse-trading by the union. Several times the union threatened to go to an arbitrator if Clegg did not render a decision favoring the AWA. Often these cases involved job security issues, such as hiring outside contractors to run the cafeteria or allowing foremen to do production work. On these occasions Clegg either decided the case in the AWA's favor or conceded on some other issue.[131]

The AWA was never a leader on the wage front. To give automotive and aircraft firms an incentive to subcontract parts production, Thompson kept pay levels a bit below those at the Big Three automakers. But this still left AWA members in a high bracket, earning as much in the late 1940s and 1950s as workers at major UAW firms like International Harvester. Percentage increases in these years moved in tandem with unionized pacesetters such as U.S. Steel and General Motors, thus belying the assertion that company unions were "less effective in handling wages and hours than in handling other matters." Because Thompson provided excellent benefits and matched union patterns on pay changes, a survey of Cleveland factory workers in 1953 rated Thompson the best-paying employer in the region.[132]

Large industrial unions dominated the labor market in these years, so the AWA kept close track of their pay gains. In 1949, for example, the AWA asked to reopen its contract as soon as a "pattern" had been set at Ford and Bethlehem Steel. Two years later, after telling management that major firms in Cleveland were matching the UAW's historic 1950 agreement with General Motors, the AWA won cost of living and annual "improvement factor" clauses in its contracts. Like the AWA, management monitored union pay developments for fear of falling out of line. When the GM-UAW cost of living formula paid two cents more than the AWA's, management was concerned that "if this differential increases much more, the company might seriously have to consider a change to the GM index."

Like other progressive employers, Thompson prided itself on offering generous fringe benefits. As industrial unions began to press for better benefits in the 1950s, Thompson improved its own plans on a regular basis. In 1955, for example, the company conducted a study of the UAW's pension plans at Ford, GM, and Ryan Aircraft and decided to align its pension plan more closely to the UAW's. The upshot of this constant competition with the UAW was that Thompson saved nothing in labor costs; if anything, it kept compensation higher than it would have been with an affiliated union.[133]

The relationship between the AWA and management was what economists call a bilateral monopoly: Thompson was the only company the AWA bargained with, and the AWA was the only union management wanted to deal with. This gave the AWA some of its bargaining power but at the same time constrained it from being too aggressive, lest management lose its preference for bargaining with a company union. Management usually met the AWA's demands, but when it did not the union was reluctant to push hard or to raise the strike threat. Because both sides had a mutual interest in keeping out the UAW and the IAM, these dynamics produced a cooperative relationship.

During organizing drives this cooperation became something closer to collusion. To defeat the UAW, the AWA and Thompson collaborated in an adroit manipulation of personnel rules. AWA members could leave work early to distribute literature on company time and property, while foremen and plant security guards were specifically instructed not to extend the same privileges to UAW supporters. When he was a BIW official, Ed Castle had a special pass giving him access to the entire Main plant; this, he said, allowed him to "knock off the new employees before the CIO would talk to them." Management bolstered the AWA's popularity by approving wage increases right before elections and by allowing the AWA to operate an in-plant patronage system that dispensed favors to the union's supporters. Sometimes the patronage was given baldly, as when the AWA's president offered one worker a better job if he joined the AWA; at other times it was more subtle, as when management chose only AWA members to head its wartime labor-management committees, including the powerful transportation committee, which distributed gas rationing cards to employees.[134]

Bargaining brought forth a more benign form of cooperation. Management regularly provided the AWA with data on Thompson's finances and production plans and even permitted the union to hire an accountant to inspect company records before negotiating a pension plan. For its part, the AWA repeatedly assured management that it was "mindful that the company faces a serious competitive situation." Because the AWA dealt solely with Thompson, it was able to make short-term concessions when Thompson had a bad year (something an affiliated local could not do if its concessions would undercut a national contract). Thus, when profits were off in 1961, the AWA allowed the company to depart from the auto industry pay pattern; in return management accepted the AWA's demand for a revamped job evaluation plan. In so doing, management showed that it, too, was interested in the other party's long-term health.[135]

During the 1950s, each of the three Cleveland plants represented by the AWA had a joint labor relations council whose monthly meetings were an important part of the AWA's relationship with management. At these meetings management regularly presented reports on corporate affairs or informed AWA officials of decisions on matters such as scheduling and layoffs. The bulk of the councils' time, however, was devoted to problems raised by AWA officials. As in the 1930s, the main concerns were working conditions (sanitation, safety, parking) and personnel matters (transfers, recalls, back pay). Typically, management promised to take care of the problem or assigned it to one of several standing joint committees, which met on a regular basis. Most issues were resolved in a single council meeting, although some discussions took months before being resolved.[136]

The council was the fourth step in the grievance procedure, prior to Lee Clegg's review. This meant that considerable time was spent debating grievances that had not been resolved at lower levels, including complaints about discipline and discharge. (For grievances on plantwide issues, the AWA could skip the procedure's lower steps and, after discussion with the plant manager, bring them directly to the council.) Usually the council could speedily resolve the grievances that came before it; difficult cases were referred to ad hoc committees composed of managers and AWA officials. Sometimes AWA officials entirely bypassed the formal procedure and initiated grievances at council meetings.[137]

A similarly thin line separated contract negotiations and council meetings. Issues regularly surfaced at the council that properly were topics for collective bargaining, such as a new pension plan, a change in the seniority system, or even wage levels. Although the AWA agreement contained the GM-UAW formula, which was designed to eliminate annual contract reopenings, that formula tended to underestimate real wage trends. Rather than waiting for the contract to expire (contracts ran for three years), council members periodically asked to renegotiate wages. Management usually agreed, since there was little chance of a strike. These supplemental wage agreements allowed the AWA to appear to "deliver the goods" on a more regular basis than national unions.[138]

"Fairness" was the key word defining the AWA's and management's expectations of one another. Each side sought to convince the other that it was not taking advantage of their shared dependence but instead was working to achieve mutually beneficial outcomes. For its part, the AWA reassured management by tying pay demands to economic conditions, by rejecting strikes, and by cooperating to improve efficiency in areas like production standards and new technology. As for management, it reciprocated in myriad ways: it kept production (and jobs) in Cleveland, never threatened to dislodge the AWA, and performed small favors like pulling strings in state government so that the AWA could legally hold parties inside the plants. There were also less tangible, almost ritualistic, expressions of mutual trust. Joint council meetings were polite, amiable, and full of reassurances that the other side "fairly considers our requests," as a management memorandum put it, or, as the AWA said of management, that it "is fair and square in all dealings with our membership." Special council meetings took place at Christmas, accompanied by skits and a party.[139]

Although it attempted to be fair, the AWA was far from obsequious. Unlike, say, a Japanese company union, the AWA assertively disagreed with management, stubbornly pressed grievances, and effectively persuaded the company to change its plans and policies. Nevertheless, the AWA's leaders rarely displayed the belligerence typical of many CIO locals. Some of this can be traced to situational incentives, such as the absorption of episodic, adversarial activities like contract negotiations into the more continuous, collaborative, and amiable atmosphere of the council meetings. (Not without reason had the old IWW slogan averred, "Feet which meet under a mahogany table don't kick.") Then there was the fact that the AWA, in contrast to an affiliated local, offered no opportunities for retiring officers to move into union staff positions. Leaders returned to their old jobs when their terms expired, unless they were promoted into management, and they knew that promotion wasn't likely if they were antagonistic.[140]

Another feature of the Thompson situation was the cushy treatment AWA officers and stewards received from the company in the 1950s. Whether this was intended to dissuade the AWA's leaders from affiliating with the UAW or to induce cooperative behavior is not clear. What is clear is that the earnings of AWA officers—from the president on down to the stewards—were far in excess of those received by workers in similar job classifications. In 1952 the differential averaged 42 percent for the AWA's top four officers; one steward managed to receive more than double his regular earnings. The excess was entirely the result of overtime pay, part of which was compensation for normal union duties such as bargaining, grievance handling, and joint committee meetings. AWA officers also received overtime for helping to administer a slew of plant organizations, including the Old Guard, the Consolidated Welfare Fund, and various recreation groups. Between union duties and these special activities, few AWA officers spent much time in their regular jobs, a fact even casual observers were aware of. A college student who spent a week at TAPCO in the early 1950s reported to management that "stewards seem to be a thorn in our side. Entirely too many of them abhor work, it seems!" Three years later an attitude survey found that Thompson workers were annoyed by the stewards' "loafing tactics." Concerned by such discontent and aware that these practices might lead to NLRB charges of illegal support, in the late 1950s management began to limit the amount of overtime paid to AWA officers.[141]

The AWA existed in isolation from other unions. It had few contacts with, and no formal ties to, company unions at Thompson plants outside Cleveland. Within Cleveland, the local AFL and CIO were contemptuous and suspicious of the AWA, which repaid those feelings in kind. Too small to train its own officers, and cut off from mainstream labor education programs, the AWA had to rely on management to meet some of its basic organizational needs. The company held classes for newly elected stewards, where they received basic information on Thompson's personnel practices, financial situation, and markets. Company managers sought to "integrate" new AWA officers by taking them to conferences of the American Management Association and by holding training sessions on technical subjects like job evaluation. Given all this, it is not surprising that when the UAW reappeared in the 1960s, its organizers castigated the AWA's "cozy relationship" with management. From a trade-union perspective, there was something odd about the AWA's isolation and its dependence on management. But the AWA seemed less peculiar when viewed from within, that is, when set in the context of Thompson's evolving welfare capitalism.[142]

Company unionism at Thompson in the 1950s was embedded in a larger ensemble of welfare practices emphasizing horizontal cohesion (what might be called, to paraphrase Lizabeth Cohen's description of the CIO, a "corporate culture of unity"). Elements of this culture can be traced back to the 1920s, when Thompson first began its welfare programs as a supplement to the security offered by extended families and benevolent associations. By the 1950s, Thompson—like Sears and Kodak—was forced to adapt its culture to new social realities: a prosperous economy, suburbanizing families, vigorous unions, and a growing welfare state.

During the 1950s, job security remained a fundamental part of Thompson's culture of unity. In fact, steady postwar growth in the automotive and defense industries permitted management to emphasize security more explicitly than in earlier years. Thompson now promised to minimize layoffs (by transfers and keeping work in-house) and, if layoffs were unavoidable, to reduce their impact (by using Old Guard funds to supplement unemployment insurance benefits, an approach borrowed from the steel and auto unions). Off the shop floor, Thompson's social and athletic programs continued with the same intensity as in the early 1930s—the roster of events in September 1955 included an Old Guard clambake, bowling and baseball leagues, a steak roast, and a golf day for women—although here, too, changes were afoot. To deemphasize paternalism and to steer clear of the NLRB, the company adopted a policy whereby all social activities had to be "planned and managed by employee committees with only broad policy guidance from the company." Another change was the emphasis on pecuniary, as opposed to in-kind, fringe benefits. Thompson's ever-increasing expenditures on pensions and health insurance were due to growing competition from unions (a phenomenon also seen at Kodak) and to a postwar social drift toward more individualized and monetized forms of security. By 1954, Thompson's benefit costs exceeded those of other auto-parts manufacturers and were well above the U.S. manufacturing average.[143]

Communications programs remained an important part of Thompson's effort to maintain a corporate Gemeinschaft in the 1950s. One change in the 1950s was the expansion of human relations efforts to office employees, a group management feared might become the next target of union organizing activity. Supervisors were told that office workers needed to be treated as people, needed to feel that their work was important, and needed "vocal, personal, and individual contact . . . as much as possible." Except for this change, however, much continued as before. Lunches and dinners that brought together workers and managers, folksy publications, family events, solicitous supervision, regular visits to the shop floor by top management—all of these continued to project an image of Thompson as an industrial community. Overall, then, Thompson's corporate culture meshed smoothly with company unionism in the 1950s, perhaps even more so than before the war.[144]

But company unionism was hardly a risk-free strategy. There was always the danger that a company union would become militant or would be taken over by a national union. Company-union members made tempting organizing targets for national unions because, unlike nonunion workers, they already were a collectivity and were familiar with the arcana of contracts and grievance procedures. Ten percent of all company unions experienced an organizing raid each year in the 1950s, surely an annoyance to managers. Even without raids, bargaining and contract administration were time-consuming procedures that limited management's ability to make prompt and unquestioned decisions. And if the Thompson experience was at all typical (and evidence suggests that it was), company unions did not come cheap. Wages at Thompson's company-union plants were roughly the same, and sometimes higher, than those at similar plants represented by national unions.[145]

One result of all this was a loss of interest in company unions at several firms—most of them large—that had managed to preserve such unions through the Second World War. Take, for example, the experience of Du

Pont, a giant, multiplant employer. Throughout the Depression and the war, Du Pont established company unions at its U.S. facilities; by 1946, 85 percent of its employees were represented by them. After the war, however, Du Pont made a strategic shift: over the course of the next decade it opened twenty-five new plants, many in the South, and all without company unions. By 1960, company unions represented only 59 percent of Du Pont's employees.[146]

Why did Thompson stick with the company-union strategy whereas Du Pont decided to shed it? First, unlike Du Pont, Thompson's plants were concentrated in unionism's heartland, the Midwest and Northeast, where organizing drives remained a constant threat. Second, Thompson's company unions were demonstrably less militant than Du Pont's. Between 1944 and 1959, Du Pont's company unions carried out four strikes and filed sixteen unfair labor practice charges against management, while not one of Thompson's company unions struck or complained to the NLRB. This record, as well as the AWA's willingness to cooperate in raising efficiency, convinced management that company unions raised productivity sufficiently to offset their wage costs.[147]

This is not to say that Thompson management was entirely satisfied with its company unions, however. Wage costs were high, and organizing drives—and the legal expenses that went with them—were a constant problem. In the 1950s, Thompson began to experiment with an alternative to traditional company unionism—the committee system—at three small plants acquired after the war. The committees were more decentralized and informal than a company union, making it harder for organizers to transform them into national union affiliates. Also, the committee system explicitly ruled out collective bargaining, thus eliminating the contractual rigidity and labor-cost pressures associated with company unions. On the other hand, management hoped that the new system would replicate what it saw as the positive features of company unionism: two-way communication, rapid dispute resolution, and a cooperative approach to problem solving. As at Sears and Kodak, then, Thompson was trying to create new institutions to preserve the communicative features of company unions without an excess of independence or bargaining power.

In keeping with Thompson's diversification into technology-intensive defense products, two of the three "new system" plants were electronics factories: Bell Sound Systems, a Columbus, Ohio, manufacturer of amplifiers and communications equipment, and Dage Television, which made closed-circuit televisions for the military in Michigan City, Indiana. (The third plant was an automotive valve factory in Fruitport, Michigan.) Over a three-year period, from 1953 to 1956, Ray Livingstone introduced virtually identical organizations in all three plants: the Voice of the Plant (Bell Sound), the Frontiersmen Association (Fruitport), and the Dage Employees' Association. Neither the Bell nor the Fruitport organization met directly with management. Instead, their elected officers spent their time directing the plants' numerous recreation and welfare activities. Separate from these organizations, however, were "human relations committees" that met with management to discuss problems and complaints. In order to avoid coming under NLRB purview, the purpose of the committees was described as "the exchange of ideas on matters affecting human relations . . . and good living within the company."[148]

The Dage plant, the smallest of the three, did things a bit differently. As at the other two plants, acquisition by Thompson brought a rapid expansion of employee recreational activities and regular use of advanced personnel techniques such as attitude surveys. But local management felt that the Dage employees would not be satisfied with the vagaries of the Bell-Fruitport model and pressed Cleveland officials for something that would "provide as many advantages of a union-type organization as possible in order to avoid possible outside interference." The end result, the Dage Employees' Association, was a hybrid combining some features of a company union (regular meetings with management) and others taken from the new committee system (handling welfare activities autonomously and carefully refusing to "deal" with management on wages or working conditions).[149]

Despite these precautions, a 1960 organizing drive at Dage resulted in unfair labor practice charges being filed against the new system. In a decision later upheld by the Seventh Circuit, the NLRB ruled that the Dage association was a labor organization and that it was dominated by management. Although the company asserted that the association never bargained and merely "expressed views and conveyed information to management," the board rejected the claim. With this resounding defeat, Thompson (by then TRW) shifted gears and gave up on both company unions and the new system. During the 1960s, it built or acquired thirty-nine new plants and created company unions at none of them. Instead, the 1960s saw the introduction of a yet another hybrid, this one combining a new "small group" approach (sensitivity groups and other team-building programs, which were introduced at most TRW plants, including company-union sites like the Main plant) together with a bevy of communications programs whose roots stretched back to the 1930s (attitude surveys, "sensing" sessions, and relational management). Although the new approach entailed some novel methods, its conceptual logic fit seamlessly with Thompson's previous strategy. As Ray Livingstone, still vice president for personnel, told *Business Week* in 1966, "Openness, leveling, listening therapy, conflict resolution—all this talk by behavioral scientists. Hell, we've been doing these things for 30 years. They're just elegant terms for principles we practiced years ago—old wine in new bottles."[150]

Company unions represented nearly three million workers in 1934, but by the end of the Second World War most of these workers had joined national unions. Why did Thompson's Cleveland employees choose to be different? The traditional view holds that they were bullied or misled. There was some of that, to be sure, but there was more. Thompson workers identified with the company as a result of its producerist values, its deference to seniority, its progressive personnel policies, and the folksy charisma of Fred Crawford. As for the AWA, it reinforced the company's unitary culture while permitting workers to have a voice of their own. Due to situational incentives and to pressure from government and national unions, by the 1950s the AWA had evolved into an organization that met its members' needs. Compared to a national union, it was less independent and powerful; on the other hand, it was also less bureaucratic and remote.

For its part, when it came to Thompson the UAW suffered from particularly bad timing—its own and that of national events. As the political climate shifted after the war, the UAW's Thompson drive was stymied by in-fighting and by a legal system that had become increasingly tolerant of Crawford-style campaign tactics and of company unions in general. Timing, in other words, worked to management's advantage (although, as we will see in the next chapter, Thompson managers also worked hard to take advantage of the changing climate).

By the 1950s, however, a paradox began to emerge: just when the law was making it easier for employers to start company unions, companies that already had them began to lose interest. The explanation is straightforward: with the threat from organized labor fading, the benefits of company unionism faded too; meanwhile, the growing independence of company unions made them more costly to deal with. Thompson management eventually found a cheaper alternative, one that channeled employee participation through committees and small groups instead of through elected bodies. In this way, Thompson—originally a late developer—moved modern welfare capitalism several steps beyond Kodak and Sears.

Six

Beyond the Manor: Politics and Public Opinion

WELFARE CAPITALISM broadened its ambit after 1933 to include the world beyond the workplace. What had once been private, solitary, and somewhat amateurish now depended as never before on political engagement, interemployer cooperation, and professional expertise. Sears Roebuck, for example, ran its welfare plans in the 1920s with minimal attention to external considerations. However, Sears had come to believe that the success of its personnel activities required "effective personal contact with individuals and groups likely to prove useful in future contingencies [including] key individuals in government, industry, and university groups who have firsthand experience in industrial relations."[1]

One reason for this shift was simple: government had become much more active in all areas of American life. Tempering and taming government was not something companies could do alone, however. It required coalitions and collective action, lobbying and influence peddling. A top priority for employers was reforming the Wagner Act, which they hated more than any other piece of New Deal legislation. Changing the law to check the labor movement was an effort that united diverse segments of the employer community—union and nonunion, large and small—with large nonunion firms like Du Pont and Thompson Products playing an especially important role. Another legislative effort focused on the Social Security Act. Employers—again with leadership from large nonunion firms (in this case, including Kodak)—sought to prevent the new welfare state from eliminating private benefit plans. Employers eventually discovered that suitably circumscribed public programs could coexist with—even complement—private welfare capitalism.

More threatening to business than any single piece of legislation were the ideological and political realignments that produced the New Deal itself. Businessmen were no longer seen as national heroes or as guarantors of the nation's prosperity. Instead, the country's hopes now lay with Big Labor and Big Government. The proximate cause of these changes was the Depression, whose severity permanently altered the political landscape. The Depression's impact was magnified, however, by the emergence of a more unified and assertive working class, a transformation that was under way long before the Depression hit. In the 1910s and 1920s, the children and grandchildren of immigrant workers were beginning to move out of their ethnic enclaves and into the cultural mainstream. They started shopping at chain stores, purchasing national brands, listening to radio, and watching movies. Reticence and ethnic parochialism gradually were replaced by a sense of entitlement and

Americanism, sentiments that attracted people to industrial unions and the New Deal. Thus the Depression brought a shift not only in public opinion but in the very meaning of "public."[2]

Capturing the public's confidence was an important part of welfare capitalism's expansion. Corporations began to spend huge sums on public relations, with the intent of breeding skepticism about unions and government and restoring faith in free enterprise. The same techniques that had facilitated the rise of mass consumption and mass politics—such as advertising, market research, and opinion polls—now were used to win the public back to business's point of view. Employers were pleased that the the Democratic party had begun to move in a probusiness direction by the end of the war. But they remained troubled by postwar opinion polls showing continued public support for unions and government, even for government ownership of business. Hence industry's public relations campaign remained at a fever pitch well into the 1950s.[3]

Mass communications became a highly sophisticated endeavor in the 1940s and 1950s. The field took a quantum leap during the war, when the federal government turned to the universities to help conduct psychological warfare, assess civilian and military morale, design military leadership programs, and analyze the effects of domestic and foreign propaganda. Over a fifth of the nation's psychologists—and numerous other social scientists—were employed by the federal government in these activities. After the war, the new communications methods, and the behavioral scientists who designed them, found ready employment in private industry, which was eager to apply the techniques that had helped the military win the war.

As one observer put it, postwar managers were becoming "psychologically minded," and, as they did, the workplace developed into a testing ground for programs intended to change people's attitudes. Mass communications and employee relations were two sides of a coin; the only difference was the size of the target audience. People who knew how to change consumer behavior or to churn out puff pieces critical of Big Labor could easily redeploy their talents in the workplace: raising employee morale, lowering absenteeism, or waging anti-union campaigns.

Who were these people? Some were journalists and salespeople; others were specialists trained in psychiatry, sociology, social work, anthropology, and, especially, psychology. By 1948, 30 percent of large corporations had a psychologist on staff, while many of the remaining 70 percent relied on independent consultants to supply them with behavioral expertise. Consultants with academic appointments were especially desirable, both because of their credentials (the field was filled with hucksters) and because they were willing to trade their skills in return for the opportunity to conduct on-site research. As these university-based consultants disseminated their findings in an ever-growing number of conference proceedings and research journals, companies were able to learn what constituted "best practice" in the field and, as well, what their competitors were doing. In short, the scientization of the workplace—as embodied in links between academics and managers (who themselves were evermore likely to be college-educated)—was yet another force prying open welfare capitalism.[4]

The three companies examined here each had different priorities for engaging the world beyond the workplace: for Thompson the focus was labor law reform; for Kodak it was social security; and for Sears it was the behavioral sciences. Yet despite this specialization, none of the firms ignored the other developments in the world around them. Sears, for example, lobbied for labor law reform, whereas Kodak and Thompson were heavy consumers of the behavioral sciences. Given this overlap, it is hardly surprising that the companies joined a wide range of employer organizations. All three simultaneously belonged to the conservative National Association of Manufacturers and to the politically liberal Committeee for Economic Development. Such overlap was due, in part, to conscious efforts by businessmen in the 1940s and 1950s to speak and act as a cohesive group. It also reflected modern welfare capitalism's preference for pragmatism over ideological purity.[5]

Labor Law

Although employers viewed the pro-union Wagner Act as the New Deal's "crowning assault on business," their political response initially was inchoate and ineffectual. Confident that the U.S. Supreme Court would invalidate the act, employers were shocked at the *Jones & Laughlin* decision in 1937. Before then, major business organizations had asked their members to resist complying with the law. Now they reconsidered their position. The National Association of Manufacturers was, in the late 1930s, divided between those who still wanted to see the act revoked and a more pragmatic group that thought the time had come to reform rather than repeal the act. The latter group tried to gain control of the NAM in the late 1930s and urged Congress to investigate the NLRB and revise the Wagner Act.[6]

Legislation introduced in the House by the Virginia representative Howard Smith in 1939 embodied the reform approach. In both its details and underlying philosophy of restraining the NLRB, the Smith bill anticipated the 1947 Taft-Hartley legislation. One issue raised at the Smith hearings concerned employer conduct during union election campaigns. In its early years, the NLRB insisted that employers maintain strict neutrality during organizing campaigns, on the theory that the employer's economic power was so great that, if he were to express his preferences, it would inhibit employees from making a free choice. The Smith committee called for amending the Wagner Act to allow employers "free speech" so long as it was not accompanied by intimidation or threats, a proposal that the NLRB vociferously opposed. Another issue raised by the Smith committee was that the NLRB had taken an "extremely hostile" approach to company unions and had "consistently pursued a policy aimed at the extermination of these nationally unaffiliated organizations." During (and after) the Smith hearings, employers bitterly complained about the NLRB's practice of disestablishing company unions even when they no longer received employer support. Disestablishment was a severe remedy that the NLRB did not apply to "sweetheart" locals of national unions, which were permitted on the ballot if they could prove employer support had ceased. The NLRB rationalized its more lenient treatment of affiliated locals on the grounds that—as part of large and powerful national unions—such locals never could be dominated by an employer. An affiliated local, said an NLRB official, "can hardly be said to be the creature of the employer, inasmuch as it is the creature of the parent body."[7]

In the end, the Smith bill languished in the Senate. Anti-employer sentiment still ran strong as a result of the LaFollette hearings, and business organizations like the NAM, although they threw their weight behind the bill, had not yet figured out how to orchestrate a successful legislative campaign. The NAM learned its lesson with the Smith bill, however. During World War II and immediately after, it transformed itself into an extremely effective lobbying organization, perhaps the most powerful of its day. At the heart of the NAM's transformation was Frederick Crawford, the head of Thompson Products, who served as the organization's president in 1942–1943 and as its chairman in 1944–1945.[8]

Crawford's involvement in national politics began in the late 1930s, when he was head of the Cleveland chamber of commerce and lobbied in Washington to bring aviation research dollars to Cleveland. Crawford also was active on the Conference Board and in the Associated Industries of Cleveland (AIC). Although the AIC formally was independent of the NAM, many of its officers—and more than half of its financial support—came from companies that belonged to the NAM. Historically the AIC was a bellicose advocate of the open shop, but in 1938 it became one of the first NAM affiliates to turn out in favor of amending the Wagner Act to yield "fairness and equity."[9]

Crawford's stature in the management community steadily rose as Thompson's battle with the NLRB intensified. Crawford's first clash with the NLRB came in 1938, when a court decision favoring Thompson forced the NLRB chairman J. Warren Madden to go on national radio to defend the board against charges that it was biased against employers. The following year, Thompson Products was one of the companies interviewed by the Smith committee about its experiences with the NLRB. Thompson's next encounter with the NLRB came in 1941, when the board ordered it to disestablish one of its company unions. In response, Thompson issued press releases declaring it would ignore the order and seek vindication in the courts. By 1942, Crawford was becoming renowned for his bold challenges to the NLRB. Right before a union election at Thompson that year, he paid regular visits to the shop floor, clearly declaring his anti-UAW and pro-company union views. The NLRB charged that his "paternalistic" partisanship violated the Wagner Act. Although this was a standard charge, Crawford said it violated his First Amendment right to free speech and he refused to accede. At a Conference Board roundtable held in New York, Crawford was a featured speaker, along with George W. Taylor and other experts on labor law. Crawford urged the audience to "find a way of putting into the field a greater awareness of independent unions, Wagner or not," and then assailed the NLRB for its "prejudiced attitude."[10]

By choosing Crawford as its president later that year, the NAM sent a clear signal that the organization was committed to reforming the national labor laws. This was a departure for the NAM. Between 1937 and 1942 it had authorized only one committee to study labor policy issues and draft statements for its board of directors. Under Crawford, the number of policy committees expanded to five; the Industrial Relations Program Committee set goals for the other four and pressed them to develop legislative options for the postwar period, many of which were later embodied in the Taft-Hartley Act.[11]

Crawford poured his sizable energy into the NAM. In 1943 alone he traveled 50,000 miles, made more than 130 speeches, and attended several White House conferences for major business leaders (noteworthy in light of the NAM's previous hostility to the Roosevelt administration). Crawford also found his way into several important federal agencies. He served on the Management-Labor Policy Committee of the War Manpower Commission and on a similar committee at the War Production Board. Recognizing the critical function of the War Labor Board, Crawford set up an industry committee to give advice to the employer members of the board, while naming an old AIC friend, William Frew Long, as the committee's executive assistant. "From then on," notes historian Howell Harris, "the organized business community was better placed to make the best possible presentation of industry's case and to 'whip' industry members into line behind considered conservative positions."[12]

Crawford was president of the NAM at the same time that Eric Johnston, a liberal, was head of the U.S. Chamber of Commerce. Like Crawford, Johnston was an articulate spokesperson for business, but his views on the New Deal and labor relations were diametrically opposed to Crawford's. Johnston favored a "firm but fair" policy of cooperating with unions, although he drew the line at their encroachment on areas of managerial responsibility. Crawford had no sympathy for Johnston's tolerant ecumenism, terming it "collaboration" and "appeasement." Johnston, however, thought that Crawford's "desire to hold the the CIO at arm's length—with, likely as not, a fist at the end of the arm, was antiquated." In the end, however, it was Crawford, not Johnston, who won support from employers.[13]

Crawford's accomplishments at the NAM were considerable. He gave the organization an air of respectability, he concentrated its hefty resources on reforming the law, and he mobilized diverse segments of industry in support of this objective. Even the Business Advisory Council, once a bastion of corporate liberalism, came out in favor of the NAM's labor law reforms. A handful of liberal employers were uncomfortable with the NAM's aggressive lobbying, and a die-hard faction (including the National Founders' Association) still sought repeal of the Wagner Act. But with these minor exceptions, businessmen spoke with one—loud—voice in favor of "balancing" the Wagner Act, thanks in no small part to Crawford. As *Fortune* magazine said in an adulatory article, Crawford had given "that once austere body"—the NAM—"a new zip." Crawford's most important achievement was getting the NAM's hidebound membership to accept realpolitik and admit that the world of the 1920s had passed. With Crawford having cleared the way, the NAM's executive vice president Walter Weisenberger confessed that the organization's obduracy in the 1930s had been a mistake: "How much better if business had met these problems head on and stuck its neck out with practical leadership instead of simply protesting and opposing only to end up with the doubtful satisfaction of saying 'we told you so.'"[14]

Some historians have divined the ascendance in the 1930s of a corporate liberal coalition led by mass-production, consumer-oriented firms like Sears and Kodak. The impression is not entirely mistaken. After the Depression, both Sears and Kodak became markedly more tolerant of the federal government's regulatory and fiscal policies. But when it came to labor relations, these avowedly liberal companies were no less anti-union than midsized manufacturing firms like Thompson Products. Because it was a producer-goods company, though, and did not have to worry about offending customers, Thompson had the freedom to take a more vocal and belligerent stance toward unions than Kodak or Sears. But behind the scenes at the NAM, giant consumer-goods companies were as busy giving money and time to the labor law campaign as were the NAM's smaller and more producer-oriented companies.[15]

Sears became an active member of the NAM in the 1930s and 1940s, even though the organization was composed primarily of manufacturers. General Wood had voted for Roosevelt in 1933 and had supported the National Recovery Administration's wage- and price-fixing schemes (which had given Sears an advantage over smaller retailers). But by the late 1930s Wood had turned into an implacable foe of the New Deal. In a letter to President Roosevelt, he claimed that "the majority of employers are fair . . . but the Labor Board, and apparently the Administration, refuse to recognize this fact." Anticipating the rhetoric of the Taft-Hartley debate, Wood told the president that "the pendulum has swung to the other extreme" and needed centering. During World War II, Wood served as a member of the NAM's executive committee and helped the organization establish lines of communication to the War Production Board (WPB), which was headed by one of Wood's former assistants, Donald M. Nelson. Nelson chose two NAM officials—Crawford and Malcolm Muir, the NAM's director—to serve on the WPB's management-labor council.[16]

As for Kodak, it was one of the top fifteen contributors to the NAM in the 1930s, a group that included such other welfare capitalists as Du Pont, Swift, and Standard Oil of New Jersey. When he was president of Kodak in the 1930s, Frank Lovejoy served on the NAM's Employment Relations Committee, and his successor, T. J. Hargrave, served with Wood on the NAM's executive committee. After the war, Hargrave (who happened to be close friends with Crawford) became a member of the NAM's key Industrial Relations Program Committee.[17]

Still, neither Kodak nor Sears ever dared to criticize the NLRB or oppose unions as freely and openly as Thompson did. During the war, Thompson's anti-union tactics meshed ever more closely with the NAM's political agenda, especially around the issues of free speech, company unionism, and alleged NLRB inequities. The U.S. Supreme Court's refusal in 1943 to review a pro-employer appellate decision in a free speech case (*American Tube Bending*) gave Crawford the green light to test the legal limits in this area. During the 1944 union campaign at its Cleveland plants (a rerun of the 1942 election), Thompson thumbed its nose at the NLRB and distributed literally tons of flyers, leaflets, and *Let's Have the Truth!* bulletins. Crawford gave several highly publicized captive-audience speeches. At one, Crawford declared,

> I will look any labor leader in the eye in the City of Cleveland and tell him he is a Goddamn liar if he says our wages aren't the best in town. . . . There has been a campaign for seven years of lies and mistruths about this company falling like drops of water on a stone. They have beaten into us these lies. . . . Get yourselves a cup of coffee, sit down at the kitchen table, and say, "Mother, tomorrow is the day. What is it we want in this world? Do we want quarreling and union power and outside leadership?" . . . I have talked to my little wife. She told me how to vote. I know how I would vote if I were working out there.

During the campaign, the local press took Crawford's side and emphasized the political issues at stake. The Cleveland *Plain Dealer* reprinted his speeches along with an editorial that said, "We are fighting to regain and to preserve freedom of speech." When the NLRB later ruled that Crawford's conduct was coercive and that another election should be held, the *Plain Dealer* ran an editorial terming this "NLRB Favoritism."[18]

Crawford, ever sensitive to the media and public opinion, seized the limelight when the NLRB made an ill-fated request for an injunction barring him from interfering with the second rerun election held in 1945. The NLRB petition, and the Sixth Circuit's subsequent rejection of it, gave Crawford the opportunity to press the case for reforming the NLRB and the Wagner Act. Initially Crawford told the press that the injunction request was "a perfect example of a dictatorial agency saying, 'To Hell with America. We'll play our game.'" After the appellate decision, Crawford went ahead and gave rousing anti-NLRB and anti-UAW speeches to all four shifts at Thompson's Main plant. The speeches—and the election results—were widely reprinted, usually accompanied by a photograph of Crawford carrying a striped prison suit with him to the podium. The *Plain Dealer* stated, "This was not just a private squabble at Thompson. . . . NLRB practices in the Thompson plant—and they are part of a bigger policy pursued in Washington for more than a decade—must, unless checked, destroy constitutional liberties."[19]

As before, the NLRB refused to certify the election, ruling that management's energetic campaign was coercive. To this the *Plain Dealer* acidly responded, "It seems to us that a good case of coercion could be made against the NLRB." Events then unfolded much as they had before. The NLRB scheduled a third rerun election for May 1947; Crawford, as usual, refused to stay out of the campaign; and the local press excoriated the NLRB. But there was one important difference this time around: at the very moment the NLRB announced the 1947 election date, Congress was in the midst of its hearings on the Taft-Hartley bill. Thus, just as the statutory die was being cast, the NLRB—either bravely or foolishly—handed its enemies a stick to beat it with. A hostile editorial in the *Plain Dealer* said that Congress now had "another argument why [the NLRB] should be legislated out of existence and why long-needed labor reforms should be enacted into law."[20]

Beginning in 1946, an emboldened NAM mounted a massive effort to reform the Wagner Act, one that was estimated to have cost more than $100 million. On the public relations front, the NAM appropriated liberal catchwords—equality, rights, anti-discrimination, fairness—to legitimate its cause. Inside Congress, NAM lobbyists worked with Republicans and southern Democrats to develop the Taft-Hartley legislation. Although the NAM denied charges that it actually wrote the legislation, a comparison of the Hartley bill with the NAM's proposals reveals "amazing similarities."[21]

Discussions of Taft-Hartley often proceed as if the law's main beneficiaries were unionized employers: in the act, some union practices were declared "unfair," various kinds of strikes became unlawful, and union contracts were made enforceable in court. It is also often assumed that Taft-Hartley did little to change those parts of the Wagner Act dealing with unfair practices by management. But, in fact, nonunion employers benefited enormously from Taft-Hartley and—at least for northern employers unaffected by the law's "right to work" provisions—most of the benefits resulted from a loosening of the strictures on unfair management practices. Taft-Hartley gave management leeway to participate in election campaigns and required the NLRB to treat unaffiliated (company) unions the same as affiliated ones.[22]

As might be expected, Thompson Products played a major part in the drama that led to Taft-Hartley. Crawford left the handling of legislative details to his personnel director, Ray Livingstone, who was every bit as articulate as his boss. Livingstone first appeared before Congress in 1946, when he testified on behalf of the Ball-Burton-Hatch bill, a predecessor to Taft-Hartley. The following year, Livingstone was a key witness during the Taft-Hartley hearings. He also served that year as chairman of the NAM's powerful Industrial Relations Program Committee, which coordinated the final legislative effort on Taft-Hartley.[23]

The NLRB's policy toward company unions regularly surfaced during the Taft-Hartley hearings, often in connection with the board's Thompson decisions. Ray Livingstone testified before the House committee, as did Hugh

Sperry, an NLRB official who had investigated the 1942 Thompson elections. Dominated by conservatives, the committee gave Sperry a chilly reception. Asserting that the board was biased against independent unions, the representatives grilled Sperry as to why so many elections were held at Thompson. "Here is the way we look at it," one representative told Sperry. "In the Thompson case it just looks like the elections would never stop until the CIO won. If the CIO had won one of the elections, then the whole thing, we feel, would have been over." When Livingstone appeared before the committee, he bashed and baited the NLRB in front of a friendly audience. "For years," he said, "the NLRB has surreptitiously used a double standard, one set of rules applied to independent unions and another set of rules for international unions." Livingstone accused the board of "partisanship" and of supporting "known Communists."[24]

Livingstone's testimony probably had more of an impact on events in Cleveland than Washington. At the very moment Livingstone was testifying, the UAW was in its final drive at the Main plant and the company union was waiting for the Sixth Circuit's decision on its legal status. But this is not to say that Livingstone's testimony was superfluous. There was reluctance in Congress to reopening the Pandora's box of company unionism. To weaken that resistance, Crawford reprinted Livingstone's testimony in pamphlet form and mailed it to thousands of leading businessmen, journalists, and educators around the country. When Taft-Hartley finally was passed, its company-union provisions forbade the NLRB from discriminating between affiliated and unaffiliated unions.[25]

After Taft-Hartley's enactment, the NLRB no longer paid attention to affiliation status when judging cases of employer support to unions. Instead, the distinction was between employer domination (the remedy for which still was disestablishment) and lesser forms of illegal employer interference. If the employer stopped interfering, the NLRB allowed the union to appear on the ballot. Taft-Hartley also forced the NLRB to apply weaker fracture rules: unfair labor practices committed more than six months prior to the filing of an election petition by a company union were not allowed to bear on the petition. These changes grandfathered existing company unions and caused the formation of quite a few new ones. Between 1947 and 1953, membership in independent local unions rose from 469,000 to 705,000, with many of the new unions being formed at smaller firms and plants.[26]

Like Fred Crawford, most nonunion employers chafed under the NLRB's rule requiring them to keep out of union representation elections. Because employers construed the rule as trammeling their right to free speech, they received a more sympathetic hearing from the courts on this issue than on company-union issues. The appellate courts were the first to challenge the NLRB's neutrality rule; not surprisingly, the Sixth Circuit led the way in *Midland Steel Products* (1940), followed by the U.S. Supreme Court in *Virginia Electric and Power Co.* (1941). In this case, the Supreme Court told the NLRB to consider the totality of an employer's conduct in judging whether anti-union utterances were coercive. Two years later came *American Tube Bending*, in which the Supreme Court again overruled the NLRB in favor of the employer.[27]

Under Harry A. Millis, who headed the NLRB from 1940 to 1945, the board became responsive to external criticism and gradually backed away from requiring employer neutrality in organizing campaigns. The NLRB's reorientation accelerated under Paul Herzog, Millis's successor, who voiced strong support for free speech by employers, so long as it was not tainted by coercion. By 1947, the NLRB was giving employers considerable leeway in expressing their views, although captive-audience speeches were still illegal. The board defended its lenience by arguing that "This is 1947, not 1935; in the interim employees have learned much about protecting their own rights and making their own choices with the full facts before them." The NLRB's stance on free speech irked labor leaders like Philip Murray of the CIO, who blasted the board for its "headlong retreat" from defending workers' rights. In light of the NLRB's change of attitude, the NAM's scathing attacks on the board may seem surprising, yet by 1947 the NLRB still had not enunciated a set of unambiguous guidelines regarding free speech; employers wanted the protection of a statute. They also hoped that Taft-Hartley would extend permissible campaign conduct beyond the NLRB's limits. With so many anti-union tactics now denied them, employers viewed campaign propaganda as an essential weapon for fending off an organizing drive.[28]

Thompson Products was mentioned repeatedly when the Taft-Hartley hearings turned to the free speech issue. In the Senate, Dr. Leo Wolman, an industrial relations expert from Columbia University, cited Thompson as "the classic case" in which an employer's right to free speech was denied. The NLRB's conduct in the Thompson case, said Wolman, was "a foolish use of public power and . . . an interference with the right of an employer to go and talk to people who are intimately associated with him." In the House, the hapless Hugh Sperry again had to defend the NLRB's actions in the Thompson case. None other than Howard Smith told Sperry that "it seems to me we are going a long way when a man can walk around a plant and just reach up and grab things and say, 'That is not the truth.' I did not understand that was constitutional government." Sperry tried to explain the board's neutrality rule but had difficulty making a persuasive argument. When it was Livingstone's turn, he attacked the NLRB with the same passion he had displayed in his company-union testimony. Recalling the NLRB's abortive injunction request, he said, "During the very week that General MacArthur had proclaimed free speech in Japan for all the Japs, we witnessed the amazing spectacle of a Government agency, the National Labor Relations Board, pleading with the U.S. circuit court in Cincinnati for an injunction trying to restrain an American employer from talking to his employees."[29]

The free speech clause that finally appeared in Taft-Hartley went well beyond the prior Supreme Court decisions on the issue and flew in the face of the

NLRB. One of the first reactions to the new law came shortly after the House and Senate had approved it. In June 1947, in a long-awaited decision on the 1944 Thompson elections, the Sixth Circuit finally ruled that the company's campaign conduct was protected by "the employer's right to free speech." Other courts, too, adopted an expansive interpretation of the new law. Employers quickly adjusted to the situation, causing Archibald Cox, a young law professor at Harvard, to castigate the amendment as "a legalistic obstruction to the protection of freedom of organization."[30]

Particularly affected by Taft-Hartley were the retail unions, which were making a major push in the late 1940s and 1950s to organize chain supermarkets and department stores. After Taft-Hartley, retail employers—including Sears—became considerably more vocal during organizing drives. At an educational conference held by the Retail Clerks in 1951, union organizers reported that captive-audience speeches were "beginning to grow by leaps and bounds" at larger stores and had contributed to several major union losses. In response to these complaints, the NLRB later that year promulgated its *Bonwit Teller* rule, which held captive-audience speeches unlawful unless employers gave equal time to the union. The Clerks were pleased with the new rule—it gave them direct access to the workplace—although they still complained that the NLRB did nothing to employers whose speeches were coercive. On the other hand, employers were infuriated by *Bonwit Teller*. At the 1953 Senate hearings to consider revisions of Taft-Hartley, representatives from the American Retail Federation and other employers' groups asked Congress to nullify it.[31]

In the first years after Taft-Hartley's passage, management did not rest easy. Although the law was a great victory, employers were fearful of efforts to amend or even repeal what unions called the "Slave Labor Act." Sears' politially astute General Wood worried that the 1950 mid-term elections would lead to a realignment against those who had voted for Taft-Hartley. Addressing a group of southern textile manufacturers, Wood said that it was "the duty of every business man to take a direct personal interest in the elections of 1950, to be prepared to spend his money and time freely." Wood's personnel director, Clarence B. Caldwell, gave similar advice to the American Retail Federation's employment relations committee, which he headed. Caldwell's committee drafted a fifteen-point document of "basic" management rights, including free speech and the power of decertification, which was to guide lobbying efforts if Congress sought to revise Taft-Hartley. The following year, when President Truman proposed a reorganization of the NLRB that would have eliminated the position of the board's conservative general counsel, Robert Denham, Caldwell's committee voiced its opposition and complained that the NLRB was not appropriately enforcing Taft-Hartley.[32]

By 1951, McCarthyism and the Korean War were under way. Businessmen from the NAM and similar organizations again found themselves serving on numerous government advisory committees, as in the Second World War, although this time union representatives were excluded from many of the committees. Wood and other employers were pleasantly surprised by the 1950 elections, in which conservatives unseated many liberal Democrats. As the country shifted farther to the right, Taft-Hartley looked increasingly secure, although the NLRB continued to irk employers with its periodic pro-labor rulings.[33]

The Democrats were in a weak position during the 1952 national elections. Senator Robert Taft accused the administration of being "dominated by a policy of appeasing the Russians" and denounced liberal Democrats as "naive dupes." Yet even though the Republicans stood a good chance of winning the White House, they were divided between diehards who supported Taft for president and moderates who favored Eisenhower. Fred Crawford was one of those diehards, as was Robert Wood, who once said that Eisenhower was "a stooge for F. D. Roosevelt; at heart he is a New Dealer." On the other hand, Kodak's Marion Folsom and even some of Wood's own managers worked on the Eisenhower campaign. In the end, the election was devastating for the Democrats. Eisenhower became the first Republican president in twenty years and the Republicans had a majority in both houses for the first time since 1930.[34]

Now the Republicans got to make their first administrative appointments since the New Deal. By and large the people picked by Eisenhower were moderates, including Folsom (who initially went to the Treasury Department) and James Worthy of Sears (who was an undersecretary in the Commerce Department). As for the NLRB, there was disagreement within the administration over how to proceed. Commerce Secretary Sinclair Weeks and some small business groups wanted to repeal all national labor laws and leave the states to regulate union-management relations. Large national firms preferred to keep Taft-Hartley but also wanted either additional pro-management legislation or more employer-sensitive appointments to the NLRB. The latter goal was easier to achieve, partly because in the spring of 1953, Paul Herzog resigned from the NLRB and two other positions opened up as well; the way was clear for a major change in the board's composition. Eisenhower selected Guy Farmer, a management attorney, to head the NLRB and chose another management attorney, Albert Beeson, and an aide to Senator Taft, Philip Ray Rodgers, to fill the other slots.[35]

For the first time in its history, the NLRB had a Republican majority. The Eisenhower board immediately began revising precedents established by prior boards while establishing new standards of its own. One of its first changes was to the *Bonwit-Teller* rule; in the *Livingston Shirt* case, the NLRB decided that employers could give captive-audience speeeches without allowing the union equal time. A raft of free speech cases followed, each of which upheld the employer's position: *Chicopee Manufacturing*, which enunciated a "prophecy doctrine" permitting employers to state that voting for a union might result in a plant being moved; *Southwestern Company*, in which an employer was permitted to tell alien employees they could be deported if they joined a "Communist" union; and *Esquire*, where an employer's threat to answer a pro-union vote with lengthy legal proceedings instead of bargaining was held to be "merely an expression of the employer's legal position." Five years into the Eisenhower board, and ten years after Taft-Hartley, the economist Joseph Shister judged the act's free speech amendment to have had "a dampening effect on new union growth," especially in the retail industry and in the South. Even *Business Week* thought that it had given employers "more weapons to fight union organization."[36]

The Eisenhower board also eased up on company unionism. It was increasingly reluctant to find an independent union to be dominated by an employer and to order its disestablishment. As one appellate court said approvingly, the NLRB no longer had to "baby along employees in the direction of choosing an outside union as their bargaining representative." Rulings like this one gave a stamp of legitimacy to company unions already in existence. None of Thompson's company unions ran into NLRB problems during the 1950s, a sharp contrast to earlier years. Sears, it will be recalled, had hired Nathan Shefferman to set up a company union at its Boston store in the 1930s. When the Clerks tried to organize the store in the early 1950s, they filed charges that Sears dominated the company union. An NLRB trial examiner upheld the charges and recommended that the union be disestablished. The case, however, then went to the Eisenhower board, which overruled its own trial examiner; it refused to disestablish the union and merely ordered Sears to cease assisting it.[37]

Although the legal climate became more favorable to company unions, their establishment rate declined after the mid-1950s. This was not because employers were oblivious to the NLRB's rulings or because they had given up on the idea of using employee groups to deter national unions. Instead, as at Du Pont, employers had come to believe that company unions were too expensive and that they perversely made it easier, not harder, for employees to be persuaded to join national unions. Employers now experimented with alternatives to company unions, including Thompson's "new system" plan and Sears' "rotating committees," both of which were intended to provide a modicum of employee representation but in a form that inhibited wage bargaining and made it difficult for national unions to mount a takeover. A 1959 study of two dozen nonunion firms in an unidentified midwestern city found that nine firms (40 percent) had some kind of representation plan, although only one had a traditional company union. The others had employee committees whose rotating membership was appointed by, and met with, management on a regular basis to discuss workplace issues. Combined with attitude surveys and other psychological techniques, these alternative forms of employee participation would become the basis for the nonunion model of the 1960s and 1970s. The new model was more individualized and emotionally engaging than company unionism, but also more passive, less democratic, and less of a threat to managerial prerogatives. Still, few mourned the passing of the company union.[38]

The Welfare State

In the early 1950s, one could still find critics of social security in the business community, although they were a smaller group than those who disliked the NLRB. Nevertheless, the critics had high hopes when Eisenhower was elected in 1952. Conservative ideologues saw a chance to eliminate a program that made government appear compassionate and necessary; insurance industry executives hoped to get rid of a major competitor. The critics devised an ingenious plan to destroy social security that drew support from congressional conservatives as well as from Oveta Culp Hobby, Eisenhower's new secretary of health, education, and welfare (HEW). But the plan was opposed by administration insiders, notably Marion B. Folsom, then undersecretary of the treasury. Folsom defended social security, arguing that it restrained welfare expenditures for the indigent elderly while preserving, even encouraging, private fringe benefits—the legacy of welfare capitalism. To the critics' dismay, Eisenhower supported a proposal, enacted in 1954, to raise social security benefits and extend coverage to agriculture. Although a modest reform, Folsom judged it "particularly significant" because it "definitely put the Administration and the Republican Party on record as favoring the principles underlying the social security system."[39]

The Republicans had come a long way since 1936, when the presidential candidate Alf Landon called for a repeal of social security. Employers also had changed their positions since then. Most businessmen in the 1930s adamantly opposed social security, especially those who still clung to the welfare capitalist ideal. But by the 1950s they had accepted the idea that old-age pensions and unemployment insurance stabilized the nation's economy. Also by the 1950s, the vast majority of large firms were supplementing social security with corporate pension plans, thus proving that welfare capitalism and the welfare state could coexist.[40]

A key figure in this transformation was Marion Folsom, the self-effacing technocrat who helped design Eastman Kodak's elaborate welfare programs in the 1910s and 1920s. He went to Washington in 1933, where he was one of a handful of businessmen backing the Social Security Act. From 1935 to 1958, Folsom served as Kodak's treasurer and held various posts in government (he replaced Oveta Hobby as HEW secretary in 1955), all the while lobbying for a "mixed" approach to welfare spending,

Welfare capitalism had been badly hurt by the Depression. Private programs had run out of funds, and public opinion, particularly in the North, had shifted in favor of labor and government intervention. In the mid-1930s, it appeared that a welfare state might choke off what remained of welfare capitalism, but Folsom had the ingenuity to see how Kodak and similar companies might profit from the situation. A welfare state financed by payroll taxes would narrow costs between welfare capitalist firms like Kodak and those companies—laggards and traditionalists—that spent little or nothing on welfare benefits.

Social security could not be allowed to displace welfare capitalism, however. Government, said Folsom, should provide only "basic minimum protection and it should not be intended to cover all the needs of everyone." To ensure that workers still looked to employers for security, public benefits had to be kept low and tax incentives were needed to be provided for private programs. As a Washington insider, Folsom lobbied tirelessly to these ends; as a business leader, he tried to persuade other employers that social security was a Keynesian stabilizer, that it was preferable to radical alternatives, and that it could coexist with—and even subsidize—private efforts. That welfare capitalism's benefit plans remained alive and well in the 1950s was due in no small part to Folsom's efforts on behalf of a "basic" welfare state.[41]

In June 1934, President Roosevelt promised the American people "to further the security of the citizen and his family through social insurance . . . to provide at once against several of the disturbing factors in life—especially those that relate to unemployment and old age." Shortly thereafter, Secretary of Labor Frances Perkins appointed a study group, the Committee on Economic Security, to draw up model legislation for unemployment and old-age insurance. The committee, like the president himself, tried to steer a middle course through the political crosswinds whipped up by the Depression.[42]

Among the more radical proposals was the Townsend Old-Age Revolving Pension Plan, devised by a doctor from Southern California. Townsend proposed flat monthly payments of two hundred dollars to everyone over age sixty on the condition that they spend the money within thirty days. Despite claims that the plan made no economic sense (it was to be financed by a national sales tax), Townsend Clubs sprouted up around the nation. Some Townsendites became followers of Father Coughlin, the popular radio priest who led the National Union for Social Justice. Others backed Huey Long's Share Our Wealth plan, which offered massive aid to retirees, parents, farmers, and veterans—all to be paid for by a "soak the rich" tax program. Communists and their allies, including the prominent social worker Mary Van Kleeck, pushed for the Lundeen bill, which proposed a comprehensive welfare state as a way out of the Depression. The bill set unemployment compensation equal to average local wages and promised substantial old-age and sickness benefits for all.[43]

On the other side was the business community, which viewed social security as an abomination. Perceptions were filtered through more general hostility to the Roosevelt administration, which employers blasted for its "bungling effort to regiment American business." The only major management group to sanction social security was the Commerce Department's Business Advisory Council (BAC), made up of the leading corporate practitioners of welfare capitalism. But the council lost several members in 1934 (including managers from giant firms such as General Motors and Du Pont), who quit in a rage over the administration's alleged pro-union sympathies. Fewer than fifty corporations remained in the council, hardly a counterweight to the opposition.[44]

The distance between the two sides was huge, leaving the administration and congressional Democrats divided over how far to tilt in either direction. On the one hand were those seeking rapid relief via a European model of universal, need-based coverage. This was the approach attempted in Ohio, where a 1932 commission proposed an unemployment compensation plan financed by contributions from workers, employers, and government. Through a broad pooling of funds during prosperous times, benefits could be paid to all needy people during periods of depression. When combined with flat pensions, the Ohio plan resembled the Lundeen bill, although social welfare experts who favored the Ohio plan, including I. M. Rubinow and Abraham Epstein, were more cautious and influential than the Lundeen group.[45]

The centrist alternative to the Ohio plan came from followers of the Wisconsin economist John R. Commons, who thought that social programs should mimic private insurance—and welfare capitalism—by using incentives to reduce risk. For workers' compensation and unemployment insurance, this meant tying an employer's tax rate to the claims filed by his employees; as a firm's premiums increased, it presumably would take steps to make the workplace safer and its jobs more stable. For old-age insurance, linking a person's pension level to his previous earnings similarly created an incentive: to remain in the labor force until retirement age. In 1932, Wisconsin enacted an unemployment insurance law based on these ideas. It created separate accounts (employer reserves) for each company in the state; workers could draw only on their own employer's fund. As benefits were paid out, firms paid additional taxes to replenish their reserve accounts, a practice known as experience rating. Abraham Epstein, a sharp critic of welfare capitalism, said that reserve accounts could not reduce layoffs during a depression, nor could they pay benefits as large as those from a pooled fund. The Wisconsin group retorted that the Ohio plan subsidized unstable employers, did nothing to prevent unemployment, and blurred the distinction between social insurance and emergency relief.[46]

The Wisconsin approach essentially adapted the welfare state to welfare capitalism. It emphasized the links between corporate and social efficiency and kept the corporation as a key unit in the social welfare system. Its distinctive gradualism, and the fact that it was the nation's first unemployment insurance law, boosted the reputation of the Commons group. In New York, Governor Roosevelt favored a Wisconsin-style bill, although it failed to pass before he moved to Washington as president. A fiscal conservative, Roosevelt thought public programs should be modeled after private efforts and not along European lines, or what he called "the dole." These predilections stayed with him after he went to Washington, and it came as no surprise that Edwin Witte, a Commons protégé and key player in the battles over the Wisconsin law, was chosen to head the Committee on Economic Security. Other major posts were also taken by members of the Wisconsin group, freezing out backers of the Ohio plan.[47]

At this point social security's fate appeared to be sealed, but this was hardly the case. The Ohio plan and more radical proposals like the Townsend plan had considerable public and congressional support. So did the "do nothing" position taken by many Republicans and employers. What the administration needed were articulate spokespeople who could swing votes in Congress and sway the business community. In the fall, Frances Perkins appointed an Advisory Council on Economic Security made up of ten social welfare experts, five labor leaders, and five employers. Preoccupied with organizing drives and still prone to voluntarism, the AFL was barely involved in the council's work. Not so the employers, all of whom had been prominent welfare capitalists in the 1920s: Morris E. Leeds (Leeds and Northrup), Sam Lewisohn (Miami Copper), Gerard Swope (General Electric), Walter C. Teagle (Standard Oil), and Marion B. Folsom (Kodak). Folsom already had a national reputation for his work developing Kodak's unemployment fund and the Rochester Plan. At forty-one the youngest of the businessmen on the council, he was given the important task of running its subcommittee on unemployment insurance.[48]

In the early days of the Depression, Folsom had thought legislation to be unnecessary if all it meant was substituting a welfare state for welfare capitalism. In testimony to the U.S. Senate in 1931, he called unemployment insurance "impractical, because its administration would be under government control." As for government-funded pensions, he said, they had been tried "in a number of European countries . . . and from what I have learned of their experience, I would not be so keen about having them tried here. We may have to someday, but I do not think we are ready yet. It would simply be turning over one more thing to the State which private employers should take care of." Yet Folsom was increasingly accepting of legislation that would encourage welfare efforts by employers. At a panel sponsored by the U.S. Chamber of Commerce in 1931, several prominent businessmen, including Folsom, asked President Hoover to relax antitrust laws and promote private reserve funds. In the New York legislature, Folsom threw his weight behind a Wisconsin-style bill to require reserve funds, which would have allowed the Rochester Plan to continue while forcing other firms to share the burden.[49]

In early skirmishes between advocates of the Ohio and Wisconsin models, the Rochester Plan was powerful ammunition for the latter. Although the plan was more impressive on paper than in practice—it had failed to attract many employers—its poor showing failed to dampen Folsom's enthusiasm for such private efforts; it did, however, convince him that government had to prod the private sector into participation. Having spent much of 1933 in Washington, heading an NRA committee for the photographic industry, Folsom also became convinced that progressive employers needed to be more engaged in politics. As he told a Procter & Gamble executive, "For some time I have felt that legislation of unemployment insurance might be forestalled by volunteer action on the part of employers in setting up their own plans. I now feel that such action is apt to be so slow that it will not forestall legislation. I now feel it is better for employers to cooperate in the enactment of sound legislation rather than have bills written by those who have had no practical experience."[50]

Over the next several years, Folsom did his best to see that Congress enacted "sound legislation." He pressed vigorously for employer reserves and a contributory pension system, bolstering those in the administration who liked the Wisconsin approach. But because Folsom was a businessman, his priorities differed from those of the administration's policy experts. His chief concerns were to minimize the cost of social security and to preserve an arena for private action. In practice this meant keeping taxes and public benefits to a "basic minimum" while allowing firms with private plans to get tax breaks or opt out of the system entirely. On these matters Folsom was quite persuasive, which raises an important point missed by critics of corporate liberalism: precisely because so many employers opposed social security, the few who endorsed it wielded enormous influence. As the leading spokesperson for that minority, Folsom's opinions carried great weight in Congress and the White House.[51]

In March 1934, Congress opened hearings on the Wagner-Lewis bill, the first New Deal legislation to propose unemployment insurance. Intended as a compromise between the Wisconsin and Ohio plans, the bill proposed a funding mechanism that would permit states to craft their own unemployment insurance systems while being subject to a uniform federal tax. In her efforts to drum up support for the bill, Frances Perkins had difficulty finding employers who would testify on its behalf. Marion Folsom, however, agreed to speak.

Folsom began his testimony with descriptions of Kodak's stabilization policy and the Rochester Plan, which he held out as models for government to promote. He castigated the Ohio approach as "a relief system" and said it was better "to have the employees go to the individual employer for their benefits instead of to the State"; otherwise, "you are bound to have them looking to the State to carry it all the way through." Nevertheless, Folsom recommended federal legislation to ensure that "employers in one state would not be placed at a disadvantage with competitors in other states" and to compel the involvement of smaller firms, the sort that had dropped out of the Rochester Plan. "Speaking for Kodak and for myself," he said, "we realize that legislation will be necessary before such plans are generally adopted." Although he favored federal action, Folsom thought the Wagner-Lewis bill should be delayed until business conditions improved.[52]

Testimony like Folsom's persuaded Perkins to drop the Wagner-Lewis bill and come up with something more attractive. At this point she convened the Committee on Economic Security, which labored throughout the fall of 1934 to produce a new bill. Predictably, there was bitter disagreement between backers of the Ohio and Wisconsin models. Folsom's subcommittee favored the Wisconsin approach, although a more privatized version. It recommended that firms contributing to private unemployment reserves—like Kodak—be allowed to opt out of a state's insurance plan if they met minimum standards. More controversial was Folsom's attempt to gain approval for microregulation-inspired "guaranteed employment plans"; in these, employers who promised year-round jobs, like Procter & Gamble and Sears, would not have to pay unemployment taxes. Finally Folsom focused attention on fiscal matters, urging a cut in the tax rate from 5 percent to 3 percent or less, depending on business conditions. A majority of the committee eventually approved this position.[53]

From Folsom's perspective, the bill was shaping up favorably. Although it did not mandate reserve funds, states would be free to choose between the Ohio and Wisconsin models. The bill also contained other key items, such as experience rating and low taxes, sought by Folsom. Yet in separate testimony to the House and Senate in February 1935, Folsom said the bill was flawed because of a provision—added at the last minute to placate Ohio-plan advocates—requiring firms with reserve plans to pay 1 percent of their payroll to a pooled state fund. The provision, combined with a gradual phasing-in of experience rating, would delay tax reductions for firms with stable employment. "Obviously," said Folsom, "an employer will not do very much about stabilization in 1936 and 1937 on the chance that he might get a reduction in his rate in 1946." Folsom again held up Kodak's stabilization techniques and the Rochester Plan for consideration.[54]

But Folsom's testimony fell on deaf ears in the House, which stripped from the bill all provisions for experience rating and employer reserve accounts. The steps were taken by Republicans opposed to social security and eager, as one representative put it, to "gum up the works." Major business organizations, including the NAM and the Chamber of Commerce, sanctioned these efforts. Folsom became deeply concerned that a bill might pass that offered no federal support for private plans. With the help of the Business Advisory Council, he launched a campaign to reverse the damage done by the House. In April 1935, the council sent Roosevelt a widely publicized report urging him to sanction private reserves and experience rating. Later that month, when the president gave a fireside chat endorsing those items, Folsom crowed, "I heard the president's address and of course was quite pleased at his statement in regard to providing an incentive to stabilize. I felt all along that he was in favor of this."[55]

Folsom's greatest success came in the Senate. The chairman of the Finance Committee, Pat Harrison, said Folsom was the first expert to appear who had practical experience and spoke a language the senators understood. Harrison later asked Folsom to indicate the amendments he wanted. According to Folsom, "I had prepared the wording for different amendments and I went over each one of them, which he copied into his personal copy of the bill." The committee, which included several southerners, asked Folsom, a Georgia native, to be available to confer with them during their deliberations. Although he never was called, Witte said that "Folsom's testimony was frequently quoted in the executive sessions." The senators followed most of Folsom's suggestions. They restored reserve funds and tax credits for stable employers and eliminated the provision that reserve-fund firms pay in to a pooled fund. The changes were contained in the Senate bill, which was passed in June and signed by Roosevelt in August, 1935.[56]

In the ensuing years, experience rating became common practice. By 1939, forty states permitted employers to pay lower taxes if they stabilized employment. Few states, however, went very far in the direction of employer reserve funds. Just seven states permitted such plans, and of these only Nebraska and Wisconsin actually used the system. Most disappointing to Folsom was New York's passage of an Ohio-style plan, with pooled funds, generous benefits, and no mention of reserve funds or experience rating. Folsom bitterly told Witte that as a result of the New York law, "the one plan which . . . does provide greater security to workers—the Rochester Unemployment Plan—will have to be abandoned and the workers now covered by it will receive less protection than they are now getting." The Rochester Plan ceased operation in 1937. But Folsom continued to lobby for experience rating in New York and eventually was successful.[57]

Unlike his approach to unemployment insurance, Roosevelt entered office without any specific intention of aiding the elderly. But pressure from the Townsendites and other groups forced him to develop a scheme calling for pension insurance financed by joint (employer/employee) payroll taxes. Folsom saw public pensions as inevitable but wanted them to be small and inexpensive. Like Roosevelt's advisers, he supported a contributory system because it offered greater fiscal discipline than plans financed by a sales or income tax. Other employers on the advisory council took similar positions. J. Douglas Brown, the administration's pension expert, later said that "the support of progressive industrial executives ensured that a national system of contributory old-age pensions would be recommended to the President and the Congress. . . . Their critical understanding of the need for contributory old-age annuities on a broad, national basis carried great weight with those in authority."[58]

But Folsom parted company with Brown and Witte over a contracting-out provision known as the Clark amendment, which was devised by insurance companies worried that social security would shrink the lucrative corporate pension business. Under the amendment, said Folsom, "smaller firms could turn their money over to a state fund," while bigger firms could "set up their own plans, which would have to meet certain standards." This would have placed welfare capitalists in competition with government to see who could offer better pensions. When Witte refused to include the amendment in the bill, the insurers assiduously lobbied Congress. In May 1935 the Senate added a provision permitting firms to remain outside social security if their pension plans met federal standards.[59]

By then, however, Folsom had lost his enthusiasm for the Clark amendment. The reason was revealed by Craig Cochrane, head of Kodak's personnel department, who told the American Management Association that the amendment would bring undesirable government scrutiny of private pension standards, including "careful accounting of employee contributions and adjustments in cases of separation." In the worst case, "no modification could be made in company plans without reference to Federal authority." Kodak was not the only firm harboring fears of federal regulation. J. Douglas Brown informed Senator Wagner that "key industrial executives are not interested in the proposals which the insurance groups are making for contracting out. They see that they have little, if anything, to gain and something to lose."[60]

With employers showing at most lukewarm interest, Roosevelt dug in his heels and refused to sign a bill containing the amendment. The deadlock was broken when the Senate removed the amendment and formed a committee to report on it. In the spring of 1936, when Congress reconsidered the amendment, Folsom openly opposed it, telling the Chamber of Commerce it would bring "constant supervision" of private pensions. He then outlined a different method for meshing corporate pensions with social security—"the supplemental plan"—which restructured pensions so that employers deducted from their premiums the amount paid to the government in social security taxes. Retirees then would receive two pensions, but the employer's cost would remain the same. Although insurers said firms would abandon pensions without the pressure of the Clark amendment, Folsom predicted that the supplemental approach would preserve private plans and provide an incentive to start new ones.[61]

Another dispute concerned the speed at which the social security fund would be endowed. Folsom wanted this to occur gradually, so as keep tax rates low. He was opposed by Secretary of the Treasury Henry Morgenthau, who favored full-reserve financing and higher tax rates. Morgenthau ostensibly was trying to prevent deficits in the program's later years, but the real reason he wanted higher taxes was to shrink the government's operating deficit. (Payroll taxes, as we know from recent experience, are an easy way to fund budget deficits under the guise of meeting future social security obligations.) Morgenthau convinced Congress to pass his full-reserve plan, much to Folsom's annoyance. Although Folsom staunchly defended the Social Security Act after its passage, he tempered his support with repeated calls to reduce taxes and get rid of full-reserve funding, which he called the "major defect" in the act. Republicans hammered away at the Morgenthau plan, hoping to weaken Roosevelt; the presidential candidate Alf Landon made it an issue in his 1936 campaign. After Landon's defeat, Arthur J. Altmeyer, the new social security commissioner, formed a second advisory council to look into the financing issue. Altmeyer asked Folsom to serve on the council and help select the other employer representatives. The men picked by Folsom were, like himself, critical of the act's fiscal details but well disposed to its larger aims.[62]

Inside the council and in congressional testimony, Folsom repeatedly urged pay-as-you-go financing and lower tax rates. He argued that a large reserve was deflationary and, like many others, blamed the 1937 recession on the Morgenthau plan. Although Folsom was a budding Keynesian, he parted company with those economists who wanted to supplement social security taxes with general revenue funds that could be raised or lowered to stabilize the business cycle. Folsom opposed any recourse to general revenues, fearing that this would loosen the restraints imposed by payroll taxes and allow benefits to rise above the basic level. On all these issues, the council went along with Folsom, and this time Congress did too. In 1939 it substituted a contingency fund for a full reserve, kept the system's financing contributory, and postponed scheduled tax increases from 1940 to 1943.[63]

The business community's hostility to social security verged on the hysterical. Organizations such as the U.S. Chamber of Commerce and the NAM vehemently attacked social security as an "immoral departure from the 'American way.'" More puzzling was opposition from bastions of business progressivism such as the Conference Board. In private, Folsom fumed about the board, which, he said, "has not, in the last few years, sensed what was going on in this country . . . and has consistently argued against the so-called 'social reform' measures." But the Conference Board was not entirely naive. Its opposition was intended to weaken Roosevelt, who was disliked less for his welfare programs than for his tax policies and the Wagner Act. Some employers, however, displayed a passion that went beyond rational calculation: after the Social Security Act was passed, they shunned the Social Security Board and refused to register employees for benefits.[64]

Folsom took it upon himself to convince other businessmen that they were mistaken. Addressing the Chamber of Commerce in 1936, he asked the audience to come to grips with social security and cooperate with the Social Security Board. A year later, he berated the chamber for failing to play a constructive role:

> Now, the result has been that the influence of business organizations has been somewhat discredited and we have not nearly as much to do with the writing of this legislation as we should have had. . . . As our civilization becomes more complex, it is only natural the government will have a little more to do with it than it had in the past. It seems to me the Chamber should study the present situation, see what the trends are, and try to prepare businessmen for changes which are inevitable.[65]

Folsom's efforts at persuasion were more than rhetorical. He worked with the Social Security Board to develop educational programs for business groups and a system for tracking payroll records. Despite this—and despite his success in securing legislation favorable to business—most employers continued to dislike social security. A 1939 poll found just 24 percent of corporate executives wanting to retain the Social Security Act. Of ten major New Deal laws, only three others (one being the Wagner Act) received less support.[66]

But business attitudes began to change during the Second World War. As corporations spent more on fringe benefits, they came to accept social insurance for the same competitive reasons that Kodak had. Hastening this shift was the growing receptivity of businessmen to Keynesianism, including the idea that deficit spending and social insurance programs stabilized aggregate demand. At the center of these developments was Marion Folsom.

Folsom turned out to be right when he predicted that social security would stimulate private pensions. Between 1936 and 1939, a majority of pre-1936 plans were integrated with federal benefits (Sears cut its profit sharing contributions to match social security), while more companies started new pension plans than discontinued old ones. Kodak's supplemental approach was widely publicized and served as a model for other employers. For a small outlay, a company could earn its employees' gratitude by augmenting the inadequate pension paid by the government. Folsom said that the supplemental approach was premised on government's "taking care of the minimum requirements of the individual and not beyond that. . . . If you keep [social security] on a minimum basic protection basis, the individual can supplement it from his own earnings and from any pension which he might derive from his employer."[67]

Uncertainty over tax issues held back the pace of pension-plan adoptions. One unresolved issue was whether payroll taxes had to be paid on fringe benefits like pensions and health care. The law said nothing about this, so Folsom pressed for clarification. "We wanted to do everything we could to encourage fringe benefits," said Folsom, "and if you started to tax them for social security, you'd discourage them." When he helped the Social Security Board set up its record system, he tried to prevent the inclusion of fringe benefits in the government's payroll data. Folsom later raised the issue in testimony to Congress and while serving on the second advisory council. In 1939, Congress specifically exempted fringe benefits from payroll taxes.[68]

Another issue was the tax status of supplemental pension plans. The tax code said that pension plans which discriminated in favor of high-income employees were not exempt from corporate income taxes. A supplemental plan like Kodak's had employers paying a larger pension (relative to wages) to employees earning more than the social security wage ceiling of $3,000 than to those earning less; social security equalized the disparity.[69] It was unclear, however, whether this was discriminatory. Folsom appealed directly to the Bureau of Internal Revenue, which granted Kodak a favorable private ruling in 1941. The ruling was embodied in the Revenue Act of 1942, which said that supplemental plans were nondiscriminatory, even going so far as to describe permissible methods for integrating corporate pensions and social security. The act also contained a hefty war profits tax, which employers could escape by putting excess earnings into certified pension plans. With the tax status of supplemental plans finally resolved, most employers chose to pay excess profits to employees rather than to the government. The result was a second wave of new corporate pension plans that dwarfed the wave of the late 1930s. The government certified 4,208 pension plans between 1942 and 1944, triple the number it had approved during the previous thirteen years. The bulk of these were supplemental plans of the type pioneered by Kodak.[70]

Contributing to the rapid growth of fringe benefits was the War Labor Board's ruling that reasonable health and pension plans were exempt from wartime wage controls. Facing a tight labor market, employers seized on the exemption as a way to attract and retain scarce labor. Organized labor also turned to fringe benefits during the war, especially AFL unions that had previous experience with private benefits. With wages frozen, these unions bargained for benefits and incorporated existing employer plans into their contracts.[71]

Some CIO unions, however, were reluctant to press for fringe benefits, fearing these would strengthen corporate ties at the expense of industrial solidarity. Such fears were not unwarranted. Welfare capitalism's wartime revival was caused not only by tax incentives but also by employers seeking to ward off or weaken labor unions; even old-fashioned recreation activities experienced a renaissance during the 1940s. Labor had a mixed response to this trend. On the one hand, some unions, such as the CIO's Electrical Workers, criticized corporate welfare programs as an anti-union tactic. On the other hand, when unions endorsed welfare benefits and tried to bargain over them, they found employers steadfastly insisting these were a non-negotiable managerial prerogative.[72]

Repelled by employer resistance and pushed by political proclivities, labor turned to Washington, demanding better social security benefits and national health insurance (the Wagner-Dingell-Murray bill). The CIO flexed its muscles in 1944 by creating a political action committee to funnel funds to liberal causes such as national health insurance. But the move to social unionism came just as the tide was turning against labor and liberalism. Employers—including Kodak, Sears, and Thompson—acted swiftly to preempt legislation by sweetening private benefits and lobbying for a freeze on social spending. Folsom, by now the nation's leading corporate expert on social security, criticized labor's efforts to expand social security to include health insurance. It would be better, he argued, "to encourage the more widespread adoption of voluntary plans than to have the Government enter new fields at this time." Folsom sought to delay scheduled payroll tax increases, something Congress went along with in 1943 and again in 1945, 1946, and 1947. With taxes—and thus benefits—frozen, unions gradually came to the realization that they had less political than economic power.[73]

Although he worked to limit social security, Folsom was committed to its basic structure and tried to sway other employers. An important vehicle for this was the Committee for Economic Development (CED), which Folsom founded in 1942 along with Paul G. Hoffman of Studebaker and William Benton of the University of Chicago. Espousing the belief that careful planning could prevent another depression, the CED's star-studded membership included many Business Advisory Council companies, although it went out of its way to recruit from more conservative business groups as well.[74]

To the CED, planning meant both macroeconomic controls and long-term business strategies. At the macroeconomic level, the CED espoused fiscal and monetary policies to achieve price stability and "satisfactory" levels of employment. (It shied away from saying "full employment," which connoted less unemployment than it was willing to tolerate.) Consistent with its conservative Keynesianism, the CED favored passive fiscal policies that would balance the economy with a minimum of government discretion. Such "automatic stabilizers" included unemployment insurance and federal pensions, which bolstered consumption during recessions. The CED wanted to see the duration of jobless benefits extended during recessions, an idea that originated with Folsom.[75]

The CED pumped out a slew of reports that explained to business leaders Keynesian concepts such as deficit financing and aggregate demand. Ideas also were disseminated through the field division, run by Folsom, which included nearly three thousand local groups around the country. The field division helped smaller firms to adopt corporate planning techniques of the sort Kodak developed before the Depression, including strategic marketing and employment stabilization plans. For Folsom, Keynesianism was an extension of microregulation and he hoped the CED could convince others to make the same connection. As with welfare spending, Folsom saw private and public planning as complementary; if business pursued the former, he thought, the latter would be kept within bounds. Early on, the field division encountered resistance from the NAM and the Chamber of Commerce, which feared that the CED's local groups might poach their members. So Folsom negotiated a gentleman's agreement with each organization, saying he would cooperate and also disband the field division after the war. Frederick Crawford, representing the NAM, became an official of the CED's field division, whereas Eric Johnston of the Chamber of Commerce joined the CED's board of trustees.[76]

In 1943, Johnston asked Folsom to chair a new Chamber of Commerce committee on social security. Johnston hoped the committee would prove that the chamber was willing to play a constructive role in debates over social security. In line with this, Folsom developed policy options that the chamber might pursue, including a continued freeze on payroll taxes and an extension of social security to uncovered firms. Folsom said that an extension would promote labor mobility and remove unfair competitive advantages held by uncovered firms. Although logical, his arguments failed to persuade those members who wanted social security repealed, not reformed. To undercut the opposition, Folsom asked the chamber to poll members about his proposals. A small survey was done in 1943 but the results were inconclusive. So Folsom's committee bombarded the membership with a stream of publications, including a periodical called *American Economic Security*. It also sponsored a 1944 national conference on social security and sent copies of the proceedings to every local chapter. That fall, Folsom asked the chamber's board to take another poll. At first the board refused; Folsom's opponents did not want to give him a mandate. But the board finally agreed to hold a referendum. The results, announced at a second conference held in 1945, showed over two-thirds behind the proposal to freeze tax rates and extend social security to uncovered sectors. After a decade of hostility, the chamber now was on record in favor of social security.[77]

Around this time, Crawford and others were forcing the NAM to rethink its approach to the New Deal. After the NAM had won its victory on labor law reform, it was ready to consider social security. A seventy-five-member social security committee was created in 1948, which Folsom was asked to chair. Within several months it issued a report containing many of the same proposals Folsom had made to the Chamber of Commerce four years earlier. But there was one important change—a call for larger pension benefits and higher taxes to fund them. From his service on the 1947 social security advisory council, Folsom had learned the startling fact that welfare benefits for the indigent elderly (old-age assistance) had grown larger than social security pensions. Folsom's efforts to freeze payroll taxes had contributed to this development. But now he worried that old-age assistance—which he disparaged as "charity relief"—might become a substitute for contributory pensions. The danger in this, Folsom warned the NAM, was that old-age assistance was set by the states but funded with federal revenues, making it "subject to terrific pressure for increased benefits." The advantage of contributory pensions was that they "bring home to the individual the fact that benefits are costly and that any increase in benefits would inevitably entail increased contributions on his part." To prevent a long-term increase in costs, the NAM committee went along with Folsom and recommended a hike in social security benefits.[78]

The NAM's board, however, rejected Folsom's report. Endorsing social security would have been a big enough step for the NAM, but a call for higher taxes was asking too much, even though, as Folsom noted, the same position had already been taken by the CED, the Chamber of Commerce, and the Republican party. Folsom felt that insurance companies and Lammot du Pont, an ultraconservative, had pressured the board into rejecting his report. "I doubt if the majority of the board would really agree with Mr. du Pont," he complained to Kodak's president T. J. Hargrave, then a top NAM official.[79]

Folsom did not give up easily. In 1949 his NAM committee produced a second report that spelled out in detail the argument for higher benefits. Social security, it said, "is a sound method of providing basic minimum protection for the aged. The objective should be to strengthen this contributory system so it will not be replaced by a free or relief-type plan." Again the board rejected the report, although the NAM's managing director urged Folsom to do some further work on it. After additional revisions, the board sanctioned the report—and social security—in 1950. Much of the credit for the NAM's historic turnaround must go to Folsom, but there were larger forces at work as well.[80]

In 1949, organized labor started an abrupt and unexpected drive for private pension benefits. This was triggered by a series of related events: first, in the famous *Inland Steel* case of 1948, the NLRB ruled that employers had a legal obligation to bargain with unions over pension benefits; the U.S. Supreme

Court upheld this ruling the following year. Meanwhile, the steel strike of 1949 ended when a presidential fact-finding panel recommended pensions and other benefits in lieu of wage increases. Shortly thereafter, Ford and the Automobile Workers (UAW) signed a model contract containing a pension plan. With these agreements setting the pattern, organized labor pushed for pensions on a broad front. Total coverage in 1950 was 50 percent higher than in 1945 and rose by another 70 percent between 1950 and 1955. As Folsom told a wage control board set up during the Korean War, "I felt all along that Social Security was to provide bare subsistence levels, and it was up to the company and the individual to build on that base. But it was only a year before Korea that that became accepted."[81]

Most unions followed nonunion Kodak by negotiating supplemental pensions integrated with social security. Some of the union plans, especially those in heavy industry, took a niggardly approach to integration. They fixed an overall benefit from which a worker's social security benefit was deducted. This created an incentive for employers to favor higher public pensions, because any increase in public benefits would result in lower total costs to the firm. Indeed, the large auto and steel manufacturers lined up behind a bill to raise social security benefits by about 80 percent. Regardless of the type of integrated plan, however, the spread of private pensions caused employers to see the competitive logic of broadening the social security burden. The NAM, the Chamber of Commerce, and other business groups solidly backed a 1950 plan to extend social security to more than ten million uncovered workers. By 1953, when another extension was being discussed, Folsom said, "You didn't find any business people against social security."[82]

There was one remaining issue, however: national health insurance. Back in the 1930s, Kodak—like most companies—provided few health benefits, so it had no reason to encourage government activity in this area. Folsom thought a purely voluntary approach was preferable and, as if to prove his point, Kodak announced an innovative hospital insurance plan in 1935. Anticipating the future, Folsom discussed with Arthur Altmeyer the possibility that national health insurance might someday be run like unemployment insurance, with employers given the right to contract out or be taxed less if their health "experience" was good. But this was pure speculation. When the issue came before the social security advisory council, Folsom spoke against it and no action was taken.[83]

By the early 1950s, however, competition between organized labor and nonunion firms was causing rapid improvements in private-sector health coverage. The number of unionized workers covered by health plans increased sharply during the war, more than doubled between 1945 and 1947, and rose steadily thereafter. Although Kodak had one of the most munificent private health plans in the nation, the company could not rest on its laurels. Doing so would have left it vulnerable to an organizing drive, something its executives dreaded. So Kodak initiated a major medical plan in 1953—among the nation's first for blue-collar workers—followed by retiree health benefits in 1954. At Sears, too, competition from unions over welfare benefits caused management to worry: "our lead has been considerably narrowed," said Clarence Caldwell.[84]

With private plans proliferating, Folsom shed his opposition to federal health insurance. While head of the U.S. Department of Health, Education, and Welfare from 1955 to 1958, Folsom had to toe the administration's line on retiree health insurance, but after he left HEW and returned to Rochester to serve as a Kodak director, he began to speak out in favor of it. Outraged physicians branded him a "socialist," yet Folsom's support for what later became the Medicare program grew out of a longstanding quest to have government provide basic insurance as a complement to existing private programs.[85]

In 1957, the number of social security beneficiaries reached the ten million mark, an event that prompted Folsom, then secretary of HEW, to dwell on the program's history: "Social security did not lower the standard of living or kill individual thrift, as was predicted by critics of this system in early years"; rather, he said, it "plays an important role in maintaining economic growth" and provides "a foundation upon which to build additional security through private effort." Folsom doubtless felt great satisfaction as he surveyed the development of social security; not only had he outlived many of its critics, but he had also achieved his main objective: a welfare state imbued with market principles and sufficiently parsimonious to preserve a role for private welfare capitalism.[86]

To American labor, the prospect of bargaining for benefits proved an irresistible lure. For the AFL, this turn marked a continuation of earlier voluntarist patterns, while for the CIO it was a pragmatic alternative to a European-style welfare state. That the CIO felt this way reflected attempts by Folsom and others to block payroll tax increases and national health insurance. One might think Folsom's efforts inadvertently backfired because they forced nonunion companies to compete with organized labor over fringe benefits, but nonunion employers preferred such competition to a comprehensive welfare state. Kodak, Sears, and Thompson found it easy—albeit costly—to match or exceed union benefit gains, whereas a generous welfare state would have displaced competition into areas where large nonunion firms might not so easily have won.

The Behavioral Sciences and Human Relations

For all of Folsom's genius, his efforts on behalf of private benefits boiled down to preserving traditional welfare capitalism. The "fringes" Kodak regularly rolled out in the 1950s were based on the same tenets of economic paternalism that had been around since the nineteenth century. On the other hand, the personnel activities inspired by the behavioral sciences—such as attitude surveys and nondirective interviewing—took a different and relatively new approach to securing worker loyalty and cooperation. As compared to traditional welfare capitalism, the new approach was less mercenary and paternalistic and it drew more heavily on resources outside the corporation, such as universities, private consultancies, and government-subsidized research.

In the management literature of the 1940s and 1950s, activities inspired by the behavioral sciences were lumped together as "human relations," a term associated with the Hawthorne project at Western Electric. The Hawthorne research—as popularized by Mayo, Roethlisberger, and others—was enormously influential; workplace applications of behavioral science went far beyond the Hawthorne experiments, however. Most of the industrial research and consulting done after World War II was carried out by a single professional group—psychologists—whereas the Hawthorne research had been an interdisciplinary endeavor drawing on anthropology, psychiatry, and sociology as well as psychology. Also, the most widely used psychological device in industry were employee selection tests, whose development and refinement had little to do with the Hawthorne experiments.

Nevertheless, Hawthorne was the inspiration for many of management's wide-ranging efforts to *change* employee attitudes. Some of these efforts were one-on-one activities, like nondirective interviewing and employee counseling. Less common were attempts to modify attitudes by changing the culture or structure of an entire organization (as in the work at Sears on morale and store size). The most popular activities were those focused on the middle level between the individual and the organization—the work group—which had so fascinated the Hawthorne researchers. The key figure at this level was the group leader; in practice, leadership training meant telling supervisors how to be sensitive, "employee-centered," and fair. Along with this training came experiments in employee participation and team dynamics.

Human relations touched all parts of industry, although the more innovative activities originated in the nonunion sector, where firms had the freedom to act without union consent and anticipated a potentially larger payoff from investing in behavioral science. Even so, some unionized employers recognized that human relations offered a powerful tool for corporatizing the work force and undermining workers' emotional attachments to unionism. As three prominent psychologists put it, "In the competition between employers and unions . . . whichever side achieves a more accurate and deeper understanding of the motivations involved to that extent improves its ability to accomplish its own purposes." By changing workers' minds, behavioral science could change the balance of power between unions and management as much as, if not more than, the legal doctrines defining the parties' formal relationships.[87]

The Hawthorne project originated in Elton Mayo's adroit coupling of a research site (AT&T's Western Electric division) with intellectual and monetary resources (the Harvard Business School and the Rockefeller Foundation). As other corporations and universities established similar ties, often with additional funding from government, the behavioral sciences spread rapidly throughout industry. For the principals, it was a symbiotic relationship: behavioral scientists gained financial support and research opportunities; employers received cutting-edge technical assistance and the legitimacy conferred by association with respected and avowedly neutral research institutions.

That university researchers were perceived as a third party, holding no brief for management, was helpful in overcoming what psychologists referred to as the "bias of the auspices": that is, the fact that employees are less likely to speak truthfully to their employer or someone representing him than to an impartial observer. When surveying attitudes, for example, employers took steps to encourage a sense of anonymity—locking "ballot boxes," omitting coding numbers on questionnaires, and asking employees to remove badges before entering the survey room. After the Pitney-Bowes Company hired researchers from Dartmouth's Tuck School of Business to conduct an attitude survey, workers were given a brochure containing the Tuck staff's credentials as well as photographs of the campus, of sealed questionnaire cartons being loaded into a car headed for Dartmouth, and of the Tuck researchers tabulating the survey data. When Thompson Products conducted its first survey in 1944, employees were asked to return the forms, unsigned, to Dr. Clyde Crobaugh of Fenn College so as to "insure the complete anonymity of the survey as well as to obtain an accurate, scientific tabulation of the results."[88]

The University of Chicago's Committee on Human Relations in Industry (CHRI) was one of the first university-based behavioral science consultancies modeled after the Mayo group. Organized in 1943, the CHRI had a half-dozen or so corporate supporters, local firms like Container Corporation of America, Link-Belt, and Sears. The companies paid a substantial fee in return for having faculty conduct research on their personnel problems. Initially Burleigh Gardner was CHRI's executive secretary, and W. Lloyd Warner chaired the group; other faculty members included Allison Davis, Robert J. Havighurst, Frederick H. Harbison, Everett C. Hughes, and William Foote Whyte, who took over as executive secretary in 1946. The CHRI's major contributor and customer, by far, was Sears. Burleigh Gardner's work at Sears during the mid-1940s was performed under CHRI auspices; in turn, Gardner taught his Chicago students how to conduct nondirective interviews. Gardner's old teacher, Lloyd Warner, delivered a series of evening talks to Sears' merchandising managers on "Social Class and Its Relevance to Sears," while Gardner and Warner held after-dinner seminars for the company's top executives on organizational structure, social dynamics, and employee morale. Sears was not unique in having a close relationship to social scientists in academia, although few other firms at the time cultivated those relationships as carefully as Sears did.[89]

Also supported by Sears was the Industrial Relations Center at the University of Chicago. The center was headed by Robert K. Burns, an entrepreneurial academic who understood that applied behavioral research was potentially lucrative. In addition to his job at the center, Burns was co-owner of Science Research Associates (SRA), an educational testing and publishing company that, together with Lyle Spencer, he had founded in the late 1930s with start-up capital from General Wood, among others. Around 1949, Sears approached the Industrial Relations Center for help in developing a new attitude questionnaire that would be less cumbersome to administer than the existing survey. Faced with the growing power of the Teamsters and the Clerks, Sears wanted the ability to identify quickly "the vulnerability of any operating unit to unionization in the face of a direct union threat." Sears also sought a more psychometrically refined instrument; the existing organization survey had been designed without concern for what James Worthy called "the niceties of statistical method and of questionnaire construction."[90]

Burns put together a team of Chicago faculty and graduate students to develop what came to be known as the Employee Inventory (EI). The group included L. L. Thurstone, the renowned psychologist who for years had been devising selection tests for Sears; Melany Baehr, one of Thurstone's students; and David Moore, Burleigh Gardner's former assistant at Sears and a sociology instructor at Chicago. By applying item analysis, factor analysis, and other statistical techniques, the EI team was able to produce a self-administering questionnaire, simple enough to permit Sears to survey all its employees annually. With the EI, said a Sears manager, the company would do a better job of predicting, when unionization threatened, "how many potentially might join if the right kind of appeals were made to them."[91]

As part of its agreement with Burns, Sears permitted SRA to publish the EI and sell it to other companies. By having SRA market the new questionnaire, Sears hoped to gain access to data on morale levels at other companies. SRA saw that there was no money to be made in selling reusable booklets and throw-away answer sheets, so it set up a facility for scoring the results and hired a former Sears manager to run it. Easy to use and bearing a solid academic pedigree, the inventory soon became industry's most popular employee attitude questionnaire. By 1959, the EI had already been used by more than one thousand companies. Because so many firms purchased the survey, SRA was able to develop norms that allowed Sears and other users to compare their EI scores to national averages. Other universities were quick to jump on the survey bandwagon, including Michigan, Cal Tech, and Minnesota. Minnesota's Industrial Relations Center developed its own questionnaire, the Attitude Scale, though it had less commercial success than the EI.[92]

Although universities possessed an aura of scientific neutrality, they also came freighted with research agendas that interfered with management's desire for confidentiality and quick results. Also, university personnel occasionally annoyed employers by insisting that an established union be included in the survey design or by refusing to do a survey if an organizing drive was under way. Hence employers often preferred to hire private consultants to conduct attitude surveys and run other behavioral science programs. Like academic researchers, consultants could project an image of independent professionalism that reassured employees and headed off any "bias of the auspices." Consultants also were more capable than company managers of addressing touchy subjects. As a Conference Board official explained, "being apart from management and an expert in survey matters, [the consultant] can call the shots as he sees them. He can warn of possible pitfalls and advise management of the most likely procedures to use." On the other hand, consultants—if they wanted to stay in business—had to be tactful and circumspect. As Burleigh Gardner, himself a consultant to Sears and many other firms, explained, "Frequently presidents and vice presidents talk about the need for concern for employees, yet in their daily actions on the job, it is clear that they are basically autocratic. . . . The consultant has to work with the realities of the situation, and, when change is needed, must find a way to influence the top level."[93]

In the 1940s, a number of private consulting firms—including Benge Associates, Stech Associates, and others—began selling specialized "human relations" services to industry, promising a more refined and cleaner approach than that offered by Shefferman's Labor Research Associates. Another group of consultants—those who conducted market surveys and opinion polls for industrial clients, including Opinion Research Corporation, Gallup, and Roper—extended their expertise to include employee attitude surveys. Even Industrial Relations Counselors, the welfare capitalist consultancy founded in the 1920s with Rockefeller money but tainted at the LaFollette hearings by its association with the Special Conference Committee, resurfaced in the 1950s as a provider of technical information on behavioral science developments.[94]

Some behavioral scientists entered the human relations business by setting up their own consulting outfits while maintaining their university positions. This gave them the best of both worlds: they retained the university's prestige but could give advice without either the openness or revenue sharing that characterized university research. Psychological Corporation, for example, was a consortium of academically employed psychologists who hired themselves out to industry. Another example was Social Research Incorporated, a consultancy founded in 1946 by Burleigh Gardner and W. Lloyd Warner. Although Gardner resigned his academic position to head up Social Research Incorporated, he maintained close ties to the University of Chicago through Warner and the graduate students he regularly hired to work for the consultancy. Until the mid-1950s, Social Research Incorporated derived most of its income from Sears, studying employee and customer attitudes. The consultancy also administered psychological tests to Sears managers, including an experimental program using thematic apperception tests (TATs). Whereas Psychological Corporation stuck to fairly narrow and quantitative industrial psychology, Social Research Incorporated—true to its roots—maintained an interdisciplinary orientation with a heavy emphasis on social anthropology.[95]

Companies on the psychological cutting edge—like Kodak, Sears, and IBM—occasionally branched out into the human relations business themselves by packaging their own successful programs and selling them to other firms. Essentially this is what Sears did with its EI, though it allowed SRA to market the questionnaire. Kodak, which was widely recognized as having one of industry's most advanced foreman training programs, developed a series of training films that it sold to other firms in the late 1940s and 1950s. The idea for the films originated with the Vocafilm Company, which, in the 1930s, had worked with Kodak and the National Association of Manufacturers in developing a series of sound-slide films (based on Kodak's Code of Industrial Relations) showing how a model code of personnel policies could be applied effectively. After the war, Vocafilm approached Kodak to see if it had any interest in filming its supervisory training program for use internally and at other companies. By then, Kodak had a clinical psychologist and a psychiatrist on staff, and these men, together with Allen Gates of Kodak's training department, developed a series of eight films dealing with such topics as human nature, feelings, subconscious motives, problem solving, getting ideas across, and "adjusting problems." With the films came a set of handbooks that included human relations truisms such as the following:

Pattern for Appealing to Feelings

1. Develop a thorough understanding of common human wants or urges, the things that satisfy when they are obtained and dissatisfy when they are denied.

2. In so far as possible, get to know what each individual values, so that the cause of his feelings, good or bad, can be understood.

3. Avoid doing things in such a way that feelings and attitudes will be adversely affected because of natural human wants.

4. Deal with the individual in such a way you will appeal to, rather than against, things you know he values.

5. In other words, add a "personal truth" when dealing with people.[96]

During the war, the federal government began to pursue research in the behavioral sciences, and Kodak's film series was an extension of the War Manpower Commission's highly successful Training Within Industry (TWI) plan. Developed by academic proponents of human relations such as Fritz Roethlisberger, and overseen by executives from Standard Oil and Western Electric, the TWI courses in human relations were given to nearly a half-million foremen during the war, who were told to "work with people" and "treat people as individuals." TWI boasted that the course raised war production by reducing the incidence of grievances in defense plants. At the very least, the government's underwriting of TWI meant that human relations ideas were diffused widely throughout American industry.[97]

TWI was one of many ways the federal government helped the behavioral sciences become an acceptable instrument for administering modern bureaucracies. The single largest project was refining the army's personnel classification and selection system, including its IQ tests. Other behavioral scientists joined the War Department's Morale Services Division, which conducted more than 250 surveys of soldier attitudes; many of these surveys—such as those relating troop morale to combat performance—had immediate relevance to industry. Because it was important to win the war on the home front as well as overseas, the Office of War Information employed polling organizations like Gallup and Roper, as well as academic social psychologists such as Rensis Likert, to study civilian attitudes. The Office of War Information was particularly interested in the morale of the nation's defense workers and its relationship to productivity and absenteeism, issues that Likert's group studied by surveying workers in shipyards and other defense plants.[98]

After the war, Likert's group became the core of the new Institute for Social Research at the University of Michigan, which, like similar organizations at other universities, prospered in the postwar years because of government's continued interest in subsidizing applied research in the behavioral sciences. Much of the research support came from the military, which saw troop and employee morale as analogous problems. The Office of Naval Research paid for the Ohio State leadership studies, while the air force requisitioned several major academic projects applying factor analysis to employee morale. The subjects in these studies were employees of corporations producing civilian, not military, goods. The Institute for Social Research conducted a landmark series of studies on morale, supervision, and performance that were paid for by the Office of Naval Research but carried out at companies such as Caterpillar, Studebaker, Detroit Edison, and Prudential Life Insurance. With steady funding from the government, the behavioral sciences took off in the 1950s: three times as many studies relating job factors to employee attitudes were published between 1950 and 1954 than had appeared between 1940 and 1944. The nexus of ties among government, corporations, and behavioral scientists was not unique: it resembled similar networks developing in the 1950s around other technologies such as nuclear energy, electronics, and aeronautics. Hence the proliferation of the applied behavioral sciences can be seen as yet another technological offshoot of the Cold War, a "soft" adjunct to the military-industrial complex.[99]

While conducting attitude surveys for Detroit Edison in the late 1940s, the Institute for Social Research refined the technique known as "survey feedback," which originally had been developed at Sears and Thompson Products. At Detroit Edison, survey findings were presented to employees through an interlocking chain of group meetings that took place over a two-year period following the survey. The company's top executives first discussed the findings and planned remedial actions, and they held similar meetings with their immediate subordinates. The process was repeated all the way down the hierarchy to the first-line supervisors and their work groups. According to the institute's researchers, this consultative approach was a powerful tool for changing attitudes, causing workers to identify with the survey and be more ready to accept corrective measures. The group meetings also had symbolic value, allowing management to demonstrate concern for employees and their opinions.[100]

Survey feedback developed out of the participatory management ideas of Kurt Lewin and his followers at MIT's Research Center for Group Dynamics. Lewin's research showed that democratic leadership styles and employee participation in group decision making resulted in higher productivity than did traditional styles of management. Because participation caused both morale *and* productivity to rise, the Lewinites arrived at the same conclusion as Elton Mayo and his followers had: that conflict in the workplace could be eradicated by a more enlightened, integrative approach to workplace management. This was essentially the same notion that had infused welfare capitalism since the early 1900s, although this time around it was footnoted with empirical corroboration.[101]

Mayo's human relations writings came in for a barrage of criticism in the 1950s, although the Lewin group largely escaped reproach. One obvious reason was ideological: Lewin espoused Deweyan principles of democratic participation—albeit a tightly circumscribed version of democracy—in contrast to Mayo's elitist embrace of leadership. Laborist liberals of the 1950s could find implicit support for trade unions in Lewin's theories, whereas Mayo's work, like that of earlier corporatists, denigrated unions. And whereas Mayo's laborist critics contended that "high employee morale" was merely a euphemism to describe workers who were "happy, contented, but typically docile," it was difficult to pin a charge of docility on Lewin's autonomous, participative work groups.[102]

Another reason for the different treatment of Lewin and Mayo had to do with timing: leadership training, attitude surveys, and other practices inspired by Mayo were widespread in the 1950s—especially in large nonunion firms—whereas participative groups did not take hold until after the debate on human relations had died down. One can find instances of small-group participation before the 1960s—Thompson's "new system" plants, for example, and Sears' rotating committees—but these groups did not usually permit workers to be directly involved in making decisons. Nevertheless, experience with such groups prepared companies for more radical forms of employee involvement. When small-group participation finally caught on in the 1970s, nonunion firms like Thompson (by then TRW) led the way.

Finally, the Mayoites, despite their prestigious affiliations, lacked the disciplinary credentials of the Lewin group. Lewin and his followers, nearly all of them social psychologists, documented their research in mainstream psychological journals and otherwise kept up their academic connections. The Mayoites, on the other hand, had no disciplinary mooring and presented most of their findings in popular books and magazines. This made them vulnerable to claims that their work was sloppy and tainted by unscientific, pro-management biases. "These men," charged the historian Loren Baritz in his 1960 study, *The Servants of Power*, "have been committed to aims other than those of their professional but non-industrial colleagues." Yet as Baritz no doubt realized, scientific professionalism and the objectivity imposed by academic journals in themselves did not guarantee unbiased inquiry. Those affiliated with Lewin's center and the Institute for Social Research were scientific professionals, but they also were pragmatic realists who pursued lines of research that government and industry were willing to fund. As relationships between industry and academia became increasingly articulated, academic behavioral scientists found themselves vulnerable to their own "bias of the auspices."[103]

Management's Jihad

The behavioral sciences had numerous industrial applications outside the workplace, as well as inside. Long before companies began surveying employee attitudes, they hired psychologists to conduct similar research on customers and other consumers. J. David Houser, who designed Sears' first employee survey, got his start after World War I doing consumer surveys for public utility companies. Other prominent consultants in this area included A. C. Nielsen and Market Research Corporation of America. Market researchers soon discovered that their survey methods—including causal analysis and sampling theory—could easily be extended to political opinions. George Gallup, Archibald Crossley, and Elmo Roper, all well known as pollsters today, began their careers in market research. Their reputations in the political arena were established after they successfully predicted Franklin D. Roosevelt's landslide victory in the 1936 presidential election. Like the rest of the behavioral sciences, polling got another boost during the Second World War, when the government hired Gallup, Claude Robinson, and other pollsters to assess the political views of civilians in Europe and at home.[104]

After the war, pollsters did a brisk business conducting public opinion surveys for corporations and employer organizations. Claude Robinson's Opinion Research Corporation, based in Princeton, New Jersey, surveyed the public on topics such as "Collectivist Ideology in America" and "Collectivism and Economic Ignorance," and then sold the results to private companies. Eager to cash in on a trend, other consultants—including Gallup, Psychological Corporation, and Burleigh Gardner's Social Research Incorporated—carried out customized evaluations of corporate communications activities. In the mid-1950s, Social Research did a huge survey (co-funded by Sears and AT&T) assessing public attitudes toward big business. The survey found that the public viewed Sears as "serving and unselfish" and that the company had an especially good reputation among teachers and professors.[105]

Companies like Sears had more than idle curiosity about the political views of their employees and customers. From the late 1940s through the early 1960s, American business spent millions on an ideological holy war against the twin evils of collectivism and statism. The corporate compulsion to sway public opinion was a sign that, despite the prosperity of the postwar years, employers were less confident than they had been before the Depression. Although business remained enormously powerful after the war, employers were concerned that the United States was becoming a "laboristic" society. These fears were not entirely unfounded; government spending as a percentage of the gross national product rose nearly 50 percent from 1929 to 1946, while private-sector union density increased by more than 300 percent in the same period.[106]

The Depression had tarnished industry's credibility, but the war restored some luster to businessmen's reputations. Business felt sufficiently self-assured after the war to challenge its ideological competitors. There were other factors, too, that made the postwar years an auspicious moment to mount a holy war on behalf of free enterprise. The public mood was swinging in a conservative direction, seeking a check on New Deal activism and an assertive labor movement, while the outbreak of the Cold War bolstered business's efforts to portray liberalism as a precursor to Stalinism, and labor as communistic. Most businessmen however, realized that although the historical moment was propitious to their cause, there was no chance of going back to the palmy days of welfare capitalism. Like Kodak's Marion Folsom, they understood that modern welfare capitalism would have to coexist with "big" labor and "big" government; at best, business could claim to be the most important part of the new tripartite society. This loss of authority, combined with the dark fears unleashed by the Cold War, gave business's pronouncements an often desperate and apocalyptic tone, unlike the buoyant boosterism of the 1920s.[107]

Although pollsters and psychologists contributed to the holy war, much of the propaganda was cooked up by a motley crew of consultants skilled in the arts of mass communications: advertising, media technology, and public relations. Practitioners of these arts lacked the academic credentials of the behavioral scientists, a deficiency that drove some of them to seek legitimacy through professional associations, specialized jargon, and university appointments. Advertising and public relations journals were started, along with communications departments at some universities. Edward L. Bernays, who taught the first public relations course at New York University in the 1920s, expressed these professional aspirations in his claim that "the ability to estimate group reactions on a large scale over a wide geographic and psychological area is a specialized ability which must be developed with the same painstaking self-criticism and with the same dependence on experience that are required for the development of the clinical sense in the doctor or surgeon." Nevertheless, for every Bernays who sought to professionalize public relations there were plenty of rank amateurs willing to pitch business's free-enterprise palaver.[108]

As with other efforts to solidify modern welfare capitalism, large nonunion firms were overrepresented in the campaign against collectivism. Many were led by ideologues like Thompson's Fred Crawford and Sears' General Wood, whose distaste for unionism stemmed from the same philosophical roots as their distrust of government. Nonunion firms also took the lead in developing new channels for communicating these values to their employees; although much of business's propaganda was aimed at the general public, the workplace remained a vital target in the ideological battle. Factories and offices were inundated with pamphlets, magazines, and books full of homilies on the virtues of free enterprise. Book racks of anti-Communist literature appeared in the plants, where workers also listened to lectures and watched color movies explaining how to identify subversives.

The business community's public relations campaign started in the mid-1930s, when the NAM hired Walter Weisenberger, a former journalist, to head its publicity department. Weisenberger raised funds to pay for a series of radio, magazine, and newspaper advertisements that portrayed the American employer as a self-made man under attack by the enemies of freedom. "Put *yourself* in his place!" the ads exhorted. The ads were mild by postwar standards, but the LaFollette committee nevertheless criticized them for ignoring the economy's "weaknesses and abuses" and for claiming "that nothing was wrong and that grave dangers lurked in the proposed remedies."[109]

As president of the NAM in 1942–1943, Crawford reproduced at a national level the kind of hard-hitting propaganda Thompson was known for in Cleveland. With business confidence waxing, Crawford found it easy to get other employers to support a renewed offensive against the New Deal. As one NAM publication stated, "the time is now ripe to show the public how business, successfully sold, operating under the free enterprise banner, can lead the way into a peaceful era of new opportunities and higher living standards." And Crawford was just the person to lead the way. He combined boundless energy with what one journalist described as "a religious faith in the private enterprise system." He also had the talent to translate abstract economic ideas into "simple, vivid stories which he tells to NAM audiences as well as to his own employees." Under Crawford, the NAM's economic diatribes became more personal, with allegories about the Old Prospector, Joe the Umbrella Maker, and Tony the Sweeper. For *Reader's Digest*, Crawford wrote an article, "The American Triangle of Plenty," that portrayed management as the beleaguered but essential conciliator of demands made by customers, stockholders, and employees. The NAM reprinted the article in pamphlet form and distributed more than four million copies nationwide.[110]

Stripped to bare essentials, the NAM's propaganda revealed a pre-Depression faith in the axioms of laissez-faire economics: business was the goose that laid the golden eggs, so long as she was left undisturbed by government and labor. Unlike the CED, which believed government could stabilize the economy, the NAM rejected Keynesian activism. NAM publications rarely mentioned specific legislation or political parties; economic ideas were presented as parables—Crawford's approach—or as abstract principles, as in the two-volume study commissioned when Crawford was chairman of the NAM, *The American Individual Enterprise System*, which contained contributions from conservative economists such as Ludwig von Mises. The NAM was less concerned with teaching economics, however, than with undermining the social changes wrought by the New Deal. Its publications insisted that higher corporate productivity was the only way to maintain an affluent society. Collective bargaining and social spending—the New Deal's Keynesian prescriptions for prosperity—contributed nothing to productivity and threatened to subvert the work ethic that had made America great. This was the message trumpeted by the NAM in the 1940s. As Crawford told a group of businessmen in 1944, "We can sell our products but we haven't sold the simple truths of what industry really means, within our local communities. . . . I think we are going to use public relations more and more to help the public understand . . . the process of creating wealth. . . . The old fundamental economic principles, upon which this country is built, have become so obscured that it is difficult now to even locate some of them."[111]

Under Crawford, the NAM began to teach its members many tricks of the public relations trade, including several that Crawford had pioneered at Thompson. NAM publications instructed managers to pay informal visits to the shop floor, hold open houses for workers and their families, send letters to workers' homes, and make regular use of bulletin boards, newspapers, and local advertising. Out of the NAM's national office came a steady flow of pamphlets explaining "what makes our economic system click," along with news releases, clippings, and advertising boilerplate that members could customize for their own use. The NAM appointed a committee in 1945 to analyze its public relations activities and make suggestions for improving them. After the committee recommended using public-opinion surveys to fine-tune propaganda, the NAM hired Opinion Research Corporation for this purpose. Claude Robinson presented the survey results at the 1946 NAM convention, warning the gathered executives that the public still distrusted them: "You fellows are thought to be wonderful producers. . . . Technically, you are great guys. But a large segment of the public thinks that you . . . worship the dollar sign. You are thought to be cold-blooded. You put property rights above human rights. That is one reason, says the public, why unions are necessary to protect the working-man." Robinson's conclusions were hardly startling; management had to do a better job of public relations: "Dramatize the fact that industry's goal is to serve the public. . . . Declare your devotion to the public's goals, make it perfectly clear to the public that the thing you seek is the public good. . . . Talk more about the things you are for rather than the things you are against."[112]

Although this all sounded easy enough, some employers felt uneasy speaking out. The law required unionized managers to discuss wages and working conditions only with the union and sharply limited what any manager could say during an organizing drive. Crawford urged the nation's managers to drop their inhibitions and tell "the blunt truth about the threats that are everywhere closing in upon the free way of life" in the nation. "This is still free America," he said, "and the protection of the Constitution extends to management. You have the right to speak to your people on any subject you choose, and I urge you to exercise this right of free speech." Crawford's manifest objective was to promote free enterprise, though he also hoped to build a constituency for labor law reform.[113]

The end of the war, followed by passage of Taft-Hartley, rising McCarthyism, and the desolation of the CIO's left-wing unions, had a curious effect on employers. Instead of basking in victory, they intensified their public relations campaign and began using strident anti-union rhetoric that previously had been outside the realm of mainstream discourse. The reasons for this shift had partly to do with Taft-Hartley's free-speech clause and the expansive interpretation given to it by Eisenhower's NLRB appointees. With a favorable legal environment and with radical labor on the defensive, unionized employers like General Electric felt less cautious about the remaining legal limits on their conduct. Throughout the 1950s, Lemuel Boulware, formerly a GE marketing executive, ran a massive anti-union communications program that included dramatized "road shows" (some starring Ronald Reagan) and numerous publications. Boulware based the program on survey research that told GE what its employees (its "job customers") were thinking and feeling.[114]

As employers grew self-assured, right-wing fringe groups became more visible and influential within the business community. These groups ran the gamut from specialized anti-union or isolationist organizations (for example, the American Security Council and American Action) to multi-issue lobbying groups (the John Birch Society, the American Enterprise Association, America's Future, and many others). The groups served as shock troops in business's holy war, clearing the way for more centrist organizations like the NAM and the U.S. Chamber of Commerce. Yet close ties existed between the mainstream and the fringe. Many members of the NAM's executive committee in the late 1940s and 1950s actively supported, and donated heavily to, ultraconservative groups. Nonunion employers were prominently associated with the radical right, including executives from Eli Lilly (the Committee for Constitutional Government), Du Pont (the Foundation for Economic Education), and Sears, whose chairman, General Robert E. Wood, supported nearly every right-wing group of the postwar era.[115]

Wood initially became identified with conservatism in 1940, when he agreed to head the isolationist America First Committee. Wood's involvement with America First, and his refusal to disavow an anti-Semitic speech given by Charles Lindbergh at an America First rally, quickly made him into a controversial public figure. To conservatives, Wood was a celebrity—someone who knew personally many members of the corporate elite and who donated generously to reactionary causes. (Probably because of his rising political prominence, in 1941 Wood was the first person from the retailing field to serve on the NAM's executive committee in over a decade.) To liberals, however, Wood was an anathema: Secretary of the Interior Harold Ickes accused him of being a "fellow traveler" of Nazism. Although Wood supported American participation in the war after the attack on Pearl Harbor, he reverted to isolationism and right-wing activism as soon as the war was over.[116]

Wood, a veteran of the anti-chain store battles, understood well the power of public relations. He backed conservative journalists such as George Sokolsky and Clifton Utley, and was a central figure in American Action—an organization established in 1945 to counteract the CIO's political action committees. In the early 1950s, Wood worked with Alfred Kohlberg, a New York textile magnate and charter member of the John Birch Society, to investigate the Ford Foundation and other liberal foundations that, Wood said, "have been supporting subversive and Communistic enterprises." At the same time Wood became cochairman of For America, a noninterventionist organization that was also opposed to immigration and racial integration. In 1955, Wood—together with other businessmen and several former FBI agents—organized the American Security Council, which served as a kind of private loyalty review board for tracking down alleged Communists and "statists."[117]

A major issue around which ultraconservatives and the business community coalesced was right-to-work legislation. Under Taft-Hartley, states were permitted to proscribe mandatory payment of union dues in unionized workplaces. Although the impact of right-to-work laws on union membership is a disputed issue, there is little doubt that employers—especially those who passionately disliked unions—hoped that these laws would slow labor's organizing momentum. Dr. George Stuart Benson, a southern fundamentalist and champion of right-to-work laws, received funding from various employers, including General Wood and Charles Hook, the president of ARMCO Steel, a nonunion holdout. Thompson Products also was active in this effort. Ray Livingstone testified in support of an Ohio right-to-work bill in 1947; ten years later he pressured Thompson's managers to help get a similar bill enacted.[118]

One of General Wood's favorite publicists was Nathan Shefferman, who cashed in on the free-enterprise campaign by writing banal articles and pamphlets in praise of the American business system. Shefferman ingratiated himself with Wood by regularly sending him his articles; in return, Wood would send Shefferman complimentary letters as well as money for junkets, including a trip Shefferman took to England in 1950, ostensibly to write a report on British socialism. With support from Wood and from something called the Constitutional and Free Enterprise Foundation, in 1954 Shefferman published a book entitled *Labor's Stake in Capitalism*, which was full of purple prose attacking the New Deal ("Uncle Sam is not Santa Claus"), collectivism ("socialism is anti-social"), and Communists ("the rats of humanity"). Wood privately urged the heads of the NAM and the U.S. Chamber of Commerce to hire Shefferman as a public relations consultant, saying that "the worker and his leader look with suspicion on any direct approach from the NAM and the Chamber of Commerce. That is why I think [you] should make arrangements for Mr. Shefferman's services to carry this message of free enterprise to the union leaders and the union members all over the United States."[119]

Wood's relationship with Shefferman is one example of how his political commitments affected the conduct of business at Sears. Because of the General's personal enthusiasm for Shefferman, Labor Relations Associates remained Sears' exclusive consultant on unions for nearly twenty years. This was noteworthy, given the facts that Shefferman was the son of an itinerant rabbi and the General had a reputation for being anti-Semitic. Indeed, many of Sears' top executives shared the General's extreme conservatism and, according to knowledgeable observers, his anti-Semitism as well. Another example was Wood's befriending of former senator Robert M. LaFollette, Jr., who, despite the civil liberty hearings he oversaw in the 1930s, later became a zealot for anti-Communist and anti-CIO causes. After LaFollette lost the 1946 Wisconsin primary election to Joseph McCarthy, Wood named LaFollette the first outside director of the Sears profit sharing fund and, in 1951, placed him on the company's board of directors.[120]

In other ways, too, Wood's political views seeped into Sears. Wood invited conservative luminaries to give speeches to employees at the annual Sears Forum. The journalist Clifton Utley twice spoke about the Communist influence in America, while Robert L. Johnson, the man who headed the "Little Hoover" commission on government reform (on which Wood also served), attacked "waste" in government and urged Sears' employees to help combat it. During the 1950s, Sears had one of the nation's most extensive programs for educating employees about free enterprise. Known as "The Story of Sears in America," it brought together small groups of employees for a series of eight meetings to discuss topics such as "progress through profits." Management considered "The Story of Sears" to be a huge success because internal research showed that the program caused a variety of "changes in employee attitudes." That, after all, was what the public relations jihad was all about.[121]

By the late 1950s, 84 percent of the nation's five hundred largest corporations were offering "practical politics" programs to their employees. The quantity of material printed on behalf of free enterprise was staggering. Yet some observers were skeptical that much—if any—of it was persuasive. William H. Whyte, a business journalist, wrote a hilariously sarcastic study of corporate public relations entitled *Is Anybody Listening?* Whyte's answer was "no"; he thought that industry's educational programs were too pedantic to have much impact on the audience. Joseph H. Willits, a university professor turned Rockefeller Foundation official, reached the same conclusion. Surveying the nation's economy after World War II, Willits wrote that businessmen "are ineffective in presenting their problems [and] their philosophy . . . partly because they are men of action rather than words, and partly because it is harder to present a complex case than a simple one."[122]

Take the experience of Du Pont, a large nonunion company. In 1950 it established a program, "How Our Business System Operates," which was intended to "innoculate blue-collar employees against creeping socialism." By 1953, more than eighty thousand Du Pont employees had received classroom training on the American free-enterprise system. Yet despite this enormous expenditure of time and money, the company's own surveys found that Du Pont employees remained skeptical of management's political views. The surveys revealed that only a minority of employees believed that business could be trusted to give good advice to the government or that business helped to protect individual freedom; most employees still thought that government, not business, was the guarantor of their liberty.[123]

Gradually it began to dawn on businessmen that classroom training and pithy pamphlets did not generate the kind of visceral response as when the same words were uttered by a vigorous leader. Trying to explain how some firms had successfully communicated a principled opposition to unions, the *Harvard Business Review* in the mid-1950s could still laud Fred Crawford for being "an effective showman," "a natural leader," someone with "an unusual degree of empathic sensitivity to his employees' needs." Crawford's emotional style was well suited to the age of radio and television, though it also harked back to the earliest days of welfare capitalism, when bosses shared beer and shop talk with their men. But those days were long gone. Now charisma would have to fill the cultural chasm separating workers from management. The *Harvard Business Review* had something like this in mind when it said companies ought to select as chief executives "the kind of person who can conform reasonably closely to what the workers want—a strong, effective leader who radiates security. . . . He must be the company to his employees. In effect, he must be the respected, admired, and emulated *paterfamilias*."[124]

The 1950s were the last days of the gray flannel man; from then on a CEO with a radiant personality was more desirable. For companies with lackluster leaders, however, another option existed: to routinize charisma by embedding it in daily organizational routines. That was the logic behind human relations training, attitude surveys, personality tests for managers, communications programs, and myriad other activities. At Kodak, at Sears after General Wood, and at other companies as well, psychology and symbolism were the preferred ways of engaging employees' emotions. Routinization was a more systematic, hence more reliable, route to modern welfare capitalism. But when unionized companies tried to pursue that course, they encountered numerous barriers. Over time the two sectors—union and nonunion—grew increasingly different from each other.

Seven

The Cold War of Industrial Relations

WELFARE CAPITALISM AND UNIONISM IN THE 1950s AND AFTER

BY THE 1950s, industrial unionism and modern welfare capitalism had gelled into separate but overlapping employment systems. The union approach embodied the dynamics of labor-management conflict, emphasizing legality and industrial solidarity, while welfare capitalism accented the the cooperative side of the workplace and was psychological in nature and enterprise-oriented. In many respects the two systems boiled down to classic organizational types—the mechanistic and the organic—though they regularly borrowed bits and pieces from each other. Unionized firms experimented with modernized welfare programs, whereas large nonunion firms acknowledged the post-Wagner revolution in employee rights.

The formation of a distinctive nonunion system received little attention in the 1950s. The nation still was riveted by union-management relations, partly because of their intrinsic drama, partly because a majority of Americans associated organized labor—and the New Deal more generally—with a rising standard of living. Academic observers also were fascinated by collective bargaining. This ritual was a world unto itself, possessed of arcane terminology and intricate distinctions: superseniority, capped COLAs, and hot-cargo clauses. The ultimate result of bargaining was a web of rules limiting management's discretion in the workplace, rules that were inscribed in collective agreements and enforced through the complicated legalisms of the grievance "machinery." As such rules proliferated, collective agreements grew thicker. Thick contracts meant high negotiating costs, which employers sought to reduce by lengthening contract durations and thus spreading negotiation (and strike) costs over a longer period. Contract durations rose steadily in the postwar years; three years became the norm and some contracts had even longer terms. (The historic General Motors-UAW agreement of 1950, called the Treaty of Detroit, ran for five years.) The essence of what was termed "mature" unionism was the ritualization of conflict, either channeled into the grievance procedure or expressed every three years at contract expirations.[1]

The lawyers who were the system's technicians thrived on its complexity, while industrial relations experts created elaborate classification schemes to identify the system's inner logic. The apex of this effort was *The Impact of Collective Bargaining on Management*, a 982-page study published in 1960 by the Brookings Institution. For the study's authors, collective bargaining was a self-contained entity, what they called "the American system of Industrial Relations." Their tome barely mentioned social legislation—which they judged inferior to private bargaining—nor did it say much about developments outside the union sector. The omission of nonunion practices was typical of the industrial relations literature of the period. On the few occasions when nonunion firms were mentioned, it was usually only to chart a "spillover" from the (dynamic) union sector to the (passive) nonunion hinterland. The economist Richard A. Lester's comment was typical: "Nonunion firms seem to follow, more or less closely, the hiring, seniority, and promotional patterns prevailing in similar unionized plants."[2]

Lester was at least partially correct. In the decade after 1935, large nonunion companies—like their unionized counterparts—bolstered personnel departments, stripped foremen of their disciplinary powers, and made employment security more explicit and encompassing. Partially unionized companies such as Union Carbide extended bargaining gains to their unorganized employees and promised them they would "be treated no less favorably than in the organized plants." Whereas in the 1920s Mary Follett had easily asserted the unity of employers and workers, by the 1950s a strong labor movement forced nonunion managers to acknowledge some differences of interest. The proliferation of employee complaint systems, which in the mid-1950s could be found at about a third of the nation's large nonunion companies, was one sign of managerial self-restraint; another was the steady expansion of seniority rules.[3]

Yet there was also movement in the opposite direction, from nonunion to union firms, which, with the exception of fringe benefits, was ignored by Lester and most other experts. Part of this unobserved flow consisted of behavioral science innovations, including psychological surveys and human relations-style supervision; relatedly, unionized employers began to rely more on personnel consultants and academic research. Taking their cues from firms like Sears and Thompson, unionized employers also adopted more sophisticated, aggressive anti-union tactics, such as the hiring of professional unionbusters (by the 1950s Shefferman's clients included several unionized firms seeking to rid themselves of a union or find a more compliant one) and the continual probing of the law's outer edges, as, for example, at International Harvester, which in the 1950s pushed the free-speech doctrine to its limits in an attempt to oust its Communist-dominated unions. The NLRB's statistics on unfair labor practices registered the change in norms: after showing no trend for nearly twenty years, charges against employers shot up almost 50 percent in the mid to late 1950s, a change that was extremely harmful to unions.[4]

Still, it was easier for nonunion firms to borrow from the union sector than the other way around. In unionized establishments, collective bargaining—with its stress on economic issues and contractual predictability—reinforced a bureaucratic mind-set that left managers *and* union leaders skeptical of anything "touchy-feely." And if unionized employers did try to create a corporatist Gemeinschaft, they ran into opposition from organized labor, which reflexively distrusted management and held a different—more horizontal—conception of industrial community. In the middle of all this was the rank and file. Many workers were capable of splitting their loyalty between company and union, a phenomenon that social scientists in the 1950s dubbed "dual allegiance" (and celebrated as a precursor to the end of ideology). Yet dual allegiance was unstable, subject to continual shifts and pulls, especially during strikes. If management rebuffed a union, union members responded by refusing to split their loyalty. When this happened, welfare activities premised on "integrative unity" either could not take root or, as with fringe benefits, failed to strengthen allegiances to management.[5]

Thus despite flows in both directions, there were limits to the amount of borrowing that occurred. Increasingly, large unionized and nonunion firms diverged in key areas such as management structure, commitment strategies, and employment stability. The industrial union system was, in Darwinian terms, a good adaptation to the environment of the 1930s and 1940s; it "fit" social conditions and the Tayloristic oligopolies of the era. The system's inability to assimilate key parts of modern welfare capitalism was not seen as a serious problem, either by outside experts or labor relations managers in unionized firms. But during the 1960s and especially after 1970, the business environment began to change: markets became more competitive and less predictable; educational levels rose steadily; and the work force shifted decisively away from manual labor. These changes strained the union sector: it was not easy for managers and unions to convert their emphasis from obedience to responsibility or to satisfy the aspirations of younger and more educated workers. Instead it was the nonunion sector that proved to be better suited than its rival to the postindustrial realities of the 1970s and 1980s. In those years, industrial unionism shrank rapidly while modern welfare capitalism spread beyond its borders to a new group of rapidly growing companies, many of them from technology and service industries. Some nonunion stalwarts did take their lumps in the early 1990s, including Kodak and Sears. But for every stalwart that faltered there were several newcomers—like Microsoft and Wal-Mart—to take their place. Among the nation's larger firms, modern welfare capitalism appeared to have triumphed over modern unionism.

The Dynamics of Distrust

As collective bargaining took hold in the 1950s, it wrought subtle changes in managerial priorities. Large unionized companies usually negotiated companywide or even industrywide agreements that preempted plant-level bargaining over issues covered in the master contract. Because of this, and because the master contract dealt with weighty issues like wages, managerial authority increasingly was concentrated at corporate headquarters. Even issues that could have been settled at the local level were displaced upward. Although unions preferred master agreements—they enhanced labor's prestige and solidarity—management also favored them. Synchronizing wage negotiations across plants limited a company's strike exposure, made its labor costs more predictable, and prevented the union from wangling better terms at the company's most vulnerable establishments.[6]

Despite its economic logic, the centralization of personnel decisions gradually eroded the quality of plant management in unionized firms. Every decision of importance came down from headquarters, draining initiative from local managers. Added to this were the constraints imposed by the union and its contract. The problem was easily recognized in the case of the foreman—the "man in the middle"—but the foreman's immediate superiors were equally stuck: between the executives at headquarters and the local union at home. All of this was occurring at a time when large nonunion companies were giving local managers greater responsibility and reducing the intensity of supervision. As one Sears manager said in 1949, "We have learned that an organization with with an extensively developed hierarchy is more rigid, less adaptive, and less satisfying to the employee than a flat organization, which . . . keeps supervision and formal controls to a minimum." By the 1960s, unionized plants were administratively calcified while their nonunion counterparts were relatively more open to innovative ways of managing.[7]

Another feature of the unionized workplace was its intricate web of rules. For unions, rules constituted a moral economy—a just procedure for distributing workplace "goods" (free time, steady work, easy jobs) among the membership. Employers, too, liked the legalistic approach: it clarified the line between contractual rights and managerial prerogatives and reduced disputes over inequities. During the Second World War, stability came to be highly valued in mass-production industries as engineers discovered that long, steady production runs were positively associated with product quality and reliability. Long-term union contracts helped to achieve such stability. But it was rules—and their adjudication through a grievance procedure—that made these lengthy agreements feasible.[8]

Rules and grievance procedures conferred substantial advantages for unionized workers. Success on the job no longer depended so critically on the relationship with a supervisor. Workers knew in advance what was expected of them and why they might be penalized, important elements of due process. On the other hand, grievance procedures symbolized the climate of suspicion that prevailed in unionized workplaces. The adversarial grievance structure reflected workers' distrust of management, whereas the plethora of disciplinary rules indicated that management viewed workers as incapable of exercising discretion. Rather than doing away with personal supervision, disciplinary rules made the foreman's job easier by providing him with "an impersonal crutch for his authority, screening the superiority of his power"; rules, said one personnel expert, allow the foreman to "evade responsibility" by saying, "sorry, Bill, but it's contrary to company policy."[9]

Theorists have traditionally argued that rules are an unavoidable by-product of complex organizations. But rules were less elaborate in nonunion workplaces, which suggests that they were not the inevitable result of an iron law. Large nonunion firms were more likely to pursue the indulgency pattern: that is, minimizing rules while taking an individualized, flexible approach to disciplinary problems. For example, Stanley Products, a nonunion Connecticut toolmaker, prided itself on its paucity of rules and its "lack of haste in handling personnel problems." It bent over backward to avoid dismissals, like other progressive nonunion firms. Although indulgency may have started as a union-avoidance technique, it gradually came to have a logic of its own. Employees were counseled, retrained, or transferred before being demoted or dismissed. As one manager of a nonunion firm said, "I'll try anything before starting down the road to progressive discipline. Transfers, demotions, you name it." Behavior that would have led to summary dismissal in the union sector—like drunkenness or gambling—instead became the occasion for a therapeutic inquiry into the causes of the behavior.[10]

In nonunion firms, personnel departments were a crucial part of the indulgency pattern. Functioning as a "third force," they mediated disputes between workers and line managers and often insisted that supervisors give workers the benefit of the doubt. James Worthy of Sears thought that the personnel manager should be the guarantor of the employees' "rights," including "fundamental notions of participation, human dignity [and] freedom to speak one's piece." In unionized firms, it was more difficult for personnel managers to act as a third force; adversarial industrial relations precluded independent personnel management. Instead, labor arbitrators served to some degree as the third force in the union sector. The fact that arbitrators revoked or reduced management penalties in more than half of all discipline and discharge cases between 1951 and 1967 is consistent with an independent approach. Yet arbitrators often accommodated to the behavioral assumptions prevailing among union-sector managers: in the vast majority of these discipline and discharge cases, regardless of whether their decision favored management or labor, arbitrators portrayed workers as disobedient or indolent. In the eyes of the arbitrator, a good worker followed rules and a good manager firmly and decisively disciplined those who violated them. Thus, despite the benefits that unionized workers accrued from a web of rules, it also stripped them of discretion and fostered what the British sociologist Alan Fox terms the low-trust syndrome: management is suspicious of employees and creates disciplinary rules; workers resent their lack of autonomy and seek reciprocity in restrictions on management. In other words, low trust begets low trust.[11]

Not all unionized firms were locked in this cycle, to be sure. During the late 1940s, the National Planning Association (NPA) conducted a nationwide search to find companies that were exemplars of "industrial peace" and "good union-management relations." From more than a thousand nominations, the NPA selected eighteen companies for intensive analysis. The case studies were summarized and compared in the NPA's final report, *Causes of Industrial Peace*, issued in 1955. What did the eighteen firms have in common? The report said that at each of them, labor relations "got off to a comparatively good start." There were no strikes for recognition, no violence, and no unfair labor practice charges. In other words, management accepted collective bargaining from the very beginning, which positively affected relations with the union for years to come. At all of the firms the two sides avoided contention, instead cooperating to sift out legitimate grievances and settle differences informally. To management, the main advantage of the union "was in getting ideas across to and reflecting reactions of workers."[12]

Such cooperative workplaces were, however, exceptions to the rule. Most managers reacted negatively to organizing drives, viewing any union win as a corporate loss. Subsequent relations with unions were similarly cast as a zero-sum game: if the union gained, it did so at the expense of corporate profits or managerial prerogatives. The economist Neil Chamberlain in 1948 found management in major industries "convinced that it faces a fight along a wide front to preserve its discretionary freedom in . . . basic matters." Feeling under siege, management carefully inscribed collective agreements with terms delineating its prerogatives and, instead of being a cooperative problem-solving tool, the grievance procedure became an extension of the bargaining process, a place where employers defended—and labor challenged—traditional corporate management.[13]

Blunt adversarialism did in some instances soften into a less antagonistic relationship. This happened as the parties became aware, through bitter experience, of the costs of perpetual battle. Such a breakthrough was celebrated in the industrial relations literature of the 1950s and epitomized by Richard A. Lester's 1958 opus, *As Unions Mature*. By then, claims made in the immediate postwar years that unions were challenging the right to manage appeared to be an exaggeration. The CIO had discarded its visions of industrial democracy in favor of a philosophy that portrayed labor's exclusion from corporate decision-making not as a failing but as a virtue of American unionism. Unions accepted the lines drawn by management and instead pushed where they found the least resistance; this yielded significant gains in wages and fringe benefits. Further, it seemed that a growing number of managers had accepted the idea that stability required cooperation with unions, however grudging such accommodation might be.[14]

But the onset of a prolonged recession in 1957 revealed the fragility of the shift to more cooperative labor relations. Imports were beginning to take a growing share of U.S. markets and for the first time in twenty years domestic demand was on its own, no longer fueled by massive deficit financing, by war expenditures, or by liquidated wartime savings. As the economy began to falter, employers decided that the time had come to modernize facilities and lower labor costs. Among unionized employers, the feeling was that too high a price had been paid for industrial stability. Wages were out of line with perceived ability to pay; automation could not proceed unless control of the shop floor was wrested away from unionized workers. Last but not least, there was a growing realization among managers that the labor movement had run out of steam.[15]

Starting in 1958, a wave of bitter strikes occurred that signaled the advent of the "hard line": a tougher management stance toward labor. From a 134-day strike at Pittsburgh Plate and Glass to a 116-day national steel strike, the disputes had in common aggressive demands by employers for greater flexibility and lower costs. In airlines and automobiles, employers banded together to present a more unified front to labor during disputes. Elsewhere, there was renewed interest in asserting and extending management rights in the workplace.

As in earlier years, a few firms bucked the trend and sought to solve their competitive problems by establishing less combative relations with their unions. Several major experiments in union-management cooperation took place in the late 1950s and early 1960s, notably at American Motors, Kaiser Steel, and Armour Packing. Yet as these examples suggest, companies taking the cooperative path tended to be the lesser firms in their industry. Because cooperation was a last-ditch attempt to forestall extinction, other employers disdained it as a sign of weakness. Hence the low-trust syndrome continued to cycle around. Managers in unionized establishments found themselves in a straitjacket—centralized, adversarial, legalistic—that was largely of their own making.[16]

"Yes, But Who Is Paying You?"

Unionized companies diligently extolled the virtues of free enterprise after the war. Taking their cues from business leaders like Fred Crawford and from organizations like the NAM, these companies were every bit as committed to the ideological jihad as was Du Pont or Thompson Products. If anything, having unions in a plant confirmed an employer's conviction that the New Deal had given too much power to labor and government (although the jihad usually was fought against more abstract enemies like communism and collectivism). One conservative propaganda organization established in 1947, the Foundation for Economic Education, drew its membership from the giant manufacturing companies that were the centers of CIO activity.[17]

Both union and nonunion employers funneled huge sums of money into groups like the Advertising Council, which staged a postwar media blitzkrieg on behalf of the "American Economic System." The council arranged to have a red, white, and blue locomotive, the *Spirit of 1776*, pull artifacts around the country showcasing the "American Heritage." The Freedom Train carried the original Bill of Rights, the flag that had been planted on Iwo Jima, and other patriotic icons. From 1947 to 1949, the train visited every major city in the nation. The message—shared by the nation's employers—was clear: free markets and political democracy could not survive without each other.[18]

Employers in the union sector turned their factories into front lines for the ideological crusade, just as nonunion firms did. A torrent of publications—including even comic books—rained down on unionized factory workers after the war. Asking "Who's Got Momma's Ear?" Whiting Williams, a journalist and friend of Fred Crawford, observed that unions were making overtures to working-class families and he urged organized employers to do the same. Those employers—like Thompson and Kodak before them—began reaching out by mailing letters and magazines to employees' homes and by holding corporate events such as family picnics.[19]

Down in the workplace trenches, however, unionized employers encountered something nonunion employers never had to contend with: organized opposition. In a massive propaganda effort of its own, the labor movement was busy creating newsletters, magazines, and educational programs. For AFL unions like Local 3 of the Electrical Workers, these efforts harked back to the "new unionism" of the 1910s, when the Garment Workers sought to widen the cultural horizons of their immigrant members. The CIO modeled its educational activities along similar lines, while also trying entirely new things, like political action committees, radio broadcasts, and television shows. Whether AFL or CIO, labor in the late 1940s and 1950s was aware that it was competing with employer efforts to build a corporate culture of unity. Such rivalry imparted an urgency to union efforts and at times the ideological contest was intense, causing genteel liberals like the economist Joseph Willits to wonder, "Where does it end? I don't fancy a world in which decisions are made by trying to outpropagandize the other side."[20]

Amid the barrage of information, labor seemed to hold its own in the 1950s. Union members voted solidly for the Democratic party and showed little enthusiasm for their employers. Postwar surveys of American workers found that those with the least complimentary opinions about business in general, and their own jobs in particular, were unionized, urban, blue-collar workers. Although dual-allegiance studies showed that workers could simultaneously be loyal to both company and union, this was small comfort to employers who had spent millions wooing workers away from Big Labor.[21]

One such employer was General Electric. Its elaborate anti-union campaign, engineered by Lemuel Boulware, used many of the methods perfected at Thompson Products: attitude surveys, continuous propaganda at the workplace and at home, and regular visits to the shop floor by the company's top executives. GE's unions fought back tooth and nail and, after more than a decade of litigation, they were rewarded with a favorable NLRB decision. The company's practices were unlawful, ruled the NLRB in 1962, because "their very massiveness showed that GE was trying to undermine the union by dealing with the union through the employees instead of the employees through the union." Thus the tactics that had worked so well for Fred Crawford proved less effective when challenged by a tenacious union.[22]

Transplanting the behavioral sciences to a unionized setting provoked similar problems. Suspicious of management's intent, trade unionists drubbed human relations as mere sugarcoating or as a trick to get "milk from contented cows." Psychologists and researchers who thought of themselves as altruists were taken aback by the hostile response they faced in unionized workplaces. As one union official told a conference of personnel experts, "Whereas you gentlemen present yourselves to the workers as specialists and as technicians and as detached professionals, they sort of chew at the end of their cigars, or spit after they have swallowed a little tobacco from the end of their cigarettes, and say, 'Yes, but who is paying you?' "[23]

The behavioral sciences were not as awful as labor leaders claimed nor so innocuous as their proponents contended. Attitude surveys, for example, offered particular advantages to the unionized employer, making it possible, as one consultant put it, to "give" before the union "demanded and won," and to "separate a demand by a union business agent from a request by the majority of workers." With information gleaned from a survey, an employer could safely reject any union demand that employees did not care deeply about. Because of these strategic considerations, the majority of unionized employers neither informed their unions before conducting a survey nor shared the findings with them. One manager explained that he kept surveys a secret because he feared the union "would attempt to control the views of the membership and thus defeat the true purpose of such a survey."[24]

These fears—that unions would subvert applied behavioral science—were, to a large extent, self-fulfilling. As the economist Richard Wilcock pointed out, it never occurred to most managers that a union "might be an important part of the social scheme within the factory." With unions pushed off to one side and surveys shrouded in secrecy, it was inevitable that union leaders would imagine the worst: that surveys—and behavioral science more generally—were intended to undermine the most fundamental aspects of unionism. Belligerent resistance was a rational response to the perception that the behavioral sciences were, as a union staffer put it, "stealing the prestige for the solution of problems [from grievance and bargaining processes] and arrogating it completely to a management-controlled device."[25]

Not only opposition from below but also indifference from above slowed the adoption of the behavioral sciences by unionized companies. Labor relations managers had built their careers around the esoteric details of collective bargaining, grievance handling, and labor law—all essentially administrative procedures. Steeped in bureaucratic rationality, the procedures aimed to reduce conflict, especially between groups. The behavioral sciences, however, were based on different premises—individualism and affective relationships—which labor relations managers, mostly lawyers and a few former union officials, found difficult to accept. Then, too, these managers were reluctant to try new things for fear that the union might take credit for them.[26]

Unionized companies tried to get around their labor relations managers—and their unions—by creating separate employee relations departments whose job it was to manage day-to-day employee matters exclusive of the bargaining relationship. Exceptionally effective in this regard was General Motors, the first of the Big Three automobile manufacturers to develop a coherent industrial relations strategy after the war. The GM approach was Janus-like: the company's unions faced a tough adversary in bargaining and contract administration, while the employees were shown a more human visage as the company sought to establish direct personal ties with them. The head of GM's employee relations department, Harry B. Coen, was an ardent foe of unionism. Said Coen, "I do not believe in making the union contact the only one between our employees and ourselves. . . I am hopeful that we as a staff can deal with it in such a manner that the union aspect will be only one little segment, or whatever segment it cares to be."[27]

Coen chose LaVerne N. Laseau, formerly with GM's customer research staff, to head a research section in the employee relations department. Laseau's first assignment was to design a contest in which employees were to write essays on "My Job and Why I Like It." Prominent individuals like Peter Drucker and George W. Taylor were hired to judge the essays, while GM offered more than $150,000 in prizes, including forty new cars and sixty-five refrigerators. The contest, launched in 1947, had two objectives. One was to raise morale by encouraging workers to reflect on the company's positive attributes and by creating the impression that GM was a fun place to work. Laseau distributed banners, flyers, and pamphlets to every GM plant in North America. Some local plants organized parades and parties to kick off the contest. The second objective was to ascertain employee attitudes toward GM, information that would be helpful in dealing with the union and changing policies to make GM a better place to work. GM invited university researchers to analyze the contest results. Paul Lazarsfeld, a noted survey researcher, used the data to test his method of latent structure analysis, while two Purdue University researchers gleaned from the essays an "industrial workers' word list" to guide management in communicating with its factory workers. Finally, GM hired Opinion Research Corporation to find out what GM employees thought of the contest.[28]

Although the new department solved some of GM's administrative problems, it proved an irritant to the company's relationship with the UAW. Walter Reuther, president of the UAW, was quick to condemn the "My Job" contest, calling it "a one-sided opinion poll." Local union officials also were critical; in some plants, contest posters were torn down and handbills distributed saying the contest was part of an effort to destroy the union. Another eruption occurred in 1955, this time after Opinion Research Corporation conducted hundreds of structured interviews at GM's Flint, Michigan, plant. Several survey questions pertained to the guaranteed annual wage, a benefit the UAW was planning to ask for in its upcoming bargaining with GM. Reuther again blasted GM, saying the survey was "designed to elicit answers that could be damaging to the union." Reuther was careful to say he was not opposed to surveys that were "properly and honestly applied," but he failed to alter the perception that labor disapproved of behavioral science in the workplace.[29]

Labor's position was reinforced by the intelligentsia's resoundingly negative critique of human relations. Liberal intellectuals of the 1950s were wary of large corporations, seeing in them a possible threat to liberty and democracy. For journalist William H. Whyte, the typical salaried employee had become a self-effacing "Organization Man," fixated on conformity and belonging, whereas economists like Clark Kerr and Arthur M. Ross wrote darkly of "a new industrial feudalism" that was tying workers ever more tightly to their jobs. Liberals derided the organic presumptions of behavioral science—that workers and employers comprised a corporate community. To these critics, such a commonalty connoted repression and even totalitarianism. Reinhard Bendix, a sociologist, and Lloyd H. Fisher, an economist, argued that the central fault of human relations—and of corporate management more generally—was that it "condemns all kinds of conflict." Left unchecked, human relations would, they feared, erode the limited commitments that secured independence in the modern world. Wrote Bendix and Fisher, "To demand unanimity of purpose in a society in which voluntary associations abound is to ask too much." Freedom—whether in the labor market or the polity—could be preserved only by what John Kenneth Galbraith termed "countervailing power." Because labor unions were the liberals' best hope for Galbraithian pluralism, anything that threatened them, including behavioral science, was roundly condemned.[30]

Human relations did have its defenders though, and a number of them—such as anthropologist William Foote Whyte and Douglas McGregor, formerly president of Antioch College and a management professor at MIT—counted themselves as liberals. To them, behavioral science had the potential, if properly applied, to enhance participation and democracy in the workplace. It would achieve this by heightening management's respect for the individual; by replacing authoritarian supervision and bureaucratic rules with consensual persuasion; and by seeking accommodation instead of top-down integration. Rather than strip employees of their identity, behavioral science, they believed, would rescue personality and individuality from the unfeeling clutches of Taylorism.[31]

In many respects the controversy over human relations was a reprise of the dispute, four decades earlier, between laborist and corporatist liberals. As before, the debate was Manichean and neither side would admit the other had a point. The defenders of human relations refused to concede that behavioral science could slip easily from tolerating differences to suppressing them. Nonunion employers were sensitive on this point; the president of Du Pont said in 1958 that, although "the modern era threatens to erase individualism," his company was doing all that it could to "protect personal identity." As for the laborist critics, they confused ends with means. Detesting union avoidance, they refused to see that human relations was not the cause of it. In a unionized workplace—or even within a union itself—behavioral science could lead to less bureaucracy and more satisfying forms of work organization.[32]

Behavioral science's slow progress in the union sector was evident in the 1950s and 1960s, when attitude surveys, personnel research, and psychological consultants were more prevalent in large nonunion firms. The union sector's resistance to the behavioral sciences was ill timed, since it came at precisely the moment when a growing proportion of the work force comprised educated, white-collar workers, including many women. Behavioral science, with its personal and participative orientation, corresponded to the expectations of these workers. But instead of meeting those expectations, unionized companies treated their white-collar employees much like those on the dominant—unionized—side of the company. Although this brought hefty salary and benefit gains to white-collar employees, with the spillover came a managerial mindset that was rigidly bureaucratic and economistic. Union-sector companies increasingly were unable to attract the best of the younger and college-educated workforce entrants, while nonunion firms came to be seen as more desirable and interesting places to work. Unions suffered similar problems. Because few of them acknowledged the virtues of the behavioral approach, organized labor found it increasingly difficult to attract white-collar workers—and women—to its ranks.[33]

By the 1970s, when the behavioral science gap had grown quite wide, the union sector finally began to pay attention to the "quality of working life." The initiative came too late, however, to erase the impression that unions, and the companies they bargained with, were unresponsive to the concerns of the most rapidly growing segments of the workforce.[34]

Contested Benefits

The United States in the 1950s was no longer the same industrializing society that had spawned welfare capitalism at the turn of the century. Americans had become far more affluent, educated, and mobile. Leisure increasingly was a private pursuit, as attested by ubiquitous images of families in station wagons, and public spending—on everything from highways to veterans' mortgages to old-age pensions—provided an underpinning for the celebration of private life. None of this would seem to be fertile soil for corporate welfare activities, yet, as we have seen, the new American welfare state was insufficiently generous to preclude corporate supplements. And the United States in the 1950s was, as critics noted, a place where private life remained embedded in group membership—clubs, churches, unions, and other such voluntary organizations. In a pluralistic society, corporations could offer their own group activities without appearing excessively paternalistic, although intrusive kinds of paternalism—company towns being a prime example—by then were beyond the pale of social acceptability.[35]

The 1950s marked a high point for employer spending on educational and recreational activities. Corporate membership in the National Industrial Recreation Association rose from eleven founding companies in 1941 to more than nine hundred in 1957. Activities ran the gamut from bowling to bingo and, as at Kodak and Thompson, recreation increasingly included the entire family. IBM started children's clubs at its lavish recreational facilities, and many other companies, including union strongholds like Ford and Goodyear, offered summer camps for the children of employees.[36]

As always, corporations had mixed motives for expenditures on "soft" welfare activities. A major consideration was public relations: recreational programs helped to rebuild an image of corporate benevolence in the workplace and the community. Dow Chemical, for example, opened its recreational facilities to everyone living in Midland, Michigan. Also, there was the old hope that corporate generosity outside the workplace would have salutary effects on productivity inside it. Finally, employers sought to weaken the appeal of unions, actual or potential, by encouraging workers to identify with the company and its management. Solomon Barkin, the research director for the Textile Workers, accurately observed that the intent of these soft activities was "to provide the individual worker with a feeling of membership, of status, which stems from the enterprise alone, and . . . to prevent, supercede, or outrank groups at the job level, specifically unions."[37]

In defense, unions pursued recreational activities of their own. The Auto Workers offered summer camps, drop-in centers for retirees, bars and games at local union halls, annual picnics, and other activities. Unity House, a vacation center opened by the Garment Workers in 1919, expanded during the 1950s to include a lakefront theater and accommodations for more than a thousand guests. Even the building trades started their own resorts, including one Los Angeles union that built its own health spa and recreation center. The rivalry between labor and management was frequently aggressive. At Ford's River Rouge plant in the 1950s, the union and the company had separate bowling leagues and recreation directors. Although Ford easily outspent the UAW on recreational activities, such largesse could backfire if it created the perception that a wealthy company was trying to undercut the union. And criticism from the union could easily tarnish the employer's image, as when union representatives told Ford workers to boycott an upcoming family picnic because it was "strictly a company affair."[38]

Nonunion employers rarely faced these problems. They were free to boast, as did the manager of a trucking company in Los Angeles, that "paternalism works in our organization." Union-sector managers might have believed the same thing, but they could never openly say so. Nor could they follow as comprehensive an array of activities as did nonunion companies, whether Kodak or a smaller outfit like Stanley Products, the tool manufacturer in Connecticut. At Stanley, recreational and social activities (many of them held at Stanley Park, a well-equipped grove near the plant) were tied to the company union and other indulgences, forming a paternal web. Like the manager in Los

Angeles, a Stanley official crowed that "paternalism is no longer a cussword in labor-management relations—if it's the right word." Still, this was a different kind of paternalism from forty years earlier. Rather than handle everything themselves, Stanley managers encouraged employees to run the social activities themselves (something unionized employers dared not do for fear the union would take over). And Stanley supplemented its soft welfare activities with a panoply of pecuniary fringe benefits—the impersonal, modern form of welfare capitalism.[39]

Throughout industry, the postwar years were a boom time for fringe benefits, with rapid expansion of everything from hospital insurance to eyeglass plans to old-age pensions. Initially, it will be recalled, unions rejected the concept of employer-provided benefits, which they saw as yet another device for undermining worker solidarity. The fact that employers refused to share the administration of benefit programs—or even to bargain over them—intensified labor's misgivings and gave credence to the strategy of substituting social insurance for private benefits. Between 1943 and 1948, organized labor tried repeatedly to pass a national health insurance bill and to expand the fledgling social security program, but each of these attempts failed, leading the UAW to conclude in 1949 that "on the legislative front, we can expect to win only basic national minimums for all of our members. They will require supplementation through collective bargaining." That year, labor got its green light from the U.S. Supreme Court and began to incorporate benefits into collective bargaining on a massive scale.[40]

Although the benefit boom was industrywide, nonunion employers gained more from the trend. No one contested their achievements, whereas in the union sector, labor and employers vied to claim credit for fashioning new programs. Benefits rarely were the cause of a strike, but unions nevertheless encountered considerable resistance when they asked, for example, that insurance plans cross employer lines, be jointly administered, or provide uniform benefits to employee subgroups. As unions seized the initiative, employers were placed in an awkward position. They could not oppose the proliferation of welfare benefits, although they were less enthusiastic about them than before. Management, said two experts, "dislikes establishing programs that may enhance the power and prestige of the union." This was especially the case with urban union locals whose miniature private welfare states commanded enormous loyalty from union members. Because organized employers sensed they were getting less than a full return for their welfare expenditures, they became more supportive of social security and the two-tier approach envisoned by Marion Folsom. In some cases—as with publicly funded temporary disability insurance—unionized employers were more enthusiastic about public spending than many nonunion employers.[41]

In the early years of the Wagner Act, the fringe benefits won by labor often were little more than a contractual acknowledgement of preexisting employer plans or, as in the retail industry, a replication of benefits already provided by large nonunion stores. Gradually, however, unionized and nonunion establishments diverged in the kinds of benefits they offered. Negotiated welfare benefits gave heavier weight to programs favoring older male workers with many years of seniority—the union's most influential members. Unionized workers were more likely to have generous pensions and health benefits, whereas nonunion workers had a relative advantage in fringes unrelated to seniority, either in-kind benefits (free meals and merchandise) or benefits of particular value to female workers (maternity leave with pay, paid vacations, and sick leave). Nonunion workers also were far more likely to participate in profit-sharing, thus further differentiating unionized from nonunion establishments.[42]

Profit sharing, a hallmark of traditional welfare capitalism, went into a tailspin during the early 1930s; one study estimated that 60 percent of all plans were discontinued in those years. Profit sharing's collapse was brief, though. The rise of mass unionism and the return of prosperity revivified the profit sharing movement in the mid-1930s. Companies resurrected plans or, like Westinghouse in 1936, started entirely new ones. Nearly half the profit-sharing plans in existence on the eve of the Second World War had been started during the previous six years. Enthusiastic over this turn of events, Senator Arthur Vandenberg, a Republican from Michigan, convened Senate hearings in November 1938 to determine what Congress might do to hasten profit sharing's return. Testifying at the hearings were several representatives from the vanguard of the 1920s: AT&T, Dennison, Kodak, Leeds and Northrup, Procter & Gamble, S. C. Johnson, Sears, and Socony Oil. Most of these firms still were nonunion in 1938.[43]

When Vandenberg's subcommittee produced its final report in 1939, the document contained charts and graphs purporting to show that companies with profit-sharing plans had fewer strikes. Although the correlation was open to various interpretations, even the committee's statisticians could not resist drawing the conclusion that profit sharing reduced strike rates by tempering the "conflict of interest which centers on the wage question." The subcommittee also was aware of arguments being made by Keynesian economists in the late 1930s that, because wage rigidity worsened economic conditions, anything that made wages less rigid—such as profit sharing—would curtail layoffs and reduce total unemployment. In an interview, however, Vandenberg insisted that he was not proposing profit sharing "for the stabilization of the whole national economy but for the stabilization of employer-employee relations, and that's justification enough."[44]

Nevertheless, the economy loomed large in Vandenberg's thinking about profit sharing. A fiscal conservative, Vandenberg repeatedly criticized the reserve-financing mechanism in the Social Security Act, which, he argued, would eventually generate enormous federal debts. Vandenberg hoped that deferred profit-sharing plans might brake the growth of social security by providing employees with an ersatz pension, as at Sears. (In fact, Sears had recently announced the intention to "integrate" its profit-sharing plan with social security, just as Kodak was doing with its pension plan.) Although private pension plans also could provide a check on social security, that idea was already being promoted by people like Marion Folsom, and pension plans lacked profit sharing's ideological punch—the ability to, as Vandenberg put it, "preserve the profit system of capitalism" and "maintain a partnership between capital and labor." The Senate report did not propose any new tax incentives, but it did recommend that profit-sharing contributions be exempted from payroll taxes, an idea that Congress enacted in 1939. The War Labor Board later gave another boost to profit sharing by permitting employers to transfer excess profits into deferred profit-sharing plans, just as with pensions. Of the profit-sharing plans in existence in 1947, half were adopted during the war.[45]

Unions never liked profit sharing, which they associated with the union-free world of welfare capitalism. Also, profit sharing made it difficult for unions to standardize wages across firms. At the Senate hearings, John L. Lewis, the head of the CIO, gave the traditional union response to profit sharing. It was, said Lewis, "rather a delusionary snare," just like the old sliding scale in the mining industry. Workers would be better off, Lewis testified, if companies gave them all funds destined for profit sharing; this at least would result in "immediate higher standards of living." A more nuanced retort came from the AFL's William Green, who, after noting various shortcomings of profit sharing, said that the AFL would support it if it were done "with a full understanding and in full cooperation with the representatives of the workers." To the AFL this required "books to be open"—including executive salaries and investment plans—as well as union representation on the company's board of directors.[46]

To managers, Green's conciliatory stance was more frightening than Lewis's obduracy. At the hearings, Alfred P. Sloan of General Motors said that profit sharing in a unionized setting would cause labor to become "involved in determining industry's managerial policies, and I think that that would be very objectionable and would be quite dangerous in what it might lead to." Indeed, it was not uncommon for a company with profit sharing to discontinue the plan after unionization. Terminating a plan, noted the Conference Board, foreclosed any "dispute as to how much profit has been made in the business." Nor was it uncommon for management to refuse a union request to initiate profit sharing. During the postwar years, General Motors repeatedly turned down UAW proposals for profit sharing, citing the same concerns Sloan enunciated in 1939. Thus, management's defense of its prerogatives combined with labor's misgivings to make profit sharing relatively uncommon in the postwar union sector.[47]

In the nonunion sector, however, there was a surge in profit sharing during the 1950s. One survey found that the percentage of large nonunion firms with profit-sharing plans nearly tripled between 1952 and 1962. Employers hoped simultaneously to raise morale, productivity, and teamwork, as well as loyalty to management. That profit sharing made it more difficult to organize unions is not to be doubted. A study of union elections in 1962 found that companies with profit-sharing plans had a lower union win rate (36 percent) than companies without them (62 percent). On the positive side, there was evidence that profit sharing led to higher levels of employee participation; about a quarter of all companies in 1948 had employees represented on a profit-sharing supervisory committee, and the proportion probably increased in the 1950s. Moreover, manufacturing firms with profit sharing had more stable employment than companies without it. Part of this was due to flexible compensation, though there were other reasons for this stability as well.[48]

Security: Income vs. Employment

Despite welfare capitalism's limited reach in the 1920s, it transformed social norms regarding security and fair treatment at work. As the Depression eroded welfare capitalism, workers turned to unions to recover lost ground and to conquer new territory. Unionism's great upswing brought a rapid expansion of policies intended to shield workers from unemployment, especially at unstable, traditionalist firms, which never had offered much in the way of security. Elsewhere unions took over the half-built manors that laggard employers had erected, expanding and entrenching those structures. Where use of seniority had itself been a seniority benefit in the 1920s, by the 1940s it became a fundamental principle of allocation, part of the moral economy of the labor movement. Where large industrial firms had earlier rejected employment stabilization in favor of a layoff system, unions now rationalized those systems and strengthened their dependence on seniority. With the Depression behind them, the new unions rejected *employment* security—specifically worksharing—in favor of *income* security provided by a layoff-rehire system tied to seniority and subsidized by unemployment insurance (and, in the 1950s, by private supplemental unemployment benefits or SUBs).[49]

Whereas the union sector came to emphasize income security, major nonunion firms embraced employment security through worksharing (cutting hours to spread the work) and other layoff-avoidance methods. Some of these activities predated the Depression, as at Kodak; others were a response to the post-Depression preoccupation with security. Starting in 1936, for example, Sears experimented with both "constant wage" and "guaranteed employment" plans in its mail-order houses. It extended the guaranteed employment plan to selected retail stores in 1939, promising all workers except part-timers and temporaries six full months of work each year. By the early 1950s, nonunion firms were twice as likely as unionized firms to turn first to cuts in pay and hours in order to trim labor costs; unionized firms were twice as likely to rely on layoffs. The gap widened as SUB plans became more prevalent in the union sector as a result of labor's campaign for a guaranteed annual wage. Whereas 5 percent of union contracts in 1954 called for layoffs when hours worked were below normal for four weeks or more, by 1971 that figure had risen to 43 percent. Layoff rates in the 1960s were two to four times higher in the union than the nonunion sector, and union workers were about 50 percent more likely to experience temporary layoffs.[50]

Each of these security mechanisms was part of an ensemble of distinctive employment practices. Seniority-based layoffs gave unionized firms—whose production tended to be relatively unstable to begin with—a way to cut costs rapidly when demand dropped off. But such flexibility induced rigidity in other areas, as seniority came to govern not only layoffs but also promotions and wages. The new industrial unions made seniority the basis for movement along internal job chains, each carrying its own wage rate, which solidified the division of labor and made it difficult for unionized employers to experiment with alternatives to layoff such as cross-training, transfers, and job restructuring. The end result was an ever-greater reliance on layoffs in the union sector.[51]

Also making it difficult to stabilize employment was the downward rigidity of union wages. As noted, one factor contributing to wage inflexibility was the dearth of profit sharing in the union sector. Another was the reluctance of unions to allow employers to reopen contracts for wage adjustments during recessions. As the duration of union contracts rose in the postwar era, union members' wages became insulated from the business cycle's immediate effects. With pay cuts increasingly foreclosed as an adjustment option, layoffs had to carry more of the load.[52]

In the nonunion sector, in contrast, wages were more flexible. They almost never were fixed by multi-year contracts, whereas profit sharing and bonuses were relatively common. Also, nonunion employers were more likely to supplement job-based wages with performance appraisals that tied pay to individuals instead of jobs. Kodak, for example, combined job evaluation with written appraisals that made a sizable portion of a worker's pay dependent on "merit" factors such as work quality, versatility, and dependability. Merit rating raised wage inequality and gave supervisors greater power over subordinates, but it also weakened the link between the reward structure and the job structure, making it easier to cross-train and transfer workers instead of laying them off. The same effect was achieved by the relatively loose division of labor found in large nonunion firms, which often had fewer job classifications than unionized workplaces of the same size. Sears, for example, prided itself on its "job flexibility," which permitted it to move employees around before resorting to layoffs.[53]

Economists Richard Freeman and James Medoff attribute these union-nonunion differences—both past and present—to the greater weight given to seniority in unionized settings. Using a rational choice model, they argue that unions represent the interests of the average worker whereas management is more sensitive to the interests of recently hired employees. Because the average employee has longer tenure than the recently hired one, unionized firms rely more heavily on seniority-based rules and benefits, including seniority-related layoff systems. The argument is logical and fits the facts, but in trying to account for sectorial differences, Freeman and Medoff assign too much weight to the preferences of the average worker and do so because a historical dimension is missing from their work.

The association between unionism and seniority that became so noticeable after the 1930s was, in fact, a historically contingent phenomenon. Prior to the 1930s, most unions—with the exception of the guild manorialists—were found in craft labor markets, where attachment to a given employer was weak and where firms tended to be small and short-lived. Hence seniority had less of a role to play. Only 26 percent of a sample of union contracts collected by economist Sumner Slichter in the mid-1920s mentioned seniority as a factor in layoffs, whereas 40 percent of the large nonunion firms surveyed by the Conference Board in 1927 relied on seniority when making layoffs. In other words, there was no automatic association between unionism and seniority. The link became widespread only after 1933, in part because the Depression soured existing unions on work sharing but more importantly because industrial unions took root in the cyclically unstable firms that already relied on seniority rules and layoff-rehire systems. In 1938, seniority was a factor in layoff decisions in 95 percent of unionized firms, double the proportion for what remained of the nonunion sector.[54]

Management's reaction to unions in the 1940s and 1950s had the effect of widening the sectorial gap even farther. By aggressively asserting their right to control production, managers discouraged unions from seeking employment stabilization measures that would have brought labor deep into the details of plant management. Walter Reuther's various ideas to stabilize auto employment—for example, he urged a sliding price scale that would have cut prices on cars during the slack season—were viewed by employers as an opening for worse things. One industrial relations manager said privately, "Behind the union's effort to encroach on management's authority are two things, which merge into one: a lust for power and a movement towards some form of socialism." Faced with plans like Reuther's, employers deflected unions to areas where joint control was less threatening: the realm of seniority, layoffs, wage guarantees, and SUBs. As the Brookings Institution study said in 1960, "By choosing income security as the goal, unions avoid the necessity of bargaining over such essential management decisions as production schedules, capital improvement plans, and plant location. By and large, management has retained its freedom to make these decisions." For unions, this was a forced choice, and it was one that would have fateful consequences in the years ahead.[55]

The Triumph of Welfare Capitalism?

The existence of two competing employment systems—collective bargaining and modern welfare capitalism—did not bode well for America's labor movement. Unionized employers alternately were tantalized by the success of nonunion corporatists and frustrated by their own inability to weaken labor's hold. Soft welfare activities were tried by many but never enjoyed the uncontested legitimacy they had in nonunion firms. As for collective bargaining, often it was bogged down by distrust and a mutual obsession with contractual details. Some historians see it differently, claiming, as does Steven Fraser, that the order and stability collective bargaining brought to the shop floor provided "common ground for a close collaboration between modern management and centralized industrial unionism." True, where unions were entrenched and companies could not move, employers preferred "mature" unionism to more militant varieties. But it is quite wrong to conclude that "the giants of American industry began to accept industrial unionism as a feature of modern management." The fact is, the majority of unionized employers, almost from the start, sought to circumscribe unions and circumvent the union's relationship to its members. As one labor official bitterly complained in 1950, "There is little evidence that employers are prepared to accept trade unionism as a proper and permanent feature of industrial relations."[56]

There was abundant evidence that employers anathematized unions. In addition to the battle over Taft-Hartley, what irked trade unionists most in the 1950s was industry's new strategy of transferring union jobs to regions that were relatively impervious to unionism. The postwar sale of federal defense plants and the new availability in the nation's hinterlands of cheap electricity and transportation gave unionized employers the opening they were looking for. Manufacturing facilities gradually moved from the urban centers of the Northeast and Midwest to rural areas, to the border states, and, especially, to the South. After a wartime decline, total manufacturing employment in the South steadily rose: by 2 percent between 1947 and 1952, 7 percent between 1952 and 1957, and 8 percent between 1957 and 1962. Much of this growth was the result of a geographic dispersion strategy pursued by unionized manufacturers.[57]

Typical in this regard was General Electric. In the 1930s, Gerard Swope had peacefully accepted unionism at GE's plants; the company was touted as an ideal of successful collective bargaining. After the war, however, GE began threatening its unions with a combination of Boulwarism and job loss. Employment at the militant Bridgeport, Connecticut, plant fell from 6,500 in 1947 to 2,888 in 1955, despite growing demand for the products manufactured there. The same thing happened at the company's main factory in Schenectady, New York, which lost nearly 60 percent of its jobs between 1954 and 1965. Production from these plants was shifted to various sites, including Ashboro, North Carolina, Lynchburg, Virginia, and Shelbyville, Indiana.[58]

To GE and other manufacturers, places like these offered a tempting combination of lower wages, right-to-work laws, and union-resistant workers. Proof of this last point came from Operation Dixie, the CIO's attempt to organize the South in the mid-1940s; the operation was a massive failure. Whether Southern workers were afraid of supporting unions or innately skeptical of them, or both, is not clear. Senate hearings in 1950 revealed widespread use of repressive anti-union tactics at plants throughout the South. A

1955 article in *Chemical Week*, however, asserted that "Southern wage earners really have a friendlier, more personal attitude toward management than do workers in other parts of the U.S." Whatever the reason, there is little doubt that the South was a tough place for union organizers in the 1950s. During NLRB elections held in the mid-1950s, two out of three Southern workers voted against unions; in the Northeast and Midwest, only one out of ten did so. To America's industrial giants, the hinterlands offered an inexpensive and conservative workforce; it seemed a good place to give modern welfare capitalism a try.[59]

Geographic decentralization was an end in itself as well as a way to wrest concessions from the unionized remainder of a company's work force. In the 1950s GE built a number of satellite plants to preclude disruptions arising from a strike at a sole supplying facility. Companies taking the hard line in the late 1950s often used the threat of job mobility to force unions into a defensive posture. This tactic encountered its stiffest resistance when unions knew that an employer could not decentralize because of investments sunk in costly facilities (for example, steel mills) or the need to stay in close proximity to customers (for example, grocery stores).[60]

By the mid-1960s, however, the hard line melted under the heat of an economic revival. Unemployment sank while spending on the Vietnam War rejuvenated old-line manufacturing industries. The war years were a hiatus from the economic problems that had surfaced in the late 1950s. But the respite left employers and unions ill prepared for the myriad difficulties that confronted them when the economic boom ended in 1973: slow growth, rising imports, deregulation, and new technologies hit the union sector with a wallop. Collective bargaining's emphasis on contractual stability proved a poor fit with the economic turbulence and shorter product-life cycles of the 1970s. Rapid technological change required more flexible work systems and higher training levels than existed in most unionized firms. Also working against unionism were changes in the labor force, which was becoming more youthful, female, and educated. White-collar work was on the ascendant, whereas the demand for manual labor was stagnant or declining. Finally, as the economy shifted, so did support for unions. Instead of seeing organized labor as the linchpin of mass prosperity, public opinion now blamed unions for acting selfishly and thereby helping to boost inflation.[61]

In this changing world, elements of the union approach that once had been realistic adaptations began to produce thorny problems for labor. Take income security, for example. Although seniority and SUBs helped unionized workers to maintain their income during recessions, the overall—and unintended—effect was vastly to increase their employment instability. From 1958 to 1981, employment swings in highly unionized industries were four times larger than in low-unionization industries. True, senior union members usually were immune from these swings, but younger workers were not. Compared to young nonunion workers, they had higher layoff rates and were less likely to say their job security was good. This did not endear unionism to the Lordstown generation of the 1970s, nor did it boost labor's standing with the burgeoning white-collar salariat, for whom a layoff system—and other features of the industrial union system—made little sense. As one former Steelworkers official admitted in the early 1980s, "We may have backed ourselves into a corner by settling for income security rather than dealing with the immense complexities of fashioning job security arrangements."[62]

Large nonunion firms found themselves better situated for the technological and demographic changes of the 1970s. Because employment security raised the likelihood that employees would be seen as assets instead of costs, it was positively associated with employer investments in worker training and education. Employment security made workers less fearful of new technology since, as at Kodak, it did not usually lead to layoffs. This was quite different from the union sector, where new technology threatened to upset the division of labor that was codified in the bargaining contract. Hence the new "team-based" and "high performance" work systems were rapidly adopted in nonunion establishments but met with indifference or resistance in the union sector. The difference in adoption rates could also be accounted for by the fact that the new work systems required a flexible division of labor, which predominated in nonunion establishments. And because nonunion managers were "psychologically minded," they were quick to appreciate the advantages of teams, employee involvement, and other activities with deep roots in the behavioral sciences.[63]

The ease with which nonunion companies assimilated the new work systems made them attractive places for young workers in the 1970s, who were more educated than ever before. By then nearly 60 percent of high school graduates were enrolling in institutions of higher education, and 20 percent of blue-collar workers had one or more years of postsecondary education. By historical standards, this was a major shift; two decades earlier, the proportion of blue-collar workers with some college education was only 4 percent. Job satisfaction studies done in the 1970s found that workers valued the opportunities provided by the new work systems to utilize their educational skills better.[64]

Both blue- and white-collar workers also appreciated the "single-status" policies in place at about half of all large nonunion firms in the 1970s. Under these plans, everyone—from secretary to CEO—received a salary while also sharing common benefit plans, cafeterias, and parking lots. Minimizing status distinctions had long been a part of modern welfare capitalism. Now it came to be especially attractive to ordinary employees, who sometimes had as much education as senior managers. To reduce social distance further, some nonunion firms even took up the old Thompson technique of "walking" (what Hewlett-Packard in the 1970s called "management by walking around" or "MBWA"). At one such firm, "members of top management go to coffee breaks regularly, since they consider their presence important. As one of them said, 'The ethic here has to do with informality, dignity, and lots of open spaces.'"[65]

The values of educated workers were consonant with the nonunion sector's emphasis on individual pay determination and merit. One study found that workers with at least some college education were more likely than less educated workers to view fairness as "recognition of individual abilities" instead of "equal treatment for all," an orientation that did not mesh with unionism's emphasis on standard wage rates, common rules, and seniority. Given the choice—as, say, during a union election—young, educated workers were inclined to reject the labor movement's egalitarian orientation. This was precisely the outcome that Michael D. Young predicted in his pessimistic book on meritocracy: that rising educational levels would erode social solidarity, leaving only the narrower loyalties of corporation and career.[66]

The fortuitously good fit between modern welfare capitalism and societal trends of the 1970s was responsible for the impression that large nonunion corporations were culturally "in synch," a perception that generated positive publicity for employers like Hewlett-Packard, the company lauded in such books as *Theory Z* and *The 100 Best Companies to Work for in America.* Moreover, it is likely that this kind of fit gave nonunion companies a competitive edge: they could hire the best new labor force entrants, utilize the latest technologies, and have the easiest time securing the former's commitment to the uncertainties of the latter.[67]

By the 1980s, books and articles were heralding the emergence of a "new nonunion model"; *The Economist* even termed it "the new corporate paternalism." A synthesis of these studies yields a list of eight features shared by large companies practicing the "new nonunion model":

1. *Strong organizational culture*: inspired by top management, based on treating employees fairly and securing their identification with the firm.

2. *Single-status systems*: companywide policies governing pay, benefits, and other programs, including profit sharing.

3. *Employment stability*: marked by internal hiring, training, and development; layoffs as a last resort.

4. *Generous compensation*: managers seek to pay above-average salaries and benefits.

5. *Indulgency pattern*: corrective approach to performance problems, including careful training of supervisors.

6. *Behavioral science*: extensive reliance on attitude surveys, employee involvement, team-based organization, and planned corporate cultures and value systems.

7. *Influential human resource departments*: with direct access to senior management.

8. *Use of labor-relations consultants*: to thwart union organizing drives; new-model firms range from those whose motivation has little to do with union avoidance to fervent anti-unionists.[68]

What's striking about this list is how similar it is to the practices identified in this book that define modern welfare capitalism. Rather than being new, the nonunion model of the 1970s and 1980s was but a slightly modified version of what companies like Sears, Kodak, and Thompson had been pursuing at least since the 1930s. The only difference is in the sixth item—the use of team organization and sociotechnical principles to alter the traditional division of labor. To be sure, the team approach was an important change: it transformed managerial assumptions about the relationship between efficiency and specialization. And because of its cooperative premises, the team approach flourished in nonunion companies while failing to graft easily onto the union sector. That is, the "team system" spread rapidly within nonunion firms because it was consistent with the logic of modern welfare capitalism—especially the Lewinite strand of human relations.

Why, then, did many observers assert that the nonunion model was something entirely new, a veritable "plant revolution"? The most important reason has to do with the proliferation of "new nonunion" plants in the 1970s, the number of which far surpassed anything seen during the previous three decades. Some of these plants were offshoots of partially unionized companies like General Mills, Mobil Oil, and Cummins Engine, who now found it technically feasible to move into the hinterlands and could do so with little fear that unions would follow. Other of these plants belonged to a new breed of entirely nonunion companies—such as Intel, Digital Equipment, Texas Instruments, Federal Express, and Wal-Mart—many of whom came from the booming high-technology and service-sector industries. The fact that these were youthful, dynamic, rapidly growing firms created a faddish impression that their employment policies were similarly avant-garde. What the pundits forgot is that precisely the same things had been said about Kodak and Sears in their day. By the 1970s, however, these pioneers were stuck in mature, slower-growth markets, not the sort of places likely to attract industrial trend-seekers.[69]

Despite these circumstances, a few older welfare capitalists reemerged as exemplars in the 1970s, including IBM, Procter & Gamble, S. C. Johnson, and Thompson (by then TRW). All of them were extremely profitable and, despite their age, still relatively fast-growing companies. TRW was one of the era's hottest conglomerates. It built or acquired sixty-six new factories in the 1960s and 1970s, which helped it achieve a phenomenal sales growth rate of over 1,000 percent between 1960 and 1974. Growth like this helped older welfare capitalists to stay in the limelight. Growth also made it easier to maintain traditional welfare policies like employment security, internal promotion, and profit sharing. None of this is to gainsay the fact that TRW and others were doing some innovative things in the 1970s, such as experimenting with team-based production methods. The use of these methods meant that TRW's newest plants (those built after 1960) had fewer job classifications and wage grades than its older plants. Yet the rest of TRW's policies in the 1970s—sensing sessions, quality circles, attitude surveys, employee meetings—were throwbacks to the single-status communitarianism of Fred Crawford, to the communicative intensity of Mayoism, and to the corporatist notion that employee representation was desirable so long as it stopped short of unionism.[70]

Although not as high-profile as TRW, Kodak and Sears were by no means entirely unnoticed after 1960. Kodak was slow to assimilate team methods but it continued to be a pacesetter in fringe benefits, and Sears still was recognized as an innovator in the behavioral sciences; it was a founding member of the elite Mayflower Group, a consortium comprised of IBM, AT&T, and other leading users of attitude surveys and similar devices. Yet slackened growth, managerial staidness, and sluggish financial returns kept both Kodak and Sears off the roster of the leading "new model" nonunion companies.[71]

During the late 1980s and 1990s, welfare capitalism experienced its most critical test since the Great Depression. Heightened competition and rapid technological change led to massive layoffs throughout American industry. Nonunion companies that had never previously experienced a major layoff jettisoned thousands of employees. Kodak, which by the 1980s had become the high-cost producer in markets where it previously had no competition, shed more than twelve thousand workers between 1985 and 1994. The trauma of the layoffs was deepened by Kodak's explicit abandonment of its no-layoff policy, as also occurred at Digital Equipment, IBM, and Polaroid. Sears, which never had such a policy but which had encouraged a sense of career security, cut even more deeply. Beset with aging stores and unable to compete with discount retailers employing low-wage workers, Sears laid off more than fifty thousand employees in the early 1990s.[72]

The instability of these years was a shock to those employees who thought themselves immune from job loss. To their dismay, middle-level managers found that the elimination of their jobs accounted for the chief cost savings to be realized from "restructuring"—a euphemism for the compression of the M-form corporation's bureaucratic hierarchy. It is important to put these changes in perspective, however. Although absolute security no longer exists, especially in blue-collar employment, not all jobs are in peril, nor are career jobs a relic of the past. Despite laying off thousands of workers, large corporations continue to offer career employment. Successful companies still put enormous effort into transforming new recruits into company men and women, in both the way they think and the skills they possess. In fact, economists find that most middle-aged workers currently have jobs that will last for decades; thus, despite the fashion for restructuring, there is little evidence of a secular decline in job stability.[73]

What are the reasons behind this paradox of change amid continuity? First, the U.S. labor force is huge and highly mobile; the unemployed either retire or get swallowed up in the market's constant churning. Second, the layoffs of the 1990s received enormous publicity because they represented a qualitative transformation: a shift away from high levels of security for previously protected white-collar groups. Far less attention was paid to the huge loss of thousands of blue-collar jobs in the late 1970s and early 1980s, a contraction that put a permanent dent in the labor market for blue-collar workers. Only in the 1990s, when professionals and managers were the ones at risk, did the politically influential middle class begin to feel threatened and the media take notice. This is not to deny the significance of the changes that occurred at firms like IBM and AT&T, but reports of the demise of career jobs have been exaggerated.

In order to preserve career jobs, some welfare capitalist firms have adopted "dualist" policies: they hive off what they see as their least essential parts (usually jobs held by less educated workers) so as to subsidize the cost of maintaining a nucleus of stable jobs with good benefits. Hewlett-Packard started a Flex Force made up of temporary employees, especially in clerical and service jobs, who receive no benefits or employment security. When markets slow, the Flex Force employees lose their jobs, thus cushioning Hewlett-Packard's core work force. Although this arrangement merely redistributes unemployment from "in" workers to "out" workers, it has, so far, managed to conserve career jobs for the company's core employees.

The Minneapolis-based manufacturer, 3M, took a different tack in the early 1990s. It maintained full employment by retraining and reassigning more than 3,500 workers to other corporate divisions, an employment stabilization technique dating back to the 1920s. Still, reliance on massive transfers is no guarantee that a hard-hit company can sustain core employment. IBM, for example, took extraordinary steps in the 1980s but still had to resort to large-scale layoffs. The company started by retraining and redeploying more than ten thousand workers, while offering generous early-retirement buyouts to thousands more. Digital Equipment and Kodak did the same thing, bending over backwards to avoid laying off people. When layoffs finally came, they put an end to these companies' implicit no-layoff policies. All three companies, however, continue to sustain cohesive industrial communities based on comprehensive benefits, employee involvement, and stable, albeit not permanent, jobs.[74]

Thus Kodak—despite layoffs and a long-term trend toward geographic decentralization—still has thousands of employees in the Rochester area and still calls itself an industrial "family." It spends huge amounts on training, career planning, and fringe benefits, including the wage dividend. In 1995, Kodak was one of twenty major corporations that pledged to invest millions of dollars to make child care and elder care more available for their workers. (The others included Hewlett-Packard, IBM, Mobil, and Texas Instruments.) Recreational activities remain important and employees still can purchase Kodak products at discount. And Kodak—like Sears and TRW—remains a nonunion stronghold and prides itself on that fact.[75]

It is important to remember, however, that there is more to the U.S. economy than the kind of firms I have been discussing in this book. Even at the height of the postwar economic boom, there remained areas of the labor market where unions did not reach and where employers were unconcerned with the niceties of employee commitment. In those years it appeared that the number of retrograde firms was shrinking under pressure from union organizing, federal labor standards, and labor-market competition. Today, however, instead of shrinking, this job market is growing ever larger. The reason is partly compositional: unions now represent fewer than 10 percent of private-sector employees, and the proportion is expected to decline to 5 percent by the next decade. Also, many more workers today hold temporary, part-time, or casual jobs. So-called contingent employees are disproportionately nonwhite and without high school diplomas; their pay is low and they lack pensions and health insurance. The growth of contingent employment is the result of a complex set of forces: the vacuum created by the decline of unions; an oversupply of less educated workers; and the dualistic dynamic occurring inside welfare capitalist companies.[76]

Given these trends, modern welfare capitalism may be turning back into the elite preserve that it was in the 1920s, when corporate manors housed only salaried employees and a lucky minority of hourly workers. True, such workers have more options today than in the 1920s—in the union sector and in government—and they also have the welfare state's safety net to fall back on. But the net is tattered, while the number of unionized and government jobs is growing very slowly, if at all. As for today's "salariat" of college graduates, it remains to be seen whether the progressive nonunion sector will be able to absorb large numbers of the new labor force entrants. Although hiring continues—even at companies like AT&T and Sears that recently laid off thousands—anxiety remains widespread. Indeed, welfare capitalists of the 1920s exuded a buoyant optimism that is noticeably missing today. Welfare capitalism is not about to disappear, but its future looks less bright than at any time since its postwar modernization.

Postscript

In May 1996, the White House held a conference on corporate responsibility attended by the heads of the largest and most progressive companies in the United States. Said President Bill Clinton: "The most fundamental responsibility of any business in a free-enterprise system is to make a profit. . . . But we must recognize that there are other responsibilities as well." The conference took place amid rising public anxiety about corporate downsizing and job cuts. Patrick J. Buchanan, who had stunned the Republican party a few months earlier by winning the New Hampshire primary on a platform of vilifying corporate America, had aimed his rhetoric at top executives such as Robert E. Allen, the head of AT&T, who receive huge salaries while laying off thousands of workers.

Clearly, modern welfare capitalism is in a transition period. Corporations today are less willing to shoulder risks for their employees than in earlier years. Mass layoffs are one sign of this; other indicators include outsourcing, managed-care health insurance, the shift from defined-benefit to defined-contribution pensions, and the rise of other kinds of "at risk" compensation. If these changes continue, they eventually will cause the death of welfare capitalism by a thousand cuts.

Alternatives to welfare capitalism lurk in the wings. Some hope that the recent installation of new, more militant leaders at the AFL-CIO will spark a union revival. Others pin their hopes on government, which continues to promulgate standards for regulating the workplace. Meanwhile, professional and managerial employees increasingly favor market individualism—now called "employability"—as their economic salvation. Such workers are adjusting to what they see as the new dog-eat-dog economy, having lost faith not only in welfare capitalism but in other institutions as well.[1]

Without doubt, the props undergirding modern welfare capitalism are weaker now than in the 1960s. Today's economy is more exposed to competition, both domestic and global, and to technological change. In an uncertain world, employers are reluctant to trade welfare capitalism's costs, which are felt immediately, for its longer-term benefits. Also, managers have far less to fear from organized labor than thirty years ago. The decline of unions makes it easier to renege on implicit promises of security, especially pledges made to blue-collar workers. And the notion that management is the steward of employee welfare seems rather quaint in a world where chief executives hop from firm to firm while middle-level managers worry about their own uncertain futures.

Even the demand for welfare capitalism may be slackening. As mentioned, a portion of the work force—predominantly young and educated—has grown skeptical not only of welfare capitalism but of government, unions, and other collective traditions. Believing they must have a broad range of skills to succeed in today's labor market, these "knowledge workers" expect to spend no more than brief stints at any single firm. They ask only that the firm ensure their future employability by providing learning experiences that can be added to their résumés. Like nineteenth-century craftsmen, such workers pride themselves on their skill and their footloose independence. But whereas most craftsmen felt a collective kinship with others in their trade, today's salaried professionals see themselves as solitary masters of their own fate. They seek individualized security—medical savings accounts and portable pension plans—instead of social insurance. Less concerned with job security than the generations that were touched by the Depression, they represent a throwback to an earlier era of market individualism.

Yet it is important to emphasize that despite recent changes, the dissolution of welfare capitalism is not at hand. Rather, the corporation will likely remain a central risk-bearing institution in American society. I advance this claim not out of any blind affection for modern welfare capitalism, whose exclusivity, lack of accountability, and dogged anti-unionism are deeply problematic, but because welfare capitalism continues to offer a good fit for the American environment. The United States still has a sizable sector of large, fast-growing firms for which the net economic benefits of welfare capitalism remain positive. New workers have to be trained, which makes turnover costly. Employee loyalty still matters, especially in fast-changing situations where organizational knowledge often is tacit. Even after extensive layoffs, companies like AT&T and Kodak have preserved stable jobs and progressive policies for their remaining employees. That is not surprising, because there is plenty of evidence that the practices associated with modern welfare capitalism—such as employment stability, profit sharing, single-status personnel policies, and employee involvement—are positively related to corporate performance. If welfare capitalism can outperform its more penurious rivals, then it is likely to endure.[2]

Ironically, one place where modern welfare capitalism has been growing in the 1990s is in the union sector. Managers of heavily unionized firms are pushing hard to adopt those things that make large nonunion firms distinctive: behavioral science practices, extensive use of teams, single-status policies, and profit sharing. Saturn, the new General Motors division in Tennessee, is the paradigmatic example of extensive cooperation between a union (the UAW) and management. Just as unions absorbed elements of welfare capitalism in the 1920s and 1930s, so today they are beginning to make modern welfare capitalism part of their agenda.

Cooperating with management, however, works better as a bargaining tactic than as an organizing strategy. Although cooperation has helped unions shore up their dwindling base, thus far it has not brought the labor movement very many new members. Unions might make a comeback by taking a different tack: playing on fears of job loss and resentment of widening inequalities between workers and management. These are tough times for the less educated, and unions may be the only hope for such workers to preserve a middle-class lifestyle. A more militant approach to organizing will not mesh smoothly with ongoing efforts to cooperate with management, however. And most nonunion employers remain bitterly opposed to unions; nothing so arouses managerial passions as an organizing drive. Nevertheless, although the prospects for labor's revival are not bright, it would be reckless for managers to act as if the labor movement were doomed.

Although unions have grown weaker in recent years, government has, if anything, become *more* active in regulating the workplace. Since the 1970s a plethora of federal legislation has imposed strict standards on business in such areas as pensions, family leave, health insurance coverage, workplace safety, and discrimination against the aged and the disabled (to name but a few). Corporate managers are well aware that if they let welfare capitalism wither, there will be popular pressure for government—and possibly unions—to fill the gap, just as in the 1930s. That is precisely why Buchanan's candidacy, Clinton's corporate responsibility conference, and other incidents caused a stir in the nation's executive suites.[3]

A fascinating development of the mid-1990s were proposals from Democratic legislators, including Edward Kennedy, Jeff Bingaman, and Richard Gephardt, to encourage companies to treat employees more like "stakeholders." Employers who train their workers, give them decent health, family, and pension benefits, and have measures to cushion them from layoffs would receive preferential tax and regulatory treatment. In effect, such legislation would require government to subsidize the cost of private welfare capitalism, which is precisely how Marion Folsom conceived of social security in the 1930s. Far-sighted executives like Folsom remain as rare now as they were then, but views like his may become more prevalent as progressive employers search for new ways of bearing the cost of commitments to their employees.[4]

In short, as modern welfare capitalism becomes less expansive and inclusive, it will spur the growth of alternate methods of risk-bearing and work organization. On the other hand, welfare capitalism retains its economic logic and applicability to American conditions, and its strategic objectives—keeping unions and government at bay—remain intact. Even as welfare capitalism becomes more parsimonious, it still has the power to shape employee aspirations and social norms as to what constitutes a "good" employer. Those who demand that corporations be responsible are not asking for anything outside the framework established by corporations themselves. Public outcry over corporate downsizing demonstrates that Americans retain their faith in welfare capitalism as an economic ideal.

Back in the 1930s, American workers had a similar faith and turned to the New Deal to pressure employers to fulfill promises broken during the Depression. Those who think that our present prosperity is secure and that such events are unlikely to happen again should beware of the meliorist mind-set that prevailed in the 1920s. Clinton's corporate responsibility conference was reminiscent of another White House gathering—this one convened by President Hoover a month after the 1929 stock market crash—during which Hoover sought pledges from major employers not to cut wages and to otherwise preserve welfare capitalism. Despite the many changes of the last seventy years, there remains widespread support for the notion that corporations are—or should be—the keystone of economic security in American society.

Notes

Introduction

1. Samuel C. Johnson, *The Essence of a Family Enterprise: Doing Business the Johnson Way* (Indianapolis, Ind., 1988), 24–31, 113–20; S. C. Johnson and Son, Inc., *Jonwax Journal: 75th Anniversary Issue* (Racine, Wisc., 1961), 47–50; Herbert Johnson quoted in Daniel Nelson, *Unemployment Insurance: The American Experience, 1915–1935* (Madison, Wisc., 1969), 54–55; "What Price Child Care?" *Business Week*, February 8, 1993, 104; Joel Kurtzman, "Managing when It's All in the Family," *New York Times*, April 9, 1989.

2. William S. Leiserson, "Personnel Problems Raised by the Current Crisis," *Management Review* 22 (April 1933), 114.

3. Emile Durkheim, *The Division of Labor in Society* (New York, 1933), first published in French in 1893. Durkheim thought that small-scale firms were more harmonious than large-scale because the latter's excessive division of labor weakened norms of solidarity. These norms were supplied by the employer, his employees, and by the social milieu, a mixture that today is somewhat mushily called "corporate culture." The concept has received less attention from historians than it deserves, although see Charles Dellheim, "Business in Time: The Historian and Corporate Culture," *Public Historian* 8 (Spring 1986), 9–25.

4. Daniel Nelson, "The Great Goodyear Strike of 1936," *Ohio History* 92 (1983), 14. Also see Morris Janowitz, "Black Legions on the March" in Daniel Aaron, ed., *America in Crisis* (New York, 1952), 305–26, and, for an insightful overview, Robert Zieger, *The CIO, 1935–1955* (Chapel Hill, N.C., 1995).

5. Francis X. Sutton, Seymour E. Harris, Carl Kaysen, and James Tobin, *The American Business Creed* (Cambridge, Mass., 1956), 247; Rovensky quoted in Herman E. Krooss, *Executive Opinion: What Business Leaders Said and Thought on Economic Issues* (Garden City, 1970), 397; Douglass V. Brown and Charles A. Myers, "The Changing Industrial Relations Philosophy of American Management," *Proceedings of the Ninth Annual Meeting of the Industrial Relations Research Association* (Madison, Wisc., 1957), 84–99.

6. Gavin Wright, "Labor History and Labor Economics" in Alexander J. Field, ed., *The Future of Economic History* (Boston, 1987). Although it is erroneous to believe that everything in the present is seamlessly connected to the past, the opposite and prevailing tendency (especially in the United States) is to see the present constantly reinventing itself. Here I try to remedy our historical amnesia while at the same time avoiding what might be called, following David Hackett Fischer, the "fallacy of continuity."

7. Stephen A. Marglin and Juliet Schor, eds., *The Golden Age of Capitalism* (Oxford, 1990). On the rebirth of conservatism, see Alan Brinkley, "The Problem of American Conservatism" and Leo P. Ribuffo, "Why Is There so Much Conservatism in the United States and Why Do so Few Historians Know Anything about It?" *American Historical Review* 99 (April 1994), 409–29, 438–49; and Charles W. Romney, "The Business of Unionism: Race, Politics, Capitalism, and the West Coast Teamsters, 1940–52," Ph.D. dissertation, University of California, Los Angeles, 1996.

Chapter One
The Coming of Welfare Capitalism

1. Sumner H. Slichter, *The Turnover of Factory Labor* (New York, 1919), 202; Alexander Keyssar, *Out of Work: The First Century of Unemployment in Massachusetts* (Cambridge, Mass., 1986).

2. Gerald Friedman, "Politics and Unions: Government, Ideology, and the Labor Movement in the United States and France, 1880–1914," Ph.D. dissertation, Harvard University, 1985, 30; Gosta Esping-Andersen, *The Three Worlds of Welfare Capitalism* (Princeton, N.J., 1990).

3. Alice Kessler-Harris, *Out to Work: A History of Wage-Earning Women in the United States* (New York, 1982), 239; Jurgen Kocka, *White Collar Workers in America, 1890–1940* (Beverly Hills, Cal., 1980).

4. Morton J. Horwitz, *The Transformation of American Law, 1780–1860* (Cambridge, Mass., 1977); Christopher L. Tomlins, *The State and the Unions: Labor Relations, Law, and the Organized Labor Movement in America* (Cambridge, Mass., 1985); Reinhard Bendix, *Work and Authority in Industry* (New York, 1956), 269; John G. Cawelti, *Apostles of*

the Self-Made Man (Chicago, 1965); Rowland Berthoff, "The 'Freedom to Control' in American Business History" in David Pinkney and Theodore Ropp, eds., *A Festschrift for Frederick B. Artz* (Durham, N.C., 1964), 158–80. On labor disputes, see Val R. Lorwin, "Reflections on the History of the French and American Labor Movements," *Journal of Economic History* 17 (March 1957), 37; Philip Taft and Philip Ross, "American Labor Violence: Its Causes, Character, and Outcome" in Hugh D. Graham and Ted Robert Gurr, eds., *Violence in America: Historical and Comparative Perspectives* (Washington, D.C., 1969), 221; Robert J. Goldstein, *Political Repression in 19th Century Europe* (London, 1983); Simha Landau, "Trends in Violence and Aggression: A Cross-Cultural Analysis," *International Journal of Comparative Sociology* 25 (September 1984), 133–58; and Howard M. Gitelman, "Perspectives on American Industrial Violence," *Business History Review* 47 (Spring 1973), 1–23.

5. Lloyd Ulman, "Who Wanted Collective Bargaining in the First Place?" *39th Annual Proceedings of the Industrial Relations Research Association, New York, December 1986*; Sanford M. Jacoby, "American Exceptionalism Revisited: The Importance of Management" in Jacoby, ed., *Masters to Managers: Historical and Comparative Perspectives on American Employers* (New York, 1991), 173–200.

6. Jeffrey Haydu, *Between Craft and Class: Skilled Workers and Factory Politics in the U.S. and Britain, 1890–1922* (Berkeley, Cal., 1988); Jonathan Zeitlin, "From Labor History to the History of Industrial Relations," *Economic History Review* 40 (May 1987), 159–84.

7. On industrial size structure, see Mark Granovetter, "Small Is Bountiful: Labor Markets and Establishment Size," *American Sociological Review* 49 (June 1984), 323–34; and data cited in David Marsden, *Beyond Economic Man* (Brighton, U.K., 1986), 183. On evidence that skill wage differentials were wider in the U.S. than in Europe in the early twentieth century, see E. H. Phelps Brown and Margaret Browne, *A Century of Pay: The Course of Pay and Production in Europe and the U.S.A.* (London, 1968); and Peter Lindert and Jeffrey Williamson, *American Inequality: A Macroeconomic History* (New York, 1980). On employer associations, see Geoffrey Ingham, *Strikes and Industrial Conflict* (London, 1974); Arthur M. Ross, "Prosperity and Labor Relations in Europe: The Case of West Germany," *Quarterly Journal of Economics* 76 (August 1962), 331–59; Everett M. Kassalow, *Trade Unions and Industrial Relations: An International Comparison* (New York, 1969); and Howell J. Harris, "Getting It Together: The Metal Manufacturers' Association of Philadelphia, c. 1900–1930," in Jacoby, ed., *Masters to Managers,* 111–30.

8. Gitelman, "Perspectives," 21; Jerry M. Cooper, "The Army and Civil Disorder: Federal Military Intervention in American Labor Disputes, 1877–1900," Ph.D. dissertation, University of Wisconsin, 1971; Robert Justin Goldstein, *Political Repression in Modern America* (Cambridge, Mass., 1978); David Brody, *Labor in Crisis: The Steel Strike of 1919* (Philadelphia, 1965); Jeremy Brecher, *Strike!* (Greenwich, Conn., 1972).

9. John R. Commons, *Labor and Administration* (New York, 1913), 153. Also see James Weinstein, *The Corporate Ideal in the Liberal State, 1900–1918* (Boston, 1968); Samuel P. Hays, "The Politics of Reform in Municipal Government in the Progressive Era," *Pacific Northwest Quarterly* 55 (October 1964), 157–69; Sidney Fine, "The National Erectors' Association and the Dynamiters," *Labor History* 32 (Spring 1991), 5–41. Also see Daniel Fusfeld, "Government and the Suppression of Radical Labor" in Charles Bright and Susan Harding, eds., *Statemaking and Social Movements* (Ann Arbor, Mich., 1984), 344–77; and Selig Perlman and Philip Taft, *History of Labor in the United States, 1896–1932*, vol. 4, *Labor Movements* (New York, 1935), 5.

10. Sanford M. Jacoby, "The Duration of Indefinite Employment Contracts in England and the United States: An Historical Analysis," *Comparative Labor Law* 5 (Winter 1982), 85–128; William E. Forbath, "The Shaping of the American Labor Movement," *Harvard Law Review* 102 (April 1989), 1,109–1,257; Daniel Ernst, "The Closed Shop, the Proprietary Capitalist, and the Law," in Jacoby, ed., *Masters to Managers*, 132–50. Also see Stephen Skowronek, *Building a New American State: The Expansion of Administrative Capacities, 1877–1920* (Cambridge, Mass., 1982); Christopher Lasch, "The Moral and Intellectual Rehabilitation of the Ruling Class," in Lasch, *The World of Nations* (New York, 1973), 81–99; Thomas K. McCraw, "Business and Government: The Origins of the Adversary Relationship," *California Management Review* 26 (Winter 1984), 33–52; and J. Rogers Hollingsworth, "The United States" in Raymond Grew, ed., *Crises of Political Development in Europe and the United States* (Princeton, N.J., 1978), 163–96.

11. Samuel Gompers, *Seventy Years of Life and Labor: An Autobiography*, vol. 1 (New York, 1925), 97.

12. Bruno Ramirez, *When Workers Fight: The Politics of Industrial Relations in the Progressive Era, 1898–1916* (Westport, Conn., 1978), 149; Elaine Glovka-Spencer, *Management and Labor in Imperial Germany: Ruhr Industrialists as Employers, 1896–1914* (New Brunswick, N.J., 1984); Eugene C. McCreary, "Social Welfare and Business: The Krupp Welfare Program, 1860–1914," *Business History Review* 42 (Spring 1968), 24–49; Donald Reid, "Industrial Paternalism: Discourse and Practice in Nineteenth-Century French Mining and Metallurgy," *Comparative Studies in Society and History* 27 (October 1985), 579–607; and Patrick Joyce, *Work, Society, and Politics: The Culture of the Factory in Later Victorian England* (New Brunswick, N.J., 1980).

13. Charles Dellheim, "The Creation of a Company Culture: Cadburys, 1861–1931," *American Historical Review* 92 (February 1987), 13–44; Charles S. Maier, "The Factory as Society: Ideologies of Industrial Management in the Twentieth Century," in R. J. Bullen, H. P. Von Strandmann, and A. B. Polonsky, eds., *Ideas into Politics: Aspects of European History, 1880–1950* (London, 1984), 147–63.

14. Douglas Flamming, *Creating the Modern South: Millhands and Managers in Dalton, Georgia, 1884–1984* (Chapel Hill, N.C., 1992); James B. Allen, *The Company Town in the American West* (Norman, Okla., 1966); Robert S. Smith, *Mill on the Dan: A History of Dan River Mills* (Durham, N.C., 1960); Harriet L. Herring, *Welfare Work in Mill Villages* (Chapel Hill, N.C., 1929); Stephen J. Scheinberg, "The Development of Corporation Labor Policy, 1900–1940," Ph.D. dissertation, University of Wisconsin, 1966, 49.

15. James Myers, *Representative Government in Industry* (New York, 1924), 169. Also see Margaret Crawford, *Building the Workingman's Paradise: The Design of American Company Towns* (London, 1995); Elinor T. Kelly, ed., *Welfare Work in Industry* (London, 1925); Stuart D. Brandes, *American Welfare Capitalism, 1880–1940* (Chicago, 1976), 38–51; Stanley Buder, *Pullman: An Experiment in Industrial Order and Community Planning, 1880–1930* (New York, 1967); Kim McQuaid, *A Response to Industrialism: Liberal Businessmen and the Evolving Spectrum of Capitalist Reform, 1886–1960* (New York, 1986), 24–44; Don D. Lescohier, "Working Conditions" in John R. Commons and Associates, *History of Labor in the United States*, vol. 3 (New York, 1935), 371–84.

16. Sanford M. Jacoby, *Employing Bureaucracy: Managers, Unions, and the Transformation of Work in American Industry, 1900–1945* (New York, 1985), 50–51, 62–64; U.S. Bureau of Labor Statistics, "Welfare Work for Employees in Industrial Establishments in the U.S.," bulletin no. 250 (1919).

17. Mary La Dame, *The Filene Store* (New York, 1930); Joseph H. Willits, "The Arbitration Plan of William Filene's Sons Company," *The Annals of the American Academy of Political and Social Science* 69 (January 1917), 205–7; McQuaid, *Response to Industrialism* 50–97.

18. Joyce, *Work, Society, and Politics* 64–72; Mary B. Gilson, *What's Past is Prologue: Reflections on My Industrial Experience* (New York, 1940); Daniel Nelson, *Managers and Workers: Origins of the New Factory System in the United States, 1880–1920* (Madison, Wisc., 1975), 157–58.

19. David Brody, *Steelworkers in America: The Nonunion Era* (New York, 1969); Robert Ozanne, *A Century of Labor-Management Relations at McCormick and International Harvester* (Madison, Wisc., 1967); Walter Licht, "Studying Work: Personnel Policies in Philadelphia Firms, 1850–1950," in Jacoby, ed., *Masters to Managers*, 43–73. Outside of heavy industry, similar bureaucratic systems were first used by the railroads. See Walter Licht, *Working for the Railroad: The Organization of Work in the Nineteenth Century* (Princeton, N.J., 1983), 207–16.

20. Daniel Nelson, *Managers and Workers*, 109–10, 153; Jacoby, *Employing Bureaucracy*, 47–49.

21. Robert H. Wiebe, *The Search for Order, 1877–1920* (New York, 1967).

22. Sanford Jacoby, "Progressive Discipline in American Industry: Its Origins, Development, and Consequences," *Advances in Industrial and Labor Relations* 3 (1986), 213–60; Steven Fraser, "Dress Rehearsal for the New Deal: Shop-Floor Insurgents, Political Elites, and Industrial Democracy in the Amalgamated Clothing Workers Union," in Michael Frisch and Daniel Walkowitz, eds., *Working-Class America* (Champaign, Ill., 1983), 212–55.

23. James T. Kloppenberg, *Uncertain Victory: Social Democracy and Progressivism in European and American Thought, 1870–1920* (New York, 1986), 403; R. Jeffrey Lustig, *Corporate Liberalism: The Origins of Modern American Political Theory, 1890–1920* (Berkeley, Cal., 1982), 120–21. Also see Robert Westbrook, *John Dewey and American Democracy* (Ithaca, N.Y., 1991) and Philip Selznick, *Law, Society, and Industrial Justice* (New York, 1969).

24. Steven Fraser, *Labor Will Rule: Sidney Hillman and the Rise of American Labor* (New

York, 1991); Sanford M. Jacoby, "Union-Management Cooperation in the U.S.: Lessons from the 1920s," *Industrial and Labor Relations Review* 37 (October 1983), 18–33.

25. Samuel Haber, *Efficiency and Uplift: Scientific Management in the Progressive Era, 1890–1920* (Chicago, 1964); Henry C. Metcalf, "Report of the Committee on Vocational Guidance," National Association of Corporation Schools, *Fourth Annual Proceedings* (Saranac Lake, N.Y., 1916), 297; John Dewey, *The Public and Its Problems* (New York, 1927), 155, cited in Mark Barenberg, "The Political Economy of the Wagner Act: Power, Symbol, and Workplace Cooperation," *Harvard Law Review* 106 (1993), 1,419; Charles S. Maier, "Between Taylorism and Technocracy: European Ideologies and the Vision of Industrial Productivity in the 1920s," *Journal of Contemporary History* 6 (April 1970), 27–61.

Welfare capitalism might be called "private welfare corporatism," a term originally coined to describe Japan's organization-oriented employment system, with its extensive welfare provisions and programs to involve employees in management. This type of enterprise-level representation should be distinguished from the societal-level variant found in northern Europe. Under European-style corporatism, workers lobby via their unions for statutory terms of employment and public welfare provisions. See Ronald Dore, "Where We Are Now: Musings of an Evolutionist," *Work, Employment, and Society* 3 (December 1989), 425–46; Sanford Jacoby, "Pacific Ties: Employment Systems in Japan and the United States" in H. Harris and N. Lichtenstein, eds., *Industrial Democracy in the Twentieth Century* (Cambridge, 1993), 206–48.

26. Robert B. Wolf, "Use of Financial Incentives in Industry," *ASME Journal* 40 (December 1918), 1,035–38.

27. John R. Commons, *Industrial Government* (New York, 1921), 58–69, 158–67; McQuaid, *Response to Industrialism*, 77–97.

28. Gerd Korman, *Industrialization, Immigrants, and Americanizers: The View from Milwaukee* (Madison, Wisc., 1967); Stephen Meyer, *The Five Dollar Day: Labor, Management, and Social Control in the Ford Motor Company, 1908–1921* (Albany, N.Y., 1981), chap. 7; Jacoby, *Employing Bureaucracy*, 58–59, 233; George S. Gibb and Evelyn H. Knowlton, *History of Standard Oil Company (New Jersey): The Resurgent Years, 1911–1927* (New York, 1956), 570–80.

29. Daniel Nelson, "The Company Union Movement, 1900–1937: A Reexamination," *Business History Review* 56 (Autumn 1982), 335–57; Brandes, *American Welfare Capitalism*, 119–34; Scheinberg, "Development of Corporation Labor Policy," 100–23; John N. Schacht, "Toward Industrial Unionism: Bell Telephone Workers and Company Unions, 1919–1937," *Labor History* 16 (Winter 1975), 22. Also see Howell John Harris, "Industrial Democracy and Liberal Capitalism, 1890–1925" in Harris and Lichtenstein, eds., *Industrial Democracy in the Twentieth Century*, 43–66.

30. Cyrus S. Ching, *Review and Reflection: A Half-Century of Labor Relations* (New York, 1953); Josephine Young Case and Everett Needham Case, *Owen D. Young and American Enterprise* (Boston, 1982); interview with Gerard Swope, CUOHP (New York, 1955); David Loth, *Swope of GE: The Story of Gerard Swope and General Electric in American Business* (New York, 1958).

31. Jacoby, *Employing Bureaucracy*, 137–40; Myers, *Representative Government*, 77.

32. Elliot M. Fox and L. Urwick, eds., *Dynamic Administration: The Collected Papers of Mary Parker Follett* (New York, 1977), 44, 84; Lustig, *Corporate Liberalism*, 126–27.

33. Barenberg, "Political Economy of the Wagner Act," 1,438; Donald Fleming, "Attitude: The History of a Concept," *Perspectives in American History* 1 (1967), 287–365.

34. Mary Parker Follett, *The New State* (New York, 1918); Lustig, *Corporate Liberalism*, 134.

35. Jacoby, *Employing Bureaucracy*, chap. 6.

36. Daniel Nelson, *Unemployment Insurance: The American Experience, 1915–1935* (Madison, Wisc., 1969), 166; Commons, *Industrial Government*, 345.

37. Rockefeller quoted in Irving Bernstein, *The Lean Years* (Boston, 1960), 170.

38. Howard M. Gitelman, "The Rockefeller Network in Industrial Relations," unpublished ms., Economics Department, Adelphi University, 1985; Clarence Hicks, *My Life in Industrial Relations* (New York, 1941); Jacoby, *Employing Bureaucracy*, 180–86; Selig Perlman and Philip Taft, *History of Labor in the United States*, vol. 4 (New York, 1935), 495–514.

39. Henrietta M. Larson and Kenneth W. Porter, *History of Humble Oil and Refining Company* (New York, 1959), 98; Nelson, "Company Union Movement," 350.

40. Henry S. Dennison, "Management," in Report of the Committee on Recent Economic Changes of the President's Conference on Unemployment, *Recent Economic Changes in the United States*, vol. 2 (New York, 1929), 250;

Jacoby, *Employing Bureaucracy*, 186–87, 330; Sanford M. Jacoby, "Employee Attitude Surveys in American Industry: An Historical Perspective," in Norman Metzger, ed., *Handbook of Health-Care Human Resource Management* (New York, 1990), 73–87; Arthur W. Kornhauser and Agnes A. Sharp, "Employee Attitudes: Suggestions from a Study in a Factory," *Personnel Journal* 10 (April 1932), 393–404; M. L. Putnam, "Improving Employee Relations: A Plan which Uses Data Obtained from Employees," *Personnel Journal* 8 (February 1930), 314–25; Richard Gillespie, *Manufacturing Knowledge: A History of the Hawthorne Experiments* (Cambridge, Mass., 1991), 35.

41. National Industrial Conference Board, *Experience with Works Councils in the United States* (New York, 1922), 111, 116; Ozanne, *A Century*, 116–33; David Montgomery, *The Fall of the House of Labor: The Workplace, the State, and American Labor Activism, 1865–1925* (New York, 1987), 456; John C. Rumm, "The DuPont Company and the Special Conference Committee, 1919–1939," paper presented at the Duquesne History Forum, October 1983.

42. Gompers quoted in Brandes, *American Welfare Capitalism*, 120; Ronald Schatz, *The Electrical Workers: A History of Labor at General Electric and Westinghouse, 1923–1960* (Urbana, Ill., 1983), 41–42; Daniel Nelson, *American Rubber Workers and Organized Labor, 1900–1941* (Princeton, N.J., 1988), 103–6.

43. Scheinberg, "Development of Corporation Labor Policy," 122; Schatz, *Electrical Workers*, 41; Kloppenberg, *Uncertain Victory*, 402; Leiserson quoted in Schacht, "Toward Industrial Unionism," 6.

44. The Recovery Act, an emergency measure intended to encourage economic revival, explicitly gave employees the right to join unions (section 7a of the act). The act touched off a burst of organizing by the AFL as well as a company-union countermovement by employers. Unlike the Wagner Act of 1935, the Recovery Act did not explicitly forbid employers from creating company unions.

45. Ozanne, *A Century*, 124–25; Nelson, *American Rubber Workers*, 104–7.

46. Bernstein, *Lean Years*, 179–80; Myers, *Representative Government*, 172; Gorton James, Henry S. Dennison, Henry P. Kendall, et al., *Profit Sharing and Stock Ownership for Employees* (New York, 1926), 54; Lizabeth Cohen, *Making a New Deal: Industrial Workers in Chicago, 1919–1939* (Cambridge, U.K., 1990), 173.

47. Kendall, *Profit Sharing*, 194; Myers, *Representative Government*, 174. Also see Ben M. Selekman, *Sharing Management with the Workers* (New York, 1924).

48. Brandes, *American Welfare Capitalism*, 141; Jacoby, *Employing Bureaucracy*, 181.

49. Jacoby, *Employing Bureaucracy*, 197; David Montgomery and Ronald Schatz, "Facing Layoffs" in Montgomery, *Workers' Control in America* (New York, 1979), 139–52; Ruth Milkman, *Gender at Work: The Dynamics of Job Segregation by Sex during World War II* (Urbana, Ill., 1987), 27–48.

50. Bendix, *Work and Authority*, 295.

51. Bernstein, *Lean Years*, 187; Fox and Urwick, *Dynamic Administration*, 14.

52. Eugene D. Genovese, *Roll, Jordan Roll: The World the Slaves Made* (New York, 1974), 7; Joyce, *Work, Society, and Politics*, 93; Gerald Zahavi, *Workers, Managers, and Welfare Capitalism: The Shoeworkers and Tanners of Endicott Johnson, 1890–1950* (Urbana, Ill., 1988), 99–125; Commons, *Industrial Government*, 267.

53. Kocka, *White-Collar Workers*, 96–97; Robert S. Lynd and Helen M. Lynd, *Middletown: A Study in Modern American Culture* (New York, 1929), 100–5. National Industrial Conference Board (NICB), *Layoff and Its Prevention* (New York, 1930), 56. High labor turnover rates made it difficult for many women workers to qualify for pensions. See Jill Quadagno, *The Transformation of Old Age Security: Class and Politics in the American Welfare State* (Chicago, 1988), 94.

54. Sumner H. Slichter, "The Current Labor Policies of American Industries" (1929), reprinted in Slichter, *Potentials of the American Economy* (Cambridge, U.K., 1961), 213.

55. Neil J. Mitchell, *The Generous Corporation: A Political Analysis of Economic Power* (New Haven, Conn., 1989), 41.

56. Adelaide Clara Dick, "Personnel Work in the San Francisco Bay Region," M.A. thesis, University of California, Berkeley, 1927, 20, 27; Slichter, *Turnover*, 426–31.

57. Johnson quoted in Herman E. Kroos, *Executive Opinion: What Business Leaders Said and Thought on Economic Issues, 1920s–1960s* (Garden City, N.Y., 1970), 351; Rosenwald in "Sears Roebuck's Profit Sharing Plan," *Industrial Relations* 2 (February 21, 1931), 67; Slichter, "Current Labor Policies," 189.

58. C. Canby Balderston, *Executive Guidance of Industrial Relations* (Philadelphia, 1935), 224–40; Herman Feldman, "The Outstanding Features of Dennison Management," *Industrial Management* 64 (August, Septem-

ber, and October 1922); Kim McQuaid, "Industry and the Cooperative Commonwealth: William P. Hapgood and the Columbia Conserve Company," *Labor History* 17 (Fall 1976), 510–29; Mitchell, *Generous Corporation*, 41.

59. Edward A. Filene, *The Way Out* (New York, 1924), 99; McQuaid, *Response to Industrialism*, 153–54; Kim McQuaid, "An American Owenite: Edward A. Filene, 1890–1937," *American Journal of Economics and Sociology* 35 (January 1976), 77–94; Mary La Dame, *The Filene Store* (New York, 1930), 183–88, 274, 312–21.

60. Ralph C. Epstein, *Industrial Profits in the United States* (New York, 1934), 43, 92, 168, 196–97; Balderston, *Executive Guidance*, 224–38; Michael A. Bernstein, *The Great Depression: Delayed Recovery and Economic Change in America, 1929–1939* (New York, 1987), 35. Although vanguard firms often came from Bernstein's emergent industries, the fit was not perfect. Despite high profits, automobile firms rarely pursued vanguard policies because it was too costly to develop a cadre of stable employees in an unstable industry. On the other hand, two of the slowest-growing industries from 1914 to 1929—soap and sugar—nevertheless produced several prominent vanguard firms, including Procter and Gamble, Fels, California and Hawaiian Sugar Refining, and Spreckels. In spite of slow growth, these firms had other characteristics—stable demand, imperishable products, low labor cost ratios—that supported personnel experimentation.

David F. Noble argues that the thread tying the vanguard together was applied science and sophisticated product engineering. In Noble's view, what counted at firms like GE or Du Pont was not the liberal inclinations of Swope and Young, nor the Du Pont family's controlling interests, nor high and stable profits, but instead a managerial disposition to favor science-based methods of personnel management. Noble is undoubtedly correct to identify a link between the laboratory and the workplace. But it is, at best, only a partial explanation for welfare capitalism. Noble, *America by Design: Science, Technology, and the Rise of Corporate Capitalism* (New York, 1977).

61. A. D. H. Kaplan, *The Guarantee of Annual Wages* (Washington, D.C., 1947), 65; Paul H. Douglas and Aaron Director, *The Problem of Unemployment* (New York, 1931), 113–17; Simon Kuznets, *Seasonal Variations in Industry and Trade* (New York, 1933); Herman Feldman, *The Regularization of Employment* (New York, 1925), 44–70; Nelson, *Unemployment Insurance*, 28–63. Also see Sam Lewisohn, Ernest G. Draper, John R. Commons, and Don D. Lescohier, *Can Business Prevent Unemployment?* (New York, 1925).

62. Herbert Feis, *Labor Relations: Study Made in the Procter & Gamble Company* (New York, 1928), 92–107; Alfred Lief, *"It Floats": The Story of Procter & Gamble* (New York, 1958), 76–81, 123–33; NICB, *Layoff*, 16–17; George D. Babcock and Reginald Trautschold, *The Taylor System in Franklin Management* (New York, 1917), 90–92.

63. Leo Wolman, *Ebb and Flow in Trade Unionism* (New York, 1936), 92; Feldman, *Regularization*, 283, 285–86.

64. NICB, *Industrial Pensions in the United States* (New York, 1925), 6; Nelson, "Company Union Movement," 338; Jacoby, *Employing Bureaucracy*, 233; NICB, *Layoff*, 85–86; Office of War Mobilization and Reconversion, *Guaranteed Wages* (Washington, D.C., 1947), 290. The number of workers covered by pensions in 1925 was 2,815,000, although over 40 percent of these were employed by railroads, where a tradition of granting pensions had existed since the 1870s.

65. J. David Houser, *What the Employer Thinks: Executives' Attitudes toward Employees* (Cambridge, Mass., 1927), 116. Note that the structure of personnel administration increasingly was two-tiered (corporate and divisional) in diversified M-form companies like General Motors. During the 1920s, GM had a corporate industrial relations section in Detroit, although operational power resided at the divisional and plant levels. C. S. Mott, "Organizing a Great Industrial," *Management and Administration* 7 (May 1924), 527; Irving Bernstein, *The Turbulent Years* (Boston, 1970), 515; Robert W. Dunn, *Labor and Automobiles* (New York, 1929), 149.

66. For example, although company unions were active at AT&T and Jersey Standard during the 1920s, they fell into desuetude at Colorado Fuel and Iron, site of Rockefeller's first foray into employee representation. H. A. Tiedemann, "Should Employee Representation Be Applied to Scattered Groups of Wage Earners?" *Personnel* 4 (February 1928), 93–98; John Schacht, *The Making of Telephone Unionism, 1920–1947* (New Brunswick, N.J., 1985), 14–45; Ben M. Selekman and Mary Van Kleeck, *Employees' Representation in the Coal Mines* (New York, 1924), 381–98; Ben M. Selekman, *Employees' Representation in Steel Works* (New York, 1924); 215–33.

67. Daniel Nelson, "Scientific Management and the Workplace, 1910–1935," in Jacoby,

ed., *Masters to Managers*, 74–89. Nelson points out that the pursuit of rapid throughput in the mass production industries took its toll on foremen, too. In the 1920s, foremen at General Motors connived with production workers to restrict output and slow the pace of work. Despite GM's vaunted cost accounting controls, company executives knew "virtually nothing" about these and other shop-floor practices. Dunn, *Labor and Automobiles*, 198–201. For a more idealized description of GM in the 1920s, see William Lazonick, *Competitive Advantage on the Shopfloor* (Cambridge, Mass., 1990), 261.

68. Similar conditions existed in the steel and machinery industries, where employment was even less stable than in rubber or autos. Kuznets, *Seasonal Variations*, 210, 211, 389; Jacoby, *Employing Bureaucracy*, 202; Thomas Klug, "Employers' Strategies in the Detroit Labor Market, 1900–1929," in Nelson Lichtenstein and Stephen Meyer, eds., *On the Line: Essays in the History of Auto Work* (Urbana, Ill., 1989), 63, 71; Epstein, *Industrial Profits*, 43; Nelson, *American Rubber Workers*, 93.

69. Balderston, *Executive Guidance*, 199–206; Schatz, *Electrical Workers*, 110; NICB, *Layoff*, 56.

70. Roger E. Keeran, "Communist Influence in the Automobile Industry, 1920–1933," *Labor History* 20 (Spring 1979), 216; Samuel Levin, "The Ford Unemployment Policy," *American Labor Legislation Review* 22 (June 1932), 103; Dunn, *Labor and Automobiles*, 78–116, 148; Jacoby, *Employing Bureaucracy*, 198.

71. NICB, *Industrial Relations Programs in Small Plants* (New York, 1929), 20; Licht, "Studying Work," 43–73.

72. Houser, *What the Employer Thinks*, 82; Commons, *Industrial Government*, 263, 265. For a different view, see Harris, "Getting It Together," 111–30.

73. Jacoby, "Union-Management Cooperation," 27–29; Epstein, *Industrial Profits*, 168; Bernstein, *Lean Years*, 190–215; Forbath, "The Shaping of the American Labor Movement," 1,250–57.

74. Bernstein, *Lean Years*, 187; Brandes, *American Welfare Capitalism*, 141. Also see Montgomery, *Fall of the House of Labor*, 455, and Rick Halpern, "The Iron Fist in the Velvet Glove: Welfare Capitalism in Chicago's Packinghouses, 1921–1933," *Journal of American Studies* 26 (1992), 159–83.

75. David Brody, "The Rise and Decline of Welfare Capitalism," in Brody, *Workers in Industrial America: Essays on the 20th Century Struggle* (New York, 1980), 78; Cohen, *Making a New Deal*, chap. 4. Commons made the same point in 1921—that vanguard employers were "so far ahead of the game that trade unions cannot reach them. Conditions are better, security is better, than unions [could] actually deliver to their members." Commons, *Industrial Government*, 263.

76. Cohen, *Making a New Deal*, 209, 246, 249.

77. Jacoby, *Employing Bureaucracy*, 195.

78. "The U.S. Steel Corporation: Part III," *Fortune* (May 1936), 141; Jacoby, *Employing Bureaucracy*, 219; NICB, *Layoff*, 56; Kaplan, *Guarantee of Annual Wages*, 104. In 1956, the unionization rate for production workers in the manufacture of durable goods was 80 percent as against 56 percent for those in nondurable industries. U.S. Bureau of Labor Statistics, *Handbook of Labor Statistics* (1975), tables 42, 154.

79. Brody, "Rise and Decline," 77; John Schacht, *The Making of Telephone Unionism, 1920–1947* (New Brunswick, N.J., 1985), 14–45; Nelson, *American Rubber Workers*, chap. 5.

80. John C. Rumm, "The DuPont Company and the Special Conference Committee, 1919–1939," paper presented at the Duquesne History Forum, October 1983; Henrietta Larson, Evelyn H. Knowlton, and Charles S. Popple, *History of Standard Oil Company (New Jersey): New Horizons, 1927–1950* (New York, 1971), 353–59; Cohen, *Making a New Deal*, 243–46.

Michael Piore and Charles Sabel offer a related interpretation, one that focuses on welfare capitalism's shop-floor characteristics (employment stability and flexible job/pay structures). Echoing Brody, they contend that this nexus would have become the norm in American industry had it not been for the Depression and the rise of industrial unions. Those events established a different norm—the "mass production model"—which entailed periodic layoffs, seniority rules, and rigid job structures comprising well-specified tasks. The idea has received considerable attention, especially since it makes the ascendance of the mass production model appear as an accidental, rather than an inevitable, event, a critical "branching point," as Piore and Sabel term it.

Yet the argument exaggerates the reach of welfare capitalism's vanguard and ties the mass production model too closely to the New Deal. Some American companies were stabilizing employment and developing flexible internal labor markets in the 1920s. But those experiments largely took place outside heavy industry, where employers were able to offer employment stability in exchange for loose job definitions and wage flexibility. Within heavy industry, however, the mass production model was well established by the 1920s. Some pieces of evidence: first, in 1929 over half of U.S. manufacturing workers were on some type of piece-rate or bonus wage plan; second, among firms with transfer pay policies in 1927—a rather select group—almost 85 percent tied a worker's pay to the job held after transfer, which suggests, as do the data on incentive pay, that a rigid pay-job link was already the norm in many industries; third, durable goods manufacturers took scant interest in stabilization during the 1920s; and finally, despite highly publicized efforts by President Hoover to promote work sharing and forestall wage cuts, these constituted heavy industry's main response to the Depression, just as in previous downturns. Michael Piore and Charles Sabel, *The Second Industrial Divide: Possibilities for Prosperity* (New York, 1984), 124–30; Daniel Nelson, "Scientific Management and the Workplace, 1910–1935," in Jacoby, ed., *Masters to Managers*, 74–89. For an interpretation of the 1920s similar to Piore and Sabel's—but one containing more argument than evidence—see Lazonick, *Competitive Advantage on the Shopfloor*, chap. 8.

81. Richard C. Wilcock, "Industrial Management's Policies toward Unionism" in Milton Derber and Edwin Young, eds., *Labor and the New Deal* (Madison, Wisc., 1961), 277–315; Howell John Harris, *The Right to Manage: Industrial Relations Policies of American Business in the 1940s* (Madison, Wisc., 1982), 23. A similar typology can be found in Benjamin M. Selekman, "Varieties of Labor Relations," *Harvard Business Review* 27 (March 1949), 386–408.

82. Melvyn Dubofsky, "Not So 'Turbulent Years': Another Look at the American 1930s," *Amerikastudien* 24 (1979), 5–20; Alan Brinkley, *Huey Long, Father Coughlin, and the Great Depression* (New York, 1982); Thomas J. Sugrue, "Crabgrass-Roots Politics: Race, Rights, and the Reaction against Liberalism in the Urban North, 1940–64," *Journal of American History* 82 (September 1995), 551–78.

Chapter Two
Modernizing Welfare Capitalism

1. Sumner H. Slichter, "Are We Becoming a Laboristic State?" *New York Times*, May 16, 1948, reprinted in John Dunlop, ed., *Potentials of the American Economy: Selected Papers of Sumner H. Slichter* (Cambridge, Mass., 1961), 255–62. For an imaginative but, I think, erroneous view of business and unions in the 1930s, see Colin Gordon, *New Deals: Business, Labor, and Politics in America, 1920–1935* (Cambridge, U.K., 1994).

2. Mark Barenberg, "The Political Economy of the Wagner Act: Power, Symbol, and Workplace Cooperation," *Harvard Law Review* 106 (1993), 1,452; James A. Gross, *The Making of the National Labor Relations Board* (Albany, N.Y., 1974), 60–67.

3. Robert F. Wagner, "Company Unions: A Vast Industrial Issue," *New York Times*, March 11, 1934, sec. 9, p. 1; Ellis W. Hawley, *The New Deal and the Problem of Monopoly: A Study in Economic Ambivalence* (Princeton, N.J., 1969); Robert F. Himmelberg, *The Origins of the National Recovery Administration: Business, Government, and the Trade Association Issue, 1921–33* (New York, 1976).

4. Elliot M. Fox and L. Urwick, eds., *Dynamic Administration: The Collected Papers of Mary Parker Follett* (New York, 1977); George Wolfskill, *The Revolt of the Conservatives: A History of the American Liberty League, 1934–40* (Boston, 1962).

5. All of the companies belonging to the Special Conference Committee (SCC) were nonunion in 1930, but by 1945 only DuPont and Standard Oil of New Jersey remained nonunion. Historian John Rumm emphasizes three features shared by DuPont and Jersey Standard: first, the two firms had numerous small establishments making diverse products, which made it difficult for unions to create a sense of commonality across plants. Second, the firms were capital-intensive, meaning that they could afford to pay high wages and benefits. Finally, Jersey Standard and DuPont used continuous-flow technologies associated with clean work and a skilled workforce. Rumm's factors are important, but they do not apply generally to the companies examined here. John C. Rumm, "The DuPont Company and the Special Conference Committee, 1919–1939," paper presented at the Duquesne History Forum, October 1983.

6. Daniel Nelson, *American Rubber Workers and Organized Labor, 1900–1941* (Princeton, N.J., 1988); Peter Friedlander, *The Emergence of a UAW Local, 1936–1939: A Study in Class and Culture* (Pittsburgh, Pa., 1975); Steve Babson, *Skilled Workers and Anglo-Gaelic Immigrants in the Rise of the UAW* (New Brunswick, N.J., 1991).

Unfortunately, skill data are not available for either company, so I have calculated skill composition from census data for geographic industry segments dominated by Kodak (miscellaneous durable goods manufacturing in Rochester) and Thompson (motor vehicle and aircraft manufacturing in Cleveland):

Blue-Collar Workforce Composition, 1950 (percentage)

	Crafts, Foremen	*Operatives*	*Laborers*
All U.S. Durable Goods Mfg.	32	54	14
Rochester, N.Y. Misc. Durable Goods Mfg.	37	60	3
Cleveland, Ohio Aircraft & Parts	39	57	4
Motor Vehs. & Parts	32	61	7

Note that the skill distribution in 1950 was almost identical to that which existed in 1940. U.S. Census Bureau, *17th Census of Population: 1950*, vol. 2, "Characteristics of the Population," pt. 32, 411, and pt. 35, 461.

7. Generally, see Herbert Northrup, *Organized Labor and the Negro* (New York, 1944).

8. David G. Moore, "Managerial Strategies and Organization Dynamics in Sears Retailing," Ph.D. dissertation, University of Chicago, 1954, 88; *E.E.O.C. v. Sears Roebuck & Co.*, 628 F. Supp. 1,264 (N.D. Ill., 1986), 1,335.

9. Elton Mayo and George F. F. Lombard, *Teamwork and Labor Turnover in the Aircraft Industry of Southern California* (Boston, 1944); Chester I. Barnard, *Organization and Management* (Cambridge, Mass., 1948); Chester I. Barnard, *The Functions of the Executive* (Cambridge, Mass., 1938). On Barnard and his relationship to Follett, see William G. Scott, *Chester I. Barnard and the Guardians of the Managerial State* (Lawrence, Kans., 1992).

10. James C. Worthy, "Sears Roebuck and Co.: The X–Y Study," unpublished ms., August 19, 1984, JCWP.

11. For a modern discussion of these issues, see Alan Fox, *Beyond Contract: Work, Power, and Trust Relations* (London, 1974).

12. Neil Chamberlain, *The Union Challenge to Management Control* (New York, 1948), and Sanford M. Jacoby, "Employee Attitude Surveys in American Industry: An Historical Perspective," *Industrial Relations* 27 (Winter 1988), 74–93.

13. Robert Lynd and Helen M. Lynd, *Middletown in Transition: A Study in Cultural Conflicts* (New York, 1937), 445.

14. Ibid., 74–101.

15. Other companies gradually came to the same realization. Employer unfair labor practices peaked in 1938 and subsequently declined. And companies most exposed to public scrutiny—particularly those in large cities—had lower unfair labor practice rates than those in smaller towns. Robert E. Lane, *The Regulation of Businessmen* (New Haven, Conn., 1954), 12, 101.

16. Richard N. Block and Benjamin W. Wolkinson, "Delay in the Union Election Campaign Revisited: A Theoretical and Empirical Analysis," *Advances in Industrial and Labor Relations* 3 (1986), 53. However, it is true that the decline in the union "win" rate was more significant after Taft-Hartley, and especially after 1953, when President Eisenhower changed the composition of the NLRB. See Joseph Shister, "The Impact of the Taft-Hartley Act on Union Strength and Collective Bargaining," *Industrial and Labor Relations Review* 11 (April 1958), 342; Lloyd Ulman, "Unionism in the Modern Period" in Seymour E. Harris, *American Economic History* (New York, 1961), 425; and Chapter Six below.

17. Morris S. Viteles, "Wartime Applications of Psychology: Their Value to Management," American Management Association, Personnel Series no. 93 (New York, 1945), 3–12; Ralph Canter, Jr., "Psychologists in Industry" *Personnel Psychology* 1 (Summer 1948), 150; George K. Bennett, "A New Era in Business and Industrial Psychology," *Personnel Psychology* 1 (Winter 1948), 473–77. Also see Loren Baritz, *The Servants of Power: A History of the Use of Social Science in American Industry* (Middletown, Conn., 1960); Gerald Gordon, "Industrial Psychiatry: Five Year Plant Experience," *Industrial Medicine and Surgery* 21 (December 1952), 585–88; Joseph Tiffin, "How Psychologists Serve Industry," *Personnel Journal* 36 (March 1958), 372–76. On the Rockefeller network, see Guy Alchon, *The Invisible Hand of Planning* (Princeton, N.J., 1985); and Scott, *Chester I. Barnard*, 30–32.

18. James C. Worthy, "A Personnel Man Looks at His Vocation," speech to the Chicago Theological Seminary, February 2, 1953, p. 14, JCWP. On the 1920s, see Sanford Jacoby, *Employing Bureaucracy: Managers, Unions, and the Transformation of Work in American Industry, 1900–1945* (New York, 1985), chap. 6; David Noble, *America by Design: Science, Technology, and the Rise of Corporate Capitalism* (New York, 1977).

19. "The Worker's Poll that Kicked up a Fuss," *Business Week*, February 19, 1955, 30–31.

20. A sampling of this literature includes C. W. M. Hart, "Industrial Relations Research and Social Theory," *Canadian Journal of Economics and Political Science* 15 (February 1949), 53–73; Daniel Bell, "Adjusting Men to Machines," *Commentary* 3 (June 1947), 79–88; "Deep Therapy on the Assembly Line," *Ammunition* 7 (April 1949), 47–51; Henry Landsberger, *Hawthorne Revisited: Management and the Worker, Its Critics and Developments in Human Relations in Industry* (Ithaca, N.Y., 1958); Clark Kerr and Lloyd H. Fisher, "Plant Sociology: The Elite and the Aborigines," in Mirra Komarovsky, ed., *Common Frontiers of the Social Sciences* (New York, 1957), 281–309; and William A. Koivisto, "Value, Theory, and Fact in Industrial Sociology," *American Journal of Sociology* 58 (May 1953), 564–72.

Most of this literature was theoretical rather than empirical; few critics examined what companies were actually doing, although one notable exception was Jeanne L. Wilensky and Harold L. Wilensky, "Personnel Counseling: The Hawthorne Case," *American Journal of Sociology* 38 (November 1951), 265–80.

21. James C. Worthy, "Changing Concepts of the Personnel Function," AMA Personnel Series no. 113 (New York, 1949), 7.

22. James C. Worthy, "A Working Philosophy of Personnel Management," address to the Industrial Relations Assocation of Chicago, June 11, 1951, JCWP; Worthy, "Changing Concepts of the Personnel Function," 8. Also see Worthy, "Democratic Principles in Business Management," speech to the Industrial Management Institute, Lake Forest College, May 27, 1948, SR Archives, Chicago, and comments on the speech by company chairman Robert E. Wood in a memo to Fowler B. McConnell et al., October 14, 1948, JCWP. Worthy's thinking was shaped by Burleigh Gardner, a leader of the "human relations" movement (see Chapters Four and Six below) and by neo-corporatist thinkers like Peter Drucker. See Drucker's *The End of Economic Man: A Study of the New Totalitarianism* (New York, 1939).

A correlation (r = .43) across manufacturing industries existed in 1939 between unionization levels and prior use of time and motion studies. James N. Baron, Frank R. Dobbin, and P. D. Jennings, "War and Peace: The Evolution of Modern Personnel Administration in U.S. Industry," *American Journal of Sociology* 92 (September 1986), 365.

23. "The Reminiscences of General Robert E. Wood," CUOHP (New York, 1961), 104. Also see "Sears National Personnel Department: Its Organization and Function" (Chicago, c. 1955), 26, DCCU.

24. Marion B. Folsom interview by Peter Corning, June 1965, transcript, 170, CUOHP (New York, 1970); G. H. Malone memorandum, May 17, 1955, box 117, TRW Papers; Sears Roebuck, *National Personnel Conference Record*, November 4-6, 1946, Chicago, in possession of Professor J. E. Jeuck.

25. G. B. Hattersley, "Employee Relations Policies," American Management Association Personnel Series no. 40 (1940), 10; National Industrial Conference Board (NICB), "Statements of Personnel Policy," Studies in Personnel Policy no. 169 (New York, 1959), 31; Jacoby, *Employing Bureaucracy*, chap. 8; W. W. Tudor, "Management's Expanding Challenge in Personnel Administration," address to the Industrial Relations Conference of the Hawaii Employers' Council, Honolulu, March 8, 1957, p. 8. Also see George P. Shultz, "A Nonunion Market for White Collar Labor" in National Bureau of Economic Research, *Aspects of Labor Economics: A Conference of the Universities-National Bureau Committee for Economic Research* (Princeton, N.J., 1962), 107–46.

26. *Sears-News Graphic*, October 10, 1957, and April 10, 1958.

27. Howard Vollmer, *Employee Rights and the Employment Relationship* (Berkeley, Cal., 1960), chap. 2; NICB, "Seniority Systems in Nonunionized Companies," Studies in Personnel Policy no. 110 (New York, 1950); Wallace Tudor quoted in *Sears-News Graphic*, May 8, 1958, SR Archives; Baritz, *Servants of Power*, 161; R. S. Livingstone (Thompson Products), "Policies for Promotion, Transfer, Demotion, and Discharge" in *For National Unity: Better Industrial Relations*, Proceedings of the 24th Silver Bay Industrial Conference, July 1941, 82–89.

28. On the overlap between personnel management and public relations in the 1940s, see Richard S. Tedlow, *Keeping the Corporate Image: Public Relations and Business, 1900–1950* (Greenwich, Conn., 1979).

29. Net income is defined as profits after depreciation, debt service, and federal tax charges. The industry data in Table 2.2 are derived from the largest firms in each industry; these are *not* all-industry averages.

30. "How Much 'Personnel' in Your Plant?" *Modern Industry* 11 (February 15, 1946), 35–36.

31. Alfred D. Chandler, Jr., *Strategy and Structure: Chapters in the History of the Amer-*

ican Industrial Enterprise (Cambridge, Mass., 1962); William H. Whyte, *The Organization Man* (Garden City, N.Y., 1956); Jacoby, *Employing Bureaucracy*, chap. 8.

32. Howell J. Harris, *The Right to Manage: Industrial Relations Policies of American Business in the 1940s* (Madison, Wisc., 1982), 20–24; Irving Bernstein, *The Turbulent Years* (Boston, 1970), chap. 10. On managerial pragmatism, see Douglass V. Brown and Charles A. Myers, "The Changing Industrial Relations Philosophy of American Management," *Proceedings of the Industrial Relations Research Association*, ninth annual meeting, 1957, 91–94; and, more generally, Robert L. Heilbroner, "The View from the Top: Reflections on a Changing Business Ideology" in Earl F. Cheit, ed., *The Business Establishment* (New York, 1964), 1–36. On the NAM in the 1940s, see Philip H. Burch, Jr., "The NAM as an Interest Group," *Politics and Society* 4 (Fall 1973), 98.

33. Author's interview with John R. McCarthy, vice president and director, personnel relations, Eastman Kodak, Rochester, N.Y., June 15, 1987.

34. James C. Worthy, *Shaping an American Institution: Robert E. Wood and Sears, Roebuck* (Urbana, Ill., 1984), 49, 257.

35. Quoted in Robert R. R. Brooks, *As Steel Goes: Unionism in a Basic Industry* (New Haven, Conn., 1940), 199.

36. Michael A. Bernstein, *The Great Depression: Delayed Recovery and Economic Change in America, 1929–1939* (Cambridge, U.K., 1987).

37. Glen H. Elder Jr., *Children of the Depression: Social Change in Life Experience* (Chicago, 1974), 153–201; Robert and Helen Lynd, *Middletown in Transition*, 41; Stephan Thernstrom, *The Other Bostonians* (Cambridge, U.K., 1967).

38. Lizabeth Cohen, *Making a New Deal: Industrial Workers in Chicago, 1919–1939* (Cambridge, U.K., 1990), 206.

39. Robert E. Wood, speech presented at the Council of Profit Sharing's Hiram Nicholas Award Dinner, October 15, 1959, REWP; Bernstein, *The Great Depression*, 37–39. For modern evidence on profit sharing's stabilizing effect, see Douglas Kruse, "Profitsharing and Employment Variability," *Industrial and Labor Relations Review* 44 (April 1990), 437–53.

40. The phrase is from Cohen, *Making a New Deal*, 333.

41. Earl Kahn, "A Study of Intraoccupational Mobility," Ph.D. dissertation, University of Chicago, 1947, p. 59; Clarence B. Caldwell, "Management Responsibility in a Free Society," address to the Fifteenth Annual Midwest Conference of the Industrial Relations Association of Chicago, December 3, 1948, 4, DCCU.

42. Elder, *Children of the Depression*, 186, 192; Caldwell, "Management Responsibility," p. 5.

43. The 1940s are well anlyzed in Gary Gerstle, *Working Class Americanism: The Politics of Labor in the Textile Industry, 1914–1960* (Cambridge, U.K., 1989); and Steven Fraser, *Labor Will Rule: Sidney Hillman and the Rise of American Labor* (New York, 1991), 498–570.

44. Clarence B. Caldwell to Fowler McConnell, November 9, 1949, JCWP; Heilbroner, "The View from the Top," 29.

45. C. B. Caldwell to F. McConnell, November 9, 1949.

46. For an overview of these companies, consult the following: W. David Lewis and Wesley P. Newton, *Delta: The History of an Airline* (Athens, Ga., 1979); Janet Guyon, "Family Feeling at Delta Creates Loyal Workers, Enmity of Unions," *Wall Street Journal*, July 7, 1980; Thomas J. Watson, *A Business and Its Beliefs: The Ideas that Helped Build IBM* (New York, 1963); Nancy Foy, *The Sun Never Sets on IBM* (New York, 1975); Herbert Feis, *Labor Relations: A Study Inside the Procter and Gamble Company* (New York, 1928); Alfred Lief, *It Floats: The Story of Procter and Gamble* (New York, 1958); "How Procter & Gamble Avoided Serious Labor Trouble for 60 Years," *Printers' Ink* 222 (January 2, 1948), 39–41; Ralph Hidy, George Gibb, and Henrietta Larson, *History of Standard Oil Company*, 3 vols. (New York, 1955–1971); Henrietta Larson and Kenneth W. Porter, *History of Humble Oil and Refining Company* (New York, 1959); Floyd S. Brandt, "Independent and National Unionism in the Oil Refining Industry," Ph.D. dissertation, Harvard University, 1960; Rumm, "The DuPont Company"; Julius Rezler, "Labor Organization at DuPont: A Study in Independent Unionism," *Labor History* 4 (Spring 1963), 178–95; Ernest T. Weir, *Progress through Productivity* (New York, 1952).

Chapter Three
Preserving the Past: Eastman Kodak

1. G. Harry Stine, *The Corporate Survivors* (New York, 1986), 49; C. Canby Balderston, *Executive Guidance of Industrial Relations* (Philadelphia, 1935), 229.

2. Reese V. Jenkins, *Images and Enterprise: Technology and the American Photographic Industry, 1839 to 1925* (Baltimore,

Md., 1975), chap. 9; Eastman Kodak Co., *A Brief History* (Rochester, N.Y., 1983); John E. Webber, "Romances of Industry—Kodak," *American Industries* 12 (July 1925), 9–12; Roger Butterfield, "The Prodigious Life of George Eastman," *Life* 36 (April 26, 1954), 154; Carl W. Ackerman, *George Eastman* (Boston, 1930), 40–44. Ackerman, author of the only authorized biography of Eastman, was dean of the School of Journalism at Columbia University. In the 1930s he was an ardent opponent of the New Deal and served on the advisory council of the ultra-conservative Liberty League. George Wolfskill, *The Revolt of the Conservatives: A History of the American Liberty League, 1934–1940* (Boston, 1962), 67–69.

3. Jenkins, *Images and Enterprise*, chap. 10; Personnel Data file, KA; Blake McKelvey, *Rochester: The Quest for Quality, 1890–1925* (Cambridge, Mass., 1956), 257–60.

4. "A Glimpse into the Works of Eastman Kodak Company," *Industrial Engineer* 82 (May 1924), 214–15; Ackerman, *George Eastman*, 111; Eastman Kodak Co., *A Young Man Looks at the Eastman Kodak Company* (Rochester, N.Y., 1937), 3, DCCU; Marion B. Folsom, "Proposed Annuity and Insurance Plan for Eastman Kodak Co.," July 13, 1928, 46, Folsom file, KA; National Recovery Administration (NRA), *Statement of the Secretary of the Code Committee of the Photographic Industry*, public hearing, Washington, D.C., August 4, 1933, 17, box 1, file 6, FPUR.

5. Jenkins, *Images and Enterprise*, 307–12; NRA, *Code Committee*, 5; interview with Donald McMaster, November 1, 1971, box 1, BPUR.

6. McKelvey, *Quest*, 46; Eastman Kodak Co., *F. W. Lovejoy: The Story of a Practical Idealist* (Rochester, N.Y., 1947); Jenkins, *Images and Enterprise*, 325–27; Marion B. Folsom, "A Great Man," *University of Rochester Library Bulletin* 26 (Spring 1971), 59.

7. Butterfield, "Prodigious Life," 160; McKelvey, *Quest*, 344; Jenkins, *Images and Enterprise*, 318–23.

8. Jenkins, *Images and Enterprise*, 328; author's interview with Donald E. McConville, director of industrial relations (retired), Eastman Kodak Co., June 17, 1987.

9. John E. Webber, "Making Kodaks and Contentment," *American Industries* 25 (November 1924), 28; Eastman quoted in Folsom, "Great Man," 75.

10. Industrial Management Council of Rochester, "Fiftieth Anniversary Report" (1966); Blake McKelvey, *Rochester: An Emerging Metropolis, 1925–1961* (Rochester, N.Y., 1961), 11–14.

11. O. N. Solbert, "George Eastman," reprinted by Eastman Kodak Co. from article originally appearing in *Image: The Journal of Photography of the Eastman House, Inc.* 2 (November 1953); Folsom, "Great Man," 73; Ackerman, *George Eastman*, passim; McKelvey, *Quest*, 315–23. Also see Blake McKelvey, *Rochester on the Genesee: The Growth of a City* (Syracuse, N.Y., 1973), 155–89, which recapitulates material from McKelvey's other books.

12. "Interview with Marion B. Folsom," February 22, 1940, Folsom file, KA; Ackerman, *George Eastman*, 159, 365, 369–70; author's interview with McConville, 1987; Butterfield, "Prodigious Life," 160; interviews with Milton Robinson, 1970, and Mrs. Marion Gleason, 1969, box 1, BPUR.

13. Ackerman, *George Eastman*, 148, 199; "Eastman Tells about His Plan of Profit Sharing," *New York Times*, February 4, 1923.

14. Virgil M. Palmer, "The Operation of a Suggestion System," *Mechanical Engineering* 56 (December 1934), 731–35; Edwin A. Hunger, "Suggestions from Employees Help Company Save Money," *Annals of the American Academy of Political and Social Science* 71 (May 1917), 186–90; McKelvey, *Quest*, 261; A. W. Crittenden interview, 1971, box 1, BPUR; "Kodak Park Athletic Association Recreation Programs" (August 1962), Employee Recreation file, KA; interview with Donald McMaster, BPUR; *Kodak Park Bulletin* 22 (July 1919), 10–15, KA.

15. Wyatt Brummit, "The Corporate Image," unpublished ms. (c. 1963), KA, 10–13, 20–22, 45–47; Folsom, "Great Man," 67; McKelvey, *Quest*, 259; "History of the Kodak Employees' Association (KEA)" (n.d.), Personnel Resources file, KA; Ackerman, *George Eastman*, 355–59; Eastman Kodak Co., "Synopsis of Plan for Sale of Common Stock to Employees" (c. 1919), DCCU.

16. Folsom, "Proposed Annuity and Insurance Plan"; Ackerman, *George Eastman*, 360.

17. George Eastman, "Why I Turned 1/3 of My Stock over to Employees," *Magazine of Wall Street* 51 (June 1927), 750–53.

18. Brummit, "Corporate Image," 29; Folsom, "Proposed Annuity and Insurance Plan," 5; Ackerman, *George Eastman*, 235.

19. "Gompers Is Here," *Rochester Herald*, February 1, 1901, Labor Agitation file, KA; *Rochester Post Express*, January 2, 1903, ibid.; Ackerman, *George Eastman*, 156–65; McKelvey, *Quest*, 261.

20. "Fifteen Percent Wage Reduction for Masons and Bricklayers Recommended by Mr. Eastman," 1921, Industrial Relations box, KA; author's interview with Russ McCarthy, director of Rochester Industrial Management Council (retired), June 20, 1987; author's interview with Ken D. Howard, director of Equal Employment Opportunity Affairs (retired), Eastman Kodak Co., June 16, 1987; author's interview with McConville, 1987.

21. U.S. Department of Commerce, *Census for 1940: Manufactures*, vol. 7, pt. 2, 565–67; "Suggested Labor Policy for Eastman Kodak Company," March 30, 1920, Industrial Relations box, KA; National Industrial Conference Board (NICB), "Statements of Personnel Policy," Studies in Personnel Policy no. 169 (New York, 1959), 31.

22. Personnel data file, KA; author's interview with Howard, 1987; NICB, "Statements," 31. Also see Daniel M. G. Raff, "Ford Welfare Capitalism in Its Economic Context" in S. M. Jacoby, ed., *Masters to Managers: Historical and Comparative Perspectives on American Employers* (New York, 1991).

23. Folsom, "Great Man," 67; "Minutes of Meeting of Superintendents of Kodak Park," May 21, 1919, Industrial Relations box, KA.

24. McKelvey, *Quest*, 261; Jenkins, *Images and Enterprise*, 319; U.S. Senate, "Extract from Hearings on Economic Security Act before the Committee on Finance: Testimony of Marion B. Folsom," 74th Cong., 1st Sess. (February 8, 1935), box 20, file 3, FPUR; Blake McKelvey to author, October 30, 1987; "History of KEA." The fact that Kodak's 1911 Welfare Fund emphasized worker safety had everything to do with liability concerns raised by New York's 1910 accident compensation law. Charles H. Thompson, "Accident Prevention Important Factor in Eastman Kodak Co." *Safety Engineering* 52 (November 1926), 229–30.

25. "Eastman Tells," *New York Times*, February 4, 1923.

26. Webber, "Making Kodaks," 28. Several of Eastman's colleagues may have shared his racialist views. Frank Lovejoy and other Kodak executives told Eastman in 1918 that Kodak should hire only employees who were "100% American in spirit and aims." One person I interviewed in Rochester, who wished to remain anonymous, said that in the 1930s and 1940s it was simply "understood" that a Jew would never rise into top management at Kodak. F. W. Lovejoy et al. to G. Eastman, November 15, 1918, KA.

27. Author's interview with Howard, 1987. An interesting but unstudied question concerns the relative prevalence of firms like Kodak, which maintained an ethnically homogeneous workforce, as compared to those like International Harvester or U.S. Steel, whose workers were ethnically and racially diverse as a result of a conscious "divide-and-conquer" hiring strategy to head off potential labor unrest. See David Gordon, Richard Edwards, and Michael Reich, *Segmented Work, Divided Workers* (Cambridge, U.K., 1982). On republicanism, see Joyce Appleby, *Capitalism and a New Social Order: The Republican Vision of the 1790s* (New York 1984), and John L. Thomas, *Alternative America: Henry George, Edward Bellamy, H. D. Lloyd, and the Adversary Tradition* (Cambridge, Mass., 1983).

28. "Interview with Folsom," 1940, Folsom file, KA; Folsom, "Great Man," 63–64, 76–77; Frank W. Lovejoy to Henry G. Pearson, December 18, 1935, Lovejoy file, KA.

29. On testing, see Raymond Callahan, *Education and the Cult of Efficiency* (Chicago, 1962); Loren Baritz, *Servants of Power: The Use of Social Science in Industrial Relations* (Middletown, Conn., 1960); David F. Noble, *America by Design: Science, Technology, and the Rise of Corporate Capitalism* (New York, 1977). On Kodak, see Balderston, *Executive Guidance*, 76–77; "Kodak Employment," pamphlet (c. 1922), Industrial Relations box, KA; "Interview with Folsom," 1940, 3–4; Sanford M. Jacoby, *Employing Bureaucracy: Managers, Unions, and the Transformation of Work in American Industry, 1900–1950* (New York, 1985), 330 note 53.

30. Speech by Frank W. Lovejoy, November 1939, Lovejoy file, KA.

31. Evan B. Metcalf, "Economic Stabilization by American Business in the Twentieth Century," Ph.D. dissertation, University of Wisconsin, 1972, 51–70. Employment stabilization was endorsed by the Federated American Engineering Societies and its president, Herbert Hoover, in the report, *Waste in Industry* (New York, 1921). Also see Samuel Haber, *Efficiency and Uplift: Scientific Management in the Progressive Era* (Chicago, 1962).

32. A. H. Robinson, "The Control of Seasonal Employment," May 1, 1937, box 17, file 4, FPUR; M. B. Folsom, "Rochester Civic Committee on Unemployment," paper presented at Silver Bay Conference on Industrial Relations, August 28, 1930, Speeches, vol. 1, FPUR; "Minutes of Meeting of the Managers and Heads of Departments of Camera, Premo, Hawk-Eye, and Century Plants and State Street Office, May 28, 1919, Industrial Relations box, KA. Also see Malcolm C. Rorty, "The

Statistical Control of Business Activities," *Harvard Business Review* 1 (1923), 144–66. To manage his home, Eastman hired a professional housekeeper who supplied him with monthly reports on the yields of his barn animals and garden. Butterfield, "Prodigious Life," 161.

33. Interview with Marion B. Folsom, CUOHP (New York, 1967), 6; Ackerman, *George Eastman*, 368; H. D. Haight to F. W. Lovejoy, November 23, 1921, box 39, FPUR; M. B. Folsom, "Program of Stabilized Production and Employment," December 1930, Speeches, vol. 1, FPUR; Daniel Nelson, *Unemployment Insurance: The American Experience, 1915–1935* (Madison, Wisc., 1969).

34. H. D. Haight to F. W. Lovejoy, March 2, 1922, box 39, file 1, FPUR.

35. Interview with Craig P. Cochrane, 1971, BPUR; "Minutes of the Meeting of the Unemployment Committee," June 6, 1922, box 39, file 2, FPUR. On George Eastman's construction stabilization plan, see *Rochester Chronicle*, June 27, 1922, and *Geneva (N.Y.) Times*, December 17, 1926, clippings in Labor Agitation file, KA; and Ackerman, *George Eastman*, 369–70.

36. Harry D. Haight, "Outline of a Plan to Secure Greater Interest, Efficiency and Production through Vocational Training," March 16, 1920, Industrial Relations box, KA; "Suggested Educational Program for Eastman Kodak Co.," March 30, 1920, KA; Frank W. Lovejoy et al. to George Eastman, November 15, 1918, Automation file, KA.

37. "Industrial Relations Policies—Eastman Kodak Co.," March 25, 1919, Industrial Relations box, KA; Webber, "Making Kodaks," 28; "Minutes of Meeting of Superintendents of Kodak Park," May 21, 1919, Industrial Relations box, KA.

Eastman was a man quite different from George F. Johnson, the president of Endicott Johnson. "Daddy" Johnson, as he was known, "carefully cultivated the image of a 'father.'" He encouraged the company's shoeworkers to come to him with their financial and personal problems and in return expected a high degree of personal and corporate loyalty (they amounted to the same thing). After his death, Johnson's sons and nephew tried to continue this kind of modern seigniorage. Eastman, however, did not consciously try to play the role of corporate patriarch, possibly because of Kodak's greater size, its heavier reliance on native-born workers, or simply because of Eastman's taciturn personality. Workers occasionally came to Eastman with their problems—one wrote to him in 1920 asking for a loan—but these were irregular occurrences. Eastman wanted and encouraged loyalty, but to Kodak rather than to himself. When he died there were no heirs to inherit the corporate mantle. See the fascinating account written by Gerald Zahavi, *Workers, Managers, and Welfare Capitalism: The Shoeworkers and Tanners of Endicott Johnson, 1890–1950* (Urbana, Ill., 1988), 44–45, 211–12; A. Johnville to G. Eastman, September 25, 1920, Industrial Relations box, KA.

38. "Anti-Bolshevistic Program" (c. 1919), Labor Agitation file, KA; McKelvey, *Quest*, 347; author's interview with Hugh Harley, former organizer and vice president, United Electrical, Radio, and Machine Workers of America (UE), November 10, 1987; George Eastman to Kodak employees, August 15, 1919, Labor Agitation file, KA.

39. Lovejoy et al. to G. Eastman, November 15, 1918, KA; Brummit, "Corporate Image," 22, 38; Craig P. Cochrane to author, April 24, 1987. Eastman justified the stock sale by noting that "as labor conditions grow more difficult, it will be greatly to the advantage of the company to be a leader, not a follower. One of the great advantages of bringing this to a head now is that it was not done under force of any circumstances. Our employees are well satisfied and loyal, and this can only act to make them more so." Ackerman, *George Eastman*, 359.

40. "Industrial Relations Policies—Eastman Kodak Co." March 25, 1919; "Superintendents of Kodak Park Plant," May 21, 1919; "Employee Organization of the Camera Works," December 31, 1919; and "Minutes of Meeting of Managers and Department Heads of Camera, Premo, Hawk-Eye, and Century Plants, and State Street Office," May 28, 1919, all in Industrial Relations box, KA.

41. Brummit, "Corporate Image," 23–25; "Employees' Representation Meeting Minutes," November 16, 1921, KA; NICB, *Experience with Works Councils in the U.S.*, Research Report no. 50 (1926), 74–75; Joint Committee Minutes, Camera Works, December 16, 1919 and December 19, 1919, Industrial Relations box, KA; "Eastman Tells," *New York Times*, February 4, 1923.

42. Form letter approved by George Eastman, December 24, 1919; F. W. Lovejoy et al. to G. Eastman, November 15, 1918; W. H. Cameron to George Eastman, August 1, 1919; "Labor Policy—Eastman Kodak Co," January 2, 1923, all in Industrial Relations box, KA; Eastman Kodak Co., "Employees' Guidebook: Kodak Park" (c. 1929), DCCU.

43. "Superintendents of Kodak Park Plant," May 21, 1919, p. 3; *Kodakery* 10 (July 3, 1952), University of Rochester Library (URL); Balderston, *Executive Guidance*, 78; *Kodak* 11 (February 1931), URL.

44. "The Eastman Kodak Company and What It Stands For" (c. 1925), Industrial Relations box, KA; *Kodak* 19 (May 1939); Peter F. O'Shea, "Showing Employees How They Can Profit by Helping Each Other," *Factory* 29 (December 1922), 677–78; Norman J. Ashenburg, "The Conscience of a Corporation: Kodak's Occupational Health Program" (n.d.), Medical file, KA; *Kodak* 17 (June 1938); *Kodak* 7 (March 1928); Eastman in NICB, "Statements," 31. In 1933, Koda-Vista homeowners pleaded with the company for mortgage relief. As a result of this, Kodak got out of the home-building business as soon as the depression was over. H. D. Haight to J. D. Brown, February 3, 1932, DCCU; T. F. Hooker to J. L. Gorham, April 26, 1933, Personnel Resources file, KA.

45. Folsom interview, Columbia University, 3–4; U.S. Senate, "Hearings on Economic Security Act: Testimony of Marion B. Folsom," 1.

Of 8,000 employees on the Rochester payroll in 1918, 37 percent were still employed at Kodak ten years later, a figure that rose to 48 percent for males. Yet only 16 percent of all U.S. workers had an average job duration of ten years or more in 1928. As for turnover, annual separation rates in Kodak's Rochester plants from 1925 to 1929 averaged 29 percent; the corresponding figure for the U.S. manufacturing sector was 43 percent. Folsom, "Proposed Annuity and Insurance Plan," July 13, 1928, 1, 5–7; "All Rochester Employees Labor Turnover" (n.d.), box 17, file 1, FPUR; W. S. Woytinsky, *Three Aspects of Labor Dynamics* (Washington, D.C., 1942), 70. On the economic logic of pensions as a device to induce retirement, see Edward Lazear, "Why Is There Mandatory Retirement?" *Journal of Political Economy* 87 (December 1979), 1,261–84.

46. Marion Folsom, "Industrial Pensions and Group Life Insurance," June 28, 1928, Folsom file, KA, 23; Eastman Kodak Co., "Kodak Retirement Annuity, Life Insurance, and Disability Benefit Plan" (1929), DCCU; American Management Association, "Retirement Annuity Plan" General Management Series no. 108 (New York, 1929); Jill Quadagno, *The Transformation of Old Age Security* (Chicago, 1988), 77–96; Folsom interview, CUOHP, 5, 10, 46; Folsom, "Pensions and Group Life," 12; "Eastman Employees in Huge Insurance," *New York Times*, December 21, 1928.

47. Brummit, "Corporate Image," 77–79; *Kodak Worker*, February and May 1928, Labor Agitation file, KA; clipping from *Rochester Democrat and Chronicle*, January 30, 1962, KA.

48. M. B. Folsom, "Rochester Civic Committee on Unemployment," paper presented at Silver Bay Conference on Industrial Relations, August 28, 1930, Speeches, vol. 1, FPUR; W. G. Stuber, "Stabilization Methods Used by Eastman Kodak Company," radio broadcast on WHEC, January 6, 1931, DCCU.

49. Stuber, "Stabilization," 3; M. B. Folsom, "Program of Stabilized Production and Employment," December 1930, Speeches, vol. 1, FPUR; "Eastman Advances Wage Bonus Dates," *New York Times*, February 14, 1931; *Kodak* 11 (March 1931), 1.

50. Stuber, "Stabilization," 4; "Scheduling of Production Stabilizes Employment," *Iron Age* 127 (February 26, 1931), 697.

51. McKelvey, *Emerging Metropolis*, 57–59; Folsom, "Civic Committee," 4–5; President's Emergency Committee for Employment, *Outline of Industrial Policies and Practices in Time of Reduced Operation and Management* (Washington, D.C., 1931).

52. F. W. Lovejoy to M. B. Folsom, July 8, 1930, August 2, 1930; M. B. Folsom to F. W. Lovejoy, August 19, 1930, box 18, FPUR; Anice Whitney, "Operation of Unemployment Benefit Plans in the United States up to 1934," *Monthly Labor Review* 38 (June 1934), 1,316–17.

53. Nelson, *Unemployment Insurance*, 61–62; "The Rochester Unemployment Benefit Plan," *Industrial Relations* 2 (March 21, 1931), 121–23; Rochester Chamber of Commerce, Industrial Management Council, "Rochester Unemployment Benefit Plan" (1931), DCCU; H. D. Haight to M. B. Folsom, December 16, 1932, box 39, FPUR; M. B. Folsom to R. K. Brodie, December 13, 1933, box 18, FPUR; M. B. Folsom to M. W. Alexander, June 3, 1931, box 18, FPUR; U.S. Senate, "Testimony of Marion B. Folsom," 30.

54. F. W. Lovejoy to F. Perkins, March 20, 1931, box 1, FPUR; Metcalf, "Economic Stabilization," 329; M. B. Folsom, "The Rochester Unemployment Benefit Plan," Silver Bay Industrial Relations Conference, August 27, 1931, Speeches, vol. 1, pp. 4, 12, FPUR; M. B. Folsom to M. W. Alexander, June 3, 1931, box 18, FPUR; Chapin Hoskins, "Will the 'Rochester Plan' Solve Unemployment?" *Forbes* 27 (June 1, 1931), 28. One critic of the plan was John A. Fitch, who told

New York's Marcy Committee that the plan was defective for leaving final decisions in the hands of management without providing assurance that employee views would be taken into account. (All of the participating companies were nonunion.) Privately, Folsom told Fitch that some of the participating companies would administer the plan jointly with employee representatives. Although Fitch said he was pleased to hear this, neither Kodak nor the other companies ever adopted joint administration. J. A. Fitch to M. B. Folsom, November 23, 1931, and February 6, 1932; M. B. Folsom to J. A. Fitch, Feburary 3, 1932, box 18, FPUR.

55. Folsom, "Rochester Plan," 10; M. B. Folsom to F. W. Lovejoy, September 25, 1933, box 1; Whitney, "Operation of Plans," 1,305–7.

56. U.S. Senate, "Testimony of Marion B. Folsom," 30. The Rochester Plan continued to pay benefits through 1937, after which the New York unemployment insurance law superceded the plan. See Chapter Six below.

57. A. H. Robinson, "Control of Seasonal Employment," 4–5, 13; M. B. Folsom to F. W. Lovejoy, February 2, 1933, box 18; F. W. Lovejoy to Wilson C. Bloomer, October 3, 1932, box 1, FPUR; NRA, *Code Committee*, scheds. I and IV. While one might harbor the suspicion that Kodak intentionally reduced employment in 1932 to cut its costs under the Rochester Plan, there is no evidence to support this and, moreover, many of those laid off in 1932 would have been ineligible for benefits in 1933. M. B. Folsom to Constance M. Kiehl, March 4, 1935, box 20, FPUR.

58. Michael A. Bernstein, *The Great Depression: Delayed Recovery and Economic Change in America, 1929–1939* (Cambridge, U.K., 1987), 144–69; "Eastman Kodak's Growth Likely to Continue," *Barron's* 24 (September 18, 1944), 21–22; R. H. Wood, "The Principles and Practices of Profit Sharing," Ph.D. dissertation, Princeton University, 1942, 53. As for profits, Kodak ranked in the top quartile of all U.S. firms for the years 1929 to 1932. Balderston, *Executive Guidance*, 229.

Some economists were skeptical of Folsom's claims. In an article for the AFL's *American Federationist*, Richard A. Lester, a young economist at Princeton, criticized Folsom for having made overly optimistic statements to Congress about the Rochester Plan's achievements. After the article was reprinted in the *Congressional Record*, Folsom wrote to J. Douglas Brown, head of Princeton's Industrial Relations Section, to complain that Lester had been unfair. Two years later, Folsom still claimed that stabilization and the Rochester Plan were responsible for Kodak's salutary depression experience. Richard A. Lester, "Merit Rating and the Unemployed," *American Federationist* 44 (April 1937), 392–95; J. D. Brown to M. B. Folsom, May 12, 1937, and R. A. Lester to M. B. Folsom, May 14, 1937, box 1, FPUR; M. B. Folsom, "Stabilization of Employment and Income," *Management Record* 1 (February 1939), 24.

59. "Eastman Kodak's Growth," *Barron's* 20 (September 2, 1940), 13; author's interview with McConville, 1987.

60. "Wage Dividends," Benefit File, KA; memo from Craig P. Cochrane, January 5, 1938, Personnel Data file, KA; "Eastman Kodak Plants—Labor Turnover" (n.d.), box 2, file 6, FPUR; Bureau of Labor Statistics, *Handbook of Labor Statistics*, bulletin 1,865 (Washington, D.C., 1975).

61. "All Rochester Employees: Labor Turnover" (n.d.), box 17, file 1, FPUR; McKelvey, *Emerging Metropolis*, 66.

62. Frederick C. Mosher et al., *City Manager Government in Rochester* (Chicago, 1940), 5; author's interview with Professor Morris Neufeld, June 20, 1987. Haloid workers took over the plant in a 1936 sit-down strike and then turned to the ACWA for help. The firm's top management was split between conservative company chairman Gilbert Mosher and the liberal Wilsons—father ("Joe," the company president) and son ("Junior," president-to-be). The Wilsons immediately recognized the new union—partly to wrest control of the firm away from Mosher, partly because young Joe Wilson, Jr., believed that collective bargaining was the proper new way of doing business. John H. Dessauer, *My Years with Xerox* (Garden City, N.Y., 1971), 3–20; author's interview with Alice Grant, June 14, 1987.

63. Eastman Kodak, *The Company in War* (Rochester, N.Y., 1943), DCCU; *Kodakery* 3 (1945), various issues; McKelvey, *Emerging Metropolis*, 152; Eastman Kodak, *Annual Report for 1945*, KA.

64. Interviews with James White, Dr. A. K. Chapman, and Dr. Lee Davy, 1971, BPUR.

65. "Kodak's Growth," *Barron's* 24 (September 18, 1944), 21–22.

66. NICB, "Statements of Personnel Policy," Studies in Personnel Policy no. 169 (New York, 1959), 30. *Kodakery* 4 (August 15, 1946); "Eastman Kodak Enlarged," *Fortune* 50 (July 1954), 76.

67. U.S. Senate, Subcommittee on Antitrust and Monopoly, "Concentration in American Industry" (Washington, D.C., 1957), table

41; "Eastman Kodak: What Makes It Click?" *Forbes* 91 (April 1, 1963), 23–24.

68. Ward Gates, "Companies Showing Sustained Growth without Mergers or Acquisitions," *Magazine of Wall Street and Business Analyst* 100 (July 6, 1957), 492; William S. Vaughn, "Eastman Kodak Company Today and Tomorrow," speech to the Boston Security Analysts Society, October 16, 1961, DCCU; "Eastman Kodak Enlarged," 152; interview with Donald McMaster, 1971, BPUR.

Although Kodak's various consent decrees never seriously hurt the company, they did leave an unfortunate legacy for business historians. When the Justice Department investigated Kodak in 1947, it issued a subpoena covering all business records going back to 1921. William ("Wild Bill") Donovan, the company's lawyer and former head of the Office of Strategic Services, denounced the subpoena as "broad, sweeping, vague and indefinite." Donovan claimed that the government was demanding 643 tons of printed material. Even if this was hyperbole, Kodak realized that it was vulnerable as a result of never having cleaned its files in over fifty years. After the company got the subpoena quashed by a friendly judge in Buffalo, it purged all of its old records and set up a discard schedule for new material. *Kodakery* 5 (March 6, 1947); interview with Arthur L. Stern, 1971, BPUR.

69. "Personnel Data File," KA; author's interview with John R. McCarthy, vice president and director, personnel relations, Eastman Kodak, June 15, 1987.

70. Interviews with Donald McMaster and J. C. Mulder, 1971, BPUR; *Wall Street Journal*, November 15, 1972; Eastman Kodak Co., "Noteworthy Facts and Helpful Rules," (September 1956), 5, 8, DCCU; "Eastman Kodak Enlarged," 152.

71. "Employee Benefit Increases on Upswing in Chemical Industry," *Chemical and Engineering News* 28 (November 20, 1950), 4,082; "Chemical Workers Are Getting Top Fringe Benefits," *Oil, Paint, and Drug Reporter* 170 (October 1, 1956), 3; U.S. Chamber of Commerce, *The Hidden Payroll: Nonwage Labor Costs of Doing Business* (Washington, D.C., 1949); U.S. Chamber of Commerce, *Fringe Benefits: 1961* (Washington, D.C., 1962); Marion Folsom, "Kodak Benefit Plan," address delivered at Princeton University, September 7, 1950, Speeches, vol. 5, FPUR.

72. Sumner H. Slichter, James Healey, and E. Robert Livernash, *The Impact of Collective Bargaining on Management* (Washington, D.C., 1960), 376, 405; U.S. Bureau of Labor Statistics, "Wages and Related Benefits in 40 Labor Markets," Bulletin 1,113 (Washington, D.C., 1952), table 8b.

73. W. A. Sawyer, "Group Medicine," in *Employee Rating, Regularization, and Group Medicine*, AMA Personnel Series no. 39 (New York, 1939), 42; *Kodak* 15 (August 1935), 11; W. A. Sawyer to J. Douglas Brown, May 20, 1936, and H. D. Haight to J. D. Brown, January 31, 1936, DCCU.

74. "Eastman to Raise Worker Insurance," *New York Times*, September 13, 1937; Eastman Kodak, "Announcement of Kodak Additional Group Life Insurance Plan" (1937), DCCU; "Industrial Relations Chronology" (n.d.), KA; "Positive Principles Broadly Applied at Kodak," *American Business* 19 (May 1949), 58.

75. *Kodakery* 6 (June 10, 1948); Folsom, "Kodak Benefit Plans," 2; U.S. Senate, Committee on Finance, "Survey of Experiences in Profit Sharing and Possibilities of Incentive Taxation: Testimony of Marion B. Folsom," 75th Cong., 3rd Sess. (November 1938), 35.

76. Tennessee Eastman, *The Wage Dividend* (Kingsport, Tenn., 1940), 10, DCCU. For example, if common stock dividends were $6.00 per share, the basis would be $2.50 (that is, $6.00 less $3.50). The wage dividend rate for that year would be one-half percent (.005) multipled by 2.5, making the wage-dividend rate one and one-quarter percent (0.125).

77. Wood, "Principles and Practices of Profit Sharing," 78; James S. Bruce, "Extra Pay for Extra Work," Presentation to the Profit Sharing Council of America, October 22, 1981, KA; William S. Vaughn interview, 1971, BPUR. Note that the wage/stock dividend ratio of 50 percent excludes the "base" dividend of $3.50 paid to stockholders before the wage dividend kicked in. Including these base stock dividends, the ratio ranged from 10 to 35 percent. Leigh S. Plummer, *Getting along with Labor* (New York, 1939), 57; author's interview with M. B. Bael, director of corporate benefits, Eastman Kodak, June 18, 1987.

78. Eastman Kodak, "Your Wage Dividend" (various years, 1947–1961), DCCU; interview with R. W. Miller, BPUR; *Kodakery* 5 (March 6, 1947); author's interview with M. B. Bael. Kodak's largest stockholders in the 1950s were the British government and the University of Rochester.

79. Eastman Kodak, "You and the Years Ahead" (1957), DCCU; *Kodakery* 17 (August 1, 1959); Eastman Kodak, "Some Aspects of Kodak's Retirement Program" (September 1955), KA.

80. "Kodak Park Athletic Association History" (n.d.), KA; "Kodak Park Recreation Pro-

grams (August 1972), KA; *Kodakery* 17 (January 8, 1959). Also see Elizabeth Fones-Wolf, "Industrial Recreation, the Second World War, and the Revival of Welfare Capitalism," *Business History Review* 60 (Summer 1986), 232–57.

81. Author's interview with Donald E. McConville, June 1987; *Kodakery* 19 (December 14, 1961).

82. Interview with William S. Vaughn, BPUR; M. B. Folsom interview, Columbia University, 165.

83. M. B. Folsom, "Retirement Plans Pay Dividends," address to the joint meeting of the U.S. Chamber of Commerce and the Philadelphia Chamber of Commerce, Philadelphia, November 8, 1946, Speeches, vol. 4, FPUR; E. H. Hartman memorandum, August 1957, Benefits file, KA. The data for Kodak are taken from the Census figures for "other durable goods operatives in Rochester," nearly all of whom were employed by Kodak.

Age of Employees as a Percentage of Work Force

	Ages 25–54	*Over 55*
Rochester, other durable goods operatives		
Female	76	7
Male	74	15
New York State, all workers		
Female	64	13
Male	68	20

Source: U.S. Bureau of the Census, *17th Census of Population: 1950*, vol. 2, pt. 32, "Population Characteristics of New York," table 76.

84. Folsom, "Kodak Benefit Plans," 2; U.S. Senate, "Profit Sharing," 35.

85. Interview with Craig P. Cochrane, 1971, BPUR; Royal Commission on Trade Unions and Employers' Associations, "Minutes of Evidence: Kodak Ltd." July 25, 1967 (London, 1968), 2,901; interview with Brian Shemmings, organizer, Association of Cinematograph, Television, and Allied Technicians, February 1967, Bain Papers, Modern Records Centre, University of Warwick Library, Coventry (hereafter Bain Papers); American Institute of Management, *Management Audit: Eastman Kodak Company* no. 160 (April 1959), 12; "Kodak's Growth," *Barron's* 24 (September 18, 1944), 21.

In 1958, production labor payroll as a ratio of value added (the labor-cost ratio) was .27 in New York's photographic equipment industry (most of which consisted of Kodak employees) versus .35 elsewhere in manufacturing; roughly the same was true in 1939 and 1954. As for "earnings" (calculated as payroll divided by employment), in 1958 production workers in New York's photographic equipment industry were paid 32 percent more than the U.S. manufacturing average; for nonproduction workers the premium was 26 percent. In both cases the premium was slightly higher than in 1939, meaning that Kodak's wages rose faster than they did elsewhere in industry between 1939 and 1958. See U.S. Bureau of the Census, *1940 Census: Manufactures—1939*, vol. 2, pt. 2, 565–67; *1954 Census of Manufactures*, vol. 2, pt. 1, 4–5, 20–21; *1958 Census of Manufactures*, vol. 2, pt. 38, B–6.

86. "Statements of Personnel Policy," 30; Edmund R. King, "Eastman Kodak: Adapting Company Operations to a Changing Environment" in American Management Association, *Company Organization for Economic Forecasting* (New York, 1957), 33–56; J. F. Teegardin to A. K. Chapman, June 25, 1947, box 2, FPUR; Donald McMaster interview, 1971, BPUR; author's interview with M. B. Bael, 1987.

87. Eastman Kodak, "How Does Kodak Handle Attrition and the Displaced Worker?" (1958), and Monte Dill, "Proposed Press Release," June 9, 1959, both in Automation file, KA; interview of E. W. Schlosser, manager of Kodak Park Roll Film Department, 1971, BPUR.

88. Folsom, "Retirement Plan Pays," 6; author's interview with John McCarthy, 1987.

89. Curt Gerling, *Smugtown U.S.A.* (Webster, N.Y., 1957), 6; author's interview with Marjorie Gootnick, June 17, 1987; *Kodakery* 2 (April 9, 1943); author's interview with Alice Grant; Royal Commission, "Kodak Ltd.," 2,904; author's interview with Leonard Sayles, 1987; interview with James White, October 1971, BPUR.

Kodak employed about 60 percent of Rochester's "other durable goods operatives" in 1950, so the proportion of blacks in this category is a good indicator of the proportion of blacks employed in semiskilled jobs at Kodak. Black males made up .4 percent of other durable goods operatives in 1950, while they accounted for 1.3 percent of Rochester's total employment; the corresponding figures for black women were .8 and 1.8 percent. In other words, blacks were underrepresented at Kodak by a factor of at least 50 percent. U.S. Bureau of the Census, *17th Census of Population*, vol. 2, pt. 32, "Population Characteristics, New York," table 77.

90. In 1950, the proportion of women employed was as follows:

All U.S. Manufacturing	26%
Operatives-durables	26
Operatives-nondurables	41
Rochester Manufacturing	34
Operatives	43
Rochester Photographic Equipment	32
Operatives	35

Operatives were about 40 percent of Kodak's Rochester work force, and craft trades accounted for an additional 20 percent. Author's interview with Leonard Sayles; U.S. Bureau of the Census, *17th Census of Population*, vol. 2, pt. 32, tables 73–74 and vol. 4, pt. 1, "Occupation by Industry," special report P–E, no. 1–C, table 2.

91. A. B. Gates, "A New Technique in Executive Training," American Management Association, Personnel Series no. 24 (New York, 1936), 23–43; Allen B. Gates, "The Development of Supervisory Leadership," paper presented before the Pittsburgh chapter of the American Society of Training Directors (October 6, 1948), 4–5, DCCU; Allen B. Gates and N. David Hubbell, "A Management Approach to Problems of Individual Adjustment," unpublished paper (1950), 4, DCCU.

92. Donald McMaster, "Kodak Looks Ahead: A Description of Management Development Activities at Eastman Kodak Company," talk given to the American Management Association (January 27, 1955), 6, DCCU; Gates and Hubbell, "A Management Approach," 17; Eastman Kodak, *Principles of Supervision: Management Problems, Management Methods, and Human Nature* (revised) (July 21, 1947), 20, DCCU; C. P. Cochrane, "Kodak's Industrial Relations Objectives and Where We Stand" (October 27, 1953), 10, DCCU.

93. Gates and Hubbell, "A Management Approach," 5; Tom Miller speech to the Monroe County Bar Association (1962), quoted in Brummit, "Corporate Image," 74–75.

94. Howell John Harris, *The Right to Manage* (Madison, Wisc., 1982), 267; Cochrane, "Kodak's Objectives," 3, 15. To get superintendents to take foreman training seriously, Kodak asked them to design and direct training programs in their divisions. With superintendents in charge, they were less likely to tell foremen to "get back from your foreman training class as soon as possible." T. H. Miller, "Some Notes on the Industrial Relations Function, with Particular Reference to EK Co." (February 9, 1961), KA.

95. Eastman Kodak, "The Supervisor and the Suggestion System" (1944), 3–4, DCCU; author's interview with D. E. McConville, 1987; Eastman Kodak, "Encouraging Employees to Submit Suggestions," specially prepared for the Executives' Service Bulletin (1950), DCCU.

96. Author's interview with D. E. McConville, 1987; author's interview with Alice Grant, 1987; *Kodakery*, passim.

97. Author's interview with John McCarthy, 1987; Miller, "Some Notes," 3. In many respects, Kodak's approach to personnel management resembled the early "liberal" model, which called for a high degree of staff involvement in line activities. See Jacoby, *Employing Bureaucracy*, chapters 5 and 6.

98. Interview with A. E. Amor, August 1971, BPUR; C. P. Cochrane, "Industrial Relations" (September 6, 1940), KA; Balderston, *Executive Guidance*, 66; interview with Craig P. Cochrane, 1971, BPUR; Miller, "Some Notes," 2, 5; author's interviews with Ken D. Howard and John McCarthy, 1987.

99. Royal Commission, "Kodak Ltd." 2,909; author's interview with D. E. McConville, 1987; interview with Craig P. Cochrane, BPUR. Kodak's Canadian plant was organized by the International Chemical Workers Union, an AFL affiliate that Kodak managers viewed as a passively cooperative union; author's interview with K. D. Howard; Arnold R. Weber, "Competitive Unionism in the Chemical Industry," *Industrial and Labor Relations Review* 13 (October 1959), 21.

100. Royal Commission, "Kodak Ltd." 2,904; G. S. Bain, "Kodak Limited and Trade Union Recognition" (May 1967), 7; interview with A. E. Amor, deputy chairman, Kodak Ltd., June 1966, Bain Papers. In many respects, the WRC system was similar to the Camera Works representation plan of 1919.

101. A. B. Gates, "Employee-Employer Relationships," speech to the Sodus Rotary Club (October 26, 1937), KA (emphasis in original); "Why Are There No Unions at Kodak?" (c. 1960), KA; author's interview with John McCarthy, 1987; author's interview with K. D. Howard, 1987.

102. Gerling, *Smugtown*, 7; interview with Dr. Louis K. Eilers, June 1972, BPUR; American Institute of Management, *Management Audit*, 15; Frank W. Lovejoy, "What is 'The Company'?" (undated), KA.

103. Interviews with Donald McConville, 1987 and 1971, BPUR; *Prentice-Hall Pension and Profit Sharing Report* 12 (December 3, 1948), 3–4.

104. NICB, "Statements," 32–33.

105. Craig P. Cochrane, "Kodak's 'Open Door' Policy" (November 27, 1956), 5–6, DCCU; Cochrane, "Kodak's Objectives," 16; Eastman Kodak, "The Square Deal," 1956, DCCU; author's interviews with K. D. Howard and D. E. McConville; D. E. McConville interview, BPUR.

Kodak and Endicott Johnson used the same phrase—"the Square Deal"—in their corporate publications, but gave it different meanings. As the motto for Endicott Johnson's entire employee relations program, the phrase was supposed to connote a businesslike exchange of good wages and fair treatment in return for loyalty and hard work. Workers and managers at Endicott Johnson "negotiated" in various ways over the precise nature of what was being exchanged; each side ultimately felt cheated: one, by the rise of unions and the other, by the company's expansion into Mississippi and Puerto Rico. At Kodak, however, "square deal" simply referred to an employee's right to complain if he felt mistreated. The lack of contractual imagery may have helped Kodak avert the perpetual haggling that went on at Endicott Johnson. "Cooperation," which was Kodak's motto, connoted a more diffuse acceptance of managerial authority than the tit-for-tat approach of Endicott Johnson. Zahavi, *Workers, Managers, and Welfare Capitalism*, 40–41, 108–111, 213.

106. Author's interview with K. D. Howard. Kodak offered other "relief valves" than the open door procedure, such as its athletic directors and medical department staff, who were encouraged to hear employee complaints.

107. Barbara S. Griffith, *The Crisis of American Labor: Operation Dixie and the Defeat of the CIO* (Philadelphia, 1988), 26; "How Southern Plants Are Meeting Operation Dixie," *Modern Industry* 12 (August 1946), 51–64; interview with James White, BPUR.

108. Gates and Hubbell, "A Management Approach," 4; interviews with James White, Dr. Lee Davy, and Dr. A. K. Chapman, BPUR. At Kodak, none of the three choices on the ballot—AFL, CIO, or "no union"—received a majority in the first election. A runoff was held between the AFL and "no union" (the two top choices), which the AFL lost.

109. McKelvey, *Emerging Metropolis*, 195; David L. Hardisky, "The Rochester General Strike of 1946," Ph.D. dissertation, University of Rochester, 1983, 31–46, 140–142.

110. Hardisky, "Rochester General Strike," 186–90; Norman Ross and Murray Savage, "The Rochester General Strike," *Political Affairs* 25 (1946), 614–24; Rochester *Labor News*, May 31, 1946 in Hardisky, 195.

111. Letter to author from Dr. Mark McCulloch, UE Archives, University of Pittsburgh, July 24, 1987; author's interview with Hugh Harley, 1987; Ronald Schatz, *The Electrical Workers: A History of Labor at General Electric and Westinghouse, 1923–1960* (Urbana, Ill., 1983), 207, 216.

112. Author's interview with Hugh Harley; McColloch letter to author; "Kodak Refutes UE Charges," *Rochester Sun*, February 27, 1947; McConville interview, BPUR.

113. Author's interview with Hugh Harley; author's interview with Russell McCarthy, former director of the Rochester Industrial Management Council, June 20, 1987; Cochrane interview, BPUR; UE flyer, "Union Organization Forces Camera Works to Offer Raise" (February 14, 1947), Labor Agitation file, KA.

114. "Proposed letter for reference material" (February 17, 1947), Labor Agitation file, KA; "Kodak Refutes," *Rochester Sun*, Feburary 27, 1947.

115. Author's interview with Alice Grant; Hardisky, "Rochester General Strike," 51, 89; Mosher, *City Manager*, 6–7; *Kodakery* 5 (March 13, 1947); author's interviews with Russell McCarthy and Hugh Harley, 1987.

116. Other Rochester employers—including Aeolian Piano, Stromberg-Carlson, Hickok Belt, and a Du Pont branch plant—dealt with independent local unions, that had been set up as company unions in the 1930s or earlier. Seven of these unions joined together to form the Rochester Alliance of Independent Unions, which had 9,000 members in the 1950s. In later years, the unionization rate in Buffalo, a branch-plant city, was 40 percent; in Rochester it was 20 percent. Leo Troy, "The Course of Company and Local Independent Unions," Ph.D. dissertation, Columbia University, 1958, 154; New York State School of Industrial and Labor Relations, Cornell University, *Handbook on Human Resources and Industrial and Labor Relations in the Rochester Industrial Area* (Ithaca, N.Y., 1954), 9; Edward C. Kokklenberg and Donna Sockell, "Union Membership in the U.S., 1973–81," *Industrial and Labor Relations Review* 38 (July 1985), 536.

117. The city's business community was proud of Rochester Products, which, although it was a General Motors subsidiary, refused to recognize the UAW and was one of GM's last nonunion factories. GM eventually decided that there were few benefits to having a lone nonunion plant and allowed the UAW to organize it in the early 1950s. The Rochester business community was aghast but could exert little influence over the giant national firm.

Author's interviews with Professor George Strauss, University of California, Berkeley, 1987, and Russell McCarthy, 1987; McKelvey, *Emerging Metropolis*, 195–96.

118. In 1947, the Association of Catholic Trade Unionists (ACTU) began cooperating with the House Committee on Un-American Activities to discredit the UE's leaders, while working with the FBI to "nail Communist officers" at the local level. Whether the ACTU was involved in the Kodak campaign is not known. In Rochester as in other places, bitter disputes took place in the 1950s between the UE and IUE, including fights at GM's Delco plant and at General Railway Signal, which Hugh Harley had targeted back in 1945. Schatz, *Electrical Workers*, 167, 185; Bert Cochran, *Labor and Communism: The Conflict that Shaped American Unions* (Princeton, N.J., 1977), 289–90; McKelvey, *Emerging Metropolis*, 195–97.

119. McConville interview in BPUR; "Eastman Kodak *and* Film Technicians of the Motion Picture Industry, Local 683 of IATSE," case no. 21–RC–4218, 115 *NLRB* no. 91 (February 27, 1956); Miller, 1962, in Brummit, "Corporate Image," 74–75.

120. McConville interview, BPUR; author's interview with Julius Loos, former head of the Rochester Typographical Union, June 14, 1987; author's interview with K. D. Howard; Blake McKelvey to author, October 30, 1987.

121. Author's interviews with Grant, Gootnick, Howard, and McConville; Neil Chamberlain, *The Union Challenge to Management Control* (New York, 1948), 79; interview of E. W. Schlosser, 1971, BPUR; Alvin Gouldner, *Patterns of Industrial Bureaucracy* (New York, 1954), 53–56. Gouldner conducted his study in the late 1940s at a gypsum mine located between Buffalo and Rochester.

122. Orme Phelps, *Discipline and Discharge in the Unionized Firm* (Berkeley, Cal., 1959); Eastman Kodak, "The Supervisor and the Suggestion System" (1944), 2; Cochrane to author, 1987; Schlosser interview, BPUR; Cochrane interview, BPUR; E. M. Fox and L. Urwick, eds., *Dynamic Administration: The Collected Papers of Mary Parker Follett* (New York, 1977), 41.

123. Clinton S. Golden and Harold Ruttenberg, *The Dynamics of Industrial Democracy* (New York, 1942); John L. Lewis quoted in Irving Bernstein, *The Turbulent Years* (Boston, 1969), 535; author's interview with D. E. McConville, 1987; Cochrane, "Kodak's Objectives," 7, 18. On egalitarianism in American society, see Lynd and Lynd, *Middletown in Transition*, 445, and R. Bendix and S. Lipset, *Social Mobility and Industrial Society* (Berkeley, Cal., 1959).

124. Author's interviews with Alice Grant and Leonard Sayles; Donald B. Straus, *Hickey-Freeman Company and Amalgamated Clothing Workers of America* (Washington, D.C., 1949), 4; American Institute of Management, "Kodak," 13.

Chapter Four
Changing Styles: Sears Roebuck

1. Quotation from *Cosmopolitan* in Gordon Weil, *Sears Roebuck, U.S.A.* (Briarcliff Manor, N.Y., 1977), 2.

2. Early Sears history is discussed in Boris Emmet and John E. Jeuck, *Catalogues and Counters: A History of Sears, Roebuck Company* (Chicago, 1950) and Louis E. Asher and Edith Heal, *Send No Money* (Chicago, 1942).

3. G. Harry Stine, *The Corporate Survivors* (New York, 1986), 47–50.

4. Speech by C. D. Henderson, July 1918, Rosenwald Papers (hereafter RP), University of Chicago, box 55; "Sears Roebuck," *American Architect* 130 (August 5, 1928).

5. Factories were familiar to Sears because the company pursued a novel strategy of taking a financial interest in its suppliers. Sears usually had less than a majority stake, although it owned several firms outright. Kenneth Briegel, "Personnel Program—Meeting Mail Order Needs," *National Personnel Conference Record*, November 4–6, 1946 (hereafter *Personnel Conference 1946*), Chicago, courtesy of Professor John E. Jeuck, University of Chicago; Emmet and Jeuck, *Catalogues*, 286; W. C. Hartman, "Applications of Motion Study in Sears, Roebuck & Co." *SAM Journal* 1 (July–September 1936), 118–22; Joseph W. Towle, "Personnel Practices of Mail Order Houses," M.B.A. thesis, Northwestern University, 1938, 11–13; Louis E. Asher to Richard Sears, February 2, 1908 in Asher Papers, University of Chicago, box 1; "Extract from an article appearing in *B.Z. am Mittag*, March 2, 1925," RP, box 55.

6. M. R. Werner, *Julius Rosenwald: The Life of a Practical Humanitarian* (New York, 1939), 152; Lisa Fine, *The Souls of the Skyscraper: Female Clerical Workers in Chicago, 1870–1913* (Philadelphia, 1990), 87; Ralph Easley to Julius Rosenwald, March 3, 1913, box 26, RP; Emmet and Jeuck, *Catalogues*, 284; Alice Kessler-Harris, *Out to Work: A History of Wage-Earning Women in the U.S.* (New York, 1982), 102–5; Julius Rosenwald,

"Memorandum for a Short Talk to the Soldiers in the Trenches" (c. 1918), box 50, RP.

At $9.12 per week, women's wages at Sears were higher than at Macy's (which paid $7.94 in 1913) even though Macy's paid well. But many of the women at Sears were clericals, who were paid more—sometimes as much as twenty-five percent more—than women working in retail stores. Sarah S. Malino, "Faces across the Counter: A Social History of Female Department Store Employees," Ph.D. dissertation, Columbia University, 1982, 158; Susan Porter Benson, *Counter Cultures: Saleswomen, Managers, and Customers in American Department Stores, 1890–1940* (Urbana, Ill., 1988), 183, 190.

7. Werner, *Julius Rosenwald*, 121–36, 154, 159; Steven Fraser, *Labor Will Rule: Sidney Hillman and the Rise of American Labor* (New York, 1991), 59; Gorton James et al., *Profit Sharing and Stock Ownership for Employees* (New York, 1926), 215–18; "The Sears Roebuck Profit Sharing Plan," *The Survey* 36 (July 22, 1916), 426–27.

8. Richard H. Wood, "The Principles and Practices of Profit Sharing," Ph.D. dissertation, Princeton University, 1942, 75–98, 126; Emmet and Jeuck, *Catalogues*, 282–86; John E. Jeuck, "A Case Study in the Evolution of Personnel Management: Sears Roebuck and Company," Ph.D. dissertation, University of Chicago, 1949, 38, 158; Werner, *Julius Rosenwald*, 161–63. Because of the plan's qualifying requirements, only 49 percent of Sears employees in 1929 were covered by profit sharing as against 80 percent at Kodak.

9. Emmet and Jeuck, *Catalogues*, 280–81, 579.

10. Asher and Heal, *Send No Money*, 128–42; Emmet and Jeuck, *Catalogues*, 138–48; assorted material in box 3, Asher Papers; Henderson 1918 speech, RP; Benson, *Counter Cultures*, 142–46; "Social Service Work, Sears Roebuck and Company" (c. 1910), Labor-Management Documentation Center, Cornell University (hereafter DCCU); "Medical Work and Sanitation at the Plant of Sears, Roebuck and Co." (c. 1911), DCCU.

11. Asher and Heal, *Send No Money*, 105, 127; Emmet and Jeuck, *Catalogues*, 151; Werner, *Julius Rosenwald*, 61–63.

12. "The Reminiscences of General Robert E. Wood," CUOHP (New York, 1961) (hereafter Wood Oral History), 40–47, 103; Emmet and Jeuck, *Catalogues*, 295, 326, 485; Alfred D. Chandler, Jr., *Strategy and Structure: Chapters in the History of the American Industrial Enterprise* (Cambridge, Mass., 1962), 240.

13. Wood Oral History, 44–57, 77; Robert E. Wood, "On to Chicago," May 4, 1950, box 45, REWP; James C. Worthy, *Shaping an American Institution: Robert E. Wood and Sears, Roebuck* (Urbana, Ill., 1984), 82; James C. Worthy, "Store Openings: Sears and Wards," JCWP.

14. Emmet and Jeuck, *Catalogues*, 354, 485–87; "The Reminiscences of James Madison Barker," CUOHP (New York, 1951) (hereafter Barker Oral History) 106; Boris Emmet, *Department Stores: Recent Policies, Costs and Profits* (Stanford, Cal., 1930), 65; E. B. Weiss, "How to Sell through Department Store Chains," *Printer's Ink Monthly* 41 (July 1940), 5.

15. Among the company's key suppliers was Endicott-Johnson, the paternalistic shoe manufacturer. Wendell Endicott, a friend of Rosenwald's, was the man responsible for bringing Robert E. Wood to Rosenwald's attention. During the Wood era, Endicott was the only manufacturer on the Sears board of directors.

16. Worthy, *Shaping*, 68; Emmet and Jeuck, *Catalogues*, 403–9, 485–87; Wood Oral History, 53, 73; E. M. West to Lessing J. Rosenwald, July 17, 1934, in letters box, JMBP; Emmet, *Department Stores*, 65, 72, 78.

17. Wood Oral History, 51, 58–59, 98; Worthy, *Shaping*, 53; *Fortune* 38 (July 1948), 84; Eugene Whitmore, "Why Sears is Pushing Southern Industrial Development," *American Business* 12 (January 1942), 12–14; "What Did Happen at Wards's?" *Fortune* 53 (May 1956), 207; H. F. Travis, "Comparative Analysis of Two Great Mail Order Companies," *Magazine of Wall Street* 90 (May 3, 1952), 167; Emmet and Jeuck, *Catalogues*, 653.

Net sales at Sears rose by an average of 10.6 percent yearly from 1940 to 1959, as against an average of 6.6 percent for a control group of other large retailers (Allied Stores, Associated Dry Goods, Federated Stores, Marshall Field, Gimbel Brothers, Macy's, May Stores, J.C. Penney, Montgomery Ward, and Spiegel). Studley Shipert Statistics, *Retail Trade (Department Stores) Composite* (Boston, 1962), tables 41 and 74; *Standard and Poor, Industry Surveys: Retail Trade*, November 8, 1951, December 24, 1959, and October 4, 1962.

18. Emmet and Jeuck, *Catalogues*, 332, 487, 595, 604, 743; Werner, *Julius Rosenwald*, 239–43; Godfrey M. Lebhar, *Chain Stores in America, 1859–1950* (New York, 1952), 41; Robert E. Wood, "Address to On-to-Chicago Meeting," February 8, 1932, box 45, REWP; *Barron's* 16 (June 8, 1936), 16; *Sears News-Graphic*, May 4, 1938 and April 27, 1950, SR

Archives; *Commercial and Financial Chronicle* 31 (October 1936), 2,859.

19. Emmet and Jeuck, *Catalogues*, 5, 595; National Recovery Administration, Division of Review, "Evidence Study of Retail Trade" (Washington, D.C., August 1935), 8; *Sixteenth Census of the United State: Census of Business*, vol. 1, "Retail Trade: 1939" (hereafter *1939 Retail Census*), pt. 1 (Washington, D.C., 1943), 15–16.

20. Chains operated 65 percent of all department stores in 1939, up from 47 percent in 1929. At the national level, antichain sentiment led to the Robinson-Patman Act of 1935 (taxing chains) and the Miller-Tydings Act of 1937 (ratifying fair trade laws). Lebhar, *Chain Stores*, 99–112, 129; Alan Brinkley, *Voices of Protest: Huey Long, Father Coughlin, and the Great Depression* (New York, 1982), 144–48; Emmet and Jeuck, *Catalogues*, 606–13, 617–20; "General Robert E. Wood, President," *Fortune* 17 (May 1938), 69. Also see Maurice Lee, *Anti-Chain Store Tax Legislation* (Chicago, 1939) and material in box 55, RP.

21. Lebhar, *Chain Stores*, 161, 178; Worthy, *Shaping*, 195; Robert W. Wood, "The Company and Its Future," Speech to the Sears Forum, April 17, 1934, box 45, REWP. Wood also supported the NRA because its wage codes intensified the economic pressures felt by low-wage retailers, especially smaller stores. After the *Schechter* decision invalidating the NRA, Sears developed its own set of minimum wage rates as a way of gaining control over its national wage structure. Robert E. Wood to Franklin D. Roosevelt, May 27, 1937, box 14, REWP; Emmet and Jeuck, *Catalogues*, 80–82.

22. "The Sears Story," *Colliers* 124 (December 17, 1949), 48–49; Worthy, *Shaping*, 177; Lebhar, *Chain Stores*, 241; Barker Oral History, 151; Wood Oral History, 68; Emmet, *Department Stores*, 79. Sears also handed out hogs to southern farmers. By 1950, 90 percent of registered swine in Texas were descendants of pigs donated by the Sears Roebuck Foundation.

23. Author's interview with James C. Worthy, June 18, 1985, Evanston, Ill. For data on productivity at other members of the National Retail Dry Goods Association, see Sears Roebuck, "Post-War Personnel Program" (Chicago, 1944), 61, JCWP, and Joseph. H. Berger, "Chain Stores Improve Policies," *Personnel Journal* 19 (June 1940), 69.

24. Emmett, *Department Stores*, 46; Benson, *Counter Cultures*, 194–95; Malino, "Faces across the Counter," chap. 2; Industrial Relations Section, Princeton University, "Personnel Relations in Department Stores" (Princeton, N.J., 1931); Emmet and Jeuck, *Catalogues*, 554.

25. The figures in Table 4.1 stayed roughly the same through the 1950s. The largest change was in the proportion of women employed: in department stores this rose from 66 percent in 1940 to about 75 percent in 1950; at Sears, the percentage of retail women increased from 39 percent in 1940 to 45 percent in 1956. As for part-time employees, there was little change in their employment in department stores between 1940 and 1950, although at Sears, they rose slightly—from 33 percent in 1940 to 36 percent in 1950. Eliazbeth A. Burnham, "Key Problems of Retail Store Selling," *Harvard Business Review* 33 (January–February 1955), 106; *Sears News-Graphic* 24 (April 12, 1956), 3.

26. Women, too, probably felt more comfortable buying feminine goods from other women. For example, women accounted for 95 percent of U.S. millinery store employees in 1939. On the EEOC suit, see Ruth Milkman, "Women's History and the Sears Case," *Feminist Studies* 12 (Summer 1986), 375–400, and, for a different perspective, Thomas Haskell and Sanford Levinson, "Academic Freedom and Expert Witnessing: Historians and the *Sears* Case," *University of Texas Law Review* 66 (1988), 301–31.

27. In 1940, 86 percent of the employees in U.S. hardware stores and 93 percent in auto supply stores were male.

28. Sears Roebuck, Department 707, "Personnel Progress Report: 1948" (Chicago, 1948), 20, JCWP; David G. Moore, "Managerial Strategies and Organizational Dynamics in Sears Retailing," Ph.D. dissertation, University of Chicago, 1954, 176. During the Sears EEOC trial, the company claimed that "socialization" caused women to avoid high-pressure commission sales jobs. Yet some women wanted those jobs but could not get them, while others avoided them because they knew that male coworkers would make life miserable for them.

29. Sears Roebuck, "Testing at Sears" (Chicago, c. 1955), 33, DCCU; Sears Roebuck, "On to Chicago: Personnel Discussions: March 1939," 38, JCWP.

30. Sears Roebuck, "Post-War Personnel Program," 77–78; Sears Roebuck, "Employee Wage and Hour Policy," Bulletin 0–339 (April 1940), SR Archives; Paul A. Mertz, "Personnel Practices of Sears Roebuck & Co." *Personnel Journal* 18 (June 1939), 74–79; "Sears Forum, Season 1933–34," April 17, 1934, box 45, REWP; Jeuck, "A Case Study," 97. For

pay data, see "Personnel Progress Report: 1948" and testimony of Wallace Tudor in U.S. Senate, *Hearings before the Select Committee on Improper Activities in the Labor or Management Field*, 85th Cong., 1st Sess., pt. 15 (Washington, D.C., 1957), 6,049. The company newspaper quoted one woman who said, "Sears women think men are paid more for comparable work than they are." *Sears News-Graphic*, April 17, 1947.

31. Sears Roebuck, Department 707, "Opportunities for Women" (Chicago, c. 1941), JCWP; "Post-War Personnel Program," 93; Sears Roebuck, Dept. 707, "1949 Year End Report," 7, JCWP.

32. From 1945 to 1948, Sears retail employment rose from 65,000 to 108,000. Of the increase, no more than 15,000 were returning veterans (97 percent of whom were men). The remainder comprised 17,000 new male and 11,000 new female employees. In the late 1970s, Sears hired civil rights attorney Charls Morgan to defend the company against EEOC charges of race and sex discrimination. Morgan alleged that the government itself had created inequities in employment opportunity at Sears. Morgan's key claim was that the glut of white males at Sears in the 1970s was the product of the G.I. bill and other postwar government programs that encouraged massive hiring and rehiring of veterans. Morgan's claim was not false, but neither was it the whole truth. See "Personnel Progress Report: 1948," 24; "1949 Year End Report," 7; "Post-War Personnel Program," 18; *Sears News-Graphic*, April 27, 1950, 10; and Worthy, *Shaping*, 143.

33. *Sears News-Graphic*, 1938, passim, and May 16, 1940.

34. Sears Roebuck, "The 'Extra Problem' in Retail Stores," Special Report no. 1, Department 707 (Chicago, May 1939), 9–10, JCWP; Sears Roebuck, "Retail Personnel Practices and Plans for 1939," Department 707 (Chicago, 1938); Jeuck, "A Case Study," 6, 18.

35. *1939 Retail Census*, 57–59; Sears Roebuck, "Extra Problem," 3; "Personnel Progress Report: 1948," 24; interview with Max Steinbock reported in Ronald Michman, "Unionization of Salespeople in Department Stores in the U.S., 1888–1964," Ph.D. dissertation, New York University, 1966, 100; Weil, *Sears Roebuck U.S.A.*, 233; author's interview with Walter Johnson, president, Retail Clerks Local 1100, San Francisco, February 9, 1979; *Sears News-Graphic*, April 17, 1947; *Personnel Conference 1946* passim. Sears was an outlier even among chain stores, where 33 percent of the employees were part-timers.

36. Benson, *Counter Cultures*, 166; Emmet, *Department Stores*, 166; Edwin S. Smith, *Reducing Seasonal Employment* (New York, 1931), 171; Russel J. Doubman, *Principles of Retail Merchandising* (New York, 1936), 78. In department stores, the December peak was 165 (with average annual employment indexed to 100), whereas at Sears it rose to only 130. C. Canby Balderston, *Executive Guidance of Industrial Relations* (Philadelphia, 1935), 342; Sears Roebuck, "Extra Problem," passim.

37. Worthy, *Shaping*, 68; Emmet and Jeuck, *Catalogues*, 405, 583; Chandler, *Strategy and Structure*, 232.

38. Mertz, "Personnel Practices," 78; Sears Roebuck, "Comparison of Personnel Policies: W. T. Grant and Sears Roebuck," Department 707, Special Report no. 19 (Chicago, December 1939); Towle, "Personnel Practices of Mail Order Houses," 38; Burleigh B. Gardner, "Sears Personnel Relations Picture: A Critical Glance into the Looking Glass" in *Personnel Conference 1946*, 101–4; Donald R. Katz, *The Big Store: Inside the Crisis and Revolution at Sears* (New York, 1987), 14; author's interview with J. C. Worthy, 1985.

Department stores and Sears went separate ways during the Depression. Between 1929 and 1933, department stores laid off 35 percent of their full-time employees and raised part-time employment by 1 percent. As a result, part-timers' share of total employment shot up from 17 to 25 percent. Adding insult to injury, stores frequently ignored seniority when making layoffs, using the Depression as an excuse to replace middle-aged salespeople with "young and pretty college girls with refined accents." Thus the Depression was a disastrous experience for career department store workers, the group around whom retail unions later formed. David M. Polak, "Evidence Study of Retail Trade," NRA, Division of Review (Washington, D.C., August 1935), 8–11; Benson, *Counter Cultures*, 186–89, 203; Helen Baker, *Personnel Programs in Department Stores* (Princeton, N.J., 1935), 51.

39. Towle, "Personnel Practices of Mail Order Houses," 99; Burleigh B. Gardner, *Human Relations in Industry* (Chicago, 1945), 178–81; "Personnel Progress Report: 1948," 24. Because of its factorylike regularity, mail order could more easily smooth work hours than could retailing. As a result, it utilized fewer part-timers (22 percent, versus 34 percent in retail). Availability of full-time jobs may have offset the lack of promotional opportunities in mail order.

40. James C. Worthy, "A Study of Employee Attitudes and Morale," ms., 1942, 54, JCWP; Sears Roebuck Personnel Department, "Sears Employee Attitude Program, 1938–

1951," Personnel Report no. 22 (Chicago, February 1952), 47, JCWP; "Sears Forum, Season 1933–34," passim; *Sears News-Graphic*, April 26, 1951, and April 3, 1946.

41. Myrna Siegendorf, "Montgomery Ward versus the Union: A Case Study in Industrial Conflict," Ph.D. dissertation, University of Wisconsin, 1946, 100.

42. According to a union organizer, "Sometimes we find stores where employees have no future . . . dead end jobs, dissatified. Those types of employees are favorable to unionism." Retail Clerks, *Proceedings of the Educational Conference: San Diego, January, 21, 1951* in Organizing Department, Conference Minutes, reel 1, RCIAP.

43. George G. Kirstein, *Stores and Unions* (New York, 1950), 108; Siegendorf, "Ward versus the Union," 99.

44. Weekly earnings for retail employees at Sears were $52.10 in 1948; elsewhere in the U.S. they ranged from $54.87 in furniture stores and $51.23 in appliance stores—both male preserves—to $30.65 in variety stores, where most employees were female. Big-ticket men at Sears earned $86 per week in 1948, roughly the same as the eight-city average for big-ticket salesmen in other department stores ($84). Unlike Sears, however, these other stores were all located in major cities. A better figure for comparison is nationwide median earnings for male appliance-store salesmen, which in 1949 came to only $52 per week. Women in hourly retail jobs (sales and nonsales) at Sears earned $34 per week in 1948; elsewhere women's earnings ranged from $19 (five-and-dime stores) to $25 (grocery stores) up to $30 (general merchandise stores, including department stores). Finally, at Sears the pay ratio between men and women was .62, roughly the same as the national retail ratio, which ranged from .58 to .64. Women in sales jobs at Sears, however, earned 70 to 75 percent as much as men.

For overviews, see *U.S. Census of Business: 1948*, vol. 2, "Retail Trade," pt. 2 (Washington, D.C., 1952), 1,302; Elizabeth A. Burnham, "Key Problems of Retail Store Selling," *Harvard Business Review* 33 (January–February 1955), 106; Sears Roebuck, Department 707, "Personnel Progress Report: 1948," 20, and "Year-End Report: 1949," 9; *U.S. Census of Population: 1950*, vol. 4, Special Reports, "Occupation by Industry," pt. 1–C, table 2, and "Industrial Characteristics," pt. 1–D, 76–80 (Washington, D.C., 1954). Men's wages are found in Kermit Mohn, "Department Store Workers' Wages in 16 Cities," *Monthly Labor Review* 67 (November 1948), 485; "1949 Year End Report," 10; Siegendorf, "Ward versus the Union," 199–200; and Worthy, "Study of Employee Attitudes and Morale," 38, JCWP. On women's pay, see U.S. Department of Labor, Women's Bureau, Bulletin 209, "Women Workers in 10 Production Areas and Their Postwar Employment Plans" (Washington, D.C., 1946), 44; Women's Bureau, Bulletin 152, "Differences in the Earnings of Women and Men," (Washington, D.C., 1938), 24; U.S. Bureau of Labor Statistics, "Retail Clerks in Department Stores: Summer 1943," Bulletin 801 (1944), 5.

45. Sears spent $442 per employee on benefits in 1948, whereas department stores averaged $372. *Sears News-Graphic*, April 26, 1951; Emmet and Jeuck, *Catalogues*, 579; U.S. Chamber of Commerce, *The Hidden Payroll: Nonwage Labor Costs of Doing Business* (Washington, D.C., 1949), 19; Joseph H. Berger, "Chain Stores Improve Policies," *Personnel Journal* 19 (June 1940), 69–71; Baker, *Personnel Programs*, 67; William R. Spriegel, *Survey of Personnel Policies in Department Stores*, University of Texas, Bureau of Business Research, report no. 12 (Austin, 1959), 36; author's interview with J. C. Worthy, 1985; Clarence B. Caldwell, "Personnel Administration is Human Engineering" in Sears Roebuck, "On to Chicago: 1939," 9.

46. Clarence B. Caldwell, "Management Responsibility in a Free Society," ms., 1950, JCWP; J. C. Worthy to C. B. Caldwell, "Factors Contributing to High Morale among Sears Employees," February 18, 1949, 15, SR Archives.

47. J. C. Worthy to C. B. Caldwell, "Factors Contributing to High Morale," 17; "Personnel Progress Report: 1948," 21; Wood Oral History, 63–65; Worthy, *Shaping*, 152, 226; Emmet and Jeuck, *Catalogues*, 679–714; "The Savings and Profitsharing Pension Fund of Sears Roebuck and Co. Employees—Rules and Regulations," May 12, 1960, DCCU.

48. Wood Oral History, 35, 121–26; Earl Kahn, "A Study of Intraoccupational Mobility," Ph.D. dissertation, University of Chicago, 1947, 58; Jeuck, "A Case Study," 183–84.

49. Wood Oral History, 37–38, 103, 126; Jeuck, "A Case Study," 160, 184; Kahn, "Intraoccupational Mobility," 58; Weil, *Sears Roebuck U.S.A.*, 205; *Sears News-Graphic*, January 22, 1953; Emmet and Jeuck, *Catalogues*, 578.

50. James M. Barker to Robert E. Wood, February 23, 1953, Speeches and Papers, vol. 9, JMBP; *Wall Street Journal*, May 5, 1966, p. 5; Wood Oral History, 40–46, 107; Emmet and Jeuck, *Catalogues*, 704.

51. Wood Oral History, 71, 108; Fairchild Publications, *The Story of Sears Roebuck*

(New York, 1961), 11; Barker to Wood, February 23, 1953, JMBP. Also see J. M. Barker to Members of Sears Directors' Finance Committee, July 21, 1947; J. M. Barker to R. E. Wood, September 3, 1951; "Report of the Finance Committee to General Robert E. Wood," April 23, 1952 and December 4, 1952; and "Report to the Directors of Sears Roebuck on the Operations of the Savings and Profit Sharing Pension Fund for the Year 1957," March 25, 1958, all in Speeches and Papers, vols. 7–10, JMBP.

52. Sears National Personnel Department, "What Do Employees Like about Sears?" June 10, 1948, JCWP; Worthy, *Shaping*, 37; Kahn, "Intraoccupational Mobility," 59. For other "miracles," see *Monthly Labor Review* 34 (May 1932), 1,067; "The Sears Story," *Colliers* 124 (December 17, 1949), 50; and Wood Oral History, 104.

Rather than worry about the fund's risks, Sears' employees thought only about its fabulous returns. Fearing that any diversification would reduce the fund's earnings, employees protested when Sears invested part of the fund in its supplier companies. Moore, "Managerial Strategies," 150; J. S. Stock (Opinion Research Corporation), "How Department Stores Stand in the Public Eye" in National Retail Dry Goods Association, *Management and Personnel Forum: 1947* (New York, 1947), 206.

53. "Sears Forum Proceedings," *Sears News-Graphic*, April 21, 1955, April 11, 1957, April 21, 1949; *Sears Dixieland News*, April 9, 1959; author's interview with Walter Johnson, 1979.

54. I. R. Andrews in "On to Chicago: 1939," 59–61; "1949 Year End Report," 12–15; "Sears National Personnel Department: Its Organization and Function" (Chicago, c. 1955), 17–20, DCCU; D. M. Lockett, "The Power of a Well-Planned Personnel Program" in *Personnel Conference 1946*; *Sears News-Graphic*, May 26, 1951, and October 23, 1952.

55. Sears Roebuck, Department 707, "Minimum Essentials for an Effective Personnel Program," special report no. 23 (February 19, 1940), 3, JCWP; Worthy, "Factors Contributing," 15; Worthy, "A Personnel Man Looks at His Vocation," speech to the Chicago Theological Seminary, February 2, 1953, 14, JCWP.

56. J. David Houser to F. W. Taussig, September 6, 1924, Wertheim Fellowship Papers, Harvard University Archives (hereafter Wertheim Papers); Houser, "Measuring Consumer Attitudes," *Bulletin of the Taylor Society* 17 (April 1932), 50–52; Edward K. Strong, Jr., *Psychological Aspects of Business* (New York, 1938), 466–74; Ferdinand C. Wheeler, "New Methods and Results in Market Research," *American Marketing Journal* 2 (April 1935), 36. For popular accounts of worker attitudes, see the writings of Whiting Williams, such as *What's on the Worker's Mind: By One Who Put on Overalls to Find Out* (New York, 1920).

57. J. David Houser, *What the Employer Thinks: Executives' Attitudes toward Employees* (Cambridge, Mass., 1927), 164, 178.

58. Arthur Kornhauser and Agnes A. Sharp, "Employee Attitudes: Suggestions from a Study in a Factory," *Personnel Journal* 10 (April 1932), 393–404; Richard S. Uhrbrock, "Attitudes of 4430 Employees," *Journal of Social Psychology* 5 (August 1934), 365–77; Rex B. Hersey, "Employees Rate Plant Policies," *Personnel Journal* 16 (September 1937), 71–80; M. L. Putnam, "Improving Employee Relations: A Plan Which Uses Data Obtained from Employees," *Personnel Journal* 8 (February 1930), 314–25; Elton Mayo, *The Human Problems of an Industrial Civilization* (New York, 1933); F. J. Roethlisberger and William J. Dickson, *Management and the Worker* (Cambridge, Mass., 1939), 190–229, 270–91.

59. J. David Houser, *What People Want from Business* (New York, 1938), 1, 8, 20; Houser to F. W. Taussig, April 6, 1937, Wertheim Papers; Arthur Kolstad, "Employee Attitudes in a Department Store," *Journal of Applied Psychology* 22 (April 1938), 470–79; Richard L. Hull, "Measuring Employee Attitudes: A Proving Ground for Personnel Policy and Practices," *Management Record* 1 (November 1939), 165–72; Virginia Jones, *History of the Employee Morale Survey Program*, Sears National Personnel Department 707 (Chicago, July 1961), 4.

60. Kirstein, *Stores and Unions*, 32–36, 59, 93, 102–3; Robert K. Burns and Robert Buchele, "Unionism in Retailing," report published by the Industrial Relations Center, University of Chicago, 1949, 1, 30–53; Raulston G. Zundel, "Conflict and Cooperation among Retail Unions," *Journal of Business* 27 (October 1954), 301–11; Miriam Wise and Jess Lacklen, *Unionization in the Retail Field* (New York, 1940), 11; Michael Harrington, *The Retail Clerks* (New York, 1962), 7–9; Report of Boyd Buffett, organizer, July 10, 1937, Organizers' Mail, reel 4, RCIAP; Martin Estey, "The Strategic Alliance as a Factor in Union Growth," *Industrial and Labor Relations Review* 9 (October 1955), 47–49; Michman, "Unionization of Salespeople," 41–51, 151–57.

61. The only exception was a Sears store located in the heavily unionized mining region of southern Illinois. The Clerks had a contract

covering the area's retailers, which Sears adhered to after opening its Belleville store in the 1920s. Kirstein, *Stores and Unions*, 135.

62. Towle, "Mail Order Houses," 19, 140; Robert E. Wood to Franklin D. Roosevelt, June 17, 1937, box 14, REWP; R. E. Wood to J. M. Barker et al, October 27, 1938, JCWP; "Retail Personnel Projects 1939," 25. On San Francisco, see Kirstein, *Stores and Unions*, 37; *Union Organization of Department Store Clerks in San Francisco and California: The Story of Larry Vail*, an interview conducted by Corinne L. Gilb during 1958–1959 for the Institute of Industrial Relations, University of California, Berkeley, 124–39; *Sears Roebuck and United Retail, Wholesale, and Department Store Employees (CIO) and Sears Department Store Employees Local 1514 (AFL)*, 45 NLRB 526 (May 25, 1943). On Seattle-Tacoma, see "Western Retail Clerks Conference," August 28, 1948, in Organizing Department Conference Minutes, 1948–51, reel 1, RCIAP; Gust Anderson to W. L. Lamberton, April 15, 1938, and Cecil B. Dunlap to W. L. Lamberton, April 21, 1938, Organizing Department, Company Correspondence, reel 5, RCIAP; Wise and Lacklen, *Unionization*, 48; S. G. Lippman to Murray Plopper, July 24, 1959, in S. G. Lippman, Legal Department Miscellaneous Correspondence, reel 1, RCIAP; U.S. Bureau of Labor Statistics, "Wages in Department and Clothing Stores," bulletin 801 (Washington, D.C., 1944), 3.

63. David G. Moore, "Analysis of Overall Morale Picture," c. 1951, reprinted as Appendix Q of Jones, *History of the Survey Program*, 5; Clarence B. Caldwell to Fowler B. McConnell, February 26, 1952, JCWP; author's interview with J. C. Worthy.

64. Justus Doenecke, "General Robert E. Wood: The Evolution of a Conservative," *Journal of the Illinois State Historical Society* 71 (August 1978), 162–75; Worthy, *Shaping*, 38–54; R. E. Wood to Franklin D. Roosevelt, June 17, 1937, box 14, REWP; Clarence B. Caldwell to Fowler McConnell, November 9, 1949, JCWP.

65. Kirstein, *Stores and Unions*, 79–85; Burns and Buchele, "Unionism in Retailing," 35–36, 51–52; B. R. Canfield, "Unionization of Salesmen," *Printer's Ink* 233 (May 28, 1948), 34; Wayne A. R. Leys, *Ethics for Policy Decisions* (Englewood Cliffs, N.J., 1952), 296–97. Avery ran full-page ads in many newspapers attacking the War Labor Board for its "dictatorial" policies, after which Congressional conservatives opened hearings on the incident.

66. Leys, *Ethics*, 296, 301; Siegendorf, "Ward versus the Union," 29, 57; Robert E. Wood to R. J. Finnegan, April 28, 1944, Wood to Marshall Field, April 29, 1944, and various newspaper clippings, all in box 41, REWP; George Wolfskill, *The Revolt of the Conservatives* (New York, 1962), 229; "The Stores and the Catalogue," *Fortune* 11 (January 1935), 69–80; "The Stewardship of Sewell Avery," *Fortune* 33 (May 1946), 186.

67. Clarence B. Caldwell, "Three Year Program: Training and Related Activities" (December 19, 1944), 31, JCWP.

68. Houser Associates, "What This Is All About" (n.d.), DCCU; Worthy, "Study of Employee Attitudes and Morale," 8–14; author's interview with David G. Moore, October 2, 1985. Sears liked to boast of its high morale scores—the company average stood at 70—but most of the other companies surveyed by Houser Associates also scored at that level. Hull, "Measuring Employee Attitudes," 167; Richard L. Hull and Arthur L. Kolstad, "Morale on the Job" in Goodwin Watson, ed., *Civilian Morale* (Boston, 1942), 355.

69. Jones, *History of the Survey Program*, 5–9; Clarence B. Caldwell, "The Retail Personnel Program: 1940," 26–28, SR Archives.

70. Clarence B. Caldwell, "The Sears Survey Program," January 15, 1952, SR Archives.

71. Worthy, "Study of Employee Attitudes and Morale," 56–61; Worthy, "Factors Influencing Employee Morale," *Harvard Business Review* 28 (January 1950), 65; David G. Moore, "Problems of Low Status Employees" (1950), 4, JCWP; David G. Moore and Burleigh B. Gardner, "Factors Related to Morale" (1946), reprinted as Appendix J of Jones, *History of the Survey Program*; William Foote Whyte, "Human Relations: A Progress Report" in Amitai Etzioni, ed., *Complex Organizations: A Sociological Reader* (New York, 1961), 105. Whyte became involved in the Sears research through the University of Chicago's Committee on Human Relations in Industry; see Chapter Six below.

72. James Worthy, "Social Aspects of Industrial Relations," typescript, August 4, 1943, 33–51, SR Archives; Hull and Kolstad, "Morale on the Job," 363; David G. Moore, "How Do Our Employees Feel about Us?" in *Personnel Conference 1946*, 104.

73. Author's interview with Burleigh B. Gardner, March 23, 1985; Allison Davis, Burleigh B. Gardner, and Mary Gardner, *Deep South: A Social Anthropological Study of Caste and Class* (Chicago, 1941); W. Lloyd Warner and Allison Davis, "A Comparative Study of American Caste" in Edgar Thompson, ed., *Race Relations and the Race Problem* (Durham, N.C., 1939), 234. Like the Hawthorne research, Yankee City received funding

from the Harvard Business School and the two studies cross-fertilized each other. Warner designed the bank wiring phase at Hawthorne, developing ideas there that became the foundation for Yankee City, while Mayo and Roethlisberger gave advice on nondirective interviewing to Warner and his student assistants. The original idea for Yankee City came from Elton Mayo, who encouraged his colleague Warner to investigate the relationship between factory and community as a complement to Hawthorne's focus on the factory's internal organization. Although the area surrounding the Hawthorne plant seemed an obvious research site, Warner thought that the community of recent immigrants was too "disorganized" and "dysfunctional" to permit a satisfactory study. This pointed him toward New England and toward the South. William Lloyd Warner and Paul Lunt, *The Social Life of a Modern Community* (New Haven, Conn., 1941), 3–5, 38–39, 49–51.

74. Gardner, *Human Relations*, 4–23, 96–116, 168–200; Burleigh B. Gardner and William F. Whyte, "The Position and Problems of the Foreman," *Applied Anthropology* 4 (Spring 1945), 26; Burleigh B. Gardner, "The Factory as a Social System," in William F. Whyte, ed., *Industry and Society* (New York, 1946), 18–19.

75. Author's interview with J. C. Worthy, 1985; Worthy, "Methods and Techniques for Building a Cooperative Organization" in University of Chicago, Industrial Relations Center, *Executive Seminar Series on Industrial Relations*, 1946–1947, Session 11, April 1947, 21, SR Archives.

76. "Sears Employee Attitude Program, 1938 through 1951," Sears Personnel Department, Personnel Report no. 22 (February 1, 1952), 6–7, JCWP; author's interview with B. B. Gardner, 1985.

77. Burleigh B. Gardner, *Case Studies for Interviewing Methods and Techniques: Business 245* (Chicago, 1944), 6–7; Moore, "How Employees Feel," 106.

78. Gardner, *Case Studies*, 3–4; Worthy, "Methods and Techniques," 10–11.

79. *Personnel Conference 1946*, 116; Burleigh B. Gardner, "A Program of Research in Human Relations in Industry," American Management Association (AMA), Personnel Series no. 80 (New York, 1945), 35.

80. Sears Roebuck, National Personnel Department, "Organization Survey: Chicago Mail Order" (November 1948), Introduction, 1, JCWP.

81. Another change was the greater care taken to cultivate a favorable image for the survey program. Questionnaires were never distributed in stores anticipating layoffs or in departments that were about to dismiss an employee. Sears National Personnel Department, "Organization Survey Manual" (January 1950), 12–35, JCWP; James C. Worthy, "Discovering and Evaluating Employee Attitudes," AMA Personnel Series no. 113 (New York, 1947), 14; Worthy, "Methods and Techniques," 23; Gardner and Moore quoted in Jones, *History of the Survey Program*, 17.

82. David G. Moore to author, April 25, 1985; James C. Worthy, "The Study of Employee Attitudes and Morale," 1947, 16, SR Archives; "Interviewing," in Sears Planning Division, *Manual for Conducting Store Surveys* (c. 1949), JCWP. A concerted effort was made to involve the local store manager in the survey process. At the start of a survey, a nondirective interviewing session was held with the manager so that he could talk about his problems and release any anxiety he harbored about his store being surveyed. After the survey was over, the team reviewed the results with the store manager and his assistants. The discussion usually focused on "inversions"—atypical response patterns. Through this clinical process store managers were taught to think analytically about their employees.

83. Worthy, "Discovering and Evaluating," 14–17; Worthy, "Methods and Techniques," 12; Caldwell, "Sears Survey Program," 12; author's interview with B. B. Gardner, 1985.

84. Jones, *History of the Survey Program*, 32; author's interview with J. C. Worthy, 1985; author's interview with Frank J. Smith, March 20, 1985.

85. Author's interview with B. B. Gardner, 1985; Moore, "Analysis of Morale," 7; "Chicago Mail Order," Recommendations, 1–5. Research done at Sears bears out these claims: a correlation of .57 was found between a unit's survey score on selected items and the subsequent occurrence of unionization attempts. The survey's ability to predict union activity was not surprising, given that Sears identified high-morale employees as those who made "positive and willing adjustments to the demands of the organization" and had "ideological sentiments" akin to management's. W. Clay Hamner and Frank J. Smith, "Work Attitudes as Predictors of Unionization Activity," *Journal of Applied Psychology* 63 (August 1978), 415–21; Moore and Gardner, "Factors Related to Morale."

86. Sears National Personnel Department and Social Research Incorporated, *Big Ticket Manual* (Chicago, c. 1949), JCWP; Sears National Personnel Department, "Report on Service Stations" (October 12, 1951), and "Employee Morale in Pool Stocks and Detached

Warehouses" (n.d.), JCWP; Earl L. Kahn, "Report on Control Buyer Problems" (May 1, 1947), Department 707, JCWP.

87. Planning Division, Department 707, "Study of Area Asssistants" (April 1950), JCWP; Moore, "Managerial Strategies," 81. For a critical analysis of a similar program at Western Electric, see Jeanne L. Wilensky and Harold Wilensky, "Personnel Counselling: The Hawthorne Case," *American Journal of Sociology* 57 (November 1951), 265–80.

88. T. V. Houser, "This is Sears," 1952, 7, DCCU; Sears, "What Do Employees Like?"; James C. Worthy, "Democratic Principles in Business Management," speech to the Industrial Management Institute, Lake Forest College (May 27, 1948), SR Archives; Robert E. Wood to Fowler B. McConnell et al., October 14, 1948, JCWP.

89. Worthy, "Democratic Principles," 53; Kurt Lewin, "Group Decision and Social Change" in T. M. Newcomb and E. L. Hartley, eds., *Readings in Social Psychology* (New York, 1947), 330–44; K. Lewin, R. Lippitt, and R. K. White, "Patterns of Aggressive Behavior in Experimentally Created Social Climates," *Journal of Social Psychology* 10 (1939), 271–99. For good overviews of the history of managerial thought, see Charles Perrow, *Complex Organizations: A Critical Essay* (New York, 1979), and Michael Rose, *Industrial Behaviour: Theoretical Developments since Taylor* (London, 1975).

90. Baker, *Personnel Programs*, 76; James C. Worthy quoted in *Sears News-Graphic*, April 12, 1956; J. M. Barker, "The Financial Statement for Employees" (August 25, 1939), JMBP.

91. National Industrial Conference Board, *Profit-Sharing for Workers*, Studies in Personnel Policy no. 97 (New York, 1948), 22.

92. *Sears News-Graphic*, October 10, 1957, and April 10, 1958; author's interview with J. C. Worthy, 1985; *Retail Labor News* 879 (May 5, 1966), A–2; Jeuck, "A Case Study," 140–43. At one of the Forums, several employees—possibly activists from the Clerks—complained about management's heavy-handed control of the PSAC election procedures. *Sears News-Graphic*, 12 April 1956.

93. Kahn, "Intraoccupational Mobility," 83.

94. "What Do Employees Like?"; "On to Chicago: 1939," 48; G. B. Hattersley, "Employee Relations Policies" in American Management Association, Personnel Series no. 40 (New York, 1940), 21; "Post-War Personnel Program," 92–93.

95. "Comparison: Grant and Sears"; James C. Worthy, "Sears Roebuck and Co.: The X–Y Study," ms., August 19, 1984, JCWP; Wallace Tudor quoted in *Sears News-Graphic*, April 9, 1959. At the 1947 meetings of a retail employers' group, one speaker made this distinction: "In a department store where there are good employer-employee relationships and no union has majority representation, management can set forth a grievance procedure without fear that it will be charged with unfair practices. On the other hand, a department store which has had continuous labor difficulty is 'asking for trouble' when it publishes a grievance procedure." C. B. Potter (Lasalle and Koch Co.), "Handling Employee Grievances" in National Retail Dry Goods Association, *Management and Personnel Forum—1947* (New York, 1947), 119.

96. Emmet and Jeuck, *Catalogues*, 566; Michman, "Unionization," 73; Benson, *Counter Cultures*, 154; "Minutes of the General Board Meeting of the Retail Clerks," Lafayette, Indiana, June 7, 1950, 32, in Retail Clerks Executive Board, reel 1, RCIAP; author's interview with J. C. Worthy, 1985. Nineteen percent of department stores used sponsors in 1947. This dropped to 17 percent in 1958, which suggests that many stores besides Sears perceived weaknesses in the system. Spriegel, *Survey of Personnel Practices*, 44.

97. C. B. Caldwell to Fowler B. McConnell, February 26, 1952, 27; author's interview with J. C. Worthy, 1985. Even in the mid-1950s, only one in ten large retailers had personnel directors with the rank of vice president. Joan K. Finder, "Differences in Personnel Practices in Large Union and Nonunion Retail Stores in New York City," M.S. thesis, N.Y. State School of Industrial and Labor Relations, Cornell University, June 1957.

98. Barker Oral History, 107; Norman Beasley, *Main Street Merchant: The Story of the J.C. Penney Co.* (New York, 1948), 130–37.

99. Moore, "Managerial Strategies," 43, 227; Towle, "Personnel Practices of Mail Order Houses," 118; Clarence B. Caldwell, untitled speech (January 15, 1952), SR Archives.

100. Chandler, *Strategy and Structure*, 240–259; A. T. Kearney and Co. report to R. E. Wood and F. B. McConnell, December 1, 1947, 9, JCWP; Barker Oral History, 19–22; J. M. Barker to Boris Emmet, June 19, 1948, JMBP; T. V. Houser, "The Sears Organization: Past and Present," based on address to the Conference Board (1956), 7, DCCU; J. M. Barker, "Administration in an Extensive Retail Organization," paper presented to the Boston Conference on Distribution (September 23, 1935), JMBP. One member of the Frazer committee was J. David Houser; this is how he first became known to Sears management.

101. "Personnel Progress Report: 1948," 11; Clarence Caldwell, "The Fieldman's Job under Decentralized Management," talk before meeting of Department 632 fieldmen (July 26, 1945), JCWP; C. B. Caldwell to F. B. McConnell, February 26, 1952, JCWP.

102. Chandler, *Strategy and Structure*, 261–79; Emmet and Jeuck, *Catalogues*, 364–73; J. C. Worthy, "Psychological Studies of Labor-Management Relations," Denver (September 7, 1949), 10, SR Archives; Caldwell, "Personnel Presentation," On-to-Chicago Meeting (May 6, 1950), JCWP; Theodore V. Houser, *Big Business and Human Values* (New York, 1957), 22. One reason Wood reintroduced the M-form structure was his belief that it positioned Sears to fend off future antitrust actions: "Now the time may come when it will be said that we are getting too big and that it is not a good thing for the people of the United States to have a company as great as this, because one company will 'exercise too much power.' If that time ever comes to me or my successor, we are in a position to say, 'If you want to break us into five separate companies, it is possible.'" Like Kodak, where antitrust concerns also shaped corporate organization, Wood's remarks give credence to the view that market-power considerations were at least as strong as efficiency incentives in driving organizational evolution. This is rather different from the conventional Chandler-Williamson story. Robert E. Wood, "Address Presented at the Sears National Personnel Conference" (June 17, 1948), box 45, REWP; Neil Fligstein, *The Transformation of Corporate Control* (Cambridge, Mass., 1990).

103. Chandler, *Strategy and Structure*, 255, 269, 279. In a letter to the company's top executives, Wood said that "maintaining efficiency and discipline and yet allowing people to express themselves [and] to exercise initiative is the greatest problem for large organizations to solve." By the early 1960s, however, Sears had reverted to a more conventional M-form structure. Robert E. Wood to F. B. McConnell et al., October 14, 1948, JCWP.

104. Robert E. Wood, "Speech in Acceptance of Tobe Award," January 1, 1951, JCWP; "The General's General Store," *Time* 59 (February 25, 1952), 86; Moore, "Managerial Strategies," 76, 78; Worthy, *Shaping*, 121. Wood believed that only his personal authority would prevent Sears from becoming a bloated bureaucracy and, partly for this reason, he refused to give up the management reins until he was well into his seventies. The same paradox of organizational flexibility combined with entrenched senior leadership has recently been observed in companies trying to develop leaner, more participative, structures. Employee participation "coexist[s] with a highly charismatic CEO exercising almost mythical and despotic authority. The 'team' seems to require an authoritarian 'coach.'" Charles Heckscher, "Can Business Beat Bureaucracy?" *The American Prospect* 2 (Fall 1990), 126.

105. Emmet and Jeuck, *Catalogues*, 371–449; Houser, "Sears Organization," passim; "Personnel Progress Report: 1948," 11; *Forbes*, September 1, 1967, 18; C. B. Caldwell to F. B. McConnell, February 26, 1952, 21, JCWP; Weiss, "How to Sell," passim; Worthy, *Shaping*, 54; Clarence B. Caldwell, "Presentation," May 6, 1950, JCWP; Moore, "Managerial Strategies," 240; Barker Oral History, 151; Lebhar, *Chain Stores*, 289. Sears' store managers were better paid than those at other chains. In 1951, 12 percent of store managers had incomes in the $25,000–50,000 range, a substantial amount. D. S. Langsdorf to F. B. McConnell, January 26, 1952, JCWP.

106. James M. Barker, "The Storekpeer's Job" (c. 1940), in Misc. Talks file, JMBP; Barker, "Some Problems of Retail Administration," paper presented at the Sears Forum (November 7, 1933), 6, JMBP; J. M. Barker to R. E. Wood, January 2, 1935, and Barker to Boris Emmet, June 19, 1948, JMBP; Emmet and Jeuck, *Catalogues*, 548–63; Wood quoted by E. P. Brooks in Worthy, *Shaping*, 92.

107. Author's interview with J. C. Worthy, 1985; J. C. Worthy, "The Development of Industrial Leadership," Allerton Park Conference (June 27, 1951), JCWP; Worthy, "Planned Executive Development—The Experience of Sears Roebuck" (c. 1950), SR Archives; C. B. Caldwell, "Executive Leadership and Employee Morale," address before store manager groups on the West Coast, Sears Projects Unit, Department 707, Special Report no. 16 (November 1939), 8, JCWP; Jones, *History of the Survey Program*, 29–30; Worthy, "Methods and Techniques," 15; letter to author from David G. Moore, April 25, 1985; author's interview with F. J. Smith, 1985. Wood fully supported Barker's efforts. As he said in 1933, "Mr. Nelson buys goods at the right price; Mr. Pollock can put in a good auditing system; Mr. Carney can have a good operating system—but it all falls down if: (1) The managers are not right; and (2) The men and women in the stores are not right." Quoted in Emmet and Jeuck, *Catalogues*, 551.

108. Houser, *Big Business*, 21; author's interview with J. C. Worthy; author's interview with V. Jon Bentz, October 23, 1985; Department 707, "Minimum Essentials," 9; Wood,

"Address at National Personnel Conference" (June 17, 1948), REWP. This is not to say that middle management ignored local stores; they did not, although it was the field men who spent the most time there, again demonstrating 707's importance. James M. Barker, an MIT-trained engineer, thought that random site visits and simple quantitative indicators like morale scores were the best and cheapest way of staying on top of local conditions. "The art of administration," he once said, "is the art of spot check." Barker Oral History, 118; J. M. Barker to Boris Emmet, June 19, 1948; Chandler, *Strategy and Structure*, 263.

109. C. B. Caldwell, "Three Years Program: Training and Related Activities" (December 19, 1944), 31, JCWP; Worthy, *Shaping*, 138; L. L. Thurstone, *The Vectors of Mind* (Chicago, 1935); Thurstone, "Better Placement through Testing" *Personnel Conference 1946*; Worthy, "Methods and Techniques," 50; J. C. Worthy, "Planned Executive Development: The Experience of Sears Roebuck" (c. 1950), SR Archives; "Basic Factors in Employee-Management Relations: A Panel of Clarence Caldwell, David G. Moore, James Worthy, and V. Jon Bentz," summary prepared by the staff of the Industrial Management Institute, University of Wisconsin (October 3, 1951), 7, SR Archives. Thurstone was a pioneer in using factor analysis to identify personality traits. Impressed by the success of his battery, Sears used it on all prospective employees, who were tested for their "mental alertness" and "temperament." On an experimental basis, Burleigh Gardner and William E. Henry, a University of Chicago graduate student, gave Thematic Apperception tests (TATs) to managers being considered for the senior reserve. Gardner, "What Makes Successful and Unsuccessful Executives?" *Advanced Management* 13 (September 1948), 116–25; author's interview with William E. Henry, October 21, 1985.

110. Author's interview with J. C. Worthy; Sears Department 707, "College Training Program, 1928–1939," special report no. 33, August 1, 1940, JCWP; Wallace W. Tudor, "The Reserve Group Programs" in "On To Chicago: 1950," JCWP; Worthy, "Social Aspects," 11.

111. Moore, "Managerial Strategies," 72, 152; author's interview with J. C. Worthy; Worthy, "Factors Contributing," 3–15; Caldwell, "Sears Survey Program"; Worthy, "The X–Y Study," 120–23; David G. Moore, "Problems of Low Status Employees" (July 1950), JCWP.

112. Peter Samson, "The Department Store: Its Past and Its Future: A Review Article," *Business History Review* 55 (Spring 1981), 28; Benson, *Counter Cultures*, 131.

113. Benson, *Counter Cultures*, 128–40, 270; Moore, "Managerial Strategies," 47.

114. Moore, "Managerial Strategies," 48, 52; Emmet, *Department Stores*, 72.

115. Hattersley, "Employee Relations, 14–15; "General Robert E. Wood," *Fortune* 17 (May 1938), 110; Emmet and Jeuck, *Catalogues*, 576–77. Hourly workers periodically complained about the bonus program as well as an executive retirement plan to supplement profit sharing. Workers thought that the plans contradicted the company's egalitarian approach to benefits. At a Sears Forum, Fowler McConnell was forced to defend the executive plan by saying it was "less handsome" than those offered to executives at other companies. *Sears News-Graphic*, April 21, 1949; also see ibid., April 2, 1946, and April 17, 1947.

116. "Seminar on Problems of Organization and the Techniques of Business Leadership" (1946), JCWP; Burleigh B. Gardner, "A Program of Research in Human Relations in Industry," American Management Association, Personnel Series no. 80 (New York, 1945); Gardner, "An Approach to Management" (c. 1948), reprinted in Jones, *History of the Survey Program*, appendix J; Moore, "Managerial Strategies," 80. In 1946 Gardner resigned his position at the University of Chicago and started his own consulting group, Social Research Incorporated (SRI). SRI derived most of its income from Sears, although it also conducted one-shot surveys for other firms worried about unionization. SRI later branched out into market research and psychological testing of managers. Gardner, "Doing Business with Management," in E. M. Eddy and W. L. Partridge, eds., *Applied Anthropology in America* (New York, 1978), 245–60.

117. Worthy, "Factors Contributing," 2; J. C. Worthy, "Organizational Structure and Employee Morale," *American Sociological Review* 15 (April 1950), 169–79; "Organization Survey: Chicago Mail Order Plant" (c. 1949), JCWP; C. B. Caldwell to F. B. McConnell, February 26, 1952, 25–26, JCWP.

118. Warner in "Seminar on Problems of Organization," discussion section, 20–23; also see Gardner's comments in the same section; Worthy, "The X–Y Study," 85–89, 107–19, JCWP; Clarence B. Caldwell, "Notes for a Discussion with Zone Managers" (December 23, 1949), SR Archives. While having practical significance, the research at Sears made the important theoretical point that organizational structure and atmosphere mattered as much, if not more, than the small groups that had

engrossed the Western Electric researchers. By linking two previously distinct levels of analysis—the informal organization emphasized by Mayo and the formal organization analyzed by the classical theorists—the Sears research prefigured ideas developed in the 1960s by McGregor, Argyris, and Likert, ideas that underpin the current managerial fascination with participation and corporate culture. Worthy, "Psychological Studies of Labor-Management Relations" (Denver, September 7, 1949), SR Archives.

119. J. C. Worthy to C. B. Caldwell, "An Employee Relations Program for Sears Roebuck, 1951," JCWP. Note the striking parallel between the Sears report and radical critiques of "bureaucratic unionism."

120. Senate, *Hearings*, pt. 15, 6,043; Robert F. Kennedy, *The Enemy Within* (New York, 1960), 215.

121. D. S. Langsdorf to Fowler B. McConnell, January 26, 1952, JCWP; report by Ben B. Seligman, RCIA Research Department (October 1958), Organizing Dept., company correspondence prior to 1966, RCIAP; J. C. Worthy to C. B. Caldwell, February 2, 1951, JCWP; Senate, *Hearings*, pt. 15, 6,045; Marten S. Estey, "Patterns of Union Membership in the Retail Trades," *Industrial and Labor Relations Review* 8 (July 1955), 562; Spriegel, *Survey of Personnel Practices*, 44.

122. Nathan W. Shefferman, *Labor's Stake in Capitalism* (New York, 1954), 95; "Real Division in the U.S. Is Not between Employer and Labor Union," *The Washington Teamster*, May 30, 1947, JMBP; Shefferman, *The Shefferman Personnel Motivation Program* (Englewood Cliffs, N.J., 1961), 138–50; Shefferman, *Employment Methods* (New York, 1920); Shefferman, *The Man in the Middle* (Garden City, N.Y., 1961), 7–12.

123. "Advising on Relations," *Business Week*, December 23, 1939, 28; Senate, *Hearings*, pt. 15, 5991, 6,038. The attorneys included Nathaniel Clark (former regional director of the NLRB) and Mervin Bachman (onetime chief assistant to NLRB member John M. Houston). Among the personnel experts were Eugene Benge (like Shefferman, author of an early personnel textbook) and John Currie (previously head of personnel at Wieboldt Stores).

124. Shefferman, *Man in the Middle*, 162–63.

125. Robert F. Kennedy received much of his information on Beck from Eddie Cheyfitz, who, it later turned out, was working for Jimmy Hoffa. When Beck resigned in September 1957, Hoffa replaced him. Kennedy, *Enemy Within*, 4–7; Donald Garnel, *The Rise of Teamster Power in the West* (Berkeley, Cal., 1972), 67–77; Arthur M. Schlesinger, Jr., *Robert Kennedy and His Times* (Boston, 1978), 138; Eric Haas, *Dave Beck: Labor Merchant* (New York, 1955), 6.

126. In 1948, Clerks' president James Suffridge sent an army of certified public accountants and lawyers to take control of the "Sears RoeBeck" locals in Seattle. Beck was furious but also worried about a possible government audit. Luckily for Beck, a friendly local judge halted Suffridge's takeover attempt. Under these inauspicious circumstances, the Clerks and the Teamsters signed a pact in 1949 jointly to organize department stores around the country. The coalition scored victories in St. Louis and a few other cities, but relations were tense. Later that year, after a jurisdictional dispute at a grocery chain, Beck dissolved the coalition. Angrily denouncing the Clerks, he said the Teamsters would no longer work with them "in any capacity of cooperation." With the Clerks now their sworn enemy, the Teamsters aggressively staked out the retail sector. In Boston they defeated the Clerks at Stearns, and in St. Louis they persuaded Harold Gibbons, a former radical, to affiliate his large RWDSEA local with the Teamsters instead of the Clerks. The biggest rupture came in 1952, when the Teamsters and Clerks mounted separate national campaigns at Ward's. Sol Lippman to James A. Suffridge, August 11, 1948; James Suffridge to George W. Stack, September 10, 1948; Sol Lippman to James Suffridge, September 10, 1948; Vernon Housewright to James Suffridge, September 28, 1948; and minutes of the General Executive Board Meeting, Chicago (October 11, 1948), all on reel 4, mail of Executive Board members, RCIAP; "AFL Organizing in Eastern Stores," *Business Week*, January 22, 1949, 112; Estey, "Strategic Alliance," 49–51; "1949 Year End Report," 28; Burns and Buchele, "Unionism in Retailing," 103; "Left Wing Cracks," 103; Raulston G. Zundel, "Conflict and Cooperation among Retail Unions," *Journal of Business* 27 (October 1954), 307.

127. Shefferman, *Man in the Middle*, 165; Senate, *Hearings*, pt. 15, 2,407–16; "Western Organizing Conference, August 28, 1948," and James A. Suffridge to George W. Stack, September 7, 1948, both in Organizing Department Conference Minutes, 1948–1951, reel 1, RCIAP; Wise and Lacklen, *Unionization*, 48; C. B. Caldwell to F. B. McConnell, June 22, 1951, JCWP; *Union Organization of Department Store Clerks*, 124–39. According to company policy, "Sears does not enter into agreements with its employees, so it has no right to make agreements for them." Sears, "Retail

Personnel Program for 1939" (Chicago, 1938), 17, courtesy of John E. Jeuck.

128. In San Francisco, the Teamsters formed a strategic alliance with the Clerks as a way of preempting the ILWU. Jointly they began to organize the city's downtown stores, with the Teamsters claiming the "outside" workers (loading docks and warehouses) and the Clerks taking those on the inside. Eventually, the city's Retailers Council offered the unions a multiemployer agreement, which Sears honored but did not sign. After the war, the Teamsters agreed to help Sears get rid of the ILWU, which had represented some Sears' loading-dock workers in San Francisco since the mid-1930s. When the workers went on strike in 1947, Shefferman asked the Clerks not to respect the ILWU's picket line. The request went to Dave Beck and was then passed along the AFL hierarchy: from Beck to Dan Tobin, on to William Green, head of the AFL, over to Suffridge of the Clerks and down to the Clerk's San Francisco officers. When the Clerks broke the line, the Teamsters moved in and took away the ILWU's contracts. *The Story of Larry Vail,* 124–55; Harvey Schwartz, *The March Inland: Origins of the ILWU Warehouse Division, 1934–1938* (Los Angeles, Cal., 1978), 106–72; Dorothy Sue Cobble, *Dishing It Out: Waitresses and Their Unions in the 20th Century* (Urbana, Ill., 1991), 91; Kirstein, *Stores and Unions*, 93, 137; Wood Oral History, 101–3; Wise and Lacklen, *Unionization*, 47; "Retail Personnel Program 1939," 25.

129. Shefferman, *Man in the Middle*, 43; Senate, *Hearings*, pt. 15, 1,509–1,684, 6,563.

130. Senate, *Hearings*, pt. 15, 1,591–1,684, 6,101, 6,200, 6,406, 6,500, 6,560. Robert E. Wood to Dave Beck, July 21, 1949, box 14, REWP; Shefferman, *Man in the Middle*, 47–64; R. E. Wood to W. C. McDermid, February 16, 1951, and McDermid to Wood, March 10, 1951, box 14, REWP. Among Walter Reuther's purchases from Shefferman was a Coldspot refrigerator, whose left-handed door saved his life during an assasination attempt. Senate, *Hearings*, pt. 15, 1,651, 3,270; Shefferman, *Man in the Middle*, 211.

131. Minneapolis was the site of a fascinating episode in the Shefferman-Teamster alliance. By 1938, the ILWU had reached the city and was threatening the Sears mail-order plant there. At that time, the Minnesota Teamsters were led by Farrell Dobbs and the Dunne brothers, an improbable alliance of Trotskyites and Communists. Despite their radical politics, Dobbs and the Dunnes were willing to do almost anything to stop the ILWU from invading their territory. So they struck a deal with Shefferman: Sears would let the mail-order workers go on strike and then would sign a third-party agreement with the Teamsters. This would shut out the ILWU, while making the Teamsters look as if they had wrung a concession from Sears. The arrangement continued until 1941, when Dan Tobin, president of the Teamsters, got the attorney general to jail Dobbs and the Dunne brothers for sedition. When the ILWU returned to the mail-order plant, so did a new Teamsters local connected to Beck and Jimmy Hoffa. Beck was able to get a 1942 election overturned, and, although the ILWU local was certified in a second election in 1943, the Teamsters protested loudly and Sears refused to bargain with it. The Teamsters finally won an election in 1946. On Minneapolis, see Shefferman, *Man in the Middle*, 22–23; Irving Bernstein, *The Turbulent Years* (Boston, 1970), 780–81; Schwartz, *March Inland*; 42 NLRB 1,037, July 29, 1942; 44 NLRB 507, October 19, 1942; 49 NLRB 1,081, May 24, 1943; and 65 NLRB 1,039, February 13, 1946. On Dallas, where a similar set of events occurred, see 62 NLRB 674, June 21, 1945 and Siegendorf, "Ward versus the Union," 136.

132. Detroit and Philadelphia were the only parts of Sears where the RWDSEA had any strength. During the war, Jimmy Hoffa—who controlled the Clerks in Detroit—helped Shefferman get rid of the RWDSEA at the Detroit stores while Beck did the same in Philadelphia. By 1950, the RWDSEA did not have a single contract with Sears. The union's problems were exacerbated by internal disputes. A group of radical union officials in New York, who had opposed the wartime strike at Ward's, were suspended by Wolchok when they refused to sign non-Communist affidavits. As the infighting worsened, the CIO's Phil Murray took away the RWDSEA's retail jurisdiction, giving it first to the Clothing Workers and then, in 1951, to a retail organizing committee comprising nine CIO unions. On Detroit, see 45 NLRB 526, November 2, 1942 and 48 NLRB 1,170, April 13, 1943; on Philadelphia, see 34 NLRB 244, August 13, 1941; 35 NLRB 1,097, September 30, 1941; and 45 NLRB 961, December 2, 1942. On the RWDSEA, see Kirstein, *Stores and Unions*, 79–92; "Wolchok Front," *Business Week*, May 25, 1946, 96; "Left-Wing Cracks," *Business Week*, February 14, 1948, 102–3; "CIO Store Union," *Business Week*, March 3, 1951, 122.

133. James C. Worthy, "Union Picture 1952," ms., 4, JCWP; J. C. Worthy to C. B. Caldwell, February 2, 1951, JCWP.

134. In the early 1950s the Clerks tried, without success, to organize Sears' stores in Pittsburgh, Miami, Indianapolis, and other

cities. On Pittsburgh, see 90 NLRB 152, July 14, 1950; 106 NLRB 230, November 3, 1953; and James Suffridge to Robert Lieberman, February 25, 1950, local union mail, reel 21, RCIAP.

135. Senate, *Hearings*, pt. 15, 6,170; S.G. Lippmann to James Suffridge, September 16, 1949, Legal Department, misc. correspondence, reel 1, RCIAP; "Sears Roebuck and Sears Roebuck Employees' Council, local no. 1635, Retail Clerks," 110 NLRB 225, 233 (October 5, 1954).

136. Senate, *Hearings*, pt. 15, 6,072, 6,168–69, 6,176. Ironically, Shefferman was critical of the regular Sears survey program, citing its generality, infrequency, and anonymity. Yet these were precisely the features that allowed Sears to survey large numbers of employees without complaint. Shefferman, *Personnel Motivation*, 165–67.

137. Shefferman, *Personnel Motivation*, 120–25; Senate, *Hearings*, pt. 15, 6,074–76; Samuel J. Meyers, "Memorandum of Local 1635, Boston, Sears Elections," May 26, 1955, Organizing Department, company correspondence, reel 5, RCIAP.

138. "Advising on Relations," 28. Also see Richard L. Hull and Arthur Kolstad, "Morale on the Job" in Goodwin Watson, ed., *Civilian Morale* (Boston, 1942).

139. Planning Division, Department 707, "Study of Employee-Managment Committees," April 1950, JCWP; Senate, *Hearings*, pt. 15, 5,928, 5,958, 5,982, 6,184, 6,223, 6,380.

140. Senate, *Hearings*, pt. 15, 6,178–83; Samuel J. Meyers to Vernon Housewright, March 24, 1953, Organizing Department, company correspondence, reel 5, RCIAP; 110 NLRB 226, October 5, 1954.

141. Senate, *Hearings*, pt. 15, 6,119–24, 6,170–79, 6,185. After the Teamsters entered the campaign, Meyers wrote a desperate letter to Herbert S. Thatcher, formerly the AFL's general counsel, asking him to get the Teamsters to withdraw. While there is no evidence linking Thatcher and Shefferman, it later came out that Thatcher's predecessor, Joseph Padway, had been a "personal friend" of Shefferman's. Meyers to Thatcher, February 8, 1955, Organizing Department, company correspondence, reel 5, RCIAP; Senate, *Hearings*, pt. 15, 5,993.

142. "What Makes Sammy Run?" asked the pamphlet, implying that Meyers disobeyed the Golden Rule, unlike "500 million people who live by it and follow in the footsteps of the Man who gave his life to preserve it." "Questions the Clerks Can't Answer" (c. 1955), Organizing Department, company correspondence, reel 5, RCIAP. Also see Senate, *Hearings*, pt. 15, 6,173–74, 6,183, 6,194, 6,224, 6,307–17; Shefferman, *Man in the Middle*, 147–67.

In a memo written in the early 1950 to the managers of a Whirpool plant in rural Ohio (a key suplier to Sears), Shefferman outlined his campaign tactics:

> 1. Find lawyer and guy who will set up the [vote no] committee.
>
> 2. Little later, find out who are your leaders on inside and outside, and sway them.
>
> 3. Go to local Legion post. Get material from them. Material to use: Communism, un-Americanism, destroying our country.
>
> 4. Keep rotating committee actively going.
>
> 5. Keep your foremen meeting. We'll tell foremen what to say and do.
>
> 6. Save merchants and clergy for final drive.
>
> 7. Build case against union and get them thrown out of their building.
>
> 8. Might be wise to get a few boys from the Vote No committee—pay them for time lost—to visit homes.
>
> 9. Don't look for help from the FBI. Only chance is your own employees.

Senate, *Hearings*, pt. 15, 6,010–11.

143. Eisenhower's undersecretary of commerce was none other than James C. Worthy, formerly of Sears' Department 707. S. G. Lippman to James A. Suffridge, January 16, 1954, and September 9, 1956, and Robert Karmel to James Suffridge, June 17, 1953, Legal Department, miscellaneous correspondence, reel 1, RCIAP.

144. Samuel J. Meyers to author, February 16, 1979; *Retail Labor Reporter*, February 28, 1958, B–7; "Sears' Dealing with Shefferman," *Business Week*, March 1, 1958, 101. Sears wielded considerable political clout, which may have affected the NLRB's stance. Ever since the anti-chain battles, Sears ran an expensive public relations machine that brought it influential friends, even governors and legislators. When the NRLB ruled against the Clerks in another Sears case, the union's attorney complained about "political shenanigans in this case which demonstrate the power of Sears in high places." Worthy, "An Employee Relations Program," 11; Robert Karmel to James A. Suffridge, January 12, 1956, in S. G. Lippman, Legal Department, miscellaneous correspondence, reel 1.

145. Senate, *Hearings*, pt. 15, 6,045, 6,205; Kennedy, *Enemy Within*, 219.

146. Kennedy, *Enemy Within*, 213, 218.

147. R. E. Wood to N. W. Shefferman, June 2, 1950, April 6, 1953; R. E. Wood to Morris Sayre and R. E. Wood to E. O. Shreve, August

4, 1948, all in box 14, REWP; Nathan W. Shefferman, *Labor's Stake in Capitalism* (New York, 1954); Doenecke, "General Wood," 174. Wood had an anti-Semitic streak that played out in his relationship with Shefferman. Wood tried to keep Jews out of Sears, whether they were suppliers (he avoided doing business with RCA because of its Jewish president, David Sarnoff) or potential corporate executives (numerous Jewish managers were blocked from the top ranks and Wood personally opposed Edward Gudeman's 1958 candidacy for company president). That Shefferman, a Jew, headed up Sears' union-avoidance activities is reminiscent of the medieval practice of using Jewish moneylenders to prevent the community from contamination by usury. Weil, *Sears Roebuck U.S.A.*, 246; interview with Robert S. Adler conducted by James C. Worthy, 1979, JCWP.

148. During the McClellan hearings, Tudor tried to erase the impression that Sears got something in return for supporting the lavish lifestyle of Dave Beck. Despite Beck's friendship with Shefferman, he said, the Teamsters initiated twenty-two major organizing drives against Sears during the 1950s. If true, it meant that Sears had wasted the money it spent on Beck and other Teamster leaders. But the fact is the Teamsters never attempted a national organizing drive at Sears until after Beck resigned. The "drives" cited by Tudor were isolated events at small warehouses in places like Bangor, Maine. Indeed, Teamster membership at Sears actually fell between 1950 and 1957, from 9,000 to 7,000. J. C. Worthy to C. B. Caldwell, February 2, 1951, JCWP; Senate, *Hearings*, pt. 15, 6,199, 6,187–95, 6,204; R. E. Wood to C. E. Humm, January 18, 1950, REWP. Also see 82 NLRB 985, April 12, 1949 and 101 NLRB 665, December 1, 1952.

149. Kenneth Slocum, "Teamsters Union to Start Drive on Sears soon to Organize 70,000 Employees," *Wall Street Journal* (December 29, 1958), 5; "St. Louis Teamsters Hit Sears," *Retail Labor Report* (hereafter *RLR*), February 28, 1958, C–2; "Teamsters Prepare to Form Sears Council," *RLR*, June 27, 1958, C–1; "Teamsters Set Date for Push on Sears," *RLR*, December 5, 1958, A–2; "Teamsters Kick Off Sears Drive," *RLR*, January 23, 1959, A–13, C1–5; "Teamsters, RCIA, Get Sears Drive into High Gear," *RLR*, March 6, 1959, C1–7; "Teamsters Issue Second Sears Paper," *RLR*, June 5, 1959, A–1.

150. *The Story of Sears Roebuck*, 82; *Sears Dixieland News*, April 9, 1959, 7, SR Archives; W. W. Tudor, "Management's Expanding Challenge in Personnel Administration," address to the the Hawaii Employers' Council (March 8, 1957), DCCU (this is the same speech Tudor gave at the 1959 Forum); "Sears Doubts Success of Union Organizing Drive," *RLR*, July 11, 1958, E–1; "Sears Expands Insurance Coverage," *RLR*, December 26, 1958, A–2; "G. M. Metcalf to All Sears Employees, October 8, 1958" in Murray Plopper to all local unions, December 8, 1958, memo file of Murray Plopper, Organizing Department, directors' bulletins, reel 1, RCIAP; "Teamsters Turn Spotlight on Sears Again," *RLR*, November 6, 1959, A–9; author's interview with Frank J. Smith, 1985; Jones, *History of the Survey Program*, 51–64, 75–79; "The Utilization of the Behavioral Sciences in Sears, Roebuck" (Chicago, 1961), 16–21, DCCU; P. W. Hansen to all local union secretaries, October 13, 1958, in Organizing Department, directors' bulletins, reel 1, RCIAP.

151. See the various reports on retail organizing in *RLR*: June 19, 1959, September 3, 1960, March 10, 1961, March 30, 1962; letter to author from Norman Weintraub, chief economist, International Brotherhood of Teamsters, April 15, 1985; Worthy, *Shaping*, 167. Beck received a full pardon from President Gerald Ford in 1975.

152. Paul W. Hansen to local union secretaries, November 8, 1957, October 13, 1958, March 6, 1959, in Organizing Department, directors' bulletins, reel 1, RCIAP; "The Creature That Works in the Dark," courtesy of Samuel J. Meyers; "Teamsters, RCIA Get Sears Drive into High Gear," *RLR*, March 6, 1959, C–5; "Sears Employees Queried by RCIA," *RLR*, May 22, 1959, A–11. When *Fortune* turned down the Clerks' request to reproduce the article, the union asked Senator Hubert Humphrey to read it into the *Congressional Record* (February 19, 1958) and then reprinted it from there.

153. S. G. Lippman to Murray Plopper, July 24, 1959, S. G. Lippman to Archie McLean, September 28, 1959, and Beaverton, Oregon, decertification material in S. G. Lippman, Legal Department, miscellaneous correspondence, reel 1, RCIAP. Also see "Seattle Clerks Ask Court to Force Arbitration," *RLR*, June 3, 1960, A–8; 47 *LRRM* 2,354, November 30, 1960; "NLRB Isssues Complaints against Sears," *RLR*, July 7, 1961, A–8; 139 NLRB 471, October 25, 1962; "Clerks Put Sears Boycott on Nationwide Basis," *RLR*, July 15, 1960, A–5, D–1.

154. A. B. Crossler memo, June 26, 1956, Montgomery Ward files, reel 2, RCIAP; "Retail Clerks to Intensify Sears Boycott," *RLR*, November 18, 1960, A–8; assorted materials in National Chain Store Committee, 1960–1969 file, reel 1, Executive Office mem-

orandum files, RCIAP; S. G. Lippman to all organizing directors, July 21, 1960, in Lippman correspondence, reel 1, RCIAP; Samuel J. Meyers, "Memorandum of Local 1635, Boston, Sears Elections" (May 26, 1955), Organizing Department, company correspondence, reel 5, RCIAP; Retail Clerks International Association, *Official Proceedings: 24th International Convention, Chicago, June 24–28, 1963*, 11–12; "AFL-CIO Council Attacks Sears Roebuck for Union-Busting Methods," *RLR*, August 19, 1960, A–1; "Clerks Step-up Sears Boycott," *RLR*, October 21, 1960, A–1; "RCIA Takes Sears Story to Stockholders," *RLR*, November 25, 1960; "Retail Clerks Send Out Sears Boycott Kits," *RLR*, December 23, 1960, A–5; "AFL-CIO Protests Sears Inclusion in Trade Fair," *RLR*, October 20, 1961, A–6.

155. S. J. Meyers to Executive Office, September 20, 1962, and "Divisional Organizing Plans for 1964" in memo file, Samuel J. Meyers, Organizing Department, directors' bulletins, reel 1, RCIAP; "NLRB Balloting at Major Retail Chains," *RLR*, March 10, 1961, March 30, 1962; Charles Osterling to S. J. Meyers, November 3, 1961, and Morton H. Frank to James A. Suffridge, June 20, 1962, Organizing Department, reel 5; "Has Boycott Hit Sears' Profits?" *Electrical Merchandising Week* 92 (November 28, 1960), 2; "Labor Acts to Revitalize Sears Boycott," *RLR*, July 31, 1964, A–4; data on boycott expenditures in "National Chain Store Committee, 1960–69" reel 1, Executive Office memorandum files, RCIAP; "Retail Clerks Call off Sears Boycott," *RLR*, May 12, 1967, A–2; Samuel J. Meyers to author, February 16, 1979.

156. Although an internal Teamsters' document admitted that Sears' fringe benefits "are seldom excelled by collective bargaining agreements" and that its wages "meet the going rate in a given city plus a little bit more," the union nevertheless made higher wages and an end to profit sharing the focus of its campaign against Sears. The Clerks, however, thought that the best approach to profit sharing was "to accept the plan and argue for improvements." "Teamsters Sight Sears Target," *RLR*, August 1, 1958, C–1; "Teamsters Analyze Sears Profit-Sharing Plan," *RLR*, June 26, 1959, A–1; Ben B. Seligman to Organizing Directors, September 20, 1957, reel 1, Organizing Department, directors' bulletins, RCIAP.

157. Southwestern Division, Organizational Meeting Synopsis, Los Angeles, April 20–21, 1950, and Eastern Division Conference, Copley Plaza Hotel, Boston, March 9, 1950, in reel 1, Organizing Department, conference minutes and meetings, 1948–51, RCIAP; Paul W. Hansen to all local union secretaries, Northwest Division, October 13, 1958, reel 1, directors' bulletins, RCIAP.

158. Most of the Clerks' organizers were male and few of them believed women would join unions. One organizer complained that "young girls living at home don't have to pay rent, don't realize what it is to make and pay for their own living. Young girls working in stores have no intention of continuing working; [they] look to marriage, so to speak." The best the Clerks could come up with was a handful of what it called "girl organizers" and an organizing leaflet in the form of a romantic diary ("elimination of overtime, won by the unions, helped her get her man!"). "Report on Sears Roebuck & Company," RCIA Research Department, October 1958 in reel 5, Organizing Department, Company Correpondence, RCIAP; RCIA Educational Conference, San Diego (January 12, 1951), 10, reel 1, Organizing Department, conference minutes, RCIAP; Kirstein, *Stores and Unions*, 32–36; Burns and Buchele, "Unionism in Retailing," 57.

159. At the time of the McClellan hearings, a Gallup poll reported that 43 percent believed "corruption and graft" to be "pretty widespread" in labor unions, while 34 percent indicated that these problems were "limited to just a few unions" (and 21 percent expressed no opinion). Derek C. Bok and John T. Dunlop, *Labor and the American Community* (New York, 1970), 16.

160. Sears' "folksy" corporate culture bears a strong resemblance to Wal-Mart's, *the* successful chain retailer of the 1990s, as Sears was in the postwar years.

Chapter Five
Recasting Company Unions: Thompson Products

1. Daniel Nelson, "The Company Union Movement, 1900–1937: A Reexamination," *Business History Review* 56 (Autumn 1982), 337. On employment methods at smaller firms in the 1930s and 1940s, see Sanford M. Jacoby, *Employing Bureaucracy: Managers, Unions, and the Transformation of Work in American Industry, 1900–1945* (New York, 1985), chaps. 7 and 8.

2. Frederick C. Crawford to author, May 12, 1987.

3. David D. Van Tassel and John J. Grabowski, eds., *The Encyclopedia of Cleveland History* (Bloomington, Ind., 1987), 9–11, 57–59, 948, 966; *Friendly Forum*, January 1951, 4, 20 (Golden Anniversary issue of the

Thompson Products employee newspaper, courtesy of Professor Anil Verma).

4. Van Tassel and Grabowski, *Encyclopedia*, 10; "Fred Crawford's Company," *Fortune* 34 (December 1946), 146–51.

5. E. S. Horning, "Wage Incentive Practices," National Industrial Conference Board Studies in Personnel Policy no. 68 (New York, 1945), 35.

6. *Friendly Forum*, January 1951, 30, 48; Geneva Seybold, "Organization of Personnel Administration," National Industrial Conference Board Studies in Personnel Policy no. 73 (New York, 1946), 76.

7. John Holmfeld, "The Site Selection for the NACA Engine Research Laboratory: A Meeting of Science and Politics," Master's essay, Case Institute of Technology, 1967; Robert Sheehan, "The Way They Think at TRW," *Fortune* 72 (October 1965), 153–57.

8. Harvey Shore, "A Historical Analysis of Thompson Products' Successful Program to Discourage Employee Acceptance of Outside Unions, 1934–1947," Ph.D. dissertation, Graduate School of Business Administration, Harvard University, 1966, 101, 147, 255, 430; U.S. Census Bureau, *16th Census of Population: 1940*, vol. 3, pt. 4, 806–9. On marriage bars, see Claudia Goldin, *Understanding the Gender Gap: An Economic History of American Women* (New York, 1990).

9. Josef J. Barton, *Peasants and Strangers: Italians, Rumanians, and Slovaks in an American City* (Cambridge, Mass., 1975), 142–46, 164; Carol Poh Miller and Robert Wheeler, *Cleveland: A Concise History, 1796–1990* (Bloomington, Ind., 1990), 131–33.

10. Frank K. Dossett, "Thompson Products: A Study in New Deal Legislation" (1947), 67, TRWP; Shore, "Historical Analysis," 47–55, 115–24; newspaper clippings in box 27, TRWP.

11. R. S. Livingstone to L. Clegg, February 14, 1936, and Livingstone quoted in *Cleveland Press*, June 25, 1942, both in Shore, "Historical Analysis," 134, 431.

12. In 1950, 20 percent of the Cleveland manufacturing labor force was female, only one percentage point higher than in 1940. Female operatives made no gains in the Cleveland auto industry between 1940 and 1950, holding steady at 17 percent, while women in the city's aircraft industry showed a slight increase, from 15 to 20 percent of the labor force. U.S. Census Bureau, *17th Census of Population: 1950*, vol. 2, "Characteristics of the Population," pt. 35, table 84.

13. Shore, "Historical Analysis," 430; *Business Week*, May 9, 1942; clipping from *The Challenger*, August 26, 1944, reel 1, TPP. In 1940, fewer than 1 percent of Cleveland automotive industry operatives were black; in 1950 this figure stood at 8 percent. Thus, in Cleveland as at Thompson, black men kept the jobs they gained during the war. They remained shut out of the skilled trades, however: in all of Cleveland only 301 black men were employed as machinists in 1950, less than 2 percent of the city's total. *16th Census*, vol. 3, pt. 4, 806–9; *17th Census*, vol. 2, pt. 35, 373.

14. An alternative to the melting pot was to build a loyal majority out of a single ethnic group, as with the native Protestants employed at Kodak Park and at General Motors' Fisher Body plant in Flint, where, according to one union organizer, over 40 percent of the work force in the 1930s belonged to the Black Legion, a Klan offshoot. Wyndham Mortimer, *Organize! My Life as a Union Man* (Boston, 1971), 104, 112.

15. "Here's the Typical Old Guard Member" (Cleveland, January 20, 1947), Thompson Files, DCCU; "Results of the 1957 Spot Check of Employee Opinion," prepared by Arlen Southern (February 12, 1957), box 137, TRWP; "The Golden Key" (1955), box 133, TRWP.

16. Crawford quoted in *Friendly Forum*, April 8, 1935, box 27, TRWP; Livingstone in "Statement of Labor History of Thompson Products, Inc." August 26, 1943, 27, in box 18, TRWP (this is the transcript of an interview with Livingstone and Crawford conducted by Whiting Williams); Lisa Fine, "Our Big Factory Family: Masculinity and Paternalism at the Reo Motor Car Company of Lansing, Michigan," *Labor History* 34 (Spring 1993), 274–91; Wayne Lewchuk, "Men and Monotony: Fraternalism as a Managerial Strategy at the Ford Motor Company," *Journal of Economic History* 53 (December 1993), 824–56; David Montgomery, *Workers' Control in America* (Cambridge, U.K., 1979); Patrick Joyce, "Labour, Capital, and Compromise: A Response to Richard Price," *Social History* 9 (January 1984), 75. Also see the remarkable interview with Crawford conducted shortly after his hundredth birthday: Davis Dyer, "A Voice of Experience: An Interview with TRW's Frederick C. Crawford," *Harvard Business Review* 68 (November–December 1991), 125.

17. Crawford in "Statement of Labor History," 19; Seybold, "Organization of Personnel Administration," 76; Ben Kozman, "Fellowship and Relaxation Found by TP Gang in Varied Activities," *Friendly Forum*, January 1951, 44; Dyer, "Voice of Experience," 117–18.

18. *Thompson Products Employees' Handbook*, March 12, 1935, box 27, TRWP.

19. Horning, "Wage Incentive Practices," 35; Thompson Products, "Let's See What Makes You Tick . . . Thompson Bonus Plan" (1945), DCCU.

20. Thompson Products, "We Led with Our Chin! A Report on a Survey of Employee Opinion Conducted in the Cleveland Plants" (August 1944), 20, DCCU; R. S. Livingstone, "Memorandum on Cleveland Rate Structure," August 27, 1940, box 28, TRWP; R. S. Livingstone to F. H. Bullen, January 26, 1944, reel 3, TPP; R. J. Myers and H. Bloch, "The Level of Factory Wage Rates in Wartime," *Monthly Labor Review* 57 (October 1943), 637–46; National Industrial Conference Board, *Systems of Wage Payment* (New York, 1930), 5, 8; C. Canby Balderston, *Group Incentives* (Philadelphia, 1930), 26.

21. Balderston, *Group Incentives*, 10, 28; "Let's See What Makes You Tick," 55; "20 Questions: A Case Study in Human Engineering," *Steel* (September 1, 1952), 5, emphasis in original.

22. *Friendly Forum*, June 8, 1934, box 27, TRWP; "A Brief History of the Thompson Products Employee Association," January 19, 1934, box 27, TRWP; Dossett, "Thompson Products," 38.

23. Thompson Products, "Here's the Typical Old Guard Member" DCCU; *Friendly Forum*, April 9, 1937, box 28, TRWP.

24. "Here's the Typical Old Guard Member"; *Friendly Forum*, January 1951, 24.

25. Miller and Wheeler, *Cleveland*, 134–46.

26. "Fred Crawford's Company," 148–49; employment data from *Moody's Industrials*, various annual volumes.

27. Shore, "Historical Analysis," 101; Livingstone in "Statement of Labor History," 21; *Friendly Forum*, January 1951, 16.

28. "Fred Crawford's Company," 148–50.

29. See Table 2.3 in Chapter Two above.

30. Bert Cochran, *Labor and Communism: The Conflict That Shaped American Unions* (Princeton, N.J., 1977), 67–68, 119; Mortimer, *Organize!*, 56, 72, 77.

31. Roy Rutherford, "The Career of Fred Crawford," *Railroad Workers' Journal* 1 (June 1946), 5–11; "Fred Crawford's Company," 206–7; Dossett, "Thompson Products," 186, 403.

32. R. S. Livingstone, "Settling Disputes without Interrupting Production," *Management Record* 4 (December 1942), 386; Livingstone, "Personnel Direction: Dynamic Function of Business" in Thompson Products, "Organization of Personnel Administration and Labor Relations Policies of Thompson Products" (n.d.), 50–51, DCCU (this is a reprint of an article in the October 1943 issue of *The Clevelander*, publication of the Cleveland Chamber of Commerce).

33. *Thompson Products Employees' Handbook* (1935), box 27, TRWP; *Employee Handbook* (1940), reel 1, TPP; "Transcript of the Proceedings of the Three-Month NLRB Trial, February 23 to May 25, 1943," 435–43, reel 1B, TPP; J. D. Wright, "Memorandum re: Labor Provisions of N.R.A.," August 28, 1933, box 27, TRWP; Seybold, "Organization of Personnel Administration," 76.

34. "Story of the Thompson Products Old Guard Association," pamphlet (1951), DCCU; "Constitution of the Old Guard of Thompson Products," January 7, 1934, and *Friendly Forum*, June 8, 1934, in box 27, TRWP; "In the Matter of Thompson Products and United Automobile Workers of America," case no. C–190, August 16, 1937, 337–38.

35. "Story of the Old Guard"; "Here's the Typical Old Guard Member." As this suggests, the company union was attuned to the interests of its senior members, a point explored in Richard Freeman and James Medoff, *What Do Unions Do?* (New York, 1984).

36. Lee M. Clegg to Frederick C. Crawford, March 6, 1936, quoted in Loren Baritz, *Servants of Power: A History of the Use of Social Science in American Industry* (Middletown, Conn., 1960), 232; L. M. Clegg to F. C. Crawford, April 17, 1934, box 17, TRWP; Elizabeth Fones-Wolf, "Industrial Recreation, the Second World War, and the Revival of Welfare Capitalism, 1934–1960," *Business History Review* 60 (Summer 1986), 232–57.

37. Thompson, *Industrial Relations Manual*, 16–17.

38. The 1935 incident—in which Thompson rejected the suggestions of a conciliator and stuck to what one manager called its "righteous course" (company unionism)—is described in Dossett, "Thompson Products," 72–74.

39. Frank Dossett, "Handling Grievances under Government Supervision" (n.d.), 34, reel 1, TPP; R. S. Livingstone, "Program Started with Wish to Be Fair to People," *Friendly Forum*, January 1951, 24.

40. Livingstone, "Settling Disputes," 388.

41. Dossett, "Thompson Products," 254. Crawford, said *Fortune* magazine, "loves to discuss with such industrial bigwigs as Alfred Sloan or J. Howard Pew the virtues of doing what every Thompson executive is expected to do frequently—get down onto the floor of the plant and say hello to a few hundred workers." "Fred Crawford's Company," 211.

42. Rutherford, "The Career of Fred Crawford," 10. Years later Crawford still maintained that "during my many years of management experience, human relations was my special interest." F. C. Crawford to author, May 12, 1987.

43. F. C. Crawford in "Proceedings of the Second Annual Public Relations Conference Sponsored by the National Association of Manufacturers," New York, (December 6–7, 1943), 87–88; and "Proceedings of the Indiana Executives' Conference on Public Relations," Indianapolis (April 14, 1944), 35–36, both in box 82, N.A.M. Records, Hagley Library, Wilmington, Delaware.

44. F. C. Crawford quoted in *Friendly Forum*, April 8, 1935, box 27, TRWP.

45. "Can There Be Industrial Peace with Unionism?" transcript of a debate between A. E. Stevenson and R. S. Livingstone, Euclid, Ohio (November 12, 1945), DCCU.

46. F. C. Crawford quoted in Dossett, "Handling Grievances," 45–54; Thompson, *Industrial Relations Manual*, 9; "Can There be Industrial Peace?" DCCU.

47. Irving Bernstein, *The Turbulent Years* (Boston, 1970), chaps. 2, 10, and 11; Harry A. Millis and Royal Montgomery, *Organized Labor* (New York, 1945), 840–55; Julius Rezler, "Labor Organization at DuPont: A Study in Independent Unionism," *Labor History* 4 (Spring 1963), 178–95; John Schacht, *The Making of Telephone Unionism, 1920–47* (New Brunswick, N.J., 1985).

48. Millis and Montgomery, *Organized Labor*, 841, 847; U.S. Bureau of Labor Statistics, *Characteristics of Company Unions*, bulletin no. 634 (Washington, D.C., 1937), 54, 204–6; Robert R. R. Brooks, *As Steel Goes . . . Unionism in a Basic Industry* (New Haven, Conn., 1940); Steve Jefferys, *Management and Managed: Fifty Years of Crisis at Chrysler* (Cambridge, U.K., 1986).

49. Bernstein, *Turbulent Years*, 319; Millis and Montgomery, *Organized Labor*, 850; Burton Crager, "Company Unions under the National Labor Relations Act," *Michigan Law Review* 40 (April 1942), 835; Joseph Rosenfarb, *The National Labor Policy and How It Works* (New York, 1940), chap. 5.

50. David J. Saposs, "Organizational and Procedural Changes in Employee Representation Plans," *Journal of Political Economy* 44 (December 1936), 807; Daniel Nelson, *American Rubber Workers and Organized Labor, 1900–1941* (Princeton, N.J., 1988), 176; Ronald W. Schatz, *The Electrical Workers: A History of Labor at General Electric and Westinghouse, 1923–60* (Urbana, Ill., 1983), 66; U.S. Bureau of Labor Statistics, *Characteristics of Company Unions*, 205.

51. Bernstein, *Turbulent Years*, 455–66; Nelson, *Rubber Workers*, 177, 252–3.

52. Saposs, "Changes in Representation Plans," 803; Leo Troy, "Local Independent and National Unions: Competitive Labor Organizations," *Journal of Political Economy* 68 (October 1960), 489. Skilled workers held leadership positions in Thompson's company unions, a phenomenon that also occurred in many industrial unions. But there is no evidence that Thompson's skilled workers enjoyed larger wage premiums than their industrial-union counterparts; in fact, the unskilled fared better under Thompson's company unions than did the highly skilled. Also, among large Midwestern industrial cities, Cleveland did not pay notably high wages. Sanford M. Jacoby and Anil Verma, "Enterprise Unions in the United States," *Industrial Relations* 31 (Winter 1992), 152–53.

53. Mark Barenberg, "The Political Economy of the Wagner Act: Power, Symbol, and Workplace Cooperation," *Harvard Law Review* 106 (1993), 1,443; Rosenfarb, *The National Labor Policy*, 131; U.S. Senate, "Statement of Paul Herzog," *Hearings before the Committee on Labor and Public Welfare*, 80th Cong., 1st Sess., pt. 4 (Washington, D.C., 1947), 1,912; National Labor Relations Board, Division of Economic Research, "Characteristics of 60 Company-Dominated Unions," research memorandum no. 10 (December 1939), 2. Barenberg argues that the company-union ban was unjustified: "If, as Wagner was convinced, [the NLRA] machinery was adequate to safeguard workers from direct managerial reprisals for their choice of an outside union over no union, why was it not adequate to safeguard the choice between a company union and either of those two options?"

54. Troy, "Local Independent Unions and the American Labor Movement," *Industrial and Labor Relations Review* 14 (April 1961), 339; F. Ray Marshall, "Independent Unions in the Gulf Coast Petroleum Refining Industry," *Labor Law Journal* 12 (September 1961), 823–40; U.S. Department of Labor, Bureau of Labor Statistics, "Unaffiliated Local and Single-Employer Unions in the United States: 1961," bulletin no. 1,348 (Washington, D.C., 1962), 7; Leo Troy, "The Course of Company and Local Independent Unions," Ph.D. dissertation, Columbia University, 1958, 187–98. On Weirton, see Teresa Ankney, "The Pendulum of Control: The Evolution of the Weirton Steel Company, 1907–51," Ph.D. dissertation, Catholic University of America, 1993.

55. "Old Guard Committee to All Thompson Product Employees" (January 13, 1934), "A Brief History of the Thompson Products Employees' Association" (January 19, 1934), and "Minutes of the First Meeting of the TPEA" (February 19, 1934), all in box 34, TRWP; *Thompson Products and UAW Local 300 (CIO)*, 33 NLRB 1,033 (August 1941); Shore, "Historical Analysis," 41–155.

56. "TPEA Manual for Employee Representatives" (January 1, 1936), 1, quoted in Shore, "Historical Analysis" 132.

57. "Constitution of the TPEA," February 13, 1934, box 27, TRWP; U.S. Bureau of Labor Statistics, *Characteristics of Company Unions*, 154; "Transcript of NLRB Trial 1943," 691–92; E. A. McBride to L. M. Clegg, May 7, 1935, and R. S. Livingstone to Management Representatives, December 3, 1934, box 27, TRWP; minutes of Joint Council Meeting, May 10, 1935, August 9, 1935, box 27, and March 3, 1937, box 28, TRWP.

58. Dossett, "Thompson Products," 122–23; R. S. Livingstone, "Employees' Association Secretarial Report: 1934" in "Transcript of NLRB Trial 1943," 608; R. S. Livingstone to P. B. Lerch, January 10, 1935, and minutes of the Joint Council Meeting, March 1, 1936, July 2, 1936, and November 11, 1936, box 27, TRWP.

59. Memo from R. S. Livingstone to management representatives on the Joint Council, December 3, 1934, box 27, TRWP.

60. Bill Hoffman in *Friendly Forum*, April 2, 1934, and May 10, 1934, box 27, TRWP; J. M. Kerwin to F. Ritter et al., June 6, 1935, box 27, TRWP.

61. Shortly after Thompson acquired the Los Angeles valve plant, Livingstone paid a visit. He warned workers that the plant would be closed if a national union organized it. Local managers gave Livingstone the name of a worker who could be trusted to do management's bidding. Livingstone promised the man a lifetime job if he succeeded in forming an "inside" union, which he did. Shore, "Historical Analysis," 184–88; 46 NLRB 514.

62. R. S. Livingstone to John R. Cox, February 24, 1936, box 142, TRWP; *Friendly Forum*, July 5, August 3, August 31, September 14, 1934, and March 15, 1935, and "Constitution of the Michigan Plant Council of Thompson Products" (September 1934), all in box 27, TRWP.

63. Sidney Fine, *Sit-down: The General Motors Strike of 1936–37* (Ann Arbor, Mich., 1969), 323; *Detroit News*, February 22, 1937; J. David Wright memorandum, February 27, 1937, box 142, TRWP; *Detroit Free Press*, February 26, 1937; *Automotive Industries* 76 (March 13, 1937), 4. Wright was later replaced as plant personnel manager by none other than Bill Goltz, a machinist who had led the 1937 UAW drive.

64. Cochran, *Labor and Communism*, 119–20, 348; Mortimer, *Organize!*, 125; Van Tassel and Grabowski, *Encyclopedia*, 404; Sidney Fine, *Sit-down*, 142–43.

65. Various UAW bulletins in box 28, TRWP; Dossett, "Thompson Products," 139; Shore, "Historical Analysis," 167.

66. Shore, "Historical Analysis," 193, 196; UAW bulletin, August 3, 1937, box 28, TRWP.

67. Van Tassel and Grabowski, *Encyclopedia*, 641; John Gunther, *Inside USA* (New York, 1947), 445; Jerold S. Auerbach, *The LaFollette Committee and the New Deal* (Indianapolis, Ind., 1966), 137–39; U.S. Senate, "Violations of Free Speech and Rights of Labor," *Hearings before a Subcommittee of the Committee on Education and Labor*, 75th Cong., 3rd Sess., pt. 21 (Washington, D.C., 1938), 9,108.

68. "Violations of Free Speech," pt. 21, 9,115, 9,289; pt. 22, 9,363–64; and pt. 38, 15,052–61, 15,112–15; Shore, "Historical Analysis," 47–55, 115–23; Dossett, "Thompson Products," 67–97; Ralph Lind to Thompson Products Co., January 23, 1934, Ralph G. Gordon to Frederick C. Crawford, July 15, 1935, and *Cleveland Ohio News*, August 12, 15, 23, 1935, clippings, all in box 27, TRWP. Thompson remained a client of the Service Bureau until 1938, when the LaFollette Committee exposed the arrangement.

69. *Friendly Forum*, May 7, 1937, box 142, TRWP; "Violations of Free Speech," pt. 28, 15,116–20. Beaudry later became head of security at the Detroit plant and, as of 1939, still had most of his arsenal intact. A. Beaudry to R. S. Livingstone, September 14, 1939, box 142, TRWP.

70. Dossett, "Thompson Products," 139, 209–213; Shore, "Historical Analysis," 230–32.

71. In defense of the Cleveland dismissals, Thompson claimed that two of the men were fired for producing excessive scrap while the third had stolen a small lamp at an Old Guard party in March (though nearly everyone at the event was drunk and said to be "sportively taking souvenirs" from the caterer). *Thompson Products and United Automobile Workers*, 3 NLRB 332, 338 (August 16, 1937); Stanley and Smoyer (attorneys) to Frederick C. Crawford, October 24, 1945, reel 4, TPP; *Toledo Blade*, May 20, 21, 22, 1937 (courtesy of Tana Mosier Porter, Toledo-Lucas County Public Library).

72. Auerbach, *LaFollette*, 144; Van Tassel and Grabowski, *Encyclopedia*, 639; Bernstein, *Lean Years*, 482.

73. Dossett, "Thompson Products," 213; Livingstone quoted in Shore, "Historical Analysis," vi.

74. *Cleveland News*, May 11, 1938, and *New York Times*, May 14, 1938, clippings in box 28, TRWP; *NLRB v. Thompson Products*, 97 F. 2d 13 (6 CCA, 1938); Dossett, "Thompson Products," 190–93, 204–37; James A. Gross, *The Reshaping of the National Labor Relations Board: National Labor Policy in Transition, 1937–1947* (Albany, N.Y., 1981), 109–86.

75. Cochran, *Labor and Communism*, 119–20; Mortimer, *Organize!*, 125; Ralph G. Gordon to H. W. Brown (IAM official in Washington, D.C.), September 3, 1935, Thompson Products file, International Association of Machinists Papers, State Historical Society of Wisconsin, Madison.

76. "Chronicle of Relationships with Independent Union: Preliminary History," typescript, no date; "Thompson Products Chronology," typescript, May 14, 1940; APW flyer, September 18, 1937; Matt Graham to Local 247, October 15, 1937; R. S. Livingstone to J. D. Wright, April 2, 1938; R. S. Livingstone to William F. Goltz, May 24, 1939; W. F. Goltz to R. S. Livingstone, May 26, 1939, all in box 142, TRWP; "Statement of William Goltz," August 2, 1940, and "Complaint of the UAW to the NLRB," 7th Region, case C–386, July 13, 1940, box 143, TRWP.

77. Richard C. Wilcock, "Industrial Management's Policies toward Unionism" in Milton Derber and Edwin Young, eds., *Labor and the New Deal* (Madison, Wisc., 1961), 296–97; "Independent Unions: An Analysis and Survey," *NAM Labor Relations Bulletin* 23 (July 23, 1937), 3, 16–17; NLRB, Division of Economic Research, "Statistical Analysis of 85 'Independent' Unions and Readapted Company Unions" (Washington, D.C., 1938) and NLRB, Division of Economic Research, "Characteristics of 60 Company-Dominated Unions" (Washington, D.C., 1939).

78. 33 NLRB 1,033, 1,041; "In the Matter of Thompson Products and UAW Local 300, and AAWA: Transcript of Evidence, December 2, 1940" reprinted in U.S. Circuit Court of Appeals for Sixth District, *Transcript of Record, NLRB v. Thompson Products and AAWA, Inc.* (April 1942) (hereafter *Transcript: 1942*), 294, reel 1, TPP.

79. Sixth Circuit, *Transcript: 1942*, 668; *Cleveland News*, January 20, 1942, clipping in box 20, TRWP. Attorney Harry E. Smoyer privately said that Roemisch was a "true believer" in the cause of company unionism. Smoyer to Frank P. Darin, August 13, 1940, box 143, TRWP.

80. Sixth Circuit, *Transcript: 1942*, 489–500; 1943 trial examiner's report reproduced in "Thompson Products, Thompson Aircraft Products, and UAW-CIO," 57 NLRB 151 (August 4, 1944), 941–42, 1,016–18; "Transcript of NLRB Trial 1943," 72, 527, reel 1B, TPP; NLRB, Trial Examiners' Division, "Exceptions of Respondent M. A. Roemisch," October 12, 1943, 4, reel 3, TPP.

81. "Transcript of the Meeting of Employees of Thompson Products" (September 16, 1942), reel 2, TPP.

82. M. A. Roemisch, "Special Instructions to Delegates and Representatives" (n.d.), box 28, TRWP; "Transcript of NLRB hearing, December 2, 1940" reprinted in Sixth Circuit, *Transcript: 1942*, 580–688; R. S. Livingstone to F. C. Crawford, June 21, 1937, box 28, TRWP; 33 NLRB 1,033, 1,039–48.

83. Labor Relations Council (LRC) minutes, October 4, 1937, April 10, 1940, September 13, 1937; Executive Committee minutes, September 15, 1938, box 28, TRWP.

84. LRC minutes, March 7, 1938, April 4, 1938, June 13, 1938, January 4, 1939, February 16, 1939, March 27, 1939, March 14, 1940, and April 10, 1940, box 28, TRWP.

85. Dossett, "Thompson Products," 274; M. A. Roemisch to R. S. Livingstone and F. C. Crawford, October 7, 1940; R. S. Livingstone, "Memorandum on Cleveland Rate Structure" August 27, 1940; LRC minutes, September 6, 1940, October 22, 1940, and November 2, 1940, box 28, TRWP.

86. 33 NLRB 1,033, 1,050.

87. *NLRB v. Thompson Products*, 11 LRRM 521, 526 (6 CCA, August 28, 1942); Millis and Montgomery, *Organized Labor*, 107–8.

88. "Thompson, Union, Will Resist NLRB," *Cleveland Plain Dealer*, August 3, 1941; *Cleveland Press*, November 14, 1941, January 14 and 30, 1942, and February 10, 1942, clippings in box 30, TRWP; *Friendly Forum*, January 1951, 5.

89. Roger Keeran, *The Communist Party and the Auto Workers Unions* (Bloomington, Ind. 1980), 141, 153; Fine, *Sit-down*, 78, 323; Proceedings of the 1941 Convention of the International Union, United Automobile Workers of America (Buffalo, N.Y., August 4–16), 171.

90. *Cleveland News*, November 4, 1941, January 21 and 30, 1942, clippings on reel 1, TPP; Dossett, "Handling Grievances" 23–24; UAW-CIO, "Brief Submitted to National War

Labor Board on Thompson Products, February 1, 1942," box 30, TRWP.

91. National War Labor Board (NWLB), "Report of the Mediator in the Matter of Thompson Products and the UAW," case no. 20 (February 26, 1942), 10, reel 1, TPP; F. C. Crawford in "Statement of Labor History," 42–49; F. C. Crawford to NWLB, Feb. 25, 1942, Walter C. Teagle to F. C. Crawford, April 18, 1942, F. C. Crawford to Frank P. Graham, April 21, 1942, and *Cleveland Plain Dealer*, April 3 and 23, 1942, all in box 30, TRWP; testimony of Victor Reuther in "Transcript of NLRB Trial, 1943," 2,942–94, reel 2B, TPP. The War Labor Board allowed the Machinists to appear on the ballot at Main even though the union could produce only 64 signature cards (out of about 4,000 workers). Crawford was angered by this, fearing that the AFL union would draw votes away from the company union and thus give the UAW two chances to win. The NWLB felt compelled to put the Machinists on the ballot to avoid charges of pro-CIO favoritism. Although the incident suggests that the NWLB was sensitive to these charges, the board's conduct in the Thompson case runs counter to the claim that it "used its power and prestige to uphold the authority of management over its employees and that of cooperative union leaders over their often rebellious rank and file." If anything, the board's behavior was consistent with its own appraisal of its mission: to reduce wartime disputes by promoting "unrestricted collective bargaining." Nelson Lichtenstein, *Labor's War at Home: The CIO in World War II* (Cambridge, U.K., 1982), 178; NWLB, *Termination Report,* vol. 1 (Washington, D.C., 1948), 64.

92. "Report of Radio Program Sponsored by UAW, Broadcast over WADC," January 14, 1942; *The Organizer*, January 6 and May 1, 1942, box 30, TRWP.

93. *Let's Have the Truth!*, January 16, 1942; "Report of Radio Program," January 14 and March 4, 1942, all in box 30, TRWP.

94. Various AAWA flyers, April to August 1941, box 29; LRC minutes, October 20, 1941, box 29, and March 11, 1942, box 30, TRWP; *Cleveland News*, March 27, 1941; Thompson Products, "Collective Bargaining Procedures" (April 12, 1941), box 29, TRWP; M. A. Roemisch to R. S. Livingstone, January 5, 1942, and AAWA's *Square Deal*, various issues from 1941 and 1942 in box 30, TRWP; "Transcript of the Meeting of Employees," September 16, 1942, reel 2, TPP.

95. *Cleveland Press*, May 2, 1942, clipping in box 30, TRWP; "Objections of the UAW-CIO to the Election Held May 1, 1942 among the Employees of Thompson Products, Inc." and NLRB, "Decision Order and Second Direction of Election, August 4, 1944," both on reel 1, TPP.

96. "Transcript of NLRB Trial 1943," 443, 534–40, reel 1B, TPP; *AAWA Bulletin*, August 31, 1942, box 30, TRWP.

97. "Transcript of the Meeting of Employees of Thompson Products, Inc., September 16, 1942," reel 2, TPP. During the meeting, UAW supporters heckled Roemisch, questioning his sincerity. Calling them "stooges," Roemisch said that he took only $600 annually for representing the AAWA and that he never had received money from Thompson Products. Indeed, no evidence of such support was ever found.

98. 1943 Trial Examiner's Report in 57 NLRB 151 (1944), 998–1,000; *Cleveland Plain Dealer*, November 5, 1942; "Transcript of NLRB trial 1943," 534–40, reel 1B and 9,219–24, reel 5B, TPP.

99. "Transcript of NLRB Trial 1943," 9,201–5, 9,213, reel 5B, TPP; 1943 Trial Examiner's Report, 1,007; "Exceptions of Respondent M. A. Roemisch," October 12, 1943, 8, reel 3, TPP.

100. 1943 Trial Examiner's Report, 1,015; "NLRB Favoritism," *Cleveland Plain Dealer*, August 8, 1944, clipping on reel 1, TPP.

101. "We Led with Our Chin," 24; 57 NLRB 151 (1944), 995; minutes of the meeting to form the AWA (November 12, 1941), and P. W. Howard to TAPCO, December 11, 1941, both reel 1, TPP; UAW-CIO, "Brief Submitted to the NWLB" (February 1942), 4; *TAPCO Bulletin*, January 13, 1942, and M. A. Roemisch to R. S. Livingstone, January 5, 1942, box 30, TRWP; "Referee OKs AWA Plea to Hike Pay," *Friendly Forum*, September 17, 1943, R. S. Livingstone to Frederick H. Bullen (regional director, War Labor Board), January 26, 1944, and *TAPCO Bulletin*, July 31, 1944, all reel 3, TPP. As of the election date in 1942, there were 3,972 workers at TAPCO. Of these, 2,786 had been transferred to TAPCO from Thompson and 2,748 had been hired from the outside (the difference reflects turnover in both groups). R. S. Livingstone to Hugh E. Sperry (regional NLRB director), June 15, 1942, reel 1, TPP.

102. In 1944 the UAW received 22 percent of the vote at TAPCO, a sharp drop from 1942. At Main, its share of the vote was 36 percent in 1944, 34 percent in 1945, and 32 percent in 1947. Robert A. Lorton to R. S. Livingstone, May 8, 1944, reel 3, TPP; NLRB, *In the Matter of Thompson Products and UAW Local No.*

300, Second Supplemental Decision and Order, 60 NLRB 3,181 (March 1945); Dossett, "Handling Grievances," 46, 57; TAPCO, *Supervisory Bulletin*, September 13, 1944, box 38, TRWP; *Cleveland Plain Dealer*, October 20, 21, and 22, 1945, clippings on reel 4, TPP; NLRB, Eighth Region, case no. 8–R–1,989, "Report on Objections," June 3, 1946, box 39, TRWP.

103. About 10 percent of Main plant participated in the 1943 strike, which is discussed in the strike correspondence file, box 138, TRWP and in *Cleveland Plain Dealer*, April 14, 1943; Joseph Coniglio and Ed Castle testimony in "Transcript of NLRB Trial 1943," 1,383, 1,408, reel 1B, and 9,150, reel 5B, TPP; 57 NLRB 151 (1944), 936, 967.

104. "Transcript of NLRB Trial 1943," 4,034–63, reel 3B, and 9,186, reel 5B, TPP. Thompson hired the black women in response to pressure from a coalition of black community organizations that had threatened to sue Thompson and several other firms (including unionized Warner and Swasey) for not hiring black women into war jobs. Although Cleveland's black population rose by 75 percent in the 1940s, the city escaped the kind of racial violence that plagued cities like Detroit. At the Detroit plant, management played the race card during the 1945 campaign, when letters were sent to all "colored" employees signed by a committee of "prominent Negros," including George Johnson and Jimmy Williams, urging them to not vote for the UAW. *Cleveland News*, November 3, November 14 and December 16, 1942, and *Cleveland Press*, December 8, 1942, clippings on reel 1, TPP; Van Tassel and Grabowski, *Encyclopedia*, 1,073; August Meier and Elliott Rudwick, *Black Detroit and the Rise of the UAW* (New York, 1979); and R. S. Livingstone, "General Procedures—Detroit Election" (March 5, 1945) box 144, TRWP.

105. Shore, "Historical Analysis," 448, 453; *Call Post*, April 3, 1943, and *The Challenger*, August 26, 1944, clippings on reel 1, TPP; "Decision of Arbitrator Arthur T. Martin, May 27, 1943," reel 2, and R. S. Livingstone to Arthur T. Martin, October 8, 1943, reel 3, TPP. The UAW also published an anti-Semitic flyer that said, "Floor Inspector Freeman of the first shift in Dept. 06: I feel sorry for you, "Fagin" Freeman because you are so disliked by your fellow workers. . . . You squeal on your fellow workers and you lie to everyone that you come in contact with." Quoted in Dossett, "Handling Grievances," 53. On race and the white working class, see Thomas J. Sugrue, "Crabgrass-Roots Politics: Race, Rights, and the Reaction against Liberalism in the Urban North, 1940–64," *Journal of American History* 82 (September 1995), 551–78.

106. R. S. Livingstone, "Labor Relations in a Nonunionized Company," paper presented at the American Management Association (Chicago, February 1946), DCCU; Baritz, *Servants of Power*, 144; Livingstone, "Settling Disputes," 391.

107. Livingstone, "Settling Disputes," 389; Seybold, "Organization of Personnel Administration," 80; Thompson Products, "Duties of the Personnel Supervisor" (February 1943), 3, reel 2, TPP; "Transcript of NLRB Trial 1943," 1,408, reel 1B, TPP. In a throwback to the era of "home visiting," each Thompson plant had a supervisor of employee services who assisted employees with their transportation problems and brought flowers and candy to sick employees. Seybold, "Organization of Personnel Administration," 84.

108. "We Led with Our Chin," passim; *Friendly Forum*, November 12, 1943, reel 3; Dossett, "Thompson Products," 654–55; Baritz, *Servants of Power*, 152; "Fred Crawford's Company," 208; "Stopping Grievances before They Grow," *Modern Industry* (February 15, 1947), reprint, DCCU.

109. Seybold, "Organization of Personnel Administration," 83–84; *Friendly Forum* (January 1951), 39–45; Rutherford, "The Career of Fred Crawford," 9; "Two-Way Information Flow Pays Off," *Factory Management and Maintenance* 104 (May 1946), 108–12; Dossett, "Thompson Products," 244–46; "Family Mass Meetings" (n.d.), box 28, TRWP; Shore, "Historical Analysis," 329; R. S. Livingstone, "20 Questions: A Case Study in Human Engineering," *Steel* (September 1, 1952), 3–7.

110. Jacoby, "Employee Attitude Surveys in American Industry: An Historical Perspective," *Industrial Relations* 27 (Winter 1988); Thompson Products, *Annual Report to Employees: 1940*, box 28, TRWP; *Annual Report to Employees: 1942*, reel 6, TPP; *Annual Report to Employees: 1946*, box 39, TRWP; Shore, "Historical Analysis," 520; Livingstone, "20 Questions," 7.

111. Various issues of *Let's Have the Truth!* and *Labor Relations Bulletin* in boxes 28–30, TRWP; "Two-Way Flow," 109; Livingstone, "General Procedures: Detroit Election," March 5, 1945, box 144, TRWP. As demonstrated by its radio shows, the UAW was familiar with modern public relations techniques. It rented sound trucks and regularly parked them at the front and rear gates of Main plant. On another occasion, it issued a pamphlet called *Let's Have the the REAL*

Truth, the first page of which said, "Read what the TP and the AWA have done and will do for you!" The rest of the pamphlet was blank. Box 30, TRWP.

112. Dyer, "Voice of Experience," 122; *Cleveland Plain Dealer*, April 2, 1944, quoted in Dossett, "Handling Grievances," 70.

113. "Supervisory Newsletter," July 15, 1946, box 39, TRWP; *Cleveland Union Leader*, August 29, 1947, reel 6, TPP; *Friendly Forum*, May 2, 1947, and May 30, 1947, box 41, TRWP; "Thompson Raises Wages $3 Million; Beats New Pattern," *Cleveland Plain Dealer*, October 22, 1945, April 26, 1946, April 29, 1947, May 16, 1947, July 25, 1947, clippings in boxes 30 and 41, TRWP; *NLRB v. Thompson Products, Inc.*, 20 LRRM 2,291, 2,297 (6CCA, 1947); G. H. Malone, "Memo of Meeting Held on April 7, 1948," box 110, TRWP.

114. "Statement of Paul Herzog" in U.S. Senate, *Hearings before the Committee on Labor and Public Welfare*, 80th Cong., 1st sess., pt. 4 (1947), 1,912.

115. "Statement of Hugh Sperry," U.S. House of Representatives, *Hearings before the Committee on Education and Labor*, 80th Cong., 1st sess., 1947, vol. 3, 3,472; "We Led with our Chin," passim; Arlen Southern, "Results of the 1957 Spot Check of Employee Opinion," February 12, 1957, 8, box 137, TRWP. There are parallels here to the recent debate over the effect of employer campaign conduct on union election outcomes. See J. Getman, S. Goldberg, and J. Herman, *Union Representation Elections: Law and Reality* (New York, 1976), and Paul Weiler, "Promises to Keep: Securing Workers' Right to Self-Organization under the NLRA," *Harvard Law Review* 96 (June 1983), 1,769–1,827.

116. Ed Hall quoted in *Cleveland Press*, November 28, 1941, clipping in box 30, TRWP; 57 NLRB 151 (1944), 938; *The Recorder* (UAW Local 826, Cleveland), May 15, 1947, box 40, TRWP; Dossett, "Thompson Products," 345; author's interview with Oscar Lockard, former AWA president, November 11, 1987.

117. "Thompson Products Chronononology" (May 1940), and UAW, "Complaint to the NLRB, 7th Region," July 13, 1940, box 143, TRWP; 47 NLRB 83 (1943), 619; Harry Millis and Emily Clark Brown, *From the Wagner Act to Taft-Hartley: A Study of National Labor Policy and Labor Relations* (Chicago, 1950), 200; 72 NLRB 886 (1947); Livingstone, "Chronology: Detroit Strike"; "General Procedure-Detroit Election" (March 5, 1945); and Plant Bulletin, March 1, 1945, all box 144, TRWP; 60 NLRB 150 (1945), 885; 70 NLRB 3 (1946) 13.

118. After a one-week strike at Toledo in 1945 (which included some damage to company property), Thompson moved the plant's production lines to Cleveland. A warehouse was left open, but the move eliminated the UAW from the Toledo facility. "Toledo Shop Committee Gains Respect of Plant's Employees," *Friendly Forum*, April 23, 1937, reel 1, TPP; *Toledo Blade*, November 13, 16, 20, 24, 27, 29, 1945; Stanley and Smoyer to F. C. Crawford, October 24, 1945, reel 4, TPP; various Toledo files, box 146, TRWP; and F. C. Crawford to author, May 12, 1987.

119. Daniel Nelson, "How the UAW Grew," *Labor History* 35 (Winter 1994), 19; R. S. Livingstone to Bill Goltz, May 24, 1939; UAW flyer, January 1941; and R. S. Livingstone to John Cox, February 24, 1936, all in box 142, TRWP.

120. *The Recorder*, May 6, 1947, and "Outline of Meeting for Supervisors of Special Products," May 2, 1947, both box 40, TRWP. This debate continued into the 1960s. For example, when the UAW tried to organize TAPCO in 1967, the company published data showing that TAPCO's wages and benefits were equal to or higher than those paid under the UAW contract at its Detroit plant (now located in Warren, Michigan). "TRW Election Bulletin," April 25, 1967, box 141, TRWP. Also see Leon Nies memo, March 9, 1959, box 118, TRWP; and Jacoby and Verma, "Enterprise Unions," passim.

121. "Public Hearing before the National War Labor Board" (November 20, 1942), reel 2, TPP; NWLB Directive Order, case no. 516 (November 25, 1942), and William H. Chamberlain to R. S. Livingstone, September 2, 1943, reel 3, TPP; NWLB, "Meeting of the Regional Board, Region V: Excerpts of Proceedings" (April 13, 1943), 111, "Decisions of Impartial Arbitrator Arthur T. Martin" (June 16, 1943), and R. S. Livingstone to Martin, July 21, 1943, all on reel 2, TPP; Steven Fraser, *Labor Will Rule: Sidney Hillman and the Rise of American Labor* (New York, 1991), 456.

122. Elizabeth Hawes, *Hurry Up Please It's Time* (New York, 1946), 181–84. More generally, see Cochran, *Labor and Communism*, chaps. 6–10, and Keeran, *The Communist Party and the Auto Unions*. Information from William (Bill) Grant's FBI file kindly provided by Professor Judith Stepan-Norris. Similar problems affected the CIO's Cleveland Industrial Union Council (CIUC), which, until the mid-1940s, had been a staunch supporter of the Thompson drive. Factional splits in the CIUC presented a propaganda opportunity for Thompson management: to discredit the head of the CIUC (A. E. Stevenson, who was tied to

the Communists and to the Thompson drive) by quoting his CIO critics. Van Tassel and Grabowski, *Encyclopedia*, 243; Dossett, "Thompson Products," 610–11; "On the Labor Front," *Cleveland Plain Dealer*, March 2, 1947, clipping in box 40, TRWP; R. S. Livingstone, "Can There Be Industrial Peace with Unionism?" (Livingstone's remarks in a public debate with A. E. Stevenson, November 1946), DCCU.

123. Cochran, *Labor and Communism*, 272–96; Victor Riesel and Aaron Levenstein, "How to Wreck a Labor Union," *Look* 11 (April 29, 1947); Stephen Meyer, *"Stalin Over Wisconsin": The Making and Unmaking of Militant Unionism, 1900–1950* (New Brunswick, N.J., 1992); *Cleveland News*, September 17, 1947, clipping on reel 6, TPP; Walter Reuther, "Report of the President" in *Proceedings of the Eleventh Convention of the UAW-CIO, Atlantic City, November 1947*, Part I, 26–28; *Supervisory Newsletter*, July 15, 1946, and *Friendly Forum*, December 12, 1947, box 40, TRWP.

124. *Cleveland Press*, November 28, 1941, clipping in box 29; UAW flyer (April 8, 1941), quoted in Shore, "Historical Analysis," 74.

125. Gross, *The Reshaping of the National Labor Relations Board*, 187–259.

126. Jacoby and Verma, "Enterprise Unions," 140.

127. R. D. Lundy, vice president, TRW, to author, December 19, 1986; Philip Taft, "Independents and the Merger," *Industrial and Labor Relations Review* 9 (April 1956), 445; Millis and Montgomery, *Organized Labor*, 886–89.

128. AWA Publicity Committee, flyer (May 17, 1954), and "Contract Negotiations" (July 22, 1955), box 117, TRWP; Peter F. Drucker, "Labor in Industrial Society," *Annals of the American Academy of Political and Social Science* 274 (March 1951), 145. Thanks to Professor Alan Derrickson for bringing this article to my attention.

129. "Transcript of NLRB Trial 1943," 620, reel 1B, TPP; Labor Relations Council minutes, Main plant, October 11, 1949, box 120, TRWP and June 27, 1949, box 70, TRWP; M. A. Roemisch to Lee Clegg, March 1, 1949, box 118, TRWP; Schacht, *The Making of Telephone Unionism*, 73; Millis and Montgomery, *Organized Labor*, 884. The Detroit company union's attorney was Frank Amprim, who, like Roemisch, represented other Detroit-area company unions, including the Down River Seamen's Union, which defeated the National Maritime Union in 1940.

130. A. Sheahen to R. S. Livingstone, June 21, 1951, box 117, TRWP; minutes of the Main plant personnel meeting, January 17, 1958, box 133, TRWP; LRC minutes, Main plant, June 7, 1961, box 127, TRWP; Main plant grievance files, 1944–1958, boxes 110, 111, and 112, TRWP. My tally of grievances is calculated from the index to the LRC minutes, 1950–1958, box 121, TRWP. The precise mixture of adversarialism and cooperation varied across Thompson's company unions. During the 1970s, for example, a TRW company union in Pennsyvlania was a quiescent organization: it never struck, filed few grievances, and only once in ten years protested a grievance all the way through to arbitration. On the other hand, an aggressive TRW company union in Ohio (not the AWA) in most respects resembled a TRW-UAW local in Connecticut. The two locals had the same number of strikes and wildcats, and, although the UAW local filed more grievances, the Ohio company union pressed a greater number through to arbitration. Jacoby and Verma, "Enterprise Unions," 144, 153.

131. Author's interview with Oscar Lockard; minutes of the Cleveland Personnel Committee, July 2, 1962, box 125, M. A. Roemisch to R. S. Livingstone, June 6, 1951; and "Grievance Report" (May 17, 1954), box 117, TRWP; R. N. Morse to M. A. Roemisch, June 7, 1949, box 118, TRWP; and LRC minutes, Main plant, February 10, 1949, box 120, TRWP. In 1951, when the AWA still had separate contracts for Main and TAPCO, Main workers were annoyed that their pay rates were below TAPCO's. After the AWA threatened to have an arbitrator rule on the issue, management agreed to reopen the contract and insert language stating that the company's "long term policy" was to "work toward entirely uniform wage scales" at its Cleveland plants. M. A. Roemisch to H. D. Bubb et al., June 20, 1951, box 117, TRWP.

132. Millis and Montgomery, *Organized Labor*, 883. LRC minutes, Cleveland area, June 2, 1961, box 125, TRWP; *Friendly Forum*, March 1, 1946, box 39, TRWP; "Comparison of Average Wages, Main plant, with U.S. CPI and Average Straight Time Wages in Durable Goods Manufacturing 1948–1960," box 141, TRWP; and *Cleveland Profiles-Cuyahoga County* (May 1953), 1–10, box 128, TRWP; Robert Ozanne, *Wages in Practice and Theory* (Madison, Wisc., 1968), 136. One IAM organizer admitted in private correspondence that Thompson was difficult to organize because it paid prevailing wages. E. H. White to S. L. Newman, April 15, 1950, reel 218, international president's file, IAM Papers, State Historical Society of Wisconsin, Madison.

133. LRC minutes, Main plant, June 28, 1949, and M. A. Roemisch to R. S. Livingstone, January 11, 1950, box 120, TRWP; M. A. Roemisch to R. S. Livingstone, July 10, 1951, box 117, TRWP; H. E. Stevens to J. W. Drake et al., May 5, 1955, G. H. Malone memorandum, May 17, 1955, and "Contract Negotiations," July 22, 1955, all box 117, TRWP; minutes of the Main plant personnel meeting, April 26, 1957, box 133, TRWP. Most unionists considered the AWA to be parasitic, although its behavior was no different from the wage imitation practiced by small national unions that were within the orbit of a major pattern-setter like the UAW. Joel A. Seidman, *Company Unions: A Study Outline with Special Reference to the ILGWU* (New York, 1935), 5.

134. "Sworn Statement of Ed Castle," January 20, 1944, and R. S. Livingstone, "Personnel Memo," May 1, 1944, reel 3, TPP; "Transcript of NLRB Trial 1943," 188–93, 490–523, 1,116, 1,153, reel 1B, and 9,185–86, reel 5B, TPP; NWLB, "Transcript of Proceedings Before Arthur T. Martin, Arbitrator," January 30, 1943, reel 2, TPP.

135. LRC minutes, Main plant, June 28, 1949, and October 11, 1949, box 120, TRWP; LRC minutes, Cleveland area, June 2, 1961, box 125, TRWP; "AWA 1961–62" file, box 126, TRWP.

136. This discussion is based on LRC minutes from Main plant and the Cleveland area 1948–1969, boxes 120–21 and 127–28, TRWP. A tally for the years 1950 to 1958 shows that the most commonly discussed topics were physical plant conditions (23 percent), personnel matters (21 percent), wage rates and standards (10 percent), business outlook and plans (10 percent), safety (7 percent), and parking (6 percent).

137. LRC minutes, Main plant, January 23, 1949, Feburary 17, 1952, April 13, 1950, September 11, 1952, January 6, 1960, all in box 120, TRWP; LRC minutes, Cleveland area, July 17, 1958, box 121, TRWP.

138. LRC minutes, Main plant, July 16, 1948, May 5, 1949, April 13, 1950, September 13, 1951, box 120, TRWP; supplemental agreements in boxes 117 and 118, TRWP. On the GM-UAW formula, see J. W. Garbarino, "The Economic Significance of Automatic Wage Adjustments" in Harold W. Davey, ed., *New Dimensions in Collective Bargaining* (New York, 1959).

139. *AWA News Bulletin*, April 2, 1953, box 117; minutes of Main plant personnel meeting, November 10, 1961, box 133, TRWP; LRC minutes, Main plant: May 5, 1949, June 28, 1949, December 2, 1949, box 120, and December 7, 1960, box 121, TRWP; R. S. Livingstone to Cleveland Factory Supervision, March 21, 1958, box 117, TRWP; G. H. Malone memo, December 9, 1949, box 118, TRWP.

140. "Chronology of Relationships," box 142, TRWP; 57 NLRB 151 (1944), 957; "Transcript of NLRB Trial 1943," 559, 684, reel 1B and NWLB, "Transcript of Proceedings before Arthur T. Martin" (January 30, 1943), 1,072, reel 2, TPP. On Japanese enterprise unions, see Ronald Dore, *British Factory-Japanese Factory* (Berkeley, Cal., 1973), and Taishiro Shirai, "A Theory of Enterprise Unionism" in Shirai, ed., *Contemporary Industrial Relations in Japan* (Madison, Wisc., 1983).

141. Karl Heilman, Jr., to G. H. Malone, August 19, 1952, box 133, and Arlen Southern, "Results of the 1957 Spot Check of Employee Opinion," February 12, 1957, box 137, TRWP. Data on pay appear in Eugene Schwartz memorandum, December 8, 1953, box 117, and in G. H. Malone to R. G. McCarty, November 5, 1958, box 118, TRWP. Also see Bob Hausermann to G. H. Malone, November 3, 1958, box 118, and G. H. Malone to R. L. Brown, September 2, 1958, box 133, TRWP.

142. Minutes of the Cleveland Personnel Committee: April 15, 1957, June 6, 1962, and October 1, 1962, box 125, and UAW flyer, April 27, 1967, box 141, TRWP. The UAW made an abortive organizing attempt at Main and TAPCO in 1960. It tried again in 1962 but failed to meet the 30 percent authorization-card minimum. The big drive came in 1967, when the UAW received 44 percent of the votes in a hotly contested election that was marked by precisely the same irregularities that had occurred in the 1940s. After its 1967 defeat, the UAW charged that TRW gave the AWA free rein in the plants while denying UAW supporters similar opportunities. Although a rerun was held, the UAW lost again, in part because the company turned to another old tactic: it gave a 5 percent wage increase a month before the second election. "UAW 1967" file, box 141, TRWP; UAW, "Objections to Election," NLRB case no. 8–RC–6714, *TRW Inc. and UAW, AFL-CIO* (May 1967), box 141, and assorted materials in boxes 126, 133, and 140, TRWP.

143. G. H. Malone, "Rules for Subcontracting" (c. 1955), box 137, TRWP; minutes of personnel meeting, October 28, 1960, box 133, TRWP; Thompson Products, "Human Relations Policy" (revised July 1957), 17, DCCU;

U.S. Chamber of Commerce, *The Hidden Payroll: Nonwage Labor Costs of Doing Business* (Washington, D.C., 1949); "Confidential Supplemental Report to the Automotive Parts Manufacturers Association" (c. 1954), box 117, TRWP; Schatz, *Electrical Workers*, chapter 6.

144. Personnel Policy Conference, January 27, 1955, box 128, TRWP; George Malone to L. W. Reeves, February 4, 1957, G. H. Malone to Division Managers, February 4, 1957, and minutes of personnel meeting, December 2, 1958, all in box 133, TRWP.

145. Arthur Shostak, *America's Forgotten Labor Organization: A Survey of the Role of the Single-Firm Independent Union in American Industry* (Princeton, N.J., 1962), 115; Jacoby and Verma, "Enterprise Unions," 148–50.

146. Rezler, "Labor Organization at DuPont," 185–95. The Du Pont experience was not unusual. At Western Electric, for example, members of the white-collar independent union (the Council of Western Electric Technical and Professional Employees) were extremely loyal to the company union but *not* to management. At Thompson, on the other hand, employees were loyal both to the company union *and* to management—a form of "dual loyalty"—that reflected the blurred boundary between company and union. Theodore Purcell, *Blue Collar Man: Patterns of Dual Allegiance in Industry* (Cambridge, Mass., 1960), 252.

147. Rezler, "Labor Organization at DuPont," 190; letter to author from R. D. Lundy, vice president, public relations, TRW Inc., December 19, 1986; minutes of Cleveland Area Labor Relations Council (January-March 1959) (discussions of suggestion system), box 121, TRWP; Shore, "Historical Analysis," 560–63; Jacoby and Verma, "Enterprise Unions," 153. Note that the AWA did finally go out on strike in 1979. "TRW Hit by Strike at Cleveland Facilities," *Wall Street Journal*, November 2, 1979.

148. "Rapid Air Force Build-up Spurs Thompson Products," *Barron's* 31 (April 23, 1951), 15–16; "Constitution of the Frontiersmen Association" (1954), and "Handbook for Employees, Bell Sound Systems" (1953), in box 127, TRWP; Bill Bunce (Bell Sound) to R. S. Livingstone, March 5, 1955, box 126, TRWP; George Malone, "Minutes of First Meeting with Employee Representatives of Dage Plant," April 4, 1956, box 127, TRWP.

149. Bill Relyea to George Malone, April 16, 1956, and "Local Plant Committee Charter" (May 8, 1956), box 127, TRWP; "Thompson Ramo Wooldridge, Inc. (Dage Television Division) and General Teamsters, Chauffeurs, and Helpers, Local Union no. 298," 132 NLRB No. 80 (1961), 993–1,023.

150. "Thompson Ramo Wooldridge and Teamsters Union," 132 NLRB 80 (1961) 995, 1,006; NLRB v. Thompson Ramo Wooldridge, Inc., 50 LRRM 2,759–62 (1962); Anil Verma and Thomas A. Kochan, "The Growth and Nature of the Nonunion Sector within a Firm" in Thomas A. Kochan, ed., *Challenges and Choices Facing American Labor* (Cambridge, Mass., 1985), 93–95; Lundy letter to author; author's interviews with Jim E. Dunlap, February 2, 1988, and Dr. Simon Ramo, December 17, 1986; T. A. Wickes to G. H. Malone, March 30, 1967, box 133, TRWP (on teams at Main plant); David Oates, "Sensing Aids Candour in Aerospace Firm," *International Machinist* (UK), April 1973; "Where Diversity Is the Tie That Binds," *Business Week*, September 24, 1966, 92. Also see Thomas A. Kochan, Harry C. Katz, and Robert B. McKersie, *The Transformation of American Industrial Relations* (New York, 1986), 93–108, whose account of the new nonunion model is based on the TRW experience.

Chapter Six
Beyond the Manor: Politics and Public Opinion

1. James C. Worthy to Clarence B. Caldwell, "An Employee Relations Program for Sears Roebuck, 1951," JCWP.

2. Donald Fleming, "Attitude: The History of a Concept," *Perspectives in American History* 1 (1967), 287–365.

3. Jean M. Converse, *Survey Research in the United States: Roots and Emergence, 1890–1960* (Berkeley, Cal., 1987); Elizabeth Fones-Wolf, *Selling Free Enterprise: The Business Assault on Labor and Liberalism, 1945–60* (Urbana, Ill., 1994), 71; Alan Brinkley, *The End of Reform: New Deal Liberalism in Recession and War* (New York, 1995).

4. Ralph Canter, Jr., "Psychologists in Industry," *Personnel Psychology* 1 (Summer 1948), 145–61; George K. Bennett, "A New Era in Business and Industrial Psychology," *Personnel Psychology* 1 (Winter 1948), 473–77.

5. On business as an interest group, see Francis X. Sutton, Seymour E. Harris, Carl Kaysen, and James Tobin, *The American Business Creed* (Cambridge, Mass., 1956); and Louis Galambos, *The Public Image of Big Business in America, 1880–1940* (Baltimore, Md., 1975). Because big corporations pursued

multiple objectives and therefore belonged to diverse organizations, one cannot rely on membership lists of employer associations to infer a company's economic interests from the public activities of its managers—a common but misguided research methodology. See, for example, Thomas Ferguson, "Industrial Conflict and the Coming of the New Deal: The Triumph of Multinational Liberalism in America," in Steven Fraser and Gary Gerstle, eds., *The Rise and Fall of the New Deal Order, 1930–1980* (Princeton, N.J., 1989) or J. C. Jenkins and B. G. Brents, "Social Protest, Hegemonic Competition, and Social Reform: A Political Struggle Interpretation of the Origins of the American Welfare State," *American Sociological Review* 54 (December 1989), 891–909.

6. Robert E. Lane, *The Regulation of Businessmen* (New Haven, Conn., 1954), 40; Harry Millis and Emily Clark Brown, *From the Wagner Act to Taft-Hartley* (Chicago, 1950), 284–85. Joining the NAM in calls to investigate and reform the NLRB was the AFL, which felt that the board was biased in favor of industrial unions.

7. U.S. Congress, House, Special Committee to Investigate the National Labor Relations Board, intermediate report no. 1,902, 76th Cong., 3d Sess. (Washington, D.C., 1940); James A. Gross, *The Reshaping of the National Labor Relations Board: National Labor Policy in Transition, 1937–47* (Albany, N.Y., 1981), 180, 198; Millis and Brown, *From Wagner to Taft-Hartley*, 176, 348–53; "Statement of Paul Herzog," U.S. Senate, Committee on Labor and Public Welfare, *Hearings: Labor Relations Program*, pt. 4, 80th Cong., 1st Sess. (Washington, D.C., 1947), 1,912.

8. Millis and Brown, *From Wagner to Taft-Hartley*, 285; Howell John Harris, *The Right to Manage: Industrial Relations Policies of American Business in the 1940s* (Madison, Wisc., 1982), 39, 106.

9. Richard W. Gable, "A Political Analysis of an Employers' Association: The National Association of Manufacturers," Ph.D. dissertation, University of Chicago, Chicago, 1950, p. 178; *AIC Bulletin*, July 19, 1938, box 28, TRWP.

10. Joseph Rosenfarb, *The National Labor Policy and How It Works* (New York, 1940), 486; Howard W. Smith to Frederick C. Crawford, September 16, 1939, box 28, TRWP; Frank Dossett, "Thompson Products: A Study in New Deal Legislation," ms. (1947), 342–43, TRWP; 1943 Trial Examiner's Report in 57 NLRB 151 (1944), 990; Stanley and Smoyer, "Brief in Support of Exceptions of the Respondents, Thompson Products and TAPCO" (December 24, 1943), box 40, TRWP; *New York Times*, May 21, 1942.

11. Gable, "A Political Analysis," 135.

12. Roy Rutherford, "The Career of Fred Crawford," *Railroad Workers' Journal* 1 (December 1946), 3; Gable, "A Political Analysis," 147, 423; *Friendly Forum*, November 12, 1943, box 39, TRWP; Harris, *Right to Manage*, 108.

13. "Crawford's Fight," *Business Week*, August 31, 1946, 88–90; Eric A. Johnston, *America Unlimited ...* (Garden City, N.Y., 1944).

14. Millis and Brown, *From Wagner to Taft-Hartley*, 287; Gable, "A Political Analysis," 72; John W. Scoville, *Labor Monopolies—or Freedom* (New York, 1946), 69–74; Steven Fraser, *Labor Will Rule: Sidney Hillman and the Rise of American Labor* (New York, 1991), 564; "Fred Crawford's Company," *Fortune* 54 (December 1946), 147; Walter Weisenberger quoted in Gable, "A Political Analysis," 120, 144.

15. On corporate liberalism in the 1930s and 1940s, see Ferguson, "Industrial Conflict"; Fraser, *Labor Will Rule*; and Kim McQuaid, *Uneasy Partners: Big Business in American Politics, 1945–1990* (Baltimore, Md., 1994).

16. Irving Pflaum, "The Baffling Career of Robert E. Wood," *Harper's* 208 (April 1954), 68–73; Robert E. Wood to Franklin D. Roosevelt, June 17, 1937, box 14, and Wood to General George Mosely, July 5, 1939, box 11, REWP; Gable, "A Political Analysis," 422; "The Reminiscences of General Robert E. Wood," CUOHP (New York, 1961), 110.

17. Gable, "A Political Analysis," 240, 512–13. When Kodak promulgated its Code of Industrial Relations in 1938, the NAM reprinted the code as an example of the nonunion "contract" employers should distribute to employees. "Eastman Kodak Publishes Code," *NAM Labor Relations Bulletin* 29 (January 1939), 8.

18. Millis and Brown, *From Wagner to Taft-Hartley*, 178; Crawford's speeches are reprinted in Dossett, "Handling Grievances under Government Supervision," unpublished ms., reel 1, pp. 45–54, TPP; *Cleveland Press*, August 25, 1944, *Plain Dealer*, August 26, 1944 and March 22, 1945, clippings on reel 4, TPP.

19. Cleveland *Plain Dealer*, October 20, 21, and 22, 1945, and *Cleveland Press*, October 22 and 23, 1945, clippings on reel 4, TPP; "A Message from Ray Livingstone," pamphlet (October 18, 1945), DCCU; "Crawford Wins," *Business Week*, October 27, 1945, 110.

20. NLRB 8th Region, case 8–R–1989, "Report on Objections," June 3, 1946, box 39,

TRWP; *Plain Dealer*, June 1, 1946 and April 4, 1947, reel 5, TPP.

21. Frank McCulloch and Tim Bornstein, *The National Labor Relations Board* (hereafter *The NLRB*) (New York, 1974), 39; Millis and Brown, *From Wagner to Taft Hartley*, 370; Richard W. Gable, "NAM: Influential Lobby or Kiss of Death?" *Journal of Politics* 15 (May 1953), 272–73.

22. Employers had two complaints: that the NLRB's disestablishment policy singled out company unions for harsher treatment than affiliated unions, and that the NLRB tolerated employer support to affiliated unions (paying stewards' salaries, for example) which it forbade unaffiliated unions. The NLRB was not insensitive to these complaints and to rebukes from appellate courts. In 1944, NLRB chairman Harry Millis ordered the board's regional directors not to apply the fracture rule too rigidly, a policy that marked a major shift for the board. Millis's successor, Paul Herzog, was even more tolerant of company unions, hoping that such lenience would preempt the Taft-Hartley legislation. During 1946 and 1947, out of more than 300 charges of employer domination of labor organizations, the NLRB ordered only 87 disestablishments, a much lower rate than before. The NLRB made a major concession in 1947 when it permitted an illegally supported (but not "dominated") company union to appear on the ballot. The last year of the Wagner Act saw company unions participate in about one-sixth of all NLRB elections, of which they won nearly two out of three. Theodore R. Iserman, *Industrial Peace and the Wagner Act* (New York, 1947), 41–48; "Statement of Theodore R. Iserman" in U.S. Senate, *Labor Relations Program*, pt. 1, 168–72; "Testimony of Dr. Leo Wolman," ibid., pt. 1, 98–99; Burton Crager, "Company Unions under the National Labor Relations Act," *Michigan Law Review* 40 (April 1942), 831–55; Millis and Brown, *From Wagner to Taft-Hartley*, 108–10; Gross, *Reshaping of the Board*, 226–59.

23. Gable, "NAM: Influential Lobby or Kiss of Death?" 268; "Raymond Livingstone Advocates High Court for Labor," *Plain Dealer*, February 8, 1946, clipping, box 39, TRWP; Alfred S. Cleveland, "NAM: Spokesman for Industry?" *Harvard Business Review* 26 (May 1948), 353–71.

24. "Statement of Hugh Sperry" in U.S. House of Representatives, Committee on Education and Labor, *Amendments to the National Labor Relations Act* (hereafter *Amendments to the NLRA*), 80th Cong., 1st Sess., vol. 4 (Washington, D.C., 1947), 3,281–3,478; "Statement of Raymond S. Livingstone," ibid., vol. 3, 1,489–1,531.

25. Livingstone pamphlet (April 3, 1947), box 40, TRWP.

26. "Section 8(a)(2): Employer Assistance to Plant Unions and Committees," *Stanford Law Review* 9 (March 1957), 351–65; Millis and Brown, *From Wagner to Taft-Hartley*, 425–28; Leo Troy, "Local Independent Unions and the American Labor Movement," *Industrial and Labor Relations Review* 14 (April 1961), 339.

27. *Virginia Electric* and *American Tube Bending* are analyzed in Millis and Brown, *From Wagner to Taft-Hartley*, 129, 177–80. Also see *Midland Steel Products Co. v. NLRB* (6CCA, 1940); Harris, *The Right to Manage*, 109.

28. Joel Seidman, *American Labor from Defense to Reconversion* (Chicago, 1953), 186–87, 263; *Detroit Edison Corp.*, 74 NLRB 279 (1947); Gross, *Reshaping the Board*, 248–49; Christopher Tomlins, *The State and the Unions: Labor Relations, Law, and the Organized Labor Movement in America, 1880–1960* (Cambridge, U.K., 1985), 273; "Statement of Paul Herzog" in U.S. Senate, *Labor Relations Program*, pt. 4, 1,909–10; Millis and Brown, *From Wagner to Taft-Hartley*, 183–87.

29. "Testimony of Leo Wolman" in U.S. Senate, *Labor Relations Program*, pt. 1, 109; "Statement of Hugh Sperry," *Amendments to the NLRA*, vol. 4, 3,450, 3,458, 3,470; "Statement of Raymond Livingstone," ibid., vol. 3, 1,499.

30. *NLRB v. Thompson Products, Inc.* 20 LRRM 2,291, 2,299 (6CCA, 1947); Harry Millis and Archibald Cox, "Some Aspects of the Labor Management Relations Act," *Harvard Law Review* 61 (1947–1948), 20; Millis and Brown, *From Wagner to Taft-Hartley*, 639, 648.

31. George G. Kirstein, *Stores and Unions* (New York, 1950), 126; Retail Clerks International Association (RCIA), minutes of the General Executive Board (GEB) meeting, Lafayette, Ind. (June 7, 1950), p. 33 in GEB minutes, reel 1 and "RCIA Educational Conference," San Diego, Cal. (January 12, 1951), p. 2 in Organizing Department minutes, reel 1, both in RCIA Papers, State Historical Society of Wisconsin, Madison; *NLRB v. Bonwit Teller*, 197 F.2d. 540 (1952); "Testimony of Frederick G. Atkinson" (American Retail Federation) and "Testimony of Sol Lippman" (RCIA) in U.S. Senate, Committee on Labor and Public Welfare, *Taft-Hartley Act Revisions*, 83rd Cong., 1st Sess. (Washington, D.C., 1953), pt. 6, 2,114–15, and pt. 3, 1,820–21.

32. "Business and Government," speech delivered by R. E. Wood at meeting of the Textile Merchants and Associated Industries (August 17, 1949), box 47, REWP; Clarence B. Caldwell, "Trends in Employee Relations in Retailing," speech to the American Retail Federation (October 21, 1949), p. 13, and Caldwell, "Report of the Committee on Employment Relations, American Retail Federation" (Washington, D.C. April 3, 1950), both in Caldwell Papers, SR Archives; McCulloch and Bornstein, *The NLRB*, 58–60. Wood sent a congratulatory note to Richard M. Nixon after the 1950 elections. R. E. Wood to Richard M. Nixon, November 13, 1950, box 11, REWP.

33. McQuaid, *Uneasy Partners*, 60–61. Also see Peter Irons, "American Business and the Origins of McCarthyism: The Cold War Crusade of the U.S. Chamber of Commerce" in Robert Griffith and Athan Theoharis, eds., *The Specter: Original Essays on the Cold War and the Origins of McCarthyism* (New York, 1974), 74–89, and Kim McQuaid, *Big Business and Presidential Power: From FDR to Reagan* (New York, 1982).

34. McQuaid, *Uneasy Partners*, 68; R. E. Wood to Joseph N. Pew, Jr., November 5, 1947, box 12, REWP; James C. Worthy, *Shaping an American Institution: Robert E. Wood and Sears Roebuck* (Urbana, Ill., 1984), 51; Justus D. Doenecke, "General Robert E. Wood: The Evolution of a Conservative," *Journal of the Illinois State Historical Society* 71 (August 1978), 174; author's interview with James C. Worthy, June 18, 1985, Evanston, Ill.

35. Joseph Alsop, "He Sparked a Revolution," *Saturday Evening Post* 228 (December 3, 1955), 136; McCulloch and Bornstein, *The NLRB*, 61–62. Even after Eisenhower's reconstitution of the NLRB, employers remained politically active, hoping to tighten the noose around labor's neck. William Ingles, a lobbyist for industry, told a group of Thompson managers in 1955 that employer organizations were seeking to make Taft-Hartley "more stringent." The 1959 Landrum-Griffin Act (which the NAM and other industry groups helped draft) included a ban on secondary boycotts and other antiunion restraints that the NAM had been seeking since the early 1940s. Only one major business group did not support the NAM on Landrum-Griffin: the Committee for Economic Development (CED), which in 1958 published a report written by the labor economist Clark Kerr calling for partial repeal of Taft-Hartley, including its right-to-work provisions. Several major companies immediately withdrew from the CED and the NAM excoriated it as a "traitor." McCulloch and Bornstein, *The NLRB*, chap 4; Thompson Products, "Personnel Policy Conference" (Cleveland, January 27, 1955), box 128, TRWP; Alan McAdams, *Power and Politics in Labor Legislation* (New York, 1964), 65–75; Karl Schriftgeisser, *Business and Public Policy: The Role of the Committee for Economic Development, 1942–67* (Englewood Cliffs, N.J., 1967), 163–67.

36. *Livingston Shirt*, 110 NLRB 29 (1953); *Chicopee Mfg.*, 107 NLRB 31 (1954); *Southwestern Co.*, 111 NLRB 805 (1955); and *Esquire Inc.*, 107 NLRB 1,238, 1,239 (1954), quoted in Janice E. Klein and E. David Wanger, "The Legal Setting for the Emergence of the Union Avoidance Strategy" in Thomas A. Kochan, ed., *Challenges and Choices Facing American Labor* (Cambridge, Mass., 1985), 82; Joseph Shister, "The Impact of the Taft-Hartley Act on Union Strength and Collective Bargaining," *Industrial and Labor Relations Review* 11 (April 1958), 340; "Union Recruiting Dips to New Lows," *Business Week*, July 13, 1957, 146. Adding insult to injury, the Eisenhower board issued a series of bargaining-unit decisions that made it more difficult for unions to win elections at retail stores. By revising its jurisdictional standards, the board excluded many small stores from its purview, and, in *Robert Hall* it held the relevant bargaining unit to be eighteen of the company's clothing stores in southern California, even though the union had petitioned for elections at only two of them. Such rulings as these hampered the Clerks' drive against Sears. *Proceedings of the 22nd Convention of the Retail Clerks* (New York, June 1955), 34–35; Klein and Wanger, "Legal Setting," 85; *Robert Hall Clothes* 118 NLRB 1,096 (1957); "NLRB, in Policy Reversal, Vetoes All-Inclusive Union for Chemicals," *Oil, Paint, and Drug Reporter* 165 (March 8, 1954), 81–82; *Guss vs. Utah Labor Relations Board*, 353 U.S. 1 (1957).

37. "Section 8(a)(2)," passim; *Coppus Engineering*, 39 LRRM 2,315 (1CCA, 1957); *Sears Roebuck and Sears Roebuck Employees Council*, 110 NLRB 226 (1954).

38. Eaton H. Conant, "Defenses of Nonunion Employers: A Study from Company Sources," *Labor Law Journal* 10 (February 1959), 100–9. After John F. Kennedy's election in 1960, nonunion employers became concerned that employee committees might run afoul of the NLRB, especially given Thompson's loss in the Dage Television case, which was publicized in the business press. This led to an intensified search for some kind of mechanism that would tap workers' brains and bind them to management but do so without the formalities of employee representation. James

Worthy envisioned this more passive kind of participation in a prescient remark made after the war: "The highest possible level of group participation in solving problems does not imply the necessity for management-worker councils, shop committees, or any other formal devices. All that is necessary is . . . to give [employees] a chance to express their own ideas and let them know that their thinking is needed and valued." Worthy, "Responsibility of the Personnel Administrator in Modern Business Management," 6th Annual Conference of the Personnel Association of Toronto (April 30, 1948), 23, SR Archives. Also see "Some Labor Law Implications of Employee Grievance Systems" in Industrial Relations Counselors, *White Collar Restiveness: A Growing Challenge* (New York, 1964), 64; Conference Board, *Behavioral Science: Concepts and Management Application*, Studies in Personnel Policy no. 216 (New York, 1969).

39. This section is adapted from Sanford M. Jacoby, "Employers and the Welfare State: The Role of Marion B. Folsom," *Journal of American History* 80 (September 1993), 525–56. On conservative opposition to social security, see Martha Derthick, *Policymaking for Social Security* (Washington, D.C., 1979), 136–94; Arthur J. Altmeyer, *The Formative Years of Social Security* (Madison, Wisc., 1968), 205, 221–30, 235; and Mark H. Leff, "Historical Perspectives on Old-Age Insurance: The State of the Art on the Art of the State" in Edward D. Berkowitz, ed., *Social Security after 50: Successes and Failures* (Westport, Conn., 1987), 33. The 1935 Social Security Act created insurance plans for unemployment benefits and old-age pensions, and welfare programs for indigent elders (old-age assistance) and children (AFDC).

40. Opinion Research Corporation, "Report on Free Market and Socialist Thinking," *Opinion Index for Industry* (Princeton, N.J., 1955); Sanford M. Jacoby, *Employing Bureaucracy: Managers, Unions, and the Transformation of Work in American Industry, 1900–1945* (New York, 1985), 233.

41. U.S. Congress, House Ways and Means Committee, *Hearings Relative to the Social Security Act Amendments of 1939* (hereafter *1939 Amendments Hearings*), 76th Cong., 1st sess., vol. 2 (Washington, D.C., 1939), 1,132.

42. Roosevelt quoted in Edward D. Berkowitz, *America's Welfare State: From Roosevelt to Reagan* (Baltimore, Md., 1991), 15.

43. Alan Brinkley, *Voices of Protest: Huey Long, Father Coughlin, and the Great Depression* (New York, 1982); Edwin E. Witte, *The Development of the Social Security Act* (Madison, Wisc., 1962), 86; Theda Skocpol and John Ikenberry, "The Political Formation of the American Welfare State," *Comparative Social Research* 6 (1983), 123; Jill Quadagno, "Welfare Capitalism and the Social Security Act of 1935," *American Sociological Review* 49 (December 1984), 638; Kenneth M. Casebeer, "Unemployment Insurance: American Social Wage, Labor Organization, and Legal Ideology," *Boston College Law Review* 35 (March 1994), 259–348.

44. C. B. Ames, "Listening in as Business Speaks" *Nation's Business* 23 (June 1935), 20; Ellis W. Hawley, "The New Deal and Business" in John Braeman, Robert H. Bremner, and David Brody, eds., *The New Deal: The National Level* (Columbus, Ohio, 1975), 55–78. Several of the defecting BAC members formed the American Liberty League, which worked assiduously to unseat Roosevelt. Robert F. Burk, *The Corporate State and the Broker State: The Du Ponts and American National Politics* (Cambridge, Mass., 1990), 188–91.

45. Daniel Nelson, *Unemployment Insurance, The American Experience, 1915–1935* (Madison, Wisc., 1969), 179–88; Witte, *Development*, 82–84; Edward Berkowitz and Kim McQuaid, *Creating the Welfare State*, 2nd ed. (New York, 1988), 111–15.

46. Nelson, *Unemployment Insurance*, 104–28.

47. Ibid., 166; Mark H. Leff, "Taxing the 'Forgotten Man': The Politics of Social Security Finance in the New Deal," *Journal of American History* 70 (September 1983), 372–74.

48. Perkins and Witte also created a technical board that drew the bulk of its personnel—including Bryce M. Stewart and Murray W. Latimer—from Industrial Relations Counselors, a Rockefeller-funded consultancy that offered technical assistance to practitioners of welfare capitalism. "Information Primer: The Committee on Economic Security," box 20, FPUR; Altmeyer, *Formative Years*, 8; Stephen J. Scheinberg, "The Development of Corporation Labor Policy, 1900–1940," Ph.D. dissertation, University of Wisconsin, 1966, 166–67; Berkowitz and McQuaid, *Creating the Welfare State*, 78–95; Witte, *Development*, 49, 89.

49. Alsop, "He Sparked a Revolution," 132–36; interview with Marion B. Folsom, CUOHP (New York 1967), 9 (hereafter Folsom interview); Folsom to Mark A. Daly, January 21, 1932, box 18, FPUR. The AFL in New York originally joined Folsom in backing employer reserves but later switched its support to an Ohio-type bill, fearing that reserve funds would "tie workers to their jobs and

promote company unionism." Nelson, *Unemployment Insurance*, 172.

50. M. B. Folsom to R. K. Brodie, December 13, 1933, and M. B. Folsom to F. W. Lovejoy, May 24, 1933, box 1, FPUR; Folsom interview, 110; National Recovery Administration, *Statement of the Secretary of the Code Committee of the Photographic Industry*, public hearing (Washington, D.C., August 4, 1933), box 1, FPUR.

51. Sociologists are engaged in a heated debate over corporate liberalism and the welfare state. See Jenkins and Brents, "Social Protest, Hegemonic Competition, and Social Reform"; Theda Skocpol and Edwin Amenta, "Did Capitalists Shape Social Security?" *American Sociological Review* 50 (August 1985), 572–75; and E. Amenta and S. Parikh, "Capitalists Did Not Want the Social Security Act: A Critique of the Capitalist Dominance Thesis," *American Sociological Review* 56 (February 1991), 124–29.

52. Nelson, *Unemployment Insurance*, 198–202; U.S. Congress, House Ways and Means Committee, *Hearings before a Subcommittee on Unemployment Insurance: 1934*, 73rd Cong., 2nd sess. (Washington, D.C., 1934), 70–74, 85–86.

53. Altmeyer, *Formative Years*, 22; Folsom interview, 16, 32; minutes of the Advisory Council on Economic Security, December 6, 7, 8 and 15, 1934, and Thomas H. Eliot, "Why Industries and Large Employers Operating in Several States Should Not Be Allowed Special Federal Treatment," December 3, 1934, all in box 20, FPUR; U.S. Congress, Senate, "Statement of Marion B. Folsom," in *Economic Security Act: Hearings before the Committee on Finance*, 74th Cong., 1st Sess. (Washington, D.C., February 8, 1935), (hereafter Folsom statement, 1935), 583; Witte, *Development*, 124–33; "Sears Constant Income Plans," January 25, 1939, Sears file, DCCU.

54. Folsom statement, 1935, 583; U.S. Congress, House Ways and Means Committee, *Economic Security Act: Hearings* 74th Cong., 1st Sess. (Washington, D.C., 1935), 991–92.

55. Witte, *Development*, 90; Altmeyer, *Formative Years*, 33; Herman E. Kroos, *Executive Opinion: What Business Leaders Said and Thought on Economic Issues* (Garden City, N.Y., 1970), 183; William H. Wilson, "How the Chamber of Commerce Viewed the NRA," *Mid-America* 44 (1962), 95–108; M. B. Folsom to H. W. Story, May 2, 1935, box 20, FPUR.

56. Folsom, *Executive Decision Making: Observations and Experience in Business and Government* (New York, 1962), 110–11; Witte, *Development*, 89, 141–42; Nelson, *Unemployment Insurance*, 215–18.

57. Marion Folsom, "Stabilization of Employment and Income," *Management Record*, 1 (February 1939), 24; Irving Bernstein, *A Caring Society: The New Deal, the Worker, and the Great Depression* (Boston, Mass. 1985), 177; Nelson, *Unemployment Insurance*, 171–73; M. B. Folsom to E. E. Witte, April 19, 1935 and E. E. Witte to M. B. Folsom, April 23, 1935, box 20, FPUR; *1939 Amendments Hearings*, 1,147.

58. Altmeyer, *Formative Years*, 10; M. B. Folsom to F. W. Lovejoy, October 26, 1934, box 18, FPUR; *1939 Amendments Hearings*, 1,160; Folsom statement, 1935, 21; J. Douglas Brown, *The Genesis of Social Security in America* (Princeton, N.J., 1969), 15.

59. M. B. Folsom to F. W. Lovejoy, October 26, 1934, box 18, FPUR; Altmeyer, *Formative Years*, 40–42; Towers, Perrin, Forster, and Crosby, *Bulletin on Social Security* (April 1935), 29, box 18, FPUR.

60. Craig P. Cochrane in American Management Association (AMA), *Economic Security: Pensions and Health Insurance* (New York, 1935), 20; Berkowitz and McQuaid, *Welfare State*, 125–26; Altmeyer, *Formative Years*, 40–41; Folsom statement, 1935, 37; Bernstein, *Caring Society*, 314. Strict federal supervision of private pension standards did not come until 1974, when Congress passed the Employee Retirement Income Security Act (ERISA).

61. Under Folsom's proposal, an employee would receive a larger pension than if the employer paid the same amount into a private plan. The difference reflected the return on the employee's own social security contributions. Altmeyer, *Formative Years*, 42; Folsom, "Social Security Act in Relation to Private Plans for Employees' Benefits," speech to the 24th Annual Meeting of the U.S. Chamber of Commerce (Washington, D.C., April 29, 1936) in Folsom speeches, vol. 2, FPUR; Folsom, "Company Annuity Plans and the Federal Old Age Benefit Plan," *Harvard Business Review* 14 (Summer 1936), 414–24.

62. Folsom, "The Act in Relation to Private Plans," 7; E. D. Berkowitz, "The First Advisory Council and the 1939 Amendments," in Berkowitz, ed., *Social Security after 50*, 59; Berkowitz and McQuaid, *Welfare State*, 133; Folsom interview, 87.

63. *1939 Amendments Hearings*, 1,135–38, 1,150; U.S. Congress, Senate, "Final Report of the Advisory Council on Social Security," 76th Cong, 1st Sess., December 10, 1938; Altmeyer, *Formative Years*, 91–109; Folsom in-

terview, 82, 125; Leff, "Taxing," 371; Murray W. Latimer and Karl Tufel, *Trends in Industrial Pensions* (New York, 1940), 40, 84.

64. Hawley, "The New Deal and Business," 65; Folsom interview, 66, 89; M. B. Folsom to F. W. Lovejoy, September 15, 1937, box 1, FPUR; Kroos, *Executive Opinion*, 182–83; Jill Quadagno, *The Transformation of Old Age Security: Class and Politics in the American Welfare State* (Chicago, 1988), 112–14; Charles McKinley and Robert W. Frase, *Launching Social Security: A Capture-and-Record Account, 1935–1937* (Madison, Wisc., 1970), 490. Although Folsom's boss, Frank Lovejoy, was an officer of the Conference Board and the NAM, he never interfered with Folsom's Washington activities. Like Folsom, he wanted to preserve Kodak's benefit programs as a bulwark against unionism. When it came to Roosevelt and the rest of the New Deal, however, the two men politely disagreed and tried to sway each other: Lovejoy sent Folsom a copy of *The Roots of Liberty*, written by NAM president Henning Prentiss; in return, Folsom complained to Lovejoy about business's anti-New Deal activities. Kodak—like many other companies—kept its options open by pursuing multiple political strategies. *F. W. Lovejoy: The Story of a Practical Idealist* (Rochester, N.Y., 1947), 28, 33–34; F. W. Lovejoy to M. B. Folsom, September 8, 1939 and M. B. Folsom to F. W. Lovejoy, February 14, 1939, box 2, FPUR; and M. B. Folsom to F. W. Lovejoy, September 15, 1937, box 1, FPUR.

65. "Business Attacks New Deal," *New York Times*, April 30, 1936; Folsom address to National Association of Commercial Organization Secretaries in Robert M. Collins, *The Business Response to Keynes, 1929–1964* (New York, 1981), 54.

66. McKinley and Frase, *Launching*, 347; Folsom interview, 82; Kroos, *Executive Opinion*, 193.

67. *1939 Amendments Hearings*, 1,132, 1,154; National Industrial Conference Board (NICB), *Company Pension Plans and the Social Security Act*, Studies in Personnel Policy (hereafter SPP) no. 16 (New York, 1939), 25–26. On Kodak's plan see C. P. Cochrane, "Changes Necessary in Company Pension Plans," *Personnel Journal* 14 (January–February 1936), 237–42, and Eastman Kodak, "Adjustments in Kodak Retirement Annuity Plan" (Rochester, N.Y., 1936), DCCU. Although James Worthy says that General Wood supported social security, Wood was a staunch supporter of America Action, a right-wing group opposed to the program. Worthy, *Shaping an American Institution*, 46; R. E. Wood to Merwin K. Hart, October 22, 1945, box 7, REWP.

68. Latimer and Tufel, *Trends in Industrial Pensions*, 40, 84; Folsom interview, 82; *1939 Amendments Hearings*, 1,138.

69. For example, say Kodak had two employees: A, who earns $2,000, and B, who earns $20,000. Prior to social security each received pension contributions totaling 10 percent of wages. After the introduction of a hypothetical 10 percent payroll tax (levied jointly on Kodak and its employees, up to the $3,000 ceiling), Kodak paid a tax of $100 for A and $150 for B, supplemented by private contributions of $100 for A and $1,850 for B. Thus, the supplemental approach meant relatively large pensions for high-wage workers or, to put this another way, government subsidization of private pensions for low-wage workers.

70. Richard H. Wood, "The Principles and Practices of Profit Sharing," Ph.D. dissertation, Princeton, 1942, 149; William C. Greenough and Francis P. King, *Pension Plans and Public Policy* (New York, 1976), 59–63; NICB, "Trends in Company Pension Plans," SPP no. 61 (New York, 1944), 12; Alicia Munnell, *The Economics of Private Pensions* (Washington, D.C., 1982), 10–13. Also see Frank Dobbin, "The Origins of Private Social Insurance: Public Policy and Fringe Benefits in America, 1920–1950," *American Journal of Sociology* 97 (March 1992), 1,416–50.

71. S. M. Jacoby and Daniel J. B. Mitchell, "Development of Contractual Features of the Union-Management Relationship," *Labor Law Journal* 33 (August 1982), 515; Robert J. Rosenthal, "Union-Management Welfare Plans," *Quarterly Journal of Economics* 62 (November 1947), 68–69.

72. "Kodak Refutes," *Rochester Sun*, February 27, 1947; Harris, *The Right to Manage*, 142, 170–71; Neil W. Chamberlain, *The Union Challenge to Management Control* (New York, 1948), 81; Elizabeth Fones-Wolf, "Industrial Recreation, the Second World War, and the Revival of Welfare Capitalism, 1934–1960," *Business History Review* 60 (Summer 1986), 232–57.

73. Beth Stevens, "Labor Unions, Employee Benefits, and the Privatization of the American Welfare State," *Journal of Policy History* 2 (1990), 238–45; Rosenthal, "Welfare Plans," 86–87; Folsom, "Our Own Social Security Needs," *Nation's Business*, March 1943, 76, 80; Folsom, "The Quest for Economic Security: A Point of View from Management," in National Conference of Social Work, *The Social Welfare Forum: 1950* (New

York, 1950), 112; Derthick, *Policymaking*, 429–31. One exception to Folsom's antiexpansionism was temporary disability insurance (TDI). Folsom backed TDI on the condition that employers could contract out from the government pool. They were permitted to do this under New York's 1950 TDI law, which Folsom had a hand in drafting. Folsom, "Manpower in the Postwar Era," AMA Personnel Series no. 63 (New York, 1943), 34; Derthick, *Policymaking*, 297–304; Folsom interview, 149–50; 75; Caldwell, "Trends in Employment Relations," 13.

74. Collins, *Business Response to Keynes*, 72–83. The CED originated in the BAC's economic policy committee, which Folsom headed, although CED officials included several officers of the NAM and the Chamber of Commerce. See Robert A. Brady, "The CED—What Is It and Why?" *Antioch Review* 4 (Spring 1944), 21–46.

75. Paul G. Hoffman, "Industrial Relations Problems of the Postwar World," AMA Personnel Series no. 69 (New York, 1943), 11–12; CED, "Taxes and the Budget: A Program for Prosperity in a Free Economy" (New York, 1947), 61; Herbert Stein in "Detailed Discussion Notes of the CED Research Advisory Board" (New York, May 10–11, 1946), 14, box 97, FPUR; Hawley, "New Deal and Business," 72–73.

76. Folsom, "Manpower," 25–34; Brady, "The CED," 25–29; McQuaid, *Big Business and Presidential Power,* 110–19; Folsom, "Company Policies for Promoting Stabilization," *Conference Board Business Record* 5 (February 1948), 80–82.

77. Schriftgeisser, *Business and Public Policy*, 3; Brady, "The CED," 22; Emerson P. Schmidt to M. B. Folsom, May 5, 1944, box 25, FPUR; Folsom interview, 74. In box 25, FPUR, see: T. W. Howard to M. B. Folsom, April 21, 1943; "Social Security in America," report of the U.S. Chamber of Commerce Social Security Committee (March 1944); M. B. Folsom to Board of Directors, November 17, 1944; M. B. Folsom, "Opening Remarks" in Chamber of Commerce, *Proceedings of the Second National Conference on Social Security* (January 10, 1945).

78. U.S. Congress, Senate, Committee on Finance, "Recommendations for Social Security Legislation: Report of the Advisory Council on Social Security," 80th Cong., 2d Sess. (Washington, D.C., 1949), 97; "Statement Supporting Report of the NAM Employee Benefits Committee" (August 19, 1948), box 27, FPUR; Folsom, "The Quest," 101–12.

79. M. B. Folsom to T. J. Hargrave, July 13, 1948, box 27, FPUR; Reinhard A. Hohaus to M. B. Folsom, July 1, 1948, box 27; Cleveland, "NAM: Spokesman for Industry?" 353–71.

80. NAM, Employee Benefits and Social Security Committee, "Explanatory Statement of the Recommended Statement of Principles" (March 18, 1949); M. B. Folsom to Employee Benefits and Social Security Committee, July 29, 1948 and August 24, 1948; and Earl Bunting to M. B. Folsom, May 17, 1949, all in box 27, FPUR; Folsom interview, 98. After social security benefits rose in the early 1950s, Kodak responded by cutting contributions to its supplemental pension plan. *Kodakery* 13 (January 27, 1955), DCCU.

81. Stevens, "Unions, Benefits, and Privatization," 241–43; Sumner H. Slichter, James Healey, and E. Robert Livernash, *The Impact of Collective Bargaining on Management* (Washington, D.C., 1960), 375–76; Alfred M. Skolnik and Joseph Zisman, "Growth in Employee-Benefit Plans," *Social Security Bulletin* 20 (March 1958), 10; "Transcript of CED Presentation to the Wage Stabilization Board" (Washington, D.C., January 11, 1951), box 97, FPUR.

82. M. B. Folsom, "The Pension Drive: Social and Economic Implications," speech to the 308th Meeting of the NICB (New York, November 22, 1949) in Speeches, vol. 5, FPUR; Greenough and King, *Pension Plans*, 46; Quadagno, *Old Age Security*, 161–70; M. B. Folsom, "Money after Age 65," *Atlantic Monthly* 184 (August 1949), 69–72; Folsom interview, 200. Nelson Lichtenstein argues that postwar union leaders were "naive" to think that saddling employers with pension plans would spur them to support social security. But this is precisely what happened. Lichtenstein, "From Corporatism to Collective Bargaining: Organized Labor and the Eclipse of Social Democracy in the Postwar Era" in Steven Fraser and Gary Gerstle, eds., *Rise and Fall*, 143.

83. Altmeyer, *Formative Years*, 27–33, 92–103; W. A. Sawyer to J. D. Brown, May 20, 1936, DCCU; Witte, *Development*, 173–88; Folsom interview, 163; M. B. Folsom to Altmeyer, March 26, 1935, box 20, FPUR; *1939 Amendments Hearings*, 1,134.

84. Beth Stevens, *Complementing the Welfare State: The Development of Private Pension, Health Insurance, and Other Employee Benefits in the U.S.* (Geneva, Switz., 1986), chaps. 3 and 4; Walter J. Lear, "Medical Care Insurance for Industrial Workers," *Monthly Labor Review* 73 (September 1951), 251–57;

Jacoby and Mitchell, "Development," 515; "Positive Principles Broadly Applied at Kodak," *American Business* 19 (May 1949), 58; Eastman Kodak, "Chronology of Changes: Benefit and Employee Relations Plans" (n.d.), KA; Folsom interview, 165; Sears Roebuck, Dept. 707, "1949 Year End Report," 13, JCWP.

85. Folsom interview, 175–80; James L. Sundquist, *Politics and Policy: The Eisenhower, Kennedy, and Johnson Years* (Washington, D.C., 1968), 291–92, 300; Folsom, "Status of the Nation's Economy," address given to the New York State Council on Economic Education, University of Rochester (July 18, 1960), 12; Robert Kuttner, "Health Care: Why Corporate America is Paralyzed," *Business Week*, April 8, 1991, 14. While president of Columbia University, Eisenhower had been a trustee of the CED, which is how he came to know Folsom. Although Folsom publicly agreed with Eisenhower on the disability issue, his aide Roswell Perkins said that he did so only "with considerable emotional difficulty" after having "tortured himself for weeks." Folsom went so far as to permit the social security administrator, Robert Ball, to assist the Democrats in developing a disability insurance bill. Folsom's one major success while HEW secretary was the Temporary Unemployment Compensation Act, which gave additional benefits to workers exhausting regular benefits during a recession. Derthick, *Policymaking*, 104–5; E. D. Berkowitz and D. M. Fox, "The Politics of Social Security Expansion: Social Security Disability Insurance, 1935–1986," *Journal of Policy History* 1 (1989), 233–60.

86. M. B. Folsom, "Dedication of New District Office and Presentation of 10-millionth Social Security Check" (June 6, 1957), speeches, vol. 10, FPUR; U.S. Department of Health, Education, and Welfare, *Annual Report: 1957* (Washington, D.C., 1958), 23.

87. J. R. P. French, Jr., A. Kornhauser, and A. Marrow, eds., "Conflict and Cooperation in Industry," *Journal of Social Issues* 2 (February 1946), 10. Also see Richard Gillespie, *Manufacturing Knowledge: A History of the Hawthorne Experiments* (Cambridge, Mass., 1991), chap. 8; Jacoby, *Employing Bureaucracy*, 269–72; Bruce Moore, "How Can Psychology Help Industry?" in American Management Association, *Values of Psychology in Industrial Management* (New York, 1940), 3–11; Michael Rose, *Industrial Behaviour: Theoretical Development since Taylor* (London, 1975). Some labor historians assert that the labor movement was bureaucratized and ossified by liberal academics who, as arbitrators and government officials, deracinated the radical potential of the Wagner Act and placed the labor movement in a contractual straitjacket. This argument has several faults. It misinterprets the sources of contractualism; understates the role of employers in defining the law; and fails to appreciate the deeply negative effect on unions of the applied behavioral sciences and changes in workers' attitudes. See Karl Klare, "Judicial Deradicalization of the Wagner Act and the Origins of Modern Legal Conservatism," *Minnesota Law Review* 62 (1978), 265–339; Katherine Stone, "The Postwar Paradigm in American Labor Law," *Yale Law Journal* 90 (June 1981), 1,509–80; Ronald W. Schatz, "From Commons to Dunlop? Rethinking the Field and Theory of Industrial Relations" in Howell Harris and Nelson Lichtenstein, *Industrial Democracy in America: The Ambiguous Promise* (Cambridge, U.K., 1993), 87–112. Alternative interpretations are offered in Melvyn Dubofsky, *The State and Labor in Modern America* (Chapel Hill, N.C., 1994) and David Brody, "Workplace Contractualism: A Historical/Comparative Analysis" in Brody, *In Labor's Cause* (New York, 1993), 221–50.

88. Morris Viteles, *Motivation and Morale in Industry* (New York, 1953); Marvin Dunnette and H. G. Heneman, Jr., "Influence of Scale Administrator on Employee Attitude Responses," *Journal of Applied Psychology* 40 (February 1956), 73–78; Eugene J. Benge, "Morale Survey Improves Management-Employee Relations," *Paper Industry and Paper World* 28 (November 1946), 1,141–43; Robert N. McMurry, "Management's Reaction to Employee Opinion Polls," *Journal of Applied Psychology* 30 (April 1946), 212–19; S. Avery Raube, "Experience with Employee Attitude Surveys," National Industrial Conference Board, Studies in Personnel Policy no. 115 (New York, 1951); Thompson Products, "We Led With Our Chin! A Report on a Survey of Employee Opinion Conducted in the Cleveland Plants" (August 1944), 20, DCCU.

89. Burleigh B. Gardner and William Foote Whyte, "Methods for the Study of Human Relations in Industry," *American Sociological Review* 11 (October 1946), 506–12; Burleigh B. Gardner, "Case Studies for Interviewing Methods," syllabus (February 1944), JCWP; "Seminar on Problems of Organization and the Techniques of Business Leadership" (November 25 and December 2, 1946), JCWP; W. Lloyd Warner, "The Committee on Human Relations in Industry," *Applied Anthropology* 4 (Spring 1945), 1.

90. David G. Moore to author, April 25, 1985; James C. Worthy, "An Employee Relations Program for Sears, Roebuck and Co." (Chicago, 1951), JCWP; Worthy, "Discovering and Evaluating Employee Attitudes," AMA Personnel Series no. 113 (New York, 1947), 13. The University of Chicago further bolstered Sears's standing in the academic community by lending one of its junior faculty, John Jeuck, to participate in the writing of a massive corporate history of Sears. The principal author was Boris Emmet, a former Sears retailing executive. Funding for the project—in the form of a hefty grant—came from none other than the Rockefeller Foundation. The study, published in 1950 by the University of Chicago Press, was entitled *Catalogues and Counters*. See the material in series 216, box 7, Rockefeller Foundation Archives, Pocantico Hills, N.Y.

91. Melany Baehr, "A Simplified Procedure for the Measurment of Employee Attitudes," *Journal of Applied Psychology* 37 (June 1953), 153–67; Robert K. Burns, "Employee Morale: Its Meaning and Measurement" in *Proceedings of the Industrial Relations Research Association, Boston, December 1951* (Madison, Wisc., 1952), 52–68; David G. Moore, "Managerial Strategies and Organizational Dynamics in Sears Retailing," Ph.D. dissertation, University of Chicago, 1954, 132; Clarence B. Caldwell, "The Sears Survey Program," January 15, 1952, Caldwell Papers, SR Archives.

92. David Moore to author, April 25, 1985; David G. Moore and Robert K. Burns, "How Good is Morale?" *Factory Management and Maintenance* 114 (February 1956), 130–36; Stephen Habbe, "Trends in Making Employee Attitude Surveys," *Management Record* 22 (February 1960), 16; Dale Yoder, Herbert G. Heneman, Jr., and Earl Cheit, "Triple Audit of Industrial Relations," Bulletin 11, Industrial Relations Center, University of Minnesota (Minneapolis, 1951); LaVerne Hamel and Hans Reif, "Should Attitude Questionnaires Be Signed?" *Personnel Psychology* 5 (Spring 1952), 35–40.

93. Stephen Habbe, "Attitude Surveys and Follow-Through Procedures," *Management Record* 22 (March 1960), 15; Burleigh B. Gardner, "Doing Business with Management" in Elizabeth M. Eddy and William L. Partridge, eds., *Applied Anthropology in America* (New York, 1978), 258.

94. S. Avery Raube, "Factors Affecting Employee Morale," National Industrial Conference Board, Studies in Personnel Policy no. 85 (New York, 1947); J. William Hess (Rockefeller Archive Center) to author, February 14, 1985; Industrial Relations Counselors, "White Collar Restiveness: A Growing Challenge," IRC monograph no. 22 (New York, 1963), 59–61. Also see Converse, *Survey Research*, passim.

95. Paul S. Achilles, ed., *Psychology at Work* (Freeport, N.Y., 1971); author's interview with Burleigh Gardner, Evanston, March 23, 1985; Gardner, "Doing Business with Management," 245–47.

96. Allen B. Gates, "The Development of Supervisory Leadership," presented before the Pittsburgh chapter of the American Society of Training Directors, October 6, 1948, p. 19, and Gates, "A Management Approach to Problems of Individual Adjustment: A Company Experiment in Developing Effective Employee Adjustment," presented before various groups, including the Wisconsin Society for Mental Health, Milwaukee, September 22, 1949, and the Twenty-Fourth Pacific Coast Management Conference, Berkeley, October 17, 1950, DCCU.

97. War Manpower Commission, Bureau of Training, TWI Service, "The Development of TWI: Program Development Institute" (December 15, 1944) and "The TWI Program: Management and Skilled Supervision" (June 1944); Walter Dietz, "Training New Supervisors in the Skill of Leadership," *Personnel* 19 (January 1943); War Manpower Commission, Bureau of Training, *The Training within Industry Report, 1941–1945* (Washington, D.C., 1945), 128, 204–22. TWI also included a separate course in job methods, covering topics such as statistical quality control and time study; this became quite popular in postwar Japan. See Alan G. Robinson and Dean M. Schroeder, "Training, Continuous Improvement, and Human Relations: The U.S. TWI Programs and the Japanese Management Style," *California Management Review* 35 (Winter 1993), 35–57, and Sanford Jacoby, "Pacific Ties: Industrial Relations and Employment Systems in Japan and the United States Since 1900," in Harris and Lichtenstein, eds., *Industrial Democracy in America*, 206–48.

98. Morris Viteles, "Wartime Applications of Pyschology: Their Value to Industry" in American Management Association, Personnel Series no. 93 (New York, 1945), 3–12; Jack Elinson, "Attitude Research in the Army," *Journal of Applied Pyschology* (February 1949), 1–5; Daniel Katz, "Studies in Social Psychology in World War II," *Psychological Bulletin* 48 (November 1951), 512–19; Samuel A. Stouffer and Leland C. DeVinney, *The American Soldier*, 2 vols. (Princeton, N.J., 1949); J. Harding, "The Measurement of Civilian Morale" in Hadley Cantril, ed., *Gauging*

Public Opinion (Princeton, N.J., 1944) 233–58; Donald G. Marquis, "Social Psychologists in National War Agencies," *Psychological Bulletin* 41 (February 1944), 115–26; Rensis A. Likert et al., "The Effects of Strategic Bombing on German Morale," in *U.S. Strategic Bombing Survey*, part 64 (Washington, D.C., 1947); Hans Skott, "Attitude Research in the Department of Agriculture," *Public Opinion Quarterly* 7 (Summer 1943), 280–92; Daniel Katz and Herbert Hyman, "Morale in War Industry," in Theodore Newcomb and Eugene L. Hartley, eds., *Readings in Social Psychology* (New York, 1947), 437–47. For a fascinating analysis of a wartime *Methodenstreit* between academic social psychologists and public-opinion pollsters, see Jean M. Converse, "Strong Arguments and Weak Evidence: The Open/Closed Question Controversy of the 1940s," *Public Opinion Quarterly* 48 (Spring 1984), 267–82.

99. R. G. Smith and R. J. Westen, *Studies of Morale Methodology and Criteria*, Research Bulletin 51–29, U.S. Air Force Training Command, Human Resources Research Center (San Antonio, Texas, 1951); Oakley J. Gordon, "A Factor Analysis of Human Needs and Industrial Morale," *Personnel Psychology* 8 (Spring 1955), 1–18; Rensis A. Likert and Daniel Katz, "Supervisory Practices and Organization Structures as They Affect Employee Productivity and Morale," American Management Association, Personnel Series no. 120 (New York, 1948), 14–24; Daniel Katz, "Employee Groups: What Motivates Them and How They Perform," *Advanced Management* 14 (September 1949), 119–24; Robert L. Kahn, "The Prediction of Productivity," *Journal of Social Psychology* 12: 2 (1956), 41–49; Daniel Katz and Robert L. Kahn, "Some Recent Findings in Human Relations Research," University of Michigan, Survey Research Center (Ann Arbor, Mich., 1952); "Best Workers Gripe the Most," *Business Week*, February 10, 1951, 68–72; Frederick Herzberg et al., *Job Attitudes: Review of Research and Opinion* (Pittsburgh, Pa., 1957).

100. Floyd C. Mann and Rensis Likert, "The Need for Research on the Communication of Research Results," *Human Organization* 11 (Winter 1952), 15–19; Robert E. Schwab, "Motivation and Human Relations Principles," American Management Association, Personnel Series no. 155 (New York, 1953), 30–39; Floyd C. Mann, "Studying and Creating Change" in Conrad M. Arensberg et al., eds., *Research in Industrial Human Relations* (New York, 1957).

101. Those influenced by Lewin included Douglas McGregor and Rensis Likert. Several years after Lewin's death in 1947, his research center moved to Michigan. Kurt Lewin, ed., *Resolving Social Conflicts* (New York, 1948); L. Coch and J. R. P. French, "Overcoming Resistance to Change," *Human Relations* 1 (1948), 512–34; Victor H. Vroom, "Some Personality Determinants of the Effects of Participation," *Journal of Abnormal and Social Psychology* 59 (1959), 322–27; Rensis Likert, *New Patterns of Management* (New York, 1961); Douglas McGregor, *The Human Side of Enterprise* (New York, 1960). A sense of the continuity in welfare capitalist thinking can be gleaned from the proceedings of the Silver Bay conferences, held at a YMCA facility on Lake George, New York. The conferences, started in the 1910s by the YMCA and by Standard Oil's Clarence J. Hicks, allowed high-level executives and academics to mingle and discuss the latest developments in personnel management. See, for example, the presentation of Lewin's ideas given in 1958 by Dr. Edwin R. Henry of Standard Oil of New Jersey. Edwin R. Henry, "Some Practical Implications of Human Relations Research Findings," *38th Silver Bay Industrial Conference on Human Relations in Industry, September 1958* (New York, 1959), 20–22. On Silver Bay, see Jacoby, *Employing Bureaucracy*, 60, 182.

102. Harold Wilensky, "Human Relations in the Workplace: An Appraisal of Some Recent Research" in Arensberg, ed., *Research in Human Relations*, 39. Also see Jeanne and Harold Wilensky, "Personnel Counseling: The Hawthorne Case," *American Journal of Sociology* 57 (November 1951), 265–80; Henry Landsberger, *Hawthorne Revisited* (Ithaca, N.Y., 1958); and, for a recent critique of the Lewin group, see Charles Perrow, *Complex Organizations: A Critical Essay*, 2nd ed. (Glenview, 1979), 112–32.

103. Loren Baritz, *The Servants of Power: A History of the Use of Social Science in American Industry* (Middletown, Conn., 1960), 197.

104. "Wrong 42 % of the Time," *Business Week*, September 12, 1936, 30–34; Albert Haring, "The Evolution of Marketing Research Technique," *National Marketing Review* 1 (Winter 1936), 268–72; Paul F. Lazarsfeld, *Radio and the Printed Page* (New York, 1940); Converse, *Survey Research*, chap. 3; Richard Jensen, "Democracy by the Numbers," *Public Opinion* 3 (March 1980), 53–59; Daniel Katz and Herbert Hyman, "Industrial Morale and Public Opinion Methods," *International Journal of Opinion and Attitude Research* 1 (September 1947), 13–30.

105. Viteles, *Motivation and Morale*; Social Research Institute, "Studies on Public At-

titudes toward Big Business," ms. (n.d.), JCWP.

106. David Vogel, "Why Businessmen Distrust Their State: The Political Consciousness of American Corporate Executives," *British Journal of Political Science* 8 (January 1978), 63; Harold G. Vatter, *The U.S. Economy in World War II* (New York, 1985), 150. More generally, see Joel Seidman, *American Labor from Defense to Reconversion* (Chicago, 1953); Harris, *The Right to Manage*, 177–200; Eric Goldman, *The Crucial Decade, 1945–1955* (New York, 1956); Athan Theoharis, *Seeds of Repression: Harry S. Truman and the Origins of McCarthyism* (Chicago, 1971); Ellen Schrecker, "McCarthyism and the Labor Movement: The Role of the State" in Steve Rosswurm, ed., *The CIO's Left-Led Unions* (New Brunswick, N.J., 1992), 139–57; and, for an overview, Fones-Wolf, *Selling Free Enterprise*.

107. Sutton et al., *The American Business Creed*, 392–93; Alan Wolfe, *America's Impasse: The Rise and Fall of the Politics of Growth* (New York, 1981); Seymour Martin Lipset, "Trade Unions and Social Structure," *Industrial Relations* 1 (October 1961), 75–90, and (February 1962), 89–110. In a 1946 survey intended to determine "Where are U.S. Reds?" nearly a fifth of the respondents said that "many" labor-union leaders "believe that the Russian system of government is better than ours." "The Fortune Survey," *Fortune* 34 (July 1946), 6.

108. Edward L. Bernays, *Crystallizing Public Opinion* (New York, 1923), 53; William Albig, *Public Opinion* (New York, 1939); Converse, *Survey Resarch*, passim; Richard S. Tedlow, *Keeping the Corporate Image: Public Relations and Business, 1900–1950* (Greenwich, Conn., 1979), 41–45.

109. Tedlow, *Keeping the Corporate Image*, 63, 71; Lane, *Regulation of Businessmen*, 9–11.

110. Gable, "NAM: Influential Lobby or Kiss of Death?" 265; "Fred Crawford's Company," 210; F. C. Crawford, *The American Triangle of Plenty* (New York, 1943); Rutherford, "Career of Fred Crawford," 41.

111. National Association of Manufacturers, *The American Individual Enterprise System: Its Nature, Evolution, and Future* (New York, 1946); Clark Kerr, "Employer Policies in Industrial Relations, 1945 to 1947" in Colston E. Warne, ed., *Labor in Postwar America* (Brooklyn, N.Y., 1949), 49; Gable, "A Political Analysis," 303–29; Frederick C. Crawford, "Give Workers the Common-Sense Facts behind Their Jobs," *Factory Management and Maintenance* 104 (September 1946), 100; Crawford, "Public Relations as a Tool in Postwar Programs" in *Proceedings of the Indiana Executives Conference on Public Relations, Indianapolis, April 14, 1944*, 28, 37, N.A.M. Records, box 82, Hagley Library, Wilmington, Delaware.

112. NAM, Industrial Relations Department, "Employee Communications" (New York, 1949); Gable, "A Political Analysis," 326, 336–40. Thompson Products hired Opinion Research Corporation in the late 1940s to study how its own public-relations program was affecting employees and the local community. R. S. Livingstone, "The Changing Concept of the Personnel Function" in American Management Association, "Industrial Applications of Medicine and Psychiatry," Personnel Series no. 130 (New York, 1949), 23.

113. Crawford, "Give Workers Facts," 103.

114. Schrecker, "McCarthyism and Labor," 139; L. R. Boulware, "How G.E. is Trying to Sell Employees on Giving Full Skill, Care, and Effort at Work," *Printers' Ink* 225 (December 10, 1948), 76–77; Herbert Northrup, *Boulwarism: The Labor Relations Policies of the General Electric Company* (Ann Arbor, Mich., 1964), 25–33; Ronald W. Schatz, *The Electrical Workers: A History of Labor at General Electric and Westinghouse, 1923–60* (Urbana, Ill., 1983), 171–75.

115. Philip H. Burch, Jr., "The NAM as an Interest Group," *Politics and Society* 4 (Fall 1973), 97–130; Fred J. Cook, "The Ultras," *The Nation*, June 23, 1962, 565–606; Daniel Bell, *The Radical Right: The New American Right Expanded and Updated* (Garden City, N.Y., 1963); John Roy Carlson, *The Plotters* (New York, 1946); Doenecke, "General Wood," 174.

116. Doenecke, "General Wood," 169; Pflaum, "The Baffling Career of Robert E. Wood," 68; Burch, "The NAM," 114. Ickes was a long-time friend of Julius Rosenwald and his son, Lessing, who succeeded his father as chairman of Sears in the early 1930s. Lessing Rosenwald was deeply upset when the General refused to criticize Lindbergh's anti-Semitism; Ickes's comment probably expressed Rosenwald's feelings at the time. Eventually Rosenwald severed all personal ties between himself and Wood. Worthy, *Shaping an American Institution*, 49, 78–81; Linda J. Lear, *Harold L. Ickes, The Aggressive Progressive, 1874–1933* (New York, 1981).

117. Cook, "The Ultras," 587, 592–93; R. E. Wood to Lamar Fleming, Jr., June 17, 1948, box 26; R. E. Wood to Merwin K. Hart, October 22, 1945, box 7; R. E. Wood to Robert Christenberry, November 15, 1946, box 26; Henry Regnery to R. E. Wood, June 24, 1953, box 13; R. E. Wood to Representative Joseph

W. Martin, Jr., July 3, 1953; and R. E. Wood to George Sokolsky, March 10, 1942, box 15, all in REWP.

118. Cook, "The Ultras," 590; "Transcript of Raymond Livingstone's Testimony to the Ohio House Industrial Relations Committee," 97th General Assembly, Columbus, Ohio (May 23, 1947), box 40, and "Minutes of personnel meeting, April 7, 1958," box 133, TRWP. Du Pont, a company with many similarities to Thompson, also encouraged employees to participate in politics but occasionally harassed those who took the "wrong" side (including support for Lyndon Johnson in his 1964 presidential run). James Phelan and Robert Pozen, *The Company State: Ralph Nader's Study Group on DuPont in Delaware* (New York, 1973), 61–63.

119. R. E. Wood to N. W. Shefferman, June 2, 1950; N. W. Shefferman to R. E. Wood, January 17, 1950, June 3, 1950, and March 9, 1953; R. E. Wood to E. O. Shreve and R. E. Wood to Morris Sayre, both August 4, 1948, all in box 14, REWP; Nathan W. Shefferman, *Labor's Stake in Capitalism* (New York, 1954), 122. Also see Nathan Shefferman, "Real Division in the United States Is Not Between Employer and Labor Union," *The Washington Teamster*, May 30, 1947, JMBP.

120. Patrick J. Maney, *"Young Bob" LaFollette: A Biography of Robert M. LaFollette, Jr., 1895–1953* (Columbia, Mo., 1978). Robert S. Alder, son of former Sears' merchandise manager Max Adler and nephew of Julius Rosenwald, accused the upper echelons of Sears' management under Wood of being infected by a "virus" of anti-Semitism. Interview with Robert S. Adler conducted by James C. Worthy, 1979, JCWP. Also see note 147, Chapter Four above.

121. Gordon Weil, *Sears Roebuck, U.S.A.* (Briarcliff Manor, N.Y., 1977), 101, 107; Utley material in box 17, REWP; *Sears News-Graphic*, February 21, 1952, p. 3, SR Archives; "Sears National Personnel Department: Its Organization and Function" (Chicago, c. 1955), 23, DCCU.

122. Alan F. Westin, "Anti-Communism and the Corporations," *Commentary* 36 (December 1963), 486; William H. Whyte, *Is Anybody Listening? How and Why U.S. Business Fumbles When It Talks with Human Beings* (New York, 1952); J. H. Willits to J. M. Barker, February 25, 1946, JMBP.

123. "Management Must Tell Its Story," *Chemical and Engineering News* 32 (November 8, 1954), 4,494; John C. Rumm, "Industrial Engineering at DuPont" in Daniel Nelson, ed., *A Mental Revolution: Scientific Management since Taylor* (Columbus, Ohio, 1992), 191; Phelan and Pozen, *The Company State*, 60.

124. Robert N. McMurry, "War and Peace in Labor Relations," *Harvard Business Review* 33 (November-December 1955), 48, 55.

Chapter Seven
The Cold War of Industrial Relations

1. Richard A. Lester, *As Unions Mature: An Analysis of the Evolution of American Unionism* (Princeton, N.J., 1958); Sanford Jacoby and Daniel Mitchell, "Does Implicit Contracting Explain Explicit Contracting?" *Proceedings of the 35th Annual Meeting of the Industrial Relations Research Association* New York, December 1982; Thomas A. Kochan, Harry C. Katz, and Robert B. McKersie, *The Transformation of American Industrial Relations* (New York, 1986); Nelson Lichtenstein, "The Treaty of Detroit: Old before Its Time," paper presented to the American Historical Association (Chicago, January 1995).

2. Sumner H. Slichter, James J. Healy, and E. Robert Livernash, *The Impact of Collective Bargaining on Management* (Washington, D.C., 1960); Richard Lester, *Hiring Practices and Labor Competition* (Princeton, N.J., 1954), 35.

3. S. W. Pickering, "Personnel Policies in a Non-Union Plant," *38th Silver Bay Industrial Conference on Human Relations in Industry, September 1958* (New York, 1959), 18–19; Sidney Fish, "Does Labor Prefer to be Unionized?" *Manufacturers' Record* 118 (January 1949), 34–35; National Industrial Conference Board (NICB), *Personnel Practices in Factory and Office*, Studies in Personnel Policy no. 145 (New York, 1954), 56; Howard Vollmer, *Employee Rights and the Employment Relationship* (Berkeley, Cal., 1960), 25.

4. "International Harvester's Attack on Radical Labor Leadership," *Factory Management and Maintenance* 105 (December 1947), 66–73; Michael Goldfield, *The Decline of Organized Labor in the United States* (Chicago, 1987), 196; Richard Freeman and James Medoff, *What Do Unions Do?* (New York, 1984), 232–42.

5. On dual allegiance, see Theodore Vincent Purcell, *Blue Collar Man: Patterns of Dual Allegiance in Industry* (Cambridge, Mass., 1960); Ross Stagner, "Dual Allegiance as a Problem in Modern Society: A Symposium," *Personnel Psychology* 7 (March 1954), 41–80.

6. Helen Baker, *The Determination and Administration of Industrial Relations Policies*

(Princeton, N.J., 1939), 53; Arnold Weber, ed., *The Structure of Collective Bargaining* (Glencoe, Ill., 1961).

7. See the comparison of RCA (unionized) and Pitney Bowes (nonunion) in American Management Association, *Essentials of Effective Personnel Administration* (New York, 1953); Caroll E. French, "Today's Priorities in Human Relations," *33rd Silver Bay Industrial Conference on Human Relations in Industry, September 1953* (New York, 1954), 7–10; Thomas A. Kochan and Peter Cappelli, "The Transformation of the Industrial Relations and Personnel Function" in Paul Osterman, ed., *Internal Labor Markets* (Cambridge, Mass., 1984), 133–61; James C. Worthy, "Changing Concepts of the Personnel Function," AMA Personnel Series no. 113 (New York, 1949), 8.

8. Sanford Jacoby and Daniel J. B. Mitchell, "Development of the Contractual Features of the Union-Management Relationship," *Labor Law Journal* 33 (August 1982), 512–18; Nelson Lichtenstein, "Conflict over Workers' Control: The Automobile Industry in World War II" in Michael Frisch and Daniel Walkowitz, eds., *Working-Class America: Essays on Labor, Community, and American Society* (Urbana, Ill., 1983), 284–311; Seymour Melman, *Profits without Production* (New York, 1983), 139–41; Sebastian Littauer, "Stability of Production Rates as a Determinant of Industrial Productivity Levels" in *Proceedings of the 114th Meeting of the American Statistical Association, Montreal, September 1954* (Washington, D.C., 1954), 241–48.

9. Alvin W. Gouldner, *Patterns of Industrial Bureaucracy* (Glencoe, Ill., 1954), 160; Paul Pigors and Faith Pigors, "Let's Talk Policy," *Personnel* 27 (July 1950), 9; Sanford M. Jacoby, "Progressive Discipline in American Industry," *Advances in Industrial and Labor Relations* 3 (1986), 213–60.

10. Edward Roseman, *Confronting Nonpromotability: How to Manage a Stalled Career* (New York, 1977), 23–41; Fred Foulkes, *Personnel Policies in Large Nonunion Firms* (Englewood Cliffs, N.J., 1980), 62–63; Stephen Habbe, "How Not to Have Grievances," *Management Record* 11 (June 1949), 247–49; M. J. Murphy, "A Little Paternalism Makes a Lot of Sense," *Factory Management and Maintenance* 108 (April 1950), 52–56; Robert Coulson, *The Termination Handbook* (New York, 1981), 124.

11. Worthy, "Changing Concepts of the Personnel Function," passim; Thomas A. Kirkwood, "Personnel Administration in the Nonunionized Plant," *33rd Silver Bay Conference*, 126; Ivar Berg, Marcia Freedman, and Michael Freeman, *Managers and Work Reform: A Limited Engagement* (New York, 1978), 178–81; Alan Fox, *Beyond Contract: Work, Power, and Trust Relations* (London, 1973), chap. 2.

12. John T. Dunlop, "The Growth of the Relationship," and Frederick Harbison and John Coleman, "Working Harmony in Eighteen Companies," in Clinton S. Golden and Virginia D. Parker, eds., *Causes of Industrial Peace under Collective Bargaining* (New York, 1955), 23, 333.

13. Neil W. Chamberlain, *The Union Challenge to Management Control* (New York, 1948), 3; James W. Kuhn, *Bargaining in Grievance Settlement: The Power of Industrial Relations* (New York, 1961).

14. Lester, *As Unions Mature*; Milton Derber, W. E. Chalmers, and Milton Edelstein, "Union Participation in Plant Decision Making," *Industrial and Labor Relations Review* 15 (October 1961), 83–101.

15. Sanford Jacoby, "Environmental Pressure and Union-Management Cooperation: Evidence from the United States, 1920–1965" in Eric Flamholtz, ed., *The Future Direction of Employee Relations* (Los Angeles, 1985), 23; Harold G. Vatter, *The U.S. Economy in the 1950's* (New York, 1963); Robert L. Aronson, "Automation: Challenge to Collective Bargaining?" in Harold W. Davey et al., eds., *New Dimensions in Collective Bargaining* (New York, 1959), 47–70; George Hildebrand, "The New Economic Environment of the United States and Its Meaning," *Industrial and Labor Relations Review* 16 (July 1963), 523–38; Robert L. Heilbroner, "The View from the Top: Reflections on a Changing Business Ideology" in Earl F. Cheit, ed., *The Business Establishment* (New York, 1964), 1–36.

16. Jack Barbash, "Union Response to the 'Hard Line,'" and Frank C. Pierson, "Recent Employer Alliances in Perspective," *Industrial Relations* 1 (October 1961), 25–38 and 39–55; Benson Soffer and Irwin L. Herrnstadt, "Recent Labor Disputes over 'Restrictive' Practices and 'Inflationary' Wage Increases," *Journal of Business* 34 (October 1961), 453–70; Jules Justin, "How to Preserve Management Rights under the Labor Contract," *Labor Law Journal* 11 (March 1960), 189–215; George W. Torrence, *Management's Right to Manage* (Washington, D.C., 1961); Jacoby, "Environmental Pressure and Union-Management Cooperation," 34–42.

17. Howell Harris, *The Right to Manage: Industrial Relations Policies of American Business in the 1940s* (Madison, Wisc., 1982), 196–98; Kim McQuaid, *Uneasy Partners: Big Business in American Politics, 1945–1990* (Baltimore, Md., 1994), 18–35. Along with

ideology, interlocking corporate and family ties brought union and nonunion companies together, as was true of General Motors and Du Pont, the organizers of the Foundation on Economic Education.

18. Harris, *The Right to Manage*, 192; James G. Bradsher, "Taking America's Heritage to the People: The Freedom Train Story," *Prologue* 17 (1985), 229–46; William H. Whyte, *Is Anybody Listening? How and Why U.S. Business Fumbles When It Talks With Human Beings* (New York, 1952); Francis X. Sutton et al., *The American Business Creed* (Cambridge, Mass., 1956), 296–98.

19. Whiting Williams quoted in Elizabeth Fones-Wolf, "Contested Play: Company, Union, and Industrial Recreation, 1945–1960," *Labor's Heritage* 6 (Summer 1994), 6; Fones-Wolf, "Industrial Recreation, the Second World War, and the Revival of Welfare Capitalism, 1934–1960," *Business History Review* 60 (Summer 1986), 232–57.

20. Lizabeth Cohen, *Making a New Deal: Industrial Workers in Chicago, 1919–1939* (Cambridge, U.K., 1990), 333–49; Derek C. Bok and John T. Dunlop, *Labor and American Community* (New York, 1970), 376–79; Joseph Willits to James M. Barker, February 25, 1946, JMBP.

21. Harris, *The Right to Manage*, 188; A. M. Rose, *Union Solidarity* (Minneapolis, Minn., 1952).

22. NLRB Trial Examiner's Report in Herbert Northrup, *Boulwarism: The Labor Relations Policies of the General Electric Company* (Ann Arbor, Mich., 1964), 101.

23. Daniel Bell, "Adjusting Men to Machines," *Commentary* 3 (June 1947), 79–88; "Deep Therapy on the Assembly Line," *Ammunition* 7 (April 1949), 47–51; NICB, *Principles and Applications of Job Evaluation* (New York, 1944), 7. Over the last fifty years, the diffusion of the applied behavioral sciences was generally consistent with the theory of institutionalization, although the theory pays insufficient attention to the cultural and political barriers that can hamper diffusion, as occurred with human relations in the union sector. Paul J. DiMaggio and Walter W. Powell, "The Iron Cage Revisited: Institutional Isomorphism and Collective Rationality in Organizational Fields," *American Sociological Review* 48 (April 1983), 47–160.

24. James W. Irwin, "Sampling Workers' Opinions," *Dun's Review* 53 (November 1945), 32–42; Bureau of National Affairs, "Is Management Listening?" *Personnel Policies Forum* 3 (May 1951), 4. Also see Robert N. McMurry, "Management's Reaction to Employee Opinion Polls," *Journal of Applied Psychology* 30 (April 1946), 212–19; and Harold B. Bergen, "Measuring Attitudes and Morale in Wartime," *Management Record* 4 (April 1942), 101–4. Several postwar studies found that union leaders were no better than corporate managers at predicting employee responses to surveys: both groups overemphasized monetary factors as determinants of worker morale. Although managers became better informed through the use of attitude surveys, union officials were reluctant to poll their own members and only a few union-sponsored surveys were conducted during the 1950s. NICB, *Experience with Employee Attitude Surveys* (New York, 1951); Frederick Herzberg et al., *Job Attitudes: Review of Research and Opinion* (Pittsburgh, Pa., 1957); NICB, *Following up Attitude Survey Findings* (New York, 1961).

25. Richard Wilcock, "Industrial Management's Policies toward Unionism" in Milton Derber and Edwin Young, eds., *Labor and the New Deal* (Madison, Wisc., 1961), 308; Solomon Barkin, "Discussion" in *Proceedings of the Fourth Annual Meeting of the Industrial Relations Research Association, Boston, December 1951* (Champaign, Ill., 1952), 82.

26. Kochan and Cappelli, "Transformation of the Personnel Function"; Sanford Jacoby, "Managing the Workplace: From Markets to Manors and Beyond" in Clark Kerr and Paul Staudohar, eds., *Labor Economics and Industrial Relations: Markets and Institutions* (Cambridge, Mass., 1994). For a sense of different worlds, compare two Conference Board reports: Allen Janger, *The Personnel Function* (New York, 1977) and Audrey Freeman, *Managing Labor Relations* (New York, 1979).

27. Coen quoted in Reinhard Bendix, *Work and Authority in Industry* (New York, 1956), 329. In 1946 Ford followed GM's lead—as usual—by replacing its notorious Service Department with a new Industrial Relations department, which immediately started a "human engineering program" and an employee survey. Later on, Elmo Roper conducted opinion polls for Ford. "Human Engineering Program Pays off for Ford," *Business Week*, October 30, 1948, 88–95; "Employee Opinion Survey Aids Ford in Policy Making," *Factory Management and Maintenance* 105 (June 1947), 132–33; D. G. Baird, "What Ford Gets from Its Employee Opinion Surveys," *Mill & Factory* 50 (January 1952), 141–43.

28. Chester Evans and LaVerne N. Laseau, *My Job Contest* (Washington, D.C., 1950), 29–30, 133–36; "How Do You Feel? GM Asks Its Workers," *Business Week*, December 31, 1949, 48–50. In the 1950s Laseau's group tried—unsuccessfully—to develop a selection

test to screen out individuals with liberal and pro-union attitudes. Loren Baritz, *The Servants of Power: A History of the Use of Social Science in American Industry* (Middletown, Conn., 1960), 166.

29. "Employees Tell Why They Like Their Jobs," *Mill and Factory* 452 (February 1948), 102–4; "The Workers' Poll that Kicked up a Fuss," *Business Week*, February 19, 1944, 30–31. In at least one instance, however, the UAW cooperated with the management of a small Illinois auto parts firm in conducting an attitude survey. "Joining in an Attitude Survey Proves a Move toward Peace," *Business Week*, April 14, 1956, 57–60.

30. John Kenneth Galbraith, *American Capitalism: The Concept of Countervailing Power* (Boston, 1956); Clark Kerr, "What Became of the Independent Spirit?" *Fortune* 48 (July 1953), 108–12; William H. Whyte, Jr., *The Organization Man* (Garden City, N.Y., 1957); Arthur M. Ross, "Do We Have a New Industrial Feudalism?" *American Economic Review* 48 (December 1958), 903–20; Reinhard Bendix and Lloyd H. Fisher, "The Perspectives of Elton Mayo," *Review of Economics and Statistics* 31 (November 1949), 318.

31. William F. Whyte, *Money and Motivation; An Analysis of Incentives in Industry* (New York, 1955); Douglas McGregor, *The Human Side of Enterprise* (New York, 1960); and Henry Landsberger, *Hawthorne Revisited* (Ithaca, N.Y., 1958). Also see Philip Selznick, *Law, Society, and Industrial Justice* (New York, 1969), 75–120.

32. "Individual Counts," *Chemical and Engineering News* 36 (May 26, 1958), 40.

33. H. Ellsworth Steele, William R. Myles, and Sherwood C. McIntyre, "Personnel Practices in the South," *Industrial and Labor Relations Review* 9 (January 1956), 248; Sanford M. Jacoby, "Employee Attitude Surveys in American Industry: An Historical Perspective" in Norman Metzger, ed., *Handbook of Healthcare Human Resource Management* (New York, 1990), 76, 81. In the mid to late 1950s, many employers feared that labor would soon expand beyond its blue-collar base. Although this never occurred, nonunion firms nevertheless began paying special attention to their clerical, professional, and technical employees; behavioral science was an important component of new white-collar policies. See, for example, Hugh Forster, "Human Relations for White-Collar Workers," *38th Silver Bay Industrial Conference on Human Relations in Industry, September 1958* (New York, 1959), 22–23.

34. Freeman, *Managing Labor Relations*, 71–75; Harold M. F. Rush, *Behavioral Science: Concepts and Management Application* (New York, 1969); Charles C. Heckscher, *The New Unionism: Employee Involvement in the Changing Corporation* (New York, 1988); Kochan, Katz, and McKersie, *Transformation of American Industrial Relations*, 47–80; Berg et al., *Managers and Work Reform*, 205–20.

35. Ronald Edsforth, *Class Conflict and Cultural Consensus: The Making of a Mass Consumer Society in Flint, Michigan* (New Brunswick, N.J., 1987); Marty Jezer, *The Dark Ages: Life in the United States, 1945–1960* (Boston, 1982).

36. Fones-Wolf, "Industrial Recreation," 255, and "Contested Play," 11.

37. "Company Recreation Is Good Business," *Glass Industry* 44 (April 1963), 210–11; Gerald R. Hocker, "Extra Services You Can Offer Employees without Being Paternalistic," *American Business* 30 (April 1960), 13; Fones-Wolf, "Industrial Recreation," 255–56; Solomon Barkin, "A Trade Unionist Appraises Management Personnel Philosophy," *Harvard Business Review* 28 (September 1950), 60.

38. Fones-Wolf, "Contested Play," 16; Bok and Dunlop, *Labor and the American Community*, 368–70.

39. Ronald Gordon, "Paternalism Works in Our Organization," *Administrative Management* 24 (August 1963), 40–41; Murphy, "A Little Paternalism," 55. Of course, paternalism periodically backfired in nonunion companies, and when it did, the results could be spectacular, as at Pullman in the 1890s, when a giant strike hit a paternalistic employer, and Kohler Products later on. Kohler—a plumbing supply company—had built a model company town in Kohler, Wisconsin. It had beautiful homes, parks, and playgrounds for workers and their families. Kohler's corporatism first began to unravel in 1931, when the company reneged on its no-layoff promises and let hundreds of workers go. In 1934, a strike ended tragically after the National Guard killed two workers and injured dozens more. Kohler never recovered from these events, and in 1952 its employees voted to join the UAW. Situations like Pullman and Kohler did not deter employers from experimenting with welfare capitalism but instead sensitized them to the importance of employment stability, the disadvantages of company towns, and the need to avoid labor violence at all costs. Walter H. Uphoff, *Kohler on Strike: Thirty Years of Conflict* (Boston, 1966); "Kohler's Paternalism Policy Fails to Head off Labor Trouble," *Business Week*, May 24, 1952, 169–71; Margaret Crawford, *Building the Workingman's Paradise: The Design of American Company Towns* (New York, 1995).

40. Jill Quadagno, *The Transformation of Old Age Security: Class and Politics in the American Welfare State* (Chicago, 1988), 161; Beth Stevens, "Labor Unions, Employee Benefits, and the Privatization of the American Welfare State," *Journal of Policy History* 2 (1990), 241. Also see Nelson Lichtenstein, "From Corporatism to Collective Bargaining: Organized Labor and the Eclipse of Social Democracy in the Postwar Era" in Steven Fraser and Gary Gerstle, eds., *The Rise and Fall of the New Deal Order, 1930–1980* (Princeton, N.J., 1989), 140–45; Franz Goldmann, "Labor's Attitude towards Health Insurance," *Industrial and Labor Relations Review* 2 (October 1948), 90–98.

41. Bok and Dunlop, *Labor and the American Community*, 373; Edward Berkowitz and Kim McQuaid, *Creating the Welfare State*, 2nd ed. (New York, 1988), 133, 138; Chamberlain, *The Union Challenge*, 313–14, 323–24; Slichter et al., *The Impact of Collective Bargaining*, 372–421; Edward D. Berkowitz, *Disabled Policy: America's Programs for the Handicapped* (Cambridge, U.K., 1989), 61–64.

42. Joan Finder, "Differences in Personnel Practices and Policies in Large Union and Non-Union Retail Stores in New York City," M.S. thesis, School of Labor and Industrial Relations, Cornell University, 1957, 109–10; Freeman and Medoff, *What Do Unions Do?* 67.

43. NICB, *Profit-Sharing and Other Supplementary-Compensation Plans Covering Wage Earners* (New York, 1937), 14; NICB, *Profitsharing for Workers* (New York, 1948), 5; Harold Bergen, "The Present Trend in Bonus," *Labor Relations Bulletin* (NAM), June 5, 1937, 6–7; "Analysis of Profitsharing Plans," *Labor Relations Bulletin*, September 28, 1937, 8–9; U.S. Senate, Committee on Finance, *Investigation of Profit-Sharing Systems between Employers and Employees in the United States: Hearings*, 75th Cong., 3rd Sess. (Washington, D.C., 1939).

44. U.S. Senate, Committee on Finance, *Survey of Experiences in Profit Sharing and Possibilities of Incentive Taxation: Report*, 76th Cong. 1st Sess. (Washington, D.C., 1939), 63, 115, 130, 139–60; "I Believe in Profit Sharing," *Factory Management and Maintenance* 97 (February 1939), 39. Also see Daniel Mitchell and Renae Broderick, "Flexible Pay Systems in the American Context: History, Policy, Research, and Implications," *Advances in Industrial and Labor Relations* 5 (1991), 114–17; NICB, *Profit-Sharing and Other Plans*, 12.

45. Arthur Altmeyer, *The Formative Years of Social Security* (Madison, Wisc., 1966), 88–89, 137; "I Believe in Profit Sharing," 39; "Statement of General Robert E. Wood" in Senate, *Investigation of Profit Sharing*, 43; Senate, *Survey of Experiences in Profit Sharing*, 239–76; speech given by Gen. Wood at Sears Forum Meeting, March 30, 1937, Sears file, REWP; NICB, *Profit Sharing for Workers*, 5, 10. Also see note 70, Chapter Six above.

46. C. Canby Balderston, *Profit Sharing for Wage Earners* (New York, 1937), 14–17 (a study published by Industrial Relations Counselors); "Statement of John L. Lewis" in Senate, *Survey of Experiences in Profit Sharing*, 190, 193; "Statement of William Green," ibid., 107; Hugh C. Middleton, "Co-Partnership of Labor and Industry," *American Federationist* 42 (September 1935), 963–64.

47. "Statement of Alfred P. Sloan, Jr." in *Survey of Experiences in Profit Sharing*, 475; NICB, *Profit Sharing for Workers*, 33; Mitchell and Broderick, "Flexible Pay Systems," 135.

48. Steele, Myles, and McIntyre, "Personnel Practices in the South," 248; H. Ellsworth Steele and Homer Fisher, Jr., "A Study of the Effects of Unionism in Southern Plants," *Monthly Labor Review* 87 (March 1964), 267; "But Doubts Still Linger," *Chemical Week* 76 (January 8, 1955), 22; NICB, *Profit Sharing for Workers*, 22, 24; "How Industry Looks at Profit Sharing," *Factory Management and Maintenance* 97 (February 1939), 41–42; Edgar R. Czarnecki, "Profit Sharing and Union Organizing," *Monthly Labor Review* 92 (December 1969), 61–62; Douglas L. Kruse, "Profit-Sharing and Employment Variability: Evidence on the Weitzman Theory," *Industrial and Labor Relations Review* 44 (April 1991), 437–53.

49. W. Rupert MacLaurin, "Workers' Attitudes on Work Sharing and Lay-Off Policies in a Manufacturing Firm." *Monthly Labor Review* 48 (January 1939), 47–60; Carl Gersuny and Gladis Kaufman, "Seniority and the Moral Economy of U.S. Automobile Workers," *Journal of Social History* 18 (Spring 1985), 463–75; Jacoby, *Employing Bureaucracy*, 232–49, 260.

50. George P. Shultz, "A Nonunion Market for White Collar Labor" in National Bureau of Economic Research, *Aspects of Labor Economics* (Princeton, N.J., 1962); Jacoby, *Employing Bureaucracy*, 246; Boris Emmet and John Jeuck, *Catalogues and Counters* (Chicago, 1950), 573–75; "Sears Standardizing Wage Plans," *Business Week*, April 27, 1940, 26–27; Sears Roebuck, "The Constant Wage Plan in Retail Stores: Revised to 6th Period, 1939," Labor-Management Documentation Center, Cornell University (DCCU); "The

Procter & Gamble Employment Guarantee Plan" in Office of War Mobilization and Reconversion, *Guaranteed Wages* (Washington, D.C., 1947), 307–16; J. F. Teegardin to Dr. A. K. Chapman, June 25, 1947, box 2, Marion B. Folsom Papers, University of Rochester; James Medoff, "Layoffs and Alternatives under Trade Unions in U.S. Manufacturing," *American Economic Review* 69 (June 1979), 380–95. In 1962, over a third of large unionized firms were covered by SUB plans, as compared to only about a tenth of comparable nonunion firms. Steele and Fisher, "Study of the Effects of Unionism," 269.

51. Paul Osterman, "Choice among Alternative Internal Labor Market Systems," *Industrial Relations* 26 (February 1987), 46–67; Herman Feldman, *Stabilizing Jobs and Wages through Better Business Management* (New York, 1940), 154–57, 184–89; Freeman and Medoff, *What Do Unions Do?* 124–32.

52. John T. Dunlop, *Wage Determination under Trade Unions* (New York, 1944); Jacoby and Mitchell, "Does Implicit Contracting Explain Explicit Contracting?" 325; Jacoby and Mitchell, "Development of Contractual Features," 515; Daniel J. B. Mitchell, *Unions, Wages, and Inflation* (Washington, D.C., 1980).

53. Because of acquisitions, Thompson Products in the 1960s had affiliated-union and nonunion establishments in addition to its company-union plants. The affiliated-union plants averaged 125 job classifications, whereas the company-union and nonunion plants had 82 and 65 classifications, respectively. Sanford Jacoby and Anil Verma, "Enterprise Unions in the United States," *Industrial Relations* 31 (Winter 1992), 153; Freeman and Medoff, *What Do Unions Do?* 80–81; Casey Ichniowski, John Delaney, and David Lewin, "The New Human Resource Management in US Workplaces: Is It Really New and Is It Only Nonunion?" *Relations Industrielles* 44 (Winter 1989), 97–119; Richard Freeman, "Union Wage Effects and Wage Dispersion within Establishments," *Industrial and Labor Relations Review* 36 (October 1982), 3–21; Slichter et al., *The Impact of Collective Bargaining*, 462–89; Kodak Park Works, "Individual Performance Rating (General Factory Employees)" (June 1944), DCCU; R. R. Ross, "Kodak Park Standard Practice: Performance Appraisal" (January 1, 1954), KA; Emmet and Jeuck, *Catalogues and Counters*, 574; D. Quinn Mills, *The IBM Lesson: The Profitable Art of Full Employment* (New York, 1988).

54. Sumner H. Slichter, *Union Policies and Industrial Management* (Washington, D.C., 1941), 105; Jacoby, *Employing Bureaucracy*, 245. The sort of historical contingency discussed here is what economists call "endogeneity"; for an example of this reasoning applied to unions, see Greg Duncan and Frank Stafford, "Do Union Members Receive Compensating Wage Differentials?" *American Economic Review* 70 (June 1980), 369. The stringency with which the new unions enforced seniority is, again, best seen not as a universal characteristic of unionism but as the result of another contingent phenomenon: namely, the decentralized kind of unionism found in the United States. By making the firm and its rules the focus of their strategy for protecting workers' rights, American unions magnified differences between unionized and nonunion workplaces, and between the American labor movement and its counterparts abroad.

55. Chamberlain, *The Union Challenge*, 137, 287; "The Guaranteed Wage," *Fortune* 35 (April 1947), 120–23, 140–42; Slichter et al., *The Impact of Collective Bargaining*, 448, 459. Also nudging unions and management into choosing income security was the unemployment insurance program, which favored layoffs over work sharing. Had Congress approved Marion Folsom's proposal on employment guarantee plans, the door would have opened to federal credits for work sharing in lieu of layoffs, creating less of an incentive for firms (and unions) to adopt seniority-based layoff systems. See Chapter Six above at note 53.

56. Steve Fraser, "The 'Labor' Question" in Fraser and Gerstle, *Rise and Fall of the New Deal Order*, 77; Barkin, "A Trade Unionist Appraises Management," 59.

57. *U.S. Statistical Abstract*, various years, 1947–1964; Bruce Schulman, *From Cotton Belt to Sun Belt: Federal Policy, Economic Development, and the Transformation of the South, 1938–1980* (New York, 1991).

58. Ronald Schatz, *The Electrical Workers: A History of Labor at General Electric and Westinghouse, 1923–60* (Urbana, Ill., 1983), 233–34. Also see Daniel Nelson, "The Rubber Workers' Southern Strategy: Labor Organizing in the New Deal South," *The Historian* 46 (May 1984), 319–38.

59. Barbara S. Griffith, *The Crisis of American Labor: Operation Dixie and the Defeat of the CIO* (Philadelphia, 1988); U.S. Senate, Commitee on Labor and Public Welfare, *Labor-Management Relations in the Southern Textile Manufacturing Industry: Hearings*, 81st Cong., 2nd sess. (Washington, D.C., 1950), passim (but note Rieve's testimony, 355–77); "Faith in Chemical Firms," *Chemical Week* 77 (November 12, 1955), 34; "Union Barriers are Dropping in the South," *Chemical*

Week 82 (February 1, 1958), 43; Daniel Cornfield and Mark Leners, "Unionization in the Rural South," *Research in Rural Sociology and Development* 4 (1989), 137–52.

60. Herbert Northrup, "Management's 'New Look" in Labor Relations," *Industrial Relations* 1 (October 1961), 22; Charles Killingsworth, "The Fall and Rise of the Idea of Structural Unemployment," *Proceedings of the 31st Meeting of the Industrial Relations Research Association, Chicago, 1978* (Madison, Wisc., 1979).

61. See Michael Piore and Charles Sabel, *The Second Industrial Divide* (New York, 1984), for a summary of these trends.

62. Freeman and Medoff, *What Do Unions Do?*, 73, 113, 126–27; Ben Fischer quoted in John Hoerr, "Why Job Security Is More Important than Income Security," *Business Week*, November 21, 1983, 86; John Heywood, "Do Union Members Receive Compensating Differentials? The Case of Employment Security," *Journal of Labor Research* 10 (Summer 1989), 271–84. Freeman and Medoff provide evidence that younger union members were much less likely than older members to credit the union for doing a good job in getting better fringe benefits.

63. Robert Cole, *Work, Mobility, and Participation: A Comparative Study of American and Japanese Industry* (Berkeley, Cal., 1979), 130, 213, 220; Cole, *Strategies for Learning* (Berkeley, 1989), passim; Agis Salpukas, "Unions: A New Role?" in Jerome M. Rosow, ed., *The Worker and the Job: Coping with Change* (Englewood Cliffs, N.J., 1974), 99–117; David Levine and Laura Tyson, "Participation, Productivity, and the Firm's Environment" in Alan Blinder, ed., *Paying for Productivity* (Washington, D.C., 1990); Foulkes, *Personnel Policies in Large Nonunion Firms*, 99–122.

64. James Wright and Richard Hamilton, "Blue Collars, Cap and Gown," *Dissent* 25 (Spring 1978), 219–23; Berg, Freedman, and Freeman, *Managers and Work Reform*, 104, 107; Also see Daniel Yankelovich, *The New Morality: A Profile of American Youth in the 1970s* (New York, 1974).

65. Foulkes, *Personnel Policies in Large Nonunion Firms*, 190, 216.

66. Selznick, *Law, Society, and Industrial Justice*, 188–89; Freeman and Medoff, *What Do Unions Do?*, 80, 128; Michael Young, *The Rise of the Meritocracy, 1870–2033: An Essay on Education and Equality* (Harmondsworth, U.K., 1958).

67. William G. Ouchi, *Theory Z: How American Business Can Meet the Japanese Challenge* (Reading, Mass., 1981); Robert Levering, Milton Moskowitz, and Michael Katz, *The 100 Best Companies to Work for in America* (Reading, Mass., 1984). Becker and Olson find that in the 1970s unionized firms experienced lower risk-adjusted shareholder returns than nonunion firms. Brian Becker and Craig Olson, "Labor Relations and Firm Performance" in Morris Kleiner, Richard Block, Myron Roomkin, and Sidney Salsburg, eds., *Human Resources and the Performance of the Firm* (Madison, Wisc., 1987), 43–86.

68. For a summary of these points, see Eileen Appelbaum and Rosemary Batt, *The New American Workplace: Transforming Work Systems in the United States* (Ithaca, N.Y., 1994). Also see Harry Braverman, *Labor and Monopoly Capitalism: The Degradation of Work in the Twentieth Century* (New York, 1974); Edward E. Lawler, "The New Plant Revolution," *Organizational Dynamics* 6 (Winter 1978), 2–12; D. Quinn Mills, "Management Performance" in Jack Stieber, Robert McKersie, and D. Quinn Mills, eds., *U.S. Industrial Relations, 1950–1980: A Critical Assessment* (Madison, Wisc., 1981), 99–128; "Nicely Does It," *The Economist*, March 19, 1994, 84; John J. Lawler, *Unionization and Deunionization: Strategy, Tactics, and Outcomes* (Columbia, S.C., 1990).

69. Jacoby, "Employee Attitude Surveys," 76; Leonard Schlesinger and James L. Heskett, "Enfranchisement of Service Workers," *California Management Review* 33 (Summer 1991), 83–100;

70. G. Harry Stine, *The Corporate Survivors* (New York, 1986), 120–32; Buck Rodgers, *The IBM Way* (New York, 1986); "How IBM Handles Its People," *International Management* 25 (November 1970), 38–42; Charles R. Sprull, *Conglomerates and the Evolution of Capitalism* (Carbondale, Ill., 1982), 60; Jacoby and Verma, "Enterprise Unions," 145; "The Systems Group of TRW, Inc." in Harold M. F. Rush, *Behavioral Science: Concepts and Management Application* (New York, 1969), 157–71; Kochan, Katz, and McKersie, *Transformation of American Industrial Relations*, 96–99.

71. Author's interview with Donald E. McConville, director of industrial relations (retired), Eastman Kodak Co., June 17, 1987; "Great Yellow Father," *Wall Street Journal*, November 15, 1972, 1; "Wisdom of Eastman Still Guides Kodak," *Magazine of Wall Street* 125 (November 22, 1969), 15–17; author's interview with Frank J. Smith, March 20, 1985; Barry Bluestone, Patricia Hanna, Sarah Kuhn, and Laura Moore, *The Retail Revolution: Market Transformation, Investment, and Labor in the Modern Department Store* (Boston, 1981).

72. Fred Foulkes, "Employment Security: Developments in the Nonunion Sector" in *Proceedings of the 41st Annual Winter Meeting of the Industrial Relations Research Association, New York, December 1988* (Madison, Wisc., 1989), 411–17; Claudia Deutsch, "Kodak Pays the Price for Change," *New York Times* (March 6, 1988); David Moberg, "This Sears Sale Item Is Not in the Catalogue," *In These Times*, August 2–29, 1989, 6; "Smaller but Wiser," *Business Week*, October 12, 1992, 28–30; Sanford Jacoby, "Postindustrial Possibilities and Sears Roebuck," *Los Angeles Times*, January 29, 1993. By the 1970s Sears employed more part-timers than in 1940 (80 percent versus 35 percent), most of them women. The shift to part-timers reduced the number of Sears' male (and disproportionately full-time) employees from from 61 percent in 1940 to 35 percent in the late 1970s. See Table 4.1, above, and Bernard Siskin, "Report on Sears, Roebuck and Co.'s Commission Sales Hiring and Promotion Practices, Revised," September 10, 1984, supplementary tables, copy on file at Texas Law Review, Austin, Texas.

73. Francis X. Diebold, David Neumark, and Daniel Polsky, "Job Stability in the United States," NBER working paper no. 4,859 (September 1994); "Whistling whilst They Work," *The Economist*, January 28, 1995, 25–26; Robert Samuelson, "Life is Shakier, But Not Shattered," *Los Angeles Times*, December 29, 1993, B–5. Divergent trends in job tenure by gender and age are responsible for the overall finding of little or no change in tenure. Between 1983 and 1991, the proportion of men working for their current employer ten years or longer declined for men over 35 and increased for men under 35. For women, there was an increase in this measure of job stability in every age group. Katharine G. Abraham, "Employment Relationships in Our Changing Economy," unpublished paper, U.S. Bureau of Labor Statistics, October 1995; John Cassidy, "All Worked Up: Is Downsizing Really News or Is It Just Business as Usual?" *The New Yorker* 72 (April 22, 1996), 51–56.

74. "When Layoffs Alone Don't Turn the Tide," *Business Week*, December 7, 1992, 100–1; Mills, *The IBM Lesson*; Thomas A. Kochan, John Paul MacDuffie, and Paul Osterman, "Employment Security at DEC: Sustaining Values Amid Environmental Change," working paper, Sloan School of Management, MIT, 1988.

75. Clare Ansberry and Carol Hymowitz, "Kodak Chief is Trying, for the Fourth Time, to Trim Firm's Costs," *Wall Street Journal*, September 19, 1989, A–1, A–18–21; Joan Redebaugh, "Eastman Kodak: A Picture-Perfect Workplace," *Manufacturing Engineering* 103 (July 1989), 42; "Companies Pledge to Invest $100 Million for Dependent Care," *Daily Labor Reporter*, October 4, 1995, A–5; Brian Kane, "Layoffs Spur Kodak Organizing," *Labor Notes* 136 (July 1990), 1, 13.

76. Abraham, "Employment Relationships"; Lawrence Mishel and Jared Bernstein, *The State of Working America* (Armonk, N.Y., 1994).

Postscript

1. Clay Chandler, "Ambivalent about Business," *Washington Post*, May 12, 1996, H–1; Alison Mitchell, "Clinton Prods Executives to 'Do the Right Thing'," *New York Times*, May 17, 1996, C–1.

2. Jeffrey Pfeffer, *Competitive Advantage through People* (Boston, 1994); U.S. Department of Labor, "Report on High Performance Work Practices and Firm Performance" (Washington, D.C., 1993) reprinted in *Daily Labor Report* 143 (July 28, 1993), F1–F12; Richard Stevenson, "People and Profits Go Hand in Hand?" *New York Times*, May 9, 1996, C–1; Frederick F. Reichheld, *The Loyalty Effect: The Hidden Force behind Growth, Profits, and Lasting Value* (Boston, 1996); and David Levine, *Reinventing the Workplace: How Business and Employees Can Both Win* (Washington, D.C., 1995).

3. George Neumann and Ellen Rissman, "Where Have All the Union Members Gone?" *Journal of Labor Economics* 2 (April 1984), 175–92; J. R. Sutton, F. Dobbin, J. W. Meyer, and W. R. Scott, "The Legalization of the Workplace," *American Journal of Sociology* 99 (January 1994), 944–71.

4. Robert Kuttner, "Rewarding Corporations That Really Invest in America," *Business Week*, February 26, 1996, 22; Adam Clymer, "Kennedy Introduces Measures to Cut Layoffs from Mergers," *New York Times*, April 16, 1996, A–4.

Index

About the Author

Sanford M. Jacoby is Professor of History, Management, and Public Policy at the University of California, Los Angeles. He is the author of *Employing Bureaucracy: Managers, Unions, and the Transformation of Work in American Industry,* and the editor of *Masters to Managers: Historical and Comparative Perspectives on American Employers* and *Workers of Nations: Industrial Relations in a Global Economy.*